Kensington Cleaners - next to
Corner of Kensington Rd / Crowchild

strip mall

CLASSICS OF WESTERN THOUGHT

Volume
III

The Modern World

FOURTH EDITION

CLASSICS OF WESTERN THOUGHT

Under the General Editorship of
Thomas H. Greer
Michigan State University

Volume **I**
The Ancient World
FOURTH EDITION
Edited by Donald S. Gochberg
Michigan State University

Volume **II**
Middle Ages, Renaissance, and Reformation
FOURTH EDITION
Edited by Karl F. Thompson
Michigan State University

Volume **III**
The Modern World
FOURTH EDITION
Edited by Edgar E. Knoebel
Michigan State University

Volume **IV**
The Twentieth Century
Edited by Donald S. Gochberg
Michigan State University

CLASSICS OF WESTERN THOUGHT
Volume
III

The Modern World

FOURTH EDITION

Edited by
Edgar E. Knoebel
Michigan State University

HARCOURT BRACE JOVANOVICH, PUBLISHERS
San Diego   New York   Chicago   Austin   Washington, D.C.
London   Sydney   Tokyo   Toronto

COVER: François Rude (1784–1855), *Departure of the Volunteers*, also widely known as *The Marseillaise* (1833–36). Stone relief on the Arch of Triumph, Paris; approx. 42×26 feet. Giraudon/Art Resource.

This giant sculpture expresses the militant spirit of 1792, when French volunteers of all ages hurried to defend the French Revolution against the invading armies of the monarchies to the east of France. Those heeding the call, except for a single youth, are represented as wearing Roman and medieval armor, while looking up to the fearsome goddess of war for inspiration and direction.

ISBN: 0-15-507684-1

Library of Congress Catalog Card Number: 87-81142

Printed in the United States of America

Introduction to
the *Classics* Series

Writings by the great minds of the Western tradition offer modern Westerners the best possible introduction to their humanistic heritage. To provide such an introduction, the editors of this series have brought together works that we consider classics of the Western tradition—of Western *thought*, in the broad sense. For the most part, these volumes of primary documents are intended for use in college-level courses in humanities or the history of civilization, normally in the company of a brief narrative text. One such text, designed especially for use with this series, is my *Brief History of the Western World*, Fifth Edition (Harcourt Brace Jovanovich, 1987).

The number and range of documents in Western civilization are, of course, enormous, and good reasons can always be advanced for choosing one work over another. We have sought works that are truly *classic*, that is to say, valuable both for their intrinsic merit and for having exerted a paramount influence on their own and later times—works that display judgment applied to observation as well as creative thought and literary skill. In deciding upon the length and quantity of selections, we have aimed to keep in balance two considerations: having each selection long enough to give a clear view of the author's ideas and, at the same time, offering selections from a substantial number of the foremost writers.

The documents appear for the most part in chronological order, in four manageable volumes: *The Ancient World* (Volume I); *Middle Ages, Renaissance, and Reformation* (Volume II); *The Modern World* (Volume III); and *The Twentieth Century* (Volume IV). Each document is introduced by a brief account of the author's life, his or her role in the shaping of the Western tradition, and the significance of the particular work. As in the selection of the writings themselves, we have kept student and instructor constantly in mind.

In this Fourth Edition of the first three volumes of the *Classics*, we have added a number of documents especially suited to the interests of today's readers. (These are noted specifically in the editor's preface to each of the revised volumes.) Most of the selections in the preceding edition have been kept; in several instances they now appear in attractive new translations. Clear and concise footnotes have been extended throughout these volumes in order to explain parts of documents that might otherwise be obscure. As a result of all these improvements, we believe that readers will find these *Classics*, more than ever, an enjoyable aid to understanding the Western intellectual heritage.

Thomas H. Greer
General Editor

Preface to
the Fourth Edition

This volume, the third in the *Classics of Western Thought* series, offers classic and representative expression of the main currents of Western thought during the past four hundred years (from about 1550 to 1950).* Arranged in chronological order, the selections reflect the modern mind in its variety and complexity—its history, literature, philosophy, science, and social and religious thought.

The origins of the modern mind are to be found in the great advances of the seventeenth and eighteenth centuries. These advances, mainly in mathematics and the natural sciences, effected an intellectual revolution that rejected medieval scholasticism and recast the perceptions of human beings regarding the universe and their place in it. The emergence of the modern European state system, composed of absolute, sovereign nation-states, further weakened the traditional political and economic order. Political absolutism was, in turn, challenged by the great liberal revolutions in England, America, and France. Liberalism in its many aspects found intellectual expression in the reforming gospel of the eighteenth-century Enlightenment, or Age of Reason. Based on scientific discoveries and new methods of inquiry, it embodied a confident faith in the orderliness of nature and in the ability of humans to be the masters of their own fate. Reason and order were also the shaping concepts of the neoclassical drama and poetry of the period.

In the nineteenth century, the spread of the Industrial Revolution was accompanied by the triumph of political and economic liberalism

---

*Selections from the years since 1950 are included in Volume IV of this series, *The Twentieth Century*, edited by Donald S. Gochberg.

and its impact on democratic thought and practice. Conservatism and socialism challenged this new order from the right and left respectively. Nationalism, as an emotional and social force, came to dominate the European scene. The tenets of the Age of Reason gave way before the gospel of romanticism in the fields of intellectual and artistic endeavor. The biological theory of organic evolution gave a new direction to science, and its implications were worked out in social and philosophical thought as well.

Since 1880, the Western world has undergone catastrophic change and social and intellectual ferment and dislocation. World wars, economic crises, the rise and fall of empires, the appearance of collectivist societies and ideologies, the amazing developments of science and technology, the emergence of a mass society—all have transformed the character of Western thought. The new age has wrought havoc with traditional modes of society and thought. Social and political thinkers, artists, and intellectuals have rebelled against all tradition and have sought through free experiment to give people a new sense of purpose and direction. Optimism and certainty have given way to growing doubts and pessimism. The rational tradition of centuries has been displaced by emphasis on the irrational and the emotional—while science and technology have raced ahead with unforeseen consequences.

In preparing this Fourth Edition, I have made it a principle to retain those selections that have proved their lasting and timeless value. In this context, I wish to acknowledge my indebtedness to Professor Charles Hirschfeld (1913–1975) for some of the material from earlier editions prepared by him. In order to give the reader an even broader view of modern thought, various new selections have been added. With respect to these, I am especially grateful to a number of my colleagues at Michigan State University for their excellent suggestions. With respect to some of the older selections, in which the language is unclear or now out-of-date, I have modernized the texts where permissible. Explanatory footnotes have been kept, as readers have found them helpful in better understanding certain passages or ideas. I also wish to thank Thomas H. Greer, the general editor of the *Classics* series, for the invaluable advice and assistance he gave in all matters concerning this edition.

The additional selections for *The Modern World* include new excerpts from the writings of Galileo Galilei, Jean Jacques Rousseau, Cesare Beccaria, Henry David Thoreau, John Stuart Mill, Charles Darwin, Albert Einstein, Sigmund Freud, Carl G. Jung, and Virginia Woolf.

Henrik Ibsen's *Hedda Gabler* adds a drama that continues to fascinate audiences of the Western world. In regard to writings retained from the previous edition, significant extensions have been made in the selections by Adam Smith, Alexis de Tocqueville, and Adolf Hitler. From among the many poets who gave expression to their own experience and time, new poems have been included—by William Wordsworth, Heinrich Heine, John McCrae, Siegfried Sassoon, Wilfred Owen, Ivan Goll, W. H. Auden, and Louis Untermeyer. I strongly believe that these revisions in *The Modern World* will make this Fourth Edition even more valuable to the reader than previous editions were.

Edgar E. Knoebel

Contents

CLASSICS OF WESTERN THOUGHT

Volume
III

The Modern World

FOURTH EDITION

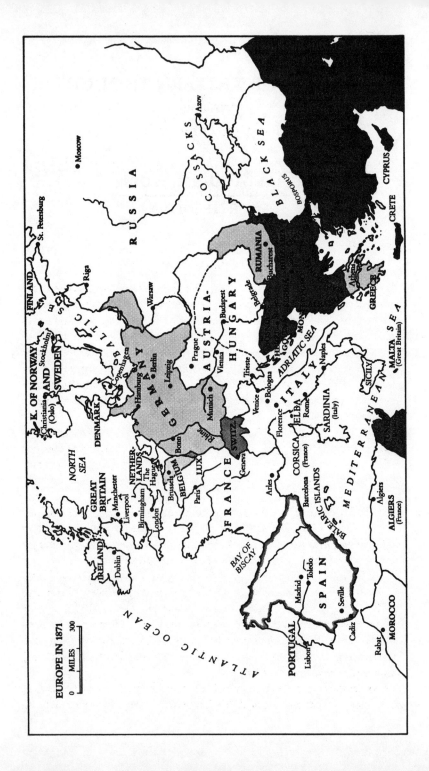

EUROPE IN 1871

0   MILES   300

ATLANTIC OCEAN

RUSSIA

• Moscow

FINLAND

St. Petersburg

K. OF NORWAY AND SWEDEN

Stockholm
Christiania (Oslo)

BALTIC SEA

Riga

Warsaw

DENMARK

Copenhagen

Hamburg • Berlin
G E R M A N Y
Leipzig

Prague •

AUSTRIA-HUNGARY

Vienna
Munich •
Budapest

Belgrade •

RUMANIA
Bucharest •

COSSACKS

BLACK SEA

BOSPORUS

Azov

CRETE

CYPRUS

Athens •
GREECE

MALTA (Great Britain)

NORTH SEA

GREAT BRITAIN

Manchester •
Liverpool •
Birmingham •
London •

IRELAND

Dublin •

NETHER-LANDS
The Hague •
Brussels •
BELGIUM
LUX.
Paris •

F R A N C E

Bonn •
Rhine
SWITZ.
Geneva •

Venice •
Trieste •
ADRIATIC SEA

Bologna •
Florence •
ELBA
Rome •
I T A L Y
Naples •

SICILY

MEDITERRANEAN SEA

CORSICA (France)
SARDINIA (Italy)

Arles •

Barcelona •
BALEARIC ISLANDS

Algiers •
ALGIERS (France)

BAY OF BISCAY

SPAIN
Madrid •
Toledo •
Seville •
Cadiz •

PORTUGAL
Lisbon •

MOROCCO
Rabat •

1

Galileo Galilei

Dialogue Concerning the Two Chief World Systems

*T*HE *major development in the Modern World that distinguishes it from all previous eras—in both the East and the West—is the Scientific Revolution of the seventeenth century. It created a different view of the earth and its place in the heavens, and a new method for finding reliable, useful knowledge. Modern science has drawn upon intellectual roots reaching back to the ancient Greek thinkers, and it has expanded enormously in technique and scope from the seventeenth century until the present. But that century was clearly the one that set Western civilization upon a new and irreversible course.*

Many inquiring minds contributed to this astonishing achievement. They did so by placing greater emphasis upon direct observation of natural phenomena and on novel ways of thinking about facts. Francis Bacon and René Descartes (see selections 2 and 3) were among the leaders in constructing the scientific method. *And one of the first to study phenomena by* direct observation, *using the just-invented telescope, was the astronomer and physicist, Galileo Galilei (1564–1642). Although he performed a great variety of scientific investigations, he is doubtless best remembered for his proofs and arguments for the heliocentric* (sun-centered) *theory of our solar system.*

The heliocentric theory had been advanced (and rejected) in ancient times, but it was revived just a century before Galileo's time by Nicolaus Copernicus (1473–1543), a Polish mathematician-astronomer. He supported it with mathematical data that others had collected, over time, concerning planetary motions. However, since Copernicus lacked conclusive observational data, and since his theory contradicted the age-old and accepted geocentric (earth-centered) *theory, his view did not take hold.*

It remained for the proud Italian, Galileo, with his simple instruments of observation, to establish proofs for the Copernican theory. For many years he kept quiet about his findings, because he had been ordered by Catholic Church authorities to refrain from teaching or defending the Copernican view. The Catholic officials, as well as the new Protestant leaders, condemned the heliocentric theory because it contradicted Holy Scripture and Christian teachings. Nevertheless, when he was about sixty years old, Galileo at last put his ideas down in writing, in the form of a pretended dialogue (debate). This four-day discourse covered a number of topics, including the merits of the two opposing theories of the solar system. He permitted this to be published in 1632—under the title Dialogue Concerning the Two Chief World Systems.

Galileo's book was promptly put on the Index (list) of works forbidden by the Church, and he was summoned to Rome to stand trial for writing it. He was, finally, condemned by the Church court and sentenced to house arrest for life. In a villa near the city of Florence, he continued his scientific investigations in physics (the laws of motion) until his death nine years later in 1642.

Galileo made his mark as a brilliant pioneer of modern science. His findings not only contributed to the emerging method, but had enormous impact upon the way humans saw themselves in the universe. His proofs for the Copernican system dissolved for all time many fundamental and deeply-held convictions in religion and philosophy, as well as in physics.

The following selection contains two excerpts from Galileo's famous Dialogue, namely, the introduction addressed "To the Discerning Reader," and the discussion on the "Third Day." In the first excerpt, Galileo comments on the concern of the Church about the Copernican theory and tells what subjects he will deal with in the dialogue. In the second excerpt, through a principal character in the discussion (Salviati), he explains and supports the Copernican theory. Interestingly, Galileo assumed that the planets travel around the sun in circular orbits, thus ignoring Johann Kepler's "First Law," published in 1609, which states that the orbits are, in fact, elliptical.

TO THE DISCERNING READER

Several years ago there was published in Rome a salutary edit[1] which, in order to obviate the dangerous tendencies of our present age, im-

[1]A Church decree to correct fault and promote truth.

DIALOGUE CONCERNING THE TWO CHIEF WORLD SYSTEMS   Galileo Galilei, Dialogue Concerning the Two Chief World Systems—Ptolemaic & Copernican, trans. Stillman Drake (Berkeley: University of California Press, 1967), 5–7, 388–92, 476. Copyright © 1962 The Regents of the University of California. Reprinted with permission.

posed a seasonable silence upon the Pythagorean[2] opinion that the earth moves. There were those who impudently asserted that this decree had its origin not in judicious inquiry, but in passion none too well informed. Complaints were to be heard that advisers who were totally unskilled at astronomical observations ought not to clip the wings of reflective intellects by means of rash prohibitions.

Upon hearing such carping insolence, my zeal could not be contained. Being thoroughly informed about that prudent determination, I decided to appear openly in the theater of the world as a witness of the sober truth. I was at that time in Rome; I was not only received by the most eminent prelates of that Court, but had their applause; indeed, this decree was not published without some previous notice of it having been given to me. Therefore I propose in the present work to show to foreign nations that as much is understood of this matter in Italy, and particularly in Rome, as transalpine diligence can ever have imagined. Collecting all the reflections that properly concern the Copernican system, I shall make it known that everything was brought before the attention of the Roman censorship, and that there proceed from this clime not only dogmas for the welfare of the soul, but ingenious discoveries for the delight of the mind as well.

To this end I have taken the Copernican side in the discourse, proceeding as with a pure mathematical hypothesis and striving by every artifice to represent it as superior to supposing the earth motionless—not, indeed, absolutely, but as against the arguments of some professed Peripatetics.[3] These men indeed deserve not even that name, for they do not walk about; they are content to adore the shadows, philosophizing not with due circumspection but merely from having memorized a few ill-understood principles.

Three principal headings are treated. First, I shall try to show that all experiments practicable upon the earth are insufficient measures for proving its mobility, since they are indifferently adaptable to an earth in motion or at rest. I hope in so doing to reveal many observations unknown to the ancients. Secondly, the celestial phenomena will be examined, strengthening the Copernican hypothesis until it might seem that this must triumph absolutely. Here new reflections are ad-

[2]Pythagoras, a Greek thinker of the sixth century B.C., was credited wrongly by Copernicus with the suggestion of a heliocentric (sun-centered) astronomy.

[3]The term applied to followers of Aristotle because of that philosopher's custom of strolling about the Lyceum while discoursing with his disciples. Meant here are the philosophers of Galileo's day.

joined which might be used in order to simplify astronomy, though not because of any necessity imposed by nature. In the third place, I shall propose an ingenious speculation. It happens that long ago I said that the unsolved problem of the ocean tides might receive some light from assuming the motion of the earth. This assertion of mine, passing by word of mouth, found loving fathers who adopted it as a child of their own ingenuity. Now, so that no stranger may ever appear who, arming himself with our weapons, shall charge us with want of attention to such an important matter, I have thought it good to reveal those probabilities which might render this plausible, given that the earth moves.

I hope that from these considerations the world will come to know that if other nations have navigated more, we have not theorized less. It is not from failing to take count of what others have thought that we have yielded to asserting that the earth is motionless, and holding the contrary to be a mere mathematical caprice, but (if for nothing else) for those reasons that are supplied by piety, religion, the knowledge of Divine Omnipotence, and a consciousness of the limitations of the human mind.

I have thought it most appropriate to explain these concepts in the form of dialogues, which, not being restricted to the rigorous observance of mathematical laws, make room also for digressions which are sometimes no less interesting than the principal argument.

Many years ago I was often to be found in the marvelous city of Venice, in discussions with Signore Giovanni Francesco Sagredo,[4] a man of noble extraction and trenchant wit. From Florence came Signore Filippo Salviati,[5] the least of whose glories were the eminence of his blood and the magnificence of his fortune. His was a sublime intellect which fed no more hungrily upon any pleasure than it did upon fine meditations. I often talked with these two of such matters in the presence of a certain Peripatetic philosopher[6] whose greatest obstacle in

---

[4]Sagredo, born at Venice in 1571, was a pupil of Galileo's at Padua and perhaps his closest friend. In the *Dialogue* he represents the educated layman for whose favorable opinion the two experts are striving.

[5]Salviati was born at Florence in 1582, of an ancient and noble family of that city. Little is known of his life. He is believed to have studied under Galileo at Padua and in the *Dialogue*, Salviati represents Galileo himself as the expert in science.

[6]A composite of the professional and amateur philosophers and literary men of Galileo's day. In the *Dialogue* his name is Simplicio; he is the expert in philosophy and the adversary of Salviati.

apprehending the truth seemed to be the reputation he had acquired by his interpretations of Aristotle.

Now, since bitter death has deprived Venice and Florence of those two great luminaries in the very meridian of their years, I have resolved to make their fame live on in these pages, so far as my poor abilities will permit, by introducing them as interlocutors in the present argument. . . . May it please those two great souls, ever venerable to my heart, to accept this public monument of my undying love. And may the memory of their eloquence assist me in delivering to posterity the promised reflections.

It happened that several discussions had taken place casually at various times among these gentlemen, and had rather whetted than satisfied their thirst for learning. Hence very wisely they resolved to meet together on certain days during which, setting aside all other business, they might apply themselves more methodically to the contemplation of the wonders of God in the heavens and upon the earth. They met in the palace of the illustrious Sagredo; and, after the customary but brief exchange of compliments, Salviati commenced. . . .

• • •

The Third Day

• • •

SALVIATI. Being at a villa of mine near Florence, I plainly observed the arrival of the sun at the summer solstice and its subsequent departure. For one evening at its setting it hid itself behind a cliff in the Pietrapana Mountains, about sixty miles away, leaving only a small shred of itself revealed to the north, the breadth of which was not the hundredth part of its diameter. But the following evening, at the same position of setting, it left a like part of itself showing which was noticeably thinner. This is a conclusive proof that it had commenced to move away from the tropic; yet the sun's return between the first and second observations surely did not amount to one second of arc along the horizon. Making the observation later with a fine telescope which would multiply the disc of the sun more than a thousandfold turned out to be pleasant and easy.

Now my idea is for us to make our observations of the fixed stars with similar instruments, utilizing some star in which the changes would be conspicuous. . . . I have already been looking by myself for a place well adapted for such observations. The place is an open plain, above which there rises to the north a very prominent mountain, at the summit of which is built a little chapel facing west and east, so that the ridgepole of its roof may cut at right angles the meridian over some house situated in the plain. I wish to affix a beam parallel to that ridgepole and about a yard above it. This done, I shall seek in the plain that place from which one of the stars of the Big Dipper is hidden by this beam which I have placed, just when the star crosses the meridian. Or else, if the beam is not large enough to hide the star, I shall find the place from which the disc of the star is seen to be cut in half by the beam—an effect which can be discerned perfectly by means of a fine telescope. It will be very convenient if there happens to be some house at the place from which this event can be perceived, but if not, then I shall drive a stick firmly into the ground and affix a mark to indicate where the eye is to be placed whenever the observation is to be repeated. I shall make the first of these observations at the summer solstice, in order to continue them from month to month, or whenever I please, until the other solstice.

By means of such observations, the star's rising or lowering can be perceived no matter how small it may be. And if in the course of these operations any such variation shall happen to become known, how great an achievement will be made in astronomy! For by this means, besides ascertaining the annual motion, we shall be able to gain a knowledge of the size and distance of that same star.

SAGREDO. I thoroughly understand the whole procedure, and the operations seem to me to be so easy and so well adapted to what is wanted, that it may very reasonably be believed that Copernicus himself, or some other astronomer, has actually performed them.

SALVIATI. It seems the other way around to me, for it is improbable that if anyone had tried this he would not have mentioned the result, whichever opinion it turned out to favor. But no one is known to have availed himself of this method, for the above or for any other purpose; and without a fine telescope it could not very well be put into effect.

SAGREDO. What you say completely satisfies me.

Now, since quite a while remains until the night, if you want me to find any rest then, I hope it will not be too much trouble for you to explain to us those problems which a little while ago you asked us to put off until tomorrow. Please give us back the reprieve which we extended to you, and abandoning all other arguments explain to us how (assuming the motions which Copernicus attributes to the earth, and keeping immovable the sun and the fixed stars) such events may follow as pertain to the elevation and lowering of the sun, the changing of the seasons, and the inequalities of nights and days, in just the way that is so easily understood to take place in the Ptolemaic system.

SALVIATI. I must not and cannot refuse anything which Sagredo pleads for. The delay that I requested was only to give me time to rearrange in my mind the premises which are useful for a clear and comprehensive explanation of the manner in which these events take place in the Copernican as well as in the Ptolemaic system. Indeed, more easily and simply in the former than in the latter, so that it may be clearly seen that the former hypothesis is as easy for nature to put into effect as it is hard for the intellect to comprehend. Nevertheless I hope, by utilizing explanations other than those resorted to by Copernicus, to make even the learning of it very much less obscure. In order to do this, I shall set forth some assumptions as known and self-evident, as follows:

First. I assume that the earth is a spherical body which rotates about its own axis and poles, and that every point on its surface traces out the circumference of a circle, greater or lesser according as the designated point is more or less distant from the poles. Of these circles, that one is greatest which is traced out by a point equidistant from the poles. All these circles are parallel to one another, and we shall refer to them as *parallels*.

Second. The earth being spherical in shape and its material being opaque, half its surface is continually lighted and the rest is dark. The boundary which separates the lighted part from the dark being a great circle, we shall call this the *boundary circle of light*.

Third. when the boundary circle of light passes through the earth's poles it will cut all the parallels into equal sections, it being a great circle; but, not passing through the poles, it will cut them all into unequal parts except the central circle; this, being also a great circle, will be cut into equal parts in any case.

Fourth. Since the earth turns about its own poles, the length of day and night is determined by the arcs of the parallels cut by the boundary circle of light. The arc which remains in the illuminated hemisphere determines the length of the day, and the remainder that of the night.

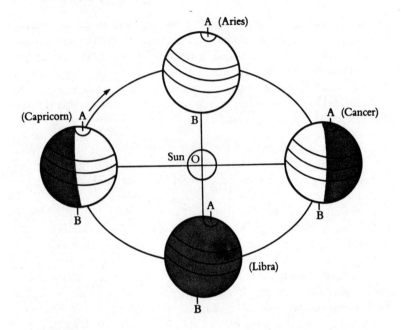

These things being set forth, we may wish to draw a diagram for a clearer understanding of what comes next. First let us indicate the circumference of a circle, to represent for us the orbit of the earth, described in the plane of the ecliptic.[7] This we may divide by two diameters into four equal parts; Capricorn, Cancer, Libra, and Aries,[8] which shall here represent at the same time the four cardinal points; that is, the two solstices[9] and the two equinoxes.[10] And in the center of this circle, let us denote the sun, O, fixed and immovable.

Now with the four points Capricorn, Cancer, Libra, and Aries as centers, we shall draw four equal circles which to us will represent the earth at these four different seasons. The center of the earth travels in the space of a year around the whole circumference Capricorn–Aries–Cancer–Libra, moving from west to east in the order of the signs of the

[7]The ecliptic is the apparent annual path of the sun among the stars, as seen from the earth.

[8]Names of four sections of the zodiac (an imaginary band around the sky, straddling the ecliptic, and divided into twelve sections).

[9]Two points in the earth's orbit when the sun is the farthest, either north or south, from the equator.

[10]Two points in the earth's orbit when the sun stands directly above the equator.

zodiac. It is already evident that when the earth is in Capricorn the sun will appear in Cancer; the earth moving along the arc from Capricorn to Aries, the sun will appear to be moving along the arc from Cancer to Libra. In a word, it will run through the signs of the zodiac in their order during the space of a year. So with this first assumption, the apparent annual motion of the sun around the ecliptic is satisfied beyond any argument.

Coming now to the other movement—that is, the diurnal [daily] motion of the earth about itself—its poles and axis must be established. These must be understood to be not perpendicularly erect to the plane of the ecliptic; that is, not parallel to the axis of the earth's orbit, but inclined from right angles about twenty-three and one-half degrees, with the North Pole toward the axis of the earth's orbit when the center of the earth is at the solstitial point in Capricorn. Assuming, then, that the center of the terrestrial globe is at that point, let us indicate the poles and the axis AB, tilted twenty-three and one-half degrees from the perpendicular on the Capricorn–Cancer diameter, . . . and this inclination must be assumed to be immutable. We shall take the upper pole, A, to be the north, and the other, B, the south.

• • •

2

Francis Bacon

The New Scientific Method

*F*RANCIS *Bacon (1561–1626), a contemporary of Shakespeare and Queen Elizabeth, was a true "man of the Renaissance." Versatile, ambitious, and unscrupulous, he was a man of affairs as well as a man of letters and a philosopher. Bacon attained the high office of Lord Chancellor under James I, but was impeached and found guilty of taking bribes, and died in disgrace. His* Essays *won him literary fame; however, his reputation rests largely on his work as the philosopher of scientific method who rejected the views of the Middle Ages and looked forward to the general acceptance of the new science, which would give human beings power over nature. A prophet of the scientific revolution of the seventeenth century, he thus helped to usher in a new age. In his philosophical works, Bacon attacked the deductive methods of scholasticism and formulated new principles of acquiring true and useful knowledge of the world through empiricism. He insisted on the necessity of direct observation of nature as the only way to know truth. The purpose of such knowledge was power, power to control nature and thereby advance the welfare of humanity. Bacon thus anticipated the eighteenth-century faith that human beings could master their own destiny.*

Bacon's New Organon *(1620), or method of scientific inquiry, was intended to replace the old* Organon *of Aristotle. In this work, which consists of a series of aphorisms, or short statements, Bacon analyzes the shortcomings of deductive, a priori methods of inquiry and proposes the inductive method, based on the direct observation of nature. While his formulation lacked precision and underrated the value of hypotheses, it was a significant attempt to free people from their barren prejudices, faulty thinking, loose use of language, and vain fictions, and to encourage them to go directly to nature to discover its secrets. The following selection features a number of Bacon's most significant aphorisms.*

Man, being the servant and interpreter of Nature, can do and understand so much and so much only as he has observed in fact or in thought of the course of nature. Beyond this he neither knows anything nor can do anything.

• • •

Human knowledge and human power meet in one; for where the cause is not known the effect cannot be produced. Nature to be commanded must be obeyed; and that which in contemplation is as the cause is in operation as the rule.

• • •

Moreover, the works already known are due to chance and experiment rather than to sciences; for the sciences we now possess are merely systems for the nice ordering and setting forth of things already invented, not methods of invention or directions for new works.

• • •

As the sciences which we now have do not help us in finding out new works, so neither does the logic which we now have help us in finding out new sciences.

• • •

The logic now in use serves rather to fix and give stability to the errors which have their foundation in commonly received notions than to help the search after truth. So it does more harm than good.

• • •

The discoveries which have hitherto been made in the sciences are such as lie close to vulgar notions,[1] scarcely beneath the surface. In order to penetrate into the inner and further recesses of nature, it is necessary that both notions and axioms[2] be derived from things by a

---

[1]Popular ideas unsupported by evidence or reason.

[2]Established principles universally recognized as true.

THE NEW SCIENTIFIC METHOD   Reprinted with permission of Macmillan Publishing Company, from Francis Bacon, *The New Organon and Related Writings* edited by Fulton H. Anderson. Copyright © 1985 by Macmillan Publishing Company. Copyright © 1960 by The Bobbs-Merrill Company, 39–45, 47–49, 66, 78, 80, 87–89, 93, 96–97, 107.

more sure and guarded way, and that a method of intellectual operation be introduced altogether better and more certain.

• • •

There are and can be only two ways of searching into and discovering truth. The one flies from the senses and particulars to the most general axioms, and from these principles, the truth of which it takes for settled and immovable, proceeds to judgment and to the discovery of middle axioms. And this way is now in fashion. The other derives axioms from the senses and particulars, rising by a gradual and unbroken ascent, so that it arrives at the most general axioms last of all. This is the true way, but as yet untried.

• • •

It cannot be that axioms established by argumentation should avail for the discovery of new works, since the subtlety of nature is greater many times over than the subtlety of argument. But axioms duly and orderly formed from particulars easily discover the way to new particulars, and thus render sciences active.

• • •

The conclusions of human reason as ordinarily applied in matters of nature, I call for the sake of distinction *Anticipations of Nature* (as a thing rash or premature). That reason which is elicited from facts by a just and methodical process, I call *Interpretation of Nature*.

• • •

For the winning of assent, indeed, anticipations are far more powerful than interpretations, because being collected from a few instances, and those for the most part of familiar occurrence, they straightway touch the understanding and fill the imagination; whereas interpretations, on the other hand, being gathered here and there from very various and widely dispersed facts, cannot suddenly strike the understanding; and therefore they must needs, in respect of the opinions of the time, seem harsh and out of tune, much as the mysteries of faith do.

• • •

One method of delivery alone remains to us which is simply this: we must lead men to the particulars themselves, and their series and order;

while men on their side must force themselves for a while to lay their notions by and begin to familiarize themselves with facts.

• • •

The doctrine of those who have denied that certainty could be attained at all has some agreement with my way of proceeding at the first setting out; but they end in being infinitely separated and opposed. For the holders of that doctrine assert simply that nothing can be known. I also assert that not much can be known in nature by the way which is now in use. But then they go on to destroy the authority of the senses and understanding; whereas I proceed to devise and supply helps for the same.

• • •

The idols and false notions which are now in possession of the human understanding, and have taken deep root therein, not only so beset men's minds that truth can hardly find entrance, but even after entrance is obtained, they will again in the very instauration[3] of the sciences meet and trouble us, unless men being forewarned of the danger fortify themselves as far as may be against their assaults.

• • •

There are four classes of Idols which beset men's minds. To these for distinction's sake I have assigned names, calling the first class *Idols of the Tribe*; the second, *Idols of the Cave*; the third, *Idols of the Market Place*; the fourth, *Idols of the Theater*.

• • •

The Idols of the Tribe have their foundation in human nature itself, and in the tribe or race of men. For it is a false assertion that the sense of man is the measure of things. On the contrary, all perceptions as well of the sense as of the mind are according to the measure of the individual and not according to the measure of the universe. And the human understanding is like a false mirror, which, receiving rays irregularly, distorts and discolors the nature of things by mingling its own nature with it.

• • •

[3]Reconstruction.

The Idols of the Cave are the idols of the individual man. For everyone (besides the errors common to human nature in general) has a cave or den of his own, which refracts and discolors the light of nature, owing either to his own proper and peculiar nature; or to his education and conversation with others; or to the reading of books, and the authority of those whom he esteems and admires; or to the differences of impressions, accordingly as they take place in a mind preoccupied and predisposed or in a mind indifferent and settled; or the like. So that the spirit of man (according as it is meted out to different individuals) is in fact a thing variable and full of perturbation, and governed as it were by chance. Whence it was well observed by Heraclitus that men look for sciences in their own lesser worlds, and not in the greater or common world.

• • •

There are also Idols formed by the . . . association of men with each other, which I call Idols of the Market Place, on account of the commerce and consort of men there. For it is by discourse that men associate, and words are imposed according to the apprehension of the vulgar. And therefore the ill and unfit choice of words wonderfully obstructs the understanding. Nor do the definitions or explanations wherewith in some things learned men are wont to guard and defend themselves, by any means set the matter right. But words plainly force and overrule the understanding, and throw all into confusion, and lead men away into numberless empty controversies and idle fancies.

• • •

Lastly, there are Idols which have immigrated into men's minds from the various dogmas of philosophies, and also from wrong laws of demonstration. These I call Idols of the Theater, because in my judgment all the received systems are but so many stage plays, representing worlds of their own creation after an unreal and scenic fashion. Nor is it only of the systems now in vogue, or only of the ancient sects and philosophies, that I speak; for many more plays of the same kind may yet be composed and in like artificial manner set forth; seeing that errors the most widely different have nevertheless causes for the most part alike. Neither again do I mean this only of entire systems, but also of many principles and axioms in science, which by tradition, credulity, and negligence have come to be received.

• • •

So much concerning the several classes of Idols and their equipage,[4] all of which must be renounced and put away with a fixed and solemn determination, and the understanding thoroughly freed and cleansed; the entrance into the kingdom of man, founded on the sciences, being not much other than the entrance into the kingdom of heaven, where-into none may enter except as a little child.

• • •

Again there is another great and powerful cause why the sciences have made but little progress, which is this. It is not possible to run a course aright when the goal itself has not been rightly placed. Now the true and lawful goal of the sciences is none other than this: that human life be endowed with new discoveries and powers. But of this the great majority have no feeling, but are merely hireling and professorial; except when it occasionally happens that some workman of acuter wit and covetous of honor applies himself to a new invention, which he mostly does at the expense of his fortunes. But in general, so far are men from proposing to themselves to augment the mass of arts and sciences, that from the mass already at hand they neither take nor look for anything more than what they may turn to use in their lectures, or to gain, or to reputation, or to some similar advantage. And if any one out of all the multitude court science with honest affection and for her own sake, yet even with him the object will be found to be rather the variety of contemplations and doctrines than the severe and rigid search after truth. And if by chance there be one who seeks after truth in earnest, yet even he will propose to himself such a kind of truth as shall yield satisfaction to the mind and understanding in rendering causes for things long since discovered, and not the truth which shall lead to new assurance of works and new light of axioms. If then the end of the sciences has not as yet been well placed, it is not strange that men have erred as to the means.

• • •

This evil, however, has been strangely increased by an opinion or conceit, which though of long standing is vain and hurtful, namely, that the dignity of the human mind is impaired by long and close intercourse with experiments and particulars, subject to sense and bound in matter; especially as they are laborious to search, ignoble to

[4]Accompanying "baggage."

meditate, harsh to deliver, illiberal to practice, infinite in number, and minute in subtlety. So that it has come at length to this, that the true way is not merely deserted, but shut out and stopped up; experience being, I do not say abandoned or badly managed, but rejected with disdain.

• • •

Neither is it to be forgotten that in every age natural philosophy has had a troublesome and hard to deal with adversary—namely, superstition, and the blind and immoderate zeal of religion. For we see among the Greeks that those who first proposed to men's then uninitiated ears the natural causes for thunder and for storms were thereupon found guilty of impiety. Nor was much more forbearance shown by some of the ancient fathers of the Christian church to those who on most convincing grounds (such as no one in his senses would now think of contradicting) maintained that the earth was round, and of consequence asserted the existence of the antipodes.[5]

Moreover, as things now are, the discourse of nature is made harder and more perilous by the summaries and systems of the schoolmen[6] who, having reduced theology into regular order as well as they were able, and fashioned it into the shape of an art, ended in incorporating the contentious and thorny philosophy of Aristotle,[7] more than was fit, with the body of religion.

To the same result, though in a different way, tend the speculations of those who have taken upon them to deduce the truth of the Christian religion from the principles of philosophers, and to confirm it by their authority, pompously solemnizing this union of the sense and faith as a lawful marriage, and entertaining men's minds with a pleasing variety of matter, but all the while disparaging things divine by mingling them with things human. Now in such mixtures of theology with philosophy only the received doctrines of philosophy are included; while new ones, albeit changes for the better, are all but expelled and exterminated.

Lastly, you will find that by the simpleness of certain divines,[8] access

---

[5] Any two places on the globe that are diametrically opposite.
[6] Medieval "scholastic" philosophers.
[7] Greek philosopher (384–322 B.C.) regarded as "The Philosopher" of antiquity.
[8] Clergy, theologians.

to any philosophy, however pure, is well-nigh closed. Some are weakly afraid lest a deeper search into nature should transgress the permitted limits of sober-mindedness, wrongfully wresting and transferring what is said in Holy Writ[9] against those who pry into sacred mysteries,[10] to the hidden things of nature, which are barred by no prohibition. Others with more subtlety surmise and reflect that if second causes are unknown everything can more readily be referred to the divine hand and rod, a point in which they think religion greatly concerned—which is in fact nothing else but to seek to gratify God with a lie. Others fear from past example that movements and changes in philosophy will end in assaults on religion. And others again appear apprehensive that in the investigation of nature something may be found to subvert or at least shake the authority of religion, especially with the unlearned. But these two last fears seem to me to savor utterly of carnal wisdom; as if men in the recesses and secret thought of their hearts doubted and distrusted the strength of religion and the empire of faith over the sense, and therefore feared that the investigation of truth in nature might be dangerous to them. But if the matter be truly considered, natural philosophy is, after the word of God, at once the surest medicine against superstition and the most approved nourishment for faith, and therefore she is rightly given to religion as her most faithful handmaid, since the one displays the will of God, the other his power. For he did not err who said, "Ye err in that ye know not the Scriptures and the power of God," thus coupling and blending in an indissoluble bond information concerning his will and meditation concerning his power. Meanwhile it is not surprising if the growth of natural philosophy is checked when religion, the thing which has most power over men's minds, has by the simpleness and incautious zeal of certain persons been drawn to take part against her.

• • •

Those who have handled sciences have been either men of experiment or men of dogmas. The men of experiment are like the ant, they only collect and use; the reasoners resemble spiders, who make cobwebs out of their own substance. But the bee takes a middle course: it gathers its material from the flowers of the garden and of the field, but

[9]Sacred Scriptures: the Bible.
[10]Profound secrets, claimed to be beyond human comprehension.

transforms and digests it by a power of its own. Not unlike this is the true business of philosophy; for it neither relies solely or chiefly on the powers of the mind, nor does it take the matter which it gathers from natural history and mechanical experiments and lay it up in the memory whole, as it finds it, but lays it up in the understanding altered and digested. Therefore from a closer and purer league between these two faculties, the experimental and the rational (such as has never yet been made), much may be hoped.

• • •

But not only is a greater abundance of experiments to be sought for and procured, and that too of a different kind from those hitherto tried; an entirely different method, order, and process for carrying on and advancing experience must also be introduced. For experience, when it wanders in its own track, is, as I have already remarked, mere groping in the dark, and confounds men rather than instructs them. But when it shall proceed in accordance with a fixed law, in regular order, and without interruption, then may better things be hoped of knowledge.

• • •

Moreover, since there is so great a number and army of particulars, and that army so scattered and dispersed as to distract and confound the understanding, little is to be hoped for from the skirmishings and slight attacks and desultory movements of the intellect, unless all the particulars which pertain to the subject of inquiry shall, by means of Tables of Discovery, apt, well arranged, and, as it were, animate, be drawn up and marshaled; and the mind be set to work upon the helps duly prepared and digested which these tables supply.

And as I do not seek to found a school, so neither do I hold out offers or promises of particular works. It may be thought, indeed, that I who make such frequent mention of works and refer everything to that end, should produce some myself by way of earnest. But my course and method, as I have often clearly stated and would wish to state again, is this—not to extract works from works or experiments from experiments (as an empiric),[11] but from works and experiments to extract causes and axioms, and again from those causes and axioms new works

---

[11] A person who relies solely on practical experience.

and experiments, as a legitimate interpreter of nature. And although in my tables of discovery, and also in the examples of particulars, and moreover in my observations on the history, any reader of even moderate sagacity and intelligence will everywhere observe indications and outlines of many noble works; still I candidly confess that the natural history which I now have, whether collected from books or from my own investigations, is neither sufficiently copious nor verified with sufficient accuracy to serve the purposes of legitimate interpretation.

• • •

3

René Descartes

Discourse on Method

*I*F *Bacon stressed the empirical element
in scientific inquiry, René Descartes (1596–1650), a French mathematician
and philosopher, established the necessity for a rigorous, rational analysis and
explanation of natural phenomena. A more profound and precise thinker than
Bacon, Descartes was the mathematical genius who worked out the new
discipline of analytic geometry. Descartes' philosophical work ranged, with
typical French clarity, over the fields of metaphysics, ethics, and psychology,
and he is generally considered the founder of modern philosophy. His emphasis
on mathematical methods of reasoning, on one hand, gave contemporary scientists a means of guaranteeing the certainty of their knowledge of the physical
universe. On the other hand, his metaphysical thought was to establish a
rational basis for religious belief. In fact, he attributed his insights, scientific and
metaphysical alike, to divine revelations made to him in a series of dreams. But
the Christian churches thought otherwise and condemned his work. What most
inspired ecclesiastical displeasure was Descartes' dualism—his belief that mind
and matter are essentially different substances subject to different laws. It was
this philosophical dualism that enabled him to separate scientific inquiry from
religious thought and to treat the world of nature as a mechanical one, operating
strictly according to mathematical law.*

The following selection from the Discourse on Method *(1637), the most
important of Descartes' philosophical writings, provides a superb demonstration
of Cartesian dualism. Descartes began his inquiry into the phenomena tangible
to human existence with the deliberate rejection of all previous knowledge,
opinions, and customs. In addition, before accepting replacements, he worked
out four steps of inquiry considered to be the true method; these were to be an
unfailing safeguard against any and all errors that might otherwise impede his
discovery of truth. For Descartes, assurance that he was not deceived in this*

process resided in his ability to doubt. *And he concluded that since he doubted, he must exist—or, even more pointedly, that since he was capable of thinking, he existed.*

At a certain point in his work, Descartes must have realized that his method was not an adequate tool for an inquiry into whether or not God exists. The strict application of the method in this specific instance might have resulted in the denial of a divine existence. Since Descartes rejected atheism, for reasons of upbringing as well as inclination, he saw himself compelled to find a way in which to prove that God exists. Thus developed the following line of thought: Descartes reasoned that it was impossible that he could have received the notion of God from nothing; nor could he accept that he had developed this notion within himself. Much rather, his ability to think of something more perfect than himself reassured him that some more perfect being existed. *In addition, the feeling that he was dependent upon this being and that he had received from it all he possessed added to his certainty about God's existence. Having investigated this topic at length, Descartes concluded that God's existence is at least as certain as any demonstration of geometry.*

The dualism in his philosophy caused Descartes to be attacked and defamed by scientists as well as by religious leaders. The former accused him of having propped up religion, while the latter, Roman Catholics and Protestants alike, charged him with having laid an ax to the very roots of Christian religion. No wonder that Descartes, who above everything else cherished a quiet existence, felt forced to spend a significant portion of his lifetime corresponding with his detractors, trying to convince them that they had either misread or misunderstood his works.

VARIOUS THOUGHTS CONCERNING THE SCIENCES

Good sense is, of all things among men, the most equally distributed; for everyone thinks himself so abundantly endowed with it, that even those who are the most difficult to satisfy in everything else, do not usually desire a larger measure of this quality than they already possess. And in this it is not likely that all are mistaken: their conviction seems rather to show that the power of judging correctly and of distin-

DISCOURSE ON METHOD   Adapted by editor, from René Descartes, *Discourse on Method*, in *The Method, Meditations and Philosophy of Descartes*, trans. John Veitch (New York: Tudor, 1901), 149, 155, 159–64, 170–76, 193–94.

guishing truth from error, which is properly called good sense or reason, is by nature equal in all men. The diversity of our opinions, consequently, does not arise from some having a larger share of reason than others, but solely from this, that we conduct our thoughts along different ways, and do not fix our attention on the same objects. For to possess a keen mind is not enough; the principal requirement is to use it correctly. The greatest minds, as they are capable of the highest virtues, are open likewise to the greatest vices; and those who travel very slowly may yet make far greater progress, provided they keep always on the straight road, than those who, while they run, take the wrong road. . . .

It is true that, while studying the customs of other men, I found here, too, scarcely any ground for firm conviction, and noticed hardly fewer contradictions among them than in the opinions of the philosophers. The greatest advantage I derived from my study was this: although observing many customs which seem extravagant and ridiculous to us, are by common consent accepted and approved by other great nations. I also learned not to hold on too firmly to those truths which I had accepted merely by example and custom. Thus I gradually liberated myself from many errors powerful enough to cloud our natural intelligence, and keep us in great measure from listening to reason. But after I had spent several years studying the book of nature, and in trying to gather some experience, I finally decided to make *myself* an object of study, and to use all the powers of my mind in choosing the paths I ought to follow. This endeavor was accompanied with greater success than it would have been had I never left my country or my books.

THE PRINCIPAL RULES OF THE METHOD

. . . I had become aware, as early as my college days, that no opinion, however absurd and incredible can be imagined, that has not been held by one of the philosophers; and afterward in the course of my travels I noticed that all those whose opinions are disagreeable to ours are not for that reason barbarians or savages, but on the contrary many of these nations make an equally good, if not a better, use of their reason than we do. I also took into account the very different character which a person exhibits, who was brought up in France or Germany, from that which this individual would have possessed had he lived always among the Chinese or among the savages. Fashions which would have pleased us ten years ago, and which may again, perhaps, please us after another ten years, appear to us at this time extravagant and ridiculous. I thus concluded that the foundation of our opinions is far more custom and example than any certain knowledge. And, finally, although this is the foundation of our opinions, I noticed that the approval by the majority is no guarantee of that truth that is difficult to discover, and in such cases it is much more likely that truth will be found by one person than by many. I could, however, select from the crowd no one whose opinions seemed worthy of preference and thus I found myself compelled to use my own reason in the conduct of my life. . . .

Among the branches of philosophy, I had, at an earlier period, given some attention to logic, and among those of mathematics, to geometrical analysis and algebra,—three arts or sciences which ought to contribute something to my design. But, on examination, I found that logic . . . is useful more in the communication of what we already know, . . . than in the investigation of the unknown; . . . These considerations caused me to seek some other method which would have the advantages of the three and not their defects. And as a multitude of laws often hampers justice, so that a state is best governed when, with few laws, these are rigidly administered; in like manner, instead of the great number of rules of which logic is composed, I believed that the four following would prove sufficient for me, provided I took the firm and unwavering resolution never in a single instance to fail in observing them.

The first was never to accept anything as true which I did not clearly know to be such; that is to say, carefully to avoid haste and prejudgment, and to accept nothing as true except what was presented to my mind so clearly and distinctly as to exclude all possibility of doubt.

The second, to divide each of the difficulties under examination into as many parts as possible, and as might be necessary for its adequate solution.

The third, to conduct my thoughts in such order that, by commencing with objects that were the simplest and easiest to know, I might rise little by little, step by step, to the knowledge of the more complex; assigning in thought a certain order even to those objects which in their own nature do not reveal a natural progression.

Finally, in every case to make enumerations so complete, and reviews so general, that I might be assured that nothing was omitted.

The long chains of simple and easy reasonings by which geometers reach the conclusions of their most difficult demonstrations, had led me

to imagine that all things, to the knowledge of which man is competent, are mutually connected in the same way. And that there is nothing
so far removed from us as to be beyond our reach, or so hidden that we
cannot discover it, provided only we refuse to accept the false for the
true, and always preserve in our thoughts the order necessary for the
deduction of one truth from another. And I had little difficulty in
determining the objects with which it was necessary to commence, for I
was already persuaded that it must be with the simplest and easiest to
know. Considering that of all those who until now have sought truth in
the sciences, the mathematicians alone have been able to find any
demonstrations, that is, any certain and evident reasons, I, therefore,
did not doubt but that such must have been the rule of their investigations. I resolved to commence, therefore, with the examination of the
simplest objects, not anticipating, however, from this any advantage
other than accustoming my mind to the love and nourishment of truth,
and to a distaste for all reasonings that were unsound. I had no intention
of attempting to master all the particular sciences commonly called
mathematics; but observing that, however different their objects, they
all agree in considering only the various relations or proportions existing among those objects. I thought it best for my purpose to consider
these proportions in the most general form possible, without referring
them to any objects in particular, except as would facilitate the knowledge of them—and without restricting them to these, that afterward I
might be better able to apply them to every other class of objects to
which they are legitimately applicable. I saw further, that in order to
understand these relations I should sometimes have to consider them
one by one, and sometimes only to bear them in mind, or embrace
them in groups. And I thought that, in order the better to consider them
individually, I should view them as straight lines, because I could find
no objects more simple, or capable of being more distinctly represented
to my imagination and senses; and on the other hand, in order to retain
them in the memory, or hold a collection of them, I should express
them by certain symbols in the briefest possible form. In this way I
believed that I could borrow all that was best both in geometrical
analysis and in algebra, and correct all the defects of the one with the
help of the other.

And, as a matter of fact, the exact observation of these few rules gave
me . . . such ease in unraveling all the questions embraced in these two
sciences, that in the two or three months I devoted to their examination, not only did I reach solutions to questions I had formerly deemed

exceedingly difficult, but even in regard to questions the solution of which I continued to be ignorant, I was enabled, as it appeared to me, to determine the means whereby a solution was possible. These results came from the fact that I commenced with the simplest and most general truths, and that each truth discovered became a rule available in the discovery of subsequent ones. Nor in this perhaps shall I appear too conceited, if it be remembered that there is one for any particular problem, and whoever grasps this truth, knows all that on that point can be known. The child, for example, who has been instructed in the basics of arithmetic, and has made a particular addition according to rule, may be assured that he has found, with respect to the sum of the numbers before him, all that in this instance is within the reach of human genius. Now, in conclusion, the method which teaches adherence to the true order, and an exact enumeration of all the conditions of the thing sought includes all that gives certainty to the rules of arithmetic.

But the chief reason for my satisfaction with this method was the assurance I had of thereby exercising my reason in all matters, if not with absolute perfection, at least as well as was possible. And, besides, I was conscious that by its use my mind was becoming gradually accustomed to clearer and more distinct conceptions of its objects; and I hoped also, from not having restricted this method to any particular matter, to apply it to the difficulties of the other sciences, with no less success than to those of algebra. I should not, however, on this account have ventured at once to examine all the difficulties of the sciences which presented themselves to me, for this would have been contrary to the order prescribed in the method. Observing that such knowledge is dependent on principles borrowed from philosophy, in which I found nothing certain, I thought it necessary, first of all to endeavor to establish its principles. And because I observed, besides, that an inquiry of this kind was of greatest importance, and one in which haste and prejudgment were most to be feared, I thought that I ought not to attempt it till I had reached a more mature age (being at that time a mere twenty-three years of age). I should first of all use much of my time in preparation for the work, by first erasing from my mind all the false opinions I had acquired and then gather a variety of experiences to provide material for my reasoning, while exercising myself in my method with a view to increase my skill in applying it.

· · ·

PROOFS OF THE EXISTENCE OF GOD
AND THE HUMAN SOUL

I doubt if it is proper to make known my first reflections on this subject, for these are so metaphysical, and so uncommon that they might not be acceptable to everyone. And yet, that it may be judged whether the foundations that I have laid are sufficiently secure, I find myself compelled to refer to them. I had long before noticed that, in regard to practice, it is sometimes necessary to adopt, as if beyond doubt, opinions which we think are highly uncertain. But as I desired to give my attention solely to the search for truth, I thought that a procedure exactly the opposite was called for, and that I ought to reject as absolutely false all opinions in which I could have the least doubt, in order to ascertain whether afterward there remained anything in my belief that was wholly certain. Accordingly, seeing that our senses sometimes deceive us, I was willing to imagine that there existed nothing precisely as it appeared to us; and because some men err in reasoning, as well as in the simplest matters of geometry, I was convinced that I was as open to error as anyone else. I therefore rejected as false all the reasonings I had formerly taken as proofs. And finally, when I considered that the very same thoughts which we experience when awake may also be experienced when we are asleep, without anyone of them being true, I imagined that all the precepts that had ever entered into my mind when awake, had in them no more reality than the illusions of my dreams. But immediately after this I observed that, while I wished to think that all was false, it was absolutely necessary that I, who thus thought, must be something; and when I observed that this truth, *I think, therefore I am,* was so certain and assured, that no reason for doubt, however extravagant, could be advanced by the sceptics to shake it, I decided that I might, without hesitation accept it as the first principle of the philosophy I was searching for.

Next, I closely examined what I was, and as I observed that I could imagine that I had no body, and that there was no world or any space in which I might be; but that I could not therefore imagine that I was not; and that, on the contrary, from the very fact that I doubted the truth of all things, it most clearly and certainly followed that I *was*. On the other hand, if I had ceased to think, although all the other precepts which I had ever imagined had been true, I would have had no reason to believe that I existed. From this I concluded that I was a substance whose whole essence or nature consists only in thinking, and which, that it may exist, has no need of space, nor is dependent on any material thing; so that I, that is to say, the soul [mind] by which I am what I am, is wholly distinct from the body. It is even more easily known than the latter, and though the latter were not, the soul would still continue to be all that it is.

After this I inquired, in general, into what is essential to the truth and certainty of a proposition; for since I had discovered one which I knew to be true, I thought that I must also be able to discover the ground of this certainty. And as I observed that in the words "I think, therefore I am," there is nothing which gives me assurance of their truth beyond this: that I see very clearly that in order to think it is necessary to exist. I then concluded that I might take, as a general rule, the principle that all the things which we very clearly and distinctly conceive are true, remembering, however, that there may be some difficulty in deciding which the things are which we conceive distinctly.

Next, from reflecting on the fact that I doubted, and that consequently my being was not wholly perfect (for I clearly saw that it was a greater perfection to know than to doubt), I was led to inquire from where I had learned to think of something more perfect than myself; and I clearly recognized that I must hold this notion from some nature which was more perfect. As for the ideas of many other things outside of me, as the sky, the earth, light, heat, and a thousand other things, I was less at a loss to know from where they came; for since I noticed in them nothing which seemed to render them superior to myself, I could believe that, if these were true, they were dependencies of my own nature, in so far as it possessed some perfection. And, if they were false, that I held them from nothing, that is to say, they were in me because of a certain imperfection of my nature. But this could not be the case with the idea of a nature more perfect than my own; for to receive it from nothing was something clearly impossible. . . . The only possibility was that it had been placed in me by a nature which was in reality more perfect than I was, and which possessed all the perfections of which I could form any idea: that is to say, in a word, God. And to this I added that, since I knew some perfections which I did not possess, I was not the only being in existence; . . . but on the contrary, that there was of necessity some other more perfect Being upon whom I was dependent, and from whom I had received all that I possessed. . . .

I was next ready to search for other truths. And when I had considered the object of the geometers, which I imagined to be a continuous body, or a space infinitely extended in length, breadth, and height or depth, divisible into various parts which can be of different figures and sizes, and can be moved or transposed in any way, . . . I went over some of their simplest demonstrations. And, immediately, I noticed that the great certainty which by common consent is accorded to these demonstrations, is founded solely upon this: that they are clearly conceived in agreement with the rules I have already laid down. Furthermore, I noticed that there was nothing in these demonstrations which could assure me of the existence of their object. For example, visualizing a triangle, I distinctly perceived that its three angles were necessarily equal to two right angles, but I did not for that reason perceive anything which could assure me that any triangle *existed*; while, on the contrary, returning to the examination of the idea of a perfect Being, I found that the existence of the Being was implied in the idea in the same way that the equality of its three angles to two right angles is implied in the idea of a triangle, or as in the idea of a sphere, the equidistance of all points on its surface from the center. Consequently, it is at least as certain that God, who is this perfect Being, is, or exists, as any demonstration of geometry can be.

The reason which causes many people to think that it is difficult to know this truth, and even also in knowing what their soul really is, is that they never raise their thoughts above material objects. They are so accustomed never to think of anything without visualizing it, which is a way of thinking limited to material objects, that all that is not imaginable seems to them not intelligible. . . . And it seems to me that they who make use of their imagination to comprehend these ideas do exactly the same thing as if, in order to hear sounds or smell odors, they try to make use of their eyes. . . .

Finally, if there are still persons who are not sufficiently persuaded of the existence of God and of their soul, by the reasons I have given, I want them to know that all the other propositions, of the truth of which they feel themselves perhaps more assured, such as having a body, and that there exist stars and an earth, and the like, are less certain. For, although we have a moral assurance of these things, which is so strong that it would be immodest of us to doubt their existence, yet at the same time no one, unless his intellect is impaired, can deny, when the question relates to a metaphysical certainty, that there is sufficient reason to exclude complete assurance. This is supported by the observation that when asleep we may imagine that we have another body and that we see other stars and another earth, when there is nothing of the kind. For how do we know that the thoughts which occur when dreaming are false rather than those which we experience when awake, since the former are often not less vivid and distinct than the latter? And though the best minds may study this question as long as they please, I do not believe that they will be able to give any sufficient reason to remove this doubt, unless they presuppose the existence of God. For to begin with, even the principle which I have already taken as a rule, namely, that all things which we clearly and distinctly conceive are true, is certain only because God is or exists, and because he is a perfect Being, and because all that we possess is derived from him. From this it follows that our ideas or notions, which to the extent of their being clear and distinct are real, and come from God, must to that extent be true. Accordingly, as we not infrequently have ideas or notions which contain some falsity, this can only be the case with those that are to some extent confused and obscure, and thus exist in us confused because we are not wholly perfect. And it is evident that it is no less repugnant that falsity or imperfection, . . . should come from God, than that truth or perfection should come from nothing. . . .

• • •

MATTERS REQUIRED FOR FURTHER ADVANCEMENT IN THE INVESTIGATION OF NATURE

• • •

I noticed, regarding experiments, that they become much more necessary the more one is advanced in knowledge. In the beginning it is better to make use only of what is presented convincingly to our senses, and of which we cannot remain ignorant, provided we give them any consideration at all, rather than to concern ourselves with more rare and obscure phenomena. The reason for this is that the more uncommon often mislead us as long as the causes of the more common are still unknown; and the circumstances upon which they depend are almost always so particular and so minute that they are very difficult to detect. Regarding this I have adopted the following procedure: first, I tried to find the principles, or first causes, of all that is or can exist in the world, without considering anything for this end but God, who has created it, and without deriving them from any source other than certain germs of truths naturally existing in our minds. Next, I examined what were the first and most common effects that could be derived from these causes; and it appears to me that, in this way, I have found heavens, stars, and earth—and even on the earth, water, air, fire, minerals, and some other things of this kind—which among all others, are the most common and simple, and therefore the easiest to know. Then, when I wished to descend to the more particular, so many different objects presented themselves to me, that I believed it impossible for the human mind to distinguish the forms or species of bodies that are upon the earth, from an infinity of others which might have been, if it had pleased God to place them there, or consequently to apply them to our use, unless we discover the causes by the effects, and avail ourselves of many particular experiments. Thereupon, turning over in my mind all the objects that had ever been presented to my senses, I can truly say that I have never observed any which I could not satisfactorily explain by the principles I had discovered. But it is necessary also to confess that the power of nature is so ample and vast, and these principles are so simple and general, that I have hardly observed any particular effect which I cannot at once recognize as capable of being deduced in many different ways. My greatest difficulty usually is to discover in which of these ways the effect depends upon them. I cannot get out of this difficulty except by seeking certain experiments, which may be such that their result is not the same, if it is to be explained in one of these ways as it would be in another. As for the rest, I am now in a position to see, as I think, with sufficient clarity which course must be taken to make the majority of those experiments which I may conduct achieve this end; but I also see that they are such and so numerous, that neither my hands nor my income, though it were a thousand times larger than it is, would be sufficient for them all. As henceforth I shall have the means of making more or fewer experiments, I shall in the same proportion make greater or less progress in the knowledge of nature. This is what I had hoped to make known by the book I had written: to show the advantage which would come to the public, and thus persuade all who truly have the common good of mankind at heart . . . to communicate to me the experiments they had already made, and to assist me in those that remain to be made. . . .

• • •

4

Thomas Hobbes

Leviathan

T*HE new seventeenth-century science found philosophical expression in the work of Thomas Hobbes (1588–1679). The patronage of the Cavendishes, a powerful, noble English family, to whom he owed his social position and his livelihood, enabled Hobbes to carry on his scientific and philosophical studies and to travel and meet the leading intellectual figures of his day. He knew the work of such scientists as Bacon, Descartes, and Galileo, and incorporated their methods and findings into his own philosophy. He completely rejected medieval scholasticism and evolved a system that was materialist and determinist. For Hobbes, human beings and their ideas were simply forms of matter in motion. Such unorthodox views brought upon him charges of impiety and atheism and earned him such epithets as the "Bugbear of the Nation" and the "Monster of Malmesbury."*

The political views held by Hobbes, which are expressed systematically in the masterpiece Leviathan *(1651), were shaped as much by his own assumptions of philosophical materialism as by the personal and political circumstances of his troubled times. Living through the bloody conflicts of the English civil wars, Hobbes was stirred by "grief for the present calamities of my country," and his primary concern was the restoration of peace and order to England. His association with royalist circles inclined him to accept a strong monarchy as the instrument of such peace.*

The Leviathan *is a vigorous and realistic argument for political absolutism. Its title, taken from the name of a terrifying sea monster referred to in the Old Testament, is meant to suggest the frightening authority Hobbes considers necessary to compel obedience and order in human society. Absolute sovereignty, Hobbes argues, is indispensable for the maintenance of order. His theories, however, pleased neither his royalist friends nor his antiroyalist enemies. For, though he favored an absolute monarchy, he was ready to accept any government powerful enough to maintain civil peace. Hobbes also rejected the traditional concepts of the divine rights of kings and the "organic" community. In his view, the origins of society were wholly secular and atomistic: society resulted from a social contract among selfish, warring individuals moved by necessity and fear. Sovereignty, once delegated, was irrevocable and indivisible. Since the seventeenth century, the influence of Hobbes and his reputation as a realistic political scientist have steadily grown: his ideas have increasingly served as a rationale for the exercise of absolute power and the glorification of the state.*

ON THE DIFFERENCE OF MANNERS

In the first place, I put as a general inclination of all mankind a perpetual and restless desire of power after power that ceases only in death. And the cause of this is not always that a man hopes for a more intensive delight than he has already attained to, or that he cannot be content with a moderate power, but because he cannot assure the power and means to live well which he already has without the acquisition of more. And from hence it is that kings, whose power is greatest, turn their endeavors to the assuring it at home by laws or abroad by wars; and when that is done, there succeeds a new desire—in some, of fame from new conquest; in others, of ease and sensual pleasure; in others, of admiration or being flattered for excellence in some art or other ability of the mind.

• • •

ON THE NATURAL CONDITION OF MANKIND AS CONCERNING THEIR HAPPINESS AND MISERY

Nature has made men so equal in the faculties of the body and mind that, though there be found one man sometimes stronger in body or of quicker mind than another, yet, when all is reckoned together, the difference between man and man is not so considerable that one man can claim for himself any benefit to which another may not put forward

LEVIATHAN   Adapted by editor, from Thomas Hobbes, *Leviathan*, in *The Ethics of Hobbes*, ed. by E. Hershey Sneath (Boston: Ginn and Company, 1898), 119, 139–46, 177–82, 319–20, 330–32, 336.

a claim as well as he. For as to the strength of body, the weakest has strength enough to kill the strongest, either by secret plotting or in alliance with others that are in the same danger. . . .

From this equality of ability arises equality of hope in the attaining of our ends. And therefore if any two men desire the same thing, which nevertheless they cannot both enjoy, they become enemies; and to achieve their end, which is principally their own preservation, and sometimes their pleasure only, endeavor to destroy or subdue one another. And from hence it comes to pass that where an invader has no more to fear than another man's single power, if one plant, sow, build, or possess an estate, others may be expected to come prepared with forces united to dispossess and deprive him, not only of the fruit of his labor, but also of his life or liberty. And the invader again is in the like danger of another. . . .

In the nature of man, we find three principal causes for quarrel: first, competition; secondly, distrust; thirdly, glory.

The first makes men invade for gain; the second, for safety; and the third for reputation. The first use violence to make themselves masters of other men's persons, wives, children, and cattle; the second, to defend them; the third, for trifles, as a word, a smile, a different opinion, and any other sign of insult, either direct to their persons or by reflection in their kindred, their friends, their nation, their profession, or their name.

It is certain, that during the time men live without a common power to keep them all in awe, they are in that condition which is called war; and such a war is of every man against every man. For war, consists not in battle only, or the act of fighting, but in a time span, where the will to fight is sufficiently known; and therefore the notion of time is to be considered in the nature of war as it is in the nature of weather. For as the nature of foul weather lies not in a shower or two of rain but in an inclination thereto over many days, so the nature of war consists not in actual fighting but in the known disposition thereto during all the time there is no assurance to the contrary. All other time is peace.

Whatsoever, therefore, follows in a time of war where every man is enemy to every man; the same follows in a time, when men live without other security than what their own strength and their own invention shall furnish them. In such condition there is no place for industry, because the fruit thereof is uncertain, and consequently no culture of the earth; no navigation nor use of the commodities that may be imported by sea; no spacious building; no instruments of moving and removing such things as require much force; no knowledge of the face of the earth; no account of time; no arts; no letters; no society; and, which is worst of all, continual fear and danger of violent death; and the life of man solitary, poor, nasty, brutish, and short.

It may seem strange to somebody who has not considered these things that nature should thus dissociate and render men apt to invade, and destroy one another; . . . But let us observe that when a man takes a journey he arms himself, and seeks to go well accompanied; when going to sleep he locks his doors; when even in his house he locks his chests, and this when he knows there are laws and public officers, armed, to revenge all injuries done to him. What opinion has he of his fellow man when he rides armed, of his fellow citizens when he locks his doors; and of his children, and servants, when he locks his chests? Does he not thereby as much accuse mankind by his actions as I do by my words? But neither of us accuse man's nature in it. The desires and other passions of man are in themselves no sin. No more are the actions that proceed from those passions till they know a law that forbids them, which, till laws are made, they cannot know, nor can any law be made till they have agreed upon the person that shall make it. . . .

To this war of every man against every man, this also follows: that nothing can be unjust. The notions of right and wrong, justice and injustice, have there no place. Where there is no common power, there is no law; where no law, no injustice. Force and fraud are in war the two cardinal virtues. Justice and injustice are none of the faculties of the body or mind. If they were, they might be in a man who was alone in the world, including his senses and passions. They are qualities that relate to men in society, not in solitude. It follows also from the same condition that there be no property, no dominion, no *mine* and *thine*; but only that is every man's what he can get, and for so long as he can keep it. And so much for the ill condition which man by mere nature is actually placed in, though with a possibility to come out of it, consisting partly in the passions, partly in his reason.

The passions that incline men to peace are fear of death, desire for such things as are necessary for comfortable living; and a hope by their labor to obtain them. And reason suggests convenient terms of peace, upon which men may be drawn to agreement. These terms are those which otherwise are called the laws of nature, whereof I shall speak more particularly. . . .

OF THE FIRST AND SECOND NATURAL LAWS

The right of nature, . . . is the liberty each man has to use his own power, as he himself desires, for the preservation of his own nature—that is to say, of his own life and consequently, of doing anything, which in his own judgment and reason, he shall believe to be the best means thereunto.

By liberty is understood, according to the proper meaning of the word, the absence of external obstructions which may take away part of a man's power to do what he desires; but cannot hinder him from using the power left him, according as his judgment, and as reason shall dictate to him.

A law of nature is a general rule, found out by reason, by which a man is forbidden to do that which is destructive of his life or takes away the means of preserving it. . . .

And because the condition of man, as has been declared before, is a state of war of every one against every one—in which every one is governed by his own reason and there is nothing he can make use of that may not be a help unto him in preserving his life against his enemies—it follows that in such a condition every man has a right to everything, even to one another's body. And therefore, as long as this natural right of every man to everything endures, there can be no security to any man, how strong or wise he may be, during the time which nature ordinarily allows men to live. And consequently it is a general rule of reason that every man ought to seek peace, as far as he has hope of obtaining it; and when he cannot obtain it, that he may seek and use all help and advantages of war. The first branch of that rule contains the first and fundamental law of nature, which is *to seek peace and follow it.* The second, the sum of the right of nature, which is, *by all means we can to defend ourselves.*

From this fundamental law of nature, by which men are commanded to seek peace, is derived this second law: that a man be willing, when others are so too, as far as for peace and defense of himself he shall judge it necessary, to lay down his right to all things; and be contented with so much liberty against other men as he would allow other men against himself. For as long as every man holds the right of doing anything he likes, so long are all men in a state of war. But if other men will not lay down their right as well as he, then there is no reason for anyone, to divest himself of his, because that would expose himself to prey, which no man is bound to, rather than to incline himself to peace. This is that law of the Gospel: *whatsoever you wish that others should do to you, that do unto them.* And that law of all men: *what you would not have done to you, do not unto them.*

. . .

OF THE CAUSES, DEVELOPMENT, AND DEFINITION OF A COMMONWEALTH

The final cause, end, or design of men, who naturally love liberty and authority over others, in the introduction of that restraint upon themselves in which we see them live in commonwealths, is the desire for their own preservation, and of a more contented life thereby; that is to say, of getting themselves out from that miserable condition of war which necessarily follows . . . from the natural passions of men when there is no visible power to keep them in awe and tie them by fear of punishment to the performance of their agreements and observation of the laws of nature. . . .

For the laws of nature, as "justice," "equity," "modesty," "mercy," and, in sum, "doing to others as we would be done to," of themselves, without the terror of some power to cause them to be observed, are contrary to our natural passions, that carry us to partiality, pride, revenge, and the like. And agreements without the sword are but words, and of no strength to secure a man at all. . . . And in all places where men have lived in small families, to rob and spoil one another has been the custom. . . . And as small families did then, so now do cities and kingdoms, which are but greater families, for their own security enlarge their dominions . . . and endeavor as much as possible to sub-due or weaken their neighbors by open force and secret arts, for lack of other protection, justly; and are remembered for it in later ages with honor.

Nor is it the joining together of a small number of men that gives them this security, because in small numbers small additions on the one side or the other make the advantage of strength so great as is sufficient to carry the victory; and therefore gives encouragement to an invasion. The multitude sufficient to confide in for our security is not determined by any certain number but by comparison with the enemy we fear; and is then sufficient when the advantage of the enemy is not so visible and conspicuous to determine the event of war as to move him to attempt it.

And should there not be so great a multitude, even if their actions be directed according to their particular judgments and particular appetites, they can expect thereby no defense nor protection, neither against a common enemy nor against the injuries of one another. For being divided in opinions concerning the best use and application of their strength, they do not help but hinder one another, and reduce their strength by mutual opposition to nothing; whereby they are easily not only subdued by a very few that agree together, but also, when there is no common enemy, they make war upon each other for their particular interests. For if we could suppose a great multitude of men to consent in the observation of justice and other laws of nature without a common power to keep them all in awe, we might as well suppose all mankind to do the same; and then there neither would be, nor need to be, any civil government or commonwealth at all, because there would be peace without subjection.

Nor is it enough for the security which men want to last all the time of their life that they be governed and directed by one judgment for a limited time, as in one battle or one war. For though they obtain a victory by their unanimous endeavor against a foreign enemy, yet afterwards, when either they have no common enemy or he that by one group is held for an enemy is by another group held for a friend, they must, by the difference of their interests, dissolve, and fall again into a war among themselves.

It is true that certain living creatures, as bees and ants, live harmoniously with each other. They are therefore called by Aristotle[1] political creatures and have no other direction, than their particular judgments and appetites; nor speech whereby one of them can signify to another what he thinks expedient for the common benefit; and therefore some man may perhaps desire to know why mankind cannot do the same. To which I answer:

First, that men are continually in competition for honor and dignity, which these creatures are not; and consequently among men there arises envy and hatred and finally war, but among these creatures not so.

Secondly, that among these creatures the common good differ not from the private; and being by nature inclined to their private, they procure thereby the common benefit. But man, whose joy consists in comparing himself with other men, can savor nothing but his own superiority.

---

[1]Greek philosopher (384–322 B.C.)

Thirdly, that these creatures, having not, as man, the use of reason, do not see nor think they see any fault, in the administration of their common business; whereas among men, there are very many that think themselves wiser and abler to govern the public better than the rest; and these strive to reform and innovate, one this way, another that way, and thereby bring it into division and civil war.

Fourthly, that these creatures, though they have some use of voice in making known to one another their desires and other affections, yet they lack that art of words by which some men can represent to others that which is good in the likeness of evil; and evil in the likeness of good; and increase or diminish the apparent greatness of good and evil, making men discontented and troubling their peace at their pleasure.

Fifthly, irrational creatures cannot distinguish between "injury" and "damage"; and, therefore, as long as they be at ease they are not offended with their fellows; whereas man is then most troublesome when he is most at ease; for then it is that he loves to show his wisdom and control the actions of them that govern the commonwealth.

Lastly, the harmony of these creatures is natural, that of men is by agreement only, which is artificial; and therefore, it is no wonder if there be something else required besides agreement to make it constant and lasting; that is, a common power to keep them in awe and to direct their actions to the common benefit.

The only way to erect such a common power which may defend them from the invasion of foreigners and the injuries of one another, and thereby to secure them so that by their own labors and by the fruits of the earth they may nourish themselves and live contentedly, is to confer all their power and strength upon one man, or upon one assembly of men that may reduce all their wills, by majority of voices, unto one will; which is as much as to say, to appoint one man or assembly of men to speak for them; and every one to accept and acknowledge himself to be author of whatsoever he that speaks for him shall act or cause to be acted in those things which concern the common peace and safety, and therein to submit their wills to his will, and their judgments to his judgment. This is more than consent or concord; it is a real unity of them all in one and the same person, made by agreement of every man with every man, in such manner as if every man should say to every man, "I authorize and give up my right of governing myself to this man, or to this assembly of men, on this condition, that you give up your right to him and authorize all his actions in like manner." This done, the multitude so united in one person is called a "commonwealth," in Latin *civitas*. This is the origin of that great "leviathan," or rather, to speak more reverently, of that "mortal god," to which we owe, under the "immortal God," our peace and defense. For by this authority, given him by every particular man in the commonwealth, he has the use of so much power and strength conferred on him that, by terror thereof, he is enabled to form the wills of them all to peace at home and mutual aid against their enemies abroad. And in him consists the essence of the commonwealth, which, to define it, is "one person, of whose acts a great multitude, by mutual covenants one with another, have made themselves the author, to the end he may use the strength and means of them all as he shall think wise for their peace and common defense."

And he that carries this person is called "sovereign" and said to have "sovereign power"; and every one besides, his "subject."

The attaining to this sovereign power is by two ways. One, by natural force, as when a man makes his children to submit themselves and their children to his rule, as being able to destroy them if they refuse; or by war subdues his enemies to his will, giving them their lives on that condition. The other is when men agree among themselves to submit to some man or assembly of men voluntarily, on confidence that they will be protected by him against all others. This latter, may be called a political commonwealth, or commonwealth by "institution," and the former, a commonwealth by "acquisition."

• • •

OF THE FUNCTION OF THE
SOVEREIGN REPRESENTATIVE

The function of the sovereign, be it a monarch or an assembly, consists in the purpose for which he was trusted with the sovereign power, namely, the securing of "the safety of the people"; to which he is obliged by the law of nature, and to render an account thereof to God, the author of that law, and to none but him. But by safety here is not meant a bare preservation but also all other contentments of life which every man by lawful labor, without danger or hurt to the commonwealth, shall acquire for himself.

And this is to be done, not by care applied to individuals further than their protection from injuries when they shall complain, but by a general provision contained in public instruction, both of doctrine and example, and in the making and executing of good laws to which individual persons may apply their own cases.

And because, if the essential rights of sovereignty . . . be taken away, the commonwealth is thereby dissolved and every man returns into the condition and calamity of a war with every other man, which is the greatest evil that can happen in this life; it is the duty of the sovereign, to maintain those rights entire, and consequently against his duty, first, to transfer to another or to remove from himself any of them. For he that deserts the means deserts the ends; and he deserts the means when, being the sovereign, he acknowledges himself subject to the civil laws and renounces supreme judicial authority or the making of war or peace by his own authority; or of judging of the necessities of the commonwealth; or of levying money and soldiers when and as much he shall judge necessary; or of making officers and ministers both of war and peace; or of appointing teachers and examining what doctrines are conformable or contrary to the defense, peace, and good of the people. Secondly, it is against his duty to let the people be ignorant or misinformed of the reasons for his essential rights, because thereby men are easy to be seduced and drawn to resist him when the commonwealth shall require their use and exercise. . . .

To the care of the sovereign belongs the making of good laws. But what is a good law? By a good law I mean not a just law; for no law can be unjust. The law is made by the sovereign power, and all that is done by such power is warranted and owned by every one of the people; and that which every man will have so, no man can say is unjust. It is in the laws of a commonwealth as in the laws of games whatsoever the players all agree on is injustice to none of them. A good law is that which is "needed" for the "good of the people" and "clearly understood."

For the use of laws, which are but rules authorized, is not to bind the people from all voluntary actions but to direct and keep them from hurting themselves by their own impulsive desires, rashness, or indiscretion; as hedges are set not to stop travelers, but to keep them in their way. And, therefore, a law that is not needed, having not the true purpose of a law, is not good. A law may be thought to be good when it is for the benefit of the sovereign, though it be not necessary for the people, but it is not so. For the good of the sovereign and people cannot be separated. It is a weak sovereign, that has weak subjects; and a weak people, whose sovereign lacks power to rule them at his will. . . .

It belongs also to the function of the sovereign to make a right application of punishments and rewards. And seeing the end of punishing is not revenge and discharge of anger, but correction, either of the offender, or of others by his example; the severest punishments are to be inflicted for those crimes that are of most danger to the public; such as are those which proceed from malice to the government established; those that spring from contempt of justice; those that provoke indignation in the multitude; and those which, unpunished, seem authorized, as when they are committed by sons, servants, or favorites of men in authority. For indignation carries men not only against the actors and authors of injustice, but against all power that is likely to protect them; as in the case of Tarquin,[2] when for the insolent act of one of his sons he was driven out of Rome and the monarchy itself dissolved.[3] But crimes which proceed from great provocation, from great fear, great need, or from ignorance, whether the fact be a great crime or not, there is often a place for leniency without prejudice to the commonwealth; and leniency, when there is such place for it, is required by the law of nature. The punishment of the leaders and teachers in a rebellion, not the poor seduced people, when they are punished, can profit the commonwealth by their example. To be severe to the people is to punish that ignorance which may in great part be blamed on the sovereign, whose fault it was that they were not better instructed.

In like manner it belongs to the duty of the sovereign, to apply his rewards so that there may arise from them benefit to the commonwealth, wherein consists their use, and purpose; and is then done when they that have well served the commonwealth are, with as little expense of the common treasure as is possible, so well recompensed as others thereby may be encouraged both to serve the same as faithfully as they can and to study the arts by which they may be enabled to do it better. . . .

Concerning the relationships of one sovereign to another, which are

---

[2]Lucius Tarquinius Superbus (that is, the "Proud," 534–510 B.C.), last of the Roman kings; said to have been a cruel despot, though a capable ruler.

[3]The offending son was Tarquinius Sextus (died *ca.* 496 B.C.). According to legend, the Romans drove his father from the throne because Sextus had raped Lucretia, the virtuous wife of his cousin, Lucius Tarquinius Collatinus. Following the successful rebellion, the Romans transformed their state into a *republic* (509 B.C.), with Lucius Tarquinius Collatinus, the wronged husband, serving as one of the first two consuls (chief executives).

included in that law commonly called the "law of nations,"[4] I need not say anything in this place because the law of nations and the law of nature is the same thing. And every sovereign has the same right, in securing the safety of his people that any particular man can have in securing the safety of his own body. And the same law that dictates to men that have no civil government what they ought to do and what to avoid in regard of one another dictates the same to commonwealths, that is, to the consciences of sovereign princes and sovereign assemblies. For there is no court of natural justice except the conscience only; where not man but God reigns whose laws, . . . since God is the author of nature, are "natural," and as God is King of kings, are "laws."

. . .

[4]International law.

5

Blaise Pascal

Thoughts

*B*LAISE Pascal (1623–1662) is *famous both as a scientist-mathematician and as a Christian thinker and defender. In his youth he was a mathematical prodigy, having written a book on conic sections by age sixteen. Later, he went on to become a colleague of Descartes and other French scientists, to formulate "Pascal's principle" in physics, to invent one of the first computers, and to make important contributions to probability theory. At age twenty-three, he underwent a mystical experience that converted him to Jansenism, that austere, almost predestinationist version of Roman Catholicism. Some years later, after the death of his father, a worsening of his own physical condition, and another conversion experience in 1654, Pascal gave up his scientific work, rejected the world in order to participate in the life of the Jansenist religious community at Port Royal, and spent the rest of his life elaborating and defending his religious views. In recent years his reputation has rested more on his role as a precursor of modern religious existentialism than on his role as a scientist. After his final conversion, Pascal was torn between his love of science and his new religious views; his Thoughts (Pensées) are essentially an attempt to reconcile the method of science with the content of religion. He accepts Descartes' method of reaching certainty through total doubt, but differs with Descartes' conclusions. Reason, according to Pascal, is indeed the key to understanding nature; but it is useless as a means of understanding and satisfying spiritual needs or of resolving the bewildering paradoxes of life. Reason cannot know God or prove his existence. The real test for such religious truths, according to Pascal, is not their rational consistency but their moral value. Moral certainty—the faith that life has some purpose and value—can come only from an act of will. Only such self-conscious choice distinguishes human beings from the rest of nature and raises them above the predicament of miserable, blundering animals.*

43

Thoughts is based on fragmentary notes for a defense of Christianity. Written by Pascal in his last years, the notes were first published, in imperfect and incomplete form, in 1670 (eight years after his death); a complete, scholarly edition appeared in 1844. Full of brilliant paradoxes and acute insights into human nature and behavior, the following excerpts embody Pascal's anguished struggle to find certainty, and his alternation between despair, mystical hope, and pious resignation. The selected excerpts include the section titles under which they appear in the original collection.

MISERY OF MAN WITHOUT GOD

Let man then contemplate the whole of nature in her full and grand majesty, and turn his vision from the low objects which surround him. Let him gaze on that brilliant light, set like an eternal lamp to illumine the universe; let the earth appear to him a point in comparison with the vast circle described by the sun; and let him wonder at the fact that this vast circle is itself but a very fine point in comparison with that described by the stars in their revolution round the firmament. But if our view be arrested there, let our imagination pass beyond; it will sooner exhaust the power of conception than nature that of supplying material for conception. The whole visible world is only an imperceptible atom in the ample bosom of nature. No idea approaches it. We may enlarge our conceptions beyond all imaginable space; we only produce atoms in comparison with the reality of things. It is an infinite sphere, the center of which is everywhere, the circumference nowhere. In short, it is the greatest sensible mark of the almighty power of God that imagination loses itself in that thought.

Returning to himself, let man consider what he is in comparison with all existence; let him regard himself as lost in this remote corner of nature; and from the little cell in which he finds himself lodged, I mean the universe, let him estimate at their true value the earth, kingdoms, cities, and himself. What is a man in the Infinite?[1]

---

[1] That having no boundaries or limits.

THOUGHTS Adapted by editor, from Blaise Pascal, *Thoughts and Minor Works*, trans. W. F. Trotter *et al.*, in *Harvard Classics* (New York: Collier, 1910), vol. 48, 25–31, 42–43, 45, 58, 62–63, 71–72, 77–79, 82–83, 88, 98–99, 120, 124, 127, 131, 134, 136–37, 145–47, 150, 157, 174–75.

But to show him another prodigy equally astonishing, let him examine the most delicate things he knows. Let a mite[2] be given him, with its minute body and parts incomparably more minute, limbs with their joints, veins in the limbs, blood in the veins, humors[3] in the blood, drops in the humors, vapors in the drops. Dividing these last things again, let him exhaust his powers of conception, and let the last object at which he can arrive be now that of our discourse. Perhaps he will think that here is the smallest point in nature. I will let him see therein a new abyss. I will paint for him not only the visible universe, but all that he can conceive of nature's immensity in the womb of this abridged atom. Let him see therein an infinity of universes, each of which has its firmament, its planets, its earth, in the same proportion as in the visible world; in each earth, animals, and in the last mites, in which he will find again all that the first had, finding still in these others the same thing without end and without cessation. Let him lose himself in wonders as amazing in their littleness as the others in their vastness. For who will not be astounded at the fact that our body, which a little while ago was imperceptible in the universe, itself imperceptible in the bosom of the whole, is now a colossus, a world, or rather a whole, in respect of the nothingness which we cannot reach? He who regards himself in this light will be afraid of himself, and observing himself sustained in the body given by nature between those two abysses of the Infinite and Nothing, will tremble at the sight of these marvels; and I think that, as his curiosity changes into admiration, he will be more disposed to contemplate them in silence than to examine them with presumption.

For, in fact, what is man in nature? A Nothing in comparison with the Infinite, an All in comparison with the Nothing, a mean between nothing and everything. Since he is infinitely removed from comprehending the extremes, the end of things and their beginning are hopelessly hidden from him in an impenetrable secret; he is equally incapable of seeing the Nothing from which he was made, and the Infinite in which he is swallowed up.

What will he do then, but perceive the appearance of the middle of things, in an eternal despair of knowing either their beginning or their end. All things proceed from the Nothing, and are borne toward the

---

[2]A tiny creature (arachnid).
[3]In seventeenth-century physiology, one of four fluids believed to be in the blood.

Infinite. Who will follow these marvellous processes? The Author of these wonders understands them. None other can do so.

Through failure to contemplate these Infinites, men have rashly rushed into the examination of nature, as though they bore some proportion to her. It is strange that they have wished to understand the beginnings of things, and thence to arrive at the knowledge of the whole, with a presumption as infinite as their object. For surely this design cannot be formed without presumption or without a capacity infinite like nature. . . .

We naturally believe ourselves far more capable of reaching the center of things than of embracing their circumference. The visible extent of the world visibly exceeds us; but as we exceed little things, we think ourselves more capable of knowing them. And yet we need no less capacity for attaining the Nothing than the All. Infinite capacity is required for both, and it seems to me that whoever shall have understood the ultimate principles of being might also attain to the knowledge of the Infinite. The one depends on the other, and one leads to the other. These extremes meet and reunite by force of distance and find each other in God, and in God alone.

Let us, then, take our compass; we are something, and we are not everything. The nature of our existence hides from us the knowledge of first beginnings which are born of the Nothing; and the littleness of our being conceals from us the sight of the Infinite.

Our intellect holds the same position in the world of thought as our body occupies in the expanse of nature.

Limited as we are in every way, this state which holds the mean between two extremes is present in all our impotence. Our senses perceive no extreme. Too much sound deafens us; too much light dazzles us; too great distance or proximity hinders our view. Too great length and too great brevity of discourse tend to obscurity; too much truth is paralyzing. . . . First principles are too self-evident for us; too much pleasure disagrees with us. Too many concords are annoying in music; too many benefits irritate us; we wish to have the means to overpay our debts. "Benefits are pleasant while it is possible to repay them; when they become much greater, they produce hatred rather than gratitude."[4] We feel neither extreme heat nor extreme cold. Excessive qualities are prejudicial to us and not perceptible by the senses; we

---

[4]Quotation from Publius Cornelius Tacitus (*ca.* 55–117). Roman politician and historian.

do not feel but suffer them. Extreme youth and extreme age hinder the mind, as also too much and too little education. In short, extremes are for us as though they were not, and we are not within their notice. They escape us, or we them.

This is our true state; this is what makes us incapable of certain knowledge and of absolute ignorance. We sail within a vast sphere, ever drifting in uncertainty, driven from end to end. When we think to attach ourselves to any point and to fasten to it, it wavers and leaves us; and if we follow it, it eludes our grasp, slips past us, and vanishes forever. Nothing stays for us. This is our natural condition and yet most contrary to our inclination; we burn with desire to find solid ground and an ultimate sure foundation whereon to build a tower reaching to the Infinite. But our whole groundwork cracks, and the earth opens to abysses.

Let us, therefore, not look for certainty and stability. Our reason is always deceived by fickle shadows; nothing can fix the finite between the two Infinites, which both enclose and fly from it.

If this be well understood, I think that we shall remain at rest, each in the state wherein nature has placed him. As this sphere which has fallen to us as our lot is always distant from either extreme, what matters it that man should have a little more knowledge of the universe? If he has it, he but gets a little higher. Is he not always infinitely removed from the end, and is not the duration of our life equally removed from eternity, even if it lasts ten years longer?

In comparison with these Infinites, all finites are equal, and I see no reason for fixing our imagination on one more than on another. The only comparison which we make of ourselves to the finite is painful to us.

If man made himself the first object of study, he would see how incapable he is of going further. How can a part know the whole? But he may perhaps aspire to know at least the parts to which he bears some proportion. But the parts of the world are all so related and linked to one another that I believe it impossible to know one without the other and without the whole.

Man, for instance, is related to all he knows. He needs a place wherein to abide, time through which to live, motion in order to live, elements to compose him, warmth and food to nourish him, air to breathe. He sees light; he feels bodies; in short, he is in a dependent alliance with everything. To know man, then, it is necessary to know how it happens that he needs air to live, and, to know the air, we must know how it is thus related to the life of man, and so on. Flame cannot exist without air; therefore, to understand the one, we must understand the other.

Since everything, then, is cause and effect, dependent and support-ing, mediate and immediate, and all is held together by a natural though imperceptible chain which binds together things most distant and most different, I hold it equally impossible to know the parts without knowing the whole and to know the whole without knowing the parts in detail. . . .

And what completes our incapability of knowing things is the fact that they are simple and that we are composed of two opposite natures, different in kind, soul and body. For it is impossible that our rational part should be other than spiritual; and if any one maintain that we are simply corporeal, this would far more exclude us from the knowledge of things, there being nothing so inconceivable as to say that matter knows itself. It is impossible to imagine how it should know itself.

So, if we are simply material, we can know nothing at all; and if we are composed of mind and matter, we cannot know perfectly things which are simple, whether spiritual or corporeal. Hence it comes that almost all philosophers have confused ideas of things, and speak of material things in spiritual terms, and of spiritual things in material terms. For they say boldly that bodies have a tendency to fall, that they seek after their center, that they fly from destruction, that they fear the void, that they have inclinations, sympathies, antipathies, all of which attributes pertain only to mind. And in speaking of minds, they consid-er them as in a place, and attribute to them movement from one place to another; and these are qualities which belong only to bodies.

Instead of receiving the ideas of these things in their purity, we color them with our own qualities, and stamp with our composite being all the simple things which we contemplate.

Who would not think, seeing us compose all things of mind and body, but that this mixture would be quite intelligible to us? Yet it is the very thing we least understand. Man is to himself the most wonderful object in nature; for he cannot conceive what the body is, still less what the mind is, and least of all how a body should be united to a mind. This is the consummation of his difficulties, and yet it is his very being. "The manner in which spirits are united to bodies cannot be understood by men, yet such is man. . . ."[5]

• • •

---

[5]Quotation from St. Augustine (354–430), philosopher, bishop, and Church Father.

There is an universal and essential difference between the actions of the will and all other actions.

The will is one of the chief factors in belief, not that it creates belief, but because things are true or false according to the aspect in which we look at them. The will, which prefers one aspect to another, turns away the mind from considering the qualities of all that it does not like to see; and thus the mind, moving in accord with the will, stops to consider the aspect which it likes and so judges by what it sees.

●   ●   ●

The nature of self-love and of this human Ego[6] is to love self only and consider self only. But what will man do? He cannot prevent this object that he loves from being full of faults and wants. He wants to be great, and he sees himself small. He wants to be happy, and he sees himself miserable. He wants to be perfect, and he sees himself full of imperfections. He wants to be the object of love and esteem among men, and he sees that his faults merit only their hatred and contempt. This embarrassment in which he finds himself produces in him the most unrighteous and criminal passion that can be imagined; for he conceives a mortal enmity against that truth which reproves him and which convinces him of his faults. He would annihilate it, but, unable to destroy it in its essence,[7] he destroys it as far as possible in his own knowledge and in that of others; that is to say, he devotes all his attention to hiding his faults both from others and from himself, and he cannot endure either that others should point them out to him, or that they should see them.

Truly it is an evil to be full of faults; but it is a still greater evil to be full of them and to be unwilling to recognize them, since that is to add the further fault of a voluntary illusion. We do not like others to deceive us; we do not think it fair that they should be held in higher esteem by us than they deserve; it is not, then, fair that we should deceive them and should wish them to esteem us more highly than we deserve.

Thus, when they discover only the imperfections and vices which we really have, it is plain they do us no wrong, since it is not they who cause them; they rather do us good, since they help us to free ourselves from an evil, namely, the ignorance of these imperfections. We ought not to be angry at their knowing our faults and despising us; it is but right that they should know us for what we are and should despise us, if

[6]The conscious self.
[7]True substance.

we are contemptible. . . . Man is, then, only disguise, falsehood, and hypocrisy, both in himself and in regard to others. He does not wish anyone to tell him the truth; he avoids telling it to others, and all these dispositions, so removed from justice and reason, have a natural root in his heart.

• • •

Men are intrusted from infancy with the care of their honor, their property, their friends, and even with the property and the honor of their friends. They are overwhelmed with business, with the study of languages, and with physical exercise; and they are made to understand that they cannot be happy unless their health, their honor, their fortune and that of their friends be in good condition, and that a single thing wanting will make them unhappy. Thus they are given cares and business which make them bustle about from break of day. It is, you will exclaim, a strange way to make them happy! What more could be done to make them miserable? Indeed! What could be done? We should only have to relieve them from all these cares; for then they would see themselves; they would reflect on what they are, whence they came, where they go, and thus we cannot employ and divert them too much. And this is why, after having given them so much business, we advise them, if they have some time for relaxation, to employ it in amusement, in play, and to be always fully occupied.

How hollow and full of ribaldry is the heart of man!

• • •

He who will know fully the vanity of man has only to consider the causes and effects of love. The cause is *I know not what*[8] and the effects are dreadful. This *I know not what*, so small an object that we cannot recognize it, agitates a whole country, princes, armies, the entire world.

Cleopatra's nose: had it been shorter, the whole aspect of the world would have been altered.

• • •

THE NECESSITY OF HOPE

We do not require great education of the mind to understand that here is no real and lasting satisfaction; that our pleasures are only vanity; that our evils are infinite; and, lastly, that death, which threatens us

---

[8]That is, an indescribable something.

every moment, must infallibly place us within a few years under the dreadful necessity of being forever either annihilated or unhappy.

There is nothing more real than this, nothing more terrible. Be as heroic as we like, that is the end which awaits the noblest life in the world. Let us reflect on this and then say whether it is not beyond doubt that there is no good in this life but in the hope of another; that we are happy only in proportion as we draw near it; and that, as there are no more woes for those who have complete assurance of eternity, so there is no more happiness for those who have no insight into it.

Surely then it is a great evil thus to be in doubt, but it is at least an indispensable duty to seek when we are in such doubt; and thus the doubter who does not seek is altogether completely unhappy and completely wrong. And if besides this he is easy and content, professes to be so, and indeed boasts of it; if it is this state itself which is the subject of his joy and vanity, I have no words to describe so silly a creature.

How can people hold these opinions? What joy can we find in the expectation of nothing but hopeless misery? What reason for boasting that we are in impenetrable darkness? . . .

* * *

Let us imagine a number of men in chains and all condemned to death, where some are killed each day in the sight of the others, and those who remain see their own fate in that of their fellows and wait their turn, looking at each other sorrowfully and without hope. It is an image of the condition of men.

* * *

When I consider the short duration of my life, swallowed up in the eternity before and after, the little space which I fill and even can see, engulfed in the infinite immensity of spaces of which I am ignorant and which know me not, I am frightened and am astonished at being here rather than there; for there is no reason why here rather than there, why now rather than then. Who has put me here? By whose order and direction have this place and time been allotted to me?

* * *

The eternal silence of these infinite spaces frightens me.

* * *

Why is my knowledge limited? Why my stature? Why my life to one hundred years rather than to a thousand? What reason has nature had for giving me such, and for choosing this number rather than another in the infinity of those from which there is no more reason to choose one than another, trying nothing else?

• • •

The last act is tragic, however happy all the rest of the play is; at the last a little earth is thrown upon our head, and that is the end forever.

• • •

We are fools to depend upon the society of our fellowmen. Wretched as we are, powerless as we are, they will not aid us; we shall die alone. We should therefore act as if we were alone, and in that case why should we build fine houses, and so on? We should seek the truth without hesitation; and, if we refuse it, we show that we value the esteem of men more than the search for truth.

• • •

Between us and heaven or hell there is only life, which is the frailest thing in the world.

• • •

This is what I see and what troubles me. I look on all sides, and I see only darkness everywhere. Nature presents to me nothing which is not matter of doubt and concern. If I saw nothing there which revealed a Divinity, I would come to a negative conclusion; if I saw everywhere the signs of a Creator, I would remain peacefully in faith. But, seeing too much to deny and too little to be sure, I am in a state to be pitied; wherefore I have a hundred times wished that if a God maintains nature, she should testify to Him unequivocally, and that, if the signs she gives are deceptive, she should suppress them altogether; that she should say everything or nothing, that I might see which cause I ought to follow. Whereas in my present state, ignorant of what I am or of what I ought to do, I know neither my condition nor my duty. My heart inclines wholly to know where is the true good, in order to follow it; nothing would be too dear to me for eternity.

I envy those whom I see living in the faith with such carelessness and who make such a bad use of a gift of which it seems to me I would make such a different use.

• • •

It is incomprehensible that God should exist, and it is incomprehensible that He should not exist, that the soul should be joined to the body, and that we should have no soul; that the world should be created, and that it should not be created, and so on; that original sin should be, and that it should not be.

• • •

We must live differently in the world, according to these different assumptions: (1) that we could always remain in it; (2) that it is certain that we shall not remain here long, and uncertain if we shall remain here one hour. This last assumption is our condition.

• • •

OF THE MEANS OF BELIEF

Reason would never submit, if it did not judge that there are some occasions on which it ought to submit. It is then right for it to submit, when it judges that it ought to submit.

• • •

If we submit everything to reason, our religion will have no mysterious and supernatural element. If we offend the principles of reason, our religion will be absurd and ridiculous.

• • •

All our reasoning reduces itself to yielding to feeling.

But fancy is like, though contrary to, feeling, so that we cannot distinguish between these contraries. One person says that my feeling is fancy, another that his fancy is feeling. We should have a rule. Reason offers itself; but it is pliable in every sense; and thus there is no rule.

• • •

The heart has its reasons, which reason does not know. We feel it in a thousand things. I say that the heart naturally loves the Universal Being, and also itself naturally, according as it gives itself to them; and it hardens itself against one or the other at its will. You have rejected the one and kept the other. Is it by reason that you love yourself?

• • •

It is the heart which experiences God, and not the reason. This, then, is faith: God felt by the heart, not by the reason.

• • •

THE PHILOSOPHERS

Thought constitutes the greatness of man.

• • •

Man is but a reed, the most feeble thing in nature, but he is a thinking reed. The entire universe need not arm itself to crush him. A vapor, a drop of water suffices to kill him. But, if the universe were to crush him, man would still be more noble than that which killed him, because he knows that he dies and the advantage which the universe has over him; the universe knows nothing of this.

• • •

It is not from space that I must seek my dignity, but from the government of my thought. I shall have no more if I possess worlds. By space the universe encompasses and swallows me up like an atom; by thought I comprehend the world.

• • •

All the dignity of man consists in thought. Thought is, therefore, by its nature a wonderful and incomparable thing. It must have strange defects to be contemptible. But it has such, so that nothing is more ridiculous. How great it is in its nature! How vile it is in its defects!

• • •

Discourses on humility are a source of pride in the vain, and of humility in the humble. So those on scepticism[9] cause believers to affirm. Few men speak humbly of humility, chastely of chastity, few doubtingly of scepticism. We are only falsehood, duplicity, contradiction; we both conceal and disguise ourselves from ourselves.

• • •

We have an incapacity of proof, insurmountable by all dogmatism.[10] We have an idea of truth, invincible to all scepticism.

• • •

[9]Perpetual doubting.
[10]Positive, authoritative assertion of opinion.

Notwithstanding the sight of all our miseries, which press upon us and take us by the throat, we have an instinct which we cannot repress and which lifts us up.

• • •

There is internal war in man between reason and the passions.
If he had only reason without passions . . .
If he had only passions without reason . . .
But having both, he cannot be without strife, being unable to be at peace with the one without being at war with the other. Thus he is always divided against and opposed to himself.

• • •

It is dangerous to make man see too clearly his equality with beasts without showing him his greatness. It is also dangerous to make him see his greatness too clearly, apart from his vileness. It is still more dangerous to leave him in ignorance of both. But it is very advantageous to show him both. Man must not think that he is on a level either with beasts or with the angels, nor must he be ignorant of both sides of his nature; but he must know both.

• • •

Let man now know his value. Let him love himself, for there is in him a nature capable of good; let him not for this reason love the vileness which is in him. Let him despise himself, for this capacity is barren; but let him not therefore despise this natural capacity. Let him hate himself, let him love himself; he has within him the capacity of knowing the truth and of being happy, but he possesses no truth, either constant or satisfactory.

I would then lead man to the desire of finding truth; to be free from passions, and ready to follow it where he may find it, knowing how much his knowledge is obscured by the passions. I would, indeed, that he should hate in himself the lust which determined his will by itself so that it may not blind him in making his choice, and may not hinder him when he has chosen.

• • •

All these contradictions, which seem most to keep me from the knowledge of religion, have led me most quickly to the true one.

• • •

MORALITY AND DOCTRINE

The chief arguments of the sceptics[11]—I pass over the lesser ones—
are that we have no certainty of the truth of these principles apart from
faith and revelation, except insofar as we naturally perceive them in
ourselves. Now this natural intuition[12] is not a convincing proof of
their truth; since, having no certainty, apart from faith, whether man
was created by a good God, or by a wicked demon, or by chance, it is
doubtful whether these principles given to us are true, or false, or
uncertain, according to our origin. Again, no person is certain, apart
from faith, whether he is awake or sleeps, seeing that during sleep we
believe that we are awake as firmly as we do when we *are* awake; we
believe that we see space, figure, and motion; we are aware of the
passage of time, we measure it; and in fact we act as if we were awake.
So that half of our life being passed in sleep, we have on our own
admission no idea of truth, whatever we may imagine. As all our
intuitions are, then, illusions, who knows whether the other half of our
life, in which we think we are awake, is not another sleep a little
different from the former, from which we awake when we suppose
ourselves asleep? . . .

These are the chief arguments on one side and the other.

I omit minor ones, such as the sceptical talk against the impressions
of custom, education, manners, country and the like. Though these
influence the majority of common folk, who dogmatize only on shallow foundations, they are upset by the least breath of the sceptics. We
have only to see their books if we are not sufficiently convinced of this,
and we shall very quickly become so, perhaps too much.

I notice the only strong point of the dogmatists,[13] namely, that,
speaking in good faith and sincerely, we cannot doubt natural principles. Against this the sceptics set up in one word the uncertainty of our
origin, which includes that of our nature. The dogmatists have been
trying to answer this objection ever since the world began.

So there is open war among men, in which each must take a part and
side either with dogmatism or scepticism. For he who thinks to remain
neutral is above all a sceptic. This neutrality is the essence of the sect; he
who is not against them is essentially for them. In this appears their
advantage. They are not for themselves; they are neutral, indifferent,
in suspense as to all things, even themselves being no exception.

[11]Persons who habitually doubt.

[12]Knowledge without resort to reason.

[13]Persons who positively assert their opinions.

What, then, shall man do in this state? Shall he doubt everything? Shall he doubt whether he is awake, whether he is being pinched, or whether he is being burned? Shall he doubt whether he doubts? Shall he doubt whether he exists? We cannot go so far as that; and I lay it down as a fact that there never has been a real complete sceptic. Nature sustains our feeble reason and prevents it raving to this extent.

Shall he, then, say, on the contrary, that he certainly possesses truth—he who, when pressed ever so little, can show no title to it and is forced to let go his hold?

What a chimera,[14] then, is man! What a novelty! What a monster, what a chaos, what a contradiction, what a prodigy! Judge of all things, imbecile worm of the earth; depositary of truth, a sink of uncertainty and error; the pride and refuse of the universe!

Who will unravel this tangle? Nature confutes the sceptics, and reason confutes the dogmatists. What, then, will you become, O men! who try to find out by your natural reason what is your true condition? You cannot avoid one of these sects, nor adhere to one of them.

Know then, proud man, what a paradox you are to yourself. Humble yourself, weak reason; be silent, foolish nature; learn that man infinitely transcends man, and learn from your Master your true condition, of which you are ignorant. Hear God.

For in fact, if man had never been corrupt, he would enjoy in his innocence both truth and happiness with assurance; and if man had always been corrupt, he would have no idea of truth or bliss. But, wretched as we are, and more so than if there were no greatness in our condition, we have an idea of happiness and cannot reach it. We perceive an image of truth and possess only a lie. Incapable of absolute ignorance and of certain knowledge, we have thus been manifestly in a degree of perfection from which we have unhappily fallen.

. . .

We desire truth, and find within ourselves only uncertainty.

We seek happiness, and find only misery and death.

We cannot but desire truth and happiness, and are incapable of certainty or happiness. This desire is left to us, partly to punish us, partly to make us perceive where from we are fallen.

. . .

[14]An imaginary animal.

We are full of things which take us out of ourselves.

Our instinct makes us feel that we must seek our happiness outside ourselves. Our passions impel us outside, even when no objects present themselves to excite them. External objects tempt us of themselves, and call to us, even when we are not thinking of them. And thus philosophers have said in vain, "Retire within yourselves, you will find your good there."[15] We do not believe them, and those who believe them are the most empty and the most foolish.

• • •

There are only two kinds of men: the righteous, who believe themselves sinners; the rest, sinners, who believe themselves righteous.

• • •

Christianity is strange. It bids man recognize that he is vile, even abominable, and bids him desire to be like God. Without such a counterpoise, this dignity would make him horribly vain, or this humiliation would make him terribly abject.

• • •

With how little pride does a Christian believe himself united to God! With how little humiliation does he place himself on a level with the worms of earth!

A glorious manner to welcome life and death, good and evil!

• • •

---

[15]Quotation from the ancient Stoic philosophers.

6

John Locke

An Essay Concerning Human Understanding

JOHN Locke *(1632–1704), the great English philosopher, was also a student of science, a practicing physician, and one of the founders of the Royal Society, the oldest scientific organization in Great Britain. As a philosopher, he carried on the empirical tradition that was so important for the development of scientific method. Through his writings he did for human nature what his contemporary Newton did for the universe, and thereby became the official philosopher of his age. He was, however, no "closet thinker." Living through the English revolutions of the seventeenth century, Locke had strong political preferences and acted on them. He opposed royal absolutism and supported the push for Parliamentary supremacy; for these activities, he suffered exile and the loss of his fortune. Philosophically, Locke was an empiricist, although he was not thoroughly consistent in his views. He said he was driven to study the process of knowing because of the fruitlessness of discussions of absolute truth and reality. For Locke, there were no absolute principles of knowledge. All knowledge was partial and tentative, formed progressively by the use of what was given by the senses. By his common-sense arguments, Locke freed the psychological process of knowing from the doctrine of inborn ideas and brought it down to earth. He thus discredited abstract rationalism, which hampered scientific investigation, and disallowed original sin and heredity as the chief sources of human behavior. This environmental psychology gave society an instrument with which to refashion the world; for, if people are the products of their environment, then by changing the environment society could remake humankind—a basic article of faith of the Enlightenment.*

In An Essay Concerning Human Understanding *(1690), Locke explores the operations of the mind and tells us what knowledge is, how it is acquired, and how valid it is. He denies the existence of inborn logical or moral principles, picturing the mind at birth as a "clean slate" on which experience and reasoning write the script. His theory, which may seem commonplace and incomplete today, was quite revolutionary in its time.*

———

NO INBORN PRINCIPLES IN THE MIND

The way shown how we come by any knowledge, sufficient to prove it not inborn.—It is an established opinion among some men, that there are in the understanding certain inborn principles; some primary notions,[1] characters, as it were stamped upon the mind of man; which the soul[2] receives in its very first being, and brings into the world with it. It would be sufficient to convince unprejudiced readers of the falseness of this supposition, if I should only show (as I hope I shall in the following parts of this discourse) how men, barely by the use of their natural faculties, may attain to all the knowledge they have, without the help of any inborn impressions; and may arrive at certainty, without any such original notions or principles. For I imagine anyone will easily grant that it would be impertinent to suppose the ideas of colors inborn in a creature to whom God has given sight, and a power to receive them by the eyes from external objects: and no less unreasonable would it be to attribute several truths to the impressions of nature, and inborn characters, when we may observe in ourselves faculties fit to attain as easy and certain knowledge of them, as if they were originally imprinted on the mind. . . .

• • •

OF IDEAS IN GENERAL AND THEIR ORIGIN

Idea is the object of thinking.—Every man being conscious that he thinks, and that which his mind is applied to while thinking being the ideas that are there, it is without a doubt that men have in their minds

---

[1]Ideas unsupported by evidence or reason.

[2]By "soul," Locke means, essentially, the "mind."

AN ESSAY CONCERNING HUMAN UNDERSTANDING   Adapted by editor, from John Locke, *An Essay Concerning Human Understanding*, in *The Philosophical Works of John Locke*, ed. J. A. St. John (London: George Bell & Sons, 1892), I, 134–35, 205–08, 210–11, 221–25, 279–80.

several ideas,—such as are those expressed by the words whiteness, hardness, sweetness, thinking, motion, man, elephant, army, drunkenness, and others. It is in the first place then to be inquired, how he comes by them? I know it is an accepted doctrine that men have inborn ideas, stamped upon their minds in their very beginning. This opinion I have at large examined already; and, I suppose what I have already said . . . will be much more easily admitted, when I have shown where the understanding may get all the ideas it has; and by what ways and degrees they may come into the mind;—for which I shall appeal to every one's own observation and experience.

All ideas come from sensation or reflection.—Let us then suppose the mind to be, as we say, white paper, void of all characters, without any ideas.—How comes it to be furnished? From where comes that vast store which the busy and boundless fancy of man has painted on it with an almost endless variety? From where has it all the materials of reason and knowledge? To this I answer, in one word, from experience. On that all our knowledge is founded; and from that it is ultimately derived. Our observation, turned upon either external objects, or upon the internal operations of our minds, is that which supplies our understanding with all the materials of thinking. These two are the fountains of knowledge, from where come all the ideas we have, or naturally can have.

The objects of sensation one source of ideas.—First, our senses, acquainted with particular sensible objects, convey to the mind several distinct perceptions of things, according to those various ways wherein those objects do affect them. And thus we come by those ideas we have of yellow, white, heat, cold, soft, hard, bitter, sweet, and all those which we call sensible qualities; which when I say the senses convey to the mind, I mean, they from external objects convey to the mind what produces there those perceptions. This great source of most of the ideas we have, depending wholly upon our senses, and derived by them to the understanding, I call sensation.

The operations of our minds, the other source of them.—Secondly, the other fountain from which experience furnishes the understanding with ideas is the perception of the operations of our own mind within us, when it considers the ideas it has got. These operations, as the soul comes to reflect on and consider, furnish the understanding with another set of ideas, which could not be had from external things. And such are perception, thinking, doubting, believing, reasoning, knowing, willing, and all the different notions of our own minds;—which we being conscious of, and observing in ourselves, do from these receive into our understandings as distinct ideas as we do from bodies affecting our senses. This source of ideas every man has wholly in himself; and though it be not sense, as having nothing to do with external objects, yet it is very like it, and might properly enough be called internal sense. But as I call the other *sensation*, so I call this *reflection*, the ideas being such only as the mind gets by reflecting on its own operations within itself. By reflection then, in the following part of this discourse, I would have understood to mean that observation which the mind takes of its own operations. . . . These two, I say, namely, external material things, as the objects of sensation, and the operations of our own minds within, as the objects of reflection are to me the only origin from where all our ideas take their beginnings. The term operations here I use in a large sense, as including not merely the actions of the mind about its ideas, but some sort of passions arising sometimes from them, such as is the satisfaction or uneasiness arising from any thought.

All our ideas are of the one or the other of these.—The understanding seems to me not to have the least glimmering of any ideas which it does not receive from one of these two. External objects furnish the mind with the ideas of sensible qualities, which are all those different perceptions they produce in us; and the mind furnishes the understanding with ideas of its own operations.

These, when we have taken a full survey of them, and their several modes, combinations, and relations, we shall find to contain all our whole stock of ideas; and that we have nothing in our minds which did not come in one of these two ways. Let anyone examine his own thoughts, and thoroughly search into his understanding; and then let him tell me, whether all the original ideas he has there, are any other than of the objects of his senses, or of the operations of his mind, considered as objects of his reflection. And how great a mass of knowledge soever he imagines to be lodged there, he will, upon taking a strict view, see that he has not any idea in his mind but what one of these two have imprinted;—though perhaps, with infinite variety compounded and enlarged by the understanding, as we shall see hereafter. . . .

The soul begins to have ideas when it begins to perceive.—To ask, at what time a man has first any ideas, is to ask, when he begins to perceive;— having ideas, and perception, being the same thing. I know it is an opinion, that the soul always thinks, and that it has the actual perception of ideas in itself constantly, as long as it exists; and that actual thinking is as inseparable from the soul as actual extension is from the body; which if true, to inquire about the beginning of a man's ideas is the same as to inquire after the beginning of his soul. For, by this account, soul and its ideas, as body and its extension, will begin to exist both at the same time. . . .

No ideas but from sensation and reflection, evident, if we observe children.—I see no reason, therefore, to believe that the soul thinks before the senses have furnished it with ideas to think about. And as those are increased and retained, so it comes, by exercise, to improve its faculty of thinking in the several parts of it; as well as, afterward by compounding those ideas, and reflecting on its own operations, it increases its stock, as well as facility in remembering, imagining, reasoning, and other modes of thinking.

State of a child in the mother's womb.—He that will suffer himself to be informed by observation and experience, and not make his own theory the rule of nature, will find few signs of a soul accustomed to much thinking in a newborn child, and much fewer of any reasoning at all. And yet it is hard to imagine that the rational soul should think so much, and not reason at all. And he that will consider that infants newly come into the world spend the greatest part of their time in sleep, and are seldom awake but when either hunger calls, or some pain (the most demanding of all sensations), or some other violent impression on the body forces the mind to perceive and attend to it;—he, I say, who considers this, will perhaps find reason to imagine that a fetus in the mother's womb differs not much from the state of a vegetable. It passes the greatest part of its time without perception or thought; doing very little but sleeping in a place where it needs not seek food, and is surrounded by liquid, always equally soft, and nearly of the same temperature. There the eyes have no light and the ears are so shut up as to hear few sounds, and there is little or no variety or change of objects to stimulate the senses.

The mind thinks in proportion to the matter it gets from experience to think about.—Follow a child from its birth, and observe the alterations that time makes, and you shall find, as the mind by the senses comes more and more to be furnished with ideas, it comes to be more and more awake. It thinks more, the more it has matter to think about. After some time it begins to know the objects which, being most familiar with it, have made lasting impressions. Thus it comes by degrees to know the persons it daily converses with, and distinguishes them from strangers. . . . And so we may observe how the mind, by degrees, improves; and it advances to the exercise of those other faculties by enlarging, compounding, and abstracting its ideas, and of reasoning about them, and reflecting upon all these. . . .

A man begins to have ideas when he first has sensation. What sensation is.—If it is asked, when does a man begin to have any ideas, I think the true answer is,—when he first has any sensation. For, since there appear not to be any ideas in the mind before the senses have conveyed any in, I conceive that ideas in the understanding are concurrent with sensation—which is such an impression or motion made in some part of the body, that produces some perception in the understanding. It is about these impressions made on our senses by outward objects that the mind seems first to engage itself, in such operations as we call perception, remembering, consideration, reasoning, and so forth.

The origin of all our knowledge.—In time the mind comes to reflect on its own operations about the ideas gotten by sensation, and thereby stores itself with a new set of ideas, which I call ideas of reflection. These are the impressions that are made on our senses by outward objects that are external to the mind; and its own operations, proceeding from powers internal and belonging to itself, which, when reflected on by the mind, become also objects of its thought. They are, as I have said, the origin of all knowledge. Thus the first capacity of human intellect is—that the mind is fitted to receive the impressions made on it; either through the senses by outward objects, or by its own operations when it reflects on them. This is the first step a man makes toward the discovery of anything, and the groundwork whereon to build all those notions which ever he shall have in this world. All those sublime thoughts which tower above the clouds, and reach as high as heaven itself, take their rise and footing here. In all that vast space wherein the mind wanders, in those far-out speculations it may seem to be occupied with, it matters not one bit beyond those ideas which sense or reflection have offered for its consideration.

In the reception of simple ideas, the understanding is for the most part passive.—In this part the understanding is merely passive; and whether or not it will have these beginnings and, as it were, materials of knowledge, is not in its own power. For the objects of our senses do, many of them, thrust their particular ideas upon our minds whether we will or not; and the operations of our minds will not let us be without, at least, some obscure notions of them. No man can be wholly ignorant of what he does when he thinks. These simple ideas, when offered to the mind, the understanding can no more refuse to have, nor alter when they are imprinted, nor blot them out and make new ones itself, than a mirror can refuse, alter, or obliterate the images or ideas which the objects set before it produce. As the bodies that surround us variously affect our organs, the mind is forced to receive the impressions; and cannot avoid the perception of those ideas that are joined to them.

OF SIMPLE IDEAS

Uncompounded appearances.—The better to understand the nature, manner, and extent of our knowledge, one thing is carefully to be observed concerning the ideas we have; and that is, that some of them are simple and some complex.

Though the qualities that affect our senses are, in the things themselves, so united and blended, that there is no separation, no distance between them; yet it is plain, the ideas they produce in the mind enter by the senses simple and unmixed. For, though the sight and touch often take in from the same object, at the same time, different ideas;— as a man sees at once motion and color; the hand feels softness and warmth in the same piece of wax; yet the simple ideas thus united in the same subject are as perfectly distinct as those that come in by different senses. The coldness and hardness which a man feels in a piece of ice are as distinct ideas in the mind as the smell and whiteness of a lily; or as the taste of sugar, and smell of a rose. And nothing can be plainer to a man than the clear and distinct perception he has of those simple ideas; which, being each in itself uncompounded, contains in it nothing but one uniform appearance in the mind, and is not distinguishable into different ideas.

The mind can neither make nor destroy them.—These simple ideas, the materials of all our knowledge, are suggested and furnished to the mind only by those two ways above mentioned, which are sensation and reflection. When the understanding is once stored with these simple ideas, it has the power to repeat, compare, and unite them, even to an almost infinite variety, and so can make at pleasure new complex ideas. But it is not in the power of the most exalted wit, or enlarged understanding, by any quickness or variety of thought, to invent or frame even one new simple idea in the mind, which is not taken in by the ways before mentioned: nor can any force of the understanding destroy those that are there. The power of man, in this little world of his own understanding being much the same as it is in the great world of visible things: wherein his power, however managed by art and skill, reaches no farther than to compound and divide the materials that are at his hand. He can do nothing toward the making the least particle of new matter, or destroying one atom of what is already in existence. The same inability everyone will find in himself, if he tries to fashion in his understanding one simple idea, not received by his senses from external objects, or by reflection from the operations of his own mind about them. I would have anyone try to imagine any taste which had never touched his palate; or frame the idea of a scent he had never smelled. If he can do this, I will also conclude that a blind man has ideas of colors, and a deaf man true distinct notions of sounds. . . .

• • •

OF COMPLEX IDEAS

Made by the mind out of simple ones.—We have up to now considered those ideas, in the reception of which the mind is only passive, and which come from sensation and reflection. . . . But as the mind is wholly passive in the reception of all its simple ideas, so it exerts several acts of its own—whereby out of its simple ideas, as the materials and foundations of the rest, the others are framed. The acts of the mind, wherein it exerts its power over its simple ideas, are chiefly these three: (1) Combining several simple ideas into one compound one; and thus all complex ideas are made. (2) The bringing of two ideas, whether simple or complex, together, and setting them by one another, so as to take a view of them at once, without uniting them into one; by which way it gets all its ideas of relations. (3) Separating them from all other ideas that accompany them in their real existence: this is called abstraction, and thus all its general ideas are made. This shows man's power, and its ways of operation, to be much the same in the material and intellectual world. For the materials in both being such as he has no power over, either to make or destroy, all that man can do is either to unite them together, or to set them by one another, or wholly separate them. I shall here begin with the first of these in the consideration of complex ideas, and come to the other two in their due places. As simple ideas are observed to exist in several combinations united together, so the mind has the power to consider several of them united together as one idea; and that not only as they are united in external objects, but as the mind has joined them together. Ideas thus made up of several simple ones put together, I call complex;—such as are beauty, gratitude, a man, an army, the universe; which, though consisting of various simple ideas, or complex ideas made up of simple ones, yet are, when the mind pleases, considered each by itself, as one entire thing, and called by one name.

Made voluntarily.—In this capacity for repeating and joining together its ideas, the mind has great power in varying and multiplying the objects of its thoughts, infinitely beyond what sensation or reflection furnished it with; but all this is still confined to those simple ideas which it received from those two sources, and which are the ultimate materials of all its compositions. For simple ideas are all from things themselves, and of these the mind can have no more, nor other than what are suggested to it. It can have no other ideas of sensible qualities than what come from without by the senses; nor any ideas of other kind of operations of thinking than what it finds in itself. But when it has once got these simple ideas, it is not confined barely to observation, and what offers itself from without; it can, by its own power, put together those ideas it has, and make new complex ones, which it never received so united. . . .

• • •

7

John Locke

Of Civil Government

*L*OCKE *opposed dogmatism not only in philosophy but also in religion and politics. He favored a greater degree of freedom in religion and education; in political thought, he provided the philosophical basis of classical liberalism—the theory and practice of limited, representative government. He wished to liberate society from the unnatural restrictions imposed by royal absolutism and to free the individual for maximum development according to the laws of nature. Locke's political ideas, set down in* Two Treatises of Government *(1690), served as a justification of the English "Glorious Revolution" of 1688 and strongly influenced the eighteenth-century revolutions in America and France and, subsequently, the development of constitutional democracy. The first treatise attacked the theory of absolute monarchy; the second treatise,* Of Civil Government—*from which the following selection is taken—was written, as Locke says in the preface, "to establish the throne of our great restorer, our present King William; to make good his title in the consent of the people . . ., and to justify to the world the people of England whose love of their just and natural rights, with their resolution to preserve them, saved the nation. . . ." Although the second treatise sounds like a response to events of 1688 and 1689, it was actually written some years before, probably in 1681. In this work, Locke based all government on the "natural rights" of the individual and on the "social contract." Specifically, this meant that government should rest on the consent of the governed and be limited in its powers. It is important to note the secular origin of government in Locke's theory as well as its fundamental individualism, which held that human beings were free moral agents—who existed prior to the establishment of government and were the very basis of it. Locke thus denied the superior authority of the state; he placed sovereignty in the individuals who make up the state and held that no government might intrude into their private affairs.*

OF THE STATE OF NATURE

To understand political power correctly, and derive it from its origins, we must consider what state all men are naturally in: a state of perfect freedom to order their actions and dispose of their possessions and persons as they think fit, within the bounds of the law of nature, without asking permission or depending upon the will of any other man.

A state also of equality, wherein all the power and jurisdiction is mutual, no one having more than another; there being nothing more evident than that creatures of the same species, born to all the same advantages of nature and the use of the same faculties, should also be equal one among another without subordination or subjection; unless the Lord and Master of them all should, by an open declaration of his will, set one above another, and confer on him by an evident and clear appointment an undoubted right to rule over others.

But though this be a state of liberty, yet it is not a state of license;[1] though man in that state has an unrestricted liberty to dispose of his person or possessions, yet he has not liberty to destroy himself, or any creature under his control. . . . The state of nature has a law of nature to govern it which obliges every one; and *reason*, which is that law, teaches all mankind who will but consult it that, being all equal and independent, no one ought to harm another in his life, health, liberty, or possessions. Since all men are the creation of one omnipotent and infinitely wise Maker, all are the servants of one sovereign Master, sent into the world by his order, and doing his work; they are his property, made to live for his, not one another's, pleasure; and being furnished with like faculties, sharing all in one community of nature, there cannot be supposed any such subordination among us that may authorize us to destroy another—as if we were made for one another's uses as the inferior ranks of creatures are for ours. Every one, as he is bound to preserve himself, . . . so by the like reason, when his own preservation is not in jeopardy, ought, as much as he can, to preserve the rest of mankind. He may not, unless it be to do justice to an offender, take away or impair the life, or what tends to the preservation of life: the liberty, health, limb, or goods of another.

---

[1]Abuse of liberty.

OF CIVIL GOVERNMENT   Adapted by editor, from John Locke, *Two Treatises of Government*, in *The Works of John Locke* (London: Thomas Tegg, 1823), V, 339–42, 353–54, 357, 387–89, 394–96, 411–13, 416–17, 423–24, 457, 459, 469–72, 483–85.

And that all men may be restrained from invading others' rights and from doing hurt to one another, and the law of nature be observed which wills the peace and preservation of all mankind, the execution of the law of nature is, in that state, put into every man's hands, whereby every one has a right to punish the breakers of that law to such a degree as may hinder its violation. For the law of nature would, as all other laws that concern men in this world, be in vain, if there were nobody that in the state of nature had a power to execute that law and thereby preserve the innocent and restrain offenders. And if any one in the state of nature may punish another for any evil he has done, every one may do so; for in that state of perfect equality, where naturally there is no superiority or jurisdiction of one over another, what any may do in prosecution of that law, every one must have a right to do.

And thus in the state of nature one man takes power over another; but yet no absolute or arbitrary power to abuse a criminal, when he has got him in his hands, according to the intensity of anger or whims of his own will; but only to punish him, so far as calm reason and conscience dictate, according to his crime. . . . In breaking the law of nature, the offender declares himself to live by another rule than that of reason and justice, which is that measure God has set to the actions of men for their mutual security; and so he becomes dangerous to mankind, the tie which is to secure them from injury and violence being slighted and broken by him. Which being a trespass against the whole species and the peace and safety of it provided for by the law of nature, every man upon this reason, by the right he has to preserve mankind in general, may restrain, or, where it is necessary, destroy things harmful to them. He thus may bring such evil on any one who has broken that law, in order to make him repent the doing of it and thereby deter him, and by his example others, from doing the like harm. And in this case, and upon this ground, every man has a right to punish the offender and be executioner of the law of nature. . . .

• • •

OF PROPERTY

God, who has given the world to men in common, has also given them reason to make use of it to the best advantage of life and convenience. The earth and all that is therein, is given to men for the support and comfort of their being. And though all the fruits it naturally produces and beasts it feeds belong to mankind in common, as they are produced by the spontaneous hand of nature; and nobody has *originally* a private estate exclusive of the rest of mankind, in any of them, since they are in their natural state; yet, being given for the use of men, there must be a means to take them some way or other before they can be of any use or at all beneficial to any particular man. The fruit or venison which nourishes the wild Indian, who knows no enclosure[2] and is still a tenant in common,[3] must be his, and so his, that is, a part of him, that another can no longer have any right to it before it can do him any good for the support of his life.

Though the earth and all inferior creatures be common to all men, yet every man has a property in his own person; this nobody has any right to but himself. The labor of his body and the work of his hands, we may say, are properly his. Whatsoever then he removes out of the state that nature has provided and left it in, he has mixed his labor with, and joined to it something that is his own, and thereby makes it his *property*. It being by him removed from the common state nature has placed it in, it has by this labor something added to it that excludes the common right of other men. For this labor being the unquestionable property of the laborer, no man but he can have a right to what that is once joined to, at least where there is enough and as good left in common for others. . . .

God gave the world to men in common; but since he gave it them for their benefit and the greatest conveniences of life they were capable to draw from it, it cannot be supposed he meant it should always remain common and uncultivated. He gave it to the use of the industrious and rational—and labor was to be his title to it—not to the whim or greed of the quarrelsome. . . .

· · ·

OF POLITICAL OR CIVIL SOCIETY

Man, being born, as has been proved, with a title to perfect freedom and an unrestricted enjoyment of all the rights and privileges of the law of nature equally with any other man or number of men in the world,

[2]Boundary enclosing private property.
[3]Sharing ownership with others.

has by nature a power not only to preserve his property[4]—that is, his life, liberty, and estate[5]—against the injuries and attempts of other men, but also to judge and punish the violations of that law by others as he is persuaded the offense deserves—even with death itself in those crimes where the heinousness in his opinion requires it. But because no political society can exist without having the power to preserve the property and also to punish the offenses of all those of that society, there and there only is political society where every one of the members has given up his natural power, surrendered it into the hands of the community. . . . And thus, all private judgment of every particular member being excluded, the community comes to be umpire by settled standing rules, impartial and the same to all parties, and by men having authority from the community for the execution of those rules. The community decides all the differences that may happen between any members of that society concerning any matter of right, and punishes those offenses which any member has committed against the society with such penalties as the law has established; whereby it is easy to see who are, and who are not, in political society together. Those who are united into one body and have a common established law and courts to appeal to, with authority to decide controversies between them and punish offenders, are in civil society one with another; but those who have no such common appeal are still in the state of nature, each being, where there is no other, judge for himself and executioner, which is, as I have before shown it, the perfect state of nature.

And thus the commonwealth[6] receives power to set down what punishment shall fit the various crimes committed by the members of that society—which is the power of making laws—as well as it has the power to punish any injury done unto any of its members by any one that is not of it—which is the power of war and peace—and all this for the preservation of the property of all the members of that society as far as is possible. But though every man who has entered into civil society and has become a member of any commonwealth has thereby surrendered his power to punish offenses against the law of nature in prosecution of his own private judgment, yet, with the judgment of offenses which he has given up to the legislative . . . he has given a right to the commonwealth to employ his force for the execution of the judgments

[4]Whatever belongs to an individual.
[5]Material possessions.
[6]Political community (state).

of the commonwealth, whenever he shall be called to it. These are, indeed, his own judgments, they being made by himself or his representative. And herein we have the origin of the legislative and executive power of civil society which is to judge by standing laws how far offenses are to be punished when committed within the commonwealth, and also to determine, by occasional judgments founded on the present circumstances of the fact, how far injuries from without are to be punished, and in both these to employ all the force of all the members when there shall be need.

Whenever, therefore, any number of men are so united into one society, and when every one gives up his executive power of the law of nature and surrenders it to the public, there and there only is a political or civil society. And this is done wherever any number of men, in the state of nature, enter into society to make one people, one body politic, under one supreme government, or else when any one joins himself to any government already made; for hereby he authorizes the society or, which is the same, the legislative thereof, to make laws for him as the public good of the society shall require. . . . And this puts men out of a state of nature into that of a commonwealth by setting up a judge on earth, with authority to determine all the controversies and redress the injuries that may happen to any member of the commonwealth; which judge is the legislative, or magistrates appointed by it. And wherever there are any number of men, however associated, that have no such decisive power to appeal to, there they are still in the state of nature. . . .

OF THE BEGINNING OF POLITICAL SOCIETIES

Men being, as has been said, by nature all free, equal, and independent, no one can be put out of this condition and subjected to the political power of another without his own consent. The only way whereby any one divests himself of his natural liberty, and puts on the bonds of civil society, is by agreeing with other men to join and unite into a community for their comfortable, safe, and peaceable living one among another, in a secure enjoyment of their properties and a greater security against any that are not of it. This any number of men may do, because it injures not the freedom of the rest; they are left as they were in the liberty of the state of nature. When any number of men have so consented to make one community or government, they are thereby incorporated and make one body politic wherein the majority have a right to act and govern the rest.

For when any number of men have, by the consent of every individual, made a community, they have thereby made that community one body, with a power to act as one body, which is only by the will and determination of the *majority*. For that which moves any community, which is the consent of the individuals of it, and it being necessary to that which is one body to move one way, it is necessary the body should move that way where the greater force carries it, which is the consent of the majority; or else it is impossible it should act or continue one body, one community, which the consent of every individual that united into it agreed that it should. Therefore, every one is bound by that consent to be governed by the majority. And therefore we see that in assemblies empowered to act by positive laws, where no other number is set by that positive law which empowers them, the act of the majority passes for the act of the whole. . . .

And thus every man, by consenting with others to make one body politic under one government, puts himself under an obligation to every one of that society to submit to the determination of the majority, and to be governed by it; or else this original compact, whereby he with others incorporates into one society, would signify nothing, and be no compact, if he be left free and under no other ties than he was in before in the state of nature. For what appearance would there be of any compact? What new engagement if he were no further tied by any decrees of the society than he himself thought fit and did actually consent to? This would be still as great a liberty as he himself had before his compact, or any one else in the state of nature has who may submit himself and consent to any acts of it if he thinks fit.

For if the consent of the majority shall not for good reason be accepted as the will of the whole and govern every individual, nothing but the consent of every individual can make any thing to be the act of the whole; but such a consent is next to impossible ever to be had if we consider the infirmities of health and duties of business which in a number, though much less than that of a commonwealth, will necessarily keep many away from the public assembly. To which, if we add the variety of opinions and diversities of interests which unavoidably happen in all groups of men, the entering into society upon such terms would be only like Cato's[7] entering into the theater, only to go out

---

[7]Marcus Porcius Cato (234–149 B.C.), also known as "Cato the Elder," was a Roman statesman and orator. He endeavored to keep alive the ancient Roman virtues such as austerity, simplicity, discipline, and obedience to authority. He loathed Greek philosophy and demonstrated his contempt for the theater by walking ostentatiously through it without sitting down for a moment.

again. Such a constitution as this would make the mighty leviathan[8] of a shorter duration than the feeblest creatures, and not let it outlast the day it was born in; which cannot be supposed that rational creatures should desire and constitute societies only to be dissolved; for where the majority cannot govern the rest, there they cannot act as one body, and consequently will be immediately dissolved again.

Whosoever, therefore, out of a state of nature unite into a community must be understood to give up all the power necessary for the purposes for which they unite into society to the majority of the community, unless they expressly agreed in any number greater than the majority. And this is done by simply agreeing to unite into one political society, which is all the compact that is, or needs be, between the individuals that enter into or make up a commonwealth. And thus that which begins and actually constitutes any political society is nothing but the consent of any number of freemen capable of a majority to unite and incorporate into such a society. And this is that, and that only, which did or could give beginning to any lawful government in the world. . . .

OF THE ENDS OF POLITICAL SOCIETY AND GOVERNMENT

If man in the state of nature be so free, as has been said, if he be absolute lord of his own person and possessions, equal to the greatest, and subject to nobody, why will he part with his freedom, why will he give up his independence and subject himself to the rule and control of any other power? To which it is obvious to answer that though in the state of nature he has such a right, yet the enjoyment of it is very uncertain and constantly exposed to the attacks of others; for all being kings as much as he, every man his equal, and the greater part no strict observers of equity and justice, the enjoyment of the property he has in this state is very unsafe, very insecure. This makes him willing to give up a condition which, however free, is full of fears and continual dangers; and it is not without reason that he seeks out and is willing to join in society with others, who are already united, or have a mind to unite, for the mutual preservation of their lives, liberties, and estates, which I call by the general name "property."

The great and chief end, therefore, of men's uniting into commonwealths and putting themselves under government, is the preserva-

---

[8]A legendary monster; the term used by Hobbes and others to symbolize the awesome power of the state.

tion of their property. To which in the state of nature there are many things lacking:

First, there lacks an established, settled, known law, received and allowed by common consent to be the standard of right and wrong and the common measure to decide all controversies between them; for though the law of nature be plain and intelligible to all rational creatures, yet men, being biased by their interest as well as ignorant for lack of studying it, are not apt to allow it as a law binding to them in the application of it to their particular cases.

Secondly, in the state of nature there lacks a known and impartial judge with authority to determine all differences according to the established law; for every one in that state being both judge and executioner of the law of nature, men being partial to themselves, passion and revenge is very apt to carry them too far and with too much intensity of feeling in their own cases, as well as negligence and unconcernedness to make them too remiss in other men's.

Thirdly, in the state of nature, there often lacks power to back and support the sentence when right, and to give it due execution. And they who by any injustice offend will seldom fail, where they are able, by force, to make good their injustice; such resistance many times makes their punishment dangerous and frequently destructive to those who attempt it.

Thus mankind, notwithstanding all the privileges of the state of nature, being but in an ill condition while they remain in it, are quickly driven into society. Hence it comes to pass that we seldom find any number of men to live any time together in this state. The inconveniences that they are therein exposed to by the irregular and uncertain exercise of the power every man has of punishing the transgressions of others make them take protection under the established laws of government and therein seek the preservation of their property. It is this that makes every one of them so willing to give up his single power of punishing, to be exercised by such alone as shall be appointed; and by such rules as the community, or those authorized by them for that purpose, shall agree on. And in this we have the origin of the right of both the legislative and executive power, as well as of the governments and societies themselves. . . .

OF THE EXTENT OF THE LEGISLATIVE POWER

The great purposes of men's entering into society being the enjoyment of their properties in peace and safety, and the great instrument and means of that being the laws established in that society, the first and fundamental positive law of all commonwealths is the establishment of the legislative power. The first and fundamental natural law which is to govern even the legislative itself, is the preservation of the society and, as far as will agree with the public good, of every person in it. This legislative is not only the supreme power of the commonwealth, but sacred and unalterable in the hands where the community has once placed it; nor can any edict of anybody else, in whatever form conceived or by whatever power backed, have the force and obligation of a law which has not its approval from that legislative which the public has chosen and appointed. Nor without this the law could not have that which is absolutely necessary to its being a law: the consent of the society over whom nobody can have a power to make laws, but by their own consent and by authority received from them. And therefore all the obedience, which by the most solemn ties any one can be obliged to pay, ultimately ends in this supreme power and is directed by those laws which it enacts. Nor can any oaths to any foreign power, or any domestic lesser power, free any member of the society from his obedience to the legislative acting pursuant to their trust, nor oblige him to any obedience contrary to the laws so enacted. . . .

These are the bounds which the trust that is put in them by the society and the law of God and nature have set to the legislative power of every commonwealth, in all forms of government:

First, they are to govern by published established laws, not to be varied in particular cases, but to have one rule for rich and poor, for the favorite at court and the farmer at his plow.

Secondly, these laws also ought to be designed for no other purpose than the good of the people.

Thirdly, they must not raise taxes on the property of the people without the consent of the people, given by themselves or their representatives. . . .

Fourthly, the legislative cannot transfer the power of making laws to anybody else, or place it anywhere but where the people have placed it.

• • •

OF TYRANNY

As *usurpation* is the exercise of power which another has a right to, so *tyranny* is the exercise of power beyond right, which nobody can have a right to. And this is making use of the power any one has in his hands, not for the good of those who are under it, but for his own private advantage—when the executive officer makes not the law, but his will, the rule, and his commands and actions are not directed to the preservation of the properties of his people, but the satisfaction of his own ambition, revenge, greed, or any other unlawful passion. . . .

Wherever law ends tyranny begins, if the law be violated to another's harm. And whosoever in authority exceeds the power given him by the law, and makes use of the force he has under his command to enforce that upon the subject which the law does not allow, ceases in that to be a legitimate official and, acting without authority, may be opposed as any other man who by force invades the right of another. This is acknowledged in minor officials. He who has authority to seize my person in the street may be opposed as a thief and a robber if he endeavors to break into my house to serve a warrant, notwithstanding that I know he has such a warrant and such a legal authority as will impower him to arrest me in the street. And why should this not hold in the highest as well as in the lowest official? I would gladly be informed. Is it reasonable that the eldest brother, because he has the greatest part of his father's estate, should thereby have a right to take away any of his younger brother's portions? Or that a rich man who possessed a whole country should have a right to seize, when he pleased, the cottage and garden of his poor neighbor? Having great power and riches . . . can be no excuse or reason for plunder and oppression. . . . Exceeding the bounds of authority is no more a right in a great than in a petty officer, no more justifiable in a king than a constable;[9] and is so much the worse in him because he has more trust put in him, has already a much greater share than his fellow citizens, and is supposed, from the advantages of his education, work, and advisers, to be more knowing in matters of right and wrong. . . .

OF THE DISSOLUTION OF GOVERNMENT

The reason why men enter into society is the preservation of their property; and the aim of their choosing and authorizing a legislative is that there may be laws made and rules set as guards and fences for the properties of all the members of the society in order to limit and moderate the power of every part and member of the society. For it can never be supposed to be the will of the society that the legislative should have a power to destroy that which every one aims to secure by entering into society, and for which the people submitted themselves to

[9]A minor official, empowered to make arrests.

legislators of their own making. Whenever the legislators endeavor to take away and destroy the property of the people, or to reduce them to slavery under arbitrary power, they put themselves into a state of war with the people who are thereupon freed from any further obedience, and are left to the common shelter which God has provided for all men against force and violence. Whenever, therefore, the legislative shall break this fundamental rule of society, and either by ambition, fear, folly, or corruption, endeavor to grasp for themselves, or put into the hands of any other, an absolute power over the lives, liberties, and estates of the people, by this breach of trust they forfeit the power the people had put into their hands for quite contrary ends. It reverts then to the people, who have a right to resume their original liberty, and, by the establishment of a new legislative, such as they shall think fit, provide for their own safety and security, which is the purpose for which they are in society. What I have said here concerning the legislative in general holds true also concerning the supreme executive, who having a double trust put in him—both to have a part in the legislative and the supreme execution of the law—acts against both when he goes about to set up his own arbitrary will as the law of the society. He acts also contrary to his trust when he either employs the force, money, and offices of the society to corrupt the representatives and win them to his purposes, or openly manipulates the electors and prescribes to their choice such whom he has by bribes, threats, promises, or otherwise won to his schemes, and employs them to bring in those who have promised beforehand how to vote and what to enact. Thus to regulate candidates and electors, and alter the ways of elections, what is it but to destroy the government by the roots, and poison the very fountain of public security? For the people, having reserved to themselves the choice of their representatives, for the protection of their properties, could do it for no other end but that they might always be freely chosen, and, so chosen, freely act and advise as the necessity of the commonwealth and the public good should upon examination and mature debate be judged to require. This, those who give their votes before they hear the debate and have weighed the reasons on all sides, are not capable of doing. To prepare such an assembly as this, and endeavor to set up appointed supporters of his own choosing for the true representatives of the people and lawmakers of society, is certainly as great a breach of trust and a perfect declaration of a scheme to subvert the government. . . .

To this perhaps it will be said that, the people being ignorant and always discontented, to lay the foundation of government in the unsteady opinion and uncertain temperament of the people is to expose it to certain ruin; and no government will be able to endure long if the people may set up a new legislative whenever they take offense at the old one. To this I answer: Quite the contrary. People are not so easily got out of their old forms as some are apt to suggest. They are hardly to be moved to change the acknowledged faults in the circumstances they have been accustomed to. And if there be any original defects, or accidental ones introduced by time or corruption, it is not an easy thing to get them changed, even when all the world sees there is an opportunity for it. This slowness and aversion in the people to abandon their old constitutions has in the many revolutions which have been seen in this kingdom, in this and former ages, . . . still brought us back to our old legislative of king, lords, and commons;[10] and whatever provocations caused the crown to be taken from some of our princes' heads, they never carried the people so far as to place it on another dynasty.

But it will be said this theory lays the foundation for frequent rebellion. To which I answer:

First, no more than any other theory; for when the people are made miserable, and find themselves exposed to the abuses of arbitrary power, revere their governors as sons of Jupiter,[11] let them be sacred or divine, descended, or authorized from heaven, give them out for whom or what you please, the same will happen. The people generally ill-treated, and contrary to right, will be ready upon any occasion to ease themselves of a burden that sits heavy upon them. They will wish and seek for the opportunity, which in the change, weakness, and accidents of human affairs seldom delays long to offer itself. He must have lived but a little while in the world who has not seen examples of this in his time, and he must have read very little who cannot produce examples of it in all sorts of governments in the world.

Secondly, I answer, such revolutions happen not upon every little mismanagement in public affairs. Great mistakes of the ruling party, many wrong and inconvenient laws, and all the slips of human frailty will be borne by the people without mutiny or murmur. But if a long train of abuses, lies, and tricks, all tending the same way, make the scheme visible to the people, and they cannot but feel what they are subjected to and see where they are going, it is not to be wondered that they should then rouse themselves and endeavor to put the rule into

---

[10]Representatives of the non-noble classes of England (House of Commons).
[11]The principal Roman god.

such hands which may secure to them the ends for which government was at first formed. . . .

Thirdly, I answer that this doctrine of a power in the people of providing for their safety anew by a new legislative, when their legislators have acted contrary to their trust by invading their property, is the best defense against rebellion, and the most likely means to hinder it. For rebellion is an opposition, not to persons, but authority which is founded only on the constitutions and laws of the government; those, whoever they may be, who by force break through, and by force justify their violation of them, are truly and properly the *rebels*. . . .

Here, probably, the common question will be asked: Who shall be judge whether the prince or legislative act contrary to their trust? This, perhaps, ill-affected and devisive men may spread among the people, when the prince only makes use of his due prerogative. To this I reply: The people shall be judge; for who shall be judge whether his trustee or deputy acts well and according to the trust placed in him but he who hired him and must, by having hired him, have still the power to discard him when he fails in his trust? If this be reasonable in particular cases of private men, why should it be otherwise in that of the greatest moment where the welfare of millions is concerned, and also where the evil, if not prevented, is greater and the redress very difficult, costly, and dangerous? . . .

If a controversy should arise between a prince and some of the people in a matter where the law is silent or doubtful, and the matter is of great consequence, I should think the proper umpire in such a case should be the body of the people. For in cases where the prince has a trust placed in him and is exempted from the common ordinary rules of the law, there, if any men find themselves aggrieved and think the prince acts contrary to or beyond that trust, who is so proper to judge as the body of the people (who, at first, placed that trust in him) as to how far they meant it should extend? But if the prince, or whoever they may be in the administration, decline that way of decision, the appeal then lies nowhere but with heaven. Force between persons, who have no known superior on earth or which permits no appeal to a judge on earth, is properly a state of war wherein the appeal lies only to heaven; and in that state the injured party must judge for himself when he will think fit to make use of that appeal and put himself to it.

To conclude, the power that every individual gave the society when he entered into it can never revert to the individuals again as long as the society lasts, but will always remain in the *community*, because without this there can be no community, no commonwealth, which is contrary to the original agreement. So also when the society has placed the legislative in any assembly of men, to continue in them and their successors with direction and authority for providing such successors, the legislative can never revert to the people while that government lasts, because having provided a legislative with power to continue forever, they have given up their political power to the legislative and cannot reclaim it. But if they have set limits to the duration of their legislative and made this supreme power in any person or assembly only temporary, or else when by the miscarriages of those in authority it is forfeited, upon the forfeiture, or at the determination of the time set, it reverts to the society. The people then have a right to act as supreme and continue the legislative in themselves, or erect a new form, or under the old form place it in new hands, as they think good.

8

Alexander Pope

Essay on Man

*T*HE European Enlightenment, or *Age of Reason, was characterized by views on God, the world, and humanity that were rooted in the scientific outlook of the seventeenth century. The leading thinkers and artists of the Age of Reason accepted the concept of a rational, benevolent, natural order, which had been created by God and whose meaning and mode of operation could be understood by rational individuals as a guide to the good life. They stated this ideal in a moderate way, inspired by ancient, classical models; thus they expressed, they felt, the old, timeless truths in a manner appropriate to their own times. One of the best representatives of this rationalistic, neoclassical tendency in literature was Alexander Pope, the English poet (1688–1744). He may, indeed, be considered the spokesman in verse of the Age of Reason. For, despite an unpleasant personality, a physical disability, and a religious handicap (he was a professing Roman Catholic in a country that still legally discriminated against that faith), Pope achieved great popular success, and the income from the sale of his works enabled him to devote his life to literature.*

Above all, Pope was a poet, a great English poet. Rarely lyrical or personal, his verse was mainly a vehicle for the expression of profound moral truths and common sense about nature and humanity. Following the accepted neoclassical rules of the craft, his verse exhibited a polished elegance, yet transcended social conformity and poetic commonplaces. His carefully wrought poetic lines and balanced rhythms contain paradox, wit, satire, and even deep feeling, which raised them to the level of great, imaginative art.

Pope's Essay on Man *(1734) is a poem written in the form of four epistles (letters) addressed to the English rationalist-deist Henry St. John, Lord Bolingbroke. Its "heroic couplets"—consisting of clear, short lines—that often balance contrasting ideas—have the effect of epigrams. The poem deals with the problem of evil in the world and with the individual's moral duty. Pope affirms that the universe, though rational, is not wholly intelligible, and individuals can find fulfillment in the cosmic order only if they avoid the faulty reasoning that leads to false pride and discontent. Feeling the need to express important philosophical beliefs of his time, Pope presents in this work a good statement of natural religion, or deism. Epistle I and the opening stanza of Epistle II are reprinted here.*

EPISTLE I

Awake, my St. John![1] leave all meaner things
To low ambition, and the pride of Kings.
Let us (since Life can little more supply
Than just to look about us and to die)
Expatiate[2] free o'er all this scene of Man;
A mighty maze![3] but not without a plan;
A Wild, where weeds and flow'rs promiscuous shoot,
Or Garden, tempting with forbidden fruit.
Together let us beat this ample field,
Try what the open, what the covert yield;
The latent tracts,[4] the giddy heights, explore
Of all who blindly creep, or sightless soar;
Eye Nature's walks, shoot Folly as it flies,
And catch the Manners[5] living as they rise;
Laugh where we must, be candid where we can;
But vindicate[6] the ways of God to Man.

    I. Say first, of God above, or Man below,
What can we reason, but from what we know?

---

[1]Henry St. John, first Viscount Bolingbroke (1678–1751). He was a friend to Pope, a guide, a philosopher, and of great inspiration to the poet.

[2]To roam or wander; to discuss at length.

[3]A confusing network of pathways.

[4]Hidden regions.

[5]Rules of behavior.

[6]Justify, defend.

ESSAY ON MAN   Alexander Pope, *Essay on Man*, in *Poetical Works of Alexander Pope* (Boston: Little, Brown, 1854), II, 36–48.

Of Man, what see we but his station here,
From which to reason, or to which refer?
Thro' worlds unnumber'd[7] tho' the God be known,
'T is ours to trace him only in our own.
He, who thro' vast immensity can pierce,
See worlds on worlds compose one universe,
Observe how system into system runs,
What other planets circle other suns,
What vary'd Being peoples ev'ry star,
May tell why Heav'n has made us as we are.
But of this frame the bearings, and the ties,
The strong connections, nice dependencies,
Gradations just, has thy pervading soul
Look'd thro'? or can a part contain the whole?
   Is the great chain, that draws all to agree,
And drawn supports, upheld by God, or thee?

   II. Presumptuous Man! the reason wouldst thou find,
Why form'd so weak, so little, and so blind?
First, if thou canst, the harder reason guess,
Why form'd no weaker, blinder, and no less?
Ask of thy mother earth, why oaks are made
Taller or stronger than the weeds they shade?
Or ask of yonder argent fields[8] above,
Why Jove's satellites are less than Jove?[9]
   Of Systems possible, if 'tis confest
That Wisdom infinite must form the best,
Where all must full or not coherent be,
And all that rises, rise in due degree;
Then, in the scale of reas'ning life, 'tis plain,
There must be, somewhere, such a rank as Man;
And all the question (wrangle e'er so long)
Is only this, if God has plac'd him wrong?
   Respecting Man, whatever wrong we call,
May, must be right, as relative to all.[10]

[7]Endless.
[8]Silvery fields—that is, the heavens.
[9]The planet Jupiter.
[10]Concerning human beings, what seems defective in itself may be advantageous in
relation to the hidden ends they are intended to serve.

In human works, tho' labour'd on with pain,
A thousand movements scarce one purpose gain;
In God's, one single can its end produce;
Yet serves to second too some other use.
So Man, who here seems principal alone,
Perhaps acts second to some sphere unknown,
Touches some wheel, or verges to some goal;
'Tis but a part we see, and not a whole.
    When the proud steed shall know why Man restrains
His fiery course, or drives him o'er the plains:
When the dull Ox, why now he breaks the clod,
Is now a victim, and now Egypt's god:[11]
Then shall Man's pride and dulness comprehend
His actions', passions', being's, use and end;
Why doing, suff'ring, check'd, impell'd; and why
This hour a slave, the next a deity.
    Then say not Man's imperfect, Heav'n in fault;
Say rather, Man's as perfect as he ought;
His knowledge measur'd to his state and place;
His time a moment, and a point his space.
If to be perfect in a certain sphere,
What matter, soon or late, or here or there?
The blest today is as completely so,
As who began a thousand years ago.

    III. Heav'n from all creatures hides the book of Fate,
All but the page prescrib'd, their present state;
From brutes[12] what men, from men what spirits[13] know:
Or who could suffer Being here below?
The lamb thy riot dooms to bleed today,
Had he thy Reason, would he skip and play?
Pleas'd to the last, he crops the flow'ry food,
And licks the hand just rais'd to shed his blood.
Oh blindness to the future! kindly giv'n,
That each may fill the circle mark'd by Heav'n;
Who sees with equal eye, as God of all,

---

[11]Some ancient Egyptians worshiped the sacred bull, Apis, who was connected with the god Ptah, creator of gods and humans.

[12]Animals.

[13]Angels.

A hero perish, or a sparrow fall,
Atoms or systems into ruin hurl'd,
And now a bubble burst, and now a world.

Hope humbly then; with trembling pinions soar;
Wait the great teacher Death; and God adore!
What future bliss, he gives not thee to know,
But gives that Hope to be thy blessing now.
Hope springs eternal in the human breast:
Man never Is, but always To be blest:[14]
The soul, uneasy and confin'd from home,[15]
Rests and expatiates in a life to come.

Lo! the poor Indian! whose untutor'd mind
Sees God in clouds, or hears him in the wind;
His soul, proud Science never taught to stray
Far as the solar walk, or milky way;
Yet simple Nature to his hope has giv'n,
Behind the cloud-topt hill, an humbler heav'n;
Some safer world in depth of woods embrac'd,
Some happier island in the wat'ry waste,
Where slaves once more their native land behold,
No fiends torment, no Christians thirst for gold!
To Be, contents his natural desire,
He asks no Angel's wing, no Seraph's[16] fire;
But thinks, admitted to that equal sky,
His faithful dog shall bear him company.

IV. Go, wiser thou! and, in thy scale of sense,
Weigh thy Opinion against Providence;[17]
Call imperfection what thou fancy'st such,
Say, here he gives too little, there too much:
Destroy all Creatures for the sport or gust,[18]
Yet cry, If Man's unhappy, God's unjust;
If Man alone engross not Heav'n's high care,
Alone made perfect here, immortal there:

[14]To enjoy divine favor.
[15]The soul's origin and destination (God).
[16]The highest order of angels.
[17]Sensory perception weighed against God's wisdom.
[18]Personal pleasure.

Snatch from his hand the balance[19] and the rod,[20]
Re-judge his justice, be the God of God!
In Pride, in reas'ning Pride, our error lies;
All quit their sphere, and rush into the skies.
Pride still is aiming at the blest abodes,
Men would be Angels, Angels would be Gods.
Aspiring to be Gods, if Angels fell,
Aspiring to be Angels, Men rebel:
And who but wishes to invert the laws
Of Order, sins against th' Eternal Cause.

V. Ask for what end the heav'nly bodies shine,
Earth for whose use? Pride answers, "'Tis for mine:
For me kind Nature wakes her genial[21] Pow'r,
Suckles each herb, and spreads out ev'ry flow'r;
Annual for me, the grape, the rose renew
The juice nectareous, and the balmy dew;
For me, the mine a thousand treasures brings;
For me, health gushes from a thousand springs;
Seas roll to waft[22] me, suns to light me rise;
My foot-stool earth, my canopy[23] the skies."
But errs not Nature from this gracious end,
From burning suns when livid deaths descend,
When earthquakes swallow, or when tempests sweep
Towns to one grave, whole nations to the deep?
"No, ('tis reply'd) the first Almighty Cause
Acts not by partial, but by gen'ral laws;
Th' exceptions few; some change since all began,
And what created perfect?"—Why then Man?
If the great end be human Happiness,
Then Nature deviates;[24] and can Man do less?
As much that end a constant course requires
Of show'rs and sun-shine, as of Man's desires;
As much eternal springs and cloudless skies,

[19]The scales of justice.
[20]The instrument of punishment.
[21]Generative.
[22]Carry.
[23]Ornamental cover (such as that often placed above a throne).
[24]Errs.

As Men for ever temp'rate, calm, and wise.
If plagues or earthquakes break not Heav'n's design,
Why then a Borgia,[25] or a Catiline?[26]
Who knows but he, whose hand the lightning forms,
Who heaves old Ocean, and who wings the storms;
Pours fierce Ambition in a Caesar's[27] mind,
Or turns young Ammon[28] loose to scourge mankind?
From pride, from pride, our very reas'ning springs;
Account for moral, as for nat'ral[29] things:
Why charge we Heav'n in those, in these acquit?
In both, to reason right is to submit.
   Better for Us, perhaps, it might appear,
Were there all harmony, all virtue here;
That never air or ocean felt the wind;
That never passion discompos'd the mind.
But all subsists by elemental strife;
And Passions are the elements of Life.
The gen'ral Order, since the whole began,
Is kept in Nature, and is kept in Man.

   VI. What would this Man? Now upward will he soar,
And little less than Angel,[30] would be more;
Now looking downwards, just as griev'd appears
To want the strength of bulls, the fur of bears.
Made for his use all creatures if he call,
Say what their use, had he the pow'rs of all?
Nature to these, without profusion, kind,
The proper organs, proper pow'rs assign'd;

[25]Caesar Borgia (*ca.* 1476–1507), son of Pope Alexander VI, soldier, and sometime cardinal. To achieve his ends he unscrupulously used cruelty, bloodshed, terror, and assassination.

[26]Lucius Sergius Catilina (*ca.* 108–62 B.C.), a Roman politician and conspirator against the Roman government. His conspiracy did not succeed and he suffered a violent death.

[27]Gaius Julius Caesar (100–44 B.C.), Roman general and statesman, who is said to have had the ambition to be crowned King of Rome.

[28]Alexander the Great (356–323 B.C.), heir of Macedonia and conqueror of Persia and Egypt. While in Egypt, he traveled to the Siwah oasis on the western border of Egypt. During his worshiping there, it was supposedly revealed to him that his true father was not King Philip, but the Egyptian god Ammon.

[29]Natural.

[30]"Thou hast made him [man] a little lower than the angels, and hast crowned him with glory and honor." Psalm 8:5 (King James version).

Each seeming want compensated of course,
Here with degrees of swiftness, there of force;
All in exact proportion to the state;
Nothing to add, and nothing to abate.
Each beast, each insect, happy in its own;
Is Heav'n unkind to Man, and Man alone?
Shall he alone, whom rational we call,
Be pleas'd with nothing, if not bless'd with all?
    The bliss of Man (could Pride that blessing find)
Is not to act or think beyond mankind;
No pow'rs of body or of soul to share,
But what his nature and his state can bear.
Why has not Man a microscopic eye?
For this plain reason, Man is not a Fly.
Say what the use, were finer optics giv'n,
T' inspect a mite,[31] not comprehend the heav'n?
Or touch, if tremblingly alive all o'er,
To smart and agonize at every pore?
Or quick effluvia[32] darting thro' the brain,
Die of a rose in aromatic pain?
If nature thunder'd in his op'ning ears,
And stunn'd him with the music of the spheres,[33]
How would he wish that Heav'n had left him still
The whisp'ring Zephyr,[34] and the purling rill?[35]
Who finds not Providence all good and wise,
Alike in what it gives, and what denies?

    VII. Far as Creation's ample range extends,
The scale of sensual, mental pow'rs ascends:
Mark how it mounts, to Man's imperial race,[36]
From the green myriads in the peopled grass:
What modes of sight betwixt each wide extreme,

---

[31]A tiny creature (arachnid).

[32]Vapors (particles) which communicate the odors to the brain.

[33]It was once held that the planets, while rolling along their spheres, emitted music. This music, should it reach the ears, was believed to be as unbearable as direct sunlight to the eye.

[34]The gentle west wind of Greek mythology.

[35]A murmuring brook.

[36]Ruling species.

The mole's dim curtain, and the lynx's beam:
Of smell, the headlong lioness between,
And hound sagacious[37] on the tainted[38] green:
Of hearing, from the life that fills the flood,[39]
To that which warbles thro' the vernal[40] wood:
The spider's touch, how exquisitely fine!
Feels at each thread, and lives along the line:
In the nice[41] bee, what sense so subtly true
From pois'nous herbs extracts the healing dew?[42]
How Instinct varies in the grov'ling swine,
Compar'd, half-reas'ning elephant, with thine!
'Twixt that, and Reason,[43] what a nice barrier,
For ever sep'rate, yet for ever near!
Remembrance[44] and Reflection[45] how ally'd;
What thin partitions Sense from Thought divide:
And Middle natures,[46] how they long to join,
Yet never pass th' insuperable line!
Without this just gradation, could they be
Subjected, these to those, or all to thee?
The pow'rs of all subdu'd by thee alone,
Is not thy Reason all these pow'rs in one?

    VIII. See, thro' this air, this ocean, and this earth,
All matter quick, and bursting into birth.
Above, how high progressive life may go!
Around, how wide! how deep extend below!
Vast chain of Being! which from God began,
Natures ethereal,[47] human, angel, man,
Beast, bird, fish, insect, what no eye can see,

[37]Having a keen sense of smell.
[38]Containing the odor of the hunted animal.
[39]Ocean. (Pope thought that fish were capable of hearing.)
[40]Springlike, green.
[41]Cautious.
[42]Honey, which was supposed to possess medicinal properties—as some moderns agree.
[43]A faculty believed denied by Nature to all animals except humans.
[44]Memory, which was thought common to most animals.
[45]The power of contemplating one's own thought, believed to belong only to humans.
[46]Creatures just below humans on the biological scale.
[47]Spiritual; heavenly.

No glass can reach; from Infinite to thee,
From thee to Nothing!—On superior pow'rs
Were we to press, inferior might on ours:
Or in the full creation leave a void,
Where, one step broken, the great scale's destroy'd:
From Nature's chain whatever link you strike,
Tenth or ten thousandth, breaks the chain alike.
   And, if each system in gradation roll[48]
Alike essential to th' amazing Whole,
The least confusion but in one, not all
That system only, but the Whole must fall.
Let Earth unbalanc'd from her orbit fly,
Planets and Suns run lawless thro' the sky;
Let ruling angels from their spheres be hurl'd,
Being on Being wreck'd, and world on world;
Heav'n's whole foundations to their centre nod,
And Nature tremble to the throne of God.
All this dread Order break—for whom? for thee?
Vile worm!—Oh Madness! Pride! Impiety!

   IX. What if the foot, ordain'd the dust to tread,
Or hand, to toil, aspir'd to be the head?
What if the head, the eye, or ear repin'd[49]
To serve mere engines to the ruling Mind?
Just as absurd for any part to claim
To be another, in this gen'ral frame:
Just as absurd, to mourn the tasks or pains,
The great directing Mind of All ordains.
   All are but parts of one stupendous whole,
Whose body Nature is, and God the soul;
That, chang'd thro' all, and yet in all the same;
Great in the earth, as in th' ethereal frame;
Warms in the sun, refreshes in the breeze,
Glows in the stars, and blossoms in the trees,
Lives thro' all life, extends thro' all extent,
Spreads undivided, operates unspent;
Breathes in our soul, informs our mortal part,

---

[48]The step-by-step progression of the interrelated parts of creation.
[49]Complained.

As full, as perfect, in a hair as heart:
As full, as perfect, in vile Man that mourns,
As the rapt Seraph that adores and burns:
To him no high, no low, no great, no small;
He fills, he bounds, connects, and equals all.

    X. Cease then, nor Order Imperfection name:
Our proper bliss depends on what we blame.
Know thy own point: This kind, this due degree
Of blindness, weakness, Heav'n bestows on thee.
Submit.—In this, or any other sphere,
Secure to be as blest as thou canst bear:
Safe in the hand of one disposing Pow'r,
Or in the natal, or the mortal hour.
All Nature is but Art,[50] unknown to thee;
All Chance, Direction, which thou canst not see;
All Discord, Harmony not understood;
All partial Evil, universal Good:
And, spite of Pride, in erring Reason's spite,
One truth is clear, WHATEVER IS, IS RIGHT.

EPISTLE II

    I. Know then thyself, presume not God to scan;[51]
The proper study of Mankind is Man.
Plac'd on this isthmus of a middle state,[52]
A Being darkly wise, and rudely great:
With too much knowledge for the Sceptic side,
With too much weakness for the Stoic's pride,[53]
He hangs between; in doubt to act, or rest;
In doubt to deem himself a God, or Beast;

---

[50]According to the English philosopher Hobbes: "Nature is the art whereby God governs the world." This idea attributes conscious design to the physical universe.

[51]Investigate, scrutinize.

[52]Between the angels (above) and the animal kingdom (below).

[53]Scepticism and Stoicism were two philosophical schools of thought in ancient Greece. Sceptics doubted the trustworthiness of a person's senses and reason; therefore, they denied human ability to gain knowledge. Stoics demanded that a person calmly accept the trials and tribulations of life.

In doubt his Mind or Body to prefer,
Born but to die, and reas'ning but to err;
Alike in ignorance, his reason such,
Whether he thinks too little, or too much:
Chaos of Thought and Passion, all confus'd;
Still by himself abus'd, or disabus'd;
Created half to rise, and half to fall;
Great lord of all things, yet a prey to all;
Sole judge of Truth, in endless Error hurl'd:[54]
The glory, jest, and riddle of the world!

• • •

9

Voltaire

Candide

FRANÇOIS Marie Arouet (1694–
1778), better known by his pen name, Voltaire, was perhaps the most characteristic and famous figure of the European Enlightenment. Born the son of a
middle-class Parisian lawyer, he was a greatly gifted and prolific writer, creating
during his long life a flood of works in history, philosophy, drama, poetry,
fiction, and biography. All of Voltaire's works, in one way or another, reflect
his belief in science, reason, and freedom; they also reflect his hatred of
superstition, intolerance, and privilege, as the main sources of evil in the world.
Voltaire eventually won fame and fortune in his lifetime, but not until after he
had suffered for his views; because of them, he was imprisoned in the ancient
Parisian fortress known as the Bastille and several times exiled. Amid his
personal misfortunes, Voltaire devoted himself to trying to clear away what he
thought was accumulated rubbish filling human minds. He popularized the
faith of the Enlightenment and became the leader and symbol of the intellectual
rebellion against traditional ideas and institutions. Toward the end of his life
Voltaire was finally acclaimed in Paris; and in 1791, the people of France, who
considered him one of the intellectual fathers of the French Revolution, en-
shrined his ashes in the Pantheon. At once liberal and conservative, deist and
agnostic, fighter and coward, generous and miserly, Voltaire was, above all, a
humanist who wished to better the world by turning nature to human use
through reason.

Candide, or Optimism (1759) was written when Voltaire was sixty-five
years old and is now the most widely read of all his works. Marked by wit and
irony and a clear, lively style, Candide is a classic story of the young innocent
learning about the wickedness of the world. But as the rollicking adventures of
the hero move along, he is shown to be a man of common sense. Many of the
other characters are symbols of contemporary ideas and institutions, which are

subjected to a withering and delightful satire. Voltaire's conclusion is that the world is mad and that sane people should concern themselves with those things that assure them of a simple, yet adequate existence—free from the envy of others.

CHAPTER 1

How Candide Was Brought Up in a Noble Castle and How He Was Expelled from the Same

In the castle of Baron Thunder-ten-tronckh[1] in Westphalia[2] there lived a youth, endowed by Nature with the most gentle character. His face was the expression of his soul. His judgment was quite honest and he was extremely simple-minded; and this was the reason, I think, that he was named Candide.[3] Old servants in the house suspected that he was the son of the Baron's sister and a decent honest gentleman of the neighborhood, whom this young lady would never marry because he could only prove seventy-one quarterings,[4] and the rest of his genealogical tree was lost, owing to the injuries of time.

The Baron was one of the most powerful lords in Westphalia, for his castle possessed a door and windows. His Great Hall was even decorated with a piece of tapestry. The dogs in his stableyards formed a pack of hounds when necessary; his grooms[5] were his huntsmen; the village

---

[1]Voltaire was appalled by the vast number of lesser German nobles, most of whom lorded over small pieces of land. Though ignorant and uneducated, these nobles were generally conceited and arrogant and extremely proud of their long, and sometimes questionable, bloodlines.

[2]A German province extending eastward from the point where the Rhine River crosses into Dutch territory. On traveling through that province in 1740, Voltaire was shocked by the poverty he saw.

[3]Literally, "glowing white," or pure. Voltaire chose this name to suggest innocence and honesty of character.

[4]Numbers used to indicate the chronological span of a noble family. A family of some thirty quarterings is counted among the very oldest, since each quartering represents one generation.

[5]People who feed and care for horses.

CANDIDE From *Candide*, trans. Richard Aldington, from *The Portable Voltaire*, ed. by Ben Ray Redman. Copyright 1949, 1968 by The Viking Press, Inc. Copyright renewed © 1976 by Viking Penguin, Inc. Reprinted by permission of Viking Penguin, Inc.

curate[6] was his Grand Almoner.[7] They all called him "My Lord," and laughed heartily at his stories.

The Baroness weighed about three hundred and fifty pounds, was therefore greatly respected, and did the honors of the house with a dignity which rendered her still more respectable. Her daughter Cunegonde,[8] aged seventeen, was rosy-cheeked, fresh, plump and tempting. The Baron's son appeared in every respect worthy of his father. The tutor Pangloss[9] was the oracle of the house, and little Candide followed his lessons with all the candor of his age and character.

Pangloss taught metaphysico-theologo-cosmolo-nigology.[10] He proved admirably that there is no effect without a cause and that, in this best of all possible worlds, My Lord the Baron's castle was the best of castles and his wife the best of all possible Baronesses.

"'Tis demonstrated," said he, "that things cannot be otherwise; for, since everything is made for an end, everything is necessarily for the best end. Observe that noses were made to wear spectacles; and so we have spectacles. Legs were visibly instituted to be breeched, and we have breeches. Stones were formed to be quarried and to build castles; and My Lord has a very noble castle; the greatest Baron in the province should have the best house; and as pigs were made to be eaten, we eat pork all the year round; consequently, those who have asserted that all is well, talk nonsense; they ought to have said that all is for the best."

Candide listened attentively and believed innocently; for he thought Miss Cunegonde extremely beautiful, although he was never bold enough to tell her so. He decided that after the happiness of being born Baron of Thunder-ten-tronckh, the second degree of happiness was to be Miss Cunegonde; the third, to see her every day; and the fourth to listen to Dr. Pangloss, the greatest philosopher of the province and therefore of the whole world.

---

[6]Priest.

[7]A high-ranking clergyman of the royal court, in charge of the distribution of alms.

[8]A name inspired by Kunigunde, who died in 1033 and was canonized in 1200. The wife of the medieval German Emperor Henry II, she supposedly "kept her virginity to her death"—thus abusing the sacrament of marriage.

[9]Literally (in Greek), all tongue.

[10]Voltaire uses Pangloss as a foil for his ridicule of the optimistic assumptions and statements of the English poet Alexander Pope (1688–1744), the German philosopher Gottfried Wilhelm von Leibnitz (1646–1716), and Christian von Wolff (1679–1754), who developed and popularized Leibnitz' philosophy.

One day when Cunegonde was walking near the castle, in a little wood which was called The Park, she observed Dr. Pangloss in the bushes, giving a lesson in experimental physics to her mother's waiting-maid, a very pretty and docile brunette. Miss Cunegonde had a great inclination for science and watched breathlessly the reiterated experiments she witnessed; she observed clearly the Doctor's sufficient reason, the effects and the causes, and returned home very much excited, pensive, filled with the desire of learning, reflecting that she might be the sufficient reason of young Candide and that he might be hers.

On her way back to the castle she met Candide and blushed; Candide also blushed. She bade him good-morning in a hesitating voice; Candide replied without knowing what he was saying. Next day, when they left the table after dinner, Cunegonde and Candide found themselves behind a screen; Cunegonde dropped her handkerchief, Candide picked it up; she innocently held his hand; the young man innocently kissed the young lady's hand with remarkable vivacity, tenderness and grace; their lips met, their eyes sparkled, their knees trembled, their hands wandered. Baron Thunder-ten-tronckh passed near the screen, and, observing this cause and effect, expelled Candide from the castle by kicking him in the backside frequently and hard. Cunegonde swooned; when she recovered her senses, the Baroness slapped her in the face; and all was in consternation in the noblest and most agreeable of all possible castles.

CHAPTER 2

What Happened to Candide Among the Bulgarians[11]

Candide, expelled from the earthly paradise, wandered for a long time without knowing where he was going, turning up his eyes to Heaven, gazing back frequently at the noblest of castles which held the most beautiful of young Baronesses; he lay down to sleep supperless between two furrows in the open fields; it snowed heavily in large flakes. The next morning the shivering Candide, penniless, dying of cold and exhaustion, dragged himself toward the neighboring town,

[11]Fictional name for the Prussians. In Voltaire's time, Prussia and Austria were the states with the largest German-speaking populations.

which was called Waldberghoff-trarbkdikdorff.[12] He halted sadly at the door of an inn. Two men dressed in blue[13] noticed him.

"Comrade," said one, "there's a well-built young man of the right height."

They went up to Candide and very civilly invited him to dinner.

"Gentlemen," said Candide with charming modesty, "you do me a great honor, but I have no money to pay my share."

"Ah, sir," said one of the men in blue, "persons of your figure and merit never pay anything; are you not five feet five tall?"

"Yes, gentlemen," said he, bowing, "that is my height."

"Ah, sir, come to table; we will not only pay your expenses, we will never allow a man like you to be short of money; men were only made to help each other."

"You are in the right," said Candide, "that is what Dr. Pangloss was always telling me, and I see that everything is for the best."

They begged him to accept a few crowns,[14] he took them and wished to give them an IOU; they refused to take it and all sat down to table.

"Do you not love tenderly . . ."

"Oh, yes," said he. "I love Miss Cunegonde tenderly."

"No," said one of the gentlemen. "We were asking if you do not tenderly love the King of the Bulgarians."[15]

"Not a bit," said he, "for I have never seen him."

"What! He is the most charming of kings, and you must drink his health."

"Oh, gladly, gentlemen."

And he drank.[16]

"That is sufficient," he was told. "You are now the support, the aid, the defender, the hero of the Bulgarians; your fortune is made and your glory assured."

They immediately put irons on his legs and took him to a regiment.

[12]A suggestion of how the German language sounded to Voltaire. He thought German was ugly and dissonant, fit only for soldiers and horses.

[13]Uniforms of Prussian recruiting officers. As the army suffered heavy losses in many battles, Prussian recruiters were incessantly searching for replacements.

[14]Silver coins.

[15]Frederick II (or Frederick the Great), King of Prussia from 1740 to 1786.

[16]Accepting the toast of the recruiters and having a drink with them took the place of signing up.

He was made to turn to the right and left, to raise the ramrod[17] and return the ramrod, to take aim, to fire, to double up, and he was given thirty strokes with a stick; the next day he drilled not quite so badly, and received only twenty strokes; the day after, he only had ten and was looked on as a prodigy by his comrades.

Candide was completely mystified and could not make out how he was a hero. One fine spring day he thought he would take a walk, going straight ahead, in the belief that to use his legs as he pleased was a privilege of the human species as well as of animals. He had not gone two leagues[18] when four other heroes, each six feet tall, fell upon him, bound him and dragged him back to a cell.[19] He was asked by his judges whether he would rather be thrashed thirty-six times by the whole regiment or receive a dozen lead bullets at once in his brain. Although he protested that men's wills are free and that he wanted neither one nor the other, he had to make a choice; by virtue of that gift of God which is called *liberty*, he determined to run the gauntlet thirty-six times and actually did so twice. There were two thousand men in the regiment. That made four thousand strokes which laid bare the muscles and nerves from his neck to his backside. As they were about to proceed to a third turn, Candide, utterly exhausted, begged as a favor that they would be so kind as to smash his head; he obtained this favor; they bound his eyes and he was made to kneel down. At that moment the King of the Bulgarians came by and inquired the victim's crime; and as this King was possessed of a vast genius, he perceived from what he learned about Candide that he was a young metaphysician very ignorant in worldly matters, and therefore pardoned him with a clemency which will be praised in all newspapers and all ages. An honest surgeon healed Candide in three weeks with the ointments recommended by Dioscorides.[20] He had already regained a little skin and could walk when the King of the Bulgarians went to war with the King of the Abares.[21]

---

[17]A rod used for ramming a powder charge into a gun, thus loading it through the muzzle.

[18]A league is a unit of distance ranging from 2.4 to 4.6 miles, depending on country.

[19]Desertions were numerous in the armies of the eighteenth century, and punishment for deserting was very severe. (While visiting the court of the King of Prussia, Voltaire had become acquainted with the harshness and brutality of military life.)

[20]Penadius Dioscorides, a Greek physician of the first century A.D. Voltaire was contemptuous of the healing arts of his age, because physicians continued to use remedies and methods that had long since become outmoded.

[21]The French, who in the Seven Years' War (1756–1763), sided with the Austrians against Prussia and England.

CHAPTER 3

*How Candide Escaped from the Bulgarians and
What Became of Him*

Nothing could be smarter, more splendid, more brilliant, better drawn up than the two armies. Trumpets, fifes, hautboys,[22] drums, cannons formed a harmony such as has never been heard even in hell. The cannons first of all laid flat about six thousand men on each side; then the musketry removed from the best of worlds some nine or ten thousand blackguards[23] who infested its surface. The bayonet also was the sufficient reason for the death of some thousands of men. The whole might amount to thirty thousand souls. Candide, who trembled like a philosopher, hid himself as well as he could during this heroic butchery.

At last, while the two kings each commanded a Te Deum[24] in his camp, Candide decided to go elsewhere to reason about effects and causes. He clambered over heaps of dead and dying men and reached a neighboring village, which was in ashes; it was an Abare village which the Bulgarians had burned in accordance with international law. Here, old men dazed with blows watched the dying agonies of their murdered wives who clutched their children to their bleeding breasts; there, disembowelled girls who had been made to satisfy the natural appetites of heroes gasped their last sighs; others, half-burned, begged to be put to death. Brains were scattered on the ground among dismembered arms and legs.

Candide fled to another village as fast as he could; it belonged to the Bulgarians, and Abarian heroes had treated it in the same way. Candide, stumbling over quivering limbs or across ruins, at last escaped from the theater of war, carrying a little food in his knapsack, and never forgetting Miss Cunegonde. His provisions were all gone when he reached Holland; but, having heard that everyone in that country was rich and a Christian, he had no doubt at all but that he would be as well treated as he had been in the Baron's castle before he had been expelled on account of Miss Cunegonde's pretty eyes.

He asked an alms of several grave persons, who all replied that if he

[22]Oboes.
[23]Scoundrels.
[24]*Te Deum laudamus* (We praise Thee, O God), an ancient Christian hymn of praise to God. It is used here to suggest the service of thanksgiving (for victory) in which it was a principal part.

continued in that way he would be shut up in a house of correction to teach him how to live.[25]

He then addressed himself to a man who had been discoursing on charity in a large assembly for an hour on end. This orator, glancing at him askance, said:

"What are you doing here? Are you for the good cause?"

"There is no effect without a cause," said Candide modestly. "Everything is necessarily linked up and arranged for the best. It was necessary that I should be expelled from the company of Miss Cunegonde, that I ran the gauntlet, and that I beg my bread until I can earn it; all this could not have happened differently."

"My friend," said the orator, "do you believe that the Pope is Anti-Christ?"[26]

"I had never heard so before," said Candide, "but whether he is or isn't, I am starving."

"You don't deserve to eat," said the other. "Hence, rascal; hence, you wretch; and never come near me again."

The orator's wife thrust her head out of the window and seeing a man who did not believe that the Pope was Anti-Christ, she poured on his head a full . . . O Heavens! To what excess religious zeal is carried by ladies!

A man who had not been baptized, an honest Anabaptist[27] named Jacques, saw the cruel and ignominious treatment of one of his brothers,[28] a featherless two-legged creature with a soul;[29] he took him

---

[25]In general, Voltaire admired the Dutch for their liberty, equality, prosperity, and tolerance, as well as for their concern for the unfortunate. On the other hand, he had also noticed that on occasion they were capable of hardheartedness and greed.

[26]At least since the days of the English reformer John Wycliffe (*ca.* 1320–1384), Protestant firebrands had wanted to believe that the Pope was the Antichrist (the enemy of Christ), a term that appears in the New Testament in the first two epistles of John. Voltaire thought that preoccupation with such questions was often an escape from practicing charity.

[27]A member of a religious group that in the sixteenth century attracted a number of followers in southwestern Germany and Switzerland. The Anabaptists (literally, rebaptizers) insisted upon baptism of the *adult* believer, thus rejecting infant baptism. Voltaire admired the Anabaptists for their simple piety, hard work, love of peace, and charity. (Though today they are usually listed as Protestants, in the sixteenth century they were persecuted by Catholics and Protestants alike. Many, therefore, fled from their homelands and settled in Holland or North America, where they became known as Mennonites or Amish.)

[28]Fellow human beings.

[29]A reference to Plato's definition of a human being.

home, cleaned him up, gave him bread and beer, presented him with two florins,[30] and even offered to teach him to work at the manufacture of Persian stuffs[31] which are made in Holland. Candide threw himself at the man's feet, exclaiming:

"Dr. Pangloss was right in telling me that all is for the best in this world, for I am vastly more touched by your extreme generosity than by the harshness of the gentleman in the black cloak and his good lady."

The next day when he walked out he met a beggar covered with sores, dull-eyed, with the end of his nose fallen away, his mouth awry, his teeth black, who talked huskily, was tormented with a violent cough and spat out a tooth at every cough.

CHAPTER 4

How Candide Met His Old Master in Philosophy,
Doctor Pangloss, and What Happened

Candide, moved even more by compassion than by horror, gave this horrible beggar the two florins he had received from the honest Anabaptist, Jacques. The phantom gazed fixedly at him, shed tears and threw its arms round his neck. Candide recoiled in terror.

"Alas!" said the wretch to the other wretch, "Don't you recognize your dear Pangloss?"

"What do I hear? You, my dear master! You, in this horrible state! What misfortune has happened to you? Why are you no longer in the noblest of castles? What has become of Miss Cunegonde, the pearl of young ladies, the masterpiece of Nature?"

"I am exhausted,"[32] said Pangloss. Candide immediately took him to the Anabaptist's stable, where he gave him a little bread to eat; and when Pangloss had recovered:

"Well!" said he, "Cunegonde?"

"Dead!" replied the other.

At this word Candide swooned; his friend restored him to his senses with a little bad vinegar which happened to be in the stable. Candide opened his eyes.

---

[30]Gold coins minted in thirteenth-century Florence. They were accepted as currency throughout Europe.

[31]Persian rugs.

[32]He means that he is dying.

"Cunegonde dead! Ah! best of worlds, where are you? But what illness did she die of? Was it because she saw me kicked out of her father's noble castle?"

"No," said Pangloss. "She was disembowelled by Bulgarian soldiers, after having been raped to the limit of possibility; they broke the Baron's head when he tried to defend her; the Baroness was cut to pieces; my poor pupil was treated exactly like his sister; and as to the castle, there is not one stone standing on another, not a barn, not a sheep, not a duck, not a tree; but we were well avenged, for the Abares did exactly the same to a neighboring barony which belonged to a Bulgarian Lord."

At this, Candide swooned again; but, having recovered and having said all that he ought to say, he inquired the cause and effect, the sufficient reason which had reduced Pangloss to so piteous a state.

"Alas!" said Pangloss, "'tis love; love, the consoler of the human race, the preserver of the universe, the soul of all tender creatures, gentle love."

"Alas!" said Candide, "I am acquainted with this love, this sovereign of hearts, this soul of our soul; it has never brought me anything but one kiss and twenty kicks in the backside. How could this beautiful cause produce in you so abominable an effect?"

Pangloss replied as follows:

"My dear Candide! You remember Paquette,[33] the maid-servant of our august Baroness; in her arms I enjoyed the delights of Paradise which have produced the tortures of Hell by which you see I am devoured; she was infected[34] and perhaps is dead. Paquette received this present from a most learned monk, who had it from the source; for he received it from an old countess, who had it from a cavalry captain, who owed it to a marchioness,[35] who derived it from a page, who had received it from a Jesuit, who, when a novice, had it in a direct line from one of the companions of Christopher Columbus. For my part, I shall not give it to anyone, for I am dying."

"O Pangloss!" exclaimed Candide, "this is a strange genealogy! Wasn't the devil at the root of it?"

"Not at all," replied that great man. "It was something indispensable in this best of worlds, a necessary ingredient; for, if Columbus in an

---

[33] A name derived from the French word *pâquerette*, which means daisy.

[34] With syphilis, which had been carried to Europe from the Americas.

[35] The wife or widow of a marquis, a high-ranking nobleman.

island of America had not caught this disease, which poisons the source of generation, and often indeed prevents generation, we should not have chocolate and cochineal;[36] it must also be noticed that hitherto in our continent this disease is peculiar to us, like theological disputes. The Turks, the Indians, the Persians, the Chinese, the Siamese and the Japanese are not yet familiar with it; but there is a sufficient reason why they in their turn should become familiar with it in a few centuries. Meanwhile, it has made marvellous progress among us, and especially in those large armies composed of honest, well-bred stipendiaries[37] who decide the destiny of States; it may be asserted that when thirty thousand men fight a pitched battle against an equal number of troops, there are about twenty thousand with the pox[38] on either side."

"Admirable!" said Candide. "But you must get cured."

"How can I?" said Pangloss. "I haven't a sou,[39] my friend, and in the whole extent of this globe, you cannot be bled or receive an enema without paying or without someone paying for you."

This last speech determined Candide; he went and threw himself at the feet of his charitable Anabaptist, Jacques, and drew so touching a picture of the state to which his friend was reduced that the good easy man did not hesitate to succor Pangloss; he had him cured at his own expense. In this cure Pangloss only lost one eye and one ear. He could write well and knew arithmetic perfectly. The Anabaptist made him his bookkeeper. At the end of two months he was compelled to go to Lisbon[40] on business and took his two philosophers on the boat with him. Pangloss explained to him how everything was for the best. Jacques was not of this opinion.

"Men," said he, "must have corrupted nature a little, for they were not born wolves, and they have become wolves. God did not give them twenty-four-pounder cannons or bayonets, and they have made bayonets and cannons to destroy each other. I might bring bankruptcies[41] into the account and Justice which seizes the goods of bankrupts in order to deprive the creditors of them."

"It was all indispensable," replied the one-eyed doctor, "and private

[36]A red dye originating in Central and South America.

[37]Mercenaries.

[38]Syphilis.

[39]A small French coin of little value.

[40]The capital city and major port of Portugal.

[41]Personal loss of money due to the bankruptcies of others had been painful to Voltaire.

misfortunes make the public good, so that the more private misfortunes there are, the more everything is well."

While he was reasoning, the air grew dark, the winds blew from the four quarters of the globe and the ship was attacked by the most horrible tempest in sight of the port of Lisbon.

CHAPTER 5

Storm, Shipwreck, Earthquake, and What Happened to
Dr. Pangloss, to Candide and the Anabaptist Jacques

Half the enfeebled passengers, suffering from that inconceivable anguish which the rolling of a ship causes in the nerves and in all the humors[42] of bodies shaken in contrary directions, did not retain strength enough even to trouble about the danger. The other half screamed and prayed; the sails were torn, the masts broken, the vessel was leaking. Those worked who could, no one co-operated, no one commanded. The Anabaptist tried to help the crew a little; he was on the main-deck; a furious sailor struck him violently and stretched him on the deck; but the blow he delivered gave him so violent a shock that he fell head-first out of the ship. He remained hanging and clinging to part of the broken mast. The good Jacques ran to his aid, helped him to climb back, and from the effort he made was flung into the sea in full view of the sailor, who allowed him to drown without condescending even to look at him. Candide came up, saw his benefactor reappear for a moment and then be engulfed forever. He tried to throw himself after him into the sea; he was prevented by the philosopher Pangloss, who proved to him that the Lisbon roads had been expressly created for the Anabaptist to be drowned in them. While he was proving this *a priori*,[43] the vessel sank, and everyone perished except Pangloss, Candide and the brutal sailor who had drowned the virtuous Anabaptist; the blackguard swam successfully to the shore and Pangloss and Candide were carried there on a plank.

When they had recovered a little, they walked toward Lisbon; they had a little money by the help of which they hoped to be saved from hunger after having escaped the storm.

Weeping the death of their benefactor, they had scarcely set foot in

---

[42]Prior to the advent of modern medicine it was held that four body fluids, so-called humors (blood, phlegm, yellow bile, black bile), determine a person's disposition and health.
[43]Reasoning from an accepted presumption.

the town when they felt the earth tremble under their feet;[44] the sea rose in foaming masses in the port and smashed the ships which rode at anchor. Whirlwinds of flame and ashes covered the streets and squares; the houses collapsed, the roofs were thrown upon the foundations, and the foundations were scattered; thirty thousand inhabitants of every age and both sexes were crushed under the ruins. Whistling and swearing, the sailor said:

"There'll be something to pick up here."

"What can be the sufficient reason for this phenomenon?" said Pangloss.

"It is the last day!" cried Candide.

The sailor immediately ran among the debris, dared death to find money, found it, seized it, got drunk, and having slept off his wine, purchased the favor of the first woman of good-will he met on the ruins of the houses and among the dead and dying. Pangloss, however, pulled him by the sleeve.

"My friend," said he, "this is not well, you are disregarding universal reason, you choose the wrong time."

"Blood and 'ounds!" he retorted, "I am a sailor and I was born in Batavia;[45] four times have I stamped on the crucifix during four voyages to Japan;[46] you have found the right man for your universal reason!"

Candide had been hurt by some falling stones; he lay in the street covered with debris. He said to Pangloss:

"Alas! Get me a little wine and oil; I am dying."

"This earthquake is not a new thing," replied Pangloss. "The town of Lima felt the same shocks in America last year; similar causes produce similar effects; there must certainly be a train of sulphur underground from Lima to Lisbon."

"Nothing is more probable," replied Candide; "but, for God's sake, a little oil and wine."

---

[44]The actual Lisbon earthquake and fire occurred on November 1, 1755. The destruction of the city, with the loss of more than thirty thousand lives, confirmed for Voltaire the wisdom of his earlier rejection of philosophical optimism. The disaster also prompted him to write both *Candide* and his *Poem on the Lisbon Earthquake* (1755).

[45]A city founded by the Dutch in the early seventeenth century on the island of Java in the East Indies. Now called Djakarta, it is the capital of Indonesia.

[46]In 1638 European traders, specifically the Spanish and the Portuguese, were expelled from Japan; only the Dutch were permitted to trade there, from a small island near Nagasaki. To discourage trading and to assure that no Christian missionary might enter disguised as a trader, Dutch merchants were supposedly required to stamp on a crucifix or an image of Jesus.

"What do you mean, probable?" replied the philosopher; "I maintain that it is proved."

Candide lost consciousness, and Pangloss brought him a little water from a neighboring fountain.

Next day they found a little food as they wandered among the ruins and regained a little strength. Afterward they worked like others to help the inhabitants who had escaped death. Some citizens they had assisted gave them as good a dinner as could be expected in such a disaster; true, it was a dreary meal; the hosts watered their bread with their tears, but Pangloss consoled them by assuring them that things could not be otherwise.

"For," said he, "all this is for the best; for, if there is a volcano at Lisbon, it cannot be anywhere else; for it is impossible that things should not be where they are; for all is well."

A little, dark man, a familiar[47] of the Inquisition,[48] who sat beside him, politely took up the conversation, and said:

"Apparently you do not believe in original sin; for, if everything is for the best, there was neither fall nor punishment."

"I most humbly beg your excellency's pardon," replied Pangloss still more politely, "for the fall of man and the curse necessarily entered into the best of all possible worlds."

"Then you do not believe in free-will?" said the familiar.

"Your excellency will pardon me," said Pangloss; "free-will can exist with absolute necessity; for it was necessary that we should be free; for in short, limited will . . ."

Pangloss was in the middle of his phrase when the familiar nodded to his armed attendant who was pouring out port or Oporto wine for him.

CHAPTER 6

How a Splendid Auto-da-Fé Was Held to Prevent Earthquakes, and How Candide Was Flogged

After the earthquake which destroyed three-quarters of Lisbon, the wise men of that country could discover no more efficacious way of

---

[47]An undercover agent.

[48]The Inquisition, or the Congregation of the Holy Office (the official name), was a Roman Catholic tribunal charged with seeking out heresy (false beliefs) and punishing heretics. It was founded in the early thirteenth century and abolished in 1834. In the fifteenth and sixteenth centuries it raged most furiously in Spain, Portugal, and Italy.

preventing a total ruin than by giving the people a splendid *auto-da-fé*.[49] It was decided by the University of Coimbre[50] that the sight of several persons being slowly burned in great ceremony is an infallible secret for preventing earthquakes.

Consequently they had arrested a Biscayan[51] convicted of having married his fellow-godmother,[52] and two Portuguese who, when eating a chicken had thrown away the bacon;[53] after dinner they came and bound Dr. Pangloss and his disciple Candide, one because he had spoken and the other because he had listened with an air of approbation; they were both carried separately to extremely cool apartments, where there was never any discomfort from the sun; a week afterwards each was dressed in a sanbenito[54] and their heads were ornamented with paper mitres; Candide's mitre[55] and sanbenito were painted with flames upside down and with devils who had neither tails nor claws; but Pangloss's devils had claws and tails, and his flames were upright.[56]

Dressed in this manner they marched in procession and listened to a most pathetic sermon, followed by lovely plain-song music. Candide was flogged in time to the music, while the singing went on; the Biscayan and the two men who had not wanted to eat bacon were burned, and Pangloss was hanged, although this is not the custom. The very same day, the earth shook again with a terrible clamor.[57]

Candide, terrified, dumbfounded, bewildered, covered with blood, quivering from head to foot, said to himself:

[49]Portuguese: act of faith. The phrase refers to the public sentencing and subsequent punishment of convicted and hardened heretics. There were indeed several *auto-da-fés* following the destruction of Lisbon.

[50]A city about one hundred miles north of Lisbon, boasting one of the oldest European universities.

[51]One living near the Gulf of Biscay, off the northern coast of Spain.

[52]A reference to the supposed illicit marriage of two godparents of the same child. (Voltaire is spoofing the complicated church prohibitions regarding matrimonial union.)

[53]Thus making themselves suspect of being Jews.

[54]A cape worn by those who were to be sentenced at the *auto-da-fé*. A yellow sanbenito with flames painted on it pointing downward indicated that the heretic's life was spared; a person to be burned wore a black sanbenito with flames pointing upward.

[55]A paper hat in the shape of a beehive or cone, somewhat resembling a bishop's mitre.

[56]Candide obviously escaped the stake through confession, while Pangloss was condemned to suffer death as a stubborn heretic.

[57]Lisbon actually suffered a second earth tremor on December 21, 1755 (some seven weeks after the leveling of the city by the first quake).

"If this is the best of all possible worlds, what are the others? Let it pass that I was flogged, for I was flogged by the Bulgarians, but, O my dear Pangloss! The greatest of philosophers! Must I see you hanged without knowing why! O my dear Anabaptist! The best of men! Was it necessary that you should be drowned in port! O Miss Cunegonde! The pearl of women! Was it necessary that your belly should be slit!"

He was returning, scarcely able to support himself, preached at, flogged, absolved and blessed, when an old woman accosted him and said:

"Courage, my son, follow me."

CHAPTER 7

How an Old Woman Took Care of Candide and How He Regained That Which He Loved

Candide did not take courage, but he followed the old woman to a hovel; she gave him a pot of ointment to rub on, and left him food and drink; she pointed out a fairly clean bed; near the bed there was a suit of clothes.

"Eat, drink, sleep," said she, "and may our Lady of Atocha, my Lord Saint Anthony of Padua and my Lord Saint James of Compostella take care of you; I shall come back tomorrow."

Candide, still amazed by all he had seen, by all he had suffered, and still more by the old woman's charity, tried to kiss her hand.

"'Tis not my hand you should kiss," said the old woman, "I shall come back tomorrow. Rub on the ointment, eat and sleep."

In spite of all his misfortune, Candide ate and went to sleep. Next day the old woman brought him breakfast, examined his back and smeared him with another ointment; later she brought him dinner, and returned in the evening with supper. The next day she went through the same ceremony.

"Who are you?" Candide kept asking her. "Who has inspired you with so much kindness? How can I thank you?"

The good woman never made any reply; she returned in the evening without any supper.

"Come with me," said she, "and do not speak a word."

She took him by the arm and walked into the country with him for about a quarter of a mile; they came to an isolated house, surrounded with gardens and canals. The old woman knocked at a little door. It was opened; she led Candide up a back stairway into a gilded apartment, left him on a brocaded sofa, shut the door and went away. Candide thought he was dreaming, and felt that his whole life was a bad dream and the present moment an agreeable dream.

The old woman soon reappeared; she was supporting with some difficulty a trembling woman of majestic stature, glittering with precious stones and covered with a veil.

"Remove the veil," said the old woman to Candide. The young man advanced and lifted the veil with a timid hand. What a moment! What a surprise! He thought he saw Miss Cunegonde, in fact he was looking at her, it was she herself. His strength failed him, he could not utter a word and fell at her feet. Cunegonde fell on the sofa. The old woman dosed them with distilled waters; they recovered their senses and began to speak: at first they uttered only broken words, questions and answers at cross purposes, sighs, tears, exclamations. The old woman advised them to make less noise and left them alone.

"What! Is it you?" said Candide. "You are alive, and I find you here in Portugal! Then you were not raped? Your belly was not slit, as the philosopher Pangloss assured me?"

"Yes, indeed," said the fair Cunegonde; "but those two accidents are not always fatal."

"But your father and mother were killed?"

"'Tis only too true," said Cunegonde, weeping.

"And your brother?"

"My brother was killed too."[58]

"And why are you in Portugal? And how did you know I was here? And by what strange adventure have you brought me to this house?"

"I will tell you everything," replied the lady, "but first of all you must tell me everything that has happened to you since the innocent kiss you gave me and the kicks you received."

Candide obeyed with profound respect; and, although he was bewildered, although his voice was weak and trembling, although his back was still a little painful, he related in the most natural manner all he had endured since the moment of their separation. Cunegonde raised her eyes to Heaven; she shed tears at the death of the good Anabaptist and Pangloss, after which she spoke as follows to Candide, who did not miss a word and devoured her with his eyes.

---

[58]As Candide learns later, her brother, too recovered from his wounds.

CHAPTER 8

Cunegonde's Story

"I was fast asleep in bed when it pleased Heaven to send the Bulgarians to our noble castle of Thunder-ten-tronckh; they murdered my father and brother and cut my mother to pieces. A large Bulgarian six feet tall, seeing that I had swooned at the spectacle, began to rape me; this brought me to, I recovered my senses, I screamed, I struggled, I bit, I scratched, I tried to tear out the big Bulgarian's eyes, not knowing that what was happening in my father's castle was a matter of custom; the brute stabbed me with a knife in the left side where I still have the scar."

"Alas! I hope I shall see it," said the naive Candide.

"You shall see it," said Cunegonde, "but let me go on."

"Go on," said Candide.

She took up the thread of her story as follows:

"A Bulgarian captain came in, saw me covered with blood, and the soldier did not disturb himself. The captain was angry at the brute's lack of respect to him, and killed him on my body. Afterward, he had me bandaged and took me to his billet as a prisoner of war. I washed the few shirts he had and did the cooking; I must admit he thought me very pretty; and I will not deny that he was very well built and that his skin was white and soft; otherwise he had little wit and little philosophy; it was plain that he had not been brought up by Dr. Pangloss. At the end of three months he lost all his money and got tired of me; he sold me to a Jew named Don Issachar,[59] who traded in Holland and Portugal and had a passion for women. This Jew devoted himself to my person but he could not triumph over it; I resisted him better than the Bulgarian soldier; a lady of honor may be raped once, but it strengthens her virtue. In order to subdue me, the Jew brought me to this country house. Up till then I believed that there was nothing on earth so splendid as the castle of Thunder-ten-tronckh; I was undeceived.

"One day the Grand Inquisitor noticed me at Mass; he ogled me continually and sent a message that he wished to speak to me on secret affairs. I was taken to his palace; I informed him of my birth; he pointed

---

[59]As a people, Jews were not one of Voltaire's targets. In fact, Voltaire deplored the persecution that they had endured for so many centuries. On the other hand, he was only too quick to blame his own loss of money, due to speculation and bad judgment, on Jewish bankers and financiers.

out how much it was beneath my rank to belong to an Israelite. A proposition was made on his behalf to Don Issachar to give me up to His Lordship. Don Issachar, who is the court banker and a man of influence, would not agree. The Inquisitor threatened him with an *auto-da-fé*. At last the Jew was frightened and made a bargain whereby the house and I belong to both in common. The Jew has Mondays, Wednesdays and the Sabbath day, and the Inquisitor has the other days of the week. This arrangement has lasted for six months. It has not been without quarrels; for it has often been debated whether the night between Saturday and Sunday belonged to the old law or the new.[60] For my part, I have hitherto resisted them both; and I think that is the reason why they still love me.

"At last My Lord the Inquisitor was pleased to arrange an *auto-da-fé* to remove the scourge of earthquakes and to intimidate Don Issachar. He honored me with an invitation. I had an excellent seat; and refreshments were served to the ladies between the Mass and the execution. I was indeed horror-stricken when I saw the burning of the two Jews and the honest Biscayan who had married his fellow-godmother; but what was my surprise, my terror, my anguish, when I saw in a sanbenito and under a mitre a face which resembled Pangloss's! I rubbed my eyes, I looked carefully, I saw him hanged; and I fainted. I had scarcely recovered my senses when I saw you stripped naked; that was the height of horror, of consternation, of grief and despair. I will frankly tell you that your skin is even whiter and of a more perfect tint than that of my Bulgarian captain. This spectacle redoubled all the feelings which crushed and devoured me. I exclaimed, I tried to say: 'Stop, barbarians!' but my voice failed and my cries would have been useless. When you had been well flogged, I said to myself: 'How does it happen that the charming Candide and the wise Pangloss are in Lisbon, the one to receive a hundred lashes, and the other to be hanged, by order of My Lord the Inquisitor, whose darling I am? Pangloss deceived me cruelly when he said that all is for the best in the world.'

"I was agitated, distracted, sometimes beside myself and sometimes ready to die of faintness, and my head was filled with the massacre of my father, of my mother, of my brother, and the insolence of my horrid Bulgarian soldier, the gash he gave me, my slavery, my life as a kitchen-wench, my Bulgarian captain, my horrid Don Issachar, my abominable Inquisitor, the hanging of Dr. Pangloss, that long plain-

[60]The Old Testament or the New Testament.

song *miserere*[61] during which you were flogged, and above all the kiss I gave you behind the screen that day when I saw you for the last time. I praised God for bringing you back to me through so many trials, I ordered my old woman to take care of you and bring you here as soon as she could. She has carried out my commission very well; I have enjoyed the inexpressible pleasure of seeing you again, of listening to you, and of speaking to you. You must be very hungry; I have a good appetite; let us begin by having supper."

Both sat down to supper; and after supper they returned to the handsome sofa we have already mentioned; they were still there when Signor Don Issachar, one of the masters of the house, arrived. It was the day of the Sabbath. He came to enjoy his rights and to express his tender love.

CHAPTER 9

What Happened to Cunegonde, to Candide, to the Grand Inquisitor and to a Jew

This Issachar was the most choleric Hebrew who had been seen in Israel since the Babylonian captivity.[62]

"What!" said he. "Bitch of a Galilean,[63] isn't it enough to have the Inquisitor? Must this scoundrel share with me too?"

So saying, he drew a long dagger which he always carried and, thinking that his adversary was unarmed, threw himself upon Candide; but our good Westphalian had received an excellent sword from the old woman along with his suit of clothes. He drew his sword, and although he had a most gentle character, laid the Israelite stone-dead on the floor at the feet of the fair Cunegonde.

"Holy Virgin!" she exclaimed, "what will become of us? A man killed in my house! If the police come we are lost."

"If Pangloss had not been hanged," said Candide, "he would have given us good advice in this extremity, for he was a great philosopher. In default of him, let us consult the old woman."

She was extremely prudent and was beginning to give her advice

---

[61] A musical composition based upon the opening phrase of Psalm 51: "Have mercy upon me, O God." It is a plea to God for pardon of deadly sins.

[62] The period (598–538 B.C.) in which Jews were held captive in Babylonia.

[63] A Christian. Jesus spent his childhood in Galilee, one of the three provinces of ancient Palestine.

when another little door opened. It was an hour after midnight, and Sunday was beginning.

This day belonged to My Lord the Inquisitor. He came in and saw the flogged Candide sword in hand, a corpse lying on the ground, Cunegonde in terror, and the old woman giving advice.

At this moment, here is what happened in Candide's soul and the manner of his reasoning:

"If this holy man calls for help, he will infallibly have me burned; he might do as much to Cunegonde; he had me pitilessly lashed; he is my rival; I am in the mood to kill, there is no room for hesitation."

His reasoning was clear and swift; and, without giving the Inquisitor time to recover from his surprise, he pierced him through and through and cast him beside the Jew.

"Here's another," said Cunegonde, "there is no chance of mercy; we are excommunicated, our last hour has come. How does it happen that you, who were born so mild, should kill a Jew and a prelate in two minutes?"

"My dear young lady," replied Candide, "when a man is in love, jealous, and has been flogged by the Inquisition, he is beside himself."

The old woman then spoke up and said:

"In the stable are three Andalusian horses, with their saddles and bridles; let the brave Candide prepare them; madam has moidores[64] and diamonds; let us mount quickly, although I can only sit on one buttock, and go to Cadiz,[65] the weather is beautifully fine, and it is most pleasant to travel in the coolness of the night."

Candide immediately saddled the three horses. Cunegonde, the old woman and he rode thirty miles without stopping.

While they were riding away, the Holy Hermandad[66] arrived at the house; My Lord was buried in a splendid church and Issachar was thrown into a sewer.

Candide, Cunegonde and the old woman had already reached the little town of Aracena[67] in the midst of the mountains of the Sierra Morena,[68] and they talked in their inn as follows.

---

[64]Portuguese gold coins.

[65]A maritime city in southwestern Spain; Cadiz functioned as Spain's door to the New World.

[66]The clerical police.

[67]About one hundred miles north of Cadiz.

[68]A mountain range.

CHAPTER 10

How Candide, Cunegonde and the Old Woman Arrived at Cadiz in Great Distress, and How They Embarked

"Who can have stolen my pistoles[69] and my diamonds?" said Cunegonde, weeping. "How shall we live? What shall we do? Where shall we find Inquisitors and Jews to give me others?"

"Alas!" said the old woman, "I strongly suspect a reverend Franciscan[70] father who slept in the same inn at Badajoz[71] with us; Heaven forbid that I should judge rashly! But he twice came into our room and left long before we did."

"Alas!" said Candide, "the good Pangloss often proved to me that this world's goods are common to all men and that everyone has an equal right to them. According to these principles the monk should have left us enough to continue our journey. Have you nothing left then, my fair Cunegonde?"

"Not a maravedi,"[72] said she.

"What are we to do?" said Candide.

"Sell one of the horses," said the old woman. "I will ride pillion[73] behind Miss Cunegonde, although I can only sit on one buttock, and we will get to Cadiz."

In the same hotel there was a Benedictine friar. He bought the horse very cheap. Candide, Cunegonde and the old woman passed through Lucena, Chillas, Lebrixa, and at last reached Cadiz. A fleet was there being equipped and troops were being raised to bring to reason the reverend Jesuit fathers[74] of Paraguay, who were accused of causing the revolt of one of their tribes against the kings of Spain and Portugal near the town of Sacramento.[75] Candide, having served with the Bulgarians, went through the Bulgarian drill before the general of the little army with so much grace, celerity, skill, pride and agility, that he was

---

[69]Spanish gold coins.

[70]A member of a Roman Catholic order.

[71]A Spanish city near the Portuguese border.

[72]A small Spanish copper coin worth less than a penny.

[73]A pad or cushion attached behind a saddle to carry an extra rider.

[74]Members of the Society of Jesus, a Catholic order founded near the middle of the sixteenth century.

[75]In 1750 Spain and Portugal agreed that the city of San Sacramento in South America should pass into Portuguese hands. To forestall the transfer, the Jesuits caused the natives to rise in revolt.

given the command of an infantry company. He was now a captain; he embarked with Miss Cunegonde, the old woman, two servants, and the two Andalusian horses which had belonged to the Grand Inquisitor of Portugal.

During the voyage they had many discussions about the philosophy of poor Pangloss.

"We are going to a new world," said Candide, "and no doubt it is there that everything is for the best; for it must be admitted that one might lament a little over the physical and moral happenings in our own world."

"I love you with all my heart," said Cunegonde, "but my soul is still shocked by what I have seen and undergone."

"All will be well," replied Candide; "the sea in this new world already is better than the seas of our Europe; it is calmer and the winds are more constant. It is certainly the new world which is the best of all possible worlds."

"God grant it!" said Cunegonde, "but I have been so horribly unhappy in mine that my heart is nearly closed to hope."

"You complain," said the old woman to them. "Alas! you have not endured such misfortunes as mine."

Cunegonde almost laughed and thought it most amusing of the old woman to assert that she was more unfortunate.

"Alas! my dear," said she, "unless you have been raped by two Bulgarians, stabbed twice in the belly, have had two castles destroyed, two fathers and mothers murdered before your eyes, and have seen two of your lovers flogged in an *auto-da-fé*, I do not see how you can surpass me; moreover, I was born a Baroness with seventy-two quarterings and I have been a kitchen-wench."

"You do not know my birth," said the old woman, "and if I showed you my backside you would not talk as you do and you would suspend your judgment."

This speech aroused intense curiosity in the minds of Cunegonde and Candide. And the old woman spoke as follows.

CHAPTER 11

The Old Woman's Story

"My eyes were not always bloodshot and red-rimmed; my nose did not always touch my chin and I was not always a servant. I am the daughter of Pope Urban X[76] and the Princess of Palestrina. Until I was fourteen I was brought up in a palace to which all the castles of your German Barons would not have served as stables; and one of my dresses cost more than all the magnificence of Westphalia. I increased in beauty, in grace, in talents, among pleasures, respect and hopes; already I inspired love, my breasts were forming; and what breasts! White, firm, carved like those of the Venus de' Medici. And what eyes! What eyelids! What black eyebrows! What fire shone from my two eyeballs, and dimmed the glitter of the stars, as the local poets pointed out to me. The women who dressed and undressed me fell into ecstasy when they beheld me in front and behind; and all the men would have liked to be in their place.

"I was betrothed to a ruling prince of Massa-Carrara.[77] What a prince! As beautiful as I was, formed of gentleness and charms, brilliantly witty and burning with love; I loved him with a first love, idolatrously and extravagantly. The marriage ceremonies were arranged with unheard-of pomp and magnificence; there were continual fêtes, revels and comic operas; all Italy wrote sonnets for me, and not a good one among them.

"I touched the moment of my happiness when an old marchioness who had been my prince's mistress invited him to take chocolate with her; less than two hours afterward he died in horrible convulsions; but that is only a trifle. My mother was in despair, though less distressed than I, and wished to absent herself for a time from a place so disastrous. She had a most beautiful estate near Gaeta;[78] we embarked on a galley, gilded like the altar of St. Peter's at Rome. A Sallé[79] pirate swooped down and boarded us; our soldiers defended us like soldiers of the Pope; they threw down their arms, fell on their knees and asked the pirates for absolution *in articulo mortis*.[80]

"They were immediately stripped as naked as monkeys and my mother, our ladies of honor and myself as well. The diligence with which these gentlemen strip people is truly admirable; but I was still

---

[76]Many years after his death, the following note, left by Voltaire, was published for the first time: "Observe the author's extreme discretion, for there has not up to the present time been any pope named Urban X. He avoids attributing a bastard daughter to a known pope. What circumspection! How delicate a conscience!"

[77]A small Italian duchy, lying northwest of Pisa.

[78]A coastal town near Naples.

[79]A coastal city near Rabat, Morocco, known as a pirate stronghold.

[80]A religious rite administered at the point of death.

more surprised by their inserting a finger in a place belonging to all of us where we women usually only allow the end of a syringe. This appeared to me a very strange ceremony; but that is how we judge everything when we leave our own country. I soon learned that it was to find out if we had hidden any diamonds there; 'tis a custom established from time immemorial among the civilized nations who roam the seas. I have learned that the religious Knights of Malta[81] never fail in it when they capture Turks and Turkish women; this is an international law which has never been broken.

"I will not tell you how hard it is for a young princess to be taken with her mother as a slave to Morocco; you will also guess all we had to endure in the pirates' ship. My mother was still very beautiful; our ladies of honor, even our waiting-maids possessed more charms than could be found in all Africa; and I was ravishing, I was beauty, grace itself, and I was a virgin; I did not remain so long; the flower which had been reserved for the handsome prince of Massa-Carrara was ravished from me by a pirate captain; he was an abominable negro who thought he was doing me a great honor. The Princess of Palestrina and I must indeed have been strong to bear up against all we endured before our arrival in Morocco! But let that pass; these things are so common that they are not worth mentioning.

"Morocco was swimming in blood when we arrived. The fifty sons of the Emperor Muley Ismael[82] had each a faction; and this produced fifty civil wars, of blacks against blacks, browns against browns, mulattoes against mulattoes. There was continual carnage throughout the whole extent of the empire.

"Scarcely had we landed when the blacks of a party hostile to that of my pirate arrived with the purpose of depriving him of his booty. After the diamonds and the gold, we were the most valuable possessions. I witnessed a fight such as is never seen in your European climates. The blood of the northern peoples is not sufficiently ardent; their madness for women does not reach the point which is common in Africa. The Europeans seem to have milk in their veins; but vitriol and fire flow in the veins of the inhabitants of Mount Atlas[83] and the neighboring

---

[81] A medieval order of Christian knights.

[82] Mawlay Isma'il, sultan of Morocco, from 1673 to 1727. He is generally regarded as an effective ruler, although he employed extreme measures of cruelty and brutality to secure law and order. When he died, he left five hundred male children, all of whom possessed the right to rule, which did not contribute to the country's political stability.

[83] A North African mountain range extending from Morocco to Tunisia.

countries. They fought with the fury of the lions, tigers[84] and serpents of the country to determine who should have us. A Moor[85] grasped my mother by the right arm, my captain's lieutenant held her by the left arm; a Moorish soldier held one leg and one of our pirates seized the other. In a moment nearly all our women were seized in the same way by four soldiers. My captain kept me hidden behind him; he had a scimitar[86] in his hand and killed everybody who opposed his fury. I saw my mother and all our Italian women torn in pieces, gashed, massacred by the monsters who disputed them. The prisoners, my companions, those who had captured them, soldiers, sailors, blacks, browns, whites, mulattoes and finally my captain were all killed and I remained expiring on a heap of corpses. As everyone knows, such scenes go on in an area of more than three hundred square leagues and yet no one ever fails to recite the five daily prayers ordered by Mahomet.[87]

"With great difficulty I extricated myself from the bloody heaps of corpses and dragged myself to the foot of a large orange-tree on the bank of a stream; there I fell down with terror, weariness, horror, despair and hunger. Soon afterwards, my exhausted senses fell into a sleep which was more like a swoon than repose. I was in this state of weakness and insensibility between life and death when I felt myself oppressed by something which moved on my body. I opened my eyes and saw a white man of good appearance who was sighing and muttering between his teeth: O che sciagura d'essere senza coglioni![88]

CHAPTER 12

Continuation of the Old Woman's Misfortunes

"Amazed and delighted to hear my native language, and not less surprised at the words spoken by this man, I replied that there were greater misfortunes than that of which he complained. In a few words I informed him of the horrors I had undergone and then swooned again.

---

[84]Voltaire is not quite accurate here. Tigers are not native to Morocco.

[85]The Moors, the principal people of northwestern Africa, are Muslim by religion and ethnically of mixed Arab and African ancestry.

[86]A curved, short sword with the cutting edge on the outside of the curve.

[87]Muhammad (570–632), Arabian prophet and founder of Islam.

[88]Italian: Oh, what misfortune to have no testicles!

He carried me to a neighboring house, had me put to bed, gave me food, waited on me, consoled me, flattered me, told me he had never seen anyone so beautiful as I, and that he had never so much regretted that which no one could give back to him.

"'I was born at Naples,' he said, 'and every year they make two or three thousand children there into capons;[89] some die of it, others acquire voices more beautiful than women's, and others become the governors of States.[90] This operation was performed upon me with very great success and I was a musician in the chapel of the Princess of Palestrina.'

"'Of my mother,' I exclaimed.

"'Of your mother!' cried he, weeping. 'What! Are you that young princess I brought up to the age of six and who even then gave promise of being as beautiful as you are?'

"'I am! my mother is four hundred yards from here, cut into quarters under a heap of corpses. . . .'

"I related all that had happened to me; he also told me his adventures and informed me how he had been sent to the King of Morocco by a Christian power to make a treaty with that monarch whereby he was supplied with powder, cannons and ships to help to exterminate the commerce of other Christians.

"'My mission is accomplished,' said this honest eunuch, 'I am about to embark at Ceuta[91] and I will take you back to Italy. *Ma che sciagura d'essere senza coglioni!*'

"I thanked him with tears of gratitude; and instead of taking me back to Italy he conducted me to Algiers[92] and sold me to the Dey.[93] I had scarcely been sold when the plague which had gone through Africa, Asia, and Europe broke out furiously in Algiers. You have seen earthquakes; but have you ever seen the plague?"

"Never," replied the Baroness.

"If you had," replied the old woman, "you would admit that it is

---

[89]A capon is actually a rooster that has been castrated for better fattening, thus more tasty eating.

[90]An allusion to the famous male soprano Farinelli (1705–1782). Following a successful career as a singer, he acquired substantial influence and political power, serving two Spanish kings, Philip V and Ferdinand VI. Honored with grand titles, he retired in 1761 to a castle near Bologna, Italy.

[91]A maritime city at the northwestern tip of Africa, opposite Gibraltar.

[92]The capital of a province in north Africa, under Turkish rule.

[93]The title of the (Turkish) governor.

much worse than an earthquake. It is very common in Africa; I caught it. Imagine the situation of a Pope's daughter aged fifteen, who in three months had undergone poverty and slavery, had been raped nearly every day, had seen her mother cut into four pieces, had undergone hunger and war, and was now dying of the plague in Algiers. However, I did not die; but my eunuch and the Dey and almost all the seraglio[94] of Algiers perished.

"When the first ravages of this frightful plague were over, the Dey's slaves were sold. A merchant bought me and carried me to Tunis; he sold me to another merchant who re-sold me at Tripoli: from Tripoli I was re-sold to Alexandria, from Alexandria re-sold to Smyrna, from Smyrna to Constantinople.[95] I was finally bought by an Aga[96] of the Janizaries,[97] who was soon ordered to defend Azov[98] against the Russians who were besieging it.[99]

"The Aga, who was a man of great gallantry, took his whole seraglio with him, and lodged us in a little fort on the islands of Palus-Maeotis,[100] guarded by two black eunuchs and twenty soldiers. He killed a prodigious number of Russians, but they returned the compliment as well. Azov was given up to fire and blood, neither sex nor age was pardoned; only our little fort remained; and the enemy tried to reduce it by starving us. The twenty Janizaries had sworn never to surrender us. The extremities of hunger to which they were reduced forced them to eat our two eunuchs for fear of breaking their oath. Some days later they resolved to eat the women.

"We had with us a most pious and compassionate Imam[101] who delivered a fine sermon to them by which he persuaded them not to kill us altogether.

"'Cut,' said he, 'only one buttock from each of these ladies and you

---

[94]Harem.

[95]The capital of the Ottoman (Turkish) Empire, which ended in 1919. The name of the city was changed to Istanbul in 1930.

[96]Title of respect for a high-ranking officer or official.

[97]An elite unit of the Turkish infantry that consisted of former slaves, natives, and sons of captured Christians. The latter were pressed into service while very young and thus quickly turned into fanatical converts to Islam.

[98]A city located at the mouth of the River Don in southern Russia.

[99]A reference to the siege of Azov (1695–96) by the Russian Tsar Peter the Great (1672–1725).

[100]Latin name for the Sea of Azov.

[101]Muslim religious official.

will make very good cheer; if you have to return, there will still be as much left in a few days; Heaven will be pleased at so charitable an action and you will be saved.'

"He was very eloquent and persuaded them. This horrible operation was performed upon us; the Imam anointed us with the same balm that is used for children who have just been circumcized; we were all at the point of death.

"Scarcely had the Janizaries finished the meal we had supplied when the Russians arrived in flat-bottomed boats; not a Janizary escaped. The Russians paid no attention to the state we were in. There are French doctors everywhere; one of them who was very skilful, took care of us; he healed us, and I shall remember all my life that, when my wounds were cured, he made propositions to me. For the rest, he told us all to cheer up; he told us that the same thing had happened in several sieges and that it was a law of war.

"As soon as my companions could walk they were sent to Moscow. I fell to the lot of a Boyar[102] who made me his gardener and gave me twenty lashes a day. But at the end of two years this lord was broken on the wheel with thirty other Boyars owing to some court disturbance,[103] and I profited by this adventure; I fled; I crossed all Russia; for a long time I was servant in an inn at Riga,[104] then at Rostock, at Wismar, at Leipzig, at Cassel,[105] at Utrecht, at Leyden, at The Hague, at Rotterdam,[106] I have grown old in misery and in shame, with only half a backside, always remembering that I was the daughter of a Pope; a hundred times I wanted to kill myself, but I still loved life. This ridiculous weakness is perhaps the most disastrous of our inclinations; for is there anything sillier than to desire to bear continually a burden one always wishes to throw on the ground; to look upon oneself with horror and yet to cling to oneself; in short, to caress the serpent which devours us until he has eaten our heart?

"In the countries it has been my fate to traverse and in the inns where I have served I have seen a prodigious number of people who hated their lives; but I have only seen twelve who voluntarily put an end to their misery: three negroes, four Englishmen, four Genevans and a German

---

[102]A Russian noble of high rank.

[103]An allusion to the uprising of the Streltsy (soldiers of the Moscow garrison) in 1698.

[104]A city on the coast of Latvia.

[105]Cities in the northern half of Germany.

[106]Cities in Holland.

professor named Robeck.[107] I ended up as servant to the Jew, Don Issachar; he placed me in your service, my fair young lady; I attached myself to your fate and have been more occupied with your adventures than with my own. I should never even have spoken of my misfortunes, if you had not piqued me a little and if it had not been the custom on board ship to tell stories to pass the time. In short, Miss, I have had experience, I know the world; provide yourself with an entertainment, make each passenger tell you his story; and if there is one who has not often cursed his life, who has not often said to himself that he was the most unfortunate of men, throw me head-first into the sea."

• • •

[After arriving in the New World, Candide meets with further adventures that show the stupidity, cruelty, and greed of men. Only in El Dorado, a paradise in the interior of South America, does he find a society in which people are naturally kind, courteous, generous, and reasonable. Having lost his beloved Cunegonde to a Spanish colonial noble, he makes plans to win her back by bribery and decides to return to Europe. On the way he falls in with Martin, a disillusioned pessimist, and under the latter's influence begins to doubt Pangloss's optimism, "the mania of maintaining that everything is well when we are wretched." Martin argues that their misadventures prove that the world is evil and was created only to infuriate us. Back in Europe, Candide meets with evidence for this view in the behavior of intellectuals, prostitutes, monks, and deposed kings. Nowhere can he find a truly happy man. The following two chapters bring Candide's adventures to their conclusion. *Ed.*]

CHAPTER 29

How Candide Found Cunegonde and the Old Woman Again

While Candide, the Baron,[108] Pangloss,[109] Martin and Cacambo[110] were relating their adventures, reasoning upon contingent or noncon-

---

[107]Johann Robe(c)k (1672–1739), who maintained that the love of life was nothing but a ridiculous notion. Having written a treatise entitled "Exercise in Voluntary Death" in which he justified suicide, he faced the consequence of his conviction and drowned himself.

[108]Son of the original Baron Thunder-ten-tronckh, who appeared in Chapter 1. Candide had discovered him as a galley slave and had purchased his freedom. He was, of course, Cunegonde's long-lost brother.

[109]Pangloss, too, is present again after many adventures. He was not killed as hinted in Chapter 6, since a downpour saved his life which kept the fire from burning and the noose from tightening.

[110]Candide's valet, brought from Cadiz.

tingent events of the universe, arguing about effects and causes, moral and physical evil, free will and necessity, and the consolations to be found in the Turkish galleys, they came to the house of the Transylvanian prince on the shores of Propontis.[111] The first objects which met their sight were Cunegonde and the old woman hanging out towels to dry on the line.

At this site the Baron grew pale. Candide, that tender lover, seeing his fair Cunegonde sunburned, blear-eyed, flat-breasted, with wrinkles around her eyes and red, chapped arms, recoiled three paces in horror, and then advanced from mere politeness. She embraced Candide and her brother. They embraced the old woman; Candide bought them both.

In the neighborhood was a little farm; the old woman suggested that Candide should buy it, until some better fate befell the group. Cunegonde did not know that she had become ugly, for nobody had told her so; she reminded Candide of his promises in so peremptory a tone that the good Candide dared not refuse her. He therefore informed the Baron that he was about to marry his sister.

"Never," said the Baron, "will I endure such baseness on her part and such insolence on yours; nobody shall ever reproach me with this infamy; my sister's children could never enter the chapters[112] of Germany. No, my sister shall never marry anyone but a Baron of the Empire."

Cunegonde threw herself at his feet and bathed them in tears; but he was inflexible.

"Madman," said Candide, "I rescued you from the galleys, I paid your ransom and your sister's; she was washing dishes here, she is ugly, I am so kind as to make her my wife, and you pretend to oppose me! I should kill you again if I listened to my anger."

"You may kill me again," said the Baron, "but you shall never marry my sister while I am alive."

CHAPTER 30

Conclusion

At the bottom of his heart Candide had not the least wish to marry Cunegonde. But the Baron's extreme impertinence determined him to

[111]Sea of Marmara, situated between the Bosporus and the Dardanelles in Turkey.
[112]Knightly assemblies.

complete the marriage, and Cunegonde urged it so warmly that he could not retract. He consulted Pangloss, Martin and the faithful Cacambo. Pangloss wrote an excellent memorandum by which he proved that the Baron had no rights over his sister and that by all the laws of the empire she could make a left-handed marriage[113] with Candide. Martin advised that the Baron should be thrown into the sea; Cacambo decided that he should be returned to the Levantine[114] captain and sent back to the galleys, after which he would be returned by the first ship to the Vicar-General at Rome.[115] This was thought to be very good advice; the old woman approved it; they said nothing to the sister; the plan was carried out with the aid of a little money and they had the pleasure of duping a Jesuit and punishing the pride of a German Baron.

It would be natural to suppose that when, after so many disasters, Candide was married to his mistress, and living with the philosopher Pangloss, the philosopher Martin, the prudent Cacambo and the old woman, having brought back so many diamonds from the country of the ancient Incas, he would lead the most pleasant life imaginable. But he was so cheated by the Jews that he had nothing left but his little farm; his wife, growing uglier every day, became shrewish and unendurable; the old woman was ailing and even more bad-tempered than Cunegonde. Cacambo, who worked in the garden and then went to Constantinople to sell vegetables, was overworked and cursed his fate. Pangloss was in despair because he did not shine in some German university. As for Martin, he was firmly convinced that people are equally uncomfortable everywhere; he accepted things patiently. Candide, Martin, and Pangloss sometimes argued about metaphysics and morals. From the windows of the farm they often watched the ships going by, filled with effendis,[116] pashas,[117] and cadis,[118] who were being exiled to Lemnos, to Mitylene[119] and Erzerum.[120] They

---

[113]A marriage between persons of unequal rank in which it was understood that the lowly spouse (and any offspring) could make no claim to the other spouse's high rank or property.

[114]Pertaining to the eastern Mediterranean region.

[115]High official of the Jesuit order.

[116]Turkish title of respect for a government official.

[117]High civil or military officials.

[118]A minor magistrate.

[119]Islands in the Aegean Sea.

[120]A coastal city in northeastern Turkey.

saw other cadis, other pashas, and other effendis coming back to take the place of the exiles and to be exiled in their turn. They saw the neatly impaled heads which were taken to the Sublime Porte.[121] These sights redoubled their discussions; and when they were not arguing, the boredom was so excessive that one day the old woman dared to say to them:

"I should like to know which is worse, to be raped a hundred times by Negro pirates, to have a buttock cut off, to run the gauntlet among the Bulgarians, to be whipped and flogged in an *auto-da-fé*, to be dissected, to row in a galley, in short, to endure all the miseries through which we have passed, or to remain here doing nothing?"

"'Tis a great question," said Candide.

These remarks led to new reflections, and Martin especially concluded that man was born to live in the convulsions of distress or in the lethargy of boredom. Candide did not agree, but he asserted nothing. Pangloss confessed that he had always suffered horribly; but, having once maintained that everything was for the best, he had continued to maintain it without believing it.

One thing confirmed Martin in his detestable principles, made Candide hesitate more than ever, and embarrassed Pangloss. And it was this. One day there came to their farm Paquette and Friar Giroflée,[122] who were in the most extreme misery; they had soon wasted their three thousand piastres,[123] had left each other, made up, quarreled again, been put in prison, escaped, and finally Friar Giroflée had turned Turk. Paquette continued her occupation everywhere and now earned nothing by it.

"I foresaw," said Martin to Candide, "that your gifts would soon be wasted and would only make them the more miserable. You and Cacambo were once bloated with millions of piastres and you are no happier than Friar Giroflée and Paquette."

"Ah! Ha!" said Pangloss to Paquette, "so Heaven brings you back to us, my dear child? Do you know that you cost me the end of my nose, an eye, and an ear! What a plight you are in! Ah! What a world this is!"

This new occurrence caused them to philosophize more than ever.

---

[121]The main gate of the palace of the sultan in Constantinople; the heads of those who had been executed were often displayed there as a deterrent to others. The phrase "Sublime Porte" is also used as a reference to the government of the Ottoman Empire.

[122]A monk whom Candide had met in Venice. Literally (in French), wallflower.

[123]Turkish money.

In the neighborhood there lived a very famous Dervish,[124] who was supposed to be the best philosopher in Turkey; they went to consult him; Pangloss was the spokesman and said:

"Master, we have come to beg you to tell us why so strange an animal as man was ever created."

"What has it to do with you?" said the Dervish. "Is it your business?"

"But, reverend father," said Candide, "there is a horrible amount of evil in the world."

"What does it matter," said the Dervish, "whether there is evil or good? When his highness sends a ship to Egypt, does he worry about the comfort or discomfort of the rats in the ship?"

"Then what should we do?" said Pangloss.

"Hold your tongue," said the Dervish.

"I flattered myself," said Pangloss, "that I should discuss with you effects and causes, this best of all possible worlds, the origin of evil, the nature of the soul and pre-established harmony."

At these words the Dervish slammed the door in their faces. During this conversation the news went round that at Constantinople two viziers[125] and the mufti[126] had been strangled and several of their friends impaled. This catastrophe made a prodigious noise everywhere for several hours. As Pangloss, Candide, and Martin were returning to their little farm, they came upon an old man who was taking the air under a bower of orange-trees at his door. Pangloss, who was as curious as he was argumentative, asked him what was the name of the mufti who had just been strangled.

"I do not know," replied the old man. "I have never known the name of any mufti or of any vizier. I am entirely ignorant of the occurrence you mention; I presume that in general those who meddle with public affairs sometimes perish miserably and that they deserve it; but I never inquire what is going on in Constantinople; I content myself with sending there for sale the produce of the garden I cultivate."

Having spoken thus, he took the strangers into his house. His two daughters and his two sons presented them with several kinds of sherbet which they made themselves, caymac[127] flavored with candied

---

[124] A member of a Muslim religious order, said to be somewhat similar to the Franciscans.
[125] Ministers of state.
[126] An official interpreter of Muslim law.
[127] Turkish word for cream.

citron peel, oranges, lemons, limes, pineapples, dates, pistachios, and Mocha coffee[128] which had not been mixed with the bad coffee of Batavia and the Isles.[129] After which this good Mussulman's two daughters perfumed the beards of Candide, Pangloss, and Martin.

"You must have a vast and magnificent estate?" said Candide to the Turk.

"I have only twenty acres," replied the Turk. "I cultivate them with my children; and work keeps at bay three great evils: boredom, vice and need."

As Candide returned to his farm he reflected deeply on the Turk's remarks. He said to Pangloss and Martin:

"That good old man seems to me to have chosen an existence preferable by far to that of the six kings with whom we had the honor to sup."

"Exalted rank," said Pangloss, "is very dangerous, according to the testimony of all philosophers; for Eglon, King of the Moabites, was murdered by Ehud; Absalom was hanged by the hair and pierced by three darts; King Nadab, son of Jeroboam, was killed by Baasha; King Elah by Zimri; Ahaziah by Jehu; Athaliah by Jehoiada; the Kings Jehoiakim, Jeconiah, and Zedekiah[130] were made slaves. You know in what manner died Croesus, Astyages, Darius, Denys of Syracuse, Pyrrhus, Perseus, Hannibal, Jugurtha, Ariovistus, Caesar, Pompey, Nero, Otho, Vitellius, Domitian, Richard II of England, Edward II, Henry VI, Richard III, Mary Stuart, Charles I, the three Henrys of France, the Emperor Henry IV. You know . . ."

"I also know," said Candide, "that we should cultivate our gardens."

"You are right," said Pangloss, "for, when man was placed in the Garden of Eden, he was placed there to dress it and to keep it; which proves that man was not born for idleness."

"Let us work without theorizing," said Martin; "'tis the only way to make life endurable."

The whole small fraternity entered into this praiseworthy plan, and each started to make use of his talents. The little farm yielded well. Cunegonde was indeed very ugly, but she became an excellent pastry-cook; Paquette embroidered; the old woman took care of the linen.

---

[128]Coffee from Arabia.

[129]Presumably the East Indies.

[130]These names—of villains and victims—are mentioned in the Old Testament.

Even Friar Giroflée performed some service; he was a very good carpenter and even became a man of honor; and Pangloss sometimes said to Candide:

"All events are linked up in this best of all possible worlds; for, if you had not been expelled from the noble castle by hard kicks in your backside for love of Mademoiselle Cunegonde, if you had not been clapped into the Inquisition, if you had not wandered about America on foot, if you had not stuck your sword in the Baron, if you had not lost all your sheep from the land of El Dorado, you would not be eating candied citrons and pistachios here."

"'Tis well said," replied Candide, "but we must cultivate our gardens."

10

Jean Jacques Rousseau

On the Origin of Inequality among Men

*I*N *the midst of the middle-class liberalism of eighteenth-century France, Jean Jacques Rousseau (1712–1778) was a startling and important exception. Though sharing some of the ideas of the Enlightenment, he was violently opposed to others. Born in Geneva into a Swiss Protestant family, Rousseau remained an outsider and a rebel, a rootless vagabond who rejected any place in French society. Privately he was unhappy and impractical, an unstable personality—nevertheless a genius—whose life would end in madness. In public matters he was an emotional democrat who spoke up sincerely for the common people, formulating ideas that would exert a paramount influence on the French Revolution, especially in its radical stage. Indeed, Rousseau has been hailed as the prophet of modern democracy and nationalism; totalitarian movements have even found inspiration in his ideas regarding the sovereignty of collective authority. Rousseau was, in addition, one of the first exponents of that combination of ideas and attitudes toward life typical of the philosophical and literary movement called romanticism.*

Rousseau shared the Enlightenment belief in progress and in the goodness of human beings and their infinite perfectibility. He sharply attacked the social order of his day as artificial, corrupt, and corrupting. But he refused to accept the simple equivalence of reason and nature, an idea held by most of the "enlightened" thinkers (see introduction to selection 8). Nature was good, but, since reason was part of civilization, it was evil: reason was not the guide to truth. To achieve truth and justice, Rousseau advocated that human beings return to nature and trust their untaught feelings. The primitive and unsophisticated elements in people were, to him, the sources of the strength needed to remake the individual and society.

Despising many features of his own eighteenth-century society, such as greed and corruption, and inequality in position and wealth, Rousseau began, in midlife, to ponder the stages of the development of humankind. He wrote down his thoughts in a work called Discourse on the Origin of Inequality among Men, *published in 1755. This book shows that Rousseau had reached the prime of his intellectual creativity, a period which lasted for approximately one decade, from 1750–1762. It is considered by many scholars to be the most original and insightful political work written by Rousseau.*

When reviewing the development of humankind from the earliest days to the latter stages of civilization, Rousseau was especially interested in pointing to those moments which had steered the ship onto the wrong course. Rousseau had no doubt that humans of the earliest stage, by and large, lived happy lives. As loners being motivated by self-preservation, they roamed the primeval forests— taking for their subsistence what a benevolent nature had provided. When nature faced them with obstacles, it was for the purpose of strengthening them. In like manner, as loners, male and female met occasionally to satisfy their sexual needs and desires. Thus, this stage of natural man and woman was a state of individual freedom and equality. Abuses of one against another, Rousseau believed, were held in check by the pity (compassion) they felt for their fellow humans and by the fear of retaliation.

With the establishment of the family, this state of happiness came to an end. In becoming social *beings, humans found themselves upon a new stage of their development—one with a* dual *character. On one hand, the visible signs of the socialization of humans—such as family, huts, language, cultivated fields, and skilled crafts—brought much comfort into their lives and even made them more gentle. On the other hand, many of the sources of conflict and suffering associated with civilization had their origin at that time—private property, human exploitation, and poverty, to name a few. In short, Rousseau concluded that an increase in comfort had as its price for humans their loss of innocence.*

By asking questions about early humans and their essential nature, Rousseau has ever since stimulated scholars in anthropology, sociology, psychology, political science, and economics to re-think previous assumptions.

The first man who, having enclosed a piece of land, thought of saying 'This is mine' and found people simple enough to believe him, was the true founder of civil society. How many crimes, wars, murders; how

ON THE ORIGIN OF INEQUALITY AMONG MEN   From *A Discourse on Inequality* by Jean Jacques Rousseau, trans. Maurice Cranston, II, 109–116. Translation copyright © 1984 by Maurice Cranston. Reprinted by permission of Viking Penguin, Inc.

much misery and horror the human race would have been spared if someone had pulled up the stakes and filled in the ditch and cried out to his fellow men: 'Beware of listening to this impostor. You are lost if you forget that the fruits of the earth belong to everyone and that the earth itself belongs to no one!' But it is highly probable that by this time things had reached a point beyond which they could not go on as they were; for the idea of property, depending on many prior ideas which could only have arisen in successive stages, was not formed all at once in the human mind. It was necessary for men to make much progress, to acquire much industry and knowledge, to transmit and increase it from age to age, before arriving at this final stage of the state of nature. Let us therefore look farther back, and try to review from a single perspective the slow succession of events and discoveries in their most natural order.

Man's first feeling was that of his existence, his first concern was that of his preservation. The products of the earth furnished all the necessary aids; instinct prompted him to make use of them. While hunger and other appetites made him experience in turn different modes of existence, there was one appetite which urged him to perpetuate his own species: and this blind impulse, devoid of any sentiment of the heart, produced only a purely animal act. The need satisfied, the two sexes recognized each other no longer, and even the child meant nothing to the mother, as soon as he could do without her.

Such was the condition of nascent[1] man; such was the life of an animal limited at first to mere sensation; and scarcely profiting from the gifts bestowed on him by nature, let alone was he dreaming of wresting anything from her. But difficulties soon presented themselves and man had to learn to overcome them. The height of trees, which prevented him from reaching their fruits; the competition of animals seeking to nourish themselves on the same fruits; the ferocity of animals who threatened his life—all this obliged man to apply himself to bodily exercises; he had to make himself agile, fleet of foot, and vigorous in combat. Natural weapons—branches of trees and stones—were soon found to be at hand. He learned to overcome the obstacles of nature, to fight when necessary against other animals, to struggle for his subsistence even against other men, or to indemnify[2] himself for what he was forced to yield to the stronger.

[1]Early, developing.
[2]Compensate.

To the extent that the human race spread, men's difficulties multiplied with their numbers. Differences between soils, climates, and seasons would have forced men to adopt different ways of life. Barren years, long hard winters, scorching summers consuming everything, demanded new industry from men. Along the sea coast and river banks they invented the hook and line to become fishermen and fish eaters. In the forests they made bows and arrows, and became hunters and warriors. In cold countries they covered themselves with the skins of the beasts they killed. Lightning, a volcano, or some happy accident introduced them to fire—a fresh resource against the rigor of winter. They learned to conserve this element, then to reproduce it, and finally to use it to cook the meats they had previously eaten raw.

This repeated employment of entities distinct from himself and distinct from each other must naturally have engendered in men's minds the perception of certain relationships. Those relationships which we express by the words 'large', 'small', 'strong', 'weak', 'fast', 'slow', 'fearful', 'bold', and other similar ideas, compared when necessary and almost unthinkingly, finally produced in him some kind of reflection, or rather a mechanical prudence[3] which would indicate to him the precautions most necessary for his safety.

The new knowledge which resulted from this development increased his superiority over other animals by making him conscious of it. He practiced setting snares for them; he outwitted them in a thousand ways, and though many animals might surpass him in strength of combat or in speed of running, he became in time the master of those that might serve him and the scourge[4] of those that might hurt him. Thus the first look he directed into himself provoked his first stirring of pride; and while hardly as yet knowing how to distinguish between ranks, he asserted the priority of his species, and so prepared himself from afar to claim priority for himself as an individual.

Although his fellow men were not to him what they are to us, and although he had hardly any more dealings with them than he had with other animals, they were not forgotten in his observations. The resemblances which he learned with time to discern between them, his female and himself, led him to think of others which he did not actually perceive; and seeing that they all behaved as he himself would behave in similar circumstances, he concluded that their manner of thinking and

[3]Awareness.
[4]Punisher.

feeling entirely matched his own; and this important truth, once well rooted in his mind, made him follow, by an intuition as sure as logic and more prompt, the best rules of conduct it was suitable to observe toward them for the sake of his own advantage and safety.

Instructed by experience that love of one's own wellbeing is the sole motive of human action, he found himself in a position to distinguish the rare occasions when common interest justified his relying on the aid of his fellows, and those even rarer occasions when competition should make him distrust them. In the first case, he united with them in a herd, or at most in a sort of free association that committed no one and which lasted only as long as the passing need which had brought it into being. In the second case, each sought to grasp his own advantage, either by sheer force, if he believed he had the strength, or by cunning and subtlety if he felt himself to be the weaker.

In this way men could have gradually acquired some crude idea of mutual commitments, and of the advantages of fulfilling them; but only so far as present and perceptible[5] interests might demand, for men had no foresight whatever, and far from troubling about a distant future, they did not even think of the next day. If it was a matter of hunting a deer, everyone well realized that he must remain faithfully at his post; but if a hare happened to pass within the reach of one of them, we cannot doubt that he would have gone off in pursuit of it without scruple[6] and, having caught his own prey, he would have cared very little about having caused his companions to lose theirs.

It is easy to understand that such intercourse between them would not demand a language much more sophisticated than that of crows or monkeys, which group together in much the same way. Inarticulate cries, many gestures and some imitative noises must have been for long the universal human language; the addition to this in each country of certain articulated and conventional sounds (the institution of which, I have already said, is none too easy to explain) produced particular languages, crude and imperfect, rather like those we find today among various savage nations. I pass in a flash over many centuries, pressed by the brevity of time, the abundance of the things I have to say, and by the almost imperceptible[7] progress of the first stages—for the more slowly the events unfolded, the more speedily they can be described.

[5]Observable.
[6]Qualm, hesitation in regard to duty.
[7]Unnoticeable.

Those first slow developments finally enabled men to make more rapid ones. The more the mind became enlightened, the more industry improved. Soon, ceasing to doze under the first tree, or to withdraw into caves, men discovered that various sorts of hard sharp stones could serve as hatchets to cut wood, dig the soil, and make huts out of branches, which they learned to cover with clay and mud. This was the epoch of a first revolution, which established and differentiated families, and which introduced property of a sort from which perhaps even then many quarrels and fights were born. However, as the strongest men were probably the first to build themselves huts which they felt themselves able to defend, it is reasonable to believe that the weak found it quicker and safer to imitate them rather than try to dislodge them; and as for those who already possessed huts, no one would readily venture to appropriate his neighbor's, not so much because it did not belong to him as because it would be no use to him and because he could not seize it without exposing himself to a very lively fight with the family which occupied it.

The first movements of the heart were the effect of this new situation, which united in a common dwelling husbands and wives, fathers and children; the habit of living together generated the sweetest sentiments known to man, conjugal love and paternal love. Each family became a little society, all the better united because mutual affection and liberty were its only bonds; at this stage also the first differences were established in the ways of life of the two sexes which had hitherto been identical. Women became more sedentary and accustomed themselves to looking after the hut and the children while men went out to seek their common subsistence. The two sexes began, in living a rather softer life, to lose something of their ferocity and their strength; but if each individual became separately less able to fight wild beasts, all, on the other hand, found it easier to group together to resist them jointly.

This new condition, with its solitary and simple life, very limited in its needs, and very few instruments invented to supply them, left men to enjoy a great deal of leisure, which they used to procure many sorts of commodities unknown to their fathers; and this was the first yoke they imposed on themselves, without thinking about it, and the first source of the evils they prepared for their descendants. For not only did such commodities continue to soften both body and mind, they almost lost through habitual use their power to please, and as they had at the same time degenerated into actual needs, being deprived of them became much more cruel than the possession of them was sweet; and people were unhappy in losing them without being happy in possessing them.

Here one can see a little more clearly how the use of speech became established and improved imperceptibly in the bosom of each family, and one might again speculate as to how particular causes could have extended and accelerated the progress of language by making language more necessary. Great floods or earthquakes surrounded inhabited districts with seas or precipices;[8] revolutions of the globe broke off portions of continents into islands. One imagines that among men thus brought together, and forced to live together, a common tongue[9] must have developed sooner than it would among those who still wandered freely through the forests of the mainland. Thus it is very possible that islanders, after their first attempts at navigation, brought the use of speech to us; and it is at least very probable that society and languages were born on islands and perfected there before they came to the continent.

Everything begins to change its aspects. Men who had previously been wandering around the woods, having once adopted a fixed settlement, come gradually together, unite in different groups, and form in each country a particular nation, united by customs and character—not by rules and laws, but through having a common way of living and eating and through the common influence of the same climate. A permanent proximity cannot fail to engender in the end some relationships between different families. Young people of opposite sexes live in neighboring huts; and the transient intercourse demanded by nature soon leads, through mutual frequentation,[10] to another kind of relationship, no less sweet and more permanent. People become accustomed to judging different objects and to making comparisons; gradually they acquire ideas of merit and of beauty, which in turn produce feelings of preference. As a result of seeing each other, people cannot do without seeing more of each other. A tender and sweet sentiment insinuates itself[11] into the soul, and at the least obstacle becomes an

[8]Steep cliffs.
[9]Language.
[10]Visitation.
[11]Works its way.

inflamed fury; jealousy awakens with love; discord triumphs, and the gentlest of passions receives the sacrifice of human blood.

To the extent that ideas and feelings succeeded one another, and the heart and mind were exercised, the human race became more sociable, relationships became more extensive and bonds tightened. People grew used to gathering together in front of their huts or around a large tree; singing and dancing, true progeny[12] of love and leisure, became the amusement, or rather the occupation, of idle men and women thus assembled. Each began to look at the others and to want to be looked at himself; and public esteem came to be prized. He who sang or danced the best; he who was the most handsome, the strongest, the most adroit[13] or the most eloquent became the most highly regarded, and this was the first step toward inequality and at the same time toward vice. From those first preferences there arose, on the one side, vanity and scorn, on the other, shame and envy, and the fermentation produced by these new leavens[14] finally produced compounds fatal to happiness and innocence.

As soon as men learned to value one another and the idea of consideration was formed in their minds, everyone claimed a right to it, and it was no longer possible for anyone to be refused consideration without affront. This gave rise to the first duties of civility, even among savages: and henceforth every intentional wrong became an outrage, because together with the hurt which might result from the injury, the offended party saw an insult to his person which was often more unbearable than the hurt itself. Thus, as everyone punished the contempt shown him by another in a manner proportionate to the esteem he accorded himself, revenge became terrible, and men grew bloodthirsty and cruel. This is precisely the stage reached by most of the savage peoples known to us; and it is for lack of having sufficiently distinguished between different ideas and seen how far those peoples already are from the first state of nature that so many authors have hastened to conclude that man is naturally cruel and needs civil institutions to make him peaceable, whereas in truth nothing is more peaceable than man in his primitive state. Placed by nature at an equal distance from the stupidity of brutes[15] and the fatal enlightenment of civilized man, limited equally by reason

[12]Offspring.
[13]Skillful.
[14]Significant changes.
[15]Beasts.

and instinct to defending himself against evils which threaten him, he is restrained by natural pity from doing harm to anyone, even after receiving harm himself: for according to the wise Locke: 'Where there is no property, there is no injury.'

But it must be noted that society's having come into existence and relations among individuals having been already established meant that men were required to have qualities different from those they possessed from their primitive constitution. Morality began to be introduced into human actions, and each man, prior to laws, was the sole judge and avenger of the offenses he had received, so that the goodness suitable to the pure state of nature was no longer that which suited nascent society. It was necessary for punishments to be more severe to the extent that opportunities for offense became more frequent; and the terror of revenge had to serve in place of the restraint of laws. Thus although men had come to have less fortitude, and their natural pity had suffered some dilution, this period of the development of human faculties, the golden mean between the indolence of the primitive state and the petulant[16] activity of our own pride, must have been the happiest epoch and the most lasting. The more we reflect on it, the more we realize that this state was the least subject to revolutions, and the best for man; and that man can have left it only as the result of some fatal accident, which, for the common good, ought never to have happened. The example of savages, who have almost always been found at this point of development, appears to confirm that the human race was made to remain there always; to confirm that this state was the true youth of the world, and that all subsequent progress has been so many steps in appearance toward the improvement of the individual, but so many steps in reality toward the decrepitude[17] of the species.

As long as men were content with their rustic huts, as long as they confined themselves to sewing their garments of skin with thorns or fishbones, and adorning themselves with feathers or shells, to painting their bodies with various colors, to improving or decorating their bows and arrows; and to using sharp stones to make a few fishing canoes or crude musical instruments; in a word, so long as they applied themselves only to work that one person could accomplish alone and to arts that did not require the collaboration of several hands, they lived as free, healthy, good and happy men so far as they could be according to

[16]Restless.
[17]Weakening, worsening.

their nature and they continued to enjoy among themselves the sweetness of independent intercourse; but from the instant one man needed the help of another, and it was found to be useful for one man to have provisions enough for two, equality disappeared, property was introduced, work became necessary, and vast forests were transformed into pleasant fields which had to be watered with the sweat of men, and where slavery and misery were soon seen to germinate[18] and flourish with the crops.

• • •

[18]Sprout.

11

Jean Jacques Rousseau

On Education

ROUSSEAU *conceived his work on education, entitled Émile, in the late 1750s. This lengthy work was published in 1762, following a number of bizarre events in his life; it gradually changed in character from a study on education to a novel which, toward its end, becomes ever more charming and romantic.*

Throughout much of his life, Rousseau was interested in matters of education. While yet a young man, he had tried his hand as a teacher of music, and shortly thereafter as a tutor of two young sons of a prominent citizen of the city of Lyons, France. With such a keen interest in matters of education, it is surprising that Rousseau declined the opportunity to raise and educate his own children. In 1745, he began to live with a simple servant girl, Thérèse Le Vasseur, who in rapid succession bore him five children—all of whom he quickly turned over to a foundling hospital. Although in his autobiography, the famous Confessions *written in the late 1760s, he reproached himself severely for his shameful behavior, he nevertheless deprived himself of a chance of raising and educating his own offspring.*

Rousseau's book, therefore, is not the carefully recorded diary of a successful educational venture, but rather a general outline of how to raise a young man properly and also—toward the end of the novel—how to raise a young woman. Émile reflects much of the author's own experiences in his early years. For example, Jean Jacques did not receive his basic education with other boys in one of the good public schools of his hometown, Geneva, Switzerland; rather, he was instructed, however erratically, by his father, whose ideas he accepted willingly and trustingly. In addition, when in his twenties—urged on by a sudden outburst of curiosity and a voracious appetite for learning—he acquired a sound general education by making use of a well-stocked private library. Rousseau also developed an abiding faith in a benevolent God—who not only created this world, but is still part of it. And nature, he thought, is nothing but God's handwriting which can be read and understood by all.

It is clear, then, that the basic design of the world is for the happiness of humankind. Thus, the evils and vices of the society of his day were of human origin, and these in turn often were put into humans by a misguided education. Rousseau's towering contribution to education is the insight that a young person must be raised according to nature. In other words, what nature has placed into a human being or whatever nature unfolds in progressive stages of early life must be permitted to develop freely. Sound education, then, can never consist of filling a young mind with a large number of facts or phrases that the student does not understand. Rather, sound education progresses in harmony with the stage-by-stage unfolding of nature in a child. The process as well as the goal is education for happiness, a condition which Émile reaches at the age of twenty-five, when he is ready to take his place in this world as a self-sufficient, self-reliant, and independent human being.

Rousseau explains that education of Émile, covering the span of twenty-five years, takes place in five stages. These are determined by the plan of nature according to which human lives develop. Accordingly, stages 1 and 2 (corresponding to Books 1 and 2 of the work—and included here) cover the years through age 12. These are the years when a boy's physical development takes place, aided by his exposure to the adversities of a natural environment. Ages 12–15, or stage 3, sees development of a boy's reason and intellect. Rather than drilling standardized lessons into him, the teacher supports the boy's natural inquisitiveness and directs it to those fields which are practical and useful. Stage 4 (ages 15–20) is the stage of socialization. In these years, Émile, who has been raised until then apart from society, is introduced to those qualities which bond human society together—chiefly, friendship, sex, and religion. In stage 5 (ages 20–25) the qualifications and upbringing of a future wife for Émile are also discussed. Because of her feminine qualities and assigned tasks in life, the young woman (Sophie) cannot be equal to Émile; her principal mission in life is to please her husband.

The impact and influence of the novel has been enormous ever since its publication. The book was at first condemned by the highest court of France, by the archbishop of Paris, and by the authorities of his hometown, Geneva. These hostile judgments turned Rousseau into a refugee for almost a decade. Nevertheless, an ever-increasing number of parents raised their children according to Rousseau's idea; and over the centuries that followed, there is hardly an educator of note who has not been deeply influenced by Émile. The best known among them are the Swiss Heinrich Pestalozzi (1746–1827), the German Friedrich Froebel (1782–1852), and the Italian Maria Montessori (1870–1952).

BOOK 1

[The First Year]

God makes all things good; man meddles with them and they become evil. He forces one soil to yield the products of another, one tree to bear another's fruit. He confuses and confounds time, place, and natural conditions. He mutilates his dog, his horse, and his slave. He destroys and defaces all things; he loves all that is deformed and monstrous; he will have nothing as nature made it, not even man himself, who must learn his paces like a saddle-horse, and be shaped to his master's taste like the trees in his garden.

Yet things would be worse without this education, and mankind cannot be made by halves. Under existing conditions a man left to himself from birth would be more of a monster than the rest. Prejudice, authority, necessity, example, all the social conditions into which we are plunged, would stifle nature in him and put nothing in her place. She would be like a sapling chance sown in the midst of the highway, bent hither and thither and soon crushed by the passers-by. . . .

We are born weak, we need strength; helpless, we need aid; foolish, we need reason. All that we lack at birth, all that we need when we come to man's estate, is the gift of education.

This education comes to us from nature, from men, or from things. The inner growth of our organs and faculties is the education of nature, the use we learn to make of this growth is the education of men, what we gain by our experience of our surroundings is the education of things. . . .

Our wisdom is slavish prejudice, our customs consist in control, constraint, compulsion. Civilized man is born and dies a slave. The infant is bound up in swaddling clothes, the corpse is nailed down in his coffin. All his life long man is imprisoned by our institutions. . . .

The child has hardly left the mother's womb, it has hardly begun to move and stretch its limbs, when it is deprived of its freedom. It is wrapped in swaddling bands, laid down with its head fixed, its legs stretched out, and its arms by its sides; it is wound round with linen and bandages of all sorts so that it cannot move. . . .

The newborn child requires to stir and stretch his limbs to free them

ON EDUCATION   Adapted by editor, from *Émile* by Jean Jacques Rousseau, trans. Barbara Foxley (London: J. M. Dent & Sons, Ltd., 1911), I, 5–6, 10–11, 14–16; II, 41–44, 48–51, 53–58.

from the stiffness resulting from being curled up so long. His limbs are stretched indeed, but he is not allowed to move them. Even the head is confined by a cap. One would think they were afraid the child should look as if it were alive.

Thus the internal impulses which should lead to growth find an insurmountable obstacle in the way of the necessary movements. The child exhausts his strength in vain struggles, or he gains strength very slowly. He was freer and less constrained in the womb; he has gained nothing by birth. . . .

Is not such a cruel bondage certain to affect both health and temper? Their first feeling is one of pain and suffering; they find every necessary movement hampered; more miserable than a galley slave, in vain they struggle, they become angry, they cry. Their first words you say are tears. That is so. From birth you are always checking them, your first gifts are fetters, your first treatment, torture. Their voice alone is free; why should they not raise it in complaint? They cry because you are hurting them; if you were swaddled you would cry louder still. . . .

Fix your eyes on nature, follow the path traced by her. She keeps children at work, she hardens them by all kinds of difficulties, she soon teaches them the meaning of pain and grief. They cut their teeth and are feverish, sharp colics bring on convulsions, they are choked by fits of coughing and tormented by worms, evil secretions corrupt the blood, germs of various kinds ferment in it, causing dangerous eruptions. Sickness and danger play the chief part in infancy. One half of the children who are born die before their eighth year. The child who has overcome hardships has gained strength, and as soon as he can use his life he holds it more securely.

This is nature's law; why contradict it? Do you not see that in your efforts to improve upon her handiwork you are destroying it; her cares are wasted? To do from without what she does within is according to you to increase the danger twofold. On the contrary, it is the way to avert it; experience shows that children delicately nurtured are more likely to die. Provided we do not overdo it, there is less risk in using their strength than in sparing it. Accustom them, therefore, to the hardships they will have to face; train them to endure extremes of temperature, climate, and condition, hunger, thirst, and weariness. . . .

A child's worth increases with his years. To his personal value must be added the cost of the care bestowed upon him. For himself there is not only loss of life, but the consciousness of death. We must therefore think most of his future in our efforts for his preservation. He must be protected against the ills of youth before he reaches them: for if the value of life increases until the child reaches an age when he can be useful, what madness to spare some suffering in infancy only to multiply his pain when he reaches the age of reason. Is that what our master teaches us?

Man is born to suffer; pain is the means of his preservation. His childhood is happy, knowing only pain of body. These bodily sufferings are much less cruel, much less painful, than other forms of suffering, and they rarely lead to self-destruction. It is not the twinges of gout which make a man kill himself, it is mental suffering that leads to despair. We pity the sufferings of childhood; we should pity ourselves; our worst sorrows are of our own making.

The newborn infant cries, his early days are spent in crying. He is alternately petted and shaken by way of soothing him; sometimes he is threatened, sometimes beaten, to keep him quiet. We do what he wants or we make him do what we want, we submit to his whims or subject him to our own. There is no middle course; he must rule or obey. Thus his earliest ideas are those of the tyrant or the slave. He commands before he can speak, he obeys before he can act, and sometimes he is punished for faults before he is aware of them, or rather before they are committed. Thus early are the seeds of evil passions sown in his young heart. At a later day these are attributed to nature, and when we have taken pains to make him bad we lament his badness.

In this way the child passes six or seven years in the hands of women, the victim of his own whims or theirs, and after they have taught him all sorts of things, when they have burdened his memory with words he cannot understand, or things which are of no use to him, when nature has been stifled by the passions they have implanted in him, this sham article is sent to a tutor. The tutor completes the development of the germs of artificiality which he finds already well grown, he teaches him everything except self-knowledge and self-control, the arts of life and happiness. When at length this infant slave and tyrant, crammed with knowledge but empty of sense, feeble alike in mind and body, is flung upon the world, and his helplessness, his pride, and his other vices are displayed, we begin to lament the wretchedness and perversity of mankind. We are wrong; this is the creature of our fantasy; the natural man is cast in another mould.

Would you keep him as nature made him? Watch over him from his birth. Take possession of him as soon as he comes into the world and keep him till he is a man; you will never succeed otherwise. The real nurse is the mother and the real teacher is the father. Let them agree in the ordering of their duties as well as in their method, let the child pass from one to the other. He will be better educated by a sensible though ignorant father than by the cleverest master in the world. For zeal will atone for lack of knowledge, rather than knowledge for lack of zeal. . . .

• • •

BOOK 2

[Ages 2–12]

• • •

I shall not take pains to prevent Émile* hurting himself; far from it, I should be vexed if he never hurt himself, if he grew up unacquainted with pain. To bear pain is his first and most useful lesson. It seems as if children were small and weak on purpose to teach them these valuable lessons without danger. The child has such a short distance to fall he will not break his leg; if he knocks himself with a stick he will not break his arm; if he seizes a sharp knife he will not grasp it tight enough to make a deep wound. So far as I know, no child, left to himself, has ever been known to kill or maim itself, or even to do itself any serious harm, unless it has been foolishly left on a high place, or alone near the fire, or within reach of dangerous weapons. What is there to be said for all which the child is surrounded with to shield him on every side so that he grows up at the mercy of pain, with neither courage nor experience, so that he thinks he is killed by a pin-prick and faints at the sight of blood?

With our foolish and pedantic methods we are always preventing children from learning what they could learn much better by themselves, while we neglect what we alone can teach them. Can anything be sillier than the pains taken to teach them to walk, as if there were anyone who was unable to walk when he grows up through his nurse's neglect? How many we see walking badly all their life because they were ill taught?

Émile shall have no padded caps, no strollers, no restrainers; or at least as soon as he can put one foot before another he shall only be supported along pavements, and he shall be taken quickly across them. Instead of keeping him confined to a stuffy room, take him out into

---

*Fictitious name of the boy to be raised and educated.

nature every day; let him run about, let him frolic and fall again and again, the oftener the better; he will learn all the sooner to pick himself up. The delights of liberty will make up for many bruises. My pupil will hurt himself oftener than yours, but he will always be merry; your pupils may receive fewer injuries, but they are always restricted, constrained, and sad. I doubt whether they are any better off.

As their strength increases, children have also less need for tears. They can do more for themselves, they need the help of others less frequently. With strength comes the sense to use it. It is with this second phase that the real personal life has its beginning; it is then that the child becomes conscious of himself. During every moment of his life memory calls up the feeling of self; he becomes really one person, always the same, and therefore capable of joy or sorrow. Hence we must begin to consider him as a moral being.

Although we know approximately the limits of human life and our chances of attaining those limits, nothing is more uncertain than the length of the life of anyone of us. Very few reach old age. The chief risks occur at the beginning of life; the shorter our past life, the less we must hope to live. Of all the children who are born scarcely one half reach adolescence, and it is very likely your pupil will not live to be a man.

What is to be thought, therefore, of that cruel education which sacrifices the present to an uncertain future, that burdens a child with all sorts of restrictions and begins by making him miserable, in order to prepare him for some far-off happiness which he may never enjoy? Even if I considered that education wise in its aims, how could I view without indignation those poor wretches subjected to an intolerable slavery and condemned like galley slaves to endless toil, with no certainty that they will gain anything by it? The age of harmless fun is spent in tears, punishments, threats, and slavery. You torment the poor thing for his good; you fail to see that you are calling death to snatch him from these gloomy surroundings. Who can say how many children fall victims to the excessive care of their fathers and mothers? They are happy to escape from this cruelty; this is all that they gain from the ills they are forced to endure: they die without regretting, having known nothing of life but its sorrows.

Men, be kind to your fellow men; this is your first duty, kind to every age and station, kind to all that is not foreign to humanity. What wisdom can you find that is greater than kindness? Love childhood, indulge its sports, its pleasures, its delightful instincts. Who has not sometimes regretted that age when laughter was ever on the lips, and when the heart was ever at peace? Why rob these innocent ones of the joys which pass so quickly, of that precious gift which they cannot abuse? Why fill with bitterness the fleeting days of early childhood, days which will no more return for them than for you? Fathers, can you tell when death will call your children to him? Do not lay up sorrow for yourselves by robbing them of the short span which nature has allotted to them. As soon as they are aware of the joy of life, let them rejoice in it, so that whenever God calls them they may not die without having tasted the joy of life. . . .

Absolute good and evil are unknown to us. In this life they are blended together; we never enjoy any perfectly pure feeling, nor do we remain for more than a moment in the same state. The feelings of our minds, like the changes in our bodies, are in a continual flux. Good and ill are common to all, but in varying proportions. The happiest is he who suffers least; the most miserable is he who enjoys least. Always more sorrow than joy—this is the lot of all of us. Man's happiness in this world is but a negative state; it must be reckoned by the scarcity of his ills.

Every feeling of hardship is inseparable from the desire to escape from it; every idea of pleasure from the desire to enjoy it. All desire implies a want, and all wants are painful; hence our wretchedness consists in the disproportion between our desires and our powers. A conscious being whose powers were equal to his desires would be perfectly happy.

What then is human wisdom? Where is the path of true happiness? The mere limitation of our desires is not enough, for if they were less than our powers, part of our faculties would be idle, and we should not enjoy our whole being; neither is the mere extension of our powers enough, for if our desires were also increased we should only be the more miserable. True happiness consists in decreasing the difference between our desires and our powers, in establishing a perfect balance between the power and the will. Then only, when all its forces are employed, will the soul be at rest and man will find himself in his true position.

In this condition, nature, who does everything for the best, has placed him from the first. To begin with, she gives him only such desires as are necessary for self-preservation and such powers as are sufficient for their satisfaction. All the rest she has stored in his mind as a sort of reserve, to be drawn upon at need. It is only in this primitive condition that we find the balance between desire and power, and then alone man is not unhappy. As soon as his potential powers of mind begin to function, imagination, more powerful than all the rest, awakes, and precedes all the rest. It is imagination which enlarges the bounds of possibility for us, whether for good or ill, and therefore stimulates and feeds desires by the hope of satisfying them. But the object which seemed within our grasp flies quicker than we can follow; when we think we have grasped it, it transforms itself and is again far ahead of us. We no longer perceive the country we have traversed, and we think nothing of it; that which lies before us becomes vaster and stretches still before us. Thus we exhaust our strength, yet never reach our goal, and the nearer we are to pleasure, the further we are from happiness. . . .

Society has enfeebled man, not merely by robbing him of the right to his own strength, but still more by making his strength insufficient for his needs. This is why his desires increase in proportion to his weakness; and this is why the child is weaker than the man. If a man is strong and a child is weak it is not because the strength of the one is absolutely greater than the strength of the other, but because the one can naturally provide for himself and the other cannot. Thus the man will have more desires and the child more whims, a word which means, I take it, desires which are not true needs, desires which can only be satisfied with the help of others.

I have already given the reason for this state of weakness. Parental affection is nature's provision against it; but parental affection may be carried to excess, it may be wanting, or it may be ill applied. Parents who live under our ordinary social conditions bring their child into these conditions too soon. By increasing his needs they do not relieve his weakness; they rather increase it. They further increase it by demanding of him what nature does not demand, by subjecting to their will what little strength he has to further his own wishes, by making slaves of themselves or of him instead of recognizing that mutual dependence which should result from his weakness or their affection.

The wise man can keep his own place; but the child who does not know what his place is, is unable to keep it. There are a thousand ways out of it, and it is the business of those who have charge of the child to keep him in his place, and this is no easy task. He should be neither beast nor man, but a child. He must feel his weakness, but not suffer through it; he must be dependent, but he must not obey; he must ask, not command. He is only subject to others because of his needs, and because they see better than he what he really needs, what may help or hinder his existence. No one, not even his father, has the right to bid the child do what is of no use to him. . . .

There are two kinds of dependence: dependence on things, which is the work of nature; and dependence on men, which is the work of society. Dependence on things, being non-moral, does no injury to liberty and begets no vices; dependence on men, being out of order, gives rise to every kind of vice, and through this master and slave become mutually depraved. . . .

Keep the child dependent on things only. By this course of education you will have followed the order of nature. Let his unreasonable wishes meet with physical obstacles only, or the punishment which results from his own actions, lessons which will be recalled when the same circumstances occur again. It is enough to prevent him from wrong-doing without forbidding him to do wrong. Experience or lack of power should take the place of law. Give him, not what he wants, but what he needs. Let there be no question of obedience for him or tyranny for you. Supply the strength he lacks just so far as is required for freedom, not for power, so that he may receive your services with a sort of shame, and look forward to the time when he may dispense with them and may achieve the honor of self-help.

Nature provides for the child's growth in her own fashion, and this should never be thwarted. Do not make him sit still when he wants to run about, nor run when he wants to be quiet. If we did not spoil our children's wills by our blunders their desires would be free from whims. Let them run, jump, and shout to their heart's content. All their own activities are instincts of the body for its growth in strength; but you should regard with suspicion those wishes which they cannot carry out for themselves, those which others must carry out for them. Then you must distinguish carefully between natural and artificial needs, between the needs of budding whims and the needs which spring from the overflowing life just described. . . .

There is such a thing as excessive severity as well as excessive indulgence, and both alike should be avoided. If you let children suffer you risk their health and life; you make them miserable now; if you take too much pains to spare them every kind of uneasiness you are laying up much misery for them in the future; you are making them delicate and oversensitive; you are taking them out of their place among men, a place to which they must sooner or later return, in spite of all your pains. You will say I am falling into the same mistake as those bad fathers whom I blamed for sacrificing the present happiness of their children to a future which may never be theirs.

Not so; for the liberty I give my pupil makes up for the slight hardships to which he is exposed. I see little fellows playing in the snow, stiff and blue with cold, scarcely able to stir a finger. They could go and warm themselves if they chose, but they do not choose; if you forced them to come in they would feel the harshness of constraint a hundredfold more than the sharpness of the cold. Then what becomes of your grievance? Shall I make your child miserable by exposing him to hardships which he is perfectly ready to endure? I secure his present good by leaving him his freedom, and his future good by arming him against the evils he will have to bear. If he had his choice, would he hesitate for a moment between you and me? . . .

I return to practical matters. I have already said your child must not get what he asks, but what he needs; he must never act from obedience, but from necessity.

The very words *obey* and *command* will be excluded from his vocabulary, still more those of *duty* and *obligation*; but the words strength, necessity, weakness, and constraint must have a large place in it. Before the age of reason it is impossible to form any idea of moral beings or social relations; so avoid, as far as may be, the use of words which express these ideas, so that the child at an early age may not attach wrong ideas to them, ideas which you cannot or will not destroy when he is older. The first mistaken idea he gets into his head is the germ of error and vice; it is the first step that needs watching. Act in such a way that while he only notices external objects his ideas are confined to sensations; let him only see the physical world around him. If not, you may be sure that either he will pay no heed to you at all, or he will form fantastic ideas of the moral world of which you speak, ideas which you will never erase as long as he lives.

To reason with children was Locke's chief advice; it is in the height of fashion at present, and I hardly think it is justified by its results; those children who have been constantly reasoned with strike me as exceedingly silly. Of all man's faculties, reason, which is, so to speak, compounded of all the rest, is the last and finest growth, and it is this you would use for the child's early training. To make a man reasonable is the capstone of a good education, and yet you profess to train a child through his reason! You begin at the wrong end, you make the end the means. If children understood reason they would not need education, but by talking to them from their earliest age in a language they do not understand you accustom them to be satisfied with words, to question all that is said to them, to think themselves as wise as their teachers; you train them to be argumentative and rebellious; and whatever you think you gain from motives of reason, you really gain from greediness, fear, or vanity with which you are obliged to reinforce your reasoning. . . .

Treat your pupil according to his age. Put him in his place from the first, and keep him in it, so that he no longer tries to leave it. Then before he knows what goodness is, he will be practicing its chief lesson. Give him no orders at all, absolutely none. Do not even let him think that you claim any authority over him. Let him only know that he is weak and you are strong, that his condition and yours puts him at your mercy; let this be perceived, learned, and felt. Let him early find upon his proud neck the heavy yoke which nature has imposed upon us, the heavy yoke of necessity, under which every finite being must bow. Let him find this necessity in things, not in the whims of man; let the curb be force, not authority. If there is something he should not do, do not forbid him, but prevent him without explanation or reasoning; what you give him, give it at his first word without prayers or pleading, above all without conditions. Give willingly, refuse unwillingly, but let your refusal be irrevocable; let no pleading move you; let your "no," once uttered, be a wall of brass, against which the child may exhaust his strength some five or six times, but in the end he will try no more to overthrow it.

Thus you will make him patient, quiet, calm, and resigned, even when he does not get all he wants; for it is in man's nature to bear patiently with the nature of things, but not with the ill will of another. A child never rebels against, "There is none left," unless he thinks the reply is false. Moreover, there is no middle course; you must either make no demands on him at all, or else you must fashion him to perfect obedience. The worst education of all is to leave him hesitating between his own will and yours, constantly disputing whether you or he is master; I would rather a hundred times that he were master.

It is very strange that ever since people began to think about education they should have hit upon no other way of guiding children than rivalry, jealousy, envy, vanity, greediness, base cowardice, all the most dangerous passions, passions ever ready to ferment, ever prepared to corrupt the soul even before the body is full-grown. With every piece of premature instruction which you try to force into their minds you plant a vice in the depths of their hearts; foolish teachers think they are doing wonders when they are making their pupils wicked in order to teach them what goodness is, and then they tell us seriously, "Such is man." Yes, such is man, as you have made him. Every means has been tried except one, the very one which might succeed—well-regulated freedom. Do not undertake to bring up a child if you cannot guide him merely by the laws of what can or cannot be. The limits of the possible and the impossible are alike unknown to him, so they can be extended or contracted around him at your will. Without a murmur he is restrained, urged on, held back, by the hands of necessity alone; he is made adaptable and teachable by the mere force of things, without any chance for vice to spring up in him; for passions do not arise so long as they have accomplished nothing.

Give your pupil no verbal lessons; he should be taught by experience alone; never punish him, for he does not know what it is to do wrong; never make him say, "Forgive me," for he does not know how to do you wrong. Wholly unmoral in his actions, he can do nothing morally wrong, and he deserves neither punishment nor reproof. . . .

• • •

12

Cesare Beccaria

On Crimes and Punishments

*I*N European history, the eighteenth century was to become an age of fermentation, until finally, with the French Revolution, the "modern world" burst forth. In the course of this preparatory century, many great minds tried to visualize the new age to come which they believed would be far superior to the one into which they had been born. Rousseau, for example, hoped that political life would be regulated by a "social contract" binding upon all. For Voltaire, the words reason, tolerance, and humanity were the signs pointing to a better future. Still others dreamt of liberty, equality, and fraternity (brotherhood)—words destined to become the slogans of the French Revolution. It fell to Cesare Beccaria (1738–1794), a shy and withdrawn young man from northern Italy, to introduce a new and more humane way of dealing with crime and punishment. Concerning future legislation, he demanded that criminal law be based on reason, the social contract idea, and humanitarian feeling.

Beccaria was born in Milan in 1738, into a family of the local nobility. He received his early education in a Jesuit school; his advanced education, in the fields of law and economics, was acquired in a leading university of northern Italy. Toward the close of his university studies he began to read the writings of the brilliant French lawyer, Montesquieu (1689–1755), as well as some of the writings of the encyclopaedists. This experience made him a committed convert to Enlightenment ideas.

When back in his native Milan, Beccaria associated with a group of like-minded young men who were interested in penal reform. His book On Crimes and Punishments—begun in 1763, when he was only twenty-five years old—was the outcome of many discussions between the author and a number of his closest friends. (Through two of these, brothers who were employed in the penal administration of Milan, Beccaria gained a first-hand knowledge of the *local prison system.) Fearful of the response to his work from political and Church authorities, Beccaria had it published anonymously in a city at some distance from Milan. The book was an instant success and was hailed by leading Enlightenment figures, as well as by various monarchs of the time. It was quickly translated into the major European languages, and copies were in brisk demand. The Church authorities, however, found it too "dangerous," and two years after publication, placed it on the Catholic Index of forbidden works.*

Without doubt, On Crimes and Punishments must be listed with those books which have brought important improvements in the treatment of prisoners. Many abuses and brutalities routinely committed during the age in which Beccaria lived eventually were abolished, and many of his demands for penal reform have been met by the civilized world. For example, he gives attention to the proper relationship between crimes committed and punishments imposed— and insists that sentences be governed by law, not the whims of a judge. In all modern nations, it is now a basic right of the accused to know the accuser, and a distinction is made between being charged with a crime and being pronounced guilty of it.

Courts are also expected to fulfill Beccaria's demand for prompt and certain punishment of the guilty. The use of torture to extract confession is now generally outlawed and looked upon with disgust. However, one of Beccaria's chief concerns has not been universally met—namely, the abolition of the death penalty. He held it permissible for the state to take a human life only in rare instances—and then, not as punishment, but only to prevent great harm to the community.

The following selection features excerpts from his chapter on capital punishment and some passages revealing his interest in crime prevention—as well as his vision of a more humane approach to the problem of crime in society.

INTRODUCTION

• • •

If we open our histories, we shall see that laws which are, or should be, pacts between free men, have for the most part been only the instrument of the passions of the few, or the product of an accidental and

ON CRIMES AND PUNISHMENTS   Reprinted from *Of Crimes and Punishments* by Cesare Beccaria, trans. Jane Grigson (1964), copyright © 1964 Oxford University Press, 11–13, 42–47, 49–51, 55–56, 91–93, 95–96. Reprinted by permission of Oxford University Press.

temporary need. They have never been dictated by a cool scrutineer of human nature, able to condense to one particular the activities of a multitude of men, and consider them from this point of view: *the greatest happiness of the greatest number.*[1] Happy those rare nations who, instead of waiting for human changes . . . to proceed at their sluggish pace from the extremities of evil to the first steps in goodness, have hastened the stages in between with good laws. Worthy, too, of men's gratitude that philosopher who, from the despised obscurity of his study, had the courage to sow widely the first seeds of useful truths, fruitless for so long.

We are now aware of the right relationship between sovereign and subject, between nation and nation; trade has been quickened in the light of philosophic truths disseminated by the printing press; and there has been kindled between the nations a tacit war[2] of industry, altogether more humane, and more worthy of rational beings. Such are the fruits we owe to this enlightened [eighteenth] century. But how very few men have examined and set themselves against the cruelty of punishments and the irregularity of criminal procedure, a part of legislation so fundamental and so neglected through most of Europe. How few have blotted out, by a return to commonly-accepted principles, those errors which have accumulated through the centuries—or have attempted at least to curb, with the force of accepted truth, the unbridled advance of ill-directed power, which until our day has exhibited nothing but one long example of cold, legalized barbarity. Yet the groans of the weak, sacrificed to cruel ignorance and wealthy indifference; the barbarous tortures, multiplied with prodigal and useless severity for crimes either illusory or unproved; the filth and horrors of a prison, augmented by that most cruel tormenter of the wretched, uncertainty, ought surely to have struck home to those magisterial persons[3] who guide the opinions of mankind.

The immortal President de Montesquieu[4] has touched briefly on this matter; truth, which is indivisible, has compelled me to follow in the shining path of this great man. But thoughtful men, for whom I write, will know how to distinguish his steps from mine. I shall be happy if, like him, I also can earn, in secret, the thanks of reason's obscure and

---

[1]A principle built upon by the English philosopher and lawyer Jeremy Bentham (1748–1833).

[2]Silent war (as opposed to military conflict).

[3]Important officials and writers.

[4]Charles Louis de Secondat Montesquieu (1689–1755), French writer on politics and law.

pacific followers, if I too can inspire that sweet tremor with which feeling spirits respond to those who uphold the cause of humanity.

At this point order should lead us to examine, and distinguish between, the different kinds of crime, and the ways in which they are punished. Crimes and punishments, however, vary so much in their nature according to the differing circumstances of the age and the country, that this would involve us in too great an immensity of tiresome detail. Enough if I indicate the most general principles, and the commonest and most ruinous errors, disabusing in that way no less those who would introduce anarchy, out of a wrong conception of the love of freedom, than those others who would so willingly reduce mankind to the regularity of the cloister.

What punishment is best suited to a given crime? Is death a punishment which is really *useful*, and *necessary* for the security and good order of society? Are torture and instruments of torture *just*, and do they attain the *ends* propounded by law? What is the best way of preventing crimes? Are the same penalties always equally useful? What influence have they on social custom? These are the problems which ought to be solved with a precision so geometric that it cannot be overcome by mists of sophistry,[5] seductive eloquence, or timidity and doubt.

If it were my sole merit to be the first to make much clearer to Italy those things which other nations have dared to put into writing and now into practice, I should consider myself happy. But if, by upholding the rights of man and the rights of invincible truth, I should help also to rescue from the pains and anguish of death some hapless victim of tyranny and ignorance, which are equally fateful, then the thanks and the tears of that one innocent man, in the transports of his joy, would console me for the contempt of all men.

• • •

MILDNESS OF PUNISHMENT

. . . It is evident that the purpose of punishments is neither to torture and afflict a sentient[6] creature nor to undo a crime already done. . . . Can one suppose that the shrieks of some poor wretch will call back out of ever-advancing time actions already consummated?

The aim, then, of punishment can only be to prevent the criminal from

[5]Deceptive, false arguments.
[6]Capable of feeling and perception.

committing new crimes against his countrymen, and to keep others from doing likewise. Punishments, therefore, and the method of inflicting them, should be chosen in due proportion to the crime, so as to make the most efficacious[7] and most lasting impression on the minds of men, and the least painful of impressions on the body of the criminal. Can one read history without horror and disgust at the useless barbarity of the tortures so coldly invented and inflicted by men who were reckoned wise? Must one not shudder at the sight of thousands of unhappy men reduced by misery, either willed or tolerated by the law (which has always favored the few and outraged the many), to a desperate state of nature? The sight of thousands accused of impossible crimes, fabricated by fearfulness and ignorance, or guilty of nothing except loyalty to their own principles, whom men endowed with the same senses, and so with the same passions, have lacerated with the premeditated, protracted formalities of torture, making them a blithe show for a fanatical populace?

For a punishment to be efficacious, it is enough that the disadvantage of the punishment should exceed the advantage anticipated from the crime; in which excess should be calculated the certainty of punishment and the loss of the expected benefit. Everything beyond this, accordingly, is superfluous, and therefore tyrannical. Men regulate their conduct in response to the repeated action of the disadvantages they know, not of the disadvantages they do not know. If we take two nations, in which the scale of crime and the scale of punishment are in due proportion to each other, and if in one the heaviest punishment is perpetual servitude and in the other the wheel,[8] I say that the one will have as much fear of its maximum penalty as the other. . . .

As punishments become more cruel, men's minds, adjusting themselves like fluids to the level of surrounding objects, become increasingly hardened; and human emotion has such an always lively force that after a hundred years of cruel punishment of that kind the wheel would seem only as terrifying as the prison had been earlier on.

The worse the ill that confronts them, the more men are driven to evade it. The very savagery of a punishment has this effect, and to avoid the penalty for the one crime they have already committed, men commit other crimes. Countries and times in which punishments have been most savage have always been those of the bloodiest and

---

[7]Effective.

[8]Torture by stretching a prisoner's body on a wheel as a prelude to death.

most inhuman acts, inasmuch as the spirit of ferocity which guided the hand of the lawgiver also guided the hand of the parricide[9] and the cutthroat. . . .

Two other grievous consequences derive from cruelty of punishment, contrary to that very purpose of preventing crime. One is that cruelty makes it difficult to maintain the necessary proportion between the crime and the punishment, for however much an ingenious cruelty may have multiplied and diversified the modes of punishment, still these cannot exceed that ultimate of force which human physique and sensibility are capable of enduring. When this extreme has been reached it is impossible to find, for more damaging and more atrocious crimes, penalties correspondingly greater such as are required to prevent those crimes. The other consequence is that atrocity in punishment breeds impunity.[10] Men are hedged within certain bounds, whether of good and evil. A spectacle too atrocious for mankind can result only from a passing frenzy and can never partake of a settled system, proper to law. If the laws are indeed cruel, either they are altered or they occasion a fatal tendency not to punish.

I end with this reflection, that the weight of punishment should be relative to the condition of the nation itself. Stronger and more palpable[11] impress must be made upon the hardened minds of a people who have barely emerged from a state of savagery. A thunderbolt is required to subdue a ferocious lion which walks off at the touch of a bullet. But as men's minds become gentler from living in a state of society, so their sensibility increases; and with that increase there must be diminution in the severity of punishment, if a constant relation is to be maintained between object and feeling.

OF CAPITAL PUNISHMENT

This useless prodigality[12] of punishment, which has never made men better, drives me to ask whether death can be inflicted either usefully or justly in a well-organized state. By what right do men take it upon themselves to slaughter other men? Certainly it cannot be that right which gives birth to sovereignty and law—which are nothing but the

[9]One who kills a parent.
[10]Disdain of, and scoffing at punishment.
[11]Easily perceptible.
[12]Excess.

sum of the smallest portions of each man's personal liberty, representing the public will (which is the aggregate of individual wills). But who has ever been willing to give other men authority to kill him? How can the least possible sacrifice of each individual's liberty ever be equated with the greatest of all good things, that is with human life itself? And were it possible, how would it accord with that other principle, that a man is not master of his own life and death? Which he must be, if he has been able to give that right to others, or to the whole of society.

The penalty of death is not therefore a *right*—I have shown that it cannot be—but a war of the nation against a citizen; because it has been judged necessary or useful to destroy him. But if I shall demonstrate that his death is neither useful nor necessary, I shall have won the cause of humanity.

The death of a citizen can only be thought necessary for two reasons. First, that although he has been deprived of liberty, he still has such connections and such power that the safety of the nation is endangered—and that he can provoke by his existence a revolution dangerous to the settled form of government. The death of such a citizen, then, becomes necessary when a nation is regaining or losing its freedom, or in a period of anarchy, when disorder takes the place of law. But under the calm rule of law, under a form of government which unites the suffrages of the nation, which is secured within and without both by its strength and (perhaps more efficacious than strength itself) by public opinion, . . . I see no need to destroy a citizen, unless his death be the only true way of keeping other men from crime (which is the second reason for believing that the penalty of death can be just or necessary). . . .

It is not intensity of pain which most greatly affects the mind, but its continuance—since human sensibility is more easily and permanently influenced by very small but repeated impressions than by a strong yet transient impact. The power of habit is universal in every living creature; and just as habit helps man to walk and talk and satisfy his needs, so it takes a steady repetition of blows to impress moral ideas upon his mind. It is not the terrible but transient spectacle of a criminal's execution, but the long sustained example of a man's loss of liberty, of a man paying for his offense to society by labors resembling those of a beast of burden, which is the most powerful brake upon crime. 'If we do such misdeeds,' we say to ourselves, 'we shall be reduced to the same endless state of wretchedness.' This is efficacious, because the thought

occurs to us over and over again; and it is much more powerful than the notion of death, which is always obscurely in sight on man's horizon. . . .
⊸▷ To be just, a punishment must not exceed that degree of intensity which will deter other men from crime. Now there is no one who, on reflection, would choose the total, permanent loss of his individual liberty, no matter what advantages a crime might bring him. It follows that the severity of a sentence of imprisonment for life, substituted for the penalty of death, would be as likely to deflect the most determined spirit—indeed I should think it more likely to do so. A great many men contemplate death with a steady, tranquil gaze; some out of fanaticism, some out of vanity, . . . some out of a last desperate effort to free themselves from life and misery. But neither fanaticism nor vanity can subsist among the fetters and the chains, under the rod, or under the yoke, or in the iron cage, where the desperate man rather begins than ends his misery. . . .
⊸▷ The penalty of death is ineffectual because of the barbarity of the example it gives to men. If the passions, or the necessity of war, have taught the spilling of human blood, the law, which is the moderator of the conduct of men, ought not to augment[13] so cruel an example— made all the more grievous, the more legalized death is inflicted with deliberation and formality. To me it appears absurd that the laws, which are the expression of the public will, which detest and punish murder, should themselves commit murder; and, to deter citizens from killing, should ordain a killing in public. . . . What are men to think when they look on the wise magistrates and the solemn priests of justice, who with tranquil indifference have a criminal dragged with slow ceremony to his death; or when they see a judge, with unfeeling coldness and perhaps a secret self-satisfaction in his own power, walk past a poor creature who writhes in his last anguish and awaits the fatal blow, on his way to enjoy the comforts and the pleasures of life? 'Ah,' they say, 'these laws are nothing but the pretexts of force; and the cruel, premeditated formalities of justice are no more than a conventional language for . . . [killing]. . . . Murder, which they preach to us as so terrible a misdeed, we see them employing coolly and without aversion. . . .'

If it is objected that in almost all ages and almost all nations some crimes have been punished by death, I shall reply that the objection

---

[13]Strengthen.

vanishes in the face of truth, which triumphs over all prescription: that the history of mankind appears a vast sea of errors, among which there float a few confused truths, each one far from the next. Human sacrifices were common to almost every nation; and who would dare to excuse them? That very few societies, and only for a very brief time, have forborne to inflict death, is more favorable than contrary to my case; since it accords with the fate of all great truths, which endure for no longer than a flash, compared with that long dark night in which mankind is enveloped. . . .

The voice of a single philosopher is too weak to overcome the tumult and the cries of so great a multitude whose guide is the blindness of habit. But the few wise men scattered across the face of the earth will echo my words in their innermost hearts. . . .

• • •

PROMPTNESS OF PUNISHMENT

The more prompt the punishment and the sooner it follows the crime, the more just it will be and the more effective. I say the more just, because the guilty man will thereby be spared the useless and harrowing torments of uncertainty, which grow with the vigor of the imagination and the feeling of his own weakness; the more just, because deprivation of liberty, in itself a punishment, should not precede sentence beyond the requirements of necessity.

Custody, then, is simply the holding of a citizen until he can be judged; and this custody, which is essentially unpleasant, should last as short a time as possible, and should be as little harsh as possible. This short period should be measured both by the length of time necessary for preparing the case, and by the prior rights of those who are already awaiting trial. Confinement should be strict enough only to prevent flight or concealment of the proofs of crime. The trial itself should be over in the shortest possible time. What contrast more cruel than the indolence of a judge and the anguish of the accused? Or the convenience and pleasures of an unfeeling magistrate set against the tears and wretchedness of a prisoner? In general the weight of punishment and the consequences of a crime should have the greatest possible effect on others and an effect as little harsh as possible on the sufferer, since the only just society is one based upon the infallible principle that men's purpose in coming together was to subject themselves to as few evils as possible.

I have said that promptness of punishment is more effective, because the shorter the time between punishment and misdeed, the stronger and more durable in the human spirit is the association of these two ideas of *crime* and *punishment*; so that they come . . . to be considered, one as cause, the other as necessary and unfailing consequence. It has been shown that the association of ideas is the cement of the whole structure of the human intellect, without which pleasure and pain would be isolated sensations devoid of effect. . . .

The proximity of crime and punishment is therefore of the greatest importance, if we desire that in clumsy, commonplace minds, the seductive picture of the rewards of crime be followed at once by the associated idea of punishment. Long delay can only have the effect of separating these two ideas more and more; and any impression made by the chastisement of crime will be made less as chastisement than as spectacle—and only after the horror of a particular crime, which would have served to reinforce the idea of punishment, has weakened in the minds of the spectators. . . .

• • •

HOW CRIMES MAY BE PREVENTED

It is better to prevent crimes than to punish them. That is the chief purpose of all good legislation, which is the art of leading men—if one may apply the language of mathematics to the blessings and evils of life—toward the maximum of possible happiness and the minimum of possible misery.

But the means hitherto employed are for the most part mistaken, and contrary to the end proposed. It is impossible to reduce the turbulent activities of mankind to a geometrical order devoid of irregularity and confusion. Just as nature's immutable[14] and very simple laws do not prevent disturbance in the movement of the planets, so human laws cannot prevent disturbances and disorders in the infinite and utterly opposed attractions of pleasure and pain. Yet such is the chimera[15] entertained by men of narrow mind, who have authority in their hands. To prohibit a multitude of trivial acts is not to prevent the crimes which they may occasion, but to create new ones, and to define at pleasure virtues and vices, which we are exhorted to regard as eternal and

[14]Unchangeable.
[15]Fantasy.

immutable. What a situation it would reduce us to, if everything which might tempt us to crime were forbidden! Man would have to be deprived of the use of his sense. For every single thing that drives men to commit a single real crime, there are a thousand things which drive them to some trivial act that a bad law insists on calling a crime; and if the likelihood of crimes is proportionate to the number of motives, then to extend the sphere of crime is to increase the likelihood that they will be committed. The majority of laws are nothing but privileges, a tribute, that is to say, by all to the comfort of the few.

We want crime to be prevented? Then we must see to it that laws are clear and simple, and that the whole strength of the nation is concentrated upon their defense, and that no part of its strength is used to destroy them. We must see that the law favors individual men more than classes of men, that men fear the law and nothing but the law. Fear of the laws is salutary,[16] but fear between man and man is dangerous and productive of crime. Men in a state of slavery are more sensual, more debauched,[17] more cruel, than men who are free. Those who are free study the sciences, study the interests of the nation, look upon great things and imitate them; slaves, content with the day, seek in the clamor of debauchery a distraction from the emptiness of their lives. . . .

We want crime to be prevented? Then see to it we must that light and freedom go hand in hand. The evils born of knowledge are in inverse[18] ratio to its diffusion; the benefits in direct ratio. A daring impostor, always a man above the ordinary, wins the adulation of an ignorant people and the hisses of an enlightened one. By making comparisons easier and by multiplying points of view, knowledge opposes sentiment to sentiment and makes them modify each other, a process which becomes all the easier when different people may be expected to hold the same views or advance the same objections. When light falls profusely over a nation, slanderous ignorance is reduced to silence, authority is disarmed of its reasons and starts to tremble, and nothing can shift the forceful vigor of the law; because there exists no enlightened man who does not approve the compacts, public, open, and effective, which uphold the security of the people. . . .

Another way of preventing crime is that of rewarding virtue. On this proposition I observe a total silence in the laws of every nation at

[16]Healthy, beneficial.

[17]Self-indulgent.

[18]Opposite.

the present time. If prizes awarded by academies for the discovery of useful truths have multiplied both knowledge and good books, why should prizes distributed by the sovereign's beneficent hand not increase virtuous actions? The coin of honor is always inexhaustible and fruitful in the hands of one who distributes it wisely.

Finally, the surest but most difficult way of preventing crime is to improve education; this is too vast a subject, and one which exceeds the limits I have set myself. . . . One great man,[19] who gives light to the humanity which persecutes him, has explained in detail the principles of an education truly useful to mankind; which should comprise, not a sterile multitude of subjects, but subjects chosen with precision and care; which should substitute, both in the moral and the physical phenomena . . . [presented] to the fresh minds of the young, originals for copies; which should lead to virtue along the easy path of feeling, and divert from evil along the never-failing path of necessity and trouble, instead of using the uncertain method of command which produces no more than a momentary and counterfeit obedience.

CONCLUSION

From all I have written a very useful theorem may be deduced, little though it conforms to custom, that common lawgiver of the nations. It is this: *In order that punishment should never be an act of violence committed by one or many against a private citizen, it is essential that it be public, speedy, and necessary, as little as the circumstances will allow, proportionate to the crime, and established by law.*

---

[19]Meant here is the French writer and philosopher Jean Jacques Rousseau (1712–1778) and his educational novel, *Émile.* (See selection 11.)

13

Adam Smith

The Wealth of Nations

*A*DAM *Smith (1723–1790), a Scottish professor of philosophy and one of the greatest economists of the modern era, was the apostle of liberalism in economics, as John Locke was in political theory. Eccentric in personality and unprepossessing in appearance, Smith led an outwardly uneventful life. His intellectual point of departure was his discovery of an orderly and beneficent system operating behind the cruel, haphazard economy of eighteenth-century Britain. Smith attacked the restrictive practices of mercantilism and wished to free the economy to operate in accordance with the laws of nature. His arguments served as the basis for nineteenth-century laissez-faire theories; however, proponents of those theories carried Smith's ideas to an extreme of which he would not have approved. Smith's major work,* An Inquiry into the Nature and Causes of the Wealth of Nations *(1776), became the bible of free enterprise and the competitive system. It was the first great work in political economy; it was also an encyclopedic survey of the economic life of Great Britain in the eighteenth century, a treatise on how to run a colonial empire, and an assault (with revolutionary import) on the mercantilistic system. In* The Wealth of Nations, *Smith expounded his belief in a natural economic order that was responsible for progress and continuously increasing productivity. The natural laws governing the market were those of individual, enlightened self-interest and competition, which, if allowed to operate freely, would be harmonized by an "invisible hand" for the ultimate good of society. He opposed any artificial controls or restrictions on the free working of the market. Smith was not an apologist for any one system or class, but industrial capitalists and their supporters later used his arguments to keep industry free from any form of government regulation. The selection presented here shows Smith's detailed knowledge with respect to the division of labor and the principles that operate within free enterprise economy.*

ON THE DIVISION OF LABOR

The greatest improvement in the productive powers of labor, and the greater part of the skill, dexterity, and judgment with which it is anywhere directed, or applied, seem to have been the effects of the division of labor. . . .

This great increase of the quantity of work, which, in consequence of the division of labor, the same number of people are capable of performing, is owing to three different circumstances: first, to the increase of dexterity in every particular workman; secondly, to the saving of the time which is commonly lost in passing from one kind of work to another; and lastly, to the invention of a great number of machines which facilitate and reduce labor, and enable one man to do the work of many.

First, the improvement of the dexterity of the workman necessarily increases the quantity of the work he can perform; and the division of labor, by reducing every man's business to some one simple operation, and by making this operation the sole employment of his life, necessarily increases very much the dexterity of the workman. A common smith, who, though accustomed to handle the hammer, has never been used to make nails, if upon some particular occasion is obliged to attempt it, will scarce be able to make above two or three hundred nails in a day, and those very bad ones. A smith who has been accustomed to make nails, but whose sole or principal business has not been that of making nails, can seldom make more than eight hundred or a thousand nails in a day. I have seen several boys under twenty years of age who had never exercised any other trade but that of making nails, and who, when they exerted themselves, could make, each of them, upwards of two thousand three hundred nails in a day. The making of a nail, however, is by no means one of the simplest operations. The same person blows the bellows, stirs or tends the fire as there is occasion, heats the iron, and forges every part of the nail; forging the head too he is obliged to change his tools. The different operations into which the making of a pin, or of a metal button, is subdivided, are all of them much more simple, and the dexterity of the person, of whose life it has been the sole business to perform them, is usually much greater. The rapidity with which some of the operations of those manufactures are

THE WEALTH OF NATIONS   Adapted by editor, from Adam Smith, *The Wealth of Nations*, ed. Edwin Cannan (1904), copyright © 1937 Random House, Inc., I, 3, 7–11, 13, 15–16, 55–58, 64–69.

performed, exceeds what the human hand could be supposed capable of acquiring.

Secondly, the advantage which is gained by saving the time commonly lost in passing from one sort of work to another, is much greater than we should at first imagine. It is impossible to pass very quickly from one kind of work to another, that is carried on in a different place, and with quite different tools. A country weaver, who cultivates a small farm, must lose a good deal of time in passing from his loom to the field, and from the field to his loom. When the two trades can be carried on in the same workhouse, the loss of time is no doubt much less. It is even in this case, however, very considerable. A man commonly delays a little in turning his hand from one sort of employment to another. When he first begins the new work he is seldom very quick and steady; his mind, as they say, does not go to it, and for some time he rather trifles than applies to good purpose. The habit of delaying and of careless application, which is naturally acquired by every country workman obliged to change his work and tools every half hour, and to apply his hand in twenty different ways almost every day of his life, renders him almost always slothful and lazy, and incapable of any vigorous application even on the most pressing occasions. Independent, therefore, of his deficiency in point of dexterity, this cause alone must always reduce considerably the quantity of work which he is capable of performing.

Thirdly, and lastly, everybody must realize how much labor is facilitated and reduced by the application of proper machinery. It is unnecessary to give any example. I shall only observe, therefore, that the invention of all those machines by which labor is so much aided, seems to have been originally owing to the division of labor. Men are much more likely to discover easier and readier methods of attaining any object, when the whole attention of their minds is directed toward that single object, than when it is dissipated among a great variety of things. But in consequence of the division of labor, the whole of every man's attention comes naturally to be directed toward some one very simple object. It is naturally to be expected, therefore, that some one or other of those who are employed in each particular branch of labor should soon find out easier and readier methods of performing their own particular work, wherever the nature of it admits of such improvement. A great part of the machines made use of in those manufactures in which labor is most subdivided, were originally the inventions of common workmen, who, being employed in some very simple operation, naturally turned their thoughts toward finding out easier and readier methods of performing it. Whoever has been much accustomed to visit such manufactures, must frequently have been shown very pretty machines, which were the inventions of such workmen, in order to speed up their own particular part of the work. In the first fire engines, a boy was constantly employed to open and shut alternately the communication between the boiler and the cylinder, according as the piston either ascended or descended. One of those boys, who loved to play with his companions, observed that, by tying a string from the handle of the valve which opened this communication to another part of the machine, the valve would open and shut without his assistance, and leave him at liberty to amuse himself with his playmates. One of the greatest improvements that has been made upon this machine, since it was first invented, was in this manner the discovery of a boy who wanted to save his own labor.

All the improvements in machinery, however, have by no means been the inventions of those who had occasion to use the machines. Many improvements have been made by the ingenuity of the makers of the machines, when to make them became the business of a peculiar trade; and some by those who are called philosophers* or men of speculation, whose trade it is not to do anything, but to observe everything; and who, upon that account, are often capable of combining together the powers of the most distant and dissimilar objects. In the progress of society, philosophy or speculation becomes, like every other employment, the principal or sole trade and occupation of a particular class of citizens. Like every other employment too, it is subdivided into a great number of different branches, each of which affords occupation to a special class of philosophers; and this subdivision of employment in philosophy, as well as in every other business, improves dexterity, and saves time. Each individual becomes more expert in his own branch, more work is done upon the whole, and the quantity of science is considerably increased by it.

It is the great multiplication of the productions of all the different arts, as a consequence of the division of labor, which occasions, in a well-governed society, that universal wealth extends itself to the lowest ranks of the people. Every workman has a great quantity of his own work to dispose of beyond what he himself has need for; and every

---

*It was held by some that the water-wheel and the steam engine were invented by philosophers.

other workman being exactly in the same situation is enabled to exchange a great quantity of his own goods for a great quantity, or, what comes to the same thing, for the price of a great quantity of theirs. He supplies them abundantly with what they have need of, and they accommodate him as amply with what he needs, and a general plenty spreads through all the various ranks of the society. . . .

ON THE PRINCIPLE WHICH GIVES RISE
TO THE DIVISION OF LABOR

This division of labor, from which so many advantages are derived, is not originally the effect of any human wisdom, which foresees and intends that general wealth to which it gives rise. It is the necessary, though very slow and gradual, consequence of a certain disposition in human nature which has in view no such extensive purpose; the disposition to barter and exchange one thing for another. . . .

In a tribe of hunters or shepherds a particular person makes bows and arrows, for example, with more readiness and dexterity than any other. He frequently exchanges them for cattle or for venison with his companions; and he finds at last that he can in this manner get more cattle and venison, than if he himself went to the field to catch them. From a regard to his own interest, therefore, the making of bows and arrows grows to be his chief business, and he becomes a sort of armorer. Another excels in making the frames and covers of their little huts or moveable houses. He is accustomed to be of use in this way to his neighbors, who reward him in the same manner with cattle and with venison, till at last he finds it in his interest to dedicate himself entirely to this employment, and to become a sort of house-carpenter. In the same manner a third becomes a blacksmith or a brass-worker; a fourth a tanner or dresser of hides or skins, the principal part of the clothing of savages. And thus the certainty of being able to exchange all that surplus produce of his own labor, which is over and above his own consumption, for such parts of the produce of other men's labor as he may have need of, encourages every man to apply himself to a particular occupation—and to cultivate and bring to perfection whatever talent or genius he may possess for that particular kind of business.

The difference of natural talents in different men is, in reality, much less than we are aware of; and the very different genius which appears to distinguish men of different professions, when grown to maturity, is not upon many occasions so much the cause, as the effect of the division of labor. The difference between the most dissimilar characters, between a philosopher and a common street porter, for example, seems to arise not so much from nature, as from habit, custom, and education. When they came into the world, and for the first six or eight years of their existence, they were, perhaps, very much alike, and neither their parents nor playmates could see any noticeable difference. About that age, or soon after, they come to be employed in very different occupations. The difference of talents comes then to be taken notice of, and widens by degrees, till at last the pride of the philosopher is willing to acknowledge scarce any resemblance. But without the disposition to barter and exchange, every man must have procured to himself every necessity and convenience of life which he wanted. All must have had the same duties to perform, and the same work to do, and there could have been no such difference of employment as could alone give rise to any great difference of talents.

As it is this disposition which forms that difference of talents, so remarkable among men of different professions, so it is this same disposition which renders that difference useful. Many breeds of animals acknowledged to be all of the same species, derive from nature a much more noticeable distinction of genius, than what, prior to custom and education, appears to take place among men. By nature a philosopher is not in genius and disposition half so different from a street porter, as a mastiff is from a greyhound, or a greyhound from a spaniel, or this last from a shepherd's dog. Those different breeds of animals, however, though all of the same species, are of scarce any use to one another. The strength of the mastiff is not in the least supported either by the swiftness of the greyhound, or by the sagacity of the spaniel, or by the docility of the shepherd's dog. The effects of those different geniuses and talents, for lack of power or disposition to barter and exchange, cannot be brought into a common stock—and do not in the least contribute to the better accommodation and convenience of the species. Each animal is still obliged to support and defend itself, separately and independently, and derives no sort of advantage from that variety of talents with which nature has endowed its fellows. Among men, on the contrary, the most dissimilar geniuses are of use to one another. The different products of their respective talents, by the general disposition to barter and exchange, are brought, as it were, into a common stock, where every man may purchase whatever part of the product of other men's talents he has need of.

• • •

ON THE NATURAL AND MARKET PRICE
OF COMMODITIES

There is in every society or neighborhood an ordinary or average rate both of wages and profit in every different employment of labor and capital. This rate is naturally regulated, . . . partly by the general circumstances of the society, their riches or poverty, their advancing, stationary, or declining condition; and partly by the particular nature of each employment.

There is likewise in every society or neighborhood an ordinary or average rate of rent, which is regulated too, . . . partly by the general circumstances of the society or neighborhood in which the land is situated, and partly by the natural or improved fertility of the land.

These ordinary or average rates may be called the natural rates of wages, profit, and rent, at the time and place in which they commonly prevail.

When the price of any commodity is neither more nor less than what is sufficient to pay the rent of the land, the wages of the labor, and the profits of the capital employed in raising, preparing, and bringing it to market, according to their natural rates, the commodity is then sold for what may be called its natural price.

The commodity is then sold precisely for what it is worth, or for what it really costs the person who brings it to market; for though in common language what is called the prime cost of any commodity does not include the profit of the person who is to sell it, yet if he sells it at a price which does not allow him the ordinary rate of profit in his neighborhood, he is evidently a loser by the trade—since by employing his capital in some other way he might have made that profit. His profit, besides, is his revenue, the proper fund of his subsistence. As, while he is preparing and bringing the goods to market, he advances to his workmen their wages, or their subsistence; so he advances to himself, in the same manner, his own subsistence, which is generally suitable to the profit which he may reasonably expect from the sale of his goods. Unless they yield him this profit, therefore, they do not repay him what they may very properly be said to have really cost him.

Though the price, therefore, which leaves him this profit, is not always the lowest at which a dealer may sometimes sell his goods, it is the lowest at which he is likely to sell them for any considerable time; at least where there is perfect liberty, or where he may change his trade as often as he pleases.

The actual price at which any commodity is commonly sold is called its market price. It may either be above, or below, or exactly the same with its natural price. . . .

When the quantity brought to market is just sufficient to supply the effectual demand and no more, the market price naturally comes to be either exactly, or as nearly as can be judged of, the same with the natural price. The whole quantity on hand can be disposed of for this price, and cannot be disposed of for more. The competition of the different dealers obliges them all to accept this price, but does not oblige them to accept less.

The quantity of every commodity brought to market naturally adjusts itself to the effectual demand. It is in the interest of all those who employ their land, labor, or capital, in bringing any commodity to market, that the quantity never should exceed the effectual demand; and it is in the interest of all other people that it never should fall short of that demand.

If at any time it exceeds the effectual demand, some of the component parts of its price must be paid below their natural rate. If it is rent, the interest of the landlords will immediately prompt them to withdraw a part of their land; and if it is wages or profit, the interest of the laborers in the one case, and of their employers in the other, will prompt them to withdraw a part of their labor or capital from this employment. The quantity brought to market will soon be no more than sufficient to supply the effectual demand. All the different parts of its price will rise to their natural rate, and the whole price to its natural price.

If, on the contrary, the quantity brought to market should at any time fall short of the effectual demand, some of the component parts of its price must rise above their natural rate. If it is rent, the interest of all other landlords will naturally prompt them to prepare more land for the raising of this commodity; if it is wages or profit, the interest of all other laborers and dealers will soon prompt them to employ more labor and capital in preparing and bringing it to market. The quantity brought there will soon be sufficient to supply the effectual demand. All the different parts of its price will soon sink to their natural rate, and the whole price to its natural price.

The natural price, therefore, is, as it were, the central price, to which the prices of all commodities are continually moving. Different factors may sometimes keep them suspended a good deal above it, and sometimes force them down even somewhat below it. But whatever may be the obstacles which hinder them from settling on this center, they are constantly tending toward it.

The whole quantity of industry annually employed in order to bring any commodity to market, naturally adjusts itself in this manner to the effectual demand. It naturally aims at bringing always that precise quantity there which may be sufficient to supply, and no more than supply, that demand. . . .

ON THE WAGES OF LABOR

The product of labor constitutes the natural compensation or wages of labor.

In that original state of things, which precedes both the ownership of land and the accumulation of capital, the whole product of labor belongs to the laborer. He has neither landlord nor master to share with him.

Had this state continued, the wages of labor would have grown with all those improvements in its productive powers, to which the division of labor gives rise. All things would gradually have become cheaper. They would have been produced by a smaller quantity of labor; and as the commodities produced by equal quantities of labor would naturally in this state of things be exchanged for one another, they would have been purchased likewise with the product of a smaller quantity. . . .

But this original state of things, in which the laborer enjoyed the whole product of his own labor, could not last beyond the first introduction of the ownership of land and the accumulation of capital. It was at an end, therefore, long before the most considerable improvements were made in the productive powers of labor, and it would be to no purpose to trace further what might have been its effects upon the compensation or wages of labor.

As soon as land becomes private property, the landlord demands a share of almost all the products which the laborer can either raise, or collect from it. His rent makes the first deduction from the product of the labor which is employed upon land.

It seldom happens that the person who tills the ground has the means to support himself till he reaps the harvest. His support is generally advanced to him from the capital of a master, the farmer who employs him, and who would have no interest to employ him, unless he was to share in the produce of his labor, or unless his capital was to be returned to him with a profit. This profit makes a second deduction from the yield of the labor which is employed upon land.

The product of almost all other labor is liable to the like deduction of profit. In all arts and manufactures the greater part of the workmen stand in need of a master to advance them the materials of their work, and their wages and support till it is completed. He shares in the product of their labor, or in the value which it adds to the materials used; and in this share consists his profit.

It sometimes happens, indeed, that a single independent workman has capital sufficient both to purchase the materials for his work, and to support himself till it is completed. He is both master and workman, and enjoys the whole product of his own labor, or the whole value which it adds to the materials used. It includes what are usually two distinct revenues, belonging to two distinct persons: the profits of capital, and the wages of labor.

Such cases, however, are not very frequent, and in every part of Europe, twenty workmen serve under a master for one that is independent; and the wages of labor are everywhere understood to be what they usually are when the laborer is one person, and the owner of the capital which employs him another.

What the common wages of labor are depends everywhere upon the contract usually made between those two parties, whose interests are by no means the same. The workmen desire to get as much as possible, the masters to give as little as possible. The former are likely to combine in order to raise, the latter in order to lower the wages of labor.

It is not, however, difficult to foresee which of the two parties must, upon all ordinary occasions, have the advantage in the dispute, and force the other into a compliance with their terms. The masters, being fewer in number, can combine much more easily; and the law authorizes, or at least does not prohibit, their combinations—while it prohibits those of the workmen. We have no acts of parliament against combining to lower the price of work; but many against combining to raise it. In all such disputes the masters can hold out much longer. A landlord, a farmer, a master manufacturer, or merchant, though they did not employ a single workman, could generally live a year or two upon the capital which they have already acquired. Many workmen could not subsist a week, few could subsist a month, and scarcely any a year without employment. In the long run the workman may be as necessary to his master as his master is to him, but the necessity is not so immediate.

We rarely hear, it has been said, of the associations of masters, though frequently of those of workmen. But whoever imagines, upon this account, that masters rarely combine, is as ignorant of the world as of the subject. Masters are always and everywhere in a sort of unspoken, but constant and uniform association, not to raise the wages of labor above their actual rate. To violate this combination is everywhere a most unpopular action, and a sort of reproach to a master among his neighbors and equals. We seldom, indeed, hear of this combination, because it is the usual, and one may say, the natural state of things which nobody ever hears of. Masters, too, sometimes enter into particular associations to lower the wages of labor even below this rate. These are always conducted with the utmost silence and secrecy, until the moment of execution; and when the workmen yield, as they sometimes do, without resistance, though severely felt by them, they are never heard of by other people. Such associations, however, are frequently resisted by a contrary defensive union of the workmen who sometimes too, without any provocation of this kind, combine of their own accord to raise the price of their labor. Their usual justifications are, sometimes, the high price of foodstuff, sometimes the great profit which their masters make by their work. But whether their unions be offensive or defensive, they are always abundantly heard of. In order to bring the point to a speedy decision, they take always recourse to the loudest clamor, and sometimes to the most shocking violence and outrage. They are desperate, and act with the folly and extravagance of desperate men, who must either starve or frighten their masters into an immediate compliance with their demands. The masters upon these occasions are just as noisy and never cease to call aloud for the assistance of the civil authorities, and the rigorous execution of those laws which have been enacted with so much severity against the unions of servants, laborers, and journeymen. The workmen, accordingly, very seldom derive any advantage from the violence of those tumultuous unions, which, partly from the actions of the civil officials, partly from the superior steadiness of the masters, partly from the necessity which the greater part of the workmen are under of submitting for the sake of present subsistence, generally end in nothing but the punishment or ruin of the ring leaders.

But though in disputes with their workmen, masters must generally have the advantage, there is however a certain rate below which it seems impossible to reduce, for any considerable time, the ordinary wages even of the lowest kind of labor. . . .

There are certain circumstances, however, which sometimes give the laborers an advantage, and enable them to raise their wages considerably above this rate, evidently the lowest which is consistent with common humanity.

When in any country the demand for those who live by wages is continually increasing; when every year furnishes employment for a greater number than had been employed the year before, the workmen have no reason to combine in order to raise their wages. The scarcity of hands gives rise to competition among masters, who bid against one another in order to get workmen, and thus voluntarily break through the natural combination of masters not to raise wages.

The demand for those who live by wages, it is evident, cannot increase but in proportion to the increase of the funds which are destined for the payment of wages. These funds are of two kinds: first, the revenue which is over and above what is necessary for the maintenance; and, secondly, the capital which is over and above what is necessary for the employment of their masters.

When the landlord or monied man has a greater income than what he judges sufficient to maintain his own family, he employs either the whole or a part of the surplus in maintaining one or more household servants. Increase this surplus, and he will naturally increase the number of those servants.

When an independent workman, such as a weaver or shoemaker, has more capital than what is sufficient to purchase the materials for his own work, and to maintain himself till he can sell it, he naturally employs one or more assistants with the surplus, in order to make a profit by their work. Increase this surplus, and he will naturally increase the number of his assistants.

The demand for those who live by wages, therefore, necessarily increases with the increase of the revenue and capital of every country, and cannot possibly increase without it. The increase of revenue and capital is the increase of national wealth. The demand for those who live by wages, therefore, naturally increases with the increase of national wealth, and cannot possibly increase without it. . . .

• • •

14

Antoine Nicolas de Condorcet

The Progress of the Human Mind

*C*ONDEMNED *as an enemy of the*
revolutionary French Republic and living as a fugitive from the Reign of Terror,
Antoine Nicolas de Condorcet (1743–1794) was inspired in 1793 to put into
writing the ideas for which he had lived and was prepared to die. Thus, out of
the bloodstained chaos of the French Revolution came his Sketch for a Historical Picture of the Progress of the Human Mind, *a "passionate affirmation*
of the rationalist faith." It was to be his last testament to humanity; for soon after
it was completed, he was arrested and the next day was found dead in his cell,
presumably a suicide by poison. In 1795, the work was published by the more
moderate government that succeeded the Terror, becoming, in effect, the new
regime's declaration of revolutionary faith. Condorcet's only work of note, it is a
summation of all of his major ideas.

An aristocratic intellectual and reformer, Condorcet was a religious doubter
and an outspoken adversary of the Church. He also fought the influence of the
hereditary nobility, despite his own noble birth. His mind and efforts were
devoted to scientific enlightenment and to social and political reform. He won
fame as a mathematician, served as secretary of the Academy of Sciences, and
became a leading member of the circle of philosopher-reformers around Voltaire.
With the outbreak of the Revolution, Condorcet plunged into political activity.
As a moderate, he fell afoul of the radicals, but not before he had effectively
championed his proposals, chiefly in the field of education.

The Progress of the Human Mind, *an outline for a larger work that*
Condorcet never lived to complete, remains the best and most moving expression
of the Enlightenment's gospel of progress. Marked by a grand, historical
optimism, it raises the idea of progress to a moral absolute and it considers the
free exercise of the spirit of inquiry capable of liberating people everywhere from
ignorance, poverty, and tyranny. Condorcet describes ten stages of human

development, beginning with the first, primitive stage of tribal hunters and fishers. Stage Two saw the introduction of property and slavery. In the course of each of the first nine stages, people struggled against the adversities caused by nature, their own ignorance, lack of communication, and priestly and secular tyranny. The Tenth Stage, however, he visualized to be almost totally different from the preceding nine, because this final stage would see the speedy fruition of the highest dreams of humanity.

Condorcet believed that he stood on the threshold of this Tenth Stage, the achievements of which he did not, of course, live to see. Though his grandiose prophecy is still far from fulfillment, it is remarkable that he accurately predicted many significant developments of the present age—among them achievements in medicine, epidemiology, genetics, geriatrics, social insurance, women's rights, education, and computer technology. He also correctly saw that population might increase beyond the means of subsistence, but he anticipated that this calamity would be forestalled by the continuing advance of reason and science as applied to birth control. Nothing dimmed Condorcet's faith in the progress of the human mind as the means to human perfectibility.

INTRODUCTION

• • •

... The aim of the work that I have undertaken, and its result will be to show by appeal to reason and fact that nature has set no term to the perfection of human faculties; that the perfectibility of man is truly indefinite; and that the progress of this perfectibility, from now onward independent of any power that might wish to halt it, has no other limit than the duration of the globe upon which nature has cast us. This progress will doubtless vary in speed, but it will never be reversed as long as the earth occupies its present place in the system of the universe, and as long as the general laws of this system produce neither a general cataclysm nor such changes as will deprive the human race of its present faculties and its present resources.

THE PROGRESS OF THE HUMAN MIND   Antoine Nicolas de Condorcet, *Sketch for a Historical Picture of the Progress of the Human Mind*, trans. June Barraclough (London: Weidenfeld, Westport, Conn.: Greenwood Press, Inc. 1979), 4–7, 9–13, 127–28, 136–37, 139–44, 147–48, 162–65, 168–69, 173–77, 179–82, 184, 187–94, 199–202. Reprinted by permission of George Weidenfeld & Nicholson Ltd.

The first stage of civilization observed among human beings is that of a small society whose members live by hunting and fishing, and know only how to make rather crude weapons and household utensils and to build or dig for themselves a place in which to live, but are already in possession of a language with which to communicate their needs, and a small number of moral ideas which serve as common laws of conduct; living in families, conforming to general customs which take the place of laws, and even possessing a crude system of government.

The uncertainty of life, the difficulty man experiences in providing for his needs, and the necessary cycle of extreme activity and total idleness do not allow him the leisure in which he can indulge in thought and enrich his understanding with new combinations of ideas. The means of satisfying his needs are too dependent on chance and the seasons to encourage any occupation whose progress might be handed down to later generations, and so each man confines himself to perfecting his own individual skill and talent.

Thus the progress of the human species was necessarily very slow; it could move forward only from time to time when it was favored by exceptional circumstances. However, we see hunting, fishing, and the natural fruits of the earth replaced as a source of subsistence by food obtained from animals that man domesticates and that he learns to keep and to breed. Later, a primitive form of agriculture developed; man was no longer satisfied with the fruits or plants that he came across by chance, but learned to store them, to collect them around his dwelling, to sow or plant them, and to provide them with favorable conditions under which they could spread.

Property, which at first was limited to the animals that a man killed, his weapons, his nets, and his cooking utensils, later came to include his cattle and eventually was extended to the earth that he won from its virgin state and cultivated. On the death of the owner this property naturally passed into the hands of his family, and in consequence some people came to possess a surplus that they could keep. If this surplus was absolute, it gave rise to new needs; but if it existed only in one commodity and at the same time there was a scarcity of another, this state of affairs naturally suggested the idea of exchange, and from then onward, moral relations grew in number and increased in complexity. A life that was less hazardous and more leisured gave opportunities for meditation or, at least, for sustained observation. Some people adopted the practice of exchanging part of their surplus for labor from which they would then be absolved. In consequence there arose a class of men whose time was not wholly taken up in manual labor and whose desires extended beyond their elementary needs. Industry was born; the arts that were already known, were spread and perfected; as men became more experienced and attentive, quite casual information suggested to them new arts; the population grew as the means of subsistence became less dangerous and precarious; agriculture, which could support a greater number of people on the same amount of land, replaced the other means of subsistence; it encouraged the growth of the population and this, in its turn, favored progress; acquired ideas were communicated more quickly and were perpetuated more surely in a society that had become more sedentary, more accessible, and more intimate. Already, the dawn of science had begun to break; man revealed himself to be distinct from the other species of animals and seemed no longer confined like them to a purely individual perfection.

As human relations increased in number, scope, and complexity, it became necessary to have a method of communicating with those who were absent, of perpetuating the memory of an event with greater precision than that afforded by oral tradition, of fixing the terms of an agreement with greater certainty than that assured by the testimony of witnesses, and of registering in a more enduring manner those respected customs according to which the members of a single society had agreed to regulate their conduct. So the need for writing was felt, and writing was invented. It seems to have been at first a genuine system of representation, but this gave way to a more conventional representation which preserved merely the characteristic features of objects. Finally by a sort of metaphor[1] analogous[2] to that which had already been introduced into language, the image of a physical object came to express moral ideas. The origin of these signs, like that of words, was ultimately forgotten, and writing became the art of attaching a conventional sign to every idea, to every word, and so by extension, to every modification of ideas and words. . . .

The history of man from the time when alphabetical writing was known in Greece to the condition of the human race at the present day in the most enlightened countries of Europe is linked by an uninterrupted chain of facts and observations; and so at this point the picture of the march and progress of the human mind becomes truly historical.

[1]A figure of speech in which one thing represents another.
[2]Similar in certain respects.

Philosophy has nothing more to guess, no more hypothetical surmises to make; it is enough to assemble and order the facts and to show the useful truths that can be derived from their connections and from their totality.

When we have shown all this, there will remain one last picture for us to sketch: that of our hopes, and of the progress reserved for future generations, which the constancy of the laws of nature seems to assure them. It will be necessary to indicate by what stages what must appear to us today a fantastic hope ought in time to become possible, and even likely; to show why, in spite of the transitory successes of prejudice and the support that it receives from the corruption of governments or peoples, truth alone will obtain a lasting victory; we shall demonstrate how nature has joined together indissolubly the progress of knowledge and that of liberty, virtue and respect for the natural rights of man; and how these, the only real goods that we possess, though so often separated that they have even been held to be incompatible, must on the contrary become inseparable from the moment when enlightenment has attained a certain level in a number of nations, and has penetrated throughout the whole mass of a great people whose language is universally known and whose commercial relations embrace the whole area of the globe. Once such a close accord has been established between all enlightened men, from then onward all will be the friends of humanity, all will work together for its perfection and its happiness.

We shall reveal the origin and trace the history of those widespread errors which have somewhat retarded or suspended the progress of reason and which have, as often as forces of a political character, even caused man to fall back into ignorance. . . .

It can even be observed that, according to the general laws of the development of our faculties, certain prejudices have necessarily come into being at each stage of our progress, but they have extended their seductions or their empire long beyond their due season, because men retain the prejudices of their childhood, their country, and their age, long after they have discovered all the truths necessary to destroy them.

Finally, in all countries at all times there are different prejudices varying with the standard of education of the different classes of men and their professions. The prejudices of philosophers harm the progress of truth; those of the less enlightened classes retard the propagation of truths already known; those of certain eminent or powerful professions place obstacles in truth's way: here we see three enemies whom reason is obliged to combat without respite, and whom she vanquishes often only after a long and painful struggle. The history of these struggles, of the birth, triumph, and fall of prejudices, will occupy a great part of this work and will be neither the least important nor the least useful section of it. . . .

Everything tells us that we are now close upon one of the great revolutions of the human race. If we wish to learn what to expect from it and to procure a certain guide to lead us in the midst of its vicissitudes,[3] what could be more suitable than to have some picture of the revolutions that have gone before it and prepared its way? The present state of enlightenment assures us that this revolution will have a favorable result, but is not this only on condition that we know how to employ our knowledge and resources to their fullest extent? And in order that the happiness that it promises may be less dearly bought, that it may be diffused more rapidly over a greater area, that it may be more complete in its effects, do we not need to study the history of the human spirit to discover what obstacles we still have to fear and what means are open to us of surmounting them?

I shall divide the area that I propose to cover into nine great stages and in a tenth I shall venture to offer some observations on the future destiny of the human race.

• • •

THE NINTH STAGE: FROM DESCARTES TO THE FOUNDATION OF THE FRENCH REPUBLIC

This sketch of the progress of philosophy and of the dissemination of enlightenment, whose more general and more evident effects we have already examined, brings us up to the stage when the influence of progress upon public opinion, of public opinion upon nations or their leaders, suddenly ceases to be a slow imperceptible affair, and produces a revolution in the whole order of several nations, a certain earnest of the revolution that must one day include in its scope the whole of the human race.

After long periods of error, after being led astray by vague or incomplete theories, publicists have at last discovered the true rights of

[3]Changes of circumstances.

man and how they can all be deduced from the single truth, that *man is a sentient*[4] *being, capable of reasoning and of acquiring moral ideas.*

They have seen that the maintenance of these rights was the sole object of men's coming together in political societies, and that the social art is the art of guaranteeing the preservation of these rights and their distribution in the most equal fashion over the largest area. It was felt that in every society the means of assuring the rights of the individual should be submitted to certain common rules, but that the authority to choose these means and to determine these rules could belong only to the majority of the members of the society itself; for in making this choice the individual cannot follow his own reason without subjecting others to it, and the will of the majority is the only mark of truth that can be accepted by all without loss of equality. . . .

Up till now we have shown the progress of philosophy only in the men who have cultivated, deepened, and perfected it. It remains for us to show what have been its effects on public opinion; how reason, while it learned to safeguard itself against the errors into which the imagination and respect for authority had so often led it, at last found a sure method of discovering and recognizing truth; and how at the same time it destroyed the prejudices of the masses which had for so long afflicted and corrupted the human race.

At last man could proclaim aloud his right, which for so long had been ignored, to submit all opinions to his own reason and to use in the search for truth the only instrument for its recognition that he has been given. Every man learned with a sort of pride that nature had not forever condemned him to base his beliefs on the opinions of others; the superstitions of antiquity and the abasement of reason before the transports[5] of supernatural religion disappeared from society as from philosophy.

Soon there was formed in Europe a class of men who were concerned less with the discovery or development of the truth than with its propagation, men who while devoting themselves to the tracking down of prejudices in the hiding places where the priests, the schools, the governments, and all long-established institutions had gathered and protected them, made it their life-work to destroy popular errors rather than to drive back the frontiers of human knowledge—an indirect

[4]Having sensory perception, conscious.
[5]Influences.

way of aiding its progress which was not less fraught with peril, nor less useful.

In England Collins[6] and Bolingbroke,[7] in France Bayle,[8] Fontenelle,[9] Voltaire,[10] Montesquieu,[11] and the schools founded by these famous men, fought on the side of truth, using in turn all the weapons with which learning, philosophy, wit, and literary talent can furnish reason; using every mood from humor to pathos, every literary form from the vast erudite encyclopaedia to the novel or the broadsheet[12] of the day; covering truth with a veil that spared weaker eyes and excited one to guess what lay beyond it; skillfully flattering prejudices so as to attack them the better; seldom threatening them, and then always either only one in its entirety or several partially; sometimes conciliating the enemies of reason by seeming to wish only for a half-tolerance in religious matters, only for a half-freedom in politics; sparing despotism when tilting against the absurdities of religion, and religion when abusing tyranny; yet always attacking the principles of these two . . . even when they seemed to be against only their more revolting or ridiculous abuses, and laying their axes to the very roots of these sinister trees when they appeared to be lopping off a few stray branches; sometimes teaching the friends of liberty that superstition is the invincible shield behind which despotism shelters and should therefore be the first victim to be sacrificed, the first chain to be broken, and sometimes denouncing it to the despots as the real enemy of their power, and frightening them with stories of its secret machinations and its bloody persecutions; never ceasing to demand the independence of reason and the freedom of the press as the right and the salvation of

---

[6]Anthony Collins (1676–1729), English deist and friend of the political theorist John Locke.

[7]Henry St. John, Lord Bolingbroke (1678–1751), English politician and statesman. A friend of Alexander Pope.

[8]Pierre Bayle (1647–1706), a French philosopher who was deeply influenced by Cartesianism.

[9]Bernard Le Bovier de Fontenelle (1657–1757), French man of letters, philosopher, and scientist.

[10]The pen name used by François Marie Arouet (1694–1778), French man of letters, historian, and philosopher.

[11]Charles Louis de Secondat Montesquieu (1689–1755), French writer on politics and law.

[12]Pamphlet.

mankind; protesting with indefatigable energy against all the crimes of fanaticism and tyranny; pursuing, in all matters of religion, administration, morals, and law, anything that bore the marks of tyranny, harshness, or barbarism; invoking the name of nature to bid kings, captains, magistrates, and priests to show respect for human life; laying to their charge, with vehemence and severity, the blood their policy or their indifference still spilled on the battlefield or on the scaffold; and finally, taking for their battle cry—*reason, tolerance, humanity*. . . .

The salutary influence of the new truths with which genius had enriched philosophy, politics, and public economy, and which had been adopted more or less generally by enlightened men, was felt far afield.

The art of printing had spread so widely and had so greatly increased the number of books published; the books that were published catered so successfully for every degree of knowledge, or industry, or income; they were so proportioned to every taste, or cast of mind; they presented such easy and often such pleasant means of instruction; they opened so many doors to truth that it was no longer possible that they should all of them be closed again, that there was no class and no profession from which the truth could be withheld. And so, though there remained a great number of people condemned to ignorance either voluntary or enforced, the boundary between the cultivated and the uncultivated had been almost entirely effaced, leaving an insensible[13] gradation between the two extremes of genius and stupidity.

Thus, an understanding of the natural rights of man, the belief that these rights are inalienable and indefeasible,[14] a strongly expressed desire for liberty of thought and letters, of trade and industry, and for the alleviation of the people's suffering, for the proscription of all penal laws against religious dissenters and the abolition of torture and barbarous punishments, the desire for a milder system of criminal legislation and jurisprudence which should give complete security to the innocent, and for a simpler civil code, more in conformance with reason and nature, indifference in all matters of religion which now were relegated to the status of superstitions and political impostures, a hatred of hypocrisy and fanaticism, a contempt for prejudice, zeal for the propagation of enlightenment: all these principles, gradually filtering down from philosophical works to every class of society whose education

[13]Unfelt, slight.
[14]Not to be undone.

went beyond the catechism and the alphabet, became the common faith, the badges of all those who were neither Machiavellians[15] nor fools. In some countries these principles formed a public opinion sufficiently widespread for even the mass of the people to show a willingness to be guided by it and to obey it. For a feeling of humanity, a tender and active compassion for all the misfortunes that afflict the human race and a horror of anything that in the actions of public institutions, or governments, or individuals, adds new pains to those that are natural and inevitable, were the natural consequences of those principles; and this feeling exhaled from all the writings and all the speeches of the time, and already its happy influence had been felt in the laws, and the public institutions, even of those nations still subject to despotism. . . .

Force or persuasion on the part of governments, priestly intolerance, and even national prejudices, had all lost their deadly power to smother the voice of truth, and nothing could now protect the enemies of reason or the oppressors of freedom from a sentence to which the whole of Europe would soon subscribe. . . .

A comparison of the attitude of mind I have already described with the forms of government prevalent at that time would have made it easy to foresee that a great revolution was inevitable, and that there were only two ways in which it could come about; either the people themselves would establish the reasonable and natural principles that philosophy had taught them to admire, or governments would hasten to anticipate them and carry out what was required by public opinion. If the revolution should come about in the former way it would be swifter and more thorough, but more violent; if it should come about in the latter way, it would be less swift and less thorough, but also less violent: if in the former way, then freedom and happiness would be purchased at the price of transient evils; if in the latter, then these evils would be avoided but, it might be, at the price of long delaying the harvest of the fruits that the revolution must, nevertheless, inevitably bear. The ignorance and corruption of the governments of the time saw that it came about in the former way, and the human race was avenged by the swift triumph of liberty and reason. . . .

From the moment when the genius of Descartes[16] gave men's minds

---

[15]Persons whose conduct matches the advice given to rulers by Niccolò Machiavelli (1469–1527), Florentine writer on politics and history: crafty, deceitful.

[16]René Descartes (1596–1650), a noted French philosopher and mathematician.

that general impulse which is the first principle of a revolution in the destinies of the human race, to the happy time of complete and pure social liberty when man was able to regain his natural independence only after having lived through a long series of centuries of slavery and misery, the picture of the progress of the mathematical and physical sciences reveals an immense horizon whose different parts must be distributed and ordered if we wish to grasp the significance of the whole and properly observe its relations. . . .

If we were to confine ourselves to showing the benefits that we have derived from the sciences in their immediate uses or in their applications to the arts, either for the well-being of individuals or for the prosperity of nations, we should display only a very small portion of their blessings.

The most important of these, perhaps, is to have destroyed prejudices and to have redirected the human intelligence, which had been obliged to follow the false directions imposed on it by the absurd beliefs that were implanted in each generation in infancy with the terrors of superstition and the fear of tyranny.

All errors in politics and morals are based on philosophical errors and these in turn are connected with scientific errors. There is not a religious system nor a supernatural extravagance that is not founded on ignorance of the laws of nature. The inventors, the defenders of these absurdities could not foresee the successive perfection of the human mind. Convinced that men in their day knew everything that they could ever know and would always believe what they then believed, they confidently supported their idle dreams on the current opinions of their country and their age.

Advances in the physical sciences are all the more fatal to these errors in that they often destroy them without appearing to attack them, and that they can shower on those who defend them so obstinately the humiliating taunt of ignorance. . . .

Up to this stage, the sciences had been the birthright of very few; they were now becoming common property and the time was at hand when their elements, their principles, and their simpler methods would become truly popular. For it was then, as last, that their application to the arts and their influence on men's judgment would become of truly universal utility.

We shall follow the progress of European nations in the education both of children and of adults. This progress may appear to have been slow, if one considers only the philosophical foundations on which education has been based, for it is still in the grip of scholastic[17] superstition: but it appears swift enough if one considers the nature and the extent of the subjects taught, for these are now confined almost completely to genuine inquiries, and include the elements of nearly all the sciences; while dictionaries, abstracts, and periodicals provide men of all ages with the information they require—even if this does not always appear in an unadulterated form. We shall examine the utility of combining oral instruction in the sciences with the immediate instruction to be acquired from books and private study, and we shall also examine whether any advantage has accrued from the development of compilation[18] into an accredited profession in whose practice a man may hope to earn a livelihood; a development that has augmented the number of indifferent[19] books in circulation, but has also increased the roads to knowledge open to men of little education. We shall give an account of the influence exercised by learned societies, for these will long remain a useful bulwark against charlatanry[20] and false scholarship. Finally we shall unfold the story of the encouragement given by certain governments to the progress of knowledge, and also of the obstacles that were laid in its path often enough by these same governments, at the same time, in the same country. We shall expose, on the one hand, the prejudices and Machiavellian principles that have directed these governments in their opposition to men's progress toward the truth, and on the other, the political opinions originating either from self-interest or even from a genuine concern for the public good, that have guided them when they have seemed interested in accelerating and protecting it. . . .

Turning now our attention to the human race in general, we shall show how the discovery of the correct method of procedure in the sciences, the growth of scientific theories, their application to every part of the natural world, to the subject of every human need, the lines of communication established between one science and another, the great number of men who cultivate the sciences, and most important of all, the spread of printing, how together all these advances ensure that no science will ever fall below the point it has reached. We shall point

[17]Reflecting the educational and philosophical methods of medieval church schools.

[18]The collection of information in various fields of knowledge; for example, in an encyclopedia.

[19]Mediocre.

[20]Fraud, deception.

out that the principles of philosophy, the slogans of liberty, the recognition of the true rights of man and his real interests, have spread through far too great a number of nations, and now direct in each of them the opinions of far too great a number of enlightened men, for us to fear that they will ever be allowed to relapse into oblivion. And indeed what reason could we have for fear, when we consider that the languages most widely spoken are the languages of the two peoples who enjoy liberty to the fullest extent and who best understand its principles, and that no league of tyrants, no political intrigues, could prevent the resolute defense, in these two languages, of the rights of reason and of liberty?

But although everything tells us that the human race will never relapse into its former state of barbarism, although everything combines to reassure us against that corrupt and cowardly political theory which would condemn it to oscillate forever between truth and error, liberty and servitude, nevertheless we still see the forces of enlightenment in possession of no more than a very small portion of the globe, and the truly enlightened vastly outnumbered by the great mass of men who are still given over to ignorance and prejudice. We still see vast areas in which men groan in slavery, vast areas offering the spectacle of nations either degraded by the vices of a civilization whose progress is impeded by corruption, or still vegetating in the infant condition of early times.

We observe that the labors of recent ages have done much for the progress of the human mind, but little for the perfection of the human race; that they have done much for the honor of man, something for his liberty, but so far almost nothing for his happiness. At a few points our eyes are dazzled with a brilliant light; but thick darkness still covers an immense stretch of the horizon. There are a few circumstances from which the philosopher can take consolation, but he is still afflicted by the spectacle of the stupidity, slavery, barbarism, and extravagance of mankind; and the friend of humanity can find unmixed pleasure only in tasting the sweet delights of hope for the future.

• • •

THE TENTH STAGE: THE FUTURE PROGRESS OF THE HUMAN MIND

If man can, with almost complete assurance, predict phenomena when he knows their laws, and if, even when he does not, he can still, with great expectation of success, forecast the future on the basis of his experience of the past, why, then, should it be regarded as a fantastic undertaking to sketch, with some pretense to truth, the future destiny of man on the basis of his history? The sole foundation for belief in the natural sciences is this idea, that the general laws directing the phenomena of the universe, known or unknown, are necessary and constant. Why should this principle be any less true for the development of the intellectual and moral faculties of man than for the other operations of nature? Since beliefs founded on past experience of like conditions provide the only rule of conduct for the wisest of men, why should the philosopher be forbidden to base his conjectures on these same foundations, so long as he does not attribute to them a certainty superior to that warranted by the number, the constancy, and the accuracy of his observations?

Our hopes for the future condition of the human race can be subsumed under three important heads: the abolition of inequality between nations, the progress of equality within each nation, and the true perfection of mankind. Will all nations one day attain that state of civilization which the most enlightened, the freest, and the least burdened by prejudices, such as the French and the Anglo-Americans, have attained already? Will the vast gulf that separates these peoples from the slavery of nations under the rule of monarchs, from the barbarism of African tribes, from the ignorance of savages, little by little disappear? . . .

Is the human race to better itself, either by discoveries in the sciences and the arts, and so in the means to individual welfare and general prosperity; or by progress in the principles of conduct or practical morality; or by a true perfection of the intellectual, moral, or physical faculties of man, an improvement which may result from a perfection either of the instruments used to heighten the intensity of these faculties and to direct their use or of the natural constitution of man?

In answering these three questions we shall find in the experience of the past, in the observation of the progress that the sciences and civilization have already made, in the analysis of the progress of the human mind and of the development of its faculties, the strongest reasons for believing that nature has set no limit to the realization of our hopes.

If we glance at the state of the world today we see first of all that in Europe the principles of the French constitution are already those of all enlightened men. We see them too widely propagated, too seriously professed, for priests and despots to prevent their gradual penetration even into the hovels of their slaves; there they will soon awaken in these slaves the remnants of their common sense and inspire them with that smoldering indignation which not even constant humiliation and fear can smother in the soul of the oppressed.

As we move from nation to nation, we can see in each what special obstacles impede this revolution and what attitudes of mind favor it. We can distinguish the nations where we may expect it to be introduced gently by the perhaps belated wisdom of their governments, and those nations where its violence intensified by their resistance must involve all alike in a swift and terrible convulsion.

Can we doubt that either common sense or the senseless discords of European nations will add to the effects of the slow but inexorable progress of their colonies, and will soon bring about the independence of the New World? And then will not the European population in these colonies, spreading rapidly over that enormous land, either civilize or peacefully remove the savage nations who still inhabit vast tracts of its land?

Survey the history of our settlements and commercial undertakings in Africa or in Asia, and you will see how our trade monopolies, our treachery, our murderous contempt for men of another color or creed, the insolence of our usurpations,[21] the intrigues or the exaggerated proselytic[22] zeal of our priests, have destroyed the respect and good-will that the superiority of our knowledge and the benefits of our commerce at first won for us in the eyes of the inhabitants. But doubtless the moment approaches when, no longer presenting ourselves as always either tyrants or corrupters, we shall become for them the beneficent instruments of their freedom. . . .

These vast lands are inhabited partly by large tribes who need only assistance from us to become civilized, who wait only to find brothers among the European nations to become their friends and pupils; partly by races oppressed by sacred despots or dull-witted conquerors, and who for so many centuries have cried out to be liberated; partly by tribes living in a condition of almost total savagery in a climate whose harshness repels the sweet blessings of civilization and deters those who would teach them its benefits; and finally, by conquering hordes who know no other law but force, no other profession but piracy. The progress of these two last classes of people will be slower and stormier,

[21]Unlawful seizures of rights and power.

[22]Missionary.

and perhaps it will even be that, reduced in number as they are driven back by civilized nations, they will finally disappear imperceptibly before them or merge into them. . . .

The time will therefore come when the sun will shine only on free men who know no other master but their reason; when tyrants and slaves, priests and their stupid or hypocritical instruments will exist only in works of history and on the stage; and when we shall think of them only to pity their victims and their dupes; to maintain ourselves in a state of vigilance by thinking on their excesses; and to learn how to recognize and so to destroy, by force of reason, the first seeds of tyranny and superstition, should they ever dare to reappear among us.

In looking at the history of societies we shall have had occasion to observe that there is often a great difference between the rights that the law allows its citizens and the rights that they actually enjoy, and, again, between the equality established by political codes and that which in fact exists among individuals: and we shall have noticed that these differences were one of the principal causes of the destruction of freedom in the ancient republics, of the storms that troubled them, and of the weakness that delivered them over to foreign tyrants.

These differences have three main causes: inequality in wealth; inequality in status between the man whose means of subsistence are hereditary and the man whose means are dependent on the length of his life, or, rather, on that part of his life in which he is capable of work; and, finally, inequality in education.

We therefore need to show that these three sorts of real inequality must constantly diminish without however disappearing altogether: for they are the result of natural and necessary causes which it would be foolish and dangerous to wish to eradicate; and one could not even attempt to bring about the entire disappearance of their effects without introducing even more fecund sources of inequality, without striking more direct and more fatal blows at the rights of man. . . .

We shall point out how [inequality] can be in great part eradicated by guaranteeing people in old age a means of livelihood produced partly by their own savings and partly by the savings of others who make the same outlay, but who die before they need to reap the reward; or, again, on the same principle of compensation, by securing for widows and orphans an income which is the same and costs the same for those families which suffer an early loss and for those which suffer it later; or again by providing all children with the capital necessary for the full use of their labor, available at the age when they start work and found a family, a capital which increases at the expense of those whom premature death prevents from reaching this age. It is to the application of the calculus to the probabilities of life and the investment of money that we owe the idea of these methods which have already been successful, although they have not been applied in a sufficiently comprehensive and exhaustive fashion to render them really useful, not merely to a few individuals, but to society as a whole, by making it possible to prevent those periodic disasters which strike at so many families and which are such a recurrent source of misery and suffering. . . .

The degree of equality in education that we can reasonably hope to attain, but that should be adequate, is that which excludes all dependence, either forced or voluntary. We shall show how this condition can be easily attained in the present state of human knowledge even by those who can study only for a small number of years in childhood, and then during the rest of their life in their few hours of leisure. We shall prove that, by a suitable choice of syllabus and of methods of education, we can teach the citizen everything that he needs to know in order to be able to manage his household, administer his affairs, and employ his labor and his faculties in freedom; to know his rights and to be able to exercise them; to be acquainted with his duties and fulfill them satisfactorily; to judge his own and other men's actions according to his own sights and to be a stranger to none of the high and delicate feelings which honor human nature; not to be in a state of blind dependence upon those to whom he must entrust his affairs or the exercise of his rights; to be in a proper condition to choose and supervise them; to be no longer the dupe of those popular errors which torment man with superstitious fears and chimerical[23] hopes; to defend himself against prejudice by the strength of his reason alone; and, finally, to escape the deceits of charlatans who would lay snares for his fortune, his health, his freedom of thought, and his conscience under the pretext of granting him health, wealth, and salvation. . . .

So we might say that a well-directed system of education rectifies natural inequality in ability instead of strengthening it, just as good laws remedy natural inequality in the means of subsistence, and just as in societies where laws have brought about this same equality, liberty, though subject to a regular constitution, will be more widespread, more complete than in the total independence of savage life. Then the

[23]Imaginary, fantastic.

social art will have fulfilled its aim, that of assuring and extending to all men enjoyment of the common rights to which they are called by nature.

The real advantages that should result from this progress, of which we can entertain a hope that is almost a certainty, can have no other term than that of the absolute perfection of the human race; since, as the various kinds of equality come to work in its favor by producing ampler sources of supply, more extensive education, more complete liberty, so equality will be more real and will embrace everything which is really of importance for the happiness of human beings. . . .

If we turn now to the arts,[24] whose theory depends on these same sciences, we shall find that their progress, depending as it does on that of theory, can have no other limits; that the procedures of the different arts can be perfected and simplified in the same way as the methods of the sciences; new instruments, machines, and looms can add to man's strength and can improve at once the quality and the accuracy of his productions, and can diminish the time and labor that has to be expended on them. The obstacles still in the way of this progress will disappear, accidents will be foreseen and prevented, the insanitary conditions that are due either to the work itself or to the climate will be eliminated.

A very small amount of ground will be able to produce a great quantity of supplies of greater utility or higher quality; more goods will be obtained for a smaller outlay; the manufacture of articles will be achieved with less wastage in raw materials and will make better use of them. Every type of soil will produce those things which satisfy the greatest number of needs; of several alternative ways of satisfying needs of the same order, that will be chosen which satisfies the greatest number of people and which requires least labor and least expenditure. So, without the need for sacrifice, methods of preservation and economy in expenditure will improve in the wake of progress in the arts of producing and preparing supplies and making articles from them.

So not only will the same amount of ground support more people, but everyone will have less work to do, will produce more and satisfy his wants more fully.

With all this progress in industry and welfare which establishes a happier proportion between men's talents and their needs, each succes-

[24]Crafts; production of material goods.

sive generation will have larger possessions, either as a result of this progress or through the preservation of the products of industry; and so, as a consequence of the physical constitution of the human race, the number of people will increase. Might there not then come a moment when these necessary laws begin to work in a contrary direction; when, the number of people in the world finally exceeding the means of subsistence, there will in consequence ensue a continual diminution of happiness and population, a true retrogression, or at best an oscillation between good and bad? In societies that have reached this stage will not this oscillation be a perennial source of more or less periodic disaster? Will it not show that a point has been attained beyond which all further improvement is impossible, that the perfectibility of the human race has after long years arrived at a term beyond which it may never go?

There is doubtless no one who does not think that such a time is still very far from us; but will it ever arrive? It is impossible to pronounce about the likelihood of an event that will occur only when the human species will have necessarily acquired a degree of knowledge of which we can have no inkling. And who would take it upon himself to predict the condition to which the art of converting the elements to the use of man may in time be brought?

But even if we agree that the limit will one day arrive, nothing follows from it that is in the least alarming as far as either the happiness of the human race or its indefinite[25] perfectibility is concerned; if we consider that, before all this comes to pass, the progress of reason will have kept pace with that of the sciences, and that the absurd prejudices of superstition will have ceased to corrupt and degrade the moral code by its harsh doctrines instead of purifying and elevating it, we can assume that by then men will know that, if they have a duty toward those who are not yet born, that duty is not to give them existence but to give them happiness; their aim should be to promote the general welfare of the human race or of the society in which they live or of the family to which they belong, rather than foolishly to encumber the world with useless and wretched beings. It is, then, possible that there should be a limit to the amount of food that can be produced, and, consequently, to the size of the population of the world, without this involving that untimely destruction of some of those creatures who have been given life, which is so contrary to nature and to social prosperity. . . .

[25]Unlimited.

The application of the calculus of combinations and probabilities to these sciences promises even greater improvement, since it is the only way of achieving results of an almost mathematical exactitude and of assessing the degree of their probability or likelihood. Sometimes, it is true, the evidence upon which these results are based may lead us, without any calculation, at the first glance, to some general truth and teach us whether the effect produced by such-and-such a cause was or was not favorable, but if this evidence cannot be weighed and measured, and if these effects cannot be subjected to precise measurement, then we cannot know exactly how much good or evil they contain; or, again, if the good and evil nearly balance each other, if the difference between them is slight, we cannot pronounce with any certainty to which side the balance really inclines. Without the application of the calculus it would be almost impossible to choose with any certainty between two combinations that have the same purpose and between which there is no apparent difference in merit. Without the calculus these sciences would always remain crude and limited for want of instruments delicate enough to catch the fleeting truth, of machines precise enough to plumb the depths where so much that is of value to science lies hidden.

However, such an application, notwithstanding the happy efforts of certain geometers, is still in its earliest stages: and it will be left to the generations to come to use this source of knowledge which is as inexhaustible as the calculus itself, or as the number of combinations, relations, and facts that may be included in its sphere of operation. . . .

Until men progress in the practice as well as in the science of morality, it will be impossible for them to attain any insight into either the nature and development of the moral sentiments, the principles of morality, the natural motives that prompt their actions, or their own true interests either as individuals or as members of society. Is not a mistaken sense of interest the most common cause of actions contrary to the general welfare? Is not the violence of our passions often the result either of habits that we have adopted through miscalculation, or of our ignorance how to restrain them, tame them, deflect them, rule them? . . .

What are we to expect from the perfection of laws and public institutions, consequent upon the progress of those sciences, but the reconciliation, the identification of the interests of each with the interests of all? Has the social art any other aim save that of destroying their apparent opposition? Will not a country's constitution and laws accord best with the rights of reason and nature when the path of virtue is no longer arduous and when the temptations that lead men from it are few and feeble?

Is there any vicious habit, any practice contrary to good faith, any crime, whose origin and first cause cannot be traced back to the legislation, the institutions, the prejudices of the country wherein this habit, this practice, this crime can be observed? In short will not the general welfare that results from the progress of the useful arts once they are grounded on solid theory, or from the progress of legislation once it is rooted in the truths of political science, incline mankind to humanity, benevolence, and justice? In other words, do not all these observations which I propose to develop further in my book, show that the moral goodness of man, the necessary consequence of his constitution, is capable of indefinite perfection like all his other faculties, and that nature has linked together in an unbreakable chain truth, happiness, and virtue?

Among the causes of the progress of the human mind that are of the utmost importance to the general happiness, we must number the complete annihilation of the prejudices that have brought about an inequality of rights between the sexes, an inequality fatal even to the party in whose favor it works. It is vain for us to look for a justification of this principle in any differences of physical organization, intellect, or moral sensibility between men and women. This inequality has its origin solely in an abuse of strength, and all the later sophistical attempts that have been made to excuse it are vain.

We shall show how the abolition of customs authorized, laws dictated by this prejudice, would add to the happiness of family life, would encourage the practice of the domestic virtues on which all other virtues are based, how it would favor the progress of education, and how, above all, it would bring about its wider diffusion; for not only would education be extended to women as well as to men, but it can only really be taken proper advantage of when it has the support and encouragement of the mothers of the family. Would not this belated tribute to equity and good sense put an end to a principle only too fecund of injustice, cruelty, and crime, by removing the dangerous conflict between the strongest and most irrepressible of all natural inclinations and man's duty or the interests of society? Would it not produce what has until now been no more than a dream, national manners of a mildness and purity, formed not by proud asceticism,[26]

[26]Self-denial, religious self-discipline.

not by hypocrisy, not by the fear of shame or religious terrors but by freely contracted habits that are inspired by nature and acknowledged by reason?

Once people are enlightened they will know that they have the right to dispose of their own life and wealth as they choose; they will gradually learn to regard war as the most dreadful of scourges, the most terrible of crimes. The first wars to disappear will be those into which usurpers have forced their subjects in defense of their pretended hereditary rights.

Nations will learn that they cannot conquer other nations without losing their own liberty; that permanent confederations are their only means of preserving their independence; and that they should seek not power but security. Gradually mercantile[27] prejudices will fade away: and a false sense of commercial interest will lose the fearful power it once had of drenching the earth in blood and of ruining nations under pretext of enriching them. When at last the nations come to agree on the principles of politics and morality, when in their own better interests they invite foreigners to share equally in all the benefits men enjoy either through the bounty of nature or by their own industry, then all the causes that produce and perpetuate national animosities and poison national relations will disappear one by one; and nothing will remain to encourage or even to arouse the fury of war. . . .

All the causes that contribute to the perfection of the human race, all the means that ensure it, must by their very nature exercise a perpetual influence and always increase their sphere of action. The proofs of this we have given and in the great work they will derive additional force from elaboration. We may conclude then that the perfectibility of man is indefinite. Meanwhile we have considered him as possessing the natural faculties and organization that he has at present. How much greater would be the certainty, how much vaster the scheme of our hopes if we could believe that these natural faculties themselves and this organization could also be improved? This is the last question that remains for us to ask ourselves.

Organic perfectibility or deterioration among the various strains in the vegetable and animal kingdom can be regarded as one of the general laws of nature. This law also applies to the human race. No one can doubt that, as preventive medicine improves and food and housing become healthier, as a way of life is established that develops our physical powers by exercise without ruining them by excess, as the two

[27]Commercial.

most virulent causes of deterioration, misery and excessive wealth, are eliminated, the average length of human life will be increased and a better health and a stronger physical constitution will be ensured. The improvement of medical practice, which will become more efficacious with the progress of reason and of the social order, will mean the end of infectious and heredity diseases and illnesses brought on by climate, food, or working conditions. It is reasonable to hope that all other diseases may likewise disappear as their distant causes are discovered. Would it be absurd then to suppose that this perfection of the human species might be capable of indefinite progress; that the day will come when death will be due only to extraordinary accidents or to the decay of the vital forces, and that ultimately the average span between birth and decay will have no assignable value? Certainly man will not become immortal, but will not the interval between the first breath that he draws and the time when in the natural course of events, without disease or accident, he expires, increase indefinitely? . . .

Finally, may we not extend such hopes to the intellectual and moral faculties? May not our parents, who transmit to us the benefits or disadvantages of their constitution, and from whom we receive our shape and features, as well as our tendencies to certain physical affections, hand on to us also that part of the physical organization which determines the intellect, the power of the brain, the ardor of the soul or the moral sensibility? Is it not probable that education, in perfecting these qualities, will at the same time influence, modify, and perfect the organization itself? Analogy, investigation of the human faculties, and the study of certain facts, all seem to give substance to such conjectures[28] which would further push back the boundaries of our hopes.

These are the questions with which we shall conclude this final stage. How consoling for the philosopher who laments the errors, the crimes, the injustices which still pollute the earth and of which he is often the victim is this view of the human race, emancipated from its shackles, released from the empire of fate and from that of the enemies of its progress, advancing with a firm and sure step along the path of truth, virtue, and happiness! It is the contemplation of this prospect that rewards him for all his efforts to assist the progress of reason and the defense of liberty. He dares to regard these strivings as part of the eternal chain of human destiny; and in this persuasion he is filled with the true delight of virtue and the pleasure of having done some lasting

[28]Suggestions, guesses.

good which fate can never destroy by a sinister stroke of revenge, by calling back the reign of slavery and prejudice. Such contemplation is for him an asylum, in which the memory of his persecutors cannot pursue him; there he lives in thought with man restored to his natural rights and dignity, forgets man tormented and corrupted by greed, fear, or envy; there he lives with his peers[29] in an Elysium[30] created by reason and graced by the purest pleasures known to the love of mankind.

[29]Equals.
[30]In Greek mythology, the region where the souls of heroes enjoyed happiness.

15

Edmund Burke

Reflections on the Revolution in France

*T*HE *liberal and democratic principles of the Enlightenment found explosive realization in the French Revolution, which in turn provoked a strong reaction against them. The most famous and most influential of these intellectual counterattacks was Edmund Burke's* Reflections on the Revolution in France *(1790). Burke (1729–1797) was a British politician and publicist who served in the House of Commons for many years and emerged as the spokesman of the landed aristocracy. In his view, the fixed social and political order of late eighteenth-century England, based on class distinctions, upper-class rule, and parliamentary supremacy, was an excellent one, worthy of perpetuation. Burke saw the French Revolution, even as it got under way, as an attack on the whole social fabric. In the* Reflections, *written in the form of a letter to a resident of Paris, he warned that the Revolution's radical policies would lead ultimately to anarchy and military dictatorship. The essay was not merely a political pamphlet, however. It was a powerful, though unsystematic, critique of the rationalist theories of the Enlightenment and a statement of the basic principles of conservatism. Compounded of poetry, philosophy, religious mysticism, and socio-political analysis,* Reflections *elaborated a theory of society as a complex organism evolving slowly in the fixed channels of historical tradition. Burke rejected what he considered the abstract vagaries of individual reason as the guide to social progress. He thought that human beings, individually and in the mass, were not basically rational, but weak creatures of irrational impulse who needed to be restrained by organized society. Property, religion, custom, and "prejudices" (or social myths) were the social controls necessary to preserve tolerable order. Burke, in short, was opposed to the rational optimism and the individualism of the Enlightenment. In time, his work became the bible of conservatism, an arsenal of arguments against social and democratic reform.*

You will observe that from Magna Carta[1] to the Declaration of Right[2] it has been the uniform policy of our constitution to claim and assert our liberties as an entailed inheritance derived to us from our forefathers, and to be transmitted to our posterity—as an estate specially belonging to the people of this kingdom, without any reference whatever to any other more general or prior right. By this means our constitution preserves a unity in so great a diversity of its parts. We have an inheritable crown, an inheritable peerage,[3] and a House of Commons[4] and a people inheriting privileges, franchises, and liberties from a long line of ancestors.

This policy appears to me to be the result of profound reflection, or rather the happy effect of following nature, which is wisdom without reflection, and above it. A spirit of innovation is generally the result of a selfish temper and confined views. People will not look forward to posterity, who never look backward to their ancestors. Besides, the people of England well know that the idea of inheritance furnishes a sure principle of conservation and a sure principle of transmission, without at all excluding a principle of improvement. It leaves acquisition free, but it secures what it acquires. Whatever advantages are obtained by a state proceeding on these maxims[5] are locked fast as in a sort of family settlement, grasped as in a kind of mortmain[6] forever. By a constitutional policy, working after the pattern of nature, we receive, we hold, we transmit our government and our privileges in the same manner in which we enjoy and transmit our property and our lives. The institutions of policy, the goods of fortune, the gifts of providence are handed down to us, and from us, in the same course and order. Our political system is placed in a just correspondence and symmetry with

[1]In 1215, English feudal barons forced King John to accept the Magna Carta (Great Charter). The chief significance of this document lies in the fact that the king, too, is held subject to the law and therefore required to respect it.

[2]A document passed by Parliament in 1689, guaranteeing important political and civil rights to that body and to the English people.

[3]Nobility.

[4]The lower house of Parliament. It excludes the nobility as a body and has become the principal lawmaking body of the United Kingdom.

[5]Rules, principles.

[6]Perpetual right to a property—a right that cannot be broken or transferred (literally, a dead hand).

REFLECTIONS ON THE REVOLUTION IN FRANCE Adapted by editor, from Edmund Burke, *Reflections on the Revolution in France*, in *The Works of Edmund Burke* (Boston: Little, Brown, 1881), III, 274–80, 295–300, 311–13, 344–48, 350–52, 358–59, 454–57, 559–61.

please!,

the order of the world and with the mode of existence decreed to a permanent body composed of transitory parts, wherein, by the disposition of a stupendous wisdom, moulding together the great mysterious incorporation of the human race, the whole, at one time, is never old or middle-aged or young, but, in a condition of unchangeable constancy, moves on through the varied tenor of perpetual decay, fall, renovation, and progression. Thus, by preserving the method of nature in the conduct of the state, in what we improve we are never wholly new; in what we retain we are never wholly obsolete. By adhering in this manner and on those principles to our forefathers, we are guided not by the superstition of antiquarians, but by the spirit of philosophic analogy. In this choice of inheritance we have given to our frame of polity the image of a relation in blood, binding up the constitution of our country with our dearest domestic ties, adopting our fundamental laws into the bosom of our family affections, keeping inseparable and cherishing with the warmth of all their combined and mutually reflected charities our state, our hearths, our sepulchres, and our altars.

Through the same plan of a conformity to nature in our artificial institutions, and by calling in the aid of her unerring and powerful instincts to fortify the fallible and feeble contrivances of our reason, we have derived several other, and those no small, benefits from considering our liberties in the light of an inheritance. Always acting as if in the presence of canonized[7] forefathers, the spirit of freedom, leading in itself to misrule and excess, is tempered with an awful gravity. This idea of a liberal descent inspires us with a sense of habitual native dignity which prevents that upstart insolence almost inevitably adhering to and disgracing those who are the first acquirers of any distinction. By this means our liberty becomes a noble freedom. It carries an imposing and majestic aspect. It has a pedigree and illustrious ancestors. It has its bearings and its ensigns armorial.[8] It has its gallery of portraits, its monumental inscriptions, its records, evidences, and titles. We procure reverence to our civil institutions on the principle upon which nature teaches us to revere individual men: on account of their age, and on account of those from whom they are descended. All your sophisters[9] cannot produce anything better adapted to preserve a rational and manly freedom than the course that we have pursued, who have chosen

[7]Revered, hallowed.
[8]Symbolic designs (coats of arms) identifying family ancestors.
[9]Self-appointed "wise men."

our nature rather than our speculations, our breasts rather than our inventions, for the great conservatories and magazines[10] of our rights and privileges.

You might, if you pleased, have profited of our example, and have given to your recovered freedom a correspondent dignity. Your privileges, though discontinued, were not lost to memory. Your constitution, it is true, while you were out of possession, suffered waste and dilapidation; but you possessed in some parts the walls, and in all the foundations of a noble and venerable castle. You might have repaired those walls; you might have built on those old foundations. Your constitution was suspended before it was perfected; but you had the elements of a constitution very nearly as good as could be wished. In your old States[11] you possessed that variety of parts corresponding with the various descriptions of which your community was happily composed; you had all that combination, and all that opposition of interests, you had that action and counteraction which, in the natural and in the political world, from the reciprocal struggle of discordant powers, draws out the harmony of the universe. These opposed and conflicting interests, which you considered as so great a blemish in your old and in our present constitution, interpose a salutary check to all precipitate resolutions; they render deliberation a matter not of choice, but of necessity; they make all change a subject of *compromise*, which naturally begets moderation; they produce *temperaments*, preventing the sore evil of harsh, crude, unqualified reformations; and rendering all the headlong exertions of arbitrary power, in the few or in the many, forever impracticable. Through that diversity of members and interests, general liberty had as many securities as there were separate views in the several orders; while by pressing down the whole by the weight of a real monarchy, the separate parts would have been prevented from warping and starting from their allotted places.

You had all these advantages in your ancient States; but you chose to act as if you had never been moulded into civil society, and had everything to begin anew. You began ill, because you began by despising everything that belonged to you. You set up your trade without a capital. If the last generations of your country appeared without much

---

[10]Storehouses.

[11]Estates–General. This was the representative nationwide assembly of the three estates (social classes)—the clergy, the nobility, and the "Third Estate" (commoners: bourgeoisie and peasants)—in the centuries preceding the French Revolution of 1789.

luster in your eyes, you might have passed them by, and derived your claims from a more early race of ancestors. Under a pious predilection[12] for those ancestors, your imaginations would have realized in them a standard of virtue and wisdom, beyond the vulgar practice of the hour: and you would have risen with the example to whose imitation you aspired. Respecting your forefathers, you would have been taught to respect yourselves. You would not have chosen to consider the French as a people of yesterday, as a nation of low-born servile wretches until the emancipating year of 1789. In order to furnish, at the expense of your honor an excuse to your apologists here for several enormities of yours, you would not have been content to be represented as a gang of slaves, suddenly broke loose from the house of bondage, and therefore to be pardoned for your abuse of the liberty to which you were not accustomed and ill fitted. Would it not, my worthy friend, have been wiser to have you thought, what I, for one, always thought you, a generous and gallant nation, long misled to your disadvantage by your high and romantic sentiments of fidelity, honor, and loyalty; that events had been unfavorable to you, but that you were not enslaved through any illiberal or servile disposition; that in your most devoted submission, you were actuated by a principle of public spirit, and that it was your country you worshipped, in the person of your king? Had you made it to be understood, that in the delusion of this amiable error you had gone further than your wise ancestors; that you were resolved to resume your ancient privileges, while you preserved the spirit of your ancient and your recent loyalty and honor; or, if diffident[13] of yourselves, and not clearly discerning the almost obliterated constitution of your ancestors, you had looked to your neighbors in this land, who had kept alive the ancient principles and models of the old common law of Europe meliorated and adapted to its present state—by following wise examples you would have given new examples of wisdom to the world. You would have rendered the cause of liberty venerable in the eyes of every worthy mind in every nation. You would have shamed despotism from the earth, by showing that freedom was not only reconcileable, but as, when well disciplined it is, auxiliary to law. You would have had an unoppressive but a productive revenue. You would have had a flourishing commerce to feed it. You would have had a free constitution; a potent monarchy; a disciplined army; a

[12]Preference.
[13]Lacking confidence.

reformed and venerated clergy; a mitigated but spirited nobility, to lead your virtue, not to overlay it; you would have had a liberal order of commons, to emulate and to recruit that nobility; you would have had a protected, satisfied, laborious, and obedient people, taught to seek and to recognize the happiness that is to be found by virtue in all conditions; in which consists the true moral equality of mankind, and not in that monstrous fiction, which, by inspiring false ideas and vain expectations into men destined to travel in the obscure walk of laborious life, serves only to aggravate and imbitter that real inequality, which it never can remove; and which the order of civil life establishes as much for the benefit of those whom it must leave in an humble state, as those whom it is able to exalt to a condition more splendid, but not more happy. You had a smooth and easy career of felicity[14] and glory laid open to you, beyond any thing recorded in the history of the world; but you have shown that difficulty is good for man.

• • •

Believe me, Sir, those who attempt to level, never equalize. In all societies, consisting of various descriptions of citizens, some description must be uppermost. The levellers, therefore, only change and pervert the natural order of things; they load the edifice of society by setting up in the air what the solidity of the structure requires to be on the ground. The associations of tailors and carpenters, of which the republic (of Paris, for instance) is composed, cannot be equal to the situation into which by the worst of usurpations—and usurpation on the prerogatives of nature—you attempt to force them.

The Chancellor of France,[15] at the opening of the States, said, in a tone of oratorical flourish, that all occupations were honorable. If he meant only that no honest employment was disgraceful, he would not have gone beyond the truth. But in asserting that anything is honorable, we imply some distinction in its favor. The occupation of a hairdresser or of a working candlemaker cannot be a matter of honor to any person—to say nothing of a number of other more servile employments. Such descriptions of men ought not to suffer oppression from the state; but the state suffers oppression if such as they, either individually or collectively, are permitted to rule. In this you think you are combating prejudice, but you are at war with nature.

[14]Happiness.
[15]A high official of the king's administration.

I do not, my dear Sir, conceive you to be of that sophistical, captious spirit, or of that uncandid dulness, as to require, for every general observation or sentiment, an explicit detail of the correctives and exceptions which reason will presume to be included in all the general propositions which come from reasonable men. You do not imagine that I wish to confine power, authority, and distinction to blood and names and titles. No, Sir. There is no qualification for government but virtue and wisdom, actual or presumptive. Wherever they are actually found, they have, in whatever state, condition, profession, or trade, the passport of Heaven to human place and honor. Woe to the country which would madly and impiously reject the service of the talents and virtues, civil, military, or religious, that are given to grace and to serve it; and would condemn to obscurity everything formed to diffuse luster and glory around a state! Woe to that country, too, that, passing into the opposite extreme, considers a low education, a mean contracted view of things, a sordid, mercenary occupation, as a preferable title to command! Everything ought to be open, but not indifferently,[16] to every man. No rotation; no appointment by lot; no mode of election operating in the spirit of sortition[17] or rotation can be generally good in a government conversant in extensive objects. Because they have no tendency, direct or indirect, to select the man with a view to the duty, or to accommodate the one to the other. I do not hesitate to say that the road to eminence and power, from obscure condition, ought not to be made too easy, nor a thing too much of course. If rare merit be the rarest of all rare things, it ought to pass through some sort of probation. The temple of honor ought to be seated on an eminence.[18] If it be opened through virtue, let it be remembered, too, that virtue is never tried but by some difficulty and some struggle.

Nothing is a due and adequate representation of a state that does not represent its ability as well as its property. But as ability is a vigorous and active principle, and as property is sluggish, inert, and timid, it never can be safe from the invasion of ability, unless it be, out of all proportion, predominant in the representation. It must be represented, too, in great masses of accumulation, or it is not rightly protected. The characteristic essence of property, formed out of the combined principles of its acquisition and conservation, is to be *unequal*. The great

---

[16]Indiscriminately.
[17]Determination by lot.
[18]High or lofty ground.

masses, therefore, which excite envy and tempt rapacity must be put out of the possibility of danger. Then they form a natural rampart about the lesser properties in all their gradations. The same quantity of property, which is by the natural course of things divided among many, has not the same operation. Its defensive power is weakened as it is diffused. In this diffusion each man's portion is less than what, in the eagerness of his desires, he may flatter himself to obtain by dissipating the accumulations of others. The plunder of the few would indeed give but a share inconceivably small in the distribution to the many. But the many are not capable of making this calculation; and those who lead them to rapine never intend this distribution.

The power of perpetuating our property in our families is one of the most valuable and interesting circumstances belonging to it, and that which tends the most to the perpetuation of society itself. It makes our weakness subservient to our virtue, it grafts benevolence even upon avarice. The possessors of family wealth, and of the distinction which attends hereditary possession (as most concerned in it), are the natural securities for this transmission. With us the House of Peers[19] is formed upon this principle. It is wholly composed of hereditary property and hereditary distinction, and made, therefore, the third of the legislature[20] and, in the last event, the sole judge of all property in all its subdivisions. The House of Commons, too, though not necessarily, yet in fact, is always so composed, in the far greater part. Let those large proprietors be what they will—and they have their chance of being among the best—they are, at the very worst, the ballast in the vessel of the commonwealth. For though hereditary wealth and the rank which goes with it are too much idolized by creeping sycophants and the blind, abject admirers of power, they are too rashly slighted in shallow speculations of the petulant, assuming, shortsighted coxcombs of philosophy. Some decent, regulated preeminence, some preference (not exclusive appropriation) given to birth is neither unnatural, nor unjust, nor impolitic.

It is said that twenty-four millions ought to prevail over two hundred thousand. True; if the constitution of a kingdom be a problem of arithmetic. . . . The will of the many, and their interest must very often

---

[19]The House of Peers, or House of Lords, is the upper house of Parliament. Membership in this assembly is restricted to hereditary nobles and high-ranking clergy.

[20]The first and second thirds of the legislature (lawmaking procedure) are the king and the House of Commons.

differ, and great will be the difference when they make an evil choice. A government of five hundred country attorneys and obscure curates is not good for twenty-four millions of men, though it were chosen by forty-eight millions, nor is it the better for being guided by a dozen of persons of quality who have betrayed their trust in order to obtain that power.[21] At present, you seem in everything to have strayed out of the high road of nature.

• • •

The science of constructing a commonwealth, or renovating it, or reforming it, is, like every other experimental science, not to be taught *a priori*.[22] Nor is it a short experience that can instruct us in that practical science, because the real effects of moral causes are not always immediate; but that which in the first instance is prejudicial may be excellent in its remoter operation, and its excellence may arise even from the ill effects it produces in the beginning. The reverse also happens: and very plausible schemes, with very pleasing commencements, have often shameful and lamentable conclusions. In states there are often some obscure and almost latent causes, things which appear at first view of little moment, on which a very great part of its prosperity or adversity may most essentially depend. The science of government being therefore so practical in itself and intended for such practical purposes—a matter which requires experience, and even more experience than any person can gain in his whole life, however sagacious and observing he may be—it is with infinite caution that any man ought to venture upon pulling down an edifice which has answered in any tolerable degree for ages the common purposes of society, or on building it up again without having models and patterns of approved utility before his eyes.

These metaphysic rights entering into common life, like rays of light which pierce into a dense medium, are by the laws of nature refracted from their straight line. Indeed, in the gross and complicated mass of human passions and concerns the primitive rights of men undergo such a variety of refractions and reflections that it becomes absurd to talk of them as if they continued in the simplicity of their original direction. The nature of man is intricate; the objects of society are of the greatest

---

[21]Burke is lashing out at the small number of French noblemen who joined the cause of the Third Estate.

[22]According to prior, or previous, assumptions of truth.

possible complexity; and, therefore, no simple disposition or direction of power can be suitable either to man's nature or to the quality of his affairs. When I hear the simplicity of contrivance aimed at and boasted of in any new political constitutions, I am at no loss to decide that the artificers are grossly ignorant of their trade or totally negligent of their duty. The simple governments are fundamentally defective, to say no worse of them. If you were to contemplate society in but one point of view, all these simple modes of polity are infinitely captivating. In effect each would answer its single end much more perfectly than the more complex is able to attain all its complex purposes. But it is better that the whole should be imperfectly and anomalously answered than that, while some parts are provided for with great exactness, others might be totally neglected or perhaps materially injured by the overcare of a favorite member.

The pretended rights of these theorists are all extremes; and in proportion as they are metaphysically true, they are morally and politically false. The rights of men are in a sort of *middle*, incapable of definition, but not impossible to be discerned. The rights of men in governments are their advantages; and these are often in balances between differences of good, in compromises sometimes between good and evil, and sometimes between evil and evil. Political reason is a computing principle: adding, subtracting, multiplying, and dividing, morally and not metaphysically, or mathematically, true moral denominations.

By these theorists the right of the people is almost always sophistically confounded with their power. The body of the community, whenever it can come to act, can meet with no effectual resistance; but till power and right are the same, the whole body of them has no right inconsistent with virtue, and the first of all virtues, prudence. Men have no right to what is not reasonable and to what is not for their benefit.

· · ·

I almost venture to affirm that not one in a hundred among us participates in the "triumph" of the Revolution Society.[23] If the king and queen of France, and their children, were to fall into our hands by

---

[23]The Revolution Society gloried in the achievements of the English "Glorious Revolution" of 1688 to 1689. In November 1789, when meeting for the spectacular centennial celebration of the Revolution, the Society drafted a document that congratulated the French revolutionaries on what they had achieved so far. The Revolution Society expressed its hope for the democratization of the British Parliament in the near future.

the chance of war, in the most acrimonious of all hostilities (I deprecate such an event, I deprecate such hostility), they would be treated with another sort of triumphal entry into London. We formerly have had a king of France[24] in that situation; you have read how he was treated by the victor in the field, and in what manner he was afterwards received in England. Four hundred years have gone over us, but I believe we are not materially changed since that period. Thanks to our sullen resistance to innovation, thanks to the cold sluggishness of our national character, we still bear the stamp of our forefathers. We have not (as I conceive) lost the generosity and dignity of thinking of the fourteenth century, nor as yet have we subtilized ourselves into savages. We are not the converts of Rousseau;[25] we are not the disciples of Voltaire;[26] Helvetius[27] has made no progress among us. Atheists[28] are not our preachers; madmen are not our lawgivers. We know that we have made no discoveries, and we think that no discoveries are to be made, in morality, nor many in the great principles of government, nor in the ideas of liberty, which were understood long before we were born, altogether as well as they will be after the grave has heaped its mould upon our presumption and the silent tomb shall have imposed its law on our pert loquacity. In England we have not yet been completely embowelled of our natural entrails; we still feel within us, and we cherish and cultivate, those inbred sentiments which are the faithful guardians, the active monitors of our duty, the true supporters of all liberal and manly morals. We have not been drawn and trussed, in order that we may be filled, like stuffed birds in a museum, with chaff and rags and paltry blurred shreds of paper about the rights of man. We preserve the whole of our feelings still native and entire, unsophisticated by pedantry and infidelity. We have real hearts of flesh and blood beating in our bosoms. We fear God; we look up with awe to kings, with affection to parliaments, with duty to magistrates, with reverence

---

[24]John II (1319–1364), while held prisoner in England, was treated in the manner reserved for visiting royalty.

[25]Jean Jacques Rousseau (1712–1778), a philosopher and writer who promoted doctrines of human equality and democracy. He was born in Geneva, Switzerland, but lived chiefly in Paris after 1741.

[26]The literary name of François Marie Arouet (1694–1778). This French writer and historian was an untiring fighter against religious intolerance and suppression of free expression.

[27]Claude Adrien Helvetius (1715–1771), a French philosopher who taught that pleasure was the highest social good.

[28]Those who deny the existence of God.

to priests, and with respect to nobility. Why? Because when such ideas are brought before our minds, it is _natural_ to be so affected; because all other feelings are false and spurious and tend to corrupt our minds, to vitiate our primary morals, to render us unfit for rational liberty, and, by teaching us a servile, licentious, and abandoned insolence, to be our low sport for a few holidays, to make us perfectly fit for, and justly deserving of, slavery through the whole course of our lives.

You see, Sir, that in this enlightened age I am bold enough to confess that we are generally men of untaught feelings, that, instead of casting away all our old prejudices,[29] we cherish them to a very considerable degree, and, to take more shame to ourselves, we cherish them because they are prejudices; and the longer they have lasted and the more generally they have prevailed, the more we cherish them. We are afraid to put men to live and trade each on his own private stock of reason, because we suspect that the stock in each man is small, and that the individuals would do better to avail themselves of the general bank and capital of nations and of ages. Many of our men of speculation, instead of exploding general prejudices, employ their sagacity to discover the latent wisdom which prevails in them. If they find what they seek, and they seldom fail, they think it more wise to continue the prejudice, with the reason involved, than to cast away the coat of prejudice and to leave nothing but the naked reason; because prejudice, with its reason, has a motive to give action to that reason, and an affection which will give it permanence. Prejudice is of ready application in the emergency; it previously engages the mind in a steady course of wisdom and virtue and does not leave the man hesitating in the moment of decision skeptical, puzzled, and unresolved. Prejudice renders a man's virtue his habit, and not a series of unconnected acts. Through just prejudice, his duty becomes a part of his nature.

Your literary men and your politicians, and so do the whole clan of the enlightened among us, essentially differ in these points. They have no respect for the wisdom of others, but they pay it off by a very full measure of confidence in their own. With them it is a sufficient motive to destroy an old scheme of things because it is an old one. As to the new, they are in no sort of fear with regard to the duration of a building run up in haste, because duration is no object to those who think little or nothing has been done before their time, and who place all their hopes in discovery. They conceive, very systematically, that all things which

[29]Adherence to traditions, customs, and conventions.

give perpetuity are mischievous, and therefore they are at inexpiable war with all establishments. They think that government may vary like modes of dress, and with as little ill effect; that there needs no principle of attachment, except a sense of present convenience, to any constitution of the state. They always speak as if they were of opinion that there is a singular species of compact between them and their magistrates which binds the magistrate, but which has nothing reciprocal in it, but that the majesty of the people has a right to dissolve it without any reason but its will. Their attachment to their country itself is only so far as it agrees with some of their fleeting projects; it begins and ends with that scheme of polity which falls in with their momentary opinion.

These doctrines, or rather sentiments, seem prevalent with your new statesmen. But they are wholly different from those on which we have always acted in this country.

• • •

We know, and what is better, we feel inwardly, that religion is the basis of civil society and the source of all good and of all comfort. In England we are so convinced of this, that there is no rust of superstition with which the accumulated absurdity of the human mind might have crusted it over in the course of ages, that ninety-nine in a hundred of the people of England would not prefer to impiety. We shall never be such fools as to call in an enemy to the substance of any system to remove its corruptions, to supply its defects, or to perfect its construction. If our religious tenets should ever want a further elucidation, we shall not call on atheism to explain them. We shall not light up our temple from that unhallowed fire. It will be illuminated with other lights. It will be perfumed with other incense than the infectious stuff which is imported by the smugglers of adulterated metaphysics. If our ecclesiastical establishment[30] should need a revision, it is not avarice or rapacity, public or private, that we shall employ for the audit, or receipt, or application of its consecrated revenue. Violently condemning neither the Greek[31] nor the Armenian,[32] nor, since heats are subsided, the Roman system of religion,[33] we prefer the Protestant, not because we

[30]The Church of England.
[31]The Greek Orthodox Church.
[32]The Armenian Apostolic Church, another branch of historic Christianity.
[33]The Roman Catholic Church.

think it has less of the Christian religion in it, but because, in our judgment, it has more. We are Protestants, not from indifference, but from zeal.

We know, and it is our pride to know, that man is by his constitution a religious animal; that atheism is against, not only our reason, but our instincts; and that it cannot prevail long. But if, in the moment of riot and in a drunken delirium from the hot spirit drawn out of the alembic[34] of hell, which in France is now so furiously boiling, we should uncover our nakedness by throwing off that Christian religion which has hitherto been our boast and comfort, and one great source of civilization among us, and among many other nations, we are apprehensive (being well aware that the mind will not endure a void) that some uncouth, pernicious, and degrading superstition might take place of it.

For that reason, before we take from our establishment the natural, human means of estimation and give it up to contempt, as you have done, and in doing it have incurred the penalties you well deserve to suffer, we desire that some other may be presented to us in the place of it. We shall then form our judgment.

On these ideas, instead of quarrelling with establishments, as some do who have made a philosophy and a religion of their hostility to such institutions, we cleave closely to them. We are resolved to keep an established church, an established monarchy, an established aristocracy, and an established democracy, each in the degree it exists, and in no greater.

• • •

To avoid, therefore, the evils of inconstancy and versatility, ten thousand times worse than those of obstinacy and the blindest prejudice, we have consecrated the state that no man should approach to look into its defects or corruptions but with due caution, that he should never dream of beginning its reformation by its subversion, that he should approach to the faults of the state as to the wounds of a father, with pious awe and trembling solicitude. By this wise prejudice we are taught to look with horror on those children of their country who are prompt rashly to hack that aged parent in pieces and put him into the kettle of magicians, in hopes that by their poisonous weeds and wild

[34]Fires.

incantations they may regenerate the paternal constitution and renovate their father's life.[35]

⚓ Society is indeed a contract. Subordinate contracts for objects of mere occasional interest may be dissolved at pleasure—but the state ought not to be considered as nothing better than a partnership agreement in a trade of pepper and coffee, calico or tobacco, or some other such low concern, to be taken up for a little temporary interest, and to be dissolved by the fancy of the parties. It is to be looked on with other reverence, because it is not a partnership in things subservient only to the gross animal existence of a temporary and perishable nature. It is a partnership in all science; a partnership in all art; a partnership in every virtue and in all perfection. As the ends of such a partnership cannot be obtained in many generations, it becomes a partnership not only between those who are living, but between those who are living, those who are dead, and those who are to be born. Each contract of each particular state is but a clause in the great primeval contract of eternal society, linking the lower with the higher natures, connecting the visible and invisible world, according to a fixed compact sanctioned by the inviolable oath which holds all physical and all moral natures, each in their appointed place. This law is not subject to the will of those who, by an obligation above them, and infinitely superior, are bound to submit their will to that law.

•   •   •

It is this inability to wrestle with difficulty which has obliged the arbitrary Assembly of France[36] to commence their schemes of reform with abolition and total destruction. But is it in destroying and pulling down that skill is displayed? Your mob can do this as well at least as your assemblies. The shallowest understanding, the rudest hand is more than equal to that task. Rage and frenzy will pull down more in half an hour than prudence, deliberation, and foresight can build up in a hundred years. The errors and defects of old establishments are visible and palpable. It calls for little ability to point them out; and where

---

[35]Burke is referring to the legend in which Medea, a Greek sorceress, persuades the daughters of King Pelias to hack their father to pieces and boil him with "youth-renewing" herbs. This bizarre procedure fails to achieve the father's rejuvenation.

[36]The National Assembly (1789–91), which, assuming the right to exercise sovereign power in the name of the French people, passed the reform measures that started the French Revolution.

absolute power is given, it requires but a word wholly to abolish the vice and the establishment together. The same lazy, but restless disposition which loves sloth and hates quiet directs these politicians when they come to work for supplying the place of what they have destroyed. To make everything the reverse of what they have seen is quite as easy as to destroy. No difficulties occur in what has never been tried. Criticism is almost baffled in discovering the defects of what has not existed; and eager enthusiasm and cheating hope have all the wide field of imagination in which they may expatiate with little or no opposition.

At once to preserve and to reform is quite another thing. When the useful parts of an old establishment are kept, and what is superadded is to be fitted to what is retained, a vigorous mind, steady, persevering attention, various powers of comparison and combination, and the resources of an understanding fruitful in expedients are to be exercised; they are to be exercised in a continued conflict with the combined force of opposite vices, with the obstinacy that rejects all improvement and the levity that is fatigued and disgusted with everything of which it is in possession. But you may object—"A process of this kind is slow. It is not fit for an assembly which glories in performing in a few months the work of ages. Such a mode of reforming, possibly, might take up many years." Without question it might; and it ought. It is one of the excellences of a method in which time is among the assistants, that its operation is slow and in some cases almost imperceptible. If circumspection and caution are a part of wisdom when we work only upon inanimate matter, surely they become a part of duty, too, when the subject of our demolition and construction is not brick and timber but sentient[37] beings, by the sudden alteration of whose state, condition, and habits, multitudes may be rendered miserable. But it seems as if it were the prevalent opinion in Paris that an unfeeling heart and an undoubting confidence are the sole qualifications for a perfect legislator. Far different are my ideas of that high office. The true lawgiver ought to have a heart full of sensibility. He ought to love and respect his kind, and to fear himself. It may be allowed to his temperament to catch his ultimate object with an intuitive glance, but his movements toward it ought to be deliberate. Political arrangement, as it is a work for social ends, is to be only wrought by social means. There, mind must conspire with mind. Time is required to produce that union of minds

[37]Living, feeling (human).

which alone can produce all the good we aim at. Our patience will achieve more than our force. If I might venture to appeal to what is so much out of fashion in Paris, I mean to experience, I should tell you that in my course I have known and, according to my measure, have cooperated with great men; and I have never yet seen any plan which has not been mended by the observations of those who were much inferior in understanding to the person who took the lead in the business. By a slow, but well-sustained progress the effect of each step is watched; the good or ill success of the first gives light to us in the second; and so, from light to light, we are conducted with safety through the whole series. We see that the parts or the system do not clash. The evils latent in the most promising contrivances are provided for as they arise. One advantage is as little as possible sacrificed to another. We compensate, we reconcile, we balance. We are enabled to unite into a consistent whole the various anomalies and contending principles that are found in the minds and affairs of men. From hence arises, not an excellence in simplicity, but one far superior, an excellence in composition. Where the great interests of mankind are concerned through a long succession of generations, that succession ought to be admitted into some share in the councils which are so deeply to affect them. If justice requires this, the work itself requires the aid of more minds than one age can furnish. It is from this view of things that the best legislators have been often satisfied with the establishment of some sure, solid, and ruling principle in government—a power like that which some of the philosophers have called a plastic nature; and having fixed the principle, they have left it afterwards to its own operation.

· · ·

The effects of the incapacity shown by the popular leaders in all the great members of the commonwealth are to be covered with the "all-atoning name" of liberty. In some people I see great liberty indeed; in many, if not in the most, an oppressive, degrading servitude. But what is liberty without wisdom and without virtue? It is the greatest of all possible evils; for it is folly, vice, and madness, without tuition or restraint. Those who know what virtuous liberty is cannot bear to see it disgraced by incapable heads on account of their having high-sounding words in their mouths. Grand, swelling sentiments of liberty I am sure I do not despise. They warm the heart; they enlarge and liberalize our minds; they animate our courage in time of conflict. Old as I am, I read the fine raptures of Lucan[38] and Corneille[39] with pleasure. Neither do I wholly condemn the little arts and devices of popularity. They facilitate the carrying of many points of moment; they keep the people together; they refresh the mind in its exertions; and they diffuse occasional gaiety over the severe brow of moral freedom. Every politician ought to sacrifice to the Graces,[40] and to join compliance with reason. But in such an undertaking as that in France all these subsidiary sentiments and artifices are of little avail. To make a government requires no great prudence. Settle the seat of power, teach obedience, and the work is done. To give freedom is still more easy. It is not necessary to guide; it only requires to let go the rein. But to form a *free government*, that is, to temper together these opposite elements of liberty and restraint in one consistent work, requires much thought, deep reflection, a sagacious, powerful, and combining mind. This I do not find in those who take the lead in the National Assembly. Perhaps they are not so miserably deficient as they appear. I rather believe it. It would put them below the common level of human understanding. But when the leaders choose to make themselves bidders at an auction of popularity, their talents, in the construction of the state, will be of no service. They will become flatterers instead of legislators, the instruments, not the guides, of the people. If any of them should happen to propose a scheme of liberty, soberly limited and defined with proper qualifications, he will be immediately outbid by his competitors who will produce something more splendidly popular. Suspicions will be raised of his fidelity to his cause. Moderation will be stigmatized as the virtue of cowards, and compromise as the prudence of traitors, until, in hopes of preserving the credit which may enable him to temper and moderate, on some occasions, the popular leader is obliged to become active in propagating doctrines and establishing powers that will afterwards defeat any sober purpose at which he ultimately might have aimed.

But am I so unreasonable as to see nothing at all that deserves commendation in the indefatigable[41] labors of this assembly? I do not deny that among an infinite number of acts of violence and folly, some good may have been done. They who destroy everything certainly will

---

[38]Marcus Annaeus Lucanus (39–65), a Roman poet.

[39]Pierre Corneille (1606–1684), a French playwright.

[40]In Greek mythology, the three sister goddesses who personified pleasure, charm, elegance, and beauty.

[41]Untiring.

remove some grievance. They who make everything new, have a chance that they may establish something beneficial. To give them credit for what they have done in virtue of the authority they have usurped, or which can excuse them in the crimes by which that authority has been acquired, it must appear, that the same things could not have been accomplished without producing such a revolution. Most assuredly they might; because almost every one of the regulations made by them, which is not very equivocal, was either in the cession of the king, voluntarily made at the meeting of the States, or in the concurrent instructions to the orders. Some usages have been abolished on just grounds; but they were such that if they had stood as they were to all eternity, they would little detract from the happiness and prosperity of any state. The improvements of the National Assembly are superficial, their errors fundamental. . . .

16

Johann Wolfgang von Goethe

Faust

JOHANN *Wolfgang von Goethe (1749–1832), a genius whose full and varied career reflected the romantic spirit of the nineteenth century, was both a scientist and one of the greatest of the German lyric poets. In his scientific work, Goethe made important contributions to biology and advanced a theory of evolution. As political adviser to the Duke of Saxe-Weimar from 1775 to the end of his life, Goethe proved a responsible and forward-looking public servant. He also wrote novels and powerful dramas that influenced German and other European literature. In his varied activities and his changing intellectual positions, Goethe epitomized the confused strains of the transition from the neoclassicism of the eighteenth century to the romanticism of the nineteenth. Indeed, he thought of himself as a prophet of his time—an interpreter of the spiritual issues of his day; the central idea of his life was the oneness of humanity and nature.*

Faust, Goethe's literary masterpiece, was inspired by the "Faust legend" about a sixteenth-century magician and man of learning. But more importantly, it is a reflection of the range of the author's own intellectual career as well as a comment on the restless seeking, affirmations, and protests of his age. Part I, from which most of the following selection is taken, was written between 1774 and 1808 (when it was published), while Goethe was going through, successively, his period of youthful self-discovery and rebellion, his neoclassical phase, and his romantic phase. Part II was written during the last twenty-five years of his life and was not published until the year of his death; only its conclusion is reprinted here. Goethe presents both parts in dramatic form, but they are more suitable to reading than to performance on a stage.

Written in symbolic poetry, the drama Faust confronts its reader with numerous situations, problems, and characters. These, however, have only as much significance as each individual finds in them. The drama's ranking among the most important pieces of Western literature is due in great measure to the fact that modern readers find themselves portrayed in it. Individuals in contemporary society, like the character Faust, are products of past civilizations, epochs, and ideas—influences that do not fuse within them into a harmonious whole but leave them disjointed and divided. Thus, from scene to scene, Faust thinks, speaks, and acts differently. For example, at some times he is a romanticist, then again a rationalist, and at times he seems thoroughly medieval. In him dwell side by side the Greek age, classical and Christian mythology, and the Reformation, as well as those deep abysses of the soul that are darkly felt but generally escape psychological and philosophical identification.

Contemporary readers of the drama recognize themselves in the person of Faust because, like him, they rarely see their dreams and aspirations come true. Faust, for example, never learns what "girds the world together in its innermost being," nor is he privileged to spend the days of his adult life as a loving husband and father. Even his vision of a "free ground" inhabited by a "free people" remains just that—a vision. Like many present-day people, Faust does not foresee the varied and often disastrous results of his dreams and acts. Because of him, for instance, a family perishes, and his service to the Emperor climaxes in a bloody war. Later, his desire for a perfect piece of land causes a lovely old couple to perish in the flames of their small hut. Undoubtedly, the intentions of Faust are often honorable, and his efforts in pursuing them untiring and unrelenting; nonetheless the results are often disastrous, and his is a truly tragic existence.

The life of Faust also resembles many modern lives in that it consists of a number of seemingly unrelated episodes, each of which must be evaluated separately; it is a succession of experiences rather than a progression of them. In these experiences, Faust seems the modern-day Everyman condemned to a tragic existence, rather than the ideal hero. He is not fortunate enough to see even his last enterprise completed. Beholding his dream rather than reality, he speaks the fateful words that should deliver his soul to Hell. But if the drama had been written to end with Faust's death and damnation, the reader would be left with a depressing emptiness. Goethe, who confided that the ending caused him great trouble, chose instead to end the drama on a religious, conciliatory, and hopeful note: Although this world resembles a gruesome madhouse, might it not be comforting to assume that there exists yet another world whose foremost attributes are divine mercy and love? In contemplating his own death, however, Goethe emphatically rejected this comforting idea.

PROLOGUE IN HEAVEN

The Lord. The Heavenly Hosts. Mephistopheles following.

(The Three Archangels step forward)

RAPHAEL.   The chanting sun, as ever, rivals
　　The chanting of his brother spheres[1]
　　And marches round his destined circuit—
　　A march that thunders in our ears.
　　His aspect cheers the Hosts of Heaven
　　Though what his essence none can say;
　　These inconceivable creations
　　Keep the high state of their first day.

GABRIEL.   And swift, with inconceivable swiftness,
　　The earth's full splendor rolls around,
　　Celestial[2] radiance alternating
　　With a dread night too deep to sound;
　　The sea against the rocks' deep bases
　　Comes foaming up in far-flung force,
　　And rock and sea go whirling onward
　　In the swift spheres' eternal course.

MICHAEL.   And storms in rivalry are raging
　　From sea to land, from land to sea,
　　In frenzy forge the world a girdle
　　From which no inmost part is free.
　　The blight of lightning flaming yonder
　　Marks where the thunder-bolt will play;
　　And yet Thine envoys,[3] Lord, revere
　　The gentle movement of Thy day.

CHOIR OF ANGELS.   Thine aspect cheers the Hosts of Heaven
　　Though what Thine essence none can say,
　　And all Thy loftiest creations
　　Keep the high state of their first day.

---

[1] It was held that, as the sun and planets travel through the skies, they create a loud sound. This sound was believed to be almost unbearable to the human ear.

[2] Heavenly.

[3] Messengers; angels.

FAUST   From *Goethe's Faust*, translated by Louis MacNeice. Copyright 1951 by Louis MacNeice. Reprinted by permission of Oxford University Press, Inc., 13–21, 28–31, 43–45, 47–48, 54–62, 73–76, 112–16, 146–50, 152–54, 284–91, 293–94, 298.

(*Enter* MEPHISTOPHELES)

MEPHISTOPHELES.[4]   Since you, O Lord, once more
   approach and ask
If business down with us be light or heavy—
And in the past you've usually welcomed me—
That's why you see me also at your levee.[5]
Excuse me, I can't manage lofty words—
Not though your whole court jeer and find me low;
My pathos[6] certainly would make you laugh
Had you not left off laughing long ago.
Your suns and worlds mean nothing much to me;
How men torment themselves, that's all I see.
The little god of the world, one can't reshape, reshade him;
He is as strange to-day as that first day you made him.
His life would be not so bad, not quite,
Had you not granted him a gleam of Heaven's light;
He calls it Reason, uses it not the least
Except to be more beastly than any beast.
He seems to me—if your Honor does not mind—
Like a grasshopper—the long-legged kind—
That's always in flight and leaps as it flies along
And then in the grass strikes up its same old song.
I could only wish he confined himself to the grass!
He thrusts his nose into every filth, alas.

LORD.   Mephistopheles, have you no other news?
Do you always come here to accuse?
Is nothing ever right in your eyes on earth?

MEPHISTOPHELES.   No, Lord! I find things there as downright
   bad as ever.
I am sorry for men's days of dread and dearth;[7]
Poor things, *my* wish to plague 'em isn't fervent.

LORD.   Do you know Faust?

MEPHISTOPHELES.   The Doctor?

----

[4]Medieval name for the Devil; sometimes shortened to Mephisto.
[5]Morning reception held by a person of high rank for his courtiers.
[6]Grand manners.
[7]Scarcity (of food).

LORD.   Aye, my servant.
MEPHISTOPHELES.   Indeed! He serves you oddly enough, I think.
The fool has no earthly habits in meat and drink.
The ferment in him drives him wide and far,
That he is mad he too has almost guessed;
He demands of heaven each fairest star
And of earth each highest joy and best,
And all that is new and all that is far
Can bring no calm to the deep-sea swell of his breast.
LORD.   Now he may serve me only gropingly,
Soon I shall lead him into the light.
The gardener knows when the sapling first turns green
That flowers and fruit will make the future bright.
MEPHISTOPHELES.   What do you wager? You will lose him yet,
Provided *you* give *me* permission
To steer him gently the course I set.
LORD.   So long as he walks the earth alive,
So long as you may try what enters your head;
Men make mistakes as long as they strive.
MEPHISTOPHELES.   I thank you for that; as regards the dead,
The dead have never taken my fancy.
I favor cheeks that are full and rosy-red;
No corpse is welcome to my house;
I work as the cat does with the mouse.
LORD.   Very well; you have my full permission.
Divert this soul from its primal[8] source
And carry it, if you can seize it,
Down with you upon your course—
And stand ashamed when you must needs admit:
A good man with his groping intuitions[9]
Still knows the path that is true and fit.
MEPHISTOPHELES.   All right—but it won't last for long.
I'm not afraid my bet will turn out wrong.
And, if my aim prove true and strong,
Allow me to triumph wholeheartedly.

---

[8]Original.
[9]The grasping of knowledge without learning or reasoning.

Dust shall he eat—and greedily—
Like my cousin the Snake[10] renowned in tale and song.

LORD.   That too you are free to give a trial;
I have never hated the likes of you.
Of all the spirits of denial
The joker is the last that I eschew.[11]
Man finds relaxation too attractive—
Too fond too soon of unconditional rest;
Which is why I am pleased to give him a companion
Who lures and thrusts and must, as devil, be active.
But ye, true sons of Heaven, it is your duty
To take your joy in the living wealth of beauty.
The changing Essence which ever works and lives
Wall you around with love, serene, secure!
And that which floats in flickering appearance
Fix ye it firm in thoughts that must endure.

CHOIR OF ANGELS.   Thine aspect cheers the Hosts of Heaven
Though what Thine essence none can say,
And all Thy loftiest creations
Keep the high state of their first day.

(Heaven closes)

MEPHISTOPHELES (*alone*).   I like to see the Old One now and then
And try to keep relations on the level.
It's really decent of so great a person
To talk so humanely even to the Devil.

PART I

NIGHT *(In a high-vaulted narrow Gothic [study] FAUST,
restless, in a chair at his desk)*

FAUST.   Here stand I, ach, Philosophy
Behind me and Law and Medicine too
And, to my cost, Theology—
All these I have sweated through and through

---

[10]The serpent that seduced Eve in the Garden of Eden. Mephistopheles intends for Faust
to indulge himself in vulgar, sensual pleasure.

[11]Shun, avoid.

And now you see me a poor fool
As wise as when I entered school!
They call me Master, they call me Doctor,
Ten years now I have dragged my college
Along by the nose through zig and zag
Through up and down and round and round
And this is all that I have found—
The impossibility of knowledge!
It is this that burns away my heart;
Of course I am cleverer than the quacks,
Than master and doctor, than clerk and priest,
I suffer no scruple or doubt in the least,
I have no qualms about devil or burning,
Which is just why all joy is torn from me,
I cannot presume to make use of my learning,
I cannot presume I could open my mind
To proselytize and improve mankind.

Besides, I have neither goods nor gold,
Neither reputation nor rank in the world;
No dog would choose to continue so!
Which is why I have given myself to Magic[12]
To see if the Spirit[13] may grant me to know
Through its force and its voice full many a secret,
May spare the sour sweat that I used to pour out
In talking of what I know nothing about,
May grant me to learn what it is that girds[14]
The world together in its inmost being,
That the seeing its whole germination, the seeing
Its workings, may end my traffic in words.

O couldst thou, light of the full moon,
Look now thy last upon my pain,
Thou for whom I have sat belated
So many midnights here and waited
Till, over books and papers, thou
Didst shine, sad friend, upon my brow!

---

[12]Charms, spells, and rituals which supposedly unlock natural or supernatural secrets.
[13]Supernatural.
[14]Binds, holds.

O could I but walk to and fro
On mountain heights in thy dear glow
Or float with spirits round mountain eyries[15]
Or weave through fields thy glances[16] glean
And freed from all miasmal[17] theories
Bathe in thy dew and wash me clean!

Oh! Am I still stuck in this jail?
This God-damned dreary hole in the wall
Where even the lovely light of heaven
Breaks wanly through the painted panes!
Cooped up among these heaps of books
Gnawed by worms, coated with dust,
Round which to the top of the Gothic vault
A smoke-stained paper forms a crust.
Retorts and canisters lie pell-mell
And pyramids of instruments,
The junk of centuries, dense and mat—
Your world, man! World? They call it that!

And yet you ask why your poor heart
Cramped in your breast should feel such fear,
Why an unspecified misery
Should throw your life so out of gear?
Instead of the living natural world
For which God made all men his sons
You hold a reeking mouldering court
Among assorted skeletons.
Away! There is a world outside!
And this one book of mystic art
Which Nostradamus[18] wrote himself,
Is this not adequate guard and guide?
By this you can tell the course of the stars,
By this, once Nature gives the word,
The soul begins to stir and dawn,
A spirit by a spirit heard.

[15]Heights.
[16]The shimmering moonlight.
[17]Noxious, nauseating.
[18]Nostradamus (1503–1566), a French astrologer and author of prophecies.

In vain your barren studies here
Construe the signs of sanctity.
You Spirits, you are hovering near;
If you can hear me, answer me!

• • •

[Faust, however, learns that the Spirits will not divulge to him the secrets of the
universe, since he is not of their kind, but merely a human being. This rejection
throws him into deepest despair, and suicide seems to him the only way to
escape such a dismal existence. *Ed.*]

I am not like the gods—that I too deeply feel—
No, I am like the worm that burrows through the dust
Which, as it keeps itself alive in the dust,
Is annulled and buried by some casual heel.

Is it not dust that on a thousand shelves
Narrows this high wall round me so?
The junk that with its thousandfold tawdriness
In this moth world keeps me so low?
Shall I find here what I require?
Read maybe in a thousand books how men
Have in the general run tortured themselves,
With but a lucky one now and then?
Why do you grin at me, you hollow skull?[19]
To point out that your brain was once, like mine, confused
And looked for the easy day but in the difficult dusk,
Lusting for truth was led astray and abused?
You instruments, I know you are mocking me
With cog and crank and cylinder.
I stood at the door, you were to be the key;
A key with intricate wards—but the bolt declines to stir.
Mysterious in the light of day
Nature lets none unveil her; if she refuse
To make some revelation to your spirit
You cannot force her with levers and with screws.
You ancient gear I have never used, it is only
Because my father used you that I retain you.
You ancient scroll, you have been turning black

[19]Faust is now addressing various objects in his study.

Since first the dim lamp smoked upon this desk to stain you.
Far better to have squandered the little I have
Than loaded with that little to stay sweating here.
Whatever legacy your fathers left you,
To own it you must earn it dear.
The thing that you fail to use is a load of lead;
The moment can only use what the moment itself has bred.

But why do my eyes fasten upon that spot?
Is that little bottle a magnet to my sight?
Why do I feel of a sudden this lovely illumination
As when the moon flows round us in a dark wood at night?

Bottle, unique little bottle, I salute you
As now I devoutly lift you down. In you
I honor human invention and human skill.
You, the quintessence of all sweet narcotics,
The extract of all rare and deadly powers,
I am your master—show me your good will!
I look on you, my sorrow is mitigated,
I hold you and my struggles are abated,
The flood-tide of my spirit ebbs away, away.
The mirroring waters glitter at my feet,
I am escorted forth on the high seas,
Allured towards new shores by a new day.
A fiery chariot floats on nimble wings
Down to me and I feel myself upbuoyed
To blaze a new trail through the upper air
Into new spheres of energy unalloyed.[20]
Oh this high life, this heavenly rapture! Do *you*
Merit this, you, a moment ago a worm?
Merit it? Aye—only turn your back on the sun
Which enchants the earth, turn your back and be firm!
And brace yourself to tear asunder the gates.
Which everyone longs to shuffle past if he can;
Now is the time to act and acting prove
That God's height need not lower the merit of Man;
Nor tremble at that dark pit in which our fancy
Condemns itself to torments of its own framing,

[20]Pure, unmixed.

But struggle on and upwards to that passage
At the narrow mouth of which all hell is flaming.
Be calm and take this step, though you should fall
Beyond it into nothing—nothing at all.

And you, you loving-cup of shining crystal—
I have not given a thought to you for years—
Down you come now out of your ancient chest!
You glittered at my ancestors' junketings[21]
Enlivening the serious guest
When with you in his hand he proceeded to
    toast his neighbor—
But to-day no neighbor will take you from my hand.
Here is a juice that makes one drunk in a wink;
It fills you full, you cup, with its brown flood.
It was I who made this, I who had it drawn;
So let my whole soul now make my last drink
A high and gala greeting, a toast to the dawn!

        (He raises the cup to his mouth. There is
        an outburst of bells and choirs)

CHORUS OF ANGELS.   Christ is arisen!
           Joy to mortality
           Whom its own fatally
           Earth-bound morality
           Bound in a prison.
FAUST.   What a deep booming, what a ringing tone
    Pulls back the cup from my lips—and with such power!
    So soon are you announcing, you deep bells,
    Easter Day's first festive hour?
    You choirs, do you raise so soon the solacing hymn
    That once round the night of the grave rang out
        from the seraphim[22]
    As man's new covenant[23] and dower?[24]
CHORUS OF WOMEN.   With balm and with spices
           'Twas we laid him out,

---

[21]Feasts.
[22]Angels.
[23]Divine promise (in Christ).
[24]Gift.

                    We who tended him,
                    Faithful, devout;
                    We wound him in linen,
                    Made all clean where he lay,
                    Alas—to discover
                    Christ gone away.
CHORUS OF ANGELS.   Christ is arisen!
                    The loving one! Blest
                    After enduring the
                    Grievous, the curing, the
                    Chastening test.
FAUST.   You heavenly music, strong as you are kind,
    Why do you search me out in the dust?
    Better ring forth where men have open hearts!
    I hear your message, my faith it is that lags behind;
    And miracle is the favorite child of faith.
    Those spheres whence peals the gospel of forgiving,
    Those are beyond what I can dare,
    And yet, so used am I from childhood to this sound,
    It even now summons me back to living.
    Once I could feel the kiss of heavenly love
    Rain down through the calm and solemn Sabbath air,
    Could find a prophecy in the full-toned bell,
    A spasm of happiness in a prayer.
    An ineffably sweet longing bound me
    To quest at random through field and wood
    Where among countless burning tears
    I felt a world rise up around me.
    This hymn announced the lively games of youth, the lovely
    Freedom of Spring's own festival;
    Now with its childlike feelings memory holds me back
    From the last and gravest step of all.
    But you, sweet songs of heaven, keep sounding forth!
    My tears well up, I belong once more to earth.

                    •   •   •

[As is customary, Faust and his study assistant, Wagner, take a stroll on Easter
Sunday. While delighting in the retreating of winter and the visible arrival of
spring, Faust at some time finds himself surrounded by common folk, who
praise him for the healing ability that snatched them from the fangs of a

devouring epidemic. Their praise rings like mockery in Faust's ears since he was and remains ignorant regarding how to treat this illness. Turning homeward, Faust and Wagner notice a poodle, who, it seems, has lost his master. Thereupon, Faust invites the dog to come with him and share his abode. *Ed.*] ·

FAUST'S STUDY

(He enters with the poodle)

FAUST. I have forsaken field and meadow
Which night has laid in a deep bed,
Night that wakes our better soul
With a holy and foreboding dread.
Now wild desires are wrapped in sleep
And all the deeds that burn and break,
The love of Man is waking now,
The love of God begins to wake.

Poodle! Quiet! Don't run hither and thither!
Leave my threshold! Why are you snuffling there?
Lie down behind the stove and rest.
Here's a cushion; it's my best.
Out of doors on the mountain paths
You kept us amused by running riot;
But as my protégé at home
You'll only be welcome if you're quiet.

Ah, when in our narrow cell
The lamp once more imparts good cheer,
Then in our bosom—in the heart
That knows itself—then things grow clear.
Reason once more begins to speak
And the blooms of hope once more to spread;
One hankers for the brooks of life,
Ah, and for life's fountain head.

Don't growl, you poodle! That animal sound
Is not in tune with the holy music
By which my soul is girdled round.
We are used to human beings who jeer
At what they do not understand,
Who grouse at the good and the beautiful

Which often causes them much ado;
But must a dog snarl at it too?

But, ah, already, for all my good intentions
I feel contentment ebbing away in my breast.
Why must the stream so soon run dry
And we be left once more athirst?
I have experienced this so often;
Yet this defect has its compensation,
We learn to prize the supernatural
And hanker after revelation,
Which burns most bright and wins assent
Most in the New Testament.
I feel impelled to open the master text
And this once, with true dedication,
Take the sacred original
And make in my mother tongue my own translation.

(He opens a Bible)

It is written: In the beginning was the Word.[25]
Here I am stuck at once. Who will help me on?
I am unable to grant the Word such merit,
I must translate it differently
If I am truly illumined by the spirit.
It is written: In the beginning was the Mind.
But why should my pen scour
So quickly ahead? Consider that first line well.
Is it the Mind that effects and creates all things?
It *should* read: In the beginning was the Power.
Yet, even as I am changing what I have writ,
Something warns me not to abide by it.
The spirit prompts me, I see in a flash what I need,
And write: In the beginning was the Deed!

Dog! If we two are to share this room,
Leave off your baying,
Leave off your barking!
I can't have such a fellow staying
Around me causing all this bother.

---

[25]The Gospel according to John, Chapter 1, verse 1. The original uses the Greek word *Logos*, which in Hellenistic philosophy stood for "Divine Reason."

One of us or the other
Will have to leave the cell.
Well?
I don't really like to eject you so
But the door is open, you may go.

But what? What do I see?
Can this really happen naturally?
Is it a fact or is it a fraud?
My dog is growing so long and broad!
He raises himself mightily,
That is not a dog's anatomy!
What a phantom have I brought to my house!
He already looks like a river horse
With fiery eyes and frightful jaws—
Aha! But I can give you pause!
For such a hybrid out of hell
Solomon's Key[26] is a good spell.

•   •   •

(MEPHISTOPHELES *comes forward from behind the stove,*
dressed like a travelling scholar) because Faust is a scholar

MEPHISTOPHELES.   What is the noise about? What might the gentle-
man fancy?
FAUST.   So that is what the poodle had inside him!
A travelling scholar? That casus[27] makes me laugh.
MEPHISTOPHELES.   My compliments to the learned gentleman.
You have put me in a sweat—not half!
FAUST.   What is your name?
MEPHISTOPHELES.   The question strikes me as petty
For one who holds the Word in such low repute,
Who, far withdrawn from all mere surface,
Aims only at the Essential Root.[28]

[26]A slim book of sorcery that pretends to be the testament of the Jewish King Solomon.
Intended for his son Roboam (Rehoboam), it gives detailed instructions on how to
become "master over the Spirits" and how to unlock the door to "knowledge and the
understanding of the magical arts and sciences."

[27]Event, situation.

[28]The inner nature of things.

FAUST.   With you, you gentry, what is essential
   The name more often than not supplies,
   As is indeed only too patent
   When they call you Fly-God, Corrupter, Father of Lies.
   All right, who are you then?
MEPHISTOPHELES.   A part of that Power
   Which always wills evil, always procures good.
FAUST.   What do you mean by this conundrum?[29]
MEPHISTOPHELES.   I am the Spirit which always denies.
   And quite rightly; whatever has a beginning
   Deserves to have an undoing;
   It would be better if nothing began at all.
   Thus everything that you call
   Sin, destruction, Evil in short,
   Is my own element, my resort.

• • •

[Following a dialogue in which Mephistopheles identifies his role more closely, spirits cast a slumber on Faust during which the Devil makes his escape from Faust's study. *Ed.*]

(The same room. Later)

FAUST.   Who's knocking? Come in! *Now* who wants to annoy me?
MEPHISTOPHELES (*outside door*).
   It's I.
FAUST.   Come in!
MEPHISTOPHELES (*outside door*).
                   You must say 'Come in' three times.
FAUST.   Come in then!
MEPHISTOPHELES (*entering*).
                   Thank you; you overjoy me.
   We two, I hope, we shall be good friends;
   To chase those megrims[30] of yours away
   I am here like a fine young squire to-day,
   In a suit of scarlet trimmed with gold
   And a little cape of stiff brocade,
   With a cock's feather in my hat

[29]Riddle.
[30]Depressed feelings.

And at my side a long sharp blade,
And the most succinct advice I can give
Is that you dress up just like me,
So that uninhibited and free
You may find out what it means to live.

FAUST.   The pain of earth's constricted life, I fancy,
Will pierce me still, whatever my attire;
I am too old for mere amusement,
Too young to be without desire.
How can the world dispel my doubt?
You must do without, you must do without!
That is the everlasting song
Which rings in every ear, which rings,
And which to us our whole life long
Every hour hoarsely sings.
I wake in the morning only to feel appalled,
My eyes with bitter tears could run
To see the day which in its course
Will not fulfil a wish for me, not one;
The day which whittles away with obstinate carping
All pleasures—even those of anticipation,
Which makes a thousand grimaces to obstruct
My heart when it is stirring in creation.
And again, when night comes down, in anguish
I must stretch out upon my bed
And again no rest is granted me,
For wild dreams fill my mind with dread.
The God who dwells within my bosom
Can make my inmost soul react;
The God who sways my every power
Is powerless with external fact.
And so existence weighs upon my breast
And I long for death and life—life I detest.

MEPHISTOPHELES.   Yet death is never a wholly welcome guest.

FAUST.   O happy is he whom death in the dazzle of victory
Crowns with the bloody laurel in the battling swirl!
Or he whom after the mad and breakneck dance
He comes upon in the arms of a girl!
O to have sunk away, delighted, deleted,
Before the Spirit of the Earth, before his might!

MEPHISTOPHELES.   Yet I know someone who failed to drink
    A brown juice on a certain night.[31]
FAUST.   Your hobby is espionage—is it not?
MEPHISTOPHELES.   Oh I'm not omniscient—but I know a lot.
FAUST.   Whereas that tumult in my soul
    Was stilled by sweet familiar chimes[32]
    Which cozened[33] the child that yet was in me
    With echoes of more happy times,
    I now curse all things that encompass
    The soul with lures and jugglery
    And bind it in this dungeon of grief
    With trickery and flattery.
    Cursed in advance be the high opinion
    That serves our spirit for a cloak!
    Cursed be the dazzle of appearance
    Which bows our senses to its yoke!
    Cursed be the lying dreams of glory,
    The illusion that our name survives!
    Cursed be the flattering things we own,
    Servants and ploughs, children and wives!
    Cursed be Mammon[34] when with his treasures
    He makes us play the adventurous man
    Or when for our luxurious pleasures
    He duly spreads the soft divan!
    A curse on the balsam of the grape!
    A curse on the love that rides for a fall!
    A curse on hope! A curse on faith!
    And a curse on patience most of all!

• • •

MEPHISTOPHELES.   Stop playing with your grief which battens
    Like a vulture on your life, your mind!
    The worst of company would make you feel
    That you are a man among mankind.
    Not that it's really my proposition

---

[31]Mephistopheles here refers to the fact that Faust, after all, did not commit suicide.
[32]The bells of Easter morning.
[33]Deceived.
[34]Wealth.

To shove you among the common men;
Though I'm not one of the Upper Ten,
If you would like a coalition
With me for your career through life,
I am quite ready to fit in,
I'm yours before you can say knife.
I am your comrade;
If you so crave,
I am your servant, I am your slave.

FAUST.   And what have I to undertake in return?

MEPHISTOPHELES.   Oh it's early days to discuss what that is.

FAUST.   No, no, the devil is an egoist
And ready to do nothing gratis[35]
Which is to benefit a stranger.
Tell me your terms and don't prevaricate!
A servant like you in the house is a danger.

MEPHISTOPHELES.   I will bind myself to your service in this world,
To be at your beck and never rest nor slack;
When we meet again on the other side,
In the same coin you shall pay me back.

FAUST.   The other side gives me little trouble;
First batter this present world to rubble,
Then the other may rise—if that's the plan.
This earth is where my springs of joy have started,
And this sun shines on me when broken-hearted;
If I can first from them be parted,
Then let happen what will and can!
I wish to hear no more about it—
Whether there too men hate and love
Or whether in those spheres too, in the future,
There is a Below or an Above.

MEPHISTOPHELES.   With such an outlook you can risk it.
Sign on the line! In these next days you will get
Ravishing samples of my arts;
I am giving you what never man saw yet.

FAUST.   Poor devil, can *you* give anything ever?
Was a human spirit in its high endeavor
Even once understood by one of your breed?

---

[35]Without charge, free.

Have you got food which fails to feed?
Or red gold which, never at rest,
Like mercury runs away through the hand?
A game at which one never wins?
A girl who, even when on my breast,
Pledges herself to my neighbor with her eyes?
The divine and lovely delight of honor
Which falls like a falling star and dies?
Show me the fruits which, before they are plucked, decay
And the trees which day after day renew their green!

MEPHISTOPHELES.   Such a commission doesn't alarm me,
I have such treasures to purvey.
But, my good friend, the time draws on when we
Should be glad to feast at our ease on something good.

FAUST.   If ever I stretch myself on a bed of ease,
Then I am finished! Is that understood?
If ever your flatteries can coax me
To be pleased with myself, if ever you cast
A spell of pleasure that can hoax me—
Then let *that* day be my last!
That's my wager!

MEPHISTOPHELES.   Done!

FAUST.   Let's shake!
If ever I say to the passing moment
'Linger a while! Thou art so fair!'
Then you may cast me into fetters,
I will gladly perish then and there!
Then you may set the death-bell tolling,
Then from my service you are free,
The clock may stop, its hand may fall,
And that be the end of time for me!

MEPHISTOPHELES.   Think what you're saying, we shall
not forget it.

FAUST.   And you are fully within your rights;
I have made no mad or outrageous claim.
If I stay as I am, I am a slave—
Whether yours or another's, it's all the same.

MEPHISTOPHELES.   I shall this very day at the College Banquet
Enter your service with no more ado,
But just one point—As a life-and-death insurance
I must trouble you for a line or two.

FAUST.   So you, you pedant, you too like things in writing?
Have you never known a man? Or a man's word? Never?
Is it not enough that my word of mouth
Puts all my days in bond for ever?
Does not the world rage on in all its streams
And shall a promise hamper *me*?
Yet this illusion reigns within our hearts
And from it who would be gladly free?
Happy the man who can inwardly keep his word;
Whatever the cost, he will not be loath to pay!
But a parchment, duly inscribed and sealed,
Is a bogey from which all wince away.
The word dies on the tip of the pen
And wax and leather lord it then.
What do you, evil spirit, require?
Bronze, marble, parchment, paper?
Quill or chisel or pencil of slate?
You may choose whichever you desire.
MEPHISTOPHELES.   How can you so exaggerate
With such a hectic rhetoric?
Any little snippet is quite good—
And you sign it with one little drop of blood.
FAUST.   If that is enough and is some use,
One may as well pander to your fad.
MEPHISTOPHELES.   Blood is a very special juice.
FAUST.   Only do not fear that I shall break this contract.
What I promise is nothing more
Than what all my powers are striving for.
I have puffed myself up too much, it is only
Your sort that really fits my case.
The great Earth Spirit has despised me
And Nature shuts the door in my face.
The thread of thought is snapped asunder,
I have long loathed knowledge in all its fashions.
In the depths of sensuality
Let us now quench our glowing passions!
And at once make ready every wonder
Of unpenetrated sorcery!
Let us cast ourselves into the torrent of time,
Into the whirl of eventfulness,
Where disappointment and success,

Pleasure and pain may chop and change
As chop and change they will and can;
It is restless action makes the man.
MEPHISTOPHELES.   No limit is fixed for you, no bound;
If you'd like to nibble at everything
Or to seize upon something flying round—
Well, may you have a run for your money!
But seize your chance and don't be funny!
FAUST.   I've told you, it is no question of happiness.
The most painful joy, enamored hate, enlivening
Disgust—I devote myself to all excess.
My breast, now cured of its appetite for knowledge,
From now is open to all and every smart,
And what is allotted to the whole of mankind
That will I sample in my inmost heart,
Grasping the highest and lowest with my spirit,
Piling men's weal and woe upon my neck,
To extend myself to embrace all human selves
And to founder in the end, like them, a wreck.
MEPHISTOPHELES.   O believe *me*, who have been chewing
These iron rations many a thousand year,
No human being can digest
This stuff, from the cradle to the bier.
This universe—believe a devil—
Was made for no one but a god!
He exists in eternal light
But *us* he has brought into the darkness
While *your* sole portion is day and night.

• • •

[Shortly thereafter, Faust and Mephistopheles set out on their journey, with
Mephistopheles acting as the guide, hoping to introduce Faust to the pleasures
of life. The first stop on their way is Auerbach's Keller in Leipzig, a tavern,
where Faust and Mephistopheles join a company of jolly wine-bibbers. However, Faust finds that he has nothing in common with these people, their crude
jokes, and primitive pleasures. Apparently, his lifelong preoccupation with
learning has deadened him to the pleasures of his senses. To revive his sensuality
and at the same time to rejuvenate him, Faust is taken by Mephistopheles to the
kitchen of a witch, who prepares a brew for him. Obviously, Mephistopheles

knows the potency of this brew, because when Faust drinks it, the devil mutters:

> "With a drink like this in you, take care—
> You'll soon see Helens[36] everywhere."

Thanks to Mephistopheles's scheming, the opportunity for Faust to meet his "Helen" is close at hand. *Ed.*]

IN THE STREET

(FAUST accosts GRETCHEN as she passes)

FAUST.   My pretty young lady, might I venture
  To offer you my arm and my escort too?
GRETCHEN.   I'm not a young lady[37] nor am I pretty
  And I can get home without help from you.

(She releases herself and goes off)

FAUST.   By Heaven, she's beautiful, this child!
  I have never seen her parallel.
  So decorous, so virtuous,
  And just a little pert as well.
  The light of her cheek, her lip so red,
  I shall remember till I'm dead!
  The way that she cast down her eye
  Is stamped on my heart as with a die;
  And the way that she got rid of me
  Was a most ravishing thing to see!

(Enter MEPHISTOPHELES)

  Listen to me! Get me that girl!
MEPHISTOPHELES.   Which one?
FAUST.   The one that just went past.
MEPHISTOPHELES.   She? She was coming from her priest,
  Absolved from her sins one and all;
  I'd crept up near the confessional.
  An innocent thing. Innocent? Yes!
  At church with nothing to confess!
  Over that girl I have no power.
FAUST.   Yet she's fourteen if she's an hour.

---

[36]Helen of Troy, the ideal of feminine beauty in ancient Greek mythology.
[37]The title "lady" was restricted to women belonging to nobility.

MEPHISTOPHELES. Why, you're talking like Randy Dick *(French)*
    Who covets every lovely flower
    And all the favors, all the laurels,
    He fancies are for him to pick;
    But it doesn't always work out like that.
FAUST.   My dear Professor of Ancient Morals,
    Spare me your trite morality!
    I tell you straight—and hear me right—
    Unless this object of delight
    Lies in my arms this very night,
    At midnight we part company.
MEPHISTOPHELES.   Haven't you heard: more haste less speed?
    A fortnight is the least I need
    Even to work up an occasion.
FAUST.   If I had only seven hours clear,
    I should not need the devil here
    To bring *this* quest to consummation.
MEPHISTOPHELES.   It's almost French, your line of talk;
    I only ask you not to worry.
    Why make your conquest in a hurry?
    The pleasure is less by a long chalk
    Than when you first by hook and by crook
    Have squeezed your doll and moulded her,
    Using all manner of poppycock
    That foreign novels keep in stock.
FAUST.   I am keen enough without all that.
MEPHISTOPHELES.   Now, joking apart and without aspersion,
    You cannot expect, I tell you flat,
    This beautiful child in quick reversion.
    Immune to all direct attack— *work hard on her*
    We must lay our plots behind her back.
FAUST.   Get me something of my angel's!
    Carry me to her place of rest!
    Get me a garter of my love's!
    Get me a kerchief from her breast!
MEPHISTOPHELES.   That you may see the diligent fashion
    In which I shall abet your passion,
    We won't let a moment waste away,
    I will take you to her room to-day.
FAUST.   And shall I see her? Have her?

MEPHISTOPHELES.   No!
   She will be visiting a neighbor.
   But you in the meanwhile, quite alone,
   Can stay in her aura[38] in her room
   And feast your fill on joys to come.
FAUST.   Can we go now?
MEPHISTOPHELES.   It is still too soon.
FAUST.   Then a present for her!
   Get me one!
                              (Exit FAUST)

MEPHISTOPHELES.   Presents already? Fine. A certain hit!
   I know plenty of pretty places
   And of long-buried jewel-cases;
   I must take stock of them a bit.

                    • • •

[Faust succeeds in wooing Gretchen, last but not least, thanks to gifts of precious jewels supplied by Mephistopheles. Mephistopheles also arranges to have Faust and Gretchen date secretly in the garden of a neighbor woman—that is, without the knowledge of Gretchen's mother and brother Valentine. Mephistopheles tricks the neighbor woman, Mrs. Martha Schwerdtlein, supposedly a widow, into opening her house to him and Faust by pretending to be romantically interested in her. Ed.]

                    MARTHA'S GARDEN

GRETCHEN.   Promise me, Heinrich![39]
FAUST.   If I can!
GRETCHEN.   Tell me: how do you stand in regard to religion?   _she is pure_
   You are indeed a good, good man
   But I think you give it scant attention.
FAUST.   Leave that, my child! You feel what I feel for you;
   For those I love I would give my life and none
   Will I deprive of his sentiments and his church.
GRETCHEN.   That is not right; one must believe thereon.
FAUST.   Must one?
GRETCHEN.   If only I had some influence!
   Nor do you honor the holy sacraments.

---

[38]Surrounding atmosphere.
[39]Heinrich (Henry), Faust's first name as given by Goethe; the character's first name in the legend was Johann (John).

FAUST.   I honor them.
GRETCHEN.   Yes, but not with any zest.
When were you last at mass, when were you last confessed?
Do you believe in God?
FAUST.   My darling, who dare say:
I believe in God?
Ask professor or priest,
Their answers will make an odd
Mockery of you.
GRETCHEN.   You don't believe, you mean?
FAUST.   Do not misunderstand me, my love, my queen!
Who can name him?
Admit on the spot:
I believe in him?
And who can dare
To perceive and declare:
I believe in him not?
The All-Embracing One,
All-Upholding One,
Does he not embrace, uphold,
You, me, Himself?
Does not the Heaven vault itself above us?
Is not the earth established fast below?
And with their friendly glances do not
Eternal stars rise over us?
Do not my eyes look into yours,
And all things thrust
Into your head, into your heart,
And weave in everlasting mystery
Invisibly, visibly, around you?
Fill your heart with *this*, great as it is,
And when this feeling grants you perfect bliss,
Than call it what you will—
Happiness! Heart! Love! God!
I have no name for it!
Feeling is all;
Name is mere sound and reek[40]
Clouding Heaven's light.

[40]Smoke and vapor.

GRETCHEN.   That sounds quite good and right;
   And much as the priest might speak,
   Only not word for word.
FAUST.   It is what all hearts have heard
   In all the places heavenly day can reach,
   Each in his own speech;
   Why not I in mine?
GRETCHEN.   I could almost accept it, you make it sound so fine,
   Still there is something in it that shouldn't be;
   For you have no Christianity.
FAUST.   Dear child!

· · ·

GRETCHEN.   Now I must go.
FAUST.   Oh, can I never rest
   One little hour hanging upon your breast,
   Pressing both breast on breast and soul on soul?
GRETCHEN.   Ah, if I only slept alone!
   I'd gladly leave the door unlatched for you to-night;
   My mother, however, sleeps so light
   And if she found us there, I own
   I should fall dead upon the spot.
FAUST.   You angel, there is no fear of that.
   Here's a little flask. Three drops are all
   It needs—in her drink—to cover nature
   In a deep sleep, a gentle pall.[41]
GRETCHEN.   What would I not do for your sake!
   I hope it will do her no injury.
FAUST.   My love, do you think that of me?
GRETCHEN.   Dearest, I've only to look at you
   And I do not know what drives me to meet your will
   I have already done so much for you
   That little more is left me to fulfil.

· · ·

[The drops that were supposed to afford Gretchen's mother a deep and restful sleep do their job only too well—they dispatch the old woman into everlasting slumber. It is not long until it is rumored in town that virtuous Gretchen

[41]Cloak (of slumber).

has a lover. On a certain night, Gretchen's brother, Valentine, a soldier, who feels greatly shamed by the rumor, hides under his sister's window to catch the villain who supposedly sneaks into Gretchen's room. As Faust and Mephistopheles arrive, Valentine draws his sword. But Mephistopheles causes Valentine's hand to go suddenly lame, allowing Faust to deliver the fatal stab. Some time before the murder of her brother, Gretchen learns that she is pregnant, a discovery that evokes great anxiety in her and sends her into moments of deep depression. When her child is born, Gretchen, in a fit of despair and mental derangement, drowns it in a pond near the village. Accused of murder, she is thrown into a dungeon. Faust, having learned of her plight, and with the help of Mephistopheles, sets out to rescue her. *Ed.*]

DUNGEON (FAUST *with a bunch of keys and a lamp, in front of an iron door*)

FAUST.   A long unwonted trembling seizes me,
The woe of all mankind seizes me fast.
It is here she lives, behind these dripping walls,
Her crime was but a dream too good to last!
And *you* Faust, waver at the door?
You fear to see your love once more?
Go in at once—or her hope of life is past.

(*He tries the key.* GRETCHEN *starts singing inside*) *off key.*

GRETCHEN.   My mother, the whore, (*mad*) *singing*
Who took my life!
My father, the rogue,   *horrible, perversion of an*
Who ate my flesh!   *innocent folk ballad. of*
My little sister   *a peasant.*
My bones did lay   *invokes tradition.*
In a cool, cool glen;
And there I turned to a pretty little wren;
Fly away! Fly away!

(FAUST *opens the lock*)

FAUST.   She does not suspect that her lover is listening—
To the chains clanking, the straw rustling.

(*He enters*)

GRETCHEN.   Oh! They come! O death! It's hard! Hard!
FAUST.   Quiet! I come to set you free.

(*She throws herself at his feet*)

GRETCHEN.   If you are human, feel my misery.

FAUST.   Do not cry out—you will wake the guard.

(He takes hold of the chains to unlock them)

GRETCHEN (*on her knees*).   Who has given you this power,
    Hangman, so to grieve me?
    To fetch me at his midnight hour!
    Have pity! Oh reprieve me!
    Will to-morrow not serve when the bells are rung?

(She gets up)

    I am still so young, I am still so young!
    Is my death so near?
    I was pretty too, that was what brought me here.
    My lover was by, he's far to-day;
    My wreath[42] lies torn, my flowers have been thrown away.
    Don't seize on me so violently!
    What have I done to you? Let me be!
    Let me not vainly beg and implore;
    You know I have never seen you before.

FAUST.   Can I survive this misery?

GRETCHEN.   I am now completely in your power.
    Only let me first suckle my child.
    This night I cherished it, hour by hour;
    To torture me they took it away
    And now I murdered it, so they say.
    And I shall never be happy again.
    People make ballads about me—the heartless crew!
    An old story ends like this—
    Must mine too?

(FAUST throws himself on the ground)

FAUST.   Look! At your feet a lover lies
    To loose you from your miseries.

(GRETCHEN throws herself beside him)

GRETCHEN.   O, let us call on the saints on bended knee!
    Beneath these steps—but see—
    Beneath this sill
    The cauldron of Hell!
    And within,

[42]The bridal wreath, made of dainty flowers and greenery, crowned the bride's head as a symbol of purity. Pregnant or formerly married brides were denied such adornment.

The Evil One in his fury
Raising a din!

FAUST.   Gretchen! Gretchen!

GRETCHEN.   That was my lover's voice!

(She springs up; the chains fall off)

I heard him calling. Where can he be?
No one shall stop me. I am free!
Quick! My arms round his neck!
And lie upon his bosom! Quick!
He called 'Gretchen!' He stood at the door.
Through the whole of Hell's racket and roar,
Through the threats and jeers and from far beyond
I heard that voice so sweet, so fond.

FAUST.   It is I!

GRETCHEN.   It's you? Oh say so once again!

(She clasps him)

It is! It is! Where now is all my pain?
And where the anguish of my captivity?
It's you; you have come to rescue me!
I am saved!
The street is back with me straight away
Where I saw you that first day,
And the happy garden too
Where Martha and I awaited you.

FAUST.   Come! Come!

GRETCHEN.   Oh stay with me, oh do!
Where *you* stay, I would like to, too.

FAUST.   Hurry!
If you don't,
The penalty will be sore.

GRETCHEN.   What! Can you kiss no more?
So short an absence, dear, as this
And you've forgotten how to kiss!
Why do I feel so afraid, clasping your neck?
In the old days your words, your looks,
Were a heavenly flood I could not check
And you kissed me as if you would smother me—
Kiss me now!
Or I'll kiss you!

(She kisses him)

Oh your lips are cold as stone!
And dumb!
What has become
Of your love?
Who has robbed me of my own?

(She turns away from him)

FAUST. Come! Follow me, my love! Be bold!
I will cherish you after a thousandfold.
Only follow me now! That is all I ask of you.
GRETCHEN. And is it you then? Really? Is it true?
FAUST.   It is! But come!
GRETCHEN. You are undoing each chain,
You take me to your arms again.
How comes it you are not afraid of me?
Do you know, my love, *whom* you are setting free?
FAUST. Come! The deep night is passing by and beyond.
GRETCHEN. My mother, I have murdered her;
I drowned my child in the pond.
Was it not a gift to you and me?
To you too—You! Are you what you seem?
Give me your hand! It is not a dream!
Your dear hand—but, oh, it's wet!
Wipe it off! I think
There is blood[43] on it.
Oh God! What have you done?
Put up your sword,
I beg you to.

• • •

FAUST. Collect yourself!
One step—just one—and you are free.
GRETCHEN. If only we were past the hill!
There sits my mother on a stone—
My brain goes cold and dead—
There sits my mother on a stone—
And wags and wags her head.

---

[43]The blood of Gretchen's brother Valentine.

No sign, no nod, her head is such a weight
She'll wake no more, she slept so late.
She slept that we might sport and play.
What a time that was of holiday!

FAUST.   If prayer and argument are no resource,
I will risk saving you by force.

GRETCHEN.   No! I will have no violence! Let me go!
Don't seize me in that murderous grip!
I have done everything else for you, you know.

FAUST.   My love! My love! The day is dawning!

GRETCHEN.   Day! Yes, it's growing day! The last day breaks on me!
My wedding day it was to be!
Tell no one you had been before with Gretchen.
Alas for my garland!
There's no more chance!
We shall meet again—
But not at the dance.
The people are thronging—but silently;
Street and square
Cannot hold them there.
The bell tolls—it tolls for *me*.
How they seize me, bind me, like a slave!
Already I'm swept away to the block.
Already there jabs at every neck,
The sharp blade which jabs at mine.
The world lies mute as the grave.

FAUST.   I wish I had never been born!

(MEPHISTOPHELES *appears outside*)

MEPHISTOPHELES.   Away! Or you are lost.
Futile wavering! Waiting and prating!
My horses are shivering,
The dawn's at the door.

GRETCHEN.   What rises up from the floor?
It's he! Send him away! It's he!
What does he want in the holy place?
It is I he wants!

FAUST.   You shall live!

GRETCHEN.   Judgment of God! I have given myself to Thee!

MEPHISTOPHELES (*to* FAUST).   Come! Or I'll leave you both
in the lurch.

GRETCHEN.   O Father, save me! I am Thine!
  You angels! Hosts of the Heavenly Church,
  Guard me, stand round in serried line!
  Heinrich! I shudder to look at you.

[handwritten: pleads for redemption]

MEPHISTOPHELES.   She is condemned!

VOICE FROM ABOVE.   Redeemed!

MEPHISTOPHELES.   Follow me!

  (He vanishes with FAUST*)*

VOICE (*from within, dying away*).   Heinrich! Heinrich!

[handwritten: Ewige Weibliche - "Eternal femine" Mary can ask God to reverse judgement Catholic]

PART II

[Part II, even much more than Part I, is a continuous and rapid succession of images, people, and problems. At the beginning of this part of the drama we learn that Faust took up services with the "Emperor," which, however, did not usher in better days, but rather caused upheavals and climaxed in war. As a reward for these services the Emperor gave Faust a useless stretch of land near the sea—a swamp, to be precise. Next, Faust entered the world of classical Greece where, with beautiful Helen, he sired a son, Euphorion. Like the mythological Icarus, Euphorion rose into the air and then perished when he suddenly fell to the ground. Faust's former assistant, Wagner—now a scientist in his own right, returns in Part II. He has succeeded in creating Homunculus, an artificial man, by means of chemistry and fire. Near the close of the drama, Faust, blinded by age and nearly one hundred years old, sets out to shore up his own domain by draining the very swamp he received from the Emperor. Mephistopheles supplies him with cheap labor, so-called Lemurs, "half-alives patched up with thin sinews and skulls and femurs."[44] While the Lemurs are actually digging a grave for his body, Faust imagines that they are building an earthen dam to protect his land from the sea. *Ed.*]

[handwritten: ignorance or second sight.]

FAUST (*blinded*).   The night seems pressing in more thickly, thickly,
  Yet in my inmost heart a light shines clear;
  What I have planned, I must complete it quickly;
  Only the master's word is weighty here.
  Up and to work, my men! Each man of you!
  And bring my bold conception to full view.
  Take up your tools and toil with pick and spade!
  What has been outlined must at once be *made*.
  Good order, active diligence,
  Ensure the fairest recompense;

[44]Thigh-bones.

[handwritten: he is draining a swamp for his own good, for good of society.]

That this vast work completion find,
A thousand hands need but one mind.

MEPHISTOPHELES (*leading the way, as foreman*).   Come on, come on!
Come in, come in!
You gangling gang of Lemurs,
You half-alives patched up with thin
Sinews and skulls and femurs.

LEMURS (*in chorus*).   You call us, here we are at hand;
And, as we understand it,
We stand to win a stretch of land
Intended as our mandate.
Our pointed staves we have them here,
Our chain to measure sections,
But why you called on us, we fear,
Has slipped our recollections.

MEPHISTOPHELES.   Artistic efforts we can spare;
And just let each one's nature guide him!
Let now the longest lie his length down there,
You others prize away the turf beside him;
As for your forebears long asleep,
Dig you an oblong, long and deep.
To narrow house from palace hall
Is such a stupid way to end it all.

(*The Lemurs begin to dig, with mocking gestures*)

LEMURS.   When I was young and lived and loved,
Methought it was passing sweet;
In the merry rout and roundabout
There would I twirl my feet.

But sneaking Age has upped his crutch
And downed me unaware;
I stumbled over the door of the grave—
Why was it open *there*?

FAUST (*groping his way*).   Oh how this clink of spades rejoices me!
For that is my conscripted labor,
The earth is now her own good neighbor
And sets the waves a boundary—
Confinement strict and strenuous.

MEPHISTOPHELES (*aside*).   And yet you've only toiled for *us*
With all your damning, all your dyking—

Spreading a feast to Neptune's liking
To glut that water-demon's maw.[45]
In all respects you're lost and stranded,
The elements with us have banded—
Annihilation is the law.

FAUST.   Foreman!

MEPHISTOPHELES.   Here!

FAUST.   Use every means you can;
Bring all your gangs up and exhort them—
Threaten them if you like or court them—
But pay or woo or force each man!
And day by day send word to me, assessing
How my intended earthworks are progressing.

MEPHISTOPHELES (*half aloud*).   The word to-day, from
     what I've heard,
Is not 'intended' but 'interred'.

FAUST.   A swamp along the mountains' flank
Makes all my previous gains contaminate;
My deeds, if I could drain this sink,
Would culminate as well as terminate:
To open to the millions living space,
Not danger-proof but free to run their race.
Green fields and fruitful; men and cattle hiving
Upon this newest earth at once and thriving,
Settled at once beneath this sheltering hill
Heaped by the masses' brave and busy skill.
With such a heavenly land behind this hedge,
The sea beyond may bluster to its edge
And, as it gnaws to swamp the work of masons,
To stop the gap one common impulse hastens.
Aye! Wedded to this concept like a wife,
I find this wisdom's final form:
He only earns his freedom and his life
Who takes them every day by storm.
And so a man, beset by dangers here,
As child, man, old man, spends his manly year.
Oh to see such activity,
Treading free ground with people that are free!

[45]Stomach.

Then could I bid the passing moment:
'Linger a while, thou art so fair!'[46]   *a creative act cannot be evil.*
The traces of my earthly days can never
Sink in the aeons[47] unaware.
And I, who feel ahead such heights of bliss,
At last enjoy my highest moment—this.

> (FAUST *sinks back [and dies]; the Lemurs seize him*
> *and lay him on the ground*)

MEPHISTOPHELES.   By no joy sated, filled by no success,
Still whoring after shapes that flutter past,
This last ill moment of sheer emptiness—
The poor man yearns to hold it fast.
He who withstood me with such strength,
Time masters him and here he lies his length.
The clock stands still—

CHORUS.   Stands still! Like
midnight . . . silent . . . stilled.
Its hand drops down.

MEPHISTOPHELES.   Drops down; it is fulfilled.

LEMURS.   It is gone by.

MEPHISTOPHELES.   Gone by! A stupid phrase.
Why say gone by?
Gone by—pure naught—complete monotony.
What use these cycles of creation!
Or snatching off the creatures to negation!
'It is gone by!'—and we can draw the inference:
If it had *not* been, it would make no difference;
The wheel revolves the same, no more, no less.
I should prefer eternal emptiness.

• • •

MEPHISTOPHELES.   Here lies the corpse and if the soul would flee
At once I show the bond, the blood-signed scroll;
Though now, alas, they have so many means
To cheat the devil of a soul.
Our old procedure gives offense,

---

[46]Legalists will forever debate whether or not Faust lost the bet because, when he spoke
these fateful words (see Part I, page 240), he beheld a *vision*, rather than reality.

[47]Ages.

Our new has not yet found endorsement;
Once I'd have managed it alone,
Now I must look for reinforcement.
Come up, you devils! Make it double quick!
You straight-horned peers and crooked-horned as well,
You old and sterling devil-stock,
Come up—and bring with you the jaws of Hell!

   (The Jaws of Hell open upon the left)

The eye-teeth gape; the throat's enormous vault
Spews forth a raging fiery flow
And through the smoking cyclone of the gullet
I see the infernal city's eternal glow.
You do right well to make the sinner quake;
And yet they think it all a dream, a fake.
Now, devils, watch this body! How does it seem?
See if you see a phosphorescent gleam.
That is the little soul, Psyche with wings—
Pull out her wings and it's a noisome worm;
With my own seal I'll set my stamp upon her,
Then forth with her into the fiery storm!
Come, claw and comb the air, strain every nerve
To catch her though she flutter, though she swerve.
To stay in her old lodging gives her pain;
The genius is about to leave the brain.

   (Glory, from above, on the right)

THE HOST OF HEAVEN.   Fly, as directed,
   Heaven's elected,
   Serenely whereby
   Sin shall have pardon,
   Dust become garden;
   Stay your progression,
   Make intercession,
   Trace for all natures
   A path to the sky.
MEPHISTOPHELES.   Discords I hear, a filthy strumming tumbling
   Down from the sky with the unwelcome day;
   That is the angels' boyish-girlish fumbling,
   Their canting taste *likes* it to sound that way.
   You know how we, in hours of deep damnation,

Have schemed annihilation for mankind;
Those angels use for adoration
The greatest stigma[48] we could find.
They come so fawningly, the milksops!
They've kidnapped many souls before our eyes,
They fight us back with our own weapons;
They too are devils—in disguise.
Defeat to-day would mean disgrace eternal;
So stand around the grave and stand infernal![49]

• • •

ANGEL.   See, we approach—why do you shrink away?
We come; if you can face us—why, then, stay!

(The Angels, closing in, occupy all the space)

CHOIR OF ANGELS.   Flames of dear feeling,
Rise beyond seeing!
Self-condemned being—
Truth be its healing!
Blessed transition
Forth from perdition,[50]
Into Eternity,
Into the One!

MEPHISTOPHELES *(collecting himself)*.   Look! The damned flames are
out that caused my fall.
Now I become myself and curse you one and all!

CHOIR OF ANGELS.   Light of Creation!
Whom it embraces
Finds all the graces
Found in salvation.
Praising in unison
Rise to your goal!
Purged is the air now—
Breathe now the soul!

(They soar up, carrying away the immortal part of FAUST)

MEPHISTOPHELES *(looking around him)*.   But how is this? Where have
they moved away to?

---

[48]Mark of shame, (the Crucifix).
[49]Immovable.
[50]Eternal damnation.

You juveniles, to take me by surprise!
Flying off heavenwards—and with my prey too;
They nibbled at this grave to win this prize.
Wresting from me a great and matchless treasure,
That noble soul which gave me right of seizure
They've filched by throwing rose-dust in my eyes.
Who is there now to lend an ear to
My wrong, restore my hard-earned right?
You have been hoaxed—so late in your career too—
It's your own fault, you're in a lurid[51] plight.
Such gross mismanagement—outrageous!
Such a great outlay squandered! Oh the shame!
Erotic folly, vulgar lust, contagious
To an old devil at the game!
Experience has indulged its appetite
On such a childish-foolish level;
When all is said, the folly is not slight
Which in the end has seized the devil.

• • •

ANGELS (*floating in the higher air, carrying the immortal part of* FAUST).
Saved, saved now is that precious part
Of our spirit world from evil:
'Should a man strive with all his heart, ⎤ Moral.
Heaven can foil the devil.' ⎦
And if love also from on high
Has helped him through his sorrow,
The hallowed legions of the sky
Will give him glad good morrow.

• • •

Whoever strives with all their power, We are allowed to save.

Faust realizes nature of goodness.
- he is also redeem by eternal feminine

17

Romantic Poetry

ROMANTICISM, *an intellectual style that flourished in the Western world from about 1780 to 1850, was generally based on a faith in the value of the unseen and the ability of human beings to discover and express hidden truth by the use of imagination, emotion, and inspiration. Great art, in the romantic view, was the expression, in new, appropriate language, of the basic moral and aesthetic truths that would bring happiness to human beings. Specifically, this imaginative faith held to a belief in the surpassing goodness and glory of physical nature, in the primacy of the* individual, *and in the truth of the individual's subjective feelings. Romanticism was, at the same time, fascinated with the remote in space and time, with the dramatic and violent, and with the melancholy and terrible. Along with these feelings, the romantics rejected the world as it was and rebelled against the social, intellectual, and aesthetic standards of their time.*

Lyric poetry was the greatest literary expression of romanticism, and it has seldom been equaled in color, sensuousness, and imaginative scope. For the romantic rebels, the poem was an organic whole, expressing more than any paraphrase, and to be grasped only in terms of the unique world it had created. The poem sprang from the individual creator's mystical experience and had no basis in ordinary social discourse.

The poems reprinted here are prime examples of romantic lyric poetry. "Lines Composed a Few Miles Above Tintern Abbey" (1798), by William Wordsworth *(1770–1850), reflects the poet's lifelong conviction that truth and joy lay in the union of the individual with external nature and that this experience could be made clear to others in artistic, symbolic forms. The poem itself is a quiet reflection expressed in smooth, rolling phrases of blank verse. It describes the development of the poet's responses to nature, from childhood experiences of it to a full religious communion with its beauty and harmony.*

The second poem by Wordsworth entitled "We Are Seven," also was written in 1798 and published in the same year. Having met the young girl in 1793, and recalling that encounter, he composed this poem, which delights through its simplicity and the girl's charm and innocence. The first line of the poem was added by an associate of Wordsworth in jesting reference to a mutual friend, James Tobin ("Jim").

"Ode on a Grecian Urn," by John Keats (1795-1821), has as its themes art and life. Written in 1820, near the end of the short, tragic life of the poet, it is an example of his self-discipline and craftsmanship as well as his sensuous appeal and richness of color and forms. Keats finds, in the scenes of life carved on an ancient Grecian urn, an expression of transcendent art that resolved the para-doxes of the arrested action: the life in death, past and present, poetry and reality, beauty and truth.

Heinrich Heine (1797–1856) is viewed by many as the leading romantic poet of German tongue, whose poetry also became known in English- and French-speaking countries. This man, who was born into a Jewish family in the Rhineland and, for most of his life, was a step-child of good fortune, loved the German language and Germany. But he disliked that nation's sometimes loud and vulgar nationalism, as well as the stifling conservatism of its business class. Having come in contact early in life with liberty and the progressive ideas of the French Revolution, he felt out of place in a Germany where the shackles of restored conservatism (1815; post-Napoleonic) kept down everything progres-sive. In 1831, he moved to Paris where he continued to write German poetry, essays, and stories.

The three poems of Heine chosen here (published in 1821, 1827, and 1844) are among his most representative and best loved (the first one is a ballad). They display vivid imagery, emotional intensity, and a bittersweet melancholia. Incidentally, Heine briefly saw his mother ("Night Thoughts") for the last time in 1844. In the following year he suffered a stroke, followed by paraly-sis of the spine, a condition which tied him to his "mattress grave" until his death (1856).

The last poem is by Walt Whitman (1819–1892), a great American poet, robust man of the people, and romantic rebel. In the free-flowing verse and large rhythms of "Out of the Cradle Endlessly Rocking" (1859), he recaptures the intense sadness of the childhood experience of a lost love. This memory calls him to a poetic destiny whose fulfillment is death, which he joyfully hails as the completion of life.

WILLIAM WORDSWORTH

Lines Composed a Few Miles Above Tintern Abbey,[1] *on Revisiting the Banks of the Wye During a Tour. July 13, 1798*

Five years have past; five summers, with the length
Of five long winters! and again I hear
These waters, rolling from their mountain-springs
With a soft inland murmur.—Once again
Do I behold these steep and lofty cliffs,
That on a wild, secluded scene impress
Thoughts of more deep seclusion, and connect
The landscape with the quiet of the sky.
The day is come when I again repose
Here, under this dark sycamore, and view
These plots of cottage-ground, these orchard-tufts,
Which at this season, with their unripe fruits,
Are clad in one green hue, and lose themselves
'Mid groves and copses. Once again I see
These hedge-rows, hardly hedge-rows, little lines
Of sportive wood run wild: these pastoral farms,
Green to the very door; and wreaths of smoke
Sent up, in silence, from among the trees!
With some uncertain notice, as might seem
Of vagrant dwellers in the houseless woods,
Or of some Hermit's cave, where by his fire
The Hermit sits alone.
These beauteous forms,
Through a long absence, have not been to me
As is a landscape to a blind man's eye:
But oft, in lonely rooms, and 'mid the din
Of towns and cities, I have owed to them,
In hours of weariness, sensations sweet,
Felt in the blood, and felt along the heart;
And passing even into my purer mind,
With tranquil restoration:—feelings too

[1]A medieval monastery, whose ruins are found on a wooded hillside of the River Wye, about ten miles from its mouth. The river rises from springs in the mountains of Wales and flows southeasterly to the Bristol Channel.

ROMANTIC POETRY   "Lines Composed a Few Miles Above Tintern Abbey," in *The Poetical Works of William Wordsworth* (Boston: Houghton, Osgood, 1880), II, 186–91.

Of unremembered pleasure: such, perhaps,
As have no slight or trivial influence
On the best portion of a good man's life,
His little, nameless, unremembered acts
Of kindness and of love. Nor less, I trust,
To them I may have owed another gift,
Of aspect more sublime: that blessed mood,
In which the burden of the mystery,
In which the heavy and the weary weight
Of all this unintelligible world,
Is lightened:—that serene and blessed mood,
In which the affections gently lead us on,—
Until, the breath of this corporeal frame
And even the motion of our human blood
Almost suspended, we are laid asleep
In body, and become a living soul:
While with an eye made quiet by the power
Of harmony, and the deep power of joy,
We see into the life of things!
If this
Be but a vain belief, yet, oh! how oft—
In darkness and amid the many shapes
Of joyless daylight; when the fretful stir
Unprofitable, and the fever of the world,
Have hung upon the beatings of my heart—
How oft, in spirit, have I turned to thee,
O sylvan Wye! thou wanderer through the woods,
How often has my spirit turned to thee!

And now, with gleams of half-extinguished thought,
With many recognitions dim and faint,
And somewhat of a sad perplexity,
The picture of the mind revives again:
While here I stand, not only with the sense
Of present pleasure, but with pleasing thoughts
That in this moment there is life and food
For future years. And so I dare to hope,
Though changed, no doubt, from what I was when first
I came among these hills; when like a roe
I bounded o'er the mountains, by the sides
Of the deep rivers, and the lonely streams,

Wherever nature led: more like a man
Flying from something that he dreads, than one
Who sought the thing he loved. For nature then
(The coarser pleasures of my boyish days
And their glad animal movements all gone by)
To me was all in all.—I cannot paint
What then I was. The sounding cataract
Haunted me like a passion: the tall rock,
The mountain, and the deep and gloomy wood,
Their colors and their forms, were then to me
An appetite; a feeling and a love,
That had no need of a remoter charm
By thoughts supplied, nor any interest
Unborrowed from the eye.—That time is past,
And all its aching joys are now no more,
And all its dizzy raptures. Not for this
Faint I, nor mourn nor murmur; other gifts
Have followed; for such loss, I would believe,
Abundant recompense. For I have learned
To look on nature, not as in the hour
Of thoughtless youth; but hearing oftentimes
The still, sad music of humanity,
Nor harsh nor grating, though of ample power
To chasten and subdue. And I have felt
A presence that disturbs me with the joy
Of elevated thoughts; a sense sublime
Of something far more deeply interfused,
Whose dwelling is the light of setting suns,
And the round ocean, and the living air,
And the blue sky, and in the mind of man:
A motion and a spirit, that impels
All thinking things, all objects of all thought,
And rolls through all things. Therefore am I still
A lover of the meadows and the woods,
And mountains; and of all that we behold
From this green earth; of all the mighty world
Of eye, and ear,—both what they half create,
And what perceive; well pleased to recognize
In nature and the language of the sense,
The anchor of my purest thoughts, the nurse,

The guide, the guardian of my heart, and soul
Of all my moral being.
                              Nor perchance,
If I were not thus taught, should I the more
Suffer my genial spirits to decay:
For thou art with me here upon the banks
Of this fair river; thou my dearest Friend,
My dear, dear Friend; and in thy voice I catch
The language of my former heart, and read
My former pleasures in the shooting lights
Of thy wild eyes. O yet a little while
May I behold in thee what I was once,
My dear, dear Sister! and this prayer I make,
Knowing that Nature never did betray
The heart that loved her; 'tis her privilege,
Through all the years of this our life, to lead
From joy to joy: for she can so inform
The mind that is within us, so impress
With quietness and beauty, and so feed
With lofty thoughts, that neither evil tongues,
Rash judgments, nor the sneers of selfish men,
Nor greetings where no kindness is, nor all
The dreary intercourse of daily life,
Shall e'er prevail against us, or disturb
Our cheerful faith, that all which we behold
Is full of blessings. Therefore let the moon
Shine on thee in thy solitary walk;
And let the misty mountain-winds be free
To blow against thee: and, in after years,
When these wild ecstasies shall be matured
Into a sober pleasure; when thy mind
Shall be a mansion for all lovely forms,
Thy memory be as a dwelling-place
For all sweet sounds and harmonies; O, then,
If solitude, or fear, or pain, or grief,
Should be thy portion, with what healing thoughts
Of tender joy wilt thou remember me,
And these my exhortations! Nor, perchance,—
If I should be where I no more can hear
Thy voice, nor catch from thy wild eyes these gleams

Of past existence,—wilt thou then forget
That on the banks of this delightful stream
We stood together; and that I, so long
A worshipper of Nature, hither came
Unwearied in that service: rather say
With warmer love,—O with far deeper zeal
Of holier love. Nor wilt thou then forget,
That after many wanderings, many years
Of absence, these steep woods and lofty cliffs,
And this green pastoral landscape, were to me
More dear, both for themselves and for thy sake!

We Are Seven

A simple child, dear brother Jim,[2]
That lightly draws its breath,
And feels its life in every limb,
What should it know of death?

I met a little cottage girl:
She was eight years old, she said;
Her hair was thick with many a curl
That clustered round her head.

She had a rustic, woodland air,
And she was wildly clad;
Her eyes were fair, and very fair,
—Her beauty made me glad.

'Sisters and brothers, little Maid,
How many may you be?'
'How many? Seven in all,' she said,
And wondering looked at me.

'And where are they? I pray you tell.'
She answered, 'Seven are we;
And two of us at Conway dwell,
And two are gone to sea.

---

[2]James Tobin, a friend of Wordsworth.

ROMANTIC POETRY   "We Are Seven," in *The Poetical Works of William Wordsworth*, ed. Edward Dowden (New York: George Bell & Sons, 1892), I, 182–84.

Two of us in the church-yard lie,
My sister and my brother,
And, in the church-yard cottage, I
Dwell near them with my mother.'

'You say that two at Conway dwell,
And two are gone to sea,
Yet you are seven; I pray you tell,
Sweet Maid, how this may be?'

Then did the little Maid reply,
'Seven boys and girls are we;
Two of us in the church-yard lie,
Beneath the church-yard tree.'

'You run about, my little Maid,
Your limbs they are alive;
If two are in the church-yard laid,
Then you are only five.'

'Their graves are green, they may be seen,'
The little Maid replied,
'Twelve steps or more from my mother's door,
And they are side by side.

My stockings there I often knit,
My kerchief there I hem;
And there upon the ground I sit,
And sing a song to them.

And often after sunset, Sir,
When it is light and fair,
I take my little porringer,[3]
And eat my supper there.

The first that died was sister Jane;
In bed she moaning lay,
Till God released her of her pain,
And then she went away.

So in the church-yard she was laid,
And, when the grass was dry,

---

[3] A bowl for soup or porridge.

Together round her grave we played,
My brother John and I.

And when the ground was white with snow,
And I could run and slide,
My brother John was forced to go,
And he lies by her side.'

'How many are you, then,' said I,
'If they two are in heaven?'
Quick was the little Maid's reply,
'O Master! we are seven.'

'But they are dead; those two are dead!
Their spirits are in heaven!'
'Twas throwing words away; for still
The little Maid would have her will,
And said, 'Nay, we are seven!' _ *she has a communicate with their spirits*

JOHN KEATS

points out ideal + reality.

Ode on a Grecian Urn

Thou still unravish'd bride of quietness!
    Thou foster-child of Silence and slow Time,
Sylvan historian,[4] who canst thus express
    A flowery tale more sweetly than our rhyme:
What leaf-fringed legend haunts about thy shape
    Of deities or mortals, or of both,
        In Tempe[5] or the dales of Arcady?[6]
    What men or gods are these? What maidens loath?
What mad pursuit? What struggle to escape?
        What pipes and timbrels? What wild ecstasy?

Heard melodies are sweet, but those unheard
    Are sweeter; therefore, ye soft pipes, play on;

[4]The pictures on the urn are a record of history.

[5]Valley along the Tempe River in northern Greece.

[6]The central region of the Peloponnesus (southern Greece).

ROMANTIC POETRY   "Ode on a Grecian Urn," in the *Poetical Works of John Keats* (Boston: Little, Brown, 1854), 310–12.

Imagined music is more perfect than real ideal

Not to the sensual ear, but, more endear'd,
    Pipe to the spirit ditties of no tone:
Fair youth, beneath the trees, thou canst not leave
    Thy song, nor ever can those trees be bare;
      Bold Lover, never, never canst thou kiss,
Though winning near the goal—yet, do not grieve;
    She cannot fade, though thou hast not thy bliss,
    Forever wilt thou love, and she be fair!

Ah, happy, happy boughs! that cannot shed
    Your leaves, nor ever bid the Spring adieu;
And, happy melodist, unwearièd,
    Forever piping songs forever new;
More happy love! more happy, happy love!
    Forever warm and still to be enjoy'd,
      Forever panting and forever young;
All breathing human passion far above,
    That leaves a heart high sorrowful and cloy'd,
      A burning forehead, and a parching tongue.

Who are these coming to the sacrifice?
    To what green altar, O mysterious priest,
Lead'st thou that heifer lowing at the skies,
    And all her silken flanks with garlands drest?
What little town by river or sea-shore,
    Or mountain-built with peaceful citadel,
      Is emptied of its folk, this pious morn?
And, little town, thy streets forevermore
    Will silent be; and not a soul to tell
      Why thou art desolate, can e'er return.

O Attic[7] shape! Fair attitude! with brede[8]
    Of marble men and maidens overwrought.[9]
With forest branches and the trodden weed;
    Thou, silent form! dost tease us out of thought
As doth eternity: Cold Pastoral!
    When old age shall this generation waste,

[7]Classical, refined.
[8]As if interwoven, flowing.
[9]Moving around the surface of the urn.

Thou shalt remain, in midst of other woe
Than ours, a friend to man, to whom thou say'st,
"Beauty is truth, truth beauty,"—that is all
Ye know on earth, and all ye need to know.

perfect is beautiful; perfect + beautiful = ideal (Plato)

HEINRICH HEINE

The Grenadiers

Toward France came walking two grenadiers,[10]
They had been captives in Russia.
They hung their heads in shame and tears
When they reached quarters in Prussia;

For there they heard the woeful fate
That the power of France was shaken,
Vanquished the army, once so great—
And the Emperor, the Emperor taken.

Then wept together the grenadiers
At the doleful news they were learning;
The one said: "Brother, what cause for tears!
Oh, how my old wound is burning!"

The other spoke: "Done is the dance!
My own life I don't cherish,
But I've a wife and child in France
Who without me will perish."

"What matters wife and child to me
When our honor is lost and forsaken?
Let them go beg if they hungry be—
My Emperor, my Emperor taken.

"When I now die, grant one request,
Which, brother, keeps me worried,
Oh, take my body along, in the bless'd
French soil I want to be buried.

[10]Soldiers of the army of Napoleon I, who in 1812 invaded Russia but was defeated.

ROMANTIC POETRY   "The Grenadiers," "Loreley," from *Heinrich Heine: Lyric Poems and Ballads*, trans. Ernst Feise, 33–35, 47–49, reprinted by permission of the University of Pittsburgh Press. © 1961 by University of Pittsburgh Press.

"Lay the Legion's cross with crimson band
On my heart—do grant this favor!
And put the musket in my hand
And gird me with my saber.

"Thus shall I harken for evermore,
A sentry of our French forces,
Until I hear the cannons roar
And the neighing of galloping horses.

"Then rides my Emperor over my grave,
Our swords gunflashes reflecting,
Then shall I rise full-armed from the grave—
The Emperor, the Emperor protecting."

Loreley[11]

I do not know what haunts me,
What saddened my mind all day;
An age-old tale confounds me,
A spell I cannot allay.

The air is cool and in twilight
The Rhine's dark waters flow;
The peak of the mountain in highlight
Reflects the evening glow.

There sits a lovely maiden
Above, so wondrous fair,
With shining jewels laden,
She combs her golden hair.

It falls through her comb in a shower,
And over the valley rings
A song of mysterious power
That lovely maiden sings.

The boatman in his small skiff is
Seized by turbulent love,
No longer he marks where the cliff is,
He looks to the mountain above.

[11]A legendary maiden who sat on a high rock which extended far into the River Rhine,
Germany, thus posing a dangerous distraction to boatmen.

I think the waves must fling him
Against the reefs nearby,
And that did with her singing
The lovely Loreley.

Night Thoughts

At night I think of Germany,
And then there is no sleep for me:
I cannot shut my eyes at all,
And down my cheeks the hot tears fall.

The seasons come and pass away!
Twelve years have vanished since the day
I told my mother I must go;
My yearnings and desires grow.

My yearnings and desires swell.
I'm under the old lady's spell;
My mother's always in my mind—
May God be close to her, and kind!

My dear old lady loves me so!
And all her tender letters show
How dreadfully her hand was shaking;
And how her mother-heart is aching.

I think of her both night and day.
Full twelve long years have flown away,
Full twelve long years have drifted past
Since I embraced my mother last.

The German nation will not fail—
It is a sturdy land, and hale,
And with its towering oak and lime
Will prosper till the end of time.

I would not give it half a care
If mother weren't living there;

ROMANTIC POETRY "Night Thoughts," trans. Aaron Kramer, from *The Poetry of Heinrich Heine*, ed. Frederic Ewen (New York: Citadel Press, 1969), 134–35, reprinted by permission of Citadel Press.

The homeland never will decay;
My mother, though, might pass away.

Since my departure, many fell
Of those I knew and loved so well—
When I begin to count the toll
The blood is driven from my soul.

Yet I must count—and with the count
I feel my pangs begin to mount.
My breast is crushed, as though the dead
Roll over it. Thank God! they've fled.

Thank God! at last the morning light
Bursts through my windows: French and bright.
My wife[12] is coming—fair as day—
And smiles my German cares away.

WALT WHITMAN

Out of the Cradle Endlessly Rocking

Out of the cradle endlessly rocking,
Out of the mocking-bird's throat, the musical shuttle,
Out of the Ninth-month midnight,
Over the sterile sands and the fields beyond, where the child leaving
    his bed wander'd alone, bareheaded, barefoot,
Down from the shower'd halo,
Up from the mystic play of shadows twining and twisting as if they
    were alive,
Out from the patches of briers and blackberries,
From the memories of the bird that chanted to me,
From your memories sad brother, from the fitful risings and fallings
    I heard,
From under that yellow half-moon late-risen and swollen as if
    with tears,

---

[12]Heine met "Mathilde"—who was eighteen years younger—in 1834 and legalized their liaison in 1841. She was a simple girl from the French countryside, cheerful and light-hearted.

ROMANTIC POETRY   Walt Whitman, "Out of the Cradle Endlessly Rocking," in *Leaves of Grass* (Philadelphia: McKay, 1884), 196–201.

From those beginning notes of yearning and love there in the mist,
From the thousand responses of my heart never to cease,
From the myriad thence-arous'd words,
From the word stronger and more delicious than any,
From such as now they start the scene revisiting,
As a flock, twittering, rising, or overhead passing,
Borne hither, ere all eludes me, hurriedly,
A man, yet by these tears a little boy again,
Throwing myself on the sand, confronting the waves,
I, chanter of pains and joys, uniter of here and hereafter,
Taking all hints to use them, but swiftly leaping beyond them,
A reminiscence sing.

Once Paumanok,[13]
When the lilac-scent was in the air and Fifth-month grass
   was growing,
Up this seashore in some briers,
Two feather'd guests from Alabama, two together,
And their nest, and four light-green eggs spotted with brown,
And every day the he-bird to and fro near at hand,
And every day the she-bird crouch'd on her nest, silent, with
   bright eyes,
And every day I, a curious boy, never too close, never
   disturbing them,
Cautiously peering, absorbing, translating.

Shine! shine! shine!
Pour down your warmth, great sun!
While we bask, we two together.

Two together!
Winds blow south, or winds blow north,
Day come white, or night come black,
Home, or rivers and mountains from home,
Singing all time, minding no time,
While we two keep together.

Till of a sudden,
May-be kill'd, unknown to her mate,

---

[13]The Indian name for Long Island, New York, a place which for Whitman held strong
childhood memories.

One forenoon the she-bird crouch'd not on the nest,
Nor return'd that afternon, nor the next,
Nor ever appear'd again.

And thenceforward all summer in the sound of the sea,
And at night under the full of the moon in calmer weather,
Over the hoarse surging of the sea,
Or flitting from brier to brier by day,
I saw, I heard at intervals the remaining one, the he-bird,
The solitary guest from Alabama.

Blow! blow! blow!
Blow up sea-winds along Paumanok's shore;
I wait and I wait till you blow my mate to me.

Yes, when the stars glisten'd,
All night long on the prong of a moss-scallop'd stake,
Down almost amid the slapping waves,
Sat the lone singer wonderful causing tears.

He call'd on his mate,
He pour'd forth the meanings which I of all men know.

Yes my brother I know,
The rest might not, but I have treasur'd every note,
For more than once dimly down to the beach gliding,
Silent, avoiding the moonbeams, blending myself with the shadows,
Recalling now the obscure shapes, the echoes, the sounds and sights
   after their sorts,
The white arms out in the breakers tirelessly tossing,
I, with bare feet, a child, the wind wafting my hair,
Listen'd long and long.

Listen'd to keep, to sing, now translating the notes,
Following you my brother.

Soothe! soothe! soothe!
Close on its wave soothes the wave behind,
And again another behind embracing and lapping, every one close,
But my love soothes not me, not me.

Low hangs the moon, it rose late,
It is lagging—O I think it is heavy with love, with love.

O madly the sea pushes upon the land,
With love, with love.

O night! do I not see my love fluttering out among the breakers?
What is that little black thing I see there in the white?

Loud! loud! loud!
Loud I call to you, my love!
High and clear I shoot my voice over the waves,
Surely you must know who is here, is here,
You must know who I am, my love.

Low-hanging moon!
What is that dusky spot in your brown yellow?
O it is the shape, the shape of my mate!
O moon do not keep her from me any longer.

Land! land! O land!
Whichever way I turn, O I think you could give me my mate back again if
*   you only would,*
For I am almost sure I see her dimly whichever way I look.

O rising stars!
Perhaps the one I want so much will rise, will rise with some of you.

O throat! O trembling throat!
Sound clearer through the atmosphere!
Pierce the woods, the earth,
Somewhere listening to catch you must be the one I want.

Shake out carols!
Solitary here, the night's carols!
Carols of lonesome love! death's carols!
Carols under that lagging, yellow, waning moon!
O under that moon where she droops almost down into the sea!
O reckless despairing carols.

But soft! sink low!
Soft! let me just murmur,
And do you wait a moment you husky-nois'd sea,
For somewhere I believe I heard my mate responding to me,
So faint, I must be still, be still to listen,
But not altogether still, for then she might not come immediately to me.

Hither my love!
Here I am! here!
With this just-sustain'd note I announce myself to you,
This gentle call is for you my love, for you.

Do not be decoy'd elsewhere,
That is the whistle of the wind, it is not my voice,
That is the fluttering, the fluttering of the spray,
Those are the shadows of leaves.

O darkness! O in vain!
O I am very sick and sorrowful.

O brown halo in the sky near the moon, drooping upon the sea!
O troubled reflection in the sea!
O throat! O throbbing heart!
And I singing uselessly, uselessly all the night.

O past! O happy life! O songs of joy!
In the air, in the woods, over fields,
Loved! loved! loved! loved! loved!
But my mate no more, no more with me!
We two together no more.

The aria sinking,
All else continuing, the stars shining,
The winds blowing, the notes of the bird continuous echoing,
With angry moans the fierce old mother incessantly moaning,
On the sands of Paumanok's shore gray and rustling,
The yellow half-moon enlarged, sagging down, drooping, the face
    of the sea almost touching,
The boy ecstatic, with his bare feet the waves, with his hair the
    atmosphere dallying,
The love in the heart long pent, now loose, now at last tumultuously
    bursting,
The aria's meaning, the ears, the soul, swiftly depositing,
The strange tears down the cheeks coursing,
The colloquy there, the trio, each uttering,
The undertone, the savage old mother incessantly crying,
To the boy's soul's questions sullenly timing, some drown'd
    secret hissing,
To the outsetting bard.

Demon or bird! (said the boy's soul),
Is it indeed toward your mate you sing? or is it really to me?
For I, that was a child, my tongue's use sleeping, now I have
    heard you,
Now in a moment I know what I am for, I awake,
And already a thousand singers, a thousand songs, clearer, louder
    and more sorrowful than yours,
A thousand warbling echoes have started to life within me, never
    to die.

O you singer solitary, singing by yourself, projecting me,
O solitary me listening, never more shall I cease perpetuating you,
Never more shall I escape, never more the reverberations,
Never more the cries of unsatisfied love be absent from me,
Never again leave me to be the peaceful child I was before what
    there in the night,
By the sea under the yellow and sagging moon,
The messenger there arous'd, the fire, the sweet hell within,
The unknown want, the destiny of me.

O give me the clew![14] (it lurks in the night here somewhere,)
O if I am to have so much, let me have more!

A word then, (for I will conquer it,)
The word final, superior to all,
Subtle, sent up—what is it?—I listen;
Are you whispering it, and have been all the time, you sea-waves?
Is that it from your liquid rims and wet sands?

Whereto answering, the sea,
Delaying not, hurrying not,
Whisper'd me through the night, and very plainly before daybreak,
Lisp'd to me the low and delicious word death,
And again death, death, death, death,
Hissing melodious, neither like the bird nor like my arous'd
    child's heart,
But edging near as privately for me rustling at my feet,
Creeping thence steadily up to my ears and laving[15] me softly
    all over,
Death, death, death, death, death.

[14]Variant of clue.
[15]Bathing.

Which I do not forget,
But fuse the song of my dusky demon and brother,
That he sang to me in the moonlight on Paumanok's gray beach,
With the thousand responsive songs at random,
My own songs awaked from that hour,
And with them the key, the word up from the waves,
The word of the sweetest song and all songs,
That strong and delicious word which, creeping to my feet,
(Or like some old crone rocking the cradle, swathed in sweet
    garments, bending aside,)
The sea whisper'd me.

18

Alexis de Tocqueville

Democracy in America

*P*OLITICAL *and social democracy, as a logical extension of the principles of liberalism, developed in the Western world in the course of the nineteenth century and thereafter. The earliest and fullest manifestation of this concept was the United States of America. Alexis de Tocqueville (1805–1859), a French aristocrat, recognized this fact and, in 1830, left his minor government post under the French monarchy to visit the United States and, for some eighteen months, see the new society at work. Ostensibly, his specific purpose was to survey the American penal system; and, indeed, he later produced a report on this subject. But the major products of his visit were the two volumes of* Democracy in America *(1835, 1840), his thorough survey of American society during the Age of Jackson.*

Democracy in America *was well received in both Europe and America, and it is still the best work on the subject by any European observer. More than a scholarly travelogue, it is a shrewd and prophetic analysis of democracy in action—the practical problems and implications of social equality, public opinion, majority rule, democratic leadership, and emerging industrialization. Tocqueville not only describes but analyzes what he observed. He judges democratic society by the standards of a moderate, enlightened aristocrat; he appreciates the new order as the wave of the future but is troubled by some of its aspects. Like Burke (see selection 15), Tocqueville values the conservative ideals of freedom and order, but, unlike Burke, accepts the value of an open society based on popular liberty. His central concern, therefore, is to reconcile individual freedom with the conformity, materialism, and potential tyranny of an egalitarian order. Tocqueville's solution is an enlightened and tempered self-interest on the part of individuals and the diffusion of power among many interest groups in a pluralistic system.*

SOCIAL CONDITION OF THE ANGLO-AMERICANS

A social condition is commonly the result of circumstances, sometimes of laws, oftener still of these two causes united; but wherever it exists, it may justly be considered as the source of almost all the laws, the usages, and the ideas which regulate the conduct of nations; whatever it does not produce it modifies. It is therefore necessary, if we would become acquainted with the legislation and the manners of a nation, to begin by the study of its social condition.

Many important observations suggest themselves upon the social condition of the Anglo-Americans, but there is one which takes precedence of all the rest. The social condition of the Americans is eminently democratic; this was its character at the foundation of the Colonies, and is still more strongly marked at the present day. I have stated in the preceding chapter that great equality existed among the emigrants who settled on the shores of New England. The germ of aristocracy was never planted in that part of the Union. The only influence which obtained there was that of intellect; the people were used to reverence certain names as the emblems of knowledge and virtue. Some of their fellow citizens acquired a power over the rest which might truly have been called aristocratic, if it had been capable of transmission from father to son. . . .

In America the aristocratic element has always been feeble from its birth; and if at the present day it is not actually destroyed, it is at any rate so completely disabled that we can scarcely assign to it any degree of influence in the course of affairs. The democratic principle, on the contrary, has gained so much strength by time, by events, and by legislation, as to have become not only predominant but all-powerful. There is no family or corporate authority, and it is rare to find even the influence of individual character enjoy any durability.

America, then, exhibits in her social state a most extraordinary phenomenon. Men are there seen on a greater equality in point of fortune and intellect, or, in other words, more equal in their strength, than in any other country of the world, or in any age of which history has preserved the remembrance.

DEMOCRACY IN AMERICA   Adapted by editor, from Alexis de Tocqueville, *Democracy in America*, trans. Henry Reeve, rev. ed. (London and New York: Colonial, 1900), I, 46, 52–54, 313–14, 317, 361, 363–65, 378–81, 383–84; II, 3–5, 144–45, 147, 208–210, 221–24.

POLITICAL CONSEQUENCES OF THE SOCIAL CONDITION OF THE ANGLO-AMERICANS

The political consequences of such a social condition as this are easily deducible. It is impossible to believe that equality will not eventually find its way into the political world as it does everywhere else. To conceive of men remaining forever unequal upon one single point, yet equal on all others, is impossible; they must come in the end to be equal upon all. Now I know of only two methods of establishing equality in the political world; every citizen must be put in possession of his rights, or rights must be granted to no one. For nations which have arrived at the same stage of social existence as the Anglo-Americans, it is therefore very difficult to discover a medium between the sovereignty of all and the absolute power of one man; and it would be vain to deny that the social condition which I have been describing is equally liable to each of these consequences.

There is, in fact, a manly and lawful passion for equality which excites men to wish all to be powerful and honored. This passion tends to elevate the humble to the rank of the great; but there exists also in the human heart a depraved taste for equality, which impels the weak to attempt to lower the powerful to their own level, and reduces men to prefer equality in slavery to inequality with freedom. Not that those nations whose social condition is democratic naturally despise liberty; on the contrary, they have an instinctive love of it. But liberty is not the chief and constant object of their desires; equality is their idol: they make rapid and sudden efforts to obtain liberty, and if they miss their aim resign themselves to their disappointment; but nothing can satisfy them except equality, and rather than lose it they resolve to perish.

On the other hand, in a State where the citizens are nearly on an equality, it becomes difficult for them to preserve their independence against the aggressions of power. No one among them being strong enough to engage in the struggle with advantage, nothing but a general combination can protect their liberty. And such a union is not always to be found.

From the same social position, then, nations may derive one or the other of two great political results; these results are extremely different from each other, but they may both proceed from the same cause.

The Anglo-Americans are the first who, having been exposed to this formidable alternative, have been happy enough to escape the dominion of absolute power. They have been allowed by their circumstances, their origin, their intelligence, and especially by their moral feeling, to establish and maintain the sovereignty of the people.

• • •

PRINCIPAL CAUSES WHICH RENDER RELIGION POWERFUL IN AMERICA

The philosophers of the eighteenth century explained the gradual decay of religious faith in a very simple manner. Religious zeal, said they, must necessarily fail, the more generally liberty is established and knowledge diffused. Unfortunately, facts are by no means in accordance with their theory. There are certain populations in Europe whose unbelief is only equalled by their ignorance and their debasement, while in America one of the freest and most enlightened nations in the world fulfils all the outward duties of religious fervor.

Upon my arrival in the United States, the religious aspect of the country was the first thing that struck my attention; and the longer I stayed there the more did I perceive the great political consequences resulting from this state of things, to which I was unaccustomed. In France I had almost always seen the spirit of religion and the spirit of freedom pursuing courses diametrically opposed to each other; but in America I found that they were intimately united, and that they reigned in common over the same country. My desire to discover the causes of this phenomenon increased from day to day. In order to satisfy it I questioned the members of all the different denominations; and I more especially sought the company of the clergy, who are the depositaries of the different persuasions, and who are more especially interested in their duration. As a member of the Roman Catholic Church I was more particularly brought into contact with several of its priests, with whom I became closely acquainted. To each of these men I expressed my astonishment and I explained my doubts; I found that they differed upon matters of detail alone; and that they mainly attributed the peaceful dominion of religion in their country to the separation of Church and State. I do not hesitate to affirm that during my stay in America I did not meet with a single individual, of the clergy or of the laity, who was not of the same opinion upon this point.

This led me to examine more attentively than I had hitherto done the station which the American clergy occupy in political society. I learned with surprise that they filled no public appointments; not one of them is to be met with in the administration, and they are not even represented in the legislative assemblies. In several States the law excludes them from political life; public opinion exclude them in all. And when I came to inquire into the prevailing spirit of the clergy I found that most of its members seemed to retire of their own accord from the exercise of power, and that they made it the pride of their profession to abstain from politics.

I heard them condemn ambition and deceit, under whatever political opinions these vices might chance to lurk; but I learned from their discourses that men are not guilty in the eye of God for any opinions concerning political government which they may profess with sincerity, any more than they are for their mistakes in building a house or in driving a furrow. . . .

If the Americans, who change the head of the Government once in four years, who elect new legislators every two years, and renew the local officers every year; if the Americans, who have abandoned the political world to the attempts of innovators, had not placed religion beyond their reach, where could it abide in the ebb and flow of human opinions? where would that respect which belongs to it be paid, amid the struggles of faction? and what would become of its immortality, in the midst of perpetual decay? The American clergy were the first to perceive this truth, and to act in conformity with it. They saw that they must renounce their religious influence, if they were to strive for political power; and they chose to give up the support of the State, rather than to share its many changes.

In America, religion is perhaps less powerful than it has been at certain periods in the history of certain peoples; but its influence is more lasting. It restricts itself to its own resources, but of those none can deprive it: its circle is limited to certain principles, but those principles are entirely its own, and under its undisputed control. . . .

• • •

SITUATION OF THE BLACK POPULATION IN THE UNITED STATES, AND DANGERS WITH WHICH ITS PRESENCE THREATENS THE WHITES

The Indians will perish in the same isolated condition in which they have lived; but the destiny of the negroes is in some measure interwoven with that of the Europeans. These two races are attached to each other without intermingling, and they are alike unable entirely to separate or to combine. The most formidable of all the ills which threaten the future existence of the Union arises from the presence of a black population upon its territory; and in contemplating the cause of the present embarrassments or of the future dangers of the United States, the observer is invariably led to consider this as a primary fact. . . .

Hitherto, wherever the whites have been the most powerful, they have maintained the blacks in a subordinate or a servile position; wherever the negroes have been strongest they have destroyed the whites; such has been the only retribution which has ever taken place between the two races.

I see that in a certain portion of the territory of the United States at the present day, the legal barrier which separated the two races is tending to fall away, but not that which exists in the manners of the country; slavery recedes, but the prejudice to which it has given birth remains stationary. Whosoever has inhabited the United States must have perceived that in those parts of the Union in which the negroes are no longer slaves, they have in no way drawn nearer to the whites. On the contrary, the prejudice of the race appears to be stronger in the States which have abolished slavery, than in those where it still exists; and nowhere is it so intolerant as in those States where servitude has never been known.

It is true, that in the North of the Union, marriages may be legally contracted between negroes and whites; but public opinion would stigmatize a man who should connect himself with a negress as infamous, and it would be difficult to meet with a single instance of such a union. The electoral franchise has been conferred upon the negroes in almost all the States in which slavery has been abolished; but if they come forward to vote, their lives are in danger. If oppressed, they may bring an action at law, but they will find none but whites among their judges; and although they may legally serve as jurors, prejudice repulses them from that office. The same schools do not receive the child of the black and of the European. In the theaters, gold cannot procure a seat for the servile race beside their former masters; in the hospitals they lie apart; and although they are allowed to invoke the same divinity as the whites, it must be at a different altar, and in their own churches, with their own clergy. The gates of heaven are not closed against these unhappy beings; but their inferiority is continued to the very confines of the other world; when the negro has died, his bones are cast aside, and the distinction of condition prevails even in the equality of death. The negro is free, but he can share neither the rights, nor the pleasures, nor the labor, nor the afflictions, nor the tomb of him whose equal he has been declared to be; and he cannot meet him upon fair terms in life or in death.

In the South, where slavery still exists, the negroes are less carefully kept apart; they sometimes share the labor and the recreations of the whites; the whites consent to intermix with them to a certain extent, and although the legislation treats them more harshly, the habits of the people are more tolerant and compassionate. In the South the master is not afraid to raise his slave to his own standing, because he knows that he can in a moment reduce him to the dust at pleasure. In the North the white no longer distinctly perceives the barrier which separates him from the degraded race, and he shuns the negro with the more persistence, since he fears that they might some day be confounded together.

Among the Americans of the South, nature sometimes reasserts her rights, and restores a transient equality between the blacks and the whites; but in the North pride restrains the most imperious of human passions. The American of the Northern States would perhaps allow the negress to share his licentious pleasures, if the laws of his country did not declare that she may aspire to be the legitimate partner of his bed; but he recoils with horror from her who might become his wife.

Thus it is, in the United States, that the prejudice which repels the negroes seems to increase in proportion as they are emancipated, and inequality is sanctioned by the manners while it is erased from the laws of the country. But if the relative position of the two races which inhabit the United States is such as I have described, it may be asked why the Americans have abolished slavery in the North of the Union, why they maintain it in the South, and why they aggravate its hardships there? The answer is easily given. It is not for the good of the negroes, but for that of the whites, that measures are taken to abolish slavery in the United States. . . .

As long as the negro remains a slave, he may be kept in a condition not very far removed from that of the brutes; but, with his liberty, he cannot but acquire a degree of instruction which will enable him to appreciate his misfortunes, and to discern a remedy for them. Moreover, there exists a unique principle of relative justice which is very firmly implanted in the human heart. Men are much more forcibly struck by those inequalities which exist within the circle of the same class, than with those which may be observed between different classes. It is more easy for them to admit slavery, than to allow several millions of citizens to exist under a load of eternal infamy and hereditary wretchedness. In the North the population of freed negroes feels these hardships and resents these indignities; but its numbers and its powers are small, while in the South it would be numerous and strong.

As soon as it is admitted that the whites and the emancipated blacks are placed upon the same territory in the situation of two alien communities, it will readily be understood that there are but two alternatives for the future; the negroes and the whites must either wholly part or wholly mingle. I have already expressed the conviction which I entertain as to the latter event. I do not imagine that the white and black races will ever live in any country upon an equal footing. But I believe the difficulty to be still greater in the United States than elsewhere. An isolated individual may surmount the prejudices of religion, of his country, or of his race, and if this individual is a king he may effect surprising changes in society; but a whole people cannot rise, as it were, above itself. A despot who should subject the Americans and their former slaves to the same yoke, might perhaps succeed in intermixing their races; but as long as the American democracy remains at the head of affairs, no one will undertake so difficult a task; and it may be foreseen that the freer the white population of the United States becomes, the more isolated will it remain.

I have previously observed that the mixed race is the true bond of union between the Europeans and the Indians; just so the mulattoes are the true means of transition between the white and the negro; so that wherever mulattoes abound, the intermixture of the two races is not impossible. In some parts of America, the European and the negro races are so crossed by one another that it is rare to meet with a man who is entirely black, or entirely white: when they have arrived at this point, the two races may really be said to be combined; or rather to have been absorbed in a third race, which is connected with both without being identical with either.

Of all the Europeans the English are those who have mixed least with the negroes. More mulattoes are to be seen in the South of the Union than in the North, but still they are infinitely more scarce than in any other European colony: mulattoes are by no means numerous in the United States; they have no force peculiar to themselves, and when quarrels originating in differences of color take place, they generally side with the whites; just as the lackeys of the great, in Europe, assume the contemptuous airs of nobility to the lower orders.

The pride of origin, which is natural to the English, is singularly increased by the personal pride which democratic liberty fosters among the Americans: the white citizen of the United States is proud of his race, and proud of himself. But if the whites and the negroes do not intermingle in the North of the Union, how should they mix in the South? Can it be supposed for an instant, that an American of the Southern States, placed, as he must forever be, between the white man with all his physical and moral superiority and the negro, will ever think of preferring the latter? The Americans of the Southern States have two powerful passions which will always keep them aloof; the first is the fear of being assimilated to the negroes, their former slaves; and the second the dread of sinking below the whites, their neighbors.

If I were called upon to predict what will probably occur at some future time, I should say, that the abolition of slavery in the South will, in the common course of things, increase the aversion of the white population for the men of color. I found this opinion upon the analogous observation which I already had occasion to make in the North. I noticed there that the white inhabitants of the North avoid the negroes with increasing care, in proportion as the legal barriers of separation are removed by the legislature; and why should not the same result take place in the South? In the North, the whites are deterred from intermingling with the blacks by the fear of an imaginary danger; in the South, where the danger would be real, I cannot imagine that the fear would be less general.

If, on the one hand, it be admitted (and the fact is unquestionable) that the colored population perpetually accumulates in the extreme South, and that it increases more rapidly than that of the whites; and if, on the other hand, it be allowed that it is impossible to foresee a time at which the whites and the blacks will be so intermingled as to derive the same benefits from society; must it not be inferred that the blacks and the whites will, sooner or later, come to open strife in the Southern States of the Union? But if it be asked what the issue of the struggle is likely to be, it will readily be understood that we are here left to form a very vague surmise of the truth. The human mind may succeed in tracing a wide circle, as it were, which includes the course of future events; but within that circle a thousand various chances and circumstances may direct it in as many different ways; and in every picture of the future there is a dim spot, which the eye of the understanding cannot penetrate. . . .

The danger of a conflict between the white and the black inhabitants of the Southern States of the Union—a danger which, however remote it may be, is inevitable—perpetually haunts the imagination of the

Americans. The inhabitants of the North make it a common topic of conversation, although they have no direct injury to fear from the struggle; but they vainly endeavor to devise some means of preventing the misfortunes which they foresee. In the Southern States the subject is not discussed: the planter does not allude to the future in conversing with strangers; the citizen does not communicate his apprehensions to his friends; he seeks to conceal them from himself; but there is something more alarming in the unspoken forebodings of the South, than in the noisy fears of the Northern States. . . .

When I contemplate the condition of the South, I can only discover two alternatives which may be adopted by the white inhabitants of those States; that is, either to emancipate the negroes, and to intermingle with them; or, remaining isolated from them, to keep them in a state of slavery as long as possible. All intermediate measures seem to me likely to terminate, and that shortly, in the most horrible of civil wars, and perhaps in the destruction of one or other of the two races. Such is the view which the Americans of the South take of the question, and they act consistently with it. As they are determined not to mingle with the negroes, they refuse to emancipate them. . . .

• • •

PHILOSOPHICAL METHOD AMONG THE AMERICANS

I think that in no country in the civilized world is less attention paid to philosophy than in the United States. The Americans have no philosophical school of their own; and they care but little for all the schools into which Europe is divided, the very names of which are scarcely known to them. Nevertheless it is easy to perceive that almost all the inhabitants of the United States conduct their understanding in the same manner, and govern it by the same rules; that is to say, that without ever having taken the trouble to define the rules of a philosophical method, they are in possession of one, common to the whole people. To evade the bondage of system and habit, of family teachings, class opinions, and, in some degree, of national prejudices; to accept tradition only as a means of information, and existing facts only as a lesson used in doing otherwise, and doing better; to seek the reason of things for one's self, and in one's self alone; to tend to results without being bound to means, and to aim at the substance through the form;— such are the principal characteristics of what I shall call the philosophical method of the Americans. But if I go further, and if I seek among these characteristics that which predominates over and includes almost all the rest, I discover that in most of the operations of the mind, each American appeals to the individual exercise of his own understanding alone. America is therefore one of the countries in the world where philosophy is least studied, and where the teachings of Descartes[1] are best applied. Nor is this surprising. The Americans do not read the works of Descartes, because their social condition deters them from speculative studies; but they follow his maxims because this very social condition naturally disposes their understanding to adopt them. In the midst of the continual movement which agitates a democratic community, the tie which unites one generation to another is relaxed or broken; every man readily loses the trace of the ideas of his forefathers or takes no care about them. Nor can men living in this state of society derive their belief from the opinions of the class to which they belong, for, so to speak, there are no longer any classes, or those which still exist are composed of such mobile elements, that their body can never exercise a real control over its members. As to the influence which the intelligence of one man has on that of another, it must necessarily be very limited in a country where the citizens, placed on the footing of a general similarity, are all closely seen by each other; and where, as no signs of incontestable greatness or superiority are perceived in any one of them, they are constantly brought back to their own reason as the most obvious and proximate source of truth. It is not only confidence in this or that man which is then destroyed, but the taste for trusting the judgment of any man whatsoever. Everyone shuts himself up in his own breast, and affects from that point to judge the world.

The practice which exists among the Americans of fixing the standard of their judgment in themselves alone, leads them to other habits of mind. As they perceive that they succeed in resolving without assistance all the little difficulties which their practical life presents, they readily conclude that everything in the world may be explained, and that nothing in it transcends the limits of the understanding. Thus they fall to denying what they cannot comprehend; which leaves them but little faith for whatever is extraordinary, and an almost insurmountable distaste for whatever is supernatural. As it is on their own testimony that they are accustomed to rely, they like to discern the object which engages their attention with extreme clearness; they therefore strip off

[1]René Descartes (1596–1650), a noted French philosopher and mathematician. (See selection 3.)

as much as possible all that covers it, they rid themselves of whatever separates them from it, they remove whatever conceals it from sight, in order to view it more closely and in the broad light of day. This disposition of the mind soon leads them to scorn forms, which they regard as useless and inconvenient veils placed between them and the truth.

The Americans then have not required to extract their philosophical method from books; they have found it in themselves. . . .

• • •

CAUSES OF THE RESTLESS SPIRIT OF THE AMERICANS IN THE MIDST OF THEIR PROSPERITY

In certain remote corners of the Old World you may still sometimes stumble upon a small district which seems to have been forgotten amid the general tumult, and to have remained stationary while everything around it was in motion. The inhabitants are for the most part extremely ignorant and poor; they take no part in the business of the country, and they are frequently oppressed by the government; yet their faces are generally calm, and their spirits light. In America I saw the freest and most enlightened men, placed in the happiest circumstances which the world affords: it seemed to me as if a cloud habitually hung upon their brow, and I thought them serious and almost sad even in their pleasures. The chief reason of this contrast is that the former do not think of the ills they endure—the latter are forever brooding over advantages they do not possess. It is strange to see with what feverish ardor the Americans pursue their own welfare; and to watch the vague dread that constantly torments them, in the event that they should not have chosen the shortest path which may lead to it. A native of the United States clings to this world's goods as if he were certain never to die; and he is so hasty in grasping at all within his reach, that one would suppose he was constantly afraid of not living long enough to enjoy them. He clutches everything, he holds nothing fast, but soon loosens his grasp to pursue fresh gratifications.

In the United States a man builds a house to spend his latter years in it, and he sells it before the roof is on: he plants a garden, and rents it just as the trees are coming into bearing: he brings a field into tillage, and leaves other men to gather the crops: he embraces a profession, and gives it up: he settles in a place, which he soon afterward leaves, to carry his changeable longings elsewhere. If his private affairs leave him any leisure, he instantly plunges into the whirlpool of politics; and if at the end of a year of unremitting labor he finds he has a few days' vacation, his eager curiosity whirls him over the vast extent of the United States, and he will travel fifteen hundred miles in a few days, to shake off his happiness. Death at length overtakes him, but it is before he is weary of his bootless chase of that complete happiness which is forever on the wing.

At first sight there is something surprising in this strange unrest of so many happy men, restless in the midst of abundance. The spectacle itself is however as old as the world; the novelty is to see a whole people furnish an exemplification of it. Their taste for physical gratifications must be regarded as the original source of that secret restlessness which the actions of the Americans betray, and of that inconstancy of which they afford fresh examples every day. He who has set his heart exclusively upon the pursuit of worldly welfare is always in a hurry, for he has but a limited time at his disposal to reach it, to grasp it, and to enjoy it. The recollection of the brevity of life is a constant spur to him. Besides the good things which he possesses, he every instant fancies a thousand others which death will prevent him from trying if he does not try them soon. This thought fills him with anxiety, fear, and regret, and keeps his mind in a ceaseless state of alarm, which leads him perpetually to change his plans and his abode. If in addition to the taste for physical well-being a social condition be superadded, in which the laws and customs make no condition permanent, here is a great additional stimulant to this restlessness of temper. Men will then be seen continually to change their track, for fear of missing the shortest cut to happiness. It may readily be conceived that if men, passionately bent upon physical gratifications, desire eagerly, they are also easily discouraged: as their ultimate object is to enjoy, the means to reach that object must be prompt and easy, or the trouble of acquiring the gratification would be greater than the gratification itself. Their prevailing frame of mind then is at once ardent and relaxed, violent and enervated. Death is often less dreaded than perseverance in continuous efforts to one end. . . .

Among democratic nations men easily attain a certain equality of conditions: they can never attain the equality they desire. It perpetually retires from before them, yet without hiding itself from their sight, and in retiring draws them on. At every moment they think they are about to grasp it; it escapes at every moment from their hold. They are near enough to see its charms, but too far off to enjoy them; and before they have fully tasted its delights they die. To these causes must be attributed that strange melancholy which oftentimes will haunt the inhabitants of democratic countries in the midst of their abundance, and that disgust at life which sometimes seizes upon them in the midst of calm and easy circumstances. Complaints are made in France that the number of suicides increases; in America suicide is rare, but insanity is said to be more common than anywhere else. These are all different symptoms of the same disease. The Americans do not put an end to their lives, however disquieted they may be, because their religion forbids it; . . .

In democratic ages enjoyments are more intense than in the ages of aristocracy, and especially the number of those who partake in them is larger: but, on the other hand, it must be admitted that man's hopes and his desires are oftener blighted, the soul is more stricken and perturbed, and care itself more keen.

•   •   •

EDUCATION OF YOUNG WOMEN
IN THE UNITED STATES

No free communities ever existed without morals; and, as I observed in the former part of this work, morals are the work of woman. Consequently, whatever affects the condition of women, their habits and their opinions, has great political importance in my eyes. Among almost all Protestant nations young women are far more the mistresses of their own actions than they are in Catholic countries. This independence is still greater in Protestant countries, like England, which have retained or acquired the right of self-government; the spirit of freedom is then infused into the domestic circle by political habits and by religious opinions. In the United States the doctrines of Protestantism are combined with great political freedom and a most democratic state of society; and nowhere are young women surrendered so early or so completely to their own guidance. Long before an American girl arrives at the age of marriage, her emancipation from maternal control begins; she has scarcely ceased to be a child when she already thinks for herself, speaks with freedom, and acts on her own impulse. The great scene of the world is constantly open to her view; far from seeking concealment, it is every day disclosed to her more completely, and she is taught to survey it with a firm and calm gaze. Thus the vices and dangers of society are early revealed to her; as she sees them clearly, she views them without illusions, and braves them without fear; for she is full of reliance on her own strength, and her reliance seems to be shared by all who are near her. An American girl scarcely ever displays that virginal bloom in the midst of young desires, or that innocent and natural grace which usually attends the European woman in the transition from girlhood to youth. It is rare that an American woman at any age displays childish timidity or ignorance. Like the young women of Europe, she seeks to please, but she knows precisely the cost of pleasing. If she does not abandon herself to evil, at least she knows that it exists; and she is remarkable rather for purity of manners than for chastity of mind. I have been frequently surprised, and almost frightened, at the singular address and happy boldness with which young women in America contrive to manage their thoughts and their language amid all the difficulties of stimulating conversation; a philosopher would have stumbled at every step along the narrow path which they trod without accidents and without effort. It is easy indeed to perceive that, even amid the independence of early youth, an American woman is always mistress of herself; she indulges in all permitted pleasures, without yielding herself up to any of them; and her reason never allows the reins of self-guidance to drop, though it often seems to hold them loosely.

In France, where remnants of every age are still so strangely mingled in the opinions and tastes of the people, women commonly receive a reserved, retired, and almost cloistral education, as they did in aristocratic times; and then they are suddenly abandoned, without a guide and without assistance, in the midst of all the irregularities inseparable from democratic society. The Americans are more consistent. They have found out that in a democracy the independence of individuals cannot fail to be very great, youth premature, tastes ill-restrained, customs fleeting, public opinion often unsettled and powerless, paternal authority weak, and marital authority contested. Under these circumstances, believing that they had little chance of repressing in woman the most vehement passions of the human heart, they held that the surer way was to teach her the art of combating those passions for herself. As they could not prevent her virtue from being exposed to frequent danger, they determined that she should know how best to defend it; and more reliance was placed on the free vigor of her will than on safeguards which have been shaken or overthrown. Instead, then, of inculcating mistrust of herself, they constantly seek to enhance their confidence in her own strength of character. As it is neither possible nor desirable to keep a young woman in perpetual or complete ignorance, they hasten to give her a precocious knowledge on all subjects. Far from hiding the corruptions of the world from her, they prefer that she should see them at once and train herself to shun them; and they hold it of more importance to protect her conduct than to be over-scrupulous of her innocence.

Although the Americans are a very religious people, they do not rely on religion alone to defend the virtue of woman; they seek to arm her reason also. In this they have followed the same method as in several other respects; they first make the most vigorous efforts to bring individual independence to exercise a proper control over itself, and they do not call in the aid of religion until they have reached the utmost limits of human strength. I am aware that an education of this kind is not without danger; I am aware that it tends to invigorate the judgment at the expense of the imagination, and to make cold and virtuous women instead of affectionate wives and agreeable companions to man. Society may be more tranquil and better regulated, but domestic life has often fewer charms. These, however, are secondary evils, which may be braved for the sake of higher interests. At the stage at which we have now arrived the time for choosing is no longer within our control; a democratic education is indispensable to protect women from the dangers with which democratic institutions and manners surround them.

* * *

HOW THE AMERICANS UNDERSTAND THE EQUALITY OF THE SEXES

I have shown how democracy destroys or modifies the different inequalities which originate in society; but is this all? or does it not ultimately affect that great inequality of man and woman which has seemed, up to the present day, to be eternally based in human nature? I believe that the social changes which bring nearer to the same level the father and son, the master and servant, and superiors and inferiors generally speaking, will raise woman and make her more and more the equal of man. But here, more than ever, I feel the necessity of making myself clearly understood; for there is no subject on which the coarse and lawless fancies of our age have taken a freer range.

There are people in Europe who, confounding together the different characteristics of the sexes, would make of man and woman beings not only equal but alike. They would give to both the same functions, impose on both the same duties, and grant to both the same rights; they would mix them in all things—their occupations, their pleasures, their business. It may readily be conceived, that by thus attempting to make one sex equal to the other, both are degraded; and from so preposterous a medley of the works of nature nothing could ever result but weak men and disorderly women.

It is not thus that the Americans understand that species of democratic equality which may be established between the sexes. They admit, that as nature has appointed such wide differences between the physical and moral constitution of man and woman, her manifest design was to give a distinct employment to their various faculties; and they hold that improvement does not consist in making beings who are so different do pretty nearly the same things, but in getting each of them to fulfil their respective tasks in the best possible manner. The Americans have applied to the sexes the great principle of political economy which governs the manufactures of our age,[2] by carefully dividing the duties of man from those of woman, in order that the great work of society may be the better carried on.

In no country has such constant care been taken as in America to trace two clearly distinct lines of action for the two sexes, and to make them keep pace one with the other, but in two pathways which are always different. American women never manage the outward concerns of the family, or conduct a business, or take a part in political life; nor are they, on the other hand, ever compelled to perform the rough labor of the fields, or to make any of those laborious exertions which demand the exertion of physical strength. No families are so poor as to form an exception to this rule. If on the one hand an American woman cannot escape from the quiet circle of domestic employments, on the other hand she is never forced to go beyond it. Hence it is that the women of America, who often exhibit a masculine strength of understanding and a manly energy, generally preserve great delicacy of personal appearance and always retain the manners of women, although they sometimes show that they have the hearts and minds of men.

Nor have the Americans ever supposed that one consequence of democratic principles is the subversion of marital power, of the confusion of the natural authorities in families. They hold that every association must have a head in order to accomplish its object, and that the natural head of the conjugal association is man. They do not therefore deny him the right of directing his partner; and they maintain, that in

---

[2]For the general principle of the economic "division of labor," explained by Adam Smith, see selection 13.

the smaller association of husband and wife, as well as in the great social community, the object of democracy is to regulate and legalize the powers which are necessary, not to subvert all power. This opinion is not peculiar to one sex, and contested by the other: I never observed that the women of America consider conjugal authority as a fortunate usurpation of their rights, nor that they thought themselves degraded by submitting to it. It appeared to me, on the contrary, that they attach a sort of pride to the voluntary surrender of their own will, and make it their boast to bend themselves to the yoke, not to shake it off. Such at least is the feeling expressed by the most virtuous of their sex; the others are silent; and in the United States it is not the practice for a guilty wife to clamor for the rights of women, while she is trampling on her holiest duties.

It has often been remarked that in Europe a certain degree of contempt lurks even in the flattery which men lavish upon women: although a European frequently affects to be the slave of woman, it may be seen that he never sincerely thinks her his equal. In the United States men seldom compliment women, but they daily show how much they esteem them. They constantly display an entire confidence in the understanding of a wife, and a profound respect for her freedom; they have decided that her mind is just as fitted as that of a man to discover the plain truth, and her heart as firm to embrace it; and they have never sought to place her virtue, any more than his, under the shelter of prejudice, ignorance, and fear. It would seem that in Europe, where man so easily submits to the despotic sway of women, they are nevertheless curtailed of some of the greatest qualities of the human species, and considered as seductive but imperfect beings; and (what may well provoke astonishment) women ultimately look upon themselves in the same light, and almost consider it as a privilege that they are entitled to show themselves futile, feeble, and timid. The women of America claim no such privileges.

Again, it may be said that in our morals we have reserved strange immunities to man; so that there is, as it were, one virtue for his use, and another for the guidance of his partner; and that, according to the opinion of the public, the very same act may be punished alternately as a crime or only as a fault. The Americans know not this unfair division of duties and rights; among them the seducer is as much dishonored as his victim. It is true that the Americans rarely lavish upon women those eager attentions which are commonly paid them in Europe; but their conduct to women always implies that they suppose them to be virtuous and refined; and such is the respect entertained for the moral freedom of the sex, that in the presence of a woman the most guarded language is used, lest her ear should be offended by an expression. In America a young unmarried woman may, alone and without fear, undertake a long journey.

The legislators of the United States, who have mitigated almost all the penalties of criminal law, still make rape a capital offense, and no crime is visited with more inexorable severity by public opinion. This may be accounted for; as the Americans can conceive nothing more precious than a woman's honor, and nothing which ought so much to be respected as her independence, they hold that no punishment is too severe for the man who deprives her of them against her will. In France, where the same offense is visited with far milder penalties, it is frequently difficult to get a verdict from a jury against the prisoner. Is this a consequence of contempt of decency or contempt of women? I cannot but believe that it is a contempt of one and of the other.

Thus the Americans do not think that man and woman have either the duty or the right to perform the same offices, but they show an equal regard for both their respective parts; and though their lot is different, they consider both of them as beings of equal value. They do not give to the courage of woman the same form or the same direction as to that of man; but they never doubt her courage: and if they hold that man and his partner ought not always to exercise their intellect and understanding in the same manner, they at least believe the understanding of the one to be as sound as that of the other, and her intellect to be as clear. Thus, then, while they have allowed the social inferiority of woman to subsist, they have done all they could to raise her morally and intellectually to the level of man; and in this respect they appear to me to have excellently understood the true principle of democratic improvement. As for myself, I do not hesitate to avow that, although the women of the United States are confined within the narrow circle of domestic life, and their situation is in some respects one of extreme dependence, I have nowhere seen woman occupying a loftier position; and if I were asked, now that I am drawing to the close of this work, in which I have spoken of so many important things done by the Americans, to what the singular prosperity and growing strength of that people ought mainly to be attributed, I should reply—to the superiority of their women.

• • •

19

Henry David Thoreau

Walden AND Civil Disobedience

THE thought and writing of Henry David Thoreau (1817–1862) have had a tremendous influence upon twentieth-century America and the rest of the world. Famous movers and shakers in the realm of politics, such as Martin Luther King, Jr., and Mohandas Gandhi of India, acknowledged their indebtedness to Thoreau for his views on civil disobedience. Conservationists and ecologists have claimed him as one of their forerunners because of his appreciation of the beauty of nature. But fame and popularity accorded to Thoreau's work in the twentieth century was virtually absent in his own lifetime. Not that he cared for success or fame—more than anything else he wanted to make a modest living as a writer so that he could live his life in the way he desired.

Thoreau became one of those rare individuals in Western civilization who introduced new and powerful ideas—without ever intending to offer a total philosophy for guiding other people's lives. His own life appears to be a case in point, because it was not held together by a dominating purpose. As a result, Thoreau's friends were seldom able to tell on which side of an argument he would come out. They could, however, be sure that whatever view Thoreau expressed would be sharply focused, moral, outside the mainstream, and without regard for the immediate consequences.

Had Thoreau been a conventional man, he would have taken advantage of what a kindly fate offered him while young. His father owned but a small shop in Concord, Massachusetts, in which he worked hard making pencils; but young Henry, assisted by a scholarship, was able to study at Harvard College. After an average performance as a student, Thoreau graduated in 1837. He now possessed the necessary credentials for starting a career that would bring him recognition, esteem, and material security. But he rejected such a life course. He preferred, rather, to remain in familiar surroundings, which included teaching at a local school, helping to run a friend's landed estate, and assisting his father in pencil making. Thoreau chose this way of life because he desired to become a writer, though he knew well that income from writing was usually meager. He, however, cared little about the material goods that the marketplace had to offer. Thoreau sought quality, the intrinsic value, the genuine. He was certain he could find these without acquiring substantial sums of money.

In order to discover what he was looking for at that time in his life (he was twenty-eight), Thoreau, in July 1845, withdrew to Walden Pond. This was wilderness land, belonging to his friend Ralph Waldo Emerson. The location, less than two miles from Concord, suggests that he wished to live in solitude (alone), but not as a recluse (loner). In fact, while living there and building his cabin, he was visited by family and friends, many of whom disapproved of a life spent in contemplative idleness. Withdrawing to Walden, for whatever time period, meant that Thoreau rejected the way most people spend their lives, that is, being pushed by economic necessity ("quiet desperation") or being tempted by the lure of gain. Standards of conduct approved and honored by society—such as hard work, thrift, and becoming wealthy in the process—meant to him that the central purpose of life had been missed altogether. Living the simple life at Walden, however, held the promise of what he was looking for: to discover his soul—once the debris that civilization had heaped upon it had been cleared away—and to discover God as revealed in the beauty and endless variety of nature.

To know God, thought Thoreau, hinged upon an individual's ability to see nature, not as one probing into her secrets, but as a person who is still capable of marveling at divine greatness unfolding itself before the spectator. Such an experience was dependent upon an individual's inner ability to comprehend it. Only a few persons could be expected to have such an experience and have their lives transformed by it. Consequently, Thoreau expected to remain alone; he founded no "society," no interest group, and no school. He simply wrote of his own experience in the woods, condensing the actual period of two years into one year in his account. Following numerous revisions, the book titled Walden was finally published in 1854, and it became an American classic.

Thoreau, possessing keen perception and a fine moral conscience, could not be expected to pass through life without eventually colliding with government. (He strongly disapproved of the coercion by society of any individual.) The immediate cause for his confrontation was the fact that Thoreau had not paid his local poll-tax for a number of years. Finally, in July 1846, and in the middle of his Walden experience, he was taken to Concord jail. The moment had apparently arrived when Thoreau could make his point while people watched. Someone, however, quietly and without his knowledge, paid the tax—thus depriving him of his chance of standing up to "unjust" government.

To pay his poll-tax quietly was unacceptable to Thoreau because in doing so, government would have made him a willing accomplice to something of which he wholly disapproved. And the revenue taken in by government supported, at that time, an invasion of Mexico by the United States. Thoreau, in this as well as in later happenings, became aware of the fact that government stands for what appears to be expedient or practical, but not necessarily for what is moral. He demanded that governmental action, as well as legislation, must be anchored in morality.

Thoreau knew, of course, that most citizens are only too willing to submit to the demands of powerful government, because they are opportunistic or too cowardly to oppose it. Therefore, it is up to an individual alone to resist. The inner strength for this act of courage comes from a person's belief that the morality of one eventually will triumph over an ocean of immorality.

These thoughts of Thoreau on government appeared for the first time in print in 1849, after he had lectured twice about it the previous year. The present title, Civil Disobedience, which captivated the imagination of so many living in the twentieth century, dates back to 1866.

<hr />

WALDEN

Where I Lived, and What I Lived for

• • •

When I first took up my abode in the woods,[1] that is, began to spend my nights as well as days there, which, by accident, was on Independence day, or the Fourth of July, 1845, my house was not finished for winter. It was merely a defense against the rain, without plastering or chimney, the walls being of rough weather-stained boards, with wide cracks which made it cool at night. The upright white cut studs and freshly planed door and window casings gave it a clean and airy look, especially in the morning, when its timbers were saturated with dew, so that I fancied that by noon some sweet gum would exude from them. To my imagination it retained throughout the day more or less of this

---

[1]The woods at Walden Pond (Massachusetts), made famous by Thoreau, who lived there from July 4, 1845, to September 6, 1847.

WALDEN   Adapted by editor from *Walden and Other Writings* by Henry David Thoreau (New York: Bantam, 1981), 168–69, 171–73, 175–78, 202–203, 205–206, 343–45.

auroral[2] character, reminding me of a certain house on a mountain which I had visited the year before. This was an airy and unplastered cabin, fit to entertain a travelling god, and where a goddess might trail her garments. The winds which passed over my dwelling were such as sweep over the ridges of mountains, bearing the broken strains, or celestial[3] parts only, of terrestrial[4] music. The morning wind forever blows, the poem of creation is uninterrupted; but few are the ears that hear it. Olympus[5] is but the outside of the earth everywhere. . . .

I was seated by the shore of a small pond,[6] about a mile and a half south of the village of Concord and somewhat higher than it, in the midst of an extensive wood between that town and Lincoln. . . . I was so low in the woods that the opposite shore, half a mile off, like the rest, covered with wood, was my most distant horizon. For the first week, whenever I looked out on the pond it impressed me like a tarn[7] high up on the side of a mountain, its bottom far above the surface of other lakes. As the sun arose, I saw it throwing off its nightly clothing of mist, and here and there, by degrees, its soft ripples or its smooth reflecting surface was revealed, while the mists, like ghosts, were stealthily withdrawing in every direction into the woods, as at the breaking up of some nocturnal conventicle.[8] The very dew seemed to hang upon the trees later into the day than usual, as on the sides of mountains. . . .

Every morning was a cheerful invitation to make my life of equal simplicity, and I may say innocence, with nature herself. I have been as sincere a worshipper of Aurora[9] as the Greeks. I got up early and bathed in the pond; that was a religious exercise, and one of the best things which I did. They say that characters were engraved on the bathing tub of king Tching-thang to this effect: "Renew thyself completely each day; do it again, and again, and forever again." I can understand that. Morning brings back the heroic ages. I was as much affected by the faint hum of a mosquito making its invisible and unimaginable tour through

[2]Dawn-like.
[3]Heavenly.
[4]Earthly.
[5]The mountain abode of the Greek gods and goddesses, thus mythical, magical.
[6]Walden Pond.
[7]A small mountain lake.
[8]Religious gathering at nighttime.
[9](Goddess of) dawn.

my apartment at earliest dawn, when I was sitting with door and windows open, as I could be by any trumpet that ever sang of fame. It was Homer's hymn; itself an Iliad and Odyssey[10] in the air, singing its own wrath and wanderings. There was something cosmical about it; a standing advertisement, till forbidden, of the everlasting vigor and fertility of the world. The morning, which is the most memorable season of the day, is the awakening hour. Then there is the least sleepiness in us; and for an hour, at least, some part of us awakes which slumbers all the rest of the day and night. Little is to be expected of that day, if it can be called a day, to which we are not awakened by our talents, but by the mechanical nudgings of some servant, are not awakened by our own newly-acquired force and aspirations from within, accompanied by the sound of celestial music, instead of factory bells, and a fragrance filling the air—to a higher life than we fell asleep from; and thus the darkness bears its fruit, and proves itself to be good, no less than the light. . . . Why is it that men give so poor an account of their day if they have not been slumbering? They are not such poor calculators. If they had not been overcome with drowsiness they would have accomplished something. Millions are awake enough for physical labor; but only one in a million is awake enough for effective intellectual exertion, only one in a hundred millions to a poetic or divine life. To be awake is to be alive. I have never yet met a man who was quite awake. How could I have looked him in the face?

We must learn to reawaken and keep ourselves awake, not by mechanical aids, but by an infinite expectation of the dawn, which does not forsake us in our soundest sleep. I know of no more encouraging fact than the unquestionable ability of man to elevate his life by a conscious endeavor. It is something to be able to paint a particular picture, or to carve a statue, and so to make a few objects beautiful; but it is far more glorious to carve and paint the very atmosphere and medium through which we look, which morally we can do. To affect the quality of the day, that is the highest of arts. Every man is expected to make his life, even in its details, worthy of the contemplation of his most elevated and critical hour. . . .

I went to the woods because I wished to live deliberately, to face only the essential facts of life, and see if I could not learn what it had to teach, and not, when I came to die, discover that I had not lived. I did not wish to live what was not life, living is so dear, nor did I wish to practice

[10]Greek epic poems credited to Homer (9th century B.C.).

resignation, unless it was quite necessary. I wanted to live deep and suck out all the marrow of life, to live so sturdily and Spartan-like[11] as to put to rout all that was not life, to cut a broad swath and shave close, to drive life into a corner, and reduce it to its lowest terms. If it proved to be mean, why then to get the whole and genuine meanness of it, and publish its meanness to the world; or if it were sublime, to know it by experience, and be able to give a true account of it in my next excursion. For most men, it appears to me, are in a strange uncertainty about it, whether it is of the devil or of God, and have *somewhat hastily* concluded that it is the chief end of man here to "glorify God and enjoy him forever."

Still we live lowly lives, like ants; though the fable tells us that we were long ago changed into men; like pygmies[12] we fight with cranes; it is error upon error, and clout upon clout, and our best virtue has for its occasion a superfluous and avoidable wretchedness. Our life is frittered away by detail. An honest man has hardly need to count more than his ten fingers, or in extreme cases he may add his ten toes, and lump the rest. Simplicity, simplicity, simplicity! I say, let your affairs be as two or three, and not a hundred or a thousand; instead of a million count half a dozen, and keep your accounts on your thumb nail. . . . Simplify, simplify. Instead of three meals a day, if it be necessary eat but one; instead of a hundred dishes, five; and reduce other things in proportion. . . . The nation itself, with all its so-called internal improvements, which, by the way, are all external and superficial, is just such an unwieldy and overgrown establishment, cluttered with furniture and tripped up by its own traps, ruined by luxury and heedless expense, by want of calculation and a worthy aim, as are the million households in the land. The only cure for it as for them is in a rigid economy, a stern and more than Spartan simplicity of life and elevation of purpose. It lives too fast. Men think that it is essential that the *Nation* have commerce, and export ice, and talk through a telegraph, and ride thirty miles an hour, without a doubt, whether *they* do or not; but whether we should live like baboons or like men, is a little uncertain. . . .

For my part, I could easily do without the post-office. I think that there are very few important communications made through it. To speak critically, I never received more than one or two letters in my life—I wrote this some years ago—that were worth the postage. The

[11]Self-disciplined, frugal, simple.
[12]People of short stature.

penny-post is, commonly, an institution through which you seriously offer a man that penny for his thoughts which is so often safely offered in jest. And I am sure that I never read any memorable news in a newspaper. If we read of one man robbed, or murdered, or killed by accident, or one house burned, or one vessel wrecked, or one steamboat blown up, or one cow run over on the Western Railroad,[13] or one mad dog killed, or one lot of grasshoppers in the winter—we never need read of another. One is enough. If you are acquainted with the principle, what do you care for a thousand instances and applications? To a philosopher all *news*, as it is called, is gossip, and they who edit and read it are old women over their tea. Yet not a few are greedy after this gossip. There was such a rush, as I hear, the other day at one of the offices to learn the foreign news by the last arrival, that several large squares of plate glass belonging to the establishment were broken by the pressure—news which I seriously think a ready wit might write a twelvemonth or twelve years beforehand with sufficient accuracy. As for Spain, for instance, if you know how to throw in Don Carlos and the Infanta, and Don Pedro and Seville and Granada,[14] from time to time in the right proportions—they may have changed the names a little since I saw the papers—and serve up a bull-fight when other entertainments fail, it will be true to the letter, and give us as good an idea of the exact state of ruin of things in Spain as the most succinct and lucid[15] reports under this head in the newspapers. And as for England, almost the last significant scrap of news from that quarter was the revolution of 1649;[16] and if you have learned the history of her crops for an average year, you never need attend to that thing again, unless your speculations are of a merely pecuniary[17] character. If one may judge who rarely looks into the newspapers, nothing new does ever happen in foreign parts, a French Revolution not excepted. . . .

   Shams and delusions are esteemed for soundest truths, while reality is fictitious. If men would steadily observe realities only, and not allow themselves to be deluded,[18] life, to compare it with such things as we

---

[13]The railroad running between Massachusetts and New York.

[14]Thoreau refers to the dynastic quarrels and intrigues of Spain and Portugal in the early 19th century.

[15]Accurate and clear.

[16]King Charles I (1625–1649) was beheaded for his opposition to the Parliamentarians.

[17]Financial.

[18]Deceived.

know, would be like a fairy tale and the Arabian Nights' Entertainments.[19] If we respected only what is inevitable and has a right to be, music and poetry would resound along the streets. When we are unhurried and wise, we perceive that only great and worthy things have any permanent and absolute existence—that petty fears and petty pleasures are but the shadow of the reality. This is always exhilarating and sublime. By closing the eyes and slumbering, and consenting to be deceived by shows, men establish and confirm their daily life of routine and habit everywhere, which still is built on purely illusory foundations. Children, who play life, discern its true law and relations more clearly than men, who fail to live it worthily, but who think that they are wiser by experience, that is, by failure. . . .

Let us spend one day as deliberately as nature, and not be thrown off the track by every nutshell and mosquito's wing that falls on the rails. Let us rise early and fast, or break fast, gently and without perturbation;[20] let company come and let company go, let the bells ring and the children cry—determined to make a day of it. Why should we knock under and go with the stream? Let us not be upset and overwhelmed in that terrible rapid and whirlpool called a dinner, situated in the middle of the day. Weather this danger and you are safe, for the rest of the way is downhill. With unrelaxed nerves, with morning vigor, sail by it, looking another way. . . . If the engine whistles, let it whistle till it is hoarse for its pains. If the bell rings, why should we run? We will consider what kind of music they are like. Let us settle ourselves, and work and wedge our feet downward through the mud and slush of opinion, and prejudice, and tradition, and delusion, and appearance, that sludge which covers the globe, through Paris and London, through New York and Boston and Concord, through church and state, through poetry and philosophy and religion, till we come to a hard bottom and rocks in place, which we can call reality, and say, This is, and no mistake. . . . If you stand face to face to a fact, you will see the sun glimmer on both its surfaces, as if it were a scimitar,[21] and feel its sweet edge dividing you through the heart, and so you will happily conclude your mortal career. Be it life or death, we crave only reality. If we are really dying, let us hear the rattle in our throats and feel cold in the extremities; if we are alive, let us go about our business.

---

[19]Collection of charming stories from the Muslim world of the 10th century A.D.
[20]Disturbance.
[21]A sword with a sharply curved blade, formerly used by Muslim warriors.

✗ Time is but the stream I go a-fishing in. I drink at it; but while I drink I see the sandy bottom and detect how shallow it is. Its thin current slides away, but eternity remains. I would drink deeper; fish in the sky, whose bottom is pebbly with stars. . . . The intellect is a cleaver; it discerns and cuts its way into the secret of things. I do not wish to be any more busy with my hands than is necessary. My head is hands and feet. I feel all my best faculties concentrated in it. My instinct tells me that my head is an organ for burrowing, as some creatures use their snout and forepaws, and with it I would mine and burrow my way through these hills. I think that the richest vein is somewhere hereabouts; so by the divining rod and thin rising vapors I judge; and here I will begin to mine.

• • •

Solitude

• • •

I have observed that sometimes the most sweet and tender, the most innocent and encouraging companionship may be found in any natural object, even for the poor misanthrope[22] and most melancholy man. There can be no very black melancholy to him who lives in the midst of nature and has his senses still. There was never yet such a storm but it was music to a healthy and innocent ear. Nothing can rightly compel a simple and brave man to a vulgar sadness. So long as I enjoy the friendship of the seasons I trust that nothing can make life a burden to me. The gentle rain which waters my beans and keeps me in the house today is not dreary and melancholy, but good for me too. Though it prevents my hoeing them, it is of far more worth than my hoeing. If it should continue so long as to cause the seeds to rot in the ground and destroy the potatoes in the low lands, it would still be good for the grass on the uplands, and, being good for the grass, it would be good for me. Sometimes, when I compare myself with other men, it seems as if I were more favored by the gods than they, more than I deserved, that I am conscious of; as if I had their approval and assurance which my fellows have not, and were especially guided and guarded. I do not flatter myself, but if it be possible they flatter me. I have never felt lonesome, or in the least oppressed by a sense of solitude, but once, and

[22]A hater of humankind.

that was a few weeks after I came to the woods, when, for an hour, I
doubted if the near neighborhood of man was not essential to a serene
and healthy life. To be alone was something unpleasant. But I was at the
same time conscious of a slight insanity in my mood, and seemed to
foresee my recovery. In the midst of a gentle rain while these thoughts
prevailed, I was suddenly aware of such sweet and beneficent companionship in nature, in the very pattering of the drops, and in every sound
and sight around my house, an infinite and unaccountable friendliness
all at once like an atmosphere sustaining me, as made the imagined
advantages of human neighborhood insignificant, and I have never
thought of them since. . . .

I find it wholesome to be alone the greater part of the time. To be in
company, even with the best, is soon wearisome and wasteful. I love to
be alone. I never found the companion that was so companionable as
solitude. We are for the most part more lonely when we are among
people than when we stay at home. A man thinking or working is
always alone, let him be where he will. Solitude is not measured by the
miles of space that intervene between a man and his fellows. The really
diligent student in one of the crowded rooms of Cambridge College is
as solitary as a dervish[23] in the desert. The farmer can work alone in the
field or the woods all day, hoeing or chopping, and not feel lonesome,
because he is employed; but when he comes home at night he cannot sit
down in a room alone, at the mercy of his thoughts, but must be where
he can "see the folks," and recreate, and as he thinks to remunerate[24]
himself for his day's solitude. Hence he wonders how the student can sit
alone in the house all night and most of the day without boredom and
"the blues;" but he does not realize that the student, though in the
house, is still at work in *his* field, and chopping in *his* woods, as the
farmer in his, and in turn seeks the same recreation and companionship
that the latter does, though it may be a more condensed form of it.

Society is commonly too cheap. We meet at very short intervals, not
having had time to acquire any new value for each other. We meet at
meals three times a day, and give each other a new taste of that old
musty cheese that we are. We have had to agree on a certain set of rules,
called etiquette and politeness, to make this frequent meeting tolerable
and that we need not come to open war. We meet at the post-office, and
at the sociable, and about the fireside every night; we live thick and are

[23]A member of a Muslim religious order, who spends his life in poverty and solitude.
[24]Repay, reward.

in each other's way, and stumble over one another, and I think that we thus lose some respect for one another. Certainly less frequency would suffice for all important and hearty communications. Consider the girls in a factory—never alone, hardly in their dreams. It would be better if there were but one inhabitant to a square mile, as where I live. The value of a man is not in his skin, that we should touch him.

• • •

Conclusion

• • •

I left the woods for as good a reason as I went there.[25] Perhaps it seemed to me that I had several more lives to live, and could not spare any more time for that one. It is remarkable how easily and virtually imperceptibly we fall into a particular route, and make a beaten track for ourselves. I had not lived there a week before my feet wore a path from my door to the pond-side; and though it is five or six years since I trod it, it is still quite distinct. It is true, I fear that others may have fallen into it, and so helped to keep it open. The surface of the earth is soft and impressible by the feet of men; and so with the paths which the mind travels. How worn and dusty, then, must be the highways of the world, how deep the ruts of tradition and conformity! . . .

I learned this, at least, by my experiment; that if one advances confidently in the direction of his dreams, and endeavors to live the life which he has imagined, he will meet with unexpected success. He will put some things behind, will pass an invisible boundary; new, universal, and more liberal laws will begin to establish themselves around and within him; or the old laws be expanded, and interpreted in his favor in a more liberal sense, and he will live with the license of a higher order of beings. In proportion as he simplifies his life, the laws of the universe will appear less complex, and solitude will not be solitude, nor poverty poverty, nor weakness weakness. If you have built castles in the air, your work need not be lost; that is where they should be. Now put the foundations under them. . . .

Why level downward to our dullest perception always, and praise that as common sense? The commonest sense is the sense of men asleep,

[25]Thoreau left after approximately two years to manage the estate of his friend Ralph Waldo Emerson, while the latter was away in England.

which they express by snoring. Sometimes we are inclined to class those who are once-and-a-half witted with the half-witted, because we appreciate only a third part of their wit. Some would find fault with the red of morning, if they ever got up early enough. "They pretend," as I hear, "that the verses of Kabir[26] have four different senses; illusion, spirit, intellect, and the popular doctrine of the Vedas;"[27] but in this part of the world it is considered a ground for complaint if a man's writings allow more than one interpretation. While England endeavors to cure the potato-rot, will not any endeavor to cure the brain-rot, which prevails so much more widely and fatally?

Perhaps I have not made myself altogether clear, but I should be proud if no more fatal fault were found with my pages than was found with the Walden ice. Southern customers objected to its blue color, which is the evidence of its purity, as if it were muddy, and preferred the Cambridge ice, which is white, but tastes of weeds. The purity men love is like the mists which envelop the earth, and not like the blue sky beyond.

Some are dinning in our ears that we Americans, and moderns generally, are intellectual dwarfs compared with the ancients, or even the Elizabethan men.[28] But what is that to the purpose? A living dog is better than a dead lion. Shall a man go and hang himself because he belongs to the race of pygmies, and not be the biggest pygmy that he can? Let every one mind his own business, and endeavor to be what he was made to be.

• • •

CIVIL DISOBEDIENCE

I heartily accept the motto,—"That government is best which governs least;" and I should like to see it acted up to more rapidly and systematically. Carried out, it finally amounts to this, which also I believe—"That government is best which governs not at all;" and

---

[26]Kabir (1450–1518), Indian [Hindu] poet, a mystic of his day and one of the founders of the Sikh religion.

[27]Sacred books of Hindu religion.

[28]Individuals living in the time of Queen Elizabeth I of England (1558–1603).

CIVIL DISOBEDIENCE   Adapted by editor from *Walden and Other Writings* by Henry David Thoreau (New York: Bantam, 1981), 85–88, 90–97, 99–101, 103–104.

when men are prepared for it, that will be the kind of government which they will have. Government is at best but an expedient; but most governments are usually, and all governments are sometimes, inexpedient. The objections which have been brought against a standing army, and they are many and weighty, and deserve to prevail, may also at last be brought against a standing government. The standing army is only an arm of the standing government. The government itself, which is only the mode which the people have chosen to execute their will, is equally liable to be abused and perverted before the people can act through it. Witness the present Mexican war,[29] the work of comparatively few individuals using the standing government as their tool; for, in the outset, the people would not have consented to this measure.

This American government—what is it but a tradition, though a recent one, endeavoring to transmit itself unimpaired to posterity, but each instant losing some of its integrity? It has not the vitality and force of a single living man; for a single man can bend it to his will. It is a sort of wooden gun to the people themselves. But it is not the less necessary for this; for the people must have some complicated machinery or other, and hear its din, to satisfy that idea of government which they have. Governments show thus how successfully men can be imposed on, even impose on themselves, for their own advantage. It is excellent, we must all allow. Yet this government never of itself furthered any enterprise, but by the alacrity[30] with which it got out of its way. *It* does not keep the country free. *It* does not settle the West. *It* does not educate. The character inherent in the American people has done all that has been accomplished; and it would have done somewhat more, if the government had not sometimes got in its way. For government is an expedient by which men would fain[31] succeed in letting one another alone; and, as has been said, when it is most expedient, the governed are most let alone by it. Trade and commerce, if they were not made of India-rubber,[32] would never manage to bounce over the obstacles which legislators are continually putting in their way; and, if one were to judge these men wholly by the effects of their actions and not partly by their intentions, they would deserve to be classed and punished with those mischievous persons who put obstructions on the railroads.

[29]The Mexican-American War (1846–1848).
[30]Briskness.
[31]Preferably.
[32]Rubber, meaning bouncy and flexible.

But, to speak practically and as a citizen, unlike those who call themselves no-government men, I ask for, not at once no government, but *at once* a better government. Let every man make known what kind of government would command his respect, and that will be one step toward obtaining it.

After all, the practical reason why, when the power is once in the hands of the people, a majority are permitted, and for a long period continue, to rule is not because they are most likely to be in the right, nor because this seems fairest to the minority, but because they are physically the strongest. But a government in which the majority rule in all cases cannot be based on justice, even as far as men understand it. Can there not be a government in which majorities do not virtually decide right and wrong, but conscience?—in which majorities decide only those questions to which the rule of expediency is applicable? Must the citizen ever for a moment, or in the least degree, resign his conscience to the legislator? Why has every man a conscience, then? I think that we should be men first, and subjects afterward. It is not desirable to cultivate a respect for the law, so much as for the right. The only obligation which I have a right to assume is to do at any time what I think right. It is truly enough said, that a corporation has no conscience; but a corporation of conscientious men is a corporation *with* a conscience. Law never made men a whit more just; and, by means of their respect for it, even the well-disposed are daily made the agents of injustice. A common and natural result of an undue respect for law is, that you may see a file of soldiers, colonel, captain, corporal, privates, powder-monkeys,[33] and all, marching in admirable order over hill and dale to the wars, against their wills, indeed, against their common sense and consciences, which makes it very steep marching indeed, and produces a palpitation of the heart. They have no doubt that it is a damnable business in which they are concerned; they are all peaceably inclined. Now, what are they? Men at all? or small movable forts and magazines, at the service of some unscrupulous man in power? Visit the Navy Yard, and behold a marine, such a man as an American government can make, or such as it can make a man with its black arts—a mere shadow and reminiscence of humanity, a man laid out alive and standing, and already, as one may say, buried under arms. . . .

The mass of men serve the state thus, not as men mainly, but as machines, with their bodies. They are the standing army, and the

[33]Men who carry gunpowder from storage areas to the artillery.

militia, jailors, constables, and so on. In most cases there is no free exercise whatever of the judgment or of the moral sense; but they put themselves on a level with wood and earth and stones; and wooden men can perhaps be manufactured that will serve the purpose as well. Such command no more respect than men of straw or a lump of dirt. They have the same sort of worth only as horses and dogs. Yet such as these even are commonly esteemed good citizens. Others—as most legislators, politicians, lawyers, ministers, and office-holders—serve the state chiefly with their heads; and, as they rarely make any moral distinctions, they are as likely to serve the Devil, without *intending* it, as God. A very few, as heroes, patriots, martyrs, reformers in the great sense, and *men*, serve the state with their consciences also, and so necessarily resist it for the most part; and they are commonly treated as enemies by it. A wise man will only be useful as a man, and will not submit to be "clay," and "stop a hole to keep the wind away". . .:

> "I am too high-born to be propertied,
> To be a secondary at control,
> Or useful serving-man and instrument
> To any sovereign state throughout the world."

He who gives himself entirely to his fellow men appears to them useless and selfish; but he who gives himself partially to them is pronounced a benefactor and philanthropist.[34]

How does it become a man to behave toward this American government today? I answer, that he cannot without disgrace be associated with it. I cannot for an instant recognize that political organization as *my* government which is the *slave's* government also.[35]

All men recognize the right of revolution; that is, the right to refuse allegiance to, and to resist, the government, when its tyranny or its inefficiency are great and unendurable. But almost all say that such is not the case now. But such was the case, they think, in the Revolution of 1775. If one were to tell me that this was a bad government because it taxed certain foreign commodities brought to its ports, it is most probable that I should not make an ado about it, for I can do without them. All machines have their friction; and possibly this does enough good to counterbalance the evil. At any rate, it is a great evil to make a stir about it. But when the friction comes to have its machine, and

---

[34]A person who benefits humankind through acts of charity and goodwill.

[35]Black slavery was still legally in force in the southern United States at this time.

oppression and robbery are organized, I say, let us not have such a machine any longer. In other words, when a sixth of the population of a nation which has undertaken to be the refuge of liberty are slaves, and a whole country is unjustly overrun and conquered by a foreign army, and subjected to military law, I think that it is not too soon for honest men to rebel and revolutionize. What makes this duty the more urgent is the fact that the country so overrun is not our own, but ours is the invading army.[36]

Paley,[37] a common authority with many on moral questions in his chapter on the "Duty of Submission to Civil Government," resolves all civil obligation into expediency; and he proceeds to say, "that so long as the interest of the whole society requires it, that is, so long as the established government cannot be resisted or changed without public inconveniency, it is the will of God that the established government be obeyed, and no longer. . . . This principle being admitted, the justice of every particular case of resistance is reduced to a computation of the quantity of the danger and grievance on the one side, and of the probability and expense of redressing it on the other." Of this, he says, every man shall judge for himself. But Paley appears never to have contemplated those cases to which the rule of expediency does not apply, in which a people, as well as an individual, must do justice, cost what it may. If I have unjustly wrested a plank from a drowning man, I must restore it to him though I drown myself. This, according to Paley, would be inconvenient. But he that would save his life, in such a case, shall lose it. This people must cease to hold slaves, and to make war on Mexico, though it cost them their existence as a people. . . .

It is not a man's duty, as a matter of course, to devote himself to the eradication[38] of any, even the most enormous wrong; he may still properly have other concerns to engage him; but it is his duty, at least, to wash his hands of it, and, if he gives it thought no longer, not to give it practically his support. If I devote myself to other pursuits and contemplations, I must first see, at least, that I do not pursue them sitting upon another man's shoulders. I must get off him first, that he may pursue his contemplations too. See what gross inconsistency is tolerated. I have heard some of my townsmen say, "I should like to have them order me out to help put down an insurrection of the slaves, or to march to Mexico;—see if I would go;" and yet these very men

---

[36]Thoreau is referring here to the U.S. invasion of Mexico (1846–47).

[37]William Paley (1743–1805), English theologian and moral philosopher.

[38]Removal, destruction.

have each, directly by their allegiance, and so indirectly, at least, by their money, furnished a substitute.[39] The soldier is applauded who refuses to serve in an unjust war by those who do not refuse to support the unjust government which makes the war; he is applauded by those whose own act and authority he disregards and sets at naught. . . . Thus, under the name of Order and Civil Government, we are all made at last to pay homage to and support our own meanness. After the first blush of sin comes its indifference, and from immoral it becomes, as it were, *un*moral, and not quite unnecessary to that life which we have made. . . .

How can a man be satisfied to entertain an opinion merely, and enjoy *it*? Is there any enjoyment in it, if his opinion is that he is aggrieved? If you are cheated out of a single dollar by your neighbor, you do not rest satisfied with knowing that you are cheated, or with saying that you are cheated, or even with petitioning him to pay you your due; but you take effectual steps at once to obtain the full amount, and see that you are never cheated again. Action from principle, the perception and the performance of right, changes things and relations; it is essentially revolutionary. . . . It not only divides states and churches, it divides families; yes, it divides the *individual*, separating the diabolical[40] in him from the divine.

Unjust laws exist: shall we be content to obey them, or shall we endeavor to amend them, and obey them until we have succeeded, or shall we transgress them at once? Men generally, under such a government as this, think that they ought to wait until they have persuaded the majority to alter them. They think that, if they should resist, the remedy would be worse than the evil. But it is the fault of the government itself that the remedy *is* worse than the evil. *It* makes it worse. Why is it not more apt to anticipate and provide for reform? Why does it not cherish its wise minority? Why does it cry and resist before it is hurt? Why does it not encourage its citizens to be on the alert to point out its faults, and *do* better than it would have them? Why does it always crucify Christ, and excommunicate Copernicus[41] and Luther,[42] and pronounce Washington and Franklin rebels? . . .

If the injustice is part of the necessary friction of the machine of

---

[39]Paying for a substitute soldier was a common method of avoiding military service at that time.

[40]Devilish.

[41]Nicolaus Copernicus (1473–1543), Polish-Prussian astronomer.

[42]Martin Luther (1483–1546), German Protestant reformer.

government, let it go, let it go: perchance it will wear smooth—certainly the machine will wear out. If the injustice has a spring, or a pulley, or a rope, or a crank, exclusively for itself, then perhaps you may consider whether the remedy will not be worse than the evil; but if it is of such a nature that it requires you to be the agent of injustice to another, then, I say, break the law. Let your life be a counter friction to stop the machine. What I have to do is to see, at any rate, that I do not lend myself to the wrong which I condemn.

As for adopting the ways which the state has provided for remedying the evil, I know not of such ways. They take too much time, and a man's life will be gone. I have other affairs to attend to. I came into this world, not chiefly to make this a good place to live in, but to live in it, be it good or bad. A man has not everything to do, but something; and because he cannot do *everything*, it is not necessary that he should do *something* wrong. It is not my business to be petitioning the Governor or the Legislature any more than it is theirs to petition me; and if they should not hear my petition, what should I do then? But in this case the state has provided no way: its very Constitution is the evil. This may seem to be harsh and stubborn and unconciliatory; but it is to treat with the utmost kindness and consideration the only spirit that can appreciate or deserves it. So is all change for the better, like birth and death, which convulse the body.

I do not hesitate to say, that those who call themselves Abolitionists[43] should at once withdraw their support, both in person and property, from the government of Massachusetts[44] and not wait till they constitute a majority of one. . . . I think that it is enough if they have God on their side, without waiting for that other one. Moreover, any man more right than his neighbors constitutes a majority of one already.

I meet this American government, or its representative, the state government, directly, and face to face, once a year—no more—in the person of its tax-gatherer. This is the only way in which a man situated as I am necessarily meets it; and it then says distinctly, Recognize me; and the simplest and most effective, and, in the present posture of affairs, the most indispensable way of treating it is to deny it then. My civil neighbor, the tax-gatherer, is the very man I have to deal with—for it is, after all, with men and not with parchment that I quarrel—and

---

[43]People calling for the abolition of slavery.
[44]Thoreau was a resident of Massachusetts.

he has voluntarily chosen to be an agent of the government. How shall he ever know well what he is and does as an officer of the government, or as a man, until he is obliged to consider whether he shall treat me, his neighbor, for whom he has respect, as a neighbor and well-disposed man, or as a maniac and disturber of the peace. . . . I know this well, that if one thousand, if one hundred, if ten men whom I could name—if ten *honest* men only—yes, if *one* HONEST man, in this State of Massachusetts, *ceasing to hold slaves*, were actually to withdraw from this copartnership, and be locked up in the county jail therefor, it would be the abolition of slavery in America. For it matters not how small the beginning may seem to be: what is once well done is done forever. . . .

Under a government which imprisons any unjustly, the true place for a just man is also a prison. The proper place today, the only place which Massachusetts has provided for her freer and less desponding spirits, is in her prisons, to be put out and locked out of the State by her own act, as they have already put themselves out by their principles. It is there that the fugitive slave, and the Mexican prisoner on parole, and the Indian come to plead the wrongs of his race should find them; on that separate, but more free and honorable ground, where the State places those who are not *with* her, but *against* her—the only house in a slave State in which a free man can live with honor. If any think that their influence would be lost there, and their voices no longer afflict the ear of the State, that they would not be as an enemy within its walls, they do not know by how much truth is stronger than error, nor how much more eloquently and effectively he can combat injustice who has experienced a little in his own person. Cast your whole vote, not a strip of paper merely, but your whole influence. A minority is powerless while it conforms to the majority; it is not even a minority then; but it is irresistible when it clogs by its whole weight. If the alternative is to keep all just men in prison, or give up war and slavery, the State will not hesitate which to choose. If a thousand men were not to pay their tax-bills this year, that would not be a violent and bloody measure, as it would be to pay them, and enable the State to commit violence and shed innocent blood. This is, in fact, the definition of a peaceable revolution, if any such is possible. If the tax-gatherer, or any other public officer, asks me, as one has done, "But what shall I do?" my answer is, "If you really wish to do anything, resign your office." When the subject has refused allegiance, and the officer has resigned his office, then the revolution is accomplished. But even suppose blood should flow. Is there not a sort of blood shed when the conscience is wounded?

Through this wound a man's real manhood and immortality flow out, and he bleeds to an everlasting death. I see this blood flowing now. . . .

When I converse with the freest of my neighbors, I perceive that whatever they may say about the magnitude and seriousness of the question, and their regard for the public tranquillity,[45] the long and the short of the matter is, that they cannot spare the protection of the existing government, and they dread the consequences to their property and families of disobedience to it. For my own part, I should not like to think that I ever rely on the protection of the State. But, if I deny the authority of the State when it presents its tax-bill, it will soon take and waste all my property, and so harass me and my children without end. This is hard. This makes it impossible for a man to live honestly, and at the same time comfortably, in outward respects. It will not be worth the while to accumulate property; that would be sure to go again. You must hire or squat somewhere, and raise but a small crop, and eat that soon. You must live within yourself, and depend upon yourself always tucked up and ready for a start, and not have many interests. A man may grow rich in Turkey even, if he will be in all respects a good subject of the Turkish government. Confucius[46] said: "If a state is governed by the principles of reason, poverty and misery are subjects of shame; if a state is not governed by the principles of reason, riches and honors are the subjects of shame." No: until I want the protection of Massachusetts to be extended to me in some distant Southern port, where my liberty is endangered, or until I am bent solely on building up an estate at home by peaceful enterprise, I can afford to refuse allegiance to Massachusetts, and her right to my property and life. It costs me less in every sense to incur the penalty of disobedience to the State than it would to obey. I should feel as if I were worth less in that case. . . .

I have paid no poll-tax[47] for six years. I was put into a jail once on this account, for one night; and, as I stood considering the walls of solid stone, two or three feet thick, the door of wood and iron, a foot thick, and the iron grating which strained the light, I could not help being struck with the foolishness of that institution which treated me as if I were mere flesh and blood and bones, to be locked up. I wondered that it should have concluded at length that this was the best use it could put

---

[45]Peacefulness.

[46]Confucius (551–479 B.C.), Chinese philosopher.

[47]A tax required for the right to vote (now prohibited by a Constitutional amendment).

me to, and had never thought to avail itself of my services in some way. I saw that, if there was a wall of stone between me and my townsmen, there was a still more difficult one to climb or break through before they could get to be as free as I was. I did not for a moment feel confined, and the walls seemed a great waste of stone and mortar. I felt as if I alone of all my townsmen had paid my tax. They plainly did not know how to treat me, but behaved like persons who are underbred. In every threat and in every compliment there was a blunder; for they thought that my chief desire was to stand the other side of that stone wall. I could not but smile to see how industriously[48] they locked the door on my thoughts, which followed them out again without hindrance, and *they* were really all that was dangerous. As they could not reach me, they had resolved to punish my body; just as boys, if they cannot come at some person against whom they have a spite, will abuse his dog. I saw that the State was half-witted, that it was timid as a lone woman with her silver spoons, and that it did not know its friends from its foes, and I lost all my remaining respect for it, and pitied it.

Thus the State never intentionally confronts a man's sense, intellectual or moral, but only his body, his senses. It is not armed with superior wit or honesty, but with superior physical strength. I was not born to be forced. I will breathe after my own fashion. Let us see who is the strongest. What force has a multitude? They only can force me who obey a higher law than I. . . .

When I came out of prison—for some one interfered, and paid that tax—I did not see that great changes had taken place in the town such as observed by one who went in a youth and emerged a tottering and gray-headed man; and yet a change had to my eyes come over the scene—the town, and State, and country—greater than any that mere time could bring about. I saw yet more distinctly the State in which I lived. I saw to what extent the people among whom I lived could be trusted as good neighbors and friends; that their friendship was for summer weather only; that they did not greatly propose to do right; that they were a distinct race from me by their prejudices and superstitions; . . . that in their sacrifices to humanity they ran no risks, not even to their property. . . . This may be to judge my neighbors harshly; for I believe that many of them are not aware that they have such an institution as the jail in their village. . . .

I have never declined paying the highway tax, because I am as

[48]Diligently, skillfully.

desirous of being a good neighbor as I am of being a bad subject; and as for supporting schools, I am doing my part to educate my fellow-countrymen now. It is for no particular item in the tax-bill that I refuse to pay it. I simply wish to refuse allegiance to the State, to withdraw and stand aloof from it effectively. I do not care to trace the course of my dollar, if I could, till it buys a man or a musket to shoot with—the dollar is innocent—but I am concerned to trace the effects of my allegiance. In fact, I quietly declare war on the State, after my fashion, though I will still make what use and get what advantage of her I can, as is usual in such cases.

If others pay the tax which is demanded of me, from a sympathy with the State, they do but what they have already done in their own case, or rather they abet[49] injustice to a greater extent than the State requires. If they pay the tax from a mistaken interest in the individual taxed, to save his property, or prevent his going to jail, it is because they have not considered wisely how far they let their private feelings interfere with the public good.

This, then, is my position at present. But one cannot be too much on his guard in such a case, lest his action be biased by obstinacy[50] or an undue regard for the opinions of men. Let him see that he does only what belongs to himself and to the hour.

I think sometimes, Why, this people mean well, they are only ignorant; they would do better if they knew how: why give your neighbors this pain to treat you as they are not inclined to? But I think again, This is no reason why I should do as they do, or permit others to suffer much greater pain of a different kind. Again, I sometimes say to myself, When many millions of men, without heat,[51] without ill will, without personal feeling of any kind, demand of you a few shillings only, without the possibility, such is their constitution, of retracting or altering their present demand, and without the possibility, on your side, of appeal to any other millions, why expose yourself to this overwhelming brute force? You do not resist cold and hunger, the winds and the waves, thus obstinately; you quietly submit to a thousand similar necessities. You do not put your head into the fire. But just in proportion as I regard this as not wholly a brute force, but partly

---

[49]Assist, further.
[50]Stubbornness.
[51]Anger.

a human force, and consider that I have relations to those millions as to so many millions of men, and not of mere brute or inanimate things, I see that appeal is possible, first and instantaneously, from them to the Maker of them, and, secondly, from them to themselves. But if I put my head deliberately into the fire, there is no appeal to fire or to the Maker of fire, and I have only myself to blame. If I could convince myself that I have any right to be satisfied with men as they are, and to treat them accordingly, and not according, in some respects, to my requisitions and expectations of what they and I ought to be, then, like a . . . fatalist, I should endeavor to be satisfied with things as they are, and say it is the will of God. And, above all, there is this difference between resisting this and a purely brute or natural force, that I can resist this with some effect; but I cannot expect, like Orpheus,[52] to change the nature of the rocks and trees and beasts.

I do not wish to quarrel with any man or nation. I do not wish to split hairs, to make fine distinctions, or set myself up as better than my neighbors. I seek rather, I may say, even an excuse for conforming to the laws of the land. I am but too ready to conform to them. Indeed, I have reason to suspect myself on this head; and each year, as the tax-gatherer comes round, I find myself disposed to review the acts and position of the general and State governments, and the spirit of the people, to discover a pretext for conformity. . . .

No man with a genius for legislation has appeared in America. They are rare in the history of the world. There are orators, politicians, and eloquent men, by the thousand; but the speaker has not yet opened his mouth to speak who is capable of settling the much-vexed questions of the day. We love eloquence for its own sake, and not for any truth which it may utter, or any heroism it may inspire. Our legislators have not yet learned the comparative value of free-trade and of freedom, of union, and of rectitude,[53] to a nation. They have no genius or talent for comparatively humble questions of taxation and finance, commerce and manufactures, and agriculture. If we were left solely to the wordy wit of legislators in Congress for our guidance, uncorrected by the seasonable experience and the effective complaints of the people, America would not long retain her rank among the nations. For eight-

---

[52]Orpheus, a poet and singer of Greek mythology who, through his music, changed the nature of those who listened to it.

[53]Uprightness, strict honesty.

een hundred years, though perchance I have no right to say it, the New Testament has been written; yet where is the legislator who has wisdom and practical talent enough to avail himself of the light which it sheds on the science of legislation?

The authority of government, even such as I am willing to submit to—for I will cheerfully obey those who know and can do better than I . . .—is still an impure one: to be strictly just, it must have the sanction and consent of the governed. It can have no pure right over my person and property but what I concede to it. The progress from an absolute to a limited monarchy, from a limited monarchy to a democracy, is a progress toward a true respect for the individual. Even the Chinese philosopher[54] was wise enough to regard the individual as the basis of the empire. Is a democracy, such as we know it, the last improvement possible in government? Is it not possible to take a step further toward recognizing and organizing the rights of man? There will never be a really free and enlightened State until the State comes to recognize the individual as a higher and independent power, from which all its own power and authority are derived, and treats him accordingly. I please myself with imagining a State at last which can afford to be just to all men, and to treat the individual with respect as a neighbor; which even would not think it inconsistent with its own repose[55] if a few were to live aloof from it, not meddling with it, nor embraced by it, who fulfilled all the duties of neighbors and fellow-men. A State which bore this kind of fruit, and suffered it to drop off as fast as it ripened, would prepare the way for a still more perfect and glorious State, which also I have imagined, but not yet anywhere seen.

[54]Confucius.
[55]Dignity, honor.

20

John Stuart Mill

On Liberty AND Utilitarianism

*T*HE *full flowering of liberal thought came in the work of John Stuart Mill (1806–1873), known as "the Aristotle of the Victorian Age" because of his versatility and the reasonableness of his views. Mill was a liberal in politics who favored a democratic base for representation, an economist who balanced laissez faire and positive government, an empiricist in philosophy, and a secular humanist in religion. He was, in short, representative of middle-class England at its intellectual best in the mid-nineteenth century. Mill came to symbolize liberalism as a way of life, with its broad sympathies and its dedication to the improvement of human beings through freedom.*

The views Mill held were rooted in the doctrinaire rationalism of his father, James Mill, who rigidly directed his son's education in the principles of Jeremy Bentham's utilitarianism. In his twenties, however, the younger Mill underwent a psychological crisis brought on by his reading of romantic poets and philosophers. Exposed to their works, he rebelled against what seemed to him the barren, calculating rationalism of Bentham and adopted a more positive, complex, and flexible point of view. While receptive to the romantic and democratic currents of mid-century European thought, Mill remained dedicated to objective, rational methods and never forsook his belief in individualism. He was, at the same time, an active social reformer who worked for all the "good causes" of his day.

On Liberty (1859), Mill's greatest contribution to modern social thought, is an eloquent essay on "the nature and limits of the power which can be legitimately exercised by society over the individual," and it offers a reasoned defense of a balanced position between individual freedom and social necessity. For Mill, positive, individual liberty is essential to both the personal happiness of self-realization and the advancement of the welfare of society. He insisted, moreover, on the necessity of unrestricted competition of ideas as the social means for discovery of truth. Although the picture of society offered by Mill— an atomistic aggregation of individuals—no longer agrees with reality, his views on intellectual freedom remain enduring ideals of the Western world.

In his work Utilitarianism *(1861), Mill endeavored to offer to the individual, as well as to society, a more secure moral foundation than existed in his time. He believed that the moral system of past centuries, based chiefly on divine revelation, had run its course. As for the future, moral principles based on intuition ("inner conviction") might serve individuals adequately—but the personal nature of such principles could not provide a common bonding for society. Utilitarianism seemed to offer what was needed, that is, a moral system which would serve both the individual and society. Mill was certain that the well-spring of morality lay within each human being. Therefore, when faced with two choices, Mill believed that humans, as a rule, will give preference to the choice of higher value over that of lesser value. Consequently, the preferences of the majority can normally be accepted and trusted as sound moral choices.*

ON LIBERTY

Of the Liberty of Thought and Discussion

The time, it is to be hoped, is gone by when any defense would be necessary of the "liberty of the press" as one of the securities against corrupt or tyrannical government. No argument, we may suppose, can now be needed against permitting a legislature or an executive, not identified in interest with the people, to prescribe opinions to them and determine what doctrines or what arguments they shall be allowed to hear. This aspect of the question, besides, has been so often and so triumphantly enforced by preceding writers that it needs not be specially insisted on in this place. Though the law of England, on the subject of the press, is as servile to this day as it was in the time of the Tudors,[1] there is little danger of its being actually put in force against political discussion except during some temporary panic or fear of

[1]The Tudor royal house ruled England from 1485 to 1603.

ON LIBERTY   Adapted by editor from *Utilitarianism, Liberty, and Representative Government* by John Stuart Mill (New York: E. P. Dutton & Co., Inc., 1910), 78–83, 86–90.

insurrection. . . . And, speaking generally, it is not, in constitutional countries, to be thought that the government, whether completely responsible to the people or not, will often attempt to control the expression of opinion, except when in doing so it makes itself the instrument of the general intolerance of the public. Let us suppose, therefore, that the government is entirely at one with the people, and never thinks of exerting any power of coercion unless in agreement with what it believes to be their voice. But I deny the right of the people to exercise such coercion, either by themselves or by their government. The power itself is illegitimate. The best government has no more title to it than the worst. It is as noxious,[2] or more noxious, when exerted in accordance with public opinion than when in opposition to it. If all mankind minus one were of one opinion, and only one person were of the contrary opinion, mankind would be no more justified in silencing that one person than he, if he had the power, would be justified in silencing mankind. Were an opinion a personal possession of no value except to the owner, if to be obstructed in the enjoyment of it were simply a private injury, it would make some difference whether the injury was inflicted only on a few persons or on many. But the peculiar evil of silencing the expression of an opinion is that it is robbing the human race, posterity as well as the existing generation—those who dissent from the opinion, still more than those who hold it. If the opinion is right, they are deprived of the opportunity of exchanging error for truth; if wrong, they lose, what is almost as great a benefit, the clearer perception and livelier impression of truth produced by its collision with error.

It is necessary to consider separately these two situations, each of which has a distinct branch of the argument corresponding to it. We can never be sure that the opinion we are endeavoring to stifle is a false opinion; and if we were sure, stifling it would be an evil still.

First, the opinion which it is attempted to suppress by authority may possibly be true. Those who desire to suppress it, of course, deny its truth; but they are not infallible.[3] They have no authority to decide the question for all mankind and exclude every other person from the means of judging. To refuse a hearing to an opinion because they are sure that it is false is to assume that *their* certainty is the same thing as *absolute* certainty. All silencing of discussion is an assumption of infalli-

---

[2]Harmful, injurious.
[3]Incapable of error.

bility. Its condemnation may be allowed to rest on this common argument, not the worse for being common.

Unfortunately for the good sense of mankind, the fact of their fallibility is far from carrying the weight in their practical judgment which is always allowed to it in theory; for while everyone well knows himself to be fallible, few think it necessary to take any precautions against their own fallibility, or admit the supposition that any opinion of which they feel very certain may be one of the examples of the error to which they admit themselves to be liable. Absolute princes,[4] or others who are accustomed to unlimited deference, usually feel this complete confidence in their own opinions on nearly all subjects. People more happily situated, who sometimes hear their opinions disputed and are not wholly unused to be set right when they are wrong, place the same unbounded reliance only on such of their opinions as are shared by all who surround them, or to whom they habitually defer; for in proportion to a man's lack of confidence in his own solitary judgment does he usually rest, with implicit[5] trust, on the infallibility of "the world" in general. And the world, to each individual, means the part of it with which he comes in contact: his party, his sect, his church, his class of society; the man may be called, by comparison, almost liberal and large-minded to whom it means anything so comprehensive as his own country or his own age. Nor is his faith in this collective authority at all shaken by his being aware that other ages, countries, sects, churches, classes, and parties have thought, and even now think, the exact reverse. He places on his own world the responsibility of being in the right against the dissenting worlds of other people; and it never troubles him that mere accident has decided which of these numerous worlds is the object of his reliance, and that the same causes which make him a churchman[6] in London would have made him a Buddhist[7] or a Confucian[8] in Peking. Yet it is as evident in itself, as any amount of argument can make it, that ages are no more infallible than individuals—every age having held many opinions which subsequent[9] ages have deemed

---

[4]Rulers of 17th- and 18-century Europe who held that their decisions and actions were answerable to God *only*.

[5]Implied, complete.

[6]A member of the Church of England.

[7]A follower of the Indian religious philosopher Buddha (Gautama Siddhartha, *ca.* 563–*ca.* 483 B.C.).

[8]A follower of the Chinese philosopher Confucius (*ca.* 551–479 B.C.).

[9]Later, following.

not only false but absurd; and it is as certain that many opinions, now general, will be rejected by future ages, as it is that many, once general, are rejected by the present.

The objection likely to be made to this argument would probably take some such form as the following. There is no greater assumption of infallibility in forbidding the propagation of error than in any other thing which is done by public authority on its own judgment and responsibility. Judgment is given to men that they may use it. Because it may be used erroneously, are men to be told that they ought not to use it at all? To prohibit what they think pernicious[10] is not claiming exemption from error, but fulfilling the duty incumbent[11] on them, although fallible, of acting on their conscientious conviction. If we were never to act on our opinions, because those opinions may be wrong, we should leave all our interests uncared for, and all our duties unperformed. An objection which applies to all conduct can be no valid objection to any conduct in particular. It is the duty of governments, and of individuals, to form the truest opinions they can; to form them carefully, and never impose them upon others unless they are quite sure of being right. But when they are sure (such reasoners may say), it is not conscientiousness but cowardice to shrink from acting on their opinions and allow doctrines which they honestly think dangerous to the welfare of mankind, either in this life or in another, to be scattered about without restraint, because other people, in less enlightened times, have persecuted opinions now believed to be true. Let us take care, it may be said, not to make the same mistake; but governments and nations have made mistakes in other things which are not denied to be fit subjects for the exercise of authority: they have laid on bad taxes, made unjust wars. Ought we therefore to lay on no taxes and, under whatever provocation, make no wars? Men and governments must act to the best of their ability. There is no such thing as absolute certainty, but there is assurance sufficient for the purposes of human life. We may, and must, assume our opinion to be true for the guidance of our own conduct; and it is assuming no more when we forbid bad men to pervert society by the propagation of opinions which we regard as false and pernicious.

I answer, that it is assuming very much more. There is the greatest difference between presuming an opinion to be true because, with

[10]Evil.
[11]Resting.

every opportunity for contesting it, it has not been refuted, and assuming its truth for the purpose of not permitting its refutation. Complete liberty of contradicting and disproving our opinion is the very condition which justifies us in assuming its truth for purposes of action; and on no other terms can a being with human faculties have any rational assurance of being right.

When we consider either the history of opinion or the ordinary conduct of human life, how can it be explained that the one and the other are no worse than they are? Not certainly to the inherent force of the human understanding, for on any matter not self-evident there are ninety-nine persons totally incapable of judging of it for one who is capable; and the capacity of the hundredth person is only comparative, for the majority of the eminent men of every past generation held many opinions now known to be erroneous, and did or approved numerous things which no one will now justify. Why is it, then, that there is on the whole a preponderance[12] among mankind of rational opinions and rational conduct? If there really is this preponderance—which there must be unless human affairs are, and have always been, in an almost desperate state—it is owing to a quality of the human mind, the source of everything respectable in man either as an intellectual or as a moral being, namely, that his errors are correctible. He is capable of correcting his mistakes by discussion and experience. Not by experience alone. There must be discussion to show how experience is to be interpreted. Wrong opinions and practices gradually yield to fact and argument; but facts and arguments, to produce any effect on the mind, must be brought before it. Very few facts are able to tell their own story, without comments to bring out their meaning. The whole strength and value, then, of human judgment depending on the one fact, that it can be set right when it is wrong, reliance can be placed on it only when the means of setting it right are kept constantly at hand. In the case of any person whose judgment is really deserving of confidence, how has it become so? Because he has kept his mind open to criticism of his opinions and conduct. Because it has been his practice to listen to all that could be said against him; to profit by as much of it as was just, and to state to himself, and upon occasion to others, the fallacy of what was fallacious. Because he has felt that the only way in which a human being can make some approach to knowing the whole of a subject is by hearing what can be said about it by persons of every variety of opinion, and studying all modes in which it can be looked at

[12]Superior in influence or weight.

by every type of mind. No wise man ever acquired his wisdom in any way but this; nor is it in the nature of human intellect to become wise in any other manner. The steady habit of correcting and completing his own opinion by comparing it with those of others, so far from causing doubt and hesitation in carrying it into practice, is the only stable foundation for a just reliance on it. . . .

It is not too much to require that what the wisest of mankind, those who are best entitled to trust their own judgment, find necessary to depend upon, should be submitted to by that miscellaneous collection of a few wise and many foolish individuals called the public. The most intolerant of churches, the Roman Catholic Church, even at the canonization[13] of a saint admits, and listens patiently to, a "devil's advocate." The holiest of men, it appears, cannot be admitted to posthumous[14] honors until all that the devil could say against him is known and weighed. If even the Newtonian philosophy[15] were not permitted to be questioned, mankind could not feel as complete assurance of its truth as they now do. The beliefs of which we are most convinced have no safeguard to rest on but a standing invitation to the whole world to prove them unfounded. If the challenge is not accepted, or is accepted and the attempt fails, we are far enough from certainty still, but we have done the best that the existing state of human reason admits of: we have neglected nothing that could give the truth a chance of reaching us; if the lists are kept open, we may hope that, if there be a better truth, it will be found when the human mind is capable of receiving it. . . .

Mankind can hardly be too often reminded that there was once a man called Socrates,[16] between whom and the legal authorities and public opinion of his time there took place a memorable collision. Born in an age and country abounding in individual greatness, this man has been handed down to us by those who best knew both him and the age as the most virtuous man in it; while *we* know him as the head and model of all subsequent teachers of virtue, the source equally of the lofty inspiration of Plato[17] and the judicious utilitarianism of

---

[13]Declaring, making.

[14]After death.

[15]Isaac Newton (1642–1727), an English mathematician, physicist, and philosopher, is famous for his "Laws of Motion" and for his principles of scientific reasoning.

[16]Socrates (470?–399 B.C.), Greek moral philosopher, a native and citizen of Athens, who devoted his life to the search for knowledge.

[17]Plato (427–347 B.C.), Greek philosopher, disciple of Socrates and teacher of Aristotle.

Aristotle,[18] "the teachers of the men who know," the two headsprings of ethical as of all other philosophy. This recognized master of all the eminent thinkers who have since lived—whose fame, still growing after more than two thousand years, all but outweighs the whole remainder of the names which make his native city illustrious—was put to death by his countrymen, after a judicial conviction, for impiety and immorality. Impiety, in denying the gods recognized by the State; indeed, his accuser asserted that he believed in no gods at all. Immorality, in being, by his doctrines and instructions, a "corruptor of youth." Of these charges the tribunal,[19] there is every ground for believing, honestly found him guilty, and condemned the man who probably of all then born had deserved best of mankind to be put to death as a criminal.

To pass from this to the only other instance of judicial iniquity,[20] the mention of which, after the condemnation of Socrates, would not be an anticlimax: the event which took place on Calvary[21] more than eighteen hundred years ago. The man who left on the memory of those who witnessed his life and conversation such an impression of his moral greatness that eighteen subsequent centuries have done homage to him as the Almighty in person, was shamefully put to death, as what? As a blasphemer.[22] Men did not merely mistake their benefactor, they mistook him for the exact contrary of what he was and treated him as that person of impiety which they themselves are now held to be for their treatment of him. The feelings with which mankind now regard these lamentable judgments, especially the later of the two, render them extremely unjust in their judgment of the unhappy actors. These were, to all appearance, not bad men—not worse than men commonly are, but rather the contrary; men who possessed in a full, or somewhat more than a full measure, the religious, moral, and patriotic feelings of their time and people: the very kind of men who, in all times, our own included, have every chance of passing through life blameless and respected. The high priest who tore his garments when the words were pronounced, which, according to all the ideas of his country, constituted the blackest guilt, was in all probability quite as sincere in his horror and indignation as the generality of respectable and pious men

[18]Aristotle (384–322 B.C.), Greek philosopher and logician.

[19]Court.

[20]Wickedness.

[21]The place near Jerusalem where Jesus was crucified.

[22]One who mocks God.

now are in the religious and moral sentiments they profess; and most of those who now shudder at his conduct, if they had lived in his time, and been born Jews, would have acted precisely as he did. Orthodox[23] Christians who are tempted to think that those who stoned to death the first martyrs must have been worse men than they themselves are, ought to remember that one of those persecutors was Saint Paul. . . .

A theory which maintains that truth may justifiably be persecuted because persecution cannot possibly do it any harm cannot be charged with being intentionally hostile to the reception of new truths; but we cannot commend the generosity of its dealing with the persons to whom mankind are indebted for them. To disclose to the world something which deeply concerns it, and of which it was previously ignorant, to prove to it that it had been mistaken on some vital point of temporal or spiritual interest, is as important a service as a human being can render to his fellow creatures, and in certain cases, as in those of the early Christians and of the Reformers,[24] those who think with Dr. Johnson[25] believe it to have been the most precious gift which could be bestowed on mankind. That the authors of such splendid benefits should be repaid by martyrdom, that their reward should be to be dealt with as the vilest of criminals, is not, upon this theory, a deplorable error and misfortune for which humanity should mourn in sackcloth and ashes, but the normal and justifiable state of things. . . .

The saying that truth always triumphs over persecution is one of those pleasant falsehoods which men repeat after one another till they pass into commonplaces, but which all experience refutes. History teems with instances of truth put down by persecution. If not suppressed forever, it may be thrown back for centuries. To speak only of religious opinions: the Reformation broke out at least twenty times before Luther, and was put down. . . . It is a piece of idle sentimentality that truth, merely as truth, has any inherent power denied to error of prevailing against the dungeon and the stake. Men are not more zealous for truth than they often are for error, and a sufficient application of legal or even of social penalties will generally succeed in stopping the spread of either. The real advantage which truth has consists in this, that when an opinion is true, it may be extinguished once, twice, or many times, but in the course of ages there will generally be found persons to

---

[23]Strict, devout.

[24]The various "unsuccessful" reformers of medieval Christianity.

[25]Samuel Johnson (1709–1784), author, maker of dictionaries, and critic.

rediscover it, until some one of its reappearances falls on a time when from favorable circumstances it escapes persecution until it has made such advance as to withstand all subsequent attempts to suppress it.

It will be said that we do not now put to death the introducers of new opinions: we are not like our fathers who killed the prophets; we even build monuments to them. It is true we no longer put heretics[26] to death; and the amount of punishment which modern feeling would probably tolerate, even against the most obnoxious opinions, is not sufficient to eliminate them. But let us not flatter ourselves that we are yet free from the stain even of legal persecution. Penalties for opinion, or at least for its expression, still exist by law; and their enforcement is not, even in these times, so unusual as to make it at all incredible that they may some day be revived in full force.

• • •

UTILITARIANISM

What Utilitarianism Is

The creed which accepts as the foundation of morals "utility" or the "greatest happiness principle" holds that actions are right in proportion as they tend to promote happiness; wrong as they tend to produce the reverse of happiness. By happiness is intended pleasure and the absence of pain; by unhappiness, pain and the absence of pleasure. To give a clear view of the moral standard set up by the theory, much more requires to be said; in particular, what things it includes in the ideas of pain and pleasure, and to what extent this is left an open question. But these supplementary explanations do not affect the theory of life on which this theory of morality is grounded—namely, that pleasure and freedom from pain are the only things desirable as ends; and that all desirable things (which are as numerous in the utilitarian as in any other scheme) are desirable either for pleasure inherent[27] in themselves or as means to the promotion of pleasure and the prevention of pain.

[26]Individuals holding religious views condemned by church authorities.

[27]Inseparably a part of it.

UTILITARIANISM   Adapted by editor from *Utilitarianism, Liberty, and Representative Government* by John Stuart Mill (New York: E. P. Dutton & Co., Inc., 1910), 6–11.

Now such a theory of life arouses in many minds, and among them in some of the most estimable in feeling and purpose, intense dislike. To suppose that life has (as they express it) no higher end than pleasure— no better and nobler object of desire and pursuit—they designate as utterly mean and groveling, as a doctrine worthy only of swine, to whom the followers of Epicurus[28] were, at a very early period, contemptuously likened; and modern holders of the doctrine are occasionally made the subject of equally polite comparisons by its German, French, and English assailants.

When thus attacked, the Epicureans have always answered that it is not they, but their accusers, who represent human nature in a degrading light, since the accusation supposes human beings to be capable of no pleasures except those of which swine are capable. If this supposition were true, the charge could not be refuted, but would then be no longer an imputation;[29] for if the sources of pleasure were precisely the same to human beings and to swine, the rule of life which is good enough for the one would be good enough for the other. The comparison of the Epicurean life to that of beasts is felt as degrading, precisely because a beast's pleasures do not satisfy a human being's conceptions of happiness. Human beings have faculties more elevated than the animal appetites and, when once made conscious of them, do not regard anything as happiness which does not include their gratification.[30] I do not, indeed, consider the Epicureans to have been by any means faultless in drawing out their scheme of consequences from the utilitarian principle. To do this in any sufficient manner, many Stoic,[31] as well as Christian, elements require to be included. But there is no known Epicurean theory of life which does not assign to the pleasures of the intellect, of the feelings and imagination, and of the moral sentiments a much higher value as pleasures than to those of mere sensation. It must be admitted, however, that utilitarian writers in general have placed the superiority of mental over bodily pleasures chiefly in the greater per-

---

[28]Epicurus (342–270 B.C.), Greek (Hellenistic) philosopher who emphasized the importance of happiness and pleasure of mind and body—in *moderation. Vulgar* Epicureanism ignores this latter and most important aspect.

[29]Accusation.

[30]Satisfaction.

[31]Stoicism; Greek (Hellenistic) philosophy founded by Zeno (336–264 B.C.). Stoicism taught duty, peace of mind, and brotherhood of all humankind, as well as the calm acceptance of all hardships of human existence.

manency, safety, uncostliness, and so on, of the former—that is, in their circumstantial advantages rather than in their intrinsic[32] nature. And on all these points utilitarians have fully proved their case; but they might have taken the other and, as it may be called, higher ground with entire consistency. It is quite compatible[33] with the principle of utility to recognize the fact that some kinds of pleasure are more desirable and more valuable than others. It would be absurd that, while in estimating all other things quality is considered as well as quantity, the estimation of pleasure should be supposed to depend on quantity alone.

If I am asked what I mean by difference of quality in pleasures, or what makes one pleasure more valuable than another, merely as a pleasure, except its being greater in amount, there is but one possible answer. Of two pleasures, if there be one to which all or almost all who have experience of both give a decided preference, irrespective of any feeling of moral obligation to prefer it, that is the more desirable pleasure. If one of the two is, by those who are competently acquainted with both, placed so far above the other that they prefer it, even though knowing it to be attended with a greater amount of discontent, and would not resign it for any quantity of the other pleasure which their nature is capable of, we are justified in ascribing[34] to the preferred enjoyment a superiority in quality so far outweighing quantity as to render it, in comparison, of small account.

Now it is an unquestionable fact that those who are equally acquainted with and equally capable of appreciating and enjoying both do give a most marked preference to the manner of existence which employs their higher faculties. Few human creatures would consent to be changed into any of the lower animals for a promise of the fullest allowance of a beast's pleasures; no intelligent human being would consent to be a fool, no instructed person would be an ignoramus, no person of feeling and conscience would be selfish and base, even though they should be persuaded that the fool, the dunce, or the rascal is better satisfied with his lot than they are with theirs. They would not resign what they possess more than he for the most complete satisfaction of all the desires which they have in common with him. If they ever fancy they would, it is only in cases of unhappiness so extreme that to escape from it they would exchange their lot for almost any other, however

[32]Belonging to the very essence of a thing.
[33]Agreeable.
[34]Assigning.

undesirable in their own eyes. A being of higher faculties requires more to make him happy, is capable probably of more acute suffering, and certainly accessible to it at more points, than one of an inferior type; but in spite of these liabilities, he can never really wish to sink into what he feels to be a lower grade of existence. We may give what explanation we please of this unwillingness; we may attribute it to pride, a name which is given indiscriminately to some of the most and to some of the least estimable feelings of which mankind are capable; we may refer it to the love of liberty and personal independence, an appeal to which was with the Stoics one of the most effective means for the inculcation[35] of it; to the love of power or to the love of excitement, both of which do really enter into and contribute to it; but its most appropriate appellation[36] is a sense of dignity, which all human beings possess in one form or other. . . . Whoever supposes that this preference takes place at a sacrifice of happiness—that the superior being, in anything like equal circumstances, is not happier than the inferior—confounds the two very different ideas of happiness and contentment. It is indisputable that the being whose capacities of enjoyment are low has the greatest chance of having them fully satisfied; and a highly endowed being will always feel that any happiness which he can look for, as the world is constituted, is imperfect. But he can learn to bear its imperfections, if they are at all bearable; and they will not make him envy the being who is indeed unconscious of the imperfections. . . . It is better to be a human being dissatisfied than a pig satisfied; better to be Socrates dissatisfied than a fool satisfied. And if the fool, or the pig, are of a different opinion, it is because they only know their own side of the question. The other party to the comparison knows both sides.

It may be objected that many who are capable of the higher pleasures occasionally, under the influence of temptation, relegate them to the lower. But this is quite compatible with a full appreciation of the intrinsic superiority of the higher. Men often, from weakness of character, make their choice for the nearer good, though they know it to be the less valuable; and this no less when the choice is between two bodily pleasures than when it is between bodily and mental. They pursue sensual indulgences to the injury of health, though perfectly aware that health is the greater good. It may be further objected that many who begin with youthful enthusiasm for everything noble, as they advance

[35]Pinning down of an idea.
[36]Name or team.

in years, sink into indolence[37] and selfishness. But I do not believe that those who undergo this very common change voluntarily choose the lower description of pleasures in preference to the higher. I believe that, before they devote themselves exclusively to the one, they have already become incapable of the other. Capacity for the nobler feelings is in most natures a very tender plant, easily killed, not only by hostile influences, but by mere want of sustenance; and in the majority of young persons it speedily dies away if the occupations to which their position in life has devoted them, and the society into which it has thrown them, are not favorable to keeping that higher capacity in exercise. Men lose their high aspirations as they lose their intellectual tastes, because they have not time or opportunity for indulging them; and they addict themselves to inferior pleasures, not because they deliberately prefer them, but because they are either the only ones to which they have access or the only ones which they are any longer capable of enjoying. It may be questioned whether anyone who has remained equally susceptible[38] to both classes of pleasures ever knowingly and calmly preferred the lower, though many, in all ages, have broken down in an ineffectual[39] attempt to combine both. . . .

I have dwelt on this point as being a necessary part of a perfectly just conception of utility or happiness considered as the directive rule of human conduct. But it is by no means an indispensable condition to the acceptance of the utilitarian standard; for that standard is not the agent's own greatest happiness, but the greatest amount of happiness altogether; and if it may possibly be doubted whether a noble character is always the happier for its nobleness, there can be no doubt that it makes other people happier, and that the world in general is immensely a gainer by it. Utilitarianism, therefore, could only attain its end by the general cultivation of nobleness of character, even if each individual were only benefited by the nobleness of others. . . .

According to the greatest happiness principle, as above explained, the ultimate end, with reference to and for the sake of which all other things are desirable—whether we are considering our own good or that of other people—is an existence exempt as far as possible from pain, and as rich as possible in enjoyments, both in point of quantity and

[37]Idleness, laziness.
[38]Open, or subject, to.
[39]Unsuccessful.

quality; the test of quality and the rule for measuring it against quantity being the preference felt by those who, in their opportunities of experience, to which must be added their habits of self-consciousness and self-observation, are best furnished with the means of comparison. This, being according to the utilitarian opinion the end of human action, is necessarily also the standard of morality, which may accordingly be defined "the rules and precepts[40] for human conduct." By their observance an existence such as has been described might be, to the greatest extent possible, secured to all mankind; and not to them only, but, so far as the nature of things admits, to all feeling creatures.

• • •

[40]Teachings.

21

Georg Wilhelm Friedrich Hegel

Reason in History

GEORG *Wilhelm Friedrich Hegel (1770–1831), the most influential philosopher of the nineteenth century, incorporated into his written work many elements of romanticism. His philosophical idealism, his emphasis on change and the sweep of history, his organic theory of society, and his rejection of the abstract, mechanical rationalism of the Enlightenment—all stamp Hegel as a child of the romantic age. A university professor in Germany for most of his life, he wrote in a complex and difficult style, but nevertheless dominated European philosophy in his lifetime by reason of the universal scope and power of his intellectual system. Since that era, almost all great Western philosophies—whether idealist or materialist, pragmatic or existentialist, radical or conservative—have had to come to terms with Hegel's ideas. In this respect, the philosophy of Hegel may be considered an intellectual bridge between the eighteenth and twentieth centuries.*

Through his philosophy Hegel hoped to prove this universe to be actually one—even if views, phenomena, and facts seemed to contradict one another. He derived his conviction concerning the oneness of the world from his Lutheran faith, which taught that all creation was of divine origin; therefore, all the world, he reasoned, had to be of one divine nature. Hegel went a step further, asserting that God, or Spirit, the term he used, had become history—and not merely interfered in history. The process in which the Spirit became history had been set in motion because the Spirit sought knowledge of its own nature or potential. In order to achieve it, the Spirit had to incorporate itself into its opposite, that is, physical creation. In incorporating itself into its opposite, the Spirit became "estranged" or "alienated." World development from that moment onward, Hegel maintained, has been a creative clash between two opposites, thesis *and* antithesis, *out of which emerges a* synthesis *(containing elements of the former thesis and antithesis). Each synthesis becomes in turn, a new thesis, calling forth its own antithesis; and this "dialectical" process is repeated, each time on a higher level, endlessly. Thus, world development is not to be understood as simple and unopposed growth, but as unwilling labor against itself, that is, struggle by which the Spirit, or Idea, may more completely realize itself. To Hegel, the objects of nature were visible monuments of the various steps of the struggle. But once they become locked in their places, their subsequent history merely shows constant, though perhaps varied, cycles of repetition. Only in the realm of historic [struggling] Ideas is the new to be found. As Ideas struggle within the arena of human events, another element enters the picture: human passions and interest. Although necessarily a continuous upward movement, world history nevertheless rocks back and forth constantly within the confines of the "warp and woof" of divine Idea and human passions.*

Hegel believed that the State was the highest and purest level the divine Idea had achieved up to his time. Thus the State was not to be understood as an organization formed at will and forged by chance, but as the highest expression of divine morality. It followed that the laws of the State were of divine origin, and therefore the duty of a citizen was to submit to them. It also was prudent to be obedient to the laws because all value that people have, all spiritual morality, all chance for self-realization, they have through the State alone. Only in fusing their subjective will with the rational will of the State could citizens find true freedom. Freedom thus could never be synonymous with a person's individualistic choices and preferences ("caprice"). Hegel held that the national bourgeois states of nineteenth-century Europe in general, and the Prussian State in particular, had arrived near the last stage of the unfolding of the divine Idea: State and morality had become virtually synonymous and interchangeable terms. That a government (State) in the next century might demand obedience while performing criminal and inhuman acts was unimaginable to Hegel. Since its premise was progression, the Hegelian dialectic allowed no room for retrogression or relapse into a barbarous past.

The Philosophy of History was not written by Hegel himself. But it is a compilation of notes written by him and by students present at lectures he delivered at the University of Berlin between 1822 and 1831; it was first published in 1837, several years after his death. The following selection, taken from the introduction to the work, summarizes its general ideas.

REASON THE ESSENCE OF HISTORY

The sole thought which philosophy brings to the observation of history, is the simple idea of *Reason*: that Reason is the sovereign of the world; that the history of the world, therefore, presents us with a rational process. This conviction and insight is a theory in the field of history as such. In that of philosophy it is no theory. It is proved by speculative thought that Reason—and this term may suffice us here, without investigating its relationship to God,—is *substance*, as well as *infinite power*; its own *infinite material* underlying all the natural and spiritual life which it originates, as well as the *infinite form*,—that which sets this material in motion. On one hand, Reason is the *substance* of the universe; that is, by which and in which all reality has its being and subsistence. On the other hand, it is the *infinite energy* of the universe; since Reason is not so powerless as to be incapable of producing anything but a mere ideal, a mere intention—having its place outside reality, nobody knows where; something separate and abstract, in the minds of certain human beings. It is *the infinite content of things*, their entire essence and truth. It is its own material which it commits to its own active energy to be used; not needing, as finite action does, the conditions of an external material of given means from which it may obtain its support, and the objects of its activity. It supplies its own nourishment, and is the object of its own operations. While it is exclusively its own basis of existence, and absolute final aim, it is also the energizing power realizing this aim; developing it not only in the phenomena of the natural, but also of the spiritual universe—the history of the world. That this "Idea" or "Reason" is the *True*, the *Eternal*, the Absolutely *Power*; that it reveals itself in the world, and that in the world nothing else is revealed but this and its honor and glory—is the thesis which, as we have said, has been proved in philosophy, and herewith is regarded as demonstrated.

Regarding those persons . . . who are not yet acquainted with philosophy, I may presume, at least, the existence of a *belief* in Reason, a desire, a thirst for acquaintance with it. . . . It is in fact the wish for rational insight and not the ambition to amass a mere heap of facts that should be presumed in every case to occupy the mind of the student of the sciences. If the clear idea of Reason is not already developed in our

REASON IN HISTORY   Adapted by editor from *Lectures on the Philosophy of History* by G. W. F. Hegel, trans. J. Sibree (from the third German edition), (London: George Bell and Sons, 1884), 9–11, 17–18, 21, 23–25, 39–41, 54, 56–59, 75–77, 82.

minds, when commencing with the study of world history, we should at least have the firm, unconquerable faith that Reason *does* exist; and that the world of intelligence and conscious will is not abandoned to chance, but must show itself in the light of the self-cognizant Idea. Yet I am not obliged to make any such preliminary demand upon your faith. What I have said here provisionally, and what I shall have further to say, is, even in reference to *our* branch of science, not to be regarded as theoretical, but as a summary view of the whole; the *result of the investigation* we are about to pursue; a result which happens to be known to *me*, because I know the entire field. It is a conclusion drawn from the history of the world, that its development has been a rational process; that it represents the rational and necessary course of the World-Spirit—that Spirit whose nature is always one and the same, but which unfolds its nature in the phenomena of the world's existence. This must, as before stated, be the *result* of history. But we have to take the latter as it is. We must proceed historically—empirically. . . .

THE ULTIMATE DESIGN OF THE WORLD

The enquiry into the *essential destiny* of Reason—as far as it is considered in reference to the world—is identical with the question, *what is the ultimate design of the world?* And the expression implies that that design is destined to be realized. Two points of consideration suggest themselves: first, the ultimate purpose of this design—its destiny as such; and secondly, its *realization*.

It must be observed at the outset, that the phenomenon we investigate—world history—belongs to the realm of *Spirit*. The term "*world*" includes both physical and psychical nature. Physical nature also plays its part in the world's history, and attention will have to be paid to the fundamental natural relations thus involved. But Spirit, and the course of its development, is our substantial object. Our task does not require us to contemplate nature as a rational system in itself—though in its own proper domain it proves itself such—but simply in its relation to *Spirit*. On the stage on which we are observing it,—world history—Spirit displays itself in its most concrete reality. Notwithstanding this . . . we must introduce some abstract characteristics of the *nature of Spirit*. . . .

The nature of Spirit may be understood by a glance at its direct opposite—*Matter*. As the essence of matter is gravity, so, on the other hand, we may affirm that the substance, the essence of Spirit is Freedom. All will readily agree to the doctrine that Spirit, among other properties, is also endowed with Freedom; but philosophy teaches that all the qualities of Spirit exist only through Freedom, that all are but means for attaining Freedom, that all seek and produce this and this alone. It is a result of speculative philosophy that Freedom is the sole truth of Spirit. Matter possesses gravity in virtue of its tendency toward a central point. It is essentially composite, consisting of parts that *exclude* each other. It seeks its unity and therefore exhibits itself as self-destructive, as verging toward its opposite. If it could attain this, it would be matter no longer, it would have perished. It strives after the realization of its ideality, for in unity it exists *ideally*. Spirit, on the contrary, may be defined as that which has its center in itself. It has not a unity outside itself, but has already found it; it exists *in* and *with itself*. Matter has its essence out of itself; Spirit is *self-contained existence*. Now this is Freedom, exactly. For if I am dependent, my being is referred to something else which I am not; I cannot exist independently of something external. I am free, on the contrary, when my existence depends upon myself. This self-contained existence of Spirit is none other than self-consciousness—consciousness of one's own being. Two things must be distinguished in consciousness; first, the fact *that I know*; secondly, *what I know*. In *self*-consciousness these are merged in one; for Spirit *knows itself*. It involves an appreciation of its own nature, and also an energy enabling it to realize itself—to make itself *actually* that which it is *potentially*. According to this abstract definition, it may be said of world history that it is the exhibition of Spirit in the process of working out the knowledge of that which it is potentially. And as the germ bears in itself the whole nature of the tree and the taste and form of its fruits, so do the first traces of Spirit virtually contain the whole of history. . . .

THE REALIZATION OF THE IDEA

• • •

The question of the *means* by which Freedom develops itself into a world leads us to the phenomenon of history itself. Although Freedom is primarily an undeveloped idea, the means it uses are external and phenomenal—presenting themselves in history as we see it unfold. The first glance at history convinces us that the actions of men proceed from their needs, their passions, their characters, and talents, and impresses us with the belief that such needs, passions, and interests are the sole springs of action, the efficient forces on this scene of activity. Among these may, perhaps, be found aims of universal kind—benevolence, or noble patriotism; but such virtues and general aims are but insignificant as compared with the world and what it generates. We may perhaps see the ideal of Reason actualized in those who adopt such aims and within the sphere of their influence; but they are only small in proportion to the mass of the human race, and the extent of their influence is limited accordingly. Passions, private aims, and the satisfacti~ of selfish desires, are on the other hand, most effective springs of action. Their power lies in the fact that they respect none of the limitations which justice and morality would impose on them, and that these natural impulses have a more direct influence over man than the artificial and tedious discipline that tends toward order and self-restraint, law and morality. . . .

The *first* that we notice, and which—though already stated more than once—cannot be too often repeated, . . . is that what we call *principle, ultimate purpose, destiny,* or the nature and idea of Spirit, is something merely general and abstract. A principle, a law, is an inner essence, which *as such*—however true in itself—is not completely real. Purposes, principles, and so on, have a place in our thoughts, in our subjective design only, but not yet in the sphere of reality. That which exists for itself only is a possibility, a potentiality, but has not yet emerged into existence. A *second* element must be introduced in order to produce actuality, that is, activity, realization, whose driving force is the will, the activity of man in the broadest sense. It is only by this activity that that Idea as well as abstract characteristics generally, are realized, actualized; for of themselves they are powerless. The activity that puts them in operation, and gives them existence, is the need, instinct, inclination, and passion of man. That some idea of mine should become reality and endure is my earnest desire; I wish to assert my personality in connection with it; I wish to be satisfied by its execution. If I am to exert myself for any object, it must in some way or other be *my* object. In the accomplishment of such or such designs I must at the same time find *my* satisfaction, although the purpose for which I exert myself yields a variety of results many of which hold no interest for me. This is the absolute right of personal existence—to find *itself* satisfied in its activity and labor. If men are to interest themselves for anything, they must have part of their existence involved in it and find their individuality gratified by its attainment. . . .

Two elements, therefore, enter into the object of our investigation;

the first the Idea, the second the complex of human passions; the one the warp, the other the woof of the vast tapestry of world history. The center and union of the two is liberty, under the conditions of morality in a State. We have spoken of the Idea of Freedom as the nature of Spirit and the absolute goal of history. Passion is regarded as undesirable, as more or less evil. Man is expected to have no passions. Passion, it is true, is not quite the fitting word for what I wish to express. I mean here nothing more than human activity as resulting from private interests, with special, self-seeking designs—with this qualification: that the whole energy of will and character is devoted to their attainment. . . .

THE IDEA OF THE STATE

The point to be analyzed is, what is the object to be realized by these means, that is, what is the form it assumes in the realm of reality. We have spoken of *means*; but in the carrying out of a subjective, limited aim, we have also to take into consideration the element of a *material*, either already present or which has to be procured. Thus the question would arise: What is the material in which the ideal of Reason is realized? The primary answer would be, personality itself—human desires, subjectivity generally. In human knowledge and will as its material element, Reason attains positive existence. We have considered subjective will where it has an object which is the truth and essence of a reality, namely, where it constitutes a great world-historical passion. As a subjective will, occupied with limited passions, it is dependent, and can gratify its desires only within the limits of this dependence. But the subjective will has also a substantial life, a reality, in which it moves in the region of *essential* being, and has the essential itself as the object of its existence. This essential being is the union of the *subjective* with the *rational* will. It is the moral whole, the *State*, which is that form of reality in which the individual has and enjoys his freedom; but on the condition of his knowing, believing and willing that which is common to the whole. And this must not be understood as if the subjective will of the social unit attained its gratification and enjoyment through that common will; as if this were a means provided for its benefit; as if the individual, in his relations to other individuals, thus limited his freedom, in order that this universal limitation, the mutual constraint of all, might secure a small space of liberty for each. Rather, we affirm, that law, morality, the State, and they alone are the positive reality and completion of Freedom. Freedom which has been curtailed is mere caprice, which in turn originates in special desires.

Subjective will, passion, is that which actualizes, realizes. The Idea is the inner essence, the State is the existing, genuinely moral life. For it is the unity of the universal, essential will with that of the individual, and this is "Morality." The individual living in this unity has a moral life, possesses a value that consists in this substantiality alone. Sophocles in his Antigone,* says, "The divine commands are not of yesterday, nor of today; no, they have an infinite existence, and no one could say from where they came." The laws of morality are not accidental, but are the essentially rational. It is the very object of the State that what is essential in the practical activity of men, and in their dispositions, should be duly recognized; that it should have a manifest existence, and maintain its position. It is the absolute interest of Reason that this moral whole should exist, and herein lies the justification and merit of heroes who have founded states, however crude these may have been. In the history of the world, only those people will be noticed, who have founded a state. For it must be understood that this latter is the realization of Freedom, that is, of the absolute final purpose, and that it exists for its own sake. It must further be understood that all the value which the human being possesses, all spiritual reality, he possesses only through the State. For his spiritual reality consists in this, that his own essence, Reason, is objectively present to him, that it possesses objective immediate existence for him. Thus only is he fully conscious; thus only is he a partaker of morality, of a just and moral social and political life. For Truth is the unity of the universal and subjective will; and the universal is to be found in the State, in its laws, its universal and rational arrangements. The State is the divine Idea as it exists on earth. We have in it, therefore, the object of history in a more definite shape than before; that in which Freedom obtains objectivity, and lives in the enjoyment of this objectivity. For law is the objectivity of Spirit; will in its true form. Only that will which obeys law, is free; for it obeys itself, it is independent and free. When the State or our country becomes a community of existence; when the subjective will of man submits to laws, the dichotomy between liberty and necessity vanishes. The rational has necessary existence, as being the reality and substance of things, and we are free in recognizing it as law, and following it as the substance of our own being. The objective and the subjective will are then reconciled, and present one identical homogeneous whole. For the morality of the State is not of that ethical reflective kind, in which one's own conviction

---

*The protagonist (heroine) of the play, *Antigone*, by the Greek dramatist Sophocles (496?–406 B.C.).

rules; this latter is rather the peculiarity of the modern time, while the true and ancient morality is based on the principle of doing one's duty. An Athenian citizen did what was required of him, as if from instinct; but if I reflect on the object of my activity, I must have the consciousness that my will has been called upon. But morality is duty, substantial law, a "*second* nature" as it has been justly called; for the *first* nature of man is his primary, animal existence. . . .

Summing up what has been said of the State, we find that we have been led to call its vital principle, that impels to action the individuals who compose it—morality. The State, its laws, its arrangements, are the rights of its members; its natural features, its mountains, air, and waters, are *their* country, their fatherland, their outward material property; the history of this State, *their* deeds; what their ancestors have produced belongs to them and lives in their memory. All is their possession, just as they are possessed by it; for it constitutes their existence, their being. . . .

THE COURSE OF WORLD HISTORY

The changes which history presents have been long characterized in general as an advance to something better, more perfect. The changes that take place in nature, however varied they may be, exhibit only a perpetually self-repeating cycle; in nature there happens "nothing new under the sun," and the replay of its phenomena brings a feeling of boredom. Only in those changes which take place in the realm of Spirit does anything new arise. This peculiarity in the world of mind has given to man an altogether different destiny from that of natural objects; . . . namely, a *real* capacity for change, and that for the better, an impulse of *perfectibility*. This principle, which brings change itself under law, has met with an unfavorable reception from religions, such as the Catholic, and from States claiming as their just right a static, or at least a stable position. . . . Perfectibility indeed is almost as vague a term as changeability; it is without scope or goal, and has no standard by which to measure the changes: the improved, more perfect state of things toward which it is expected to move is altogether undetermined.

The principle of *development* implies a latent destiny, an existing potentiality striving to realize itself. This formal concept finds actual existence in Spirit which has the history of the world for its theater, its property, and realm of its realization. It is not of such a nature as to be tossed to and fro amid the superficial play of accidents, but is rather the absolute arbiter of things, entirely unmoved by contingencies which it applies and manages for its own purposes. Development, however, is also a property of organic natural objects. . . . That development (of *natural organisms*) takes place in a direct, unopposed, unhindered manner. . . . But in relation to Spirit it is quite otherwise. The realization of *its* Idea is mediated by consciousness and will. These very faculties are, in the first instance, sunk in their primary natural life; the first object and goal of their striving is the realization of their natural destiny,— which, since it is Spirit that animates it, is possessed of vast attractions, great power and richness. Thus Spirit is at war with itself; it has to overcome itself as its most formidable obstacle. That development which in the sphere of nature is a peaceful growth, is in that of Spirit, a severe, a mighty conflict with itself. What Spirit really strives for is the realization of its ideal being; but in doing so, it hides that goal from its own vision, and is proud and well satisfied in this alienation from it.

Its expansion, therefore, does not present the harmless peacefulness of mere growth, as does that of organic life, but hard unwilling labor against itself. It exhibits, moreover, not the mere formal idea of development, but the attainment of a definite result. The goal of attainment we determined at the outset: it is Spirit in its essential nature, that is, Freedom. This is the fundamental object, and therefore also the leading principle of the development, whereby it receives meaning and importance. . . . There are many important periods in history in which development seems to have been interrupted; in which, we might rather say, the whole enormous gain of previous culture appears to have been entirely lost. Afterward, a new beginning became necessary, made in the hope of regaining—by the assistance of some remains from the wreck of the former civilization, and by new and incalculable expenditures in strength and time, . . . the former level of culture. We behold also *continued* processes of growth: structures and systems of culture in particular spheres, rich in kind, and well developed in every direction. The merely formal and indeterminate view of development in general can neither assign to one form of expansion superiority over the other, nor make understandable the object of that decay of older periods of growth; but must regard such occurrences, or to speak more clearly, the retrocessions they exhibit, as external contingencies. . . .

World history shows the *gradation* in the development of that principle whose substantial *purpose* is the consciousness of Freedom. The analysis of the successive stages, in their abstract form belongs to logic; in their concrete aspect to the Philosophy of Spirit. Here it is sufficient to state that the first stage in the process presents that immersion of Spirit in nature which has been already referred to; the second stage shows it advancing to the consciousness of its freedom. But this initial separation from nature is imperfect and partial, since it is derived immediately from the merely natural state, is consequently related to it, and is still encumbered with it as an essentially connected element. The third stage is the elevation of the soul from this still limited and special form of freedom to its pure universal form; that state in which the spiritual essence attains the consciousness and feeling of itself. These stages are the basic principles of the universal process. But how each of them on the other hand involves within *itself* a process of formation, forming the links in a dialectic of transition, to detail this must be reserved for the sequel. . . .

THE UNIVERSALITY OF THE SPIRIT

World history in general is therefore the development of Spirit in *time*, as nature is the development of the Idea in *space*.

If then we cast a glance at world history in general, we see a vast picture of changes and transactions, of infinitely varied forms of people, states, individuals in restless succession. Everything that can enter into and interest the soul of man, all our sensibility to *goodness, beauty, and greatness*, is called into play. On every hand aims are adopted and pursued, which we recognize, whose accomplishment we desire—we hope and fear for them. In all these occurrences and changes we behold human action and suffering predominant; everywhere something related to ourselves exists, and therefore everywhere something arouses our interest for or against. Sometimes it attracts us by beauty, freedom, and rich variety, sometimes by energy that enables even vice to make itself important. Sometimes we see the large mass of some general interest advancing with comparative slowness, and subsequently sacrificed to an infinite complication of trifling circumstances, and then be scattered. Then, again, with a vast expenditure of power a trivial result is produced; while from what appears unimportant a tremendous issue proceeds. On every hand there is the varied throng of events drawing us within the circle of its interest, and when one combination vanishes another immediately appears in its place. . . .

If we consider Spirit in this way, regarding its changes not merely as rejuvenating transitions, that is, returns to the same form, but rather as manipulations of itself, by which it multiplies the material for future endeavors, we see it exerting itself in a variety of modes and directions. It develops and enjoys itself in an abundance which is inexhaustible, because every one of its creations, in which it has already found gratification, meets it anew as material, and is a new stimulus for shaping activity. The abstract notion of mere change gives place to the thought of Spirit manifesting, developing, and perfecting its powers in every direction which its many-sided nature can follow. What powers it inherently possesses we learn from the variety of products and formations which it originates. In this pleasurable activity, it has to do only with itself. Involved with the conditions of mere nature—internal and external—it will indeed meet in these not only opposition and hindrance, but will often see its endeavors thereby fail; often sink under the complications in which it is entangled either by nature or by itself. But in such case it perishes in fulfilling its own destiny and proper function, and even thus exhibits the spectacle of self-demonstration as spiritual activity. . . .

We have already discussed the final aim of this progression. The principles of the successive phases of Spirit that move the nations through the necessary stages are themselves only steps in the development of the one universal Spirit, which through them elevates and completes itself into a self-comprehending *totality*.

While we are thus concerned exclusively with the idea of Spirit, and in the history of the world regard everything as only its manifestation, we have, in traversing the past, however extensive its periods, only to do with what is *present*. For philosophy, as occupying itself with the True, has to do with the *eternally present*. Nothing in the past is lost for it; for the Idea is ever present; Spirit is immortal. With it there is no past, no future, but an essential *now*. This necessarily implies that the present form of Spirit comprehends within it all earlier stages. These have indeed unfolded themselves in succession independently; but what Spirit is, it has always been, essentially. The difference is only development of this essential nature. The life of the ever-present Spirit is a cycle of stages, which, looked at in one aspect still exist beside each other, and when looked at from another point of view appear as past. The moments which Spirit seems to have left behind, it still possesses in the depths of its present.

· · ·

22

Charles Darwin

The Origin of Species AND
The Descent of Man

*C*HARLES *Darwin (1809–1882)
has, with good reason, been called "the Newton of Biology." His ideas not only
revolutionized that discipline but re-formed most social thought around the
concepts of evolutionary biology. Like Newton, Darwin is one of the giant
figures in the intellectual development of the Western world; however, his
central concept, it is important to note, was not original with him. The idea of
evolution was already "in the air" during the years in which this young English
naturalist surveyed the results of his five-year trip to South America on the
research ship "Beagle" (1831–1836). Geologists and biologists, as well as philosophers and social thinkers, had already advanced the concept of developmental
growth in their fields. Darwin, however, was to give the theory a solid scientific
basis and establish it beyond quibbling by marshaling voluminous evidence in its
favor. For a time he was extremely hesitant about publishing his conclusions,
fearing that they would offend religious beliefs. But the simultaneous work
and independent exposition of organic evolution in 1858 by another biologist,
Alfred Russel Wallace, prodded Darwin into action. In 1859 he published the
results of his own findings,* The Origin of Species by Means of Natural
Selection, or the Preservation of the Favored Races in the Struggle
for Life.

    *The title underlined Darwin's novel thesis that organic evolution had taken
place by natural selection and competitive struggle, in which successive small
variations that made for survival eventually produced new species. Even this
explanation of the process had been suggested to Darwin, for in 1838 he had
read Thomas Malthus's* Essay on Population, *which describes the pressure of
population on the food supply. The* Origin of Species, *as well as Darwin's
later work* The Descent of Man *(1871), caused a great outcry. Contradicting
the Christian belief in special creation, it held humans to be part of nature and*

subject to all its laws, and it seemed to obliterate the distinction between body and mind. Darwin stood firm, however, and evolution was soon widely accepted both by scientists and by the general public.

continuously changing

The implications of the evolutionary theory were equally important for political, economic, and moral thought. By analogy, all ideas, beliefs, and institutions were conceived to be in a state of flux, a view that seemed to destroy any rational basis for absolute standards and to equate the natural and the good. By making human beings a part of nature engaged in a dramatic struggle for survival, Darwinism reinforced the perspectives of romanticism and encouraged the irrationalism of the last century. Some social thinkers used the theory to justify the competitive economic system, while others, like Marx, saw in it a rationale for the class struggle and progress toward socialism. Darwin himself never made these broader applications or ever went beyond the limits of his biological hypothesis. The organic theory of evolution still stands essentially as he stated it, with only those modifications made necessary by new discoveries in genetics, ecology, and paleontology.

THE ORIGIN OF SPECIES

As this whole volume is one long argument, it may be convenient to the reader to have the leading facts and inferences briefly recapitulated.

That many and serious objections may be advanced against the theory of descent with modification through variation and natural selection, I do not deny. I have endeavored to give to them their full force. Nothing at first can appear more difficult to believe than that the more complex organs and instincts have been perfected, not by means superior to, though analogous with, human reason, but by the accumulation of innumerable slight variations, each good for the individual possessor. Nevertheless, this difficulty, though appearing to our imagination insuperably great, cannot be considered real if we admit the following propositions, namely, that all parts of the organization and instincts offer, at least, individual differences—that there is a struggle for existence leading to the preservation of profitable deviations[1] of

[1]Variations.

THE ORIGIN OF SPECIES   Adapted by editor from *The Origin of Species by Means of Natural Selection, or the Preservation of the Favored Races in the Struggle for Life*, 6th ed., by Charles Darwin (New York: Appleton, 1892), II, 267–68, 271–82, 290–95, 298–301, 304–306.

structure or instinct—and, lastly, that gradations in the state of perfection of each organ may have existed, each good of its kind. The truth of these propositions cannot, I think, be disputed.

It is, no doubt, extremely difficult even to conjecture by what gradations many structures have been perfected, more especially among broken and failing groups of organic beings, which have suffered much extinction; but we see so many strange gradations in nature, that we ought to be extremely cautious in saying that any organ or instinct, or any whole structure, could not have arrived at its present state by many graduated steps. There are, it must be admitted, cases of special difficulty opposed to the theory of natural selection; and one of the most curious of these is the existence in the same community of two or three defined castes of workers or sterile female ants; but I have attempted to show how these difficulties can be mastered. . . .

As according to the theory of natural selection, an interminable[2] number of intermediate forms must have existed, linking together all the species in each group by gradations as fine as are our existing varieties, it may be asked, Why do we not see these linking forms all around us? Why are not all organic beings blended together in an inextricable chaos? With respect to existing forms, we should remember that we have no right to expect (excepting in rare cases) to discover *directly* connecting links between them, but only between each and some extinct and supplanted form. Even on a wide area, which has during a long period remained continuous, and of which the climatic and other conditions of life change insensibly in proceeding from a district occupied by one species into another district occupied by a closely allied species, we have no just right to expect often to find intermediate varieties in the intermediate zones. For we have reason to believe that only a few species of a genus[3] ever undergo change; the other species becoming utterly extinct and leaving no modified progeny.[4] Of the species which do change, only a few within the same country change at the same time; and all modifications are slowly effected. I have also shown that the intermediate varieties which probably at first existed in the intermediate zones, would be liable to be supplanted by the allied forms on either hand; for the latter, from existing in greater numbers, would generally be modified and im-

[2]Endless.

[3]A biological classification including a number of related *species*.

[4]Offspring.

proved at a quicker rate than the intermediate varieties, which existed in lesser numbers; so that the intermediate varieties would, in the long run, be supplanted and exterminated.

On this doctrine of the extermination of an infinity of connecting links, between the living and extinct inhabitants of the world, and at each successive period between the extinct and still older species, why is not every geological formation charged with such links? Why does not every collection of fossil remains afford plain evidence of the gradation and mutation of the forms of life? Although geological research has undoubtedly revealed the former existence of many links, bringing numerous forms of life much closer together, it does not yield the infinitely many fine gradations between past and present species required on the theory; and this is the most obvious of the many objections which may be urged against it. Why, again, do whole groups of allied species appear, though this appearance is often false, to have come in suddenly on the successive geological stages? Although we now know that organic beings appeared on this globe, at a period incalculably remote, long before the lowest bed of the Cambrian system[5] was deposited, why do we not find beneath this system great piles of strata stored with the remains of the progenitors[6] of the Cambrian fossils?[7] For on the theory, such strata must somewhere have been deposited at these ancient and utterly unknown epochs of the world's history.

I can answer these questions and objections only on the supposition that the geological record is far more imperfect than most geologists believe. The number of specimens in all our museums is absolutely as nothing compared with the countless generations of countless species which have certainly existed. The parent-form of any two or more species would not be in all its characters directly intermediate between its modified offspring, any more than the rock-pigeon is directly intermediate in crop and tail between its descendants, the pouter and fantail pigeons. We should not be able to recognize a species as the parent of another and modified species, if we were to examine the two ever so closely, unless we possessed most of the intermediate links; and owing to the imperfection of the geological record, we have no just right to expect to find so many links. If two or three, or even more linking forms were discovered, they would simply be ranked by many

[5]An early geological formation (earth stratum).
[6]Ancestors.
[7]Remains of creatures.

naturalists as so many new species, more especially if found in different geological sub-stages, let their differences be ever so slight. Numerous existing doubtful forms could be named which are probably varieties;[8] but who will pretend that in future ages so many fossil links will be discovered, that naturalists will be able to decide whether or not these doubtful forms ought to be called varieties? Only a small portion of the world has been geologically explored. Only organic beings of certain classes can be preserved in a fossil condition, at least in any great number. Many species when once formed never undergo any further change but become extinct without leaving modified descendants; and the periods, during which species have undergone modification, though long as measured by years, have probably been short in comparison with the periods during which they retained the same form. It is the dominant and widely ranging species which vary most frequently and vary most, and varieties are often at first local—both causes rendering the discovery of intermediate links in any one formation less likely. Local varieties will not spread into other and distant regions until they are considerably modified and improved; and when they have spread, and are discovered in a geological formation, they appear as if suddenly created there, and will be simply classed as new species. Most formations have been intermittent in their accumulation; and their duration has probably been shorter than the average duration of specific forms. Successive formations are in most cases separated from each other by blank intervals of time of great length; for fossiliferous formations thick enough to resist future degradation can as a general rule be accumulated only where much sediment is deposited on the subsiding bed of the sea. During the alternate periods of elevation and of stationary level the record will generally be blank. During these latter periods there will probably be more variability in the forms of life; during periods of subsidence, more extinction. . . .

That the geological record is imperfect all will admit; but that it is imperfect to the degree required by our theory, few will be inclined to admit. If we look at long enough intervals of time, geology plainly declares that species have all changed; and they have changed in the manner required by the theory, for they have changed slowly and in a graduated manner. We clearly see this in the fossil remains from consecutive formations invariably being much more closely related to each other, than are the fossils from widely separated formations. . . .

[8]Variations *within* a species.

Under domestication[9] we see much variability, caused, or at least excited, by changed conditions of life; but often in so obscure a manner, that we are tempted to consider the variations as spontaneous. Variability is governed by many complex laws,—by correlated growth, compensation, the increased use and disuse of parts, and the definite action of the surrounding conditions. There is much difficulty in ascertaining how largely our domestic productions have been modified; but we may safely infer that the amount has been large, and that modifications can be inherited for long periods. As long as the conditions of life remain the same, we have reason to believe that a modification, which has already been inherited for many generations, may continue to be inherited for an almost infinite number of generations. On the other hand, we have evidence that variability when it has once come into play, does not cease under domestication for a very long period; nor do we know that it ever ceases, for new varieties are still occasionally produced by our oldest domesticated productions.

Variability is not actually caused by man; he only unintentionally exposes organic beings to new conditions of life, and then nature acts on the organization and causes it to vary. But man can and does select the variations given to him by nature, and thus accumulates them in any desired manner. He thus adapts animals and plants for his own benefit or pleasure. He may do this methodically, or he may do it unconsciously by preserving the individuals most useful or pleasing to him without any intention of altering the breed. It is certain that he can largely influence the character of a breed by selecting, in each successive generation, individual differences so slight as to be inappreciable except by an educated eye. This unconscious process of selection has been the great agency[10] in the formation of the most distinct and useful domestic breeds. That many breeds produced by man have to a large extent the character of natural species, is shown by the inextricable doubts whether many of them are varieties or aboriginally[11] distinct species.

There is no reason why the principles which have acted so efficiently under domestication should not have acted under nature. In the survival of favored individuals and races, during the constantly recurrent Struggle for Existence, we see a powerful and everacting form of Selection. The struggle for existence inevitably follows from the high

[9]Taming and using animals to serve human purposes.
[10]Factor.
[11]From the beginning.

geometrical ratio of increase which is common to all organic beings. This high rate of increase is proved by calculation,—by the rapid increase of many animals and plants during a succession of peculiar seasons, and when naturalized in new countries. More individuals are born than can possibly survive. A grain in the balance may determine which individuals shall live and which shall die,—which variety or species shall increase in number, and which shall decrease, or finally become extinct. As the individuals of the same species come in all respects into the closest competition with each other, the struggle will generally be most severe between them; it will be almost equally severe between the varieties of the same species, and next in severity between the species of the same genus. On the other hand the struggle will often be severe between beings remote in the scale of nature. The slightest advantage in certain individuals, at any age or during any season, over those with which they come into competition, or better adaptation in however slight a degree to the surrounding physical conditions, will, in the long run, turn the balance.

With animals having separated sexes, there will be in most cases a struggle between the males for the possession of the females. The most vigorous males, or those which have most successfully struggled with their conditions of life, will generally leave most progeny. But success will often depend on the males having special weapons, or means of defense, or charms; and a slight advantage will lead to victory.

As geology plainly proclaims that each land has undergone great physical changes, we might have expected to find that organic beings have varied under nature, in the same way as they have varied under domestication. And if there has been any variability under nature, it would be an unaccountable fact if natural selection had not come into play. It has often been asserted, but the assertion is incapable of proof, that the amount of variation under nature is a strictly limited quantity. Man, though acting on external characters alone and often capriciously, can produce within a short period a great result by adding up mere individual differences in his domestic productions; and every one admits that species present individual differences. But, besides such differences, all naturalists admit that natural varieties exist which are considered sufficiently distinct to be worthy of record in systematic works. No one has drawn any clear distinction between individual differences and slight varieties; or between more plainly marked varieties and sub-species, and species. On separate continents, and on different parts of the same continent when divided by barriers of any kind, and on outlying islands, what a multitude of forms exist, which some experienced naturalists rank as varieties, others as geographical races or sub-species, and others as distinct, though closely allied species!

If, then, animals and plants do vary, let it be ever so slightly or slowly, why should not variations or individual differences, which are in any way beneficial, be preserved and accumulated through natural selection, or the survival of the fittest? If man can by patience select variations useful to him, why, under changing and complex conditions of life, should not variations useful to nature's living products often arise, and be preserved or selected? What limit can be put to this power, acting during long ages and rigidly scrutinizing the whole constitution, structure, and habits of each creature,—favoring the good and rejecting the bad? I can see no limit to this power, in slowly and beautifully adapting each form to the most complex relations of life. The theory of natural selection, even if we look no farther than this, seems to be in the highest degree probable. I have already recapitulated, as fairly as I could, the opposed difficulties and objections: now let us turn to the special facts and arguments in favor of the theory.

On the view that species are only strongly marked and permanent varieties, and that each species first existed as a variety, we can see why it is that no line of demarcation can be drawn between species, commonly supposed to have been produced by special acts of creation, and varieties which are acknowledged to have been produced by secondary laws. On this same view we can understand how it is that in a region where many species of a genus have been produced, and where they now flourish, these same species should present many varieties; for where the production of species has been active, we might expect, as a general rule, to find it still in action; and this is the case if varieties be incipient[12] species. Moreover, the species of the larger genera,[13] which afford the greater number of varieties or incipient species, retain to a certain degree the character of varieties; for they differ from each other by a less amount of difference than do the species of smaller genera. The closely allied species also of the larger genera apparently have restricted ranges, and in their affinities[14] they are clustered in little groups round other species—in both respects resembling varieties. These are strange

[12]At the beginning stage.
[13]Plural of genus (see footnote 3).
[14]Similarities.

relations on the view that each species was independently created, but are intelligible if each existed first as a variety. . . .

As natural selection acts solely by accumulating slight, successive, favorable variations, it can produce no great or sudden modifications; it can act only by short and slow steps. Hence, the canon[15] of "Natura non facit saltum,"[16] which every fresh addition to our knowledge tends to confirm, is on this theory intelligible. We can see why throughout nature the same general end is gained by an almost infinite diversity of means, for every peculiarity when once acquired is long inherited, and structures already modified in many different ways have to be adapted for the same general purpose. We can, in short, see why nature is prodigal[17] in variety, though stingy in innovation. But why this should be a law of nature if each species has been independently created, no man can explain. . . .

The fact, as we have seen, that all past and present organic beings can be arranged within a few great classes, in groups subordinate to groups, and with the extinct groups often falling in between the recent groups, is intelligible on the theory of natural selection with its contingencies of extinction and divergence of character. On these same principles we see how it is, that the mutual affinities of the forms within each class are so complex. We see why certain characters are far more serviceable than others for classification;—why adaptive characters, though of paramount importance to the beings, are of hardly any importance in classification; why characters derived from rudimentary parts, though of no service to the beings, are often of high classificatory value; and why embryological characters are often the most valuable of all. The real affinities of all organic beings, in contradistinction to their adaptive resemblances, are due to inheritance or community of descent. The Natural System is a genealogical arrangement, with the acquired grades of difference, marked by the terms, varieties, species, genera, families, and so forth; and we have to discover the lines of descent by the most permanent characters whatever they may be and of however slight vital importance.

The similar framework of bones in the hand of a man, wing of a bat, fin of the porpoise, and leg of the horse,—the same number of verte-

---

[15]Rule.

[16]Latin: nature makes no leap—that is, there are no large gaps, or jumps, in natural development.

[17]Extravagant.

brae forming the neck of the giraffe and of the elephant,—and innumerable other such facts, at once explain themselves on the theory of descent with slow and slight successive modifications. The similarity of pattern in the wing and in the leg of a bat, though used for such different purpose,—in the jaws and legs of a crab,—in the petals, stamens,[18] and pistils[19] of a flower, is likewise, to a large extent, intelligible on the view of the gradual modification of parts or organs which were aboriginally alike in an early progenitor in each of these classes. On the principle of successive variations not always appearing at an early age, and being inherited at a corresponding not early period of life, we clearly see why the embryos of mammals, birds, reptiles, and fishes should be so closely similar, and so unlike the adult forms. We may cease marvelling at the embryo of an air-breathing mammal or bird having branchial[20] slits and arteries running in loops, like those of a fish which has to breathe the air dissolved in water by the aid of well-developed branchiae.

Disuse, aided sometimes by natural selection, will often have reduced organs when rendered useless under changed habits or conditions of life; and we can understand on this view the meaning of rudimentary organs.[21] But disuse and selection will generally act on each creature, when it has come to maturity and has to play its full part in the struggle for existence, and will thus have little power on an organ during early life; hence the organ will not be reduced or rendered rudimentary at this early age. The calf, for instance, has inherited teeth, which never cut through the gums of the upper jaw, from an early progenitor having well-developed teeth; and we may believe that the teeth in the mature animal were formerly reduced by disuse, owing to the tongue and palate, or lips, having become excellently fitted through natural selection to browse without their aid; whereas in the calf, the teeth have been left unaffected, and on the principle of inheritance at corresponding ages have been inherited from a remote period to the present day. On the view of each organism with all its separate parts having been specially created, how utterly inexplicable is it that organs bearing the plain stamp of inutility, such as the teeth in the embryonic calf or the shrivelled wings under the soldered wing-covers of many

---

[18]The pollen-bearing organs.

[19]The seed-bearing organs.

[20]Gill-like.

[21]Remnants of organs no longer used.

beetles, should so frequently occur. Nature may be said to have taken pains to reveal her scheme of modification, by means of rudimentary organs, of embryological and homologous[22] structures, but we are too blind to understand her meaning.

I have now recapitulated the facts and considerations which have thoroughly convinced me that species have been modified, during a long course of descent. This has been effected chiefly through the natural selection of numerous successive, slight, favorable variations aided in an important manner by the inherited effects of the use and disuse of parts; and in an unimportant manner, that is in relation to adaptive structures, whether past or present, by the direct action of external conditions, and by variations which seem to us in our ignorance to arise spontaneously. It appears that I formerly underrated the frequency and value of these latter forms of variation, as leading to permanent modifications of structure independently of natural selection. But as my conclusions have lately been much misrepresented, and it has been stated that I attribute the modification of species exclusively to natural selection, I may be permitted to remark that in the first edition of this work, and subsequently, I placed in a most conspicuous position—namely, at the close of the Introduction—the following words: "I am convinced that natural selection has been the main but not the exclusive means of modification." This has been of no avail. Great is the power of steady misrepresentation; but the history of science shows that fortunately this power does not long endure. . . .

I see no good reason why the views given in this volume should shock the religious feelings of any one. It is satisfactory, as showing how transient such impressions are, to remember that the greatest discovery ever made by man, namely the law of the attraction of gravity, was also attacked by Leibnitz,[23] "as subversive of natural, and inferentially of revealed, religion." A celebrated author and divine[24] has written to me that "he has gradually learned to see that it is just as noble a conception of the Deity to believe that He created a few original forms capable of self-development into other and needful forms, as to believe that He required a fresh act of creation to supply the voids caused by the action of His laws."

---

[22]Organs of different species that have the same or similar embryological origin.
[23]Gottfried Wilhelm von Leibnitz (1646–1716), German philosopher and mathematician.
[24]Clergyman.

Why, it may be asked, until recently did nearly all the most eminent living naturalists and geologists disbelieve in the mutability[25] of species. It cannot be asserted that organic beings in a state of nature are subject to no variation; it cannot be proved that the amount of variation in the course of long ages is a limited quantity; no clear distinction has been, or can be, drawn between species and well-marked varieties. It cannot be maintained that species when intercrossed are invariably sterile, and varieties invariably fertile; or that sterility is a special endowment and sign of creation. The belief that species were immutable productions was almost unavoidable as long as the history of the world was thought to be of short duration; and now that we have acquired some idea of the lapse of time, we are too apt to assume, without proof, that the geological record is so perfect that it would have afforded us plain evidence of the mutation of species, if they had undergone mutation.

But the chief cause of our natural unwillingness to admit that one species has given birth to other and distinct species, is that we are always slow in admitting great changes of which we do not see the steps. The difficulty is the same as that felt by so many geologists, when Lyell[26] first insisted that long lines of inland cliffs had been formed, and great valleys excavated, by the force which we see still at work. The mind cannot possibly grasp the full meaning of the term of even a million years; it cannot add up and perceive the full effects of many slight variations, accumulated during an almost infinite number of generations. . . .

It may be asked how far I extend the doctrine of the modification of species. The question is difficult to answer, because the more distinct the forms are which we consider, by so much the arguments in favor of community of descent become fewer in number and less in force. But some arguments of the greatest weight extend very far. All the members of whole classes are connected together by a chain of affinities, and all can be classed on the same principle, in groups subordinate to groups. Fossil remains sometimes tend to fill up very wide intervals between existing orders.

Organs in a rudimentary condition plainly show that an early progenitor had the organ in a fully developed condition; and this in some

---

[25]Changeability.
[26]Charles Lyell (1797–1875), British geologist.

cases implies an enormous amount of modification in the descendants. Throughout whole classes various structures are formed on the same pattern, and at a very early age the embryos closely resemble each other. Therefore I cannot doubt that the theory of descent with modification embraces all the members of the same great class or kingdom. I believe that animals are descended from at most only four or five progenitors, and plants from an equal or lesser number.

Analogy would lead me one step farther, namely, to the belief that all animals and plants are descended from some one prototype. But analogy may be a deceitful guide. Nevertheless all living things have much in common, in their chemical composition, their cellular structure, their laws of growth, and their liability to injurious influences. We see this even in so trifling a fact as that the same poison often similarly affects plants and animals; or that the poison secreted by the gall-fly produces monstrous growths on the wild rose or oak-tree. With all organic beings, excepting perhaps some of the very lowest, sexual reproduction seems to be essentially similar. With all, as far as is at present known, the germinal vesicle[27] is the same; so that all organisms start from a common origin. If we look even to the two main divisions—namely, to the animal and vegetable kingdoms—certain low forms are so far intermediate in character that naturalists have disputed to which kingdom they should be referred. As Professor Asa Gray[28] has remarked, "the spores and other reproductive bodies of many of the lower algae may claim to have first a characteristically animal, and then an unequivocally vegetable existence." Therefore, on the principle of natural selection with divergence of character, it does not seem incredible that, from some such low and intermediate form, both animals and plants may have been developed; and, if we admit this, we must likewise admit that all the organic beings which have ever lived on this earth may be descended from some one primordial form. But this inference is chiefly grounded on analogy, and it is immaterial whether or not it be accepted. No doubt it is possible, as Mr. G. H. Lewes[29] has urged, that at the first commencement of life many different forms were evolved; but if so, we may conclude that only a very few have left modified descendants. For, as I have recently remarked in regard to the

[27]A small cavity or sac.
[28]Asa Gray (1810–1888), American botanist.
[29]George Henry Lewes (1817–1878), English philosopher and literary critic.

members of each great kingdom, such as the Vertebrata, Articulata,[30] and so forth, we have distinct evidence in their embryological, homologous, and rudimentary structures, that within each kingdom all the members are descended from a single progenitor.

When the views advanced by me in this volume, and by Mr. Wallace,[31] or when analogous views on the origin of species are generally admitted, we can dimly foresee that there will be a considerable revolution in natural history. Systematists will be able to pursue their labors as at present; but they will not be incessantly haunted by the shadowy doubt whether this or that form be a true species. This, I feel sure and I speak after experience, will be no slight relief. The endless disputes whether or not some fifty species of British brambles are good species will cease. Systematists will have only to decide (not that this will be easy) whether any form be sufficiently constant and distinct from other forms, to be capable of definition; and if definable, whether the differences be sufficiently important to deserve a specific name. This latter point will become a far more essential consideration than it is at present; for differences, however slight, between any two forms, if not blended by intermediate gradations, are looked at by most naturalists as sufficient to raise both forms to the rank of species.

Hereafter we shall be compelled to acknowledge that the only distinction between species and well-marked varieties is, that the latter are known, or believed, to be connected at the present day by intermediate gradations, whereas species were formerly thus connected. Hence, without rejecting the consideration of the present existence of intermediate gradations between any two forms, we shall be led to weigh more carefully and to value higher the actual amount of difference between them. It is quite possible that forms now generally acknowledged to be merely varieties may hereafter be thought worthy of specific names; and in this case scientific and common language will come into accordance. In short, we shall have to treat species in the same manner as those naturalists treat genera, who admit that genera are merely artificial combinations made for convenience. This may not be a cheering prospect; but we shall at least be freed from the vain search for the undiscovered and undiscoverable essence of the term species. . . .

---

[30]Invertebrates which have jointed bodies like worms, insects, spiders, and crustaceans.

[31]Alfred Russel Wallace (1823–1913), an English biologist who advanced, independently, an evolutionary view similar to that of Darwin.

Authors of the highest eminence seem to be fully satisfied with the view that each species has been independently created. To my mind it accords better with what we know of the laws impressed on matter by the Creator, that the production and extinction of the past and present inhabitants of the world should have been due to secondary causes, like those determining the birth and death of the individual. When I view all beings not as special creations, but as the lineal descendants of some few beings which lived long before the first bed of the Cambrian system was deposited, they seem to me to become ennobled. Judging from the past, we may safely infer that not one living species will transmit its unaltered likeness to a distant future. And of the species now living very few will transmit progeny of any kind to a far distant future; for the manner in which all organic beings are grouped, shows that the greater number of species in each genus, and all the species in many genera, have left no descendants, but have become utterly extinct. We can so far take a prophetic glance into the future as to fortell that it will be the common and widely-spread species, belonging to the larger and dominant groups within each class, which will ultimately prevail and procreate new and dominant species. As all the living forms of life are the lineal descendants of those which lived long before the Cambrian epoch, we may feel certain that the ordinary succession by generation has never once been broken, and that no cataclysm has desolated the whole world. Hence we may look with some confidence to a secure future of great length. And as natural selection works solely by and for the good of each being, all corporeal and mental endowments will tend to progress toward perfection.

It is interesting to contemplate a tangled bank, clothed with many plants of many kinds, with birds singing in the bushes, with various insects flitting about, and with worms crawling through the damp earth, and to reflect that these elaborately constructed forms, so different from each other, and dependent upon each other in so complex a manner, have all been produced by laws acting around us. These laws, taken in the largest sense, being Growth with Reproduction; Inheritance which is almost implied by reproduction; Variability from the indirect and direct action of the conditions of life, and from use and disuse: a Ratio of Increase so high as to lead to a Struggle for Life, and as a consequence to Natural Selection, entailing Divergence of Character and the Extinction of less-improved forms. Thus, from the war of nature, from famine and death, the most exalted object which we are capable of conceiving, namely, the production of the higher animals, directly follows. There is grandeur in this view of life, with its several powers, having been originally breathed by the Creator into a few forms or into one; and that, while this planet has gone cycling on according to the fixed law of gravity, from so simple a beginning endless forms most beautiful and most wonderful have been, and are being evolved.

THE DESCENT OF MAN

. . .

Man, like every other animal, has no doubt advanced to his present high condition through a struggle for existence resulting from his rapid multiplication; and if he is to advance still higher, it is to be feared that he must remain subject to a severe struggle. Otherwise he would sink into indolence,[32] and the more gifted men would not be more successful in the battle of life than the less gifted. Hence our natural rate of increase, though leading to many and obvious evils, must not be greatly diminished by any means. There should be open competition for all men; and the most able should not be prevented by laws or customs from succeeding best and rearing the largest number of offspring. Important as the struggle for existence has been and even still is, yet as far as the highest part of man's nature is concerned there are other factors more important. For the moral qualities are advanced, either directly or indirectly, much more through the effects of habit, the reasoning powers, instruction, religion, and so forth, than through natural selection. . . .

▷ The main conclusion arrived at in this work, namely that man is descended from some lowly organized form, will, I regret to think, be highly distasteful to many. But there can hardly be a doubt that we are descended from barbarians. The astonishment which I felt on first seeing a group of Fuegians[33] on a wild and broken shore will never be forgotten by me, for the thought at once rushed into my mind—such were our ancestors. These men were absolutely naked and smeared with paint, their long hair was tangled, their mouths frothed with

---

[32]Laziness.

[33]Native Indians of the Land of Fire, the southernmost tip of South America.

THE DESCENT OF MAN Adapted by editor from *The Descent of Man and Selection in Relation to Sex*, 2nd ed., revised, by Charles Darwin (New York: D. Appleton and Company, 1898), 633–34.

excitement, and their expression was wild, startled, and distrustful. They possessed hardly any skills, and like wild animals lived on what they could catch; they had no government, and were merciless to everyone not of their own small tribe. He who has seen a savage . . . will not feel much shame, if forced to acknowledge that the blood of some more humble creature flows in his veins. For my own part I would as soon be descended from that heroic little monkey, who braved his dreaded enemy in order to save the life of his keeper, or from that old baboon, who descending from the mountains, carried away in triumph his young comrade from a crowd of astonished dogs—as from a savage who delights to torture his enemies, offers up bloody sacrifices, practices infanticide[34] without remorse, treats his wives like slaves, knows no decency, and is haunted by the grossest superstitions.

Man may be excused for feeling some pride at having risen, though not through his own exertions, to the very summit of the organic scale; and the fact of his having thus risen, instead of having been simply placed there, may give him hope for a still higher destiny in the distant future. But we are not here concerned with hopes or fears, only with the truth as far as our reason permits us to discover it; and I have given the evidence to the best of my ability. We must, however, acknowledge, as it seems to me, that man with all his noble qualities, with sympathy which feels for the most debased, with benevolence which extends not only to other men but to the humblest living creature, with his god-like intellect which has penetrated into the movements and make-up of the solar system—with all these exalted powers—Man still bears in his bodily frame the indelible stamp of his lowly origin.

should see
females as equals

---

[34]The killing of an infant.

23

Karl Marx AND Friedrich Engels
The Communist Manifesto

*T*HE development of the Industrial *Revolution in the first half of the nineteenth century, with its gross exploitation of factory labor, gave rise to criticisms of the prevailing social and economic systems. The most thoroughgoing and influential attack was mounted in the 1840s by two young Germans, Karl Marx (1818–1883) and Friedrich Engels (1820–1895). Marx was a philosophy student turned journalist and revolutionary agitator, who was forced to flee from Germany and France. He finally settled in London in 1849, where he devoted the rest of his life to radical activities on an international scale and to writing a critical analysis of the capitalist economy. Marx worked in close collaboration with his friend and fellow radical Engels, who used his inherited wealth to underwrite his impecunious colleague's activities. The two dedicated their lives to the overthrow of capitalist society and to its replacement by a new socialist or communist order. Their chief weapon was the ideology that has come to be known as Marxism—a combination of philosophical, economic, and historical theory and revolutionary practice. Marxism has since become the chief doctrine of the international socialist and communist movements and has also influenced the thought and practice of many non-Marxists.*

The underlying philosophy of Marxism was dialectical materialism, which, like Hegel's thought (see selection 21), viewed all existence as a process evolving in a rational pattern according to the "dialectic," the real "laws of motion" of nature, society, and thought. But it rejected Hegel's idealist contention that "ideas" (Spirit) are superior to "matter" and held matter to be the ultimate stuff of reality. It embodied a theory of history that saw all social change as basically determined by technological-economic forces ("the modes of production") and moving inevitably through conflict (dialectic) to the resolution of all contradictions in the final stage of communism.

Marx and Engels wished, however, to do more than understand the world; they wished to change it. The Communist Manifesto, which they wrote in Brussels in 1847 as a platform for a radical organization, was a call to arms as well as a summary of the two men's basic social views. Its revolutionary appeal was made in the context of an outline of the history of Western Europe. Marx and Engels traced the evolution of socio-political systems in the past and projected this evolution into the future. For them, all historical change was characterized by the struggle of economic classes. The instrument for the final transformation of society was the proletariat, the class of industrial wage-earners. Once the proletariat achieved full consciousness of its role, it would organize economically and politically to overthrow the capitalist system. Though falling short of predictive accuracy, the Manifesto, as well as Marxism generally, has had wide appeal because of the cogency of its analysis, its apocalyptic quality, and its assurances of inevitable success.

A specter[1] is haunting Europe—the specter of Communism. All the powers of old Europe have entered into a holy alliance to exorcise this specter; Pope and Tsar, Metternich[2] and Guizot,[3] French radicals[4] and German police spies.

Where is the party in opposition that has not been decried as communistic by its opponents in power? Where the opposition that has not hurled back the branding reproach of Communism, against the more advanced opposition parties, as well as against its reactionary adversaries?

[1]A frightening, ghost-like image.

[2]Prince von Metternich (1773–1859), an Austrian statesman and diplomat, was largely responsible for the concept of Europe that emerged from the Congress of Vienna (1814–15). In March 1848 a rebellious Vienna mob forced Metternich to resign as minister of foreign affairs, an office that he had held since 1809.

[3]François Pierre Guillaume Guizot (1787–1874), a French historian and statesman, was prime minister (1840–48) under King Louis Philippe.

[4]Politicians seeking to replace the French monarchy with a *republic*.

THE COMMUNIST MANIFESTO   From *Manifesto of the Communist Party* by Karl Marx and Friedrich Engels, trans. Samuel Moore (New York: Socialist Labor Party, 1888), 7–21, 28.

Two things result from this fact.

1. Communism is already acknowledged by all European powers to be itself a power.

2. It is high time that Communists should openly, in the face of the whole world, publish their views, their aims, their tendencies, and meet this nursery tale of the specter of Communism with a Manifesto of the party itself.

To this end Communists of various nationalities have assembled in London, and sketched the following manifesto, to be published in the English, French, German, Italian, Flemish and Danish languages.

BOURGEOIS AND PROLETARIANS

The history of all hitherto existing society is the history of class struggles.

Freeman and slave, patrician and plebeian,[5] lord and serf, guildmaster and journeyman, in a word, oppressor and oppressed, stood in constant opposition to one another, carried on an uninterrupted, now hidden, now open fight, a fight that each time ended, either in a revolutionary reconstitution of society at large, or in the common ruin of the contending classes.

In the earlier epochs of history we find almost everywhere a complicated arrangement of society into various orders, a manifold graduation of social rank. In ancient Rome we have patricians, knights, plebeians, slaves; in the Middle Ages, feudal lords, vassals,[6] guildmasters, journeymen, apprentices, serfs; in almost all of these classes, again, subordinate gradations.

The modern bourgeois society that has sprouted from the ruins of feudal society, has not done away with class antagonisms. It has but established new classes, new conditions of oppression, new forms of struggle in place of the old ones.

Our epoch, the epoch of the bourgeoisie,[7] possesses, however, this distinctive feature: it has simplified the class antagonisms. Society

[5]A person of the lower class of freemen in ancient Rome.

[6]Medieval lords and their vassals (subordinates) made up the ruling military and land-holding aristocracy.

[7]The small class of entrepreneurs and capitalists who own and control the means of production.

as a whole is more and more splitting up into two great hostile camps, into two great classes directly facing each other: Bourgeoisie and Proletariat.[8]

From the serfs of the Middle Ages sprang the chartered burghers of the earliest towns. From these burgesses[9] the first elements of the bourgeoisie were developed.

The discovery of America, the rounding of the Cape,[10] opened up fresh ground for the rising bourgeoisie. The East Indian and Chinese markets, the colonization of America, trade with the colonies, the increase in the means of exchange and in commodities generally, gave to commerce, to navigation, to industry, an impulse never before known, and thereby, to the revolutionary element in the tottering feudal society, a rapid development.

The feudal system of industry, under which industrial production was monopolized by closed guilds,[11] now no longer sufficed for the growing wants of the new markets. The manufacturing system took its place. The guildmasters were pushed on one side by the manufacturing middle class; division of labor between the different corporate guilds vanished in the face of division of labor in each single workshop.

Meantime the markets kept ever growing, the demand, ever rising. Even manufacture no longer sufficed. Thereupon, steam and machinery revolutionized industrial production. The place of manufacture was taken by the giant, Modern Industry, the place of the industrial middle class, by industrial millionaires, the leaders of whole industrial armies, the modern bourgeois.

Modern industry has established the world market, for which the discovery of America paved the way. This market has given an immense development to commerce, to navigation, to communication by land. This development has, in its turn, reacted on the extension of industry; and in proportion as industry, commerce, navigation and railways extended, in the same proportion the bourgeoisie developed, increased its capital, and pushed into the background every class handed down from the Middle Ages.

[8]The large and ever-increasing number of wage earners who neither own nor control the means of production.

[9]Shopkeepers; townspeople.

[10]The Cape of Good Hope, at the southern tip of Africa.

[11]Medieval associations of craftsmen or merchants; they limited their own numbers and fixed prices.

We see, therefore, how the modern bourgeoisie is itself the product of a long course of development, of a series of revolutions in the modes of production and of exchange.

Each step in the development of the bourgeoisie was accompanied by a corresponding political advance of that class. An oppressed class under the sway of the feudal nobility, an armed and self-governing association in the medieval commune, here independent urban republic (as in Italy and Germany), there taxable "third estate" of the monarchy (as in France), afterwards, in the period of manufacture proper, serving either the semi-feudal or the absolute monarchy as a counterpoise against the nobility, and, in fact, cornerstone of the great monarchies in general, the bourgeoisie has at last, since the establishment of Modern Industry and of the world market, conquered for itself, in the modern representative State, exclusive political sway. The executive of the modern State is but a committee for managing the common affairs of the whole bourgeoisie.

The bourgeoisie, historically, has played a most revolutionary part.

The bourgeoisie, wherever it has got the upper hand, has put an end to all feudal, patriarchal, idyllic relations. It has pitilessly torn asunder the motley feudal ties that bound man to his "natural superiors," and has left remaining no other nexus between man and man than naked self-interest, callous "cash payment." It has drowned the most heavenly ecstasies of religious fervor, of chivalrous enthusiasm, of philistine sentimentalism, in the icy water of egotistical calculation. It has resolved personal worth into exchange value, and in place of the numberless indefeasible chartered freedoms, has set up that single, unconscionable freedom—Free Trade. In one word, for exploitation, veiled by religious and political illusions, it has substituted naked, shameless, direct, brutal exploitation.

The bourgeoisie has stripped of its halo every occupation hitherto honored and looked up to with reverent awe. It has converted the physician, the lawyer, the priest, the poet, the man of science, into its paid wage laborers.

The bourgeoisie has torn away from the family its sentimental veil, and has reduced the family relation to a mere money relation.

The bourgeoisie has disclosed how it came to pass that the brutal display of vigor in the Middle Ages, which Reactionists so much admire, found its fitting complement in the most slothful indolence. It has been the first to show what man's activity can bring about. It has accomplished wonders far surpassing Egyptian pyramids, Roman aqueducts, and Gothic cathedrals; it has conducted expeditions that put in the shade all former Exoduses of nations and crusades.

The bourgeoisie cannot exist without constantly revolutionizing the instruments of production, and thereby the relations of production, and with them the whole relations of society. Conservation of the old modes of production in unaltered form, was, on the contrary, the first condition of existence for all earlier industrial classes. Constant revolutionizing of production, uninterrupted disturbance of all social conditions, everlasting uncertainty and agitation, distinguish the bourgeois epoch from all earlier ones. All fixed, fast-frozen relations, with their train of ancient and venerable prejudices and opinions, are swept away, all new-formed ones become antiquated before they can ossify. All that is solid melts into air, all that is holy is profaned, and man is at last compelled to face with sober senses his real conditions of life and his relations with his kind.

The need of a constantly expanding market for its products chases the bourgeoisie over the whole surface of the globe. It must nestle everywhere, settle everywhere, establish connections everywhere.

The bourgeoisie has through its exploitation of the world market given a cosmopolitan character to production and consumption in every country. To the great chagrin of Reactionists, it has drawn from under the feet of industry the national ground on which it stood. All old-established national industries have been destroyed or are daily being destroyed. They are dislodged by new industries, whose introduction becomes a life and death question for all civilized nations, by industries that no longer work up indigenous raw material, but raw material drawn from the remotest zones, industries whose products are consumed, not only at home, but in every quarter of the globe. In place of the old wants, satisfied by the productions of the country, we find new wants, requiring for their satisfaction the products of distant lands and climes. In place of the old local and national seclusion and self-sufficiency, we have intercourse in every direction, universal interdependence of nations. And as in material, so also in intellectual production. The intellectual creations of individual nations become common property. National one-sidedness and narrow-mindedness become more and more impossible, and from the numerous national and local literatures there arises a world literature.

The bourgeoisie, by the rapid improvement of all instruments of production, by the immensely facilitated means of communication, draws all, even the most barbarian, nations into civilization. The cheap prices of its commodities are the heavy artillery with which it batters down all Chinese walls, with which it forces the barbarians' intensely obstinate hatred of foreigners to capitulate. It compels all nations, on pain of extinction, to adopt the bourgeois mode of production; it compels them to introduce what it calls civilization into their midst, namely, to become bourgeois themselves. In a word, it creates a world after its own image.

The bourgeoisie has subjected the country to the rule of the towns. It has created enormous cities, has greatly increased the urban population as compared with the rural, and has thus rescued a considerable part of the population from the idiocy of rural life. Just as it has made the country dependent on the towns, so it has made barbarian and semi-barbarian countries dependent on the civilized ones, nations of peasants on nations of bourgeois, the East on the West.

The bourgeoisie keeps more and more doing away with the scattered state of the population, of the means of production, and of property. It has agglomerated population, centralized means of production, and has concentrated property in a few hands. The necessary consequence of this was political centralization. Independent, or but loosely connected provinces, with separate interests, laws, governments, and systems of taxation, became lumped together in one nation, with one government, one code of laws, one national class–interest, one frontier and one customs tariff.

The bourgeoisie, during its rule of scarce one hundred years, has created more massive and more colossal productive forces than have all preceding generations together. Subjection of Nature's forces to man, machinery, application of chemistry to industry and agriculture, steam navigation, railways, electric telegraphs, clearing of whole continents for cultivation, canalization of rivers, whole populations conjured out of the ground—what earlier century had even a presentiment that such productive forces slumbered in the lap of social labor?

We see then: the means of production and of exchange on whose foundation the bourgeoisie built itself up, were generated in feudal society. At a certain stage in the development of these means of production and of exchange, the conditions under which feudal society produced and exchanged, the feudal organization of agriculture and manufacturing industry, in one word, the feudal relations of property, became no longer compatible with the already developed productive forces; they became so many fetters. They had to burst asunder; they were burst asunder.

Into their place stepped free competition, accompanied by a social and political constitution adapted to it, and by the economical and political sway of the bourgeois class.

A similar movement is going on before our own eyes. Modern bourgeois society with its relations of production, of exchange, and of property, a society that has conjured up such gigantic means of production and of exchange, is like the sorcerer, who is no longer able to control the powers of the nether world whom he has called up by his spells. For many a decade past the history of industry and commerce is but the history of the revolt of modern productive forces against modern conditions of production, against the property relations that are the conditions for the existence of the bourgeoisie and of its rule. It is enough to mention the commercial crises that by their periodical return put on its trial, each time more threateningly, the existence of the entire bourgeois society. In these crises a great part not only of the existing products, but also of the previously created productive forces, is periodically destroyed. In these crises there breaks out an epidemic that, in all earlier epochs, would have seemed an absurdity—the epidemic of overproduction. Society suddenly finds itself put back into a state of momentary barbarism; it appears as if a famine, a universal war of devastation had cut off the supply of every means of subsistence; industry and commerce seem to be destroyed; and why? Because there is too much civilization, too much means of subsistence, too much industry, too much commerce. The productive forces at the disposal of society no longer tend to further the development of the conditions of bourgeois property; on the contrary, they have become too powerful for these conditions, by which they are fettered, and so soon as they overcome these fetters, they bring disorder into the whole of bourgeois society, endanger the existence of bourgeois property. The conditions of bourgeois society are too narrow to comprise the wealth created by them. And how does the bourgeoisie get over these crises? On the one hand by enforced destruction of a mass of productive forces; on the other, by the conquest of new markets, and by the more thorough exploitation of the old ones. That is to say, by paving the way for more extensive and more destructive crises, and by diminishing the means whereby crises are prevented.

The weapons with which the bourgeoisie felled feudalism to the ground are now turned against the bourgeoisie itself.

But not only has the bourgeoisie forged the weapons that bring death to itself; it has also called into existence the men who are to wield those weapons—the modern working class—the proletarians.

In proportion as the bourgeoisie, that is, capital, is developed, in the same proportion is the proletariat, the modern working class, developed; a class of laborers, who live only so long as they find work, and who find work only so long as their labor increases capital. These laborers, who must sell themselves piecemeal, are a commodity, like every other article of commerce, and are consequently exposed to all the vicissitudes of competition, to all the fluctuations of the market.

Owing to the extensive use of machinery and to division of labor, the work of the proletarians has lost all individual character, and, consequently, all charm for the workman. He becomes an appendage of the machine, and it is only the most simple, most monotonous, and most easily acquired knack that is required of him. Hence, the cost of production of a workman is restricted, almost entirely, to the means of subsistence that he requires for his maintenance, and for the propagation of his race. But the price of a commodity, and also of labor, is equal to its cost of production. In proportion, therefore, as the repulsiveness of the work increases, the wage decreases. Nay, more, in proportion as the use of machinery and division of labor increases, in the same proportion the burden of toil also increases, whether by prolongation of the working hours, by increase of the work exacted in a given time, or by increased speed of the machinery, and so forth.

Modern industry has converted the little workshop of the patriarchal master into the great factory of the industrial capitalist. Masses of laborers, crowded into the factory, are organized like soldiers. As privates of the industrial army they are placed under the command of a perfect hierarchy of officers and sergeants. Not only are they slaves of the bourgeois class, and of the bourgeois State, they are daily and hourly enslaved by the machine, by the over-seer, and, above all, by the individual bourgeois manufacturer himself. The more openly this despotism proclaims gain to be its end and aim, the more petty, the more hateful and the more embittering it is.

The less the skill and exertion or strength is implied in manual labor, in other words, the more modern industry becomes developed, the more is the labor of men superseded by that of women. Differences of age and sex have no longer any distinctive social validity for the working class. All are instruments of labor, more or less expensive to use, according to age and sex.

No sooner is the exploitation of the laborer by the manufacturer so far at an end that he receives his wages in cash, than he is set upon by the other portions of the bourgeoisie, the landlord, the shopkeeper, the pawnbroker, and so forth.

The lower strata of the middle class—the small tradespeople, shopkeepers, and retired tradesmen generally, the handicraftsmen and peasants—all these sink gradually into the proletariat, partly because their diminutive capital does not suffice for the scale on which modern industry is carried on, and is swamped in the competition with the large capitalists, partly because their specialized skill is rendered worthless by new methods of production. Thus the proletariat is recruited from all classes of the population.

The proletariat goes through various stages of development. With its birth begins its struggle with the bourgeoisie. At first the contest is carried on by individual laborers, then by the workpeople of a factory, then by the operatives of one trade, in one locality, against the individual bourgeois who directly exploits them. They direct their attacks not against the bourgeois conditions of production, but against the instruments of production themselves; they destroy imported wares that compete with their labor, they smash to pieces machinery, they set factories ablaze, they seek to restore by force the vanished status of the workman of the Middle Ages.

At this stage the laborers still form an incoherent mass scattered over the whole country, and broken up by their mutual competition. If anywhere they unite to form more compact bodies, this is not yet the consequence of their own active union, but of the union of the bourgeoisie, which class, in order to attain its own political ends, is compelled to set the whole proletariat in motion, and is moreover yet, for a time, able to do so. At this stage, therefore, the proletarians do not fight their enemies, but the enemies of their enemies, the remnants of absolute monarchy, the landowners, the non-industrial bourgeois, the petty bourgeoisie. Thus the whole historical movement is concentrated in the hands of the bourgeoisie; every victory so obtained is a victory for the bourgeoisie.

But with the development of industry the proletariat not only increases in number; it becomes concentrated in greater masses, its strength grows and it feels that strength more. The various interests and conditions of life within the ranks of the proletariat are more and more equalized, in proportion as machinery obliterates all distinctions of labor, and nearly everywhere reduces wages to the same low level. The growing competition among the bourgeois, and the resulting commercial crises, make the wages of the workers ever more fluctuating. The unceasing improvement of machinery, ever more rapidly developing, makes their livelihood more and more precarious; the collisions between individual workmen and individual bourgeois take *clashes* more and more the character of collisions between two classes. Thereupon the workers begin to form combinations (Trades' Unions) against the bourgeois; they club together in order to keep up the rate of wages; they found permanent associations in order to make provision beforehand for these occasional revolts. Here and there the contest breaks out into riots.

Now and then the workers are victorious, but only for a time. The real fruit of their battles lies not in the immediate result, but in the ever-expanding union of the workers. This union is furthered by the improved means of communication that are created in modern industry and that place the workers of different localities in contact with one another. It was just this contact that was needed to centralize the numerous local struggles, all of the same character, into one national struggle between classes. But every class struggle is a political struggle. And that union, to attain which the burghers of the Middle Ages, with their miserable highways, required centuries, the modern proletarians, thanks to railways, achieve in a few years.

This organization of the proletarians into a class and consequently into a political party, is continually being upset again by the competition between the workers themselves. But it ever rises up again; stronger, firmer, mightier. It compels legislative recognition of particular interests of the workers, by taking advantage of the divisions among the bourgeoisie itself. Thus the ten-hour bill in England was carried.

Altogether collisions between the classes of the old society further, in many ways, the course of development of the proletariat. The bourgeoisie finds itself involved in a constant battle. At first with the aristocracy; later on, with those portions of the bourgeoisie itself whose interests have become antagonistic to the progress of industry; at all times with the bourgeoisie of foreign countries. In all these battles it sees itself compelled to appeal to the proletariat, to ask for its help, and thus to drag it into the political arena. The bourgeoisie itself, therefore, supplies the proletariat with its own elements of political and general

Proletariat are tools to be used.

education, in other words, it furnishes the proletariat with weapons for fighting the bourgeoisie.

Further, as we have already seen, entire sections of the ruling classes are, by the advance of industry, precipitated into the proletariat, or are at least threatened in their conditions of existence. These also supply the proletariat with fresh elements of enlightenment and progress.

Finally, in times when the class struggle nears the decisive hour, the process of dissolution going on within the ruling class, in fact within the whole range of old society, assumes such a violent, glaring character, that a small section of the ruling class cuts itself adrift, and joins the revolutionary class, the class that holds the future in its hands. Just as, therefore, at an earlier period, a section of the nobility went over to the bourgeoisie, so now a portion of the bourgeoisie goes over to the proletariat, and in particular, a portion of the bourgeois ideologists, who have raised themselves to the level of comprehending theoretically the historical movement as a whole.

Of all the classes that stand face to face with the bourgeoisie today, the proletariat alone is a really revolutionary class. The other classes decay and finally disappear in the face of modern industry; the proletariat is its special and essential product.

The lower middle class, the small manufacturer, the shopkeeper, the artisan, the peasant, all these fight against the bourgeoisie to save from extinction their existence as fractions of the middle class. They are, therefore, not revolutionary, but conservative. Nay, more, they are reactionary, for they try to roll back the wheel of history. If by chance they are revolutionary, they are so only in view of their impending transfer into the proletariat, they thus defend not their present, but their future interests, they desert their own standpoint to place themselves at that of the proletariat.

The "dangerous class," the social scum, that passively rotting mass thrown off by the lowest layers of old society, may, here and there, be swept into the movement by a proletarian revolution; its conditions of life, however, prepare it far more for the part of a bribed tool of reactionary intrigue.

In the conditions of the proletariat, those of old society at large are already virtually swamped. The proletarian is without property; his relation to his wife and children has no longer anything in common with the bourgeois family relations; modern industrial labor, modern subjection to capital, the same in England as in France, in America as in Germany, has stripped him of every trace of national character. Law, morality, religion, are to him so many bourgeois prejudices, behind which lurk in ambush just as many bourgeois interests.

All the preceding classes that got the upper hand sought to fortify their already acquired status by subjecting society at large to their conditions of appropriation. The proletarians cannot become masters of the productive forces of society, except by abolishing their own previous mode of appropriation, and thereby also every other previous mode of appropriation. They have nothing of their own to secure and to fortify; their mission is to destroy all previous securities for, and insurances of, individual property.

All previous historical movements were movements of minorities, or in the interest of minorities. The proletarian movement is the self-conscious, independent movement of the immense majority, in the interest of the immense majority. The proletariat, the lowest stratum of our present society, cannot stir, cannot raise itself up, without the whole superincumbent strata of official society being sprung into the air.

Though not in substance, yet in form, the struggle of the proletariat with the bourgeoisie is at first a national struggle. The proletariat of each country must, of course, first of all settle matters with its own bourgeoisie.

In depicting the most general phases of the development of the proletariat, we traced the more or less veiled civil war, raging within existing society, up to the point where that war breaks out into open revolution, and where the violent overthrow of the bourgeoisie lays the foundation for the sway of the proletariat.

Hitherto every form of society has been based, as we have already seen, on the antagonism of oppressing and oppressed classes. But in order to oppress a class certain conditions must be assured to it under which it can, at least, continue its slavish existence. The serf, in the period of serfdom, raised himself to membership in the commune, just as the petty bourgeois, under the yoke of feudal absolutism, managed to develop into a bourgeois. The modern laborer, on the contrary, instead of rising with the progress of industry, sinks deeper and deeper below the conditions of existence of his own class. He becomes a pauper, and pauperism develops more rapidly than population and wealth. And here it becomes evident that the bourgeoisie is unfit any longer to be the ruling class in society and to impose its conditions of existence upon society as an over-riding law. It is unfit to rule because it is incompetent to assure an existence to its slave within his slavery, because it cannot help letting him sink into such a state that it has to feed him instead of being fed by him. Society can no longer live under this bourgeoisie; in other words, its existence is no longer compatible with society.

The essential condition for the existence, and for the sway of the bourgeois class, is the formation and augmentation of capital; the condition for capital is wage-labor. Wage-labor rests exclusively on competition between the laborers. The advance of industry, whose involuntary promoter is the bourgeoisie, replaces the isolation of the laborers, due to competition, by their revolutionary combination, due to association. The development of modern industry, therefore, cuts from under its feet the very foundation on which the bourgeoisie produces and appropriates products. What the bourgeoisie therefore produces, above all, are its own gravediggers. Its fall and the victory of the proletariat are equally inevitable.

PROLETARIANS AND COMMUNISTS

In what relation do the Communists stand to the proletarians as a whole?

The Communists do not form a separate party opposed to other working class parties.

They have no interests separate and apart from those of the proletariat as a whole.

They do not set up any sectarian principles of their own by which to shape and mould the proletarian movement.

The Communists are distinguished from the other working class parties by this only: 1. In the national struggles of the proletarians of the different countries, they point out and bring to the front the common interests of the entire proletariat, independently of all nationality. 2. In the various stages of development which the struggle of the working class against the bourgeoisie has to pass through, they always and everywhere represent the interests of the movement as a whole.

The Communists, therefore, are on the one hand, practically, the most advanced and resolute section of the working class parties of every country, that section which pushes forward all others; on the other hand, theoretically, they have over the great mass of the proletariat the advantage of clearly understanding the line of march, the conditions, and the ultimate general results of the proletarian movement.

The immediate aim of the Communists is the same as that of all the other proletarian parties: formation of the proletariat into a class, overthrow of the bourgeois supremacy, conquest of political power by the proletariat.

The theoretical conclusions of the Communists are in no way based on ideas or principles that have been invented, or discovered, by this or that would-be universal reformer.

They merely express, in general terms, actual relations springing from an existing class struggle, from a historical movement going on under our very eyes. The abolition of existing property relations is not at all a distinctive feature of Communism.

All property relations in the past have continually been subject to historical change, consequent upon the change in historical conditions.

The French Revolution, for example, abolished feudal property in favor of bourgeois property.

The distinguishing feature of Communism is not the abolition of property generally, but the abolition of bourgeois property. But modern bourgeois private property is the final and most complete expression of the system of producing and appropriating products, that is based on class antagonism, on the exploitation of the many by the few.

In this sense the theory of the Communists may be summed up in the single sentence: Abolition of private property.

We Communists have been reproached with the desire of abolishing the right of personally acquiring property as the fruit of a man's own labor, which property is alleged to be the ground work of all personal freedom, activity and independence.

Hard-won, self-acquired, self-earned property! Do you mean the property of the petty artisan and of the small peasant, a form of property that preceded the bourgeois form? There is no need to abolish that; the development of industry has to a great extent already destroyed it, and is still destroying it daily.

Or do you mean modern bourgeois private property?

But does wage-labor create any property for the laborer? Not a bit. It creates capital, namely, that kind of property which exploits wage-labor, and which cannot increase except upon condition of getting a new supply of wage-labor for fresh exploitation. Property, in its present form, is based on the antagonism of capital and wage-labor. Let us examine both sides of this antagonism.

To be a capitalist, is to have not only a purely personal, but a social status in production. Capital is a collective product, and only by the united action of many members, nay, in the last resort, only by the united action of all members of society, can it be set in motion.

Capital is therefore not a personal, it is a social power.

When, therefore, capital is converted into common property, into the property of all members of society, personal property is not thereby transformed into social property. It is only the social character of the property that is changed. It loses its class character.

Let us now take wage-labor.

The average price of wage-labor is the minimum wage, namely, that quantum of the means of subsistence, which is absolutely requisite to keep the laborer in bare existence as a laborer. What, therefore, the wage-laborer appropriates by means of his labor, merely suffices to prolong and reproduce a bare existence. We by no means intend to abolish this personal appropriation of the products of labor, an appropriation that is made for the maintenance and reproduction of human life, and that leaves no surplus wherewith to command the labor of others. All that we want to do away with is the miserable character of this appropriation, under which the laborer lives merely to increase capital, and is allowed to live only in so far as the interest of the ruling class requires it.

In bourgeois society, living labor is but a means to increase accumulated labor. In communist society, accumulated labor is but a means to widen, to enrich, to promote the existence of the laborer.

In bourgeois society, therefore, the past dominates the present; in communist society, the present dominates the past. In bourgeois society capital is independent and has individuality, while the living person is dependent and has no individuality.

And the abolition of this state of things is called by the bourgeois, abolition of individuality and freedom! And rightly so. The abolition of bourgeois individuality, bourgeois independence, and bourgeois freedom is undoubtedly aimed at.

By freedom is meant, under the present bourgeois conditions of production, free trade, free selling and buying.

But if selling and buying disappears, free selling and buying disappears also. This talk about free selling and buying, and all the other "brave words" of our bourgeoisie about freedom in general, have a meaning, if any, only in contrast with restricted selling and buying, with the fettered traders of the Middle Ages, but have no meaning when opposed to the Communistic abolition of buying and selling, of the bourgeois conditions of production, and of the bourgeoisie itself.

You are horrified at our intending to do away with private property. But in your existing society private property is already done away with for nine-tenths of the population; its existence for the few is solely due to its non-existence in the hands of those nine-tenths. You reproach us, therefore, with intending to do away with a form of property, the necessary condition for whose existence is the non-existence of any property for the immense majority of society.

In one word, you reproach us with intending to do away with your property. Precisely so: that is just what we intend.

From the moment when labor can no longer be converted into capital, money, or rent, into a social power capable of being monopolized, that is, from the moment when individual property can no longer be transformed into bourgeois property, into capital, from that moment, you say, individuality vanishes!

You must, therefore, confess that by "individual" you mean no other person than the bourgeois, than the middle class owner of property. This person must, indeed, be swept out of the way, and made impossible.

Communism deprives no man of the power to appropriate the products of society: all that it does is to deprive him of the power to subjugate the labor of others by means of such appropriation.

It has been objected, that upon the abolition of private property all work will cease, and universal laziness will overtake us.

According to this, bourgeois society ought long ago to have gone to the dogs through sheer idleness; for those of its members who work, acquire nothing, and those who acquire anything, do not work. The whole of this objection is but another expression of the tautology: that there can no longer be any wage-labor when there is no longer any capital.

All objections against the Communistic mode of producing and appropriating material products, have, in the same way, been urged against the Communistic modes of producing and appropriating intellectual products. Just as, to the bourgeois the disappearance of class property is the disappearance of production itself, so the disappearance of class culture is to him identical with the disappearance of all culture.

That culture, the loss of which he laments, is, for the enormous majority, a mere training to act as a machine.

But don't wrangle with us so long as you apply to our intended abolition of bourgeois property, the standard of your bourgeois notions of freedom, culture, law, and so forth. Your very ideas are but the outgrowth of the conditions of your bourgeois production and bourgeois property, just as your jurisprudence is but the will of your class made into a law for all, a will, whose essential character and direction are determined by the economic conditions of existence of your class.

The selfish misconception that induces you to transform into eternal laws of nature and of reason, the social forms springing from your present mode of production and form of property—historical relations that rise and disappear in the progress of production—this misconception you share with every ruling class that has preceded you. What you see clearly in the case of ancient property, what you admit in the case of feudal property, you are of course forbidden to admit in the case of your own bourgeois form of property.

Abolition of the family! Even the most radical flare up at this infamous proposal of the Communists.

On what foundation is the present family, the bourgeois family, based? On capital, on private gain. In its completely developed form this family exists only among the bourgeoisie. But this state of things finds its complement in the practical absence of the family among the proletarians, and in public prostitution.

The bourgeois family will vanish as a matter of course when its complement vanishes, and both will vanish with the vanishing of capital.

Do you charge us with wanting to stop the exploitation of children by their parents? To this crime we plead guilty.

But, you will say, we destroy the most hallowed of relations, when we replace home education by social.

And your education! Is not that also social, and determined by the social conditions under which you educate, by the intervention, direct or indirect, of society by means of schools, and so forth? The Communists have not invented the intervention of society in education; they do but seek to alter the character of that intervention, and to rescue education from the influence of the ruling class.

The bourgeois clap-trap about the family and education, about the hallowed co-relation of parent and child, become all the more disgusting, the more, by the action of modern industry, all family ties among the proletarians are torn asunder, and their children transformed into simple articles of commerce and instruments of labor.

But you Communists would introduce community of women, screams the whole bourgeoisie in chorus.

The bourgeois sees in his wife a mere instrument of production. He hears that the instruments of production are to be exploited in common, and, naturally, can come to no other conclusion than that the lot of being common to all will likewise fall to the women.

He has not even a suspicion that the real point aimed at is to do away with the status of women as mere instruments of production.

For the rest nothing is more ridiculous than the virtuous indignation of our bourgeois at the community of women which, they pretend, is to be openly and officially established by the Communists. The Communists have no need to introduce community of women; it has existed almost from time immemorial.

Our bourgeois, not content with having the wives and daughters of their proletarians at their disposal, not to speak of common prostitutes, take the greatest pleasure in seducing each other's wives.

Bourgeois marriage is in reality a system of wives in common, and thus, at the most, what the Communists might possibly be reproached with, is that they desire to introduce, in substitution for a hypocritically concealed, an openly legalized community of women. For the rest it is self-evident that the abolition of the present system of production must bring with it the abolition of the community of women springing from that system, namely, of prostitution both public and private.

The Communists are further reproached with desiring to abolish countries and nationality.

The working men have no country. We cannot take from them what they have not got. Since the proletariat must first of all acquire political supremacy, must rise to be the leading class of the nation, must constitute itself *the* nation, it is, so far, itself national, though not in the bourgeois sense of the word.

National differences and antagonisms between peoples are daily more and more vanishing, owing to the development of the bourgeoisie, to freedom of commerce, to the world market, to uniformity in the mode of production and in the conditions of life corresponding thereto.

The supremacy of the proletariat will cause them to vanish still faster. United action, of the leading civilized countries at least, is one of the first conditions for the emancipation of the proletariat.

In proportion as the exploitation of one individual by another is put an end to, the exploitation of one nation by another will also be put an end to. In proportion as the antagonism between classes within the nation vanishes, the hostility of one nation to another will come to an end.

The charges against Communism made from a religious, a philosophical, and generally, from an ideological standpoint are not deserving of serious examination.

Does it require deep intuition to comprehend that man's ideas, views, and conceptions, in one word, man's consciousness changes with every change in the conditions of his material existence, in his social relations and in his social life?

What else does the history of ideas prove, than that intellectual production changes its character in proportion as material production is changed? The ruling ideas of each age have ever been the ideas of its ruling class.

When people speak of ideas that revolutionize society, they do but express the fact that within the old society the elements of a new one have been created, and that the dissolution of the old ideas keeps even pace with the dissolution of the old conditions of existence.

When the ancient world was in its last throes, the ancient religions were overcome by Christianity. When Christian ideas succumbed in the 18th century to rationalist ideas, feudal society fought its death battle with the then revolutionary bourgeoisie. The ideas of religious liberty and freedom of conscience merely gave expression to the sway of free competition within the domain of knowledge.

"Undoubtedly," it will be said, "religious, moral, philosophical and juridical ideas have been modified in the course of historical development. But religion, morality, philosophy, political science, and law, constantly survived this change."

"There are, besides, eternal truths, such as Freedom, Justice, and so forth, that are common to all states of society. But Communism abolishes eternal truths, it abolishes all religion, and all morality, instead of constituting them on a new basis; it therefore acts in contradiction to all past historical experience."

What does this accusation reduce itself to? The history of all past society has consisted in the development of class antagonisms, antagonisms that assume different forms at different epochs.

But whatever form they may have taken, one fact is common to all past ages, namely, the exploitation of one part of society by the other. No wonder, then, that the social consciousness of past ages, despite all the multiplicity and variety it displays, moves within certain common forms, or general ideas, which cannot completely vanish except with the total disappearance of class antagonisms.

The Communist revolution is the most radical rupture with traditional property relations; no wonder that its development involves the most radical rupture with traditional ideas.

But let us have done with the bourgeois objections to Communism.

We have seen above that the first step in the revolution by the working class is to raise the proletariat to the position of ruling class; to win the battle of democracy.

The proletariat will use its political supremacy to wrest, by degrees, all capital from the bourgeoisie; to centralize all instruments of production in the hands of the State, that is, of the proletariat organized as the ruling class; and to increase the total productive forces as rapidly as possible.

Of course, in the beginning this cannot be effected except by means of despotic inroads on the rights of property and on the conditions of bourgeois production; by means of measures, therefore, which appear economically insufficient and untenable, but which, in the course of the movement, outstrip themselves, necessitate further inroads upon the old social order and are unavoidable as a means of entirely revolutionizing the mode of production.

These measures will, of course, be different in different countries.

Nevertheless in the most advanced countries the following will be pretty generally applicable:

1. Abolition of property in land and application of all rents of land to public purposes.

2. A heavy progressive or graduated income tax.

3. Abolition of all right of inheritance.

4. Confiscation of the property of all emigrants and rebels.

5. Centralization of credit in the hands of the State, by means of a national bank with State capital and an exclusive monopoly.

6. Centralization of the means of communication and transport in the hands of the State.

7. Extension of factories and instruments of production owned by the State; the bringing into cultivation of waste lands, and the improvement of the soil generally in accordance with a common plan.

8. Equal liability of all to labor. Establishment of industrial armies, especially for agriculture.

9. Combination of agriculture with manufacturing industries: gradual abolition of the distinction between town and country, by a more equable distribution of population over the country.

10. Free education for all children in public schools. Abolition of children's factory labor in its present form. Combination of education with industrial production, and so forth.

When, in the course of development, class distinctions have disappeared and all production has been concentrated in the hands of a vast association of the whole nation, the public power will lose its political character. Political power, properly so called, is merely the organized power of one class for oppressing another. If the proletariat during its contest with the bourgeoisie is compelled, by the force of circumstances, to organize itself as a class, if, by means of a revolution, it makes itself the ruling class, and, as such, sweeps away by force the old conditions of production, then it will, along with these conditions, have swept away the conditions for the existence of class antagonisms, and of classes generally, and will thereby have abolished its own supremacy as a class.

In place of the old bourgeois society with its classes and class antagonisms we shall have an association in which the free development of each is the condition for the free development of all.

• • •

POSITION OF THE COMMUNISTS IN RELATION TO THE VARIOUS EXISTING OPPOSITION PARTIES

The Communists fight for the attainment of the immediate aims, for the enforcement of the momentary interests of the working class; but in the movement of the present, they also represent and take care of the future of that movement. In France the Communists ally themselves with the Social-Democrats, against the conservative and radical bourgeoisie, reserving, however, the right to take up a critical position in regard to phrases and illusions traditionally handed down from the great Revolution.[12] . . .

In Germany they fight with the bourgeoisie whenever it acts in a revolutionary way, against the absolute monarchy, the feudal squirearchy,[13] and the petty bourgeoisie.[14]

But they never cease, for a single instant, to instill into the working class the clearest possible recognition of the hostile antagonism between bourgeoisie and proletariat, in order that the German workers may straightway use, as so many weapons against the bourgeoisie, the social and political conditions that the bourgeoisie must necessarily introduce along with its supremacy, and in order that, after the fall of

[12]The French Revolution (1789–95).
[13]The landed gentry (small landowners).
[14]Small shopkeepers and craftspeople.

the reactionary classes in Germany, the fight against the bourgeoisie itself may immediately begin.

The Communists turn their attention chiefly to Germany, because that country is on the eve of a bourgeois revolution[15] that is bound to be carried out under more advanced conditions of European civilization, and with a more developed proletariat, than that of England was in the seventeenth, and of France in the eighteenth century, and because the bourgeois revolution in Germany will be but the prelude to an immediately following proletarian revolution.

In short, the Communists everywhere support every revolutionary movement against the existing social and political order of things.

In all these movements they bring to the front, as the leading question in each, the property question, no matter what its degree of development at the time.

Finally, they labor everywhere for the union and agreement of the democratic parties of all countries.

The Communists disdain to conceal their views and aims. They openly declare that their ends can be attained only by the forcible overthrow of all existing social conditions. Let the ruling classes tremble at a Communistic revolution. The proletarians have nothing to lose but their chains. They have a world to win.

Working men of all countries, unite!

[15]The ill-fated national and liberal revolution of 1848–49.

24

Michael Bakunin

Anarchism

*M*ARX *and Engels were not the only important social agitators of the mid- and late-nineteenth century. Of a different mold but similarly influential was the anarchist Michael Bakunin (1814–1876). His birth into a Russian family of rank and privilege assured Bakunin of a good education and prospects for a distinguished career; upon completing his education as a cadet, he became an officer of the Russian army. But after only two years of service he resigned his commission in order to pursue studies at the University of Berlin, where for a short time he studied Hegelian philosophy. Just as abruptly as he had cut his ties with the army, however, he discontinued and even repudiated his formal studies in order to throw himself into the revolutionary struggles of his day. From age thirty, he devoted his entire existence to activities related to the cause of revolution: writing, traveling, agitating, organizing—and paying for his dedication to the cause by spending over a decade either in prison or in exile.*

More than a political theorist, Bakunin was a revolutionary activist who threw himself into every situation that had even the semblance of a rebellious disturbance. Social rebellion drew him so often from his desk that most of his written legacy consists of unfinished articles, books, pamphlets, and proposed programs for action. His prime and lasting aim was revolutionary work that would bring about, at last, the total annihilation of the existing order. He was the forerunner of the anarchic "terrorist" bands that frighten and perplex the present-day world.

The anarchistic ideas of Bakunin rested upon his perception that the masses of his day were deprived of liberty and locked into servitude and exploitation. He felt that those in power would continue to use any and all means to keep the rest of the people down—laws, courts, police, conventions, morality and, above

all else, religion. Consequently, Bakunin's struggle was against every manifestation of power and privilege, even the minutest expression and vestige of the
bourgeois world. Unlike Marx, Bakunin did not hope and labor for a grand day
of world revolution, when the existing power structure would be overturned.
Rather, whenever an opportunity presented itself to weaken the existing order,
he sought to deliver the hardest blow possible against it.

The unceasing struggle against authority brought Bakunin into frequent (but
temporary) comradeship with the Marxian socialists. Though the target of their
revolt was the same, the goals of socialists and anarchists were vastly different.
Whereas the Marxists' foremost aim was economic equality for all, Bakunin's
overwhelming concern was for liberty—that is, everlasting freedom from every
kind of power, monopoly, regimentation, and control. Consequently, while
the Marxist proletariat—being petty bourgeois in spirit—in reality sought
economic and political re-enfranchisement, Bakunin and his followers aimed at
the destruction of all established institutions. Before the new society could be
built, the old had to be turned into rubble. Bakunin was convinced, further, that
only those people who had been completely rejected by bourgeois society, such as
the landless laborers and the much reviled Lumpenproletariat (the Marxian
term for the very lowest of the proletariat—that is, riff-raff, or rabble), were
capable of a genuine rebellion or revolution. He discerned such people only in
southern Europe (Italy and Spain) and in eastern Europe (Russia). Differing
with Marx, Bakunin held the industrial proletariat of England and Germany to
be incapable of truly revolutionary action.

Bakunin maintained that in their struggle for liberty the truly revolutionary
masses would find themselves assisted by "that intelligent and genuinely noble
section of youth whose open-hearted convictions and burning aspirations lead it
to embrace the cause of the people despite being born into the privileged classes."
These educated idealists (he among them) would supply leadership and guidance while at all times remaining one with the people. At no time would they
allow themselves to become a ruling elite of any sort and in this way deprive the
people of the choicest fruit of their rebellion—liberty. Bakunin suspected that
after a socialist revolution, the party elite would transform itself into a new
ruling class of government officials, functionaries, and technocrats. If this were
to happen, the people would have merely exchanged one ruling class for
another. The romantic idealist Bakunin demanded that following the anarchist
revolution, his elite should relinquish all positions of power, because liberty for
everyone was assured only when people lived together in free associations of
equals. Individuals, he visualized, would collaborate voluntarily, because they
would perceive it to be in their own best interest to do so. On the other hand,

everyone would have the right to refuse collaboration or to secede from the association. The words force, coercion, *and* compulsion *would be totally absent from the vocabulary of the future.*

While Marx viewed history as a dialectic process, Bakunin was unable to discern any blueprint for historical development. Accordingly, he felt that events happen because of human volition, certain conditions, or chance. In the 1860s Bakunin believed that the masses were intent upon making sweeping revolutionary changes in the near future. But he was sobered by the unification of Germany in 1871, which appeared to postpone the fruition of his dreams. He then adopted the view that no large-scale revolutionary changes would take place until after the mighty nation-states of Europe had clashed in a general and bloody war.

The following selection is taken from one of Bakunin's proposed programs of action, entitled Principles and Organization of the International Brotherhood. *It was written in the mid-1860s.*

PRINCIPLES AND ORGANIZATION OF THE INTERNATIONAL BROTHERHOOD

I. Aim of the Society

1. The aim of this society is the triumph of the principle of revolution in the world, and consequently the radical overthrow of all presently existing religious, political, economic and social organizations and institutions and the reconstitution first of European and subsequently of world society on the basis of *liberty, reason, justice* and *work*.

2. This kind of task cannot be achieved overnight. The association is therefore constituted for an indefinite period, and will cease to exist only on the day when the triumph of its principle throughout the world removes its *raison d'être*.[1]

---

[1]French: reason for being.

ANARCHISM   From *Principles and Organization of the International Brotherhood* by Michael Bakunin in *Michael Bakunin Selected Writings*, edited by Arthur Lehning. Copyright 1974 by Grove Press, Inc. Reprinted by permission of Grove Press, Inc. 64–69, 76–78, 82–85, 87, 90–92.

II. *Revolutionary Catechism*[2]   ~~atheists?~~

1. Denial of the existence of a real, extra-terrestrial, individual God, and consequently also of any revelation and any divine intervention in the affairs of the human world. *Abolition of the service and worship of divinity.*

2. In replacing the worship of God by *respect* and *love for humanity*, we assert *human reason* as the one criterion of truth; *human conscience* as the basis of justice; *individual and collective liberty* as the only creator of order for mankind.

3. *Liberty* is the absolute right of all adult men and women to seek no sanction for their actions except their own conscience and their own reason, to determine them only of their own free will, and consequently to be responsible for them to themselves first of all, and then to the society of which they are a part, but only in so far as they freely consent to be a part of it.

4. It is quite untrue that the freedom of the individual is bounded by that of every other individual. Man is truly free only to the extent that his own freedom, freely acknowledged and reflected as in a mirror by the free conscience of all other men, finds in their freedom the confirmation of its infinite scope. Man is truly free only among other equally free men, and since he is free only in terms of mankind, the enslavement of any one man on earth, being an offense against the very principle of humanity, is a denial of the liberty of all.

5. Every man's *liberty* can be realized, therefore, only by the *equality* of all. The realization of liberty in legal and actual equality is *justice.*

6. There is only one dogma, one law, one moral basis for men, and *that is liberty.* To respect your neighbor's liberty *is duty;* to love, help and serve him, *virtue.*

7. *Absolute rejection of any principle of authority and of raison d'État.*[3] *Human society,* which was originally a natural fact, prior to liberty and the awakening of the human mind, and which later became a religious fact, organized on the principle of divine and human authority, must now be reconstituted on the basis of liberty, henceforward to be the sole determinant of its organization, both political and economic. *Order in society must be the outcome of the greatest possible development of all local, collective and individual liberties.*

---

[2]Summary of doctrines and principles.

[3]Literally, reason of State; a measure taken by a government to ensure the very continuance of the state—sometimes contrary to individual liberty and justice.

8. The political and economic organization of society must therefore not flow downward, from high to low, and outward, from center to circumference, as it does today on the principle of unity and enforced centralization, *but upward* and *inward*, on the principle of free association and free federation.

9. *Political organization.*

It is impossible to determine a concrete, universal and compulsory norm for the internal development and political organization of nations, since the existence of each is subordinate to a host of variable historical, geographical and economic factors which never permit of the establishment of an organizational model equally applicable and acceptable to all. Furthermore, any undertaking of this nature, being utterly devoid of practical utility, would militate against the richness and spontaneity of life, which delights in infinite diversity, and would in addition be contrary to the very principle of liberty. Nevertheless, there do exist *essential, absolute conditions* without which the practical realization and organization of liberty will always be impossible. These conditions are:

9(*a*). *The radical abolition of all official religion and every privileged or state-protected, -financed or -maintained church.* Absolute freedom of conscience and propaganda for all, each man having the unlimited option of building as many temples as he pleases to his gods, whatever their denomination, and of paying and maintaining the priests of his religion.

9(*b*). Seen as religious corporations, churches shall enjoy none of the political rights which will belong to productive associations, shall be unable to inherit or possess wealth in common, excepting their houses or establishments of prayer, and shall never be allowed to participate in the upbringing of children, since their sole aim in life is the systematic negation of morality and liberty, and the practice of sorcery for profit.

9(*c*). *Abolition of monarchy, republic.*

9(*d*). *Abolition of class, rank, privilege and distinction in all its forms. Complete equality of political rights for all men and all women; universal suffrage.*

9(*e*). *Abolition,* dissolution, and moral, political, legal, bureaucratic and social bankruptcy of the *custodial, transcendental,* centralist *state,* lackey and alter ego[4] of the church, and as such the permanent source of

---

[4]Another self.

poverty, degradation and subjugation among the people. As a natural consequence, *abolition of all state universities*—public education must be the exclusive prerogative of the free communes and associations; *abolition* of *state magistracy*—all judges to be elected by the people; *abolition* of the *criminal and civil codes currently in force in Europe*—because all of these, being equally inspired by the worship of God, state, family as a religious and political entity, and property, are contrary to human rights, and because *only by liberty* can the code of liberty be created. *Abolition* of *banks*, and *all other state credit institutions*. *Abolition* of *all central administration, bureaucracies, standing armies* and *state police*.

9(*f*). Immediate and direct election of all public officials, both civil and judicial, as well of all national, provincial and communal councillors or representatives, by popular vote, which is to say by the universal suffrage of all adult men and women.

9(*g*). *Reorganization* of each region, taking as its basis and starting point *the absolute freedom of individual, productive association and commune*.

9(*h*). *Individual rights.*

(i). The right of every man or woman to be completely supported, cared for, protected, brought up and educated from birth to coming of age in all public, primary, secondary, higher, industrial, artistic and scientific schools at the expense of society.

(ii). The equal right of each to be advised and assisted by the latter, as far as possible, at the outset of the career which each new adult will freely choose, after which the society which has declared him completely free will exercise no further supervision or authority over him, decline all responsibility toward him, and owe him nothing more than respect and if necessary protection for his liberty.

(iii). The liberty of every adult man and woman must be absolute and complete freedom to come and go, openly to profess any shade of opinion, to be idle or active, immoral or moral, in other words to dispose of his own person and his own belongings as he pleases and to be answerable to no one; freedom either to live honestly, by their own labor, or shamefully, by exploiting charity or individual trust, given that such charity and trust be voluntary and be proffered by adults only.

(iv). Unconditional freedom for every variety of propaganda, whether through conversation, the press or in public or private meetings, without any constraint but the natural corrective power of public opinion. Absolute liberty of associations, not excepting those whose aims may be or seem to be immoral, and even including those whose aim is the corruption and [destruction] of individual and public liberty.

(v). Liberty cannot and should not defend itself except by means of liberty, and it is a dangerous misconception to advocate its limitation under the specious pretext of protection. Since morality has no other source, incentive, cause and object than liberty, and is itself inseparable from liberty, all restrictions imposed on the latter with the intention of safeguarding the former have always turned against it. Psychology, statistics and the entire course of history prove that individual and social immorality have always been the necessary consequence of bad public and private education, of the absence or breakdown of public opinion, which never develops or improves its moral level except by way of liberty alone, and above all of defective social organization. As the famous French statistician Quételet[5] has pointed out, experience shows that it is always society which prepares the ground for crime, and that the wrongdoer is only the predestined instrument of its commission. It is pointless, therefore, to level against social immorality the rigors of a legislation which would encroach upon the freedom of the individual. On the contrary, experience shows that repression and authoritarianism, far from preventing its excesses, have always deepened and extended it in those countries so afflicted, and that private and public morality have always gained or lost to the extent that the freedom of individuals has broadened or narrowed. So that in order to moralize present-day society, we must first embark upon the outright destruction of that entire political and social organization which is based upon inequality, privilege, divine authority and contempt for humanity. And once having rebuilt it on the basis of the utmost equality, justice, work and an education inspired exclusively by respect for humanity, we should provide it for its guardian with public opinion, and for its soul with the most absolute liberty.

(vi). Yet society must not remain totally defenseless against parasitic, mischievous and dangerous individuals. Since labor is to be the basis of all political rights, society—a province, a nation, each within its individual borders—will have the power to remove [these rights] from all adult individuals who, being neither sick, disabled nor old, live at the expense of public or private charity, together with

[5]Adolphe Lambert Jacques Quételet (1796–1874), Belgian statistician and astronomer.

the obligation to restore them as soon as they begin to live by their own labor once again.

(vii). Since the freedom of every individual is inalienable, society shall never allow any individual whatsoever legally to alienate his freedom or to engage upon any contract with another individual on any footing but the utmost equality and reciprocity. It shall not, however, have the power to disbar a man or woman so devoid of any sense of personal dignity as to contract a relationship of voluntary servitude with another individual, but it will consider them as living off private charity and therefore unfit to enjoy political rights *throughout the duration of that servitude.*

(viii). All persons who have been deprived of their political rights shall likewise lose the right to rear and keep their children. In case of infidelity to a freely contracted commitment, or in the event of an overt or proven infringement of the property, the person or especially the liberty of a citizen, whether native or foreign, society shall apply those penalties specified by its laws against the offending native or foreigner.

(ix). Absolute abolition of all cruel and degrading sentences, corporal punishment and the death penalty as sanctioned and enforced by the law. Abolition of all those indefinite or protracted punishments which leave no hope and no real possibility of rehabilitation, since crime ought to be considered as sickness, and punishment as cure rather than social retaliation.

(x). Any individual condemned by the laws of any society, commune, province or nation shall retain the right not to submit to the sentence imposed on him, by declaring that he no longer wishes to be part of that society. But in such a case the society in question shall have the concomitant right to expel him from its midst and to declare him outside its warrant and protection.

(xi). Having thus reverted to the natural law of an eye for an eye, a tooth for a tooth, at least inside the territory occupied by that society, the individual shall be liable to robbery, ill-treatment and even death without any cause for alarm. Any person will be able to dispose of him like a dangerous animal, although never to subject him or use him as a slave. . . .

10. *Social organization.*

Without political equality there is no true political liberty, but political equality will only become possible when there is *economic and social equality.*

10(*a*). Equality does not mean the levelling down of individual differences, nor intellectual, moral and physical uniformity among individuals. This diversity of ability and strength, and these differences of race, nation, sex, age and character, far from being a social evil, constitute the treasurehouse of mankind. Nor do economic and social equality mean the levelling down of individual fortunes, in so far as these are products of the ability, productive energy and thrift of an individual.

10(*b*). The sole prerequisite for equality and justice is *a form of social organization such that each human individual born into it may find—to the extent that these are dependent upon society rather than upon nature—equal means for his development from infancy and adolescence to coming of age, first in upbringing and education, then in the exercise of the various capacities with which each is endowed by nature. This equality at the outset,* which justice requires for all, will never be feasible as long as the right of succession survives.

10(*c*). Justice, as well as human dignity, demands that *each individual should be the child of his own achievements, and only those achievements.* We hotly reject the doctrine of hereditary sin,[6] disgrace and responsibility. By the same token, we must reject the illusory heredity of virtue, honors and rights—*and of wealth also.* The heir to any kind of wealth is no longer the complete child of his own achievements, and in terms of initial circumstance he is privileged.

10(*d*). *Abolition of the right of inheritance.* As long as this right continues, hereditary differences of class, rank and wealth—in other words, social inequality and privilege—will survive in fact, if not in law. But it is an inescapable social law that *de facto* inequality always produces inequality of rights: social inequality necessarily becomes political. And we have already stated that without political equality there is no liberty in the universal, human and truly democratic sense, while society will always remain split into two uneven halves, with one vast section, including the entire mass of the people, suffering the oppression and exploitation of the other. Therefore *the right of succession is contrary to the triumph of liberty,* and a society wishing to become free must abolish it.

10(*e*). *This right must be abolished because, relying as it does upon a fiction, it runs counter to the very spirit of liberty.* All individual, political and social

---

[6]Hereditary, or original, sin (in traditional Christian doctrine) is the guilt or weakness implanted in every human being at conception, due to the sinful disobedience of Adam, the first man.

rights belong to the real, the living individual. Once dead, his will does not exist any more than he himself does, and it is a fictitious will that oppresses the living in the name of the dead. If the dead person sets such store by the enforcement of his wishes, let him stand up and enforce them himself, if he can, but he has no right to ask society to bend all its strength and law to the service of his nonexistence.

10(*f*). The legitimate and positive function of the right of succession has always been that of securing for subsequent generations the means to grow and to become men. Consequently, *only the trust for public upbringing and education will have the right to inherit*, with the matching obligation to make equal provision for the maintenance, upbringing and education of every child from birth to coming of age and emancipation. In this way, all parents will be equally confident in their children's future, and since equality for all is a fundamental precondition of morality for all, and all privilege is a cradle of immorality, parents whose love for their children is rational enough to be inspired not by vanity but by human dignity will prefer them to be brought up in strict equality, even if they do have the means to leave an inheritance which would place them in a privileged position.

10(*g*). Once the inequality produced by the right of inheritance has been abolished, there will still remain (but to a far lesser degree) the inequality that arises from differences in individual ability, strength and productive capacity—a difference which, while never disappearing altogether, will be of diminishing importance under the influence of an egalitarian upbringing and social system, and which in addition will never weigh upon future generations once there is no more right of inheritance.

10(*h*). Labor is the sole producer of wealth. Everybody is free, of course, either to die of starvation or to dwell among the wild beasts of the desert or the forest, but anybody who wants to live within society should earn his living by his own work, or run the risk of being considered a parasite, an exploiter of the wealth (that is, the labor) of others, and a thief.

10(*i*). *Labor* is the fundamental basis of dignity and human rights, for it is only by means of his own free, intelligent work that man becomes a creator in his turn, wins from the surrounding world and his own animal nature his humanity and rights, and creates the world of civilization. . . .

The unequal line drawn between intellectual and manual labor must therefore be removed. The economic output of society is itself considerably impaired, because mind cut off from physical activity weakens, withers and fades, whereas the physical vigor of humanity cut off from intelligence is brutalized, and in this state of artificial divorce neither produces the half of what could and should be produced once they are restored by a new social synthesis to form an indivisible productive process. When the thinker works and the worker thinks, free, intelligent labor will emerge as humanity's highest aspiration, the basis of its dignity and law and the embodiment of its human power on earth—and humanity will be instituted.

10(k).[7] *Intelligent free labor will necessarily be associated labor.* Everybody will be free to associate or not to associate in labor, but there can be no doubt that with the exception of works of imagination, whose nature requires the inner concentration of the individual mind, in all those industrial and even scientific and artistic enterprises whose nature admits of associated labor, such association will be generally preferred for the simple reason that it would miraculously increase the productive energies of each associate member of a productive association, who will earn a great deal more in less time and with far less trouble. Once the free productive associations stop being slaves and become their own masters and the owners of the necessary capital, once they include all the specialist minds required by each enterprise as members cooperating side by side with the labor force, and once they amalgamate among themselves—still freely, in accordance with their needs and natures— then sooner or later they will expand beyond national frontiers. They will form one vast economic federation, with a parliament informed by precise, detailed statistics on a world scale, such as are not yet possible today, and will both offer and demand to control, decide and distribute the output of world industry among the various countries, so that there will no longer, or hardly ever, be commercial or industrial crises, enforced stagnation, disasters and waste of energy and capital. Human labor emancipating each and every man, will regenerate the world.

10(l). *The land, with all its natural resources, belongs to all, but will be held only by those who work it.*

10(m). Woman, *differing from man but not inferior to him, intelligent, industrious and free like him, is declared his equal both in rights and in all political and social functions and duties.*

10(n). Abolition not of the natural but of the *legal* family, based on civil law and ownership. Religious and civil marriage are replaced by *free marriage.* Two *adult* individuals of opposite sex have the right to unite and separate in accordance with their desires and mutual interests

[7]There is no sub-entry (j) in the original text.

and the promptings of their hearts, nor does society have any right either to prevent their union or to hold them to it against their will. Once the right of succession is abolished and society guarantees the upbringing of all its children, every reason previously advanced for the political and civil backing given to marital indissolubility disappears, and the union of the sexes reverts to the complete liberty which, here as elsewhere, is always the *sine qua non*[8] of genuine morality. In free marriage, man and woman must enjoy equal measure of liberty. Neither violence, passion nor the rights freely granted in the past may excuse any infringement by one party of the other's liberty, and any such infringement shall be considered criminal.

10(*o*). From the moment of conception until her child is born, a woman is entitled to a social subvention paid not for her benefit but for her child's. Any mother wishing to feed and rear her children will also receive all the costs of their maintenance and care from society.

10(*p*). Parents will have the right to keep their children at their side and to attend to their upbringing, under the guardianship and supreme supervision of society, which will always retain the right and duty to part children from their parents whenever the latter may be in a position to demoralize or even hamper their children's development, either by example or by brutal, inhuman precepts or treatment.

10(*q*). Children belong neither to their parents nor to society but to themselves and their future liberty. From infancy to coming of age they are only potentially free, and must therefore find themselves under the aegis[9] of *authority*. It is true that their parents are their natural protectors, but *the legal and ultimate protector is society*, which has the right and duty to tend them because its own future depends on the intellectual and moral guidance they receive. Society can only give liberty to adults provided it supervises the upbringing of minors.

10(*r*). *School must take the place of church*, with the immense difference that the religious education provided by the latter has no other purpose than to perpetuate the rule of human ignorance or so-called divine authority, whereas school upbringing and education will have no other purpose than the true emancipation of the children upon reaching the age of majority, and will consist of nothing less than their progressive initiation into liberty by the threefold development of their physical and mental powers and their will. Reason, truth, justice, human respect, awareness of personal dignity (inseparable from the human

---

[8]Latin: without which, not—that is, the absolutely necessary prerequisite.
[9]Protective shield or cover.

dignity of another), love of liberty for one's own sake and for others', belief in work as the basis and condition of all rights; contempt for unreason, falsehood, injustice, cowardice, slavery and idleness—these must be the keystones of public education. First it must shape men, then specialists and citizens, and, in step with the children's growth, authority must naturally make more and more room for liberty, so that by the time the adolescent has come of age and become lawfully emancipated he will have forgotten how his infancy was controlled and guided by something other than liberty. Human respect, the seed of liberty, must be present even in the harshest and most absolute behavior of authority. This is the touchstone of all moral education: inculcate that respect in children, and you create men.

After completing their primary and secondary education the children will be advised, informed, but not coerced, by their superiors with a view to choosing some higher or specialist school, according to their abilities and inclinations. At the same time, each will apply himself to the theoretical and practical study of that branch of industry which most attracts him, and whatever sums he earns by working during his apprenticeship will be made available when he comes of age.

10(s). As soon as he comes of age, the adolescent will be declared a free citizen and absolute master of his actions. In exchange for the care it has exercised during his infancy, society will ask for three things: that he remain *free*, that he *live by his own labor*, and that he *respect the liberty of others*. And because the crimes and vices by which present-day society is afflicted are the sole outcome of defective social organization, we may be sure that given a form of organization and upbringing based on reason, justice, liberty, human respect and complete equality, good will become the rule and evil a morbid exception, ever decreasing under the all-powerful influence of moralized public opinion.

10(t). The old, the disabled and the sick will be cared for and respected, enjoy all public and social rights, and be generously maintained at the common expense. . . .

III. Requisite Qualities for Membership of the International Family:

He must be an atheist. On behalf of the earth and of mankind, he must join us in laying claim to everything which religions have hauled off into the heavens and bestowed upon their gods: truth, liberty, happiness, justice, goodness. He must recognize that *morality* is totally independent of theology and divine metaphysics and has no other source than the collective conscience of man.

He must, like ourselves, be the adversary of the principle of authority and loathe all its applications and consequences in the intellectual and moral as well as in the political, economic and social spheres. . . .

He must be a revolutionary. He must understand that such a complete and radical transformation of society, which must necessarily involve the downfall of all privilege, monopoly and constituted power, will naturally not occur by peaceful means. That for the same reason it will be opposed by the rich and powerful, and supported, in every land, only by the people, together with that intelligent and genuinely noble section of youth whose open-hearted convictions and burning aspirations lead it to embrace the cause of the people despite being born into the privileged classes.

He must understand that the sole and final purpose of this revolution is the true political, economic and social emancipation of the people, and that while it may be assisted and largely organized by the above-mentioned section of youth, in the long run it will only come through the people. That history has completely exhausted all other religious, national and political questions, and that only one question remains outstanding today, subsuming all the rest and uniquely capable of mobilizing the people—*the social question.* That any so-called revolution—whether it resembles the recent Polish insurrection,[10] or the doctrine which Mazzini[11] now preaches, whether it is exclusively political, constitutional, monarchist or even republican, like the last abortive move of the Spanish progressives[12]—any such revolution, working as it does apart from the people, and consequently unable to succeed without drawing upon some privileged class and representing the interests of the latter, will necessarily work against the people and will be a retrograde, harmful, counter-revolutionary movement.

He will therefore despise any secondary movement whose immediate, direct aim is other than the political and social emancipation of the working classes, in other words the people, and will see it either as a fatal error or a shabby trick. Hostile to all compromise and concilia-

---

[10]The Second Polish Revolution (1863–64), a futile uprising of zealous Polish nationalists attempting to gain complete independence from tsarist (Russian) rule.

[11]Giuseppe Mazzini (1805–1872), an Italian patriot and devoted republican who labored a lifetime on behalf of the unification of Italy.

[12]Nineteenth-century Spanish liberals who tried and failed to overthrow the monarchy and establish a republic.

tion—henceforward impossible—and to any false coalition with those whose interests make them the natural enemies of the people, *he must see that the only salvation for his own country and for the entire world lies in social revolution.*

He must also understand that this revolution, being essentially cosmopolitan, like justice and liberty themselves, will only be able to triumph by sweeping like a universal holocaust across the flimsy barriers of nations and bringing all states tumbling in its wake, embracing first the whole of Europe, and then the world. *He must understand that the social revolution will necessarily become a European and worldwide revolution.*

That the world will inevitably split into two camps, that of the new life and of the old privileges, and that between these two opposing camps, created as in the time of the wars of religion not by national sympathies but by community of ideas and interests, a war of extermination is bound to erupt, with no quarter and no respite. That in the very interest of its own security and self-preservation the social revolution—contrary in its whole essence to that hypocritical policy of non-intervention, which is fit only for the moribund[13] and the impotent—cannot live and thrive except by growing, and will not lay down the sword until it has destroyed all states and all the old religious, political and economic institutions both in Europe and throughout the civilized world.

That this will not be a war of conquest, but of emancipation—sometimes enforced, perhaps, but salutary all the same—because its purpose and outcome will be nothing more nor less than the destruction of states and their secular roots, which have always been the basis of all slavery, with the blessing of religion.

That even in the most apparently hostile countries, once the social revolution breaks out at one point it will find keen and tenacious allies in the popular masses, who will be unable to do other than rally to its banner as soon as they understand and come in contact with its activities and purpose. That it will consequently be necessary to choose the most fertile soil for its beginning, where it has only to withstand the first assault of reaction before expanding to overwhelm the frenzies of its enemies, federalizing all the lands it has absorbed and welding them into a single indomitable revolutionary alliance. . . .

•   •   •

[13]Dying.

25
Pope Leo XIII
Concerning New Things

*T*HE *response of the papacy to the spread of industrialization and its consequent problems and disturbances was long awaited. At last in 1891 Pope Leo XIII stated the official Roman Catholic position in an encyclical known as* Rerum Novarum *(Concerning New Things). The pontiff's declaration on "The Condition of Labor" was greeted joyously by most Roman Catholics. Both clergy and laity had for some time been concerned about the plight of the industrial working classes and had sought alleviation of labor's distress; they welcomed guidance from the pope himself.*

Beyond that, even many non-Catholic humanitarians soon came to appreciate Concerning New Things *as a document that retained the positive elements of the past while, at the same time, furnishing a guide for the humane development of industrial society. The papal letter repudiated the two economic theories that had dominated much of the nineteenth century, economic liberalism and Marxian socialism. The evil fruits of the former were visible everywhere. (The pope, while serving as a prelate in Belgium, had witnessed the blight and deprivation wrought upon the population by industrialization—just as Karl Marx had observed it a few decades earlier.) The pursuit of selfish interests had not resulted in "the advantage of each and all." Rather, economic liberalism had created a small group of very rich entrepreneurs and financiers while, on the other hand, a vast number of people had been reduced to abject poverty and virtual slavery. Marxian socialism, the opposing economic theory that had made converts among the laboring masses, was criticized by the pope for preaching class hatred and for predicting that the two remaining classes of historical consequence, the proletariat and the capitalists, would meet in a clash of cataclysmic dimensions. Such a gospel of hatred, destruction, and bloodshed was abhorrent to Christian teaching. Was not reconciliation one of the noblest tasks of the Christian Church?*

The appeal of Concerning New Things *lies in the fact that it deals with the relationship between past, present, and future. Leo himself was deeply influenced by the teachings of St. Thomas Aquinas, who saw society as a living body whose members perform different functions but at the same time have a right to receive a just reward for their labor. Accordingly, Leo spoke of the right of everyone to procure for self and family what is necessary for a life of "reasonable and frugal comfort." The earnings that can be saved a laborer must be able to invest in property. Indeed, the pope desired property to be spread as widely as possible. Yet, at the same time, he accepted the fact that the amount of property people possess will vary because their abilities, circumstances, and luck vary greatly. Though all are equal before God's judgment, this life produces a fruitful inequality relative to rank and property. However, concluded the pope, the possession of any amount of property always carries the obligation of good stewardship and generosity to the poor.*

To insure that their interests were well represented, the pope encouraged workers to form labor unions. These, then, would negotiate with the employers so that each laborer might receive a fair share. The state, in turn, was to assure the peaceful and fair process of the employee-employer relationship. Leo expected the state to protect the weak from abuse by the strong whenever the need arose. At all times, however, the state was to guarantee the inviolate possession of private property.

When Concerning New Things *first appeared, Marxian socialists as well as economic liberals saw nothing new or noteworthy in it. Even many Catholic employers paid scant attention to it. Yet, as time progressed,* Rerum Novarum *was increasingly perceived as a principal guide in the development of industrial capitalism in the West. As years and decades passed, employers and employees learned to shun class warfare and to live together and bargain together with a degree of mutual respect. Leo's letter, upheld by succeeding pontiffs, contributed to this outcome.*

It is not surprising that the spirit of revolutionary change, which has long been predominant in the nations of the world, should have passed beyond politics and made its influence felt in the cognate field of

CONCERNING NEW THINGS   From *Leo XIII on The Condition of Labor (Rerum Novarum)* in *Seven Great Encyclicals* (New York: Paulist Press, 1963), 1–3, 6–11, 15, 18–24, 29–30.

practical economy. The elements of a conflict are unmistakable: the growth of industry, and the surprising discoveries of science; the changed relations of masters and workmen; the enormous fortunes of individuals and the poverty of the masses; the increased self-reliance and the closer mutual combination of the working population; and, finally, a general moral deterioration. The momentous seriousness of the present state of things just now fills every mind with painful apprehension; wise men discuss it; practical men propose schemes; popular meetings, legislatures, and sovereign princes, all are occupied with it—and there is nothing which has a deeper hold on public attention.

Therefore, Venerable Brethren,[1] as on former occasions, when it seemed opportune to refute false teaching, We[2] have addressed you in the interests of the Church and of the commonwealth, and have issued Letters on Political Power, on Human Liberty, on the Christian Constitution of the State, and on similar subjects, so now We have thought it useful to speak on

THE CONDITION OF LABOR

It is a matter on which We have touched once or twice already. But in this Letter the responsibility of the apostolic office urges Us to treat the question expressly and at length, in order that there may be no mistake as to the principles which truth and justice dictate for its settlement. The discussion is not easy, nor is it free from danger. It is not easy to define the relative rights and the mutual duties of the wealthy and of the poor, of capital and of labor. And the danger lies in this, that crafty agitators constantly make use of these disputes to pervert men's judgments and to stir up the people to sedition.

But all agree, and there can be no question whatever, that some remedy must be found, and quickly found, for the misery and wretchedness which press so heavily at this moment on the large majority of the very poor. The ancient workmen's guilds[3] were destroyed in the last century, and no other organization took their place. Public institu-

---

[1]Patriarchs, archbishops, and bishops of the Catholic world in grace and communion with the Roman papacy.

[2]Pope Leo XIII (1878–1903). It has been common for persons of royal or papal authority to refer to themselves in this plural form.

[3]Medieval associations of craftsmen.

tions and the laws have repudiated the ancient religion.[4] Hence by degrees it has come to pass that working men have been given over, isolated and defenseless, to the callousness of employers and the greed of unrestrained competition. The evil has been increased by rapacious usury,[5] which, although more than once condemned by the Church, is nevertheless, under a different form but with the same guilt, still practiced by avaricious and grasping men. And to this must be added the custom of working by contract, and the concentration of so many branches of trade in the hands of a few individuals, so that a small number of very rich men have been able to lay upon the masses of the poor a yoke little better than slavery itself.

To remedy these evils the *Socialists*, working on the poor man's envy of the rich, endeavor to destroy private property, and maintain that individual possessions should become the common property of all, to be administered by the State or by municipal bodies. They hold that, by thus transferring property from private persons to the community, the present evil state of things will be set to rights, because each citizen will then have his equal share of whatever there is to enjoy. But their proposals are so clearly futile for all practical purposes, that if they were carried out the working man himself would be among the first to suffer. Moreover they are emphatically unjust, because they would rob the lawful possessor, bring the State into a sphere that is not its own, and cause complete confusion in the community.

PRIVATE OWNERSHIP

It is surely undeniable that, when a man engages in remunerative[6] labor, the very reason and motive of his work is to obtain property, and to hold it as his own private possession. If one man hires out to another his strength or his industry, he does this for the purpose of receiving in return what is necessary for food and living; he thereby expressly proposes to acquire a full and real right, not only to the remuneration, but also to the disposal of that remuneration as he pleases. Thus, if he lives sparingly, saves money, and invests his savings, for greater security, in land, the land in such a case is only his wages in another form;

[4]Christian religion. Leo is referring to the secularization of life in a number of countries as well as to the separation of Church and State.

[5]Rates of interest in excess of what the law allows or what can be justified.

[6]Labor for wages.

and, consequently, a working man's little estate thus purchased should be as completely at his own disposal as the wages he receives for his labor. But it is precisely in this power of disposal that ownership consists, whether the property be land or movable goods. The *Socialists*, therefore, in endeavoring to transfer the possessions of individuals to the community, strike at the interests of every wage earner, for they deprive him of the liberty of disposing of his wages, and thus of all hope and possibility of increasing his stock and of bettering his condition in life.

What is of still greater importance, however, is that the remedy they propose is manifestly against justice. For every man has by nature the right to possess property as his own. This is one of the *chief points of distinction* between man and the animal creation. . . .

. . .

SOCIALISM REJECTED

The idea, then, that the civil government should, at its own discretion, penetrate and pervade the family and the household, is a great and pernicious mistake. True, if a family finds itself in great difficulty, utterly friendless, and without prospect for help, it is right that extreme necessity be met by public aid; for each family is a part of the commonwealth. In like manner, if within the walls of the household there occur grave disturbance of mutual rights, the public power must interfere to force each party to give the other what is due; for this is not to rob citizens of their rights, but justly and properly to safeguard and strengthen them. But the rulers of the State must go no further: nature bids them stop here. Paternal authority can neither be abolished by the State nor absorbed; for it has the same source as human life itself; . . . The Socialists, therefore, in setting aside the parent and introducing the providence of the State, act *against natural justice*, and threaten the very existence of family life.

And such interference is not only unjust, but is quite certain to harass and disturb all classes of citizens, and to subject them to odious and intolerable slavery. It would open the door to envy, to evil speaking, and to quarreling; the sources of wealth would themselves run dry, for no one would have any interest in exerting his talents or his industry; and that ideal equality of which so much is said would, in reality, be the leveling down of all to the same condition of misery and dishonor.

Thus it is clear *that the main tenet of Socialism, the community of goods, must be utterly rejected*; for it would injure those whom it is intended to benefit, it would be contrary to the natural rights of mankind, and it would introduce confusion, and disorder into the commonwealth. Our first and most fundamental principle, therefore, when We undertake to alleviate the condition of the masses, must be the inviolability of private property. This laid down, We go on to show where we must find the remedy that We seek.

THE CHURCH IS NECESSARY

We approach the subject with confidence, and in the exercise of the rights which belong to Us. For no practical solution of this question will ever be found without the assistance of Religion and the Church. It is We who are the chief guardian of Religion, and the chief dispenser of what belongs to the Church, and We must not by silence neglect the duty which lies upon Us. Doubtless this most serious question demands the attention and the efforts of others besides Ourselves—of the rulers of States, of employers of labor, of the wealthy, and of the working population themselves for whom We plead. But We affirm without hesitation that all the striving of men will be vain if they leave out the Church. It is the Church that proclaims from the Gospel those teachings by which the conflict can be brought to an end, or at least made far less bitter; the Church uses its efforts not only to enlighten the mind, but to direct by its precepts the life and conduct of men; the Church improves and ameliorates the condition of the working man by numerous useful organizations; does its best to enlist the services of all ranks in discussing and endeavoring to meet, in the most practical way, the claims of the working classes; and acts on the decided view that for these purposes recourse should be had, in due measure and degree, to the help of the law and of State authority.

Let it be laid down, in the first place, that humanity must remain as it is. It is impossible to reduce human society to a level. The *Socialists* may do their utmost, but all striving against nature is vain. There naturally exists among mankind innumerable differences of the most important kind; people differ in capability, in diligence, in health, and in strength; and unequal fortune is a necessary result of inequality in condition. Such inequality is far from being disadvantageous either to individuals or to the community; social and public life can only go on by the help of various kinds of capacity and the playing of many parts, and each man, as a rule, chooses the part which peculiarly suits his case. As regards bodily labor, even had man never fallen from the state of innocence, he would not have been wholly unoccupied; but that which would then have been his free choice, his delight, became afterwards compulsory, and the painful expiation[7] of his sin. "Cursed be the earth in your work; in your labor you shall eat of it all the days of your life."[8] In like manner, the other pains and hardships of life will have no end or cessation on this earth; for the consequences of sin are bitter and hard to bear, and they must be with man as long as life lasts. To suffer and to endure, therefore, is the lot of humanity, let men try as they may, no strength and no artifice will ever succeed in banishing from human life the ills and troubles which beset it. If any there are who pretend differently—who hold out to a hard-pressed people freedom from pain and trouble, undisturbed repose, and constant enjoyment—they cheat the people and impose upon them, and their lying promises will only make the evil worse than before. There is nothing more useful than to look at the world as it really is—and at the same time look elsewhere for a remedy to its troubles.

EMPLOYER AND EMPLOYEE

The great mistake that is made in the matter now under consideration, is to possess oneself of the idea that class is naturally hostile to class; that rich and poor are intended by nature to live at war with one another. So irrational and so false is this view, that the exact contrary is the truth. Just as the symmetry of the human body is the result of the disposition of the members of the body, so in a State it is ordained by nature that these two classes should exist in harmony and agreement, and should, as it were, fit into one another, so as to maintain the equilibrium of the body politic. Each requires the other; capital cannot do without labor, nor labor without capital. Mutual agreement results in pleasantness and good order; perpetual conflict necessarily produces confusion and outrage. Now, in preventing such strife as this, and in making it impossible, the efficacy of Christianity is marvelous and manifold.

First of all, there is nothing more powerful than Religion (of which the Church is the interpreter and guardian) in drawing rich and poor

[7]Making amends, atonement.
[8]Genesis 3:17.

together, by reminding each class of its duties to the other, and especially of the duties of justice. Thus Religion teaches the laboring man and the workman to carry out honestly and well all equitable agreements freely made, never to injure capital, nor to outrage the person of an employer; never to employ violence in representing his own cause, nor to engage in riot and disorder; and to have nothing to do with men of evil principles, who work upon the people with artful promises, and raise foolish hopes which usually end in disaster and in repentance when too late. Religion teaches the rich man and the employer that their work people are not their slaves; that they must respect in every man his dignity as a man and as a Christian; that labor is nothing to be ashamed of, if we listen to right reason and to Christian philosophy, but is an honorable employment, enabling a man to sustain his life in an upright and creditable way; and that it is shameful and inhuman to treat men like chattels to make money by, or to look upon them merely as so much muscle or physical power. Thus, again, Religion teaches that, as among the workmen's concerns are Religion herself, and things spiritual and mental, the employer is bound to see that he has time for the duties of piety; that he be not exposed to corrupting influences and dangerous occasions; and that he be not led away to neglect his home and family or to squander his wages. Then, again, the employer must never tax his work-people beyond their strength, nor employ them in work unsuited to their sex or age.

His great and principal obligation is to give to every one that which is just. Doubtless before we can decide whether wages are adequate many things have to be considered; but rich men and masters should remember this—that to exercise pressure for the sake of gain, upon the indigent and destitute, and to make one's profit out of the need of another, is condemned by all laws, human and divine. To defraud any one of wages that are his due is a crime which cries to the avenging anger of Heaven. "Behold, the hire of the laborers . . . which by fraud has been kept back by you, cries; and the cry of them has entered the ears of the Lord of Sabaoth."[9] Finally, the rich must religiously refrain from cutting down the workman's earnings, either by force, fraud, or by usurious dealing; and with the more reason because the poor man is weak and unprotected, and because his slender means should be sacred in proportion to their scantiness.

[9]Hosts, armies; God (James 5:4).

Were these precepts carefully obeyed and followed would not strife die out and cease?

· · ·

THE RIGHT USE OF MONEY

Therefore, those whom fortune favors are warned that freedom from sorrow and abundance of earthly riches, are no guarantee of that beatitude that shall never end, but rather the contrary; that the rich should tremble at the threatenings of Jesus Christ—threatenings so strange in the mouth of our Lord; and that a most strict account must be given to the Supreme Judge for all that we possess. . . . Private ownership, as we have seen, is the natural right of man; and to exercise that right, especially as members of society, is not only lawful but absolutely necessary. "It is lawful," says St. Thomas of Aquin,[10] "for a man to hold private property; and it is also necessary for the carrying on of human life."[11] But if the question be asked, How must one's possessions be used? the Church replies without hesitation in the words of the same holy Doctor: "Man should not consider his outward possessions as his own, but as common to all, so as to share them without difficulty when others are in need. Whence the Apostle says, Command the rich of this world . . . to give with ease, to communicate."[12] True, no one is commanded to distribute to others that which is required for his own necessities and those of his household; nor even to give away what is reasonably required to keep up becomingly his condition in life; "for no one ought to live unbecomingly."[13] But when necessity has been supplied, and one's position fairly considered, it is a duty to give to the indigent out of that which is over. "That which remains give alms."[14] It is a duty, not of justice (except in extreme cases), but of Christian charity—a duty which is not enforced by human law. . . .

· · ·

[10]St. Thomas Aquinas (*ca.* 1225–1274), a leading medieval philosopher, is sometimes referred to as the "Angelic Doctor."

[11]Thomas Aquinas, *Summa Theologica*, Book Two, Part Two, Question 66, Article 2.

[12]Ibid., Question 65, Article 2.

[13]Ibid., Question 32, Article 6.

[14]Luke 11:41.

THE STATE AND POVERTY

It cannot, however, be doubted that to attain the purpose of which We treat, not only the Church, but all human means must conspire. All who are concerned in the matter must be of one mind and must act together. It is in this, as in the Providence which governs the world; results do not happen save where all the causes co-operate.

Let us now, therefore, inquire what part the State should play in the work of remedy and relief.

By the State We here understand, not the particular form of government which prevails in this or that nation, but the State as rightly understood. . . .

The first duty, therefore, of the rulers of the State should be to make sure that the laws and institutions, the general character and administration of the commonwealth, shall be such as to produce of themselves public well-being and private prosperity. This is the proper office of wise statesmanship and the work of the heads of the State. Now a State chiefly prospers and flourishes by morality, well-regulated family life, by respect for religion and justice, by the moderation and equal distribution of public burdens, by the progress of the arts and of trade, by the abundant yield of the land—by everything which makes the citizens better and happier. Here, then, it is in the power of a ruler to benefit every order of the State, and among the rest to promote in the highest degree the interests of the poor; and this by virtue of his office, and without being exposed to any suspicion of undue interference—for it is the province of the commonwealth to consult for the common good. And the more that is done for the working population by the general laws of the country, the less need will there be to seek for particular means to relieve them. . . .

• • •

THE RIGHT OF PROTECTION

Rights must be religiously respected wherever they are found; and it is the duty of the public authority to prevent and punish injury, and to protect each one in the possession of his own. Still, when there is question of protecting the rights of individuals, the poor and helpless have a claim to special consideration. The richer population have many ways of protecting themselves, and stand less in need of help from the

State; those who are badly off have no resources of their own to fall back upon, and must chiefly rely upon the assistance of the State. And it is for this reason that wage-earners, who are, undoubtedly, among the weak and necessitous, should be specially cared for and protected by the commonwealth.

Here, however, it will be advisable to advert expressly to one or two of the more important details.

It must be borne in mind that the chief thing to be secured is the safeguarding, by legal enactment and policy, of private property. Most of all it is essential in these times of covetous greed, to keep the multitude within the line of duty; for if all may justly strive to better their condition, yet neither justice nor the common good allows anyone to seize that which belongs to another, or, under the pretext of futile and ridiculous equality, to lay hands on other people's fortunes. It is most true that by far the larger part of the people who work prefer to improve themselves by honest labor rather than by doing wrong to others. But there are not a few who are imbued with bad principles and are anxious for revolutionary change, and whose great purpose it is to stir up tumult and bring about a policy of violence. The authority of the State should intervene to put restraint upon these disturbers, to save the workmen from their seditious arts, and to protect lawful owners from spoliation.

THE WORKMAN'S RIGHTS

When work-people have recourse to a strike, it is frequently because the hours of labor are too long, or the work too hard, or because they consider their wages insufficient. The grave inconvenience of this not uncommon occurrence should be obviated[15] by public remedial measures; for such paralysis of labor not only affects the masters and their work-people, but is extremely injurious to trade, and to the general interests of the public; moreover, on such occasions, violence and disorder are generally not far off, and thus it frequently happens that the public peace is threatened. The laws should be beforehand, and prevent these troubles from arising; they should lend their influence and authority to the removal in good time of the causes which lead to conflicts between masters and those whom they employ. . . .

[15]Prevented.

HOURS OF LABOR

If we turn now to things exterior and corporal, the first concern of all is to save the poor workers from the cruelty of grasping speculators, who use human beings as mere instruments for making money. It is neither justice nor humanity so to grind men down with excessive labor as to stupefy their minds and wear out their bodies. Man's powers, like his general nature, are limited, and beyond these limits he cannot go. His strength is developed and increased by use and exercise, but only on condition of due intermission and proper rest. Daily labor, therefore, must be so regulated that it may not be protracted during longer hours than strength admits. How many and how long the intervals of rest should be, will depend upon the nature of the work, on circumstances of time and place, and on the health and strength of the workman. Those who labor in mines and quarries, and in work within the bowels of the earth, should have shorter hours in proportion, as their labor is more severe and more trying to health. Then, again, the season of the year must be taken in account; for not infrequently a kind of labor is easy at one time which at another is intolerable or very difficult. Finally, work which is suitable for a strong man cannot reasonably be required from a woman or a child.

CHILD LABOR

And in regard to children, great care should be taken not to place them in workshops and factories until their bodies and minds are sufficiently mature. For just as rough weather destroys the buds of spring, so too early an experience of life's hard work blights the young promise of a child's powers, and makes any real education impossible. Women, again, are not suited to certain trades; for a woman is by nature fitted for home-work, and it is that which is best adapted at once to preserve her modesty, and to promote the good bringing up of children and the well-being of the family. As a general principle, it may be laid down, that a workman ought to have leisure and rest in proportion to the wear and tear of his strength; for the waste of strength must be repaired by the cessation of work.

In all agreements between masters and work-people, there is always the condition, expressed or understood, that there be allowed proper rest for soul and body. To agree in any other sense would be against what is right and just; for it can never be right or just to require on the one side, or to promise on the other, the giving up of those duties which a man owes to his God and to himself.

JUST WAGES

We now approach a subject of very great importance and one on which, if extremes are to be avoided, right ideas are absolutely necessary. Wages, we are told, are fixed by free consent; and, therefore, the employer when he pays what was agreed upon, has done his part, and is not called upon for anything further. The only way, it is said, in which injustice could happen, would be if the master refused to pay the whole of the wages, or the workman would not complete the work undertaken; when this happens the State should intervene, to see that each obtains his own, but not under any other circumstances. . . .

Let it be granted, then, that, as a rule, workman and employer should make free agreements, and in particular should freely agree as to wages; nevertheless, there is a dictate of nature more imperious and more ancient than any bargain between man and man, that the remuneration must be enough to support the wage-earner in reasonable and frugal comfort. If through necessity or fear of a worse evil, the workman accepts harder conditions because an employer or contractor will give him no better, he is the victim of force and injustice. In these and similar questions, however—such as, for example, the hours of labor in different trades, the sanitary precautions to be observed in factories and workshops, and so on—in order to supersede undue interference on the part of the State, especially as circumstances, times and localities differ so widely, it is advisable that recourse be had to societies or boards such as We shall mention presently, or to some other method of safeguarding the interests of wage-earners; the State to be asked for approval and protection.

BENEFITS OF PROPERTY OWNERSHIP

If a workman's wages be sufficient to enable him to maintain himself, his wife, and his children in reasonable comfort, he will not find it difficult, if he is a sensible man, to study economy; and he will not fail, by cutting down expenses, to put by a little property: nature and reason would urge him to do this. We have seen that this great labor question cannot be solved except by assuming as a principle that private ownership must be held sacred and inviolable. The law, therefore, should favor ownership, and its policy should be to induce as many people as possible to become owners.

Many excellent results will follow from this; and first of all, property will certainly become more equitably divided. For the effect of civil change and revolution has been to divide society into two widely different castes. On the one side there is the party which holds the power because it holds the wealth; which has in its grasp all labor and all trade; which manipulates for its own benefit and its own purposes all the sources of supply, and which is powerfully represented in the councils of the State itself. On the other side there is the needy and powerless multitude, sore and suffering, always ready for disturbance. If working people can be encouraged to look forward to obtaining a share in the land, the result will be that the gulf between vast wealth and deep poverty will be bridged over, and the two orders will be brought nearer together. Another consequence will be the great abundance of the fruits of the earth. Men always work harder and more readily when they work on that which is their own; nay, they learn to love the very soil which yields in response to the labor of their hands, not only food to eat, but an abundance of the good things for themselves and those that are dear to them. It is evident how such a spirit of willing labor would add to the produce of the earth and to the wealth of the community. And a third advantage would arise from this: men would cling to the country in which they were born; for no one would exchange his country for a foreign land if his own afforded him the means of living a tolerable and happy life. These three important benefits, however, can only be expected on the condition that a man's means be not drained and exhausted by excessive taxation. The right to possess private property is from nature, not from man; and the State has only the right to regulate its use in the interests of the public good, but by no means to abolish it altogether. The State is, therefore, unjust and cruel, if, in the name of taxation, it deprives the private owner of more than is just.

WORKMEN'S ASSOCIATIONS

In the first place—employers and workmen may themselves effect much in the matter of which We treat, by means of those institutions and organizations which afford opportune assistance to those in need, and which draw the two orders more closely together. Among these may be enumerated: societies for mutual help; various foundations established by private persons for providing for the workman, and for his widow or his orphans, in sudden calamity, in sickness, and in the event of death; and what are called "patronages," or institutions for the care of boys and girls, for young people, and also for those of more mature age.

The most important of all are workmen's associations; for these virtually include all the rest. History attests what excellent results were effected by the craftman's guilds of a former day. They were the means not only of many advantages to the workmen, but in no small degree of the advancement of art, as numerous monuments remain to prove. Such associations should be adapted to the requirements of the age in which we live—an age of greater instruction, of different customs, and of more numerous requirements in daily life. It is gratifying to know that there are actually in existence not a few societies of this nature, consisting either of workmen alone, or of workmen and employers together; but it were greatly to be desired that they should multiply and become more effective. We have spoken of them more than once; but it will be well to explain here how much they are needed, to show that they exist by their own right, and to enter into their organization and their work.

The experience of his own weakness urges man to call in help from without. We read in the pages of Holy Writ: "It is better that two should be together than one; for they have the advantage of their society. If one fall he shall be supported by the other. Woe to him that is alone, for when he falls he has none to lift him up."[16] And further: "A brother that is helped by his brother is like a strong city."[17] It is this natural impulse which unites men in civil society; and it is this also which makes them band themselves together in associations of citizen with citizen; associations which, it is true, cannot be called societies in the complete sense of the word, but which are societies nevertheless. . . .

Particular societies, then, although they exist within the State, and are each a part of the State, nevertheless cannot be prohibited by the State absolutely and as such. For to enter into a "society" of this kind is the natural right of man; and the State must protect natural rights, not destroy them; and if it forbids its citizens to form associations, it contradicts the very principle of its own existence; for both they and it exist in virtue of the same principle, which is, the natural propensity of man to live in society. . . .

• • •

[16]Ecclesiastes 4:9–10.
[17]Proverbs 18:19.

CONCLUSION

We have now laid before you, Venerable Brethren, who are the persons, and what are the means, by which this most difficult question must be solved. Every one must put his hand to work which falls to his share, and that at once and immediately, lest the evil which is already so great may by delay become absolutely beyond remedy. Those who rule the State must use the law and the institutions of the country; masters and rich men must remember their duty; the poor, whose interests are at stake, must make every lawful and proper effort; since Religion alone, as We said at the beginning, can destroy the evil at its root, all men must be persuaded that the primary thing needful is to return to real Christianity, in the absence of which all the plans and devices of the wisest will be of little avail.

As far as regards the Church, its assistance will never be wanting, be the time or the occasion what it may; and it will intervene with great effect in proportion as its liberty of action is the more unfettered; let this be carefully noted by those whose office it is to provide for the public welfare. Every minister of holy Religion must throw into the conflict all the energy of his mind, and all the strength of his endurance; with your authority, Venerable Brethren, and by your example, they must never cease to urge upon all men of every class, upon the high as well as the lowly, the Gospel doctrines of Christian life; by every means in their power they must strive for the good of the people; and above all they must earnestly cherish in themselves, and try to arouse in others, charity, the mistress and queen of virtues. For the happy results we all long for must be chiefly brought about by the plenteous outpouring of charity; of that true Christian charity which is the fulfilling of the whole Gospel law, which is always ready to sacrifice itself for other's sake, and which is man's surest antidote against worldly pride and immoderate love of self; that charity whose office is described and whose Godlike features are drawn by the apostle St. Paul in these words: "Charity is patient, is kind, . . . seeks not her own, . . . suffers all things, . . . endures all things."[18]

---

[18]I Corinthians 13:4–7.

26

Fyodor Dostoevsky

(Social Conscience) [handwritten annotation]

The Brothers Karamazov:
The Grand Inquisitor

Transition: re-visioning the World [handwritten annotation]
Social [handwritten annotation]

*T*HE *contemporary era, with its concern for the irrational, unconscious springs of human behavior, with its doubts and rejection of the old certainties, may be said to have begun in the last quarter of the nineteenth century. Fyodor Dostoevsky (1821–1881), the great Russian novelist, was the literary herald of the new age, and it is significant that his genius was not truly appreciated until half a century after his death. Today he is considered one of the greatest artists and thinkers of the Western world, the writer who first laid bare the confusion in human minds and souls that grew into the intellectual chaos of the twentieth century.*

The artistry of Dostoevsky is inseparable from his ideas. In his novels, he cast these ideas in artistic form, making his characters symbols of universal truths. Although he wrote in a simple, direct style, the novels have an intricate, agitated quality that produces a disturbing emotional effect in the reader. Dostoevsky was a literary realist, but he probed beneath the surface of realistic detail into the tortured, innermost recesses of his characters. His work thus focused on the morbid aspects of human behavior and feeling, on evil and suffering. Dostoevsky saw human beings as both corrupt and capable of greatness; he felt that their salvation lay in faith in God and in His revelation through suffering, forgiveness, and love. Dostoevsky was, however, no simple believer. His faith arose from doubts and contradictions and was shaped by a sense of humanity's unending tragic quest.

In his novels, Dostoevsky suggests the tragic course of his own life and the torments of his restless mind and passionate nature. From childhood on, death, disease, and suffering pervaded his life. While in exile in Siberia as a result of his radical social views, he experienced a religious conversion. His religious feelings led him to identify with the masses of Russian peasants and to preach a gospel of mystical Russian nationalism. At the same time, he attacked the bourgeois civilization of Western Europe, with its rationalism and materialism, as decadent and doomed to destruction. Dostoevsky was not only the prophet of the irrational: he was the enemy of reason.

The Brothers Karamazov *(1880), Dostoevsky's greatest novel and the tragic tale of a middle-class Russian family, has as its theme the search for faith through struggle against evil. Presented in the following selection is the portion known as "The Grand Inquisitor," after a legend composed by one character, a rationalist and unbeliever, and told to his brother, a saintly figure living in a monastery. Essentially, the story is an allegory of the human predicament, in which individuals strive for true freedom but fear and reject it in favor of the ease and security of obedience to authority. Some have also considered the story a prophetic attack on all forms of modern authoritarianism.*

———————

[The setting is a tavern, where two of the brothers Karamazov, Ivan and Alyosha, are seated at a table. Ivan begins telling Alyosha about a "poem" he has written. *Ed.*]

"Even this must have a preface—that is, a literary preface," laughed Ivan, "and I am a poor hand at making one. You see, my action takes place in the sixteenth century, and at that time, as you probably learned at school, it was customary in poetry to bring down heavenly powers on earth. Not to speak of Dante,[1] in France clerks, as well as the monks in the monasteries, used to give regular performances in which the Madonna,[2] the saints, the angels, Christ, and God Himself were brought on the stage. In those days it was done in all simplicity. In Victor Hugo's[3] 'Notre Dame de Paris' an edifying and gratuitous spectacle was provided for the people in the Hotel de Ville[4] of Paris in

---

[1]Dante Alighieri (1265–1321), the Florentine poet who wrote the *Divine Comedy*, one of the great works of literature.

[2]The Virgin Mary, the mother of Jesus.

[3]Victor Marie Hugo (1802–1885), a prolific French writer, published his novel *Notre Dame de Paris* in 1831.

[4]City Hall.

THE BROTHERS KARAMAZOV: THE GRAND INQUISITOR   Reprinted with permission of The Macmillan Company from *The Brothers Karamazov* by F. Dostoevsky. [Trans. Constance Garnett (New York, 1951), 253–72.] First published in 1912 by William Heinemann Ltd.

the reign of Louis XI[5] in honor of the birth of the dauphin.[6] It was called *Le bon jugement de la très sainte et gracieuse Vierge Marie*,[7] and she appears herself on the stage and pronounces her *bon jugement*. Similar plays, chiefly from the Old Testament, were occasionally performed in Moscow, too, up to the times of Peter the Great.[8] But besides plays there were all sorts of legends and ballads scattered about the world, in which the saints and angels and all the powers of Heaven took part when required. In our monasteries the monks busied themselves in translating, copying, and even composing such poems—and even under the Tartars.[9] There is, for instance, one such poem (of course, from the Greek), 'The Wanderings of Our Lady Through Hell,' with descriptions as bold as Dante's. Our Lady[10] visits Hell, and the Archangel Michael leads her through the torments. She sees the sinners and their punishment. There she sees among others one noteworthy set of sinners in a burning lake; some of them sink to the bottom of the lake so that they can't swim out, and 'these God forgets'—an expression of extraordinary depth and force. And so Our Lady, shocked and weeping, falls before the throne of God and begs for mercy for all in Hell—for all she has seen there, indiscriminately. Her conversation with God is immensely interesting. She beseeches Him, she will not desist, and when God points to the hands and feet of her Son, nailed to the Cross, and asks, 'How can I forgive His tormentors?' she bids all the saints, all the martyrs, all the angels and archangels to fall down with her and pray for mercy on all without distinction. It ends by her winning from God a respite of suffering every year from Good Friday till Trinity day,[11] and the sinners at once raise a cry of thankfulness from Hell, chanting, 'Thou art just, O Lord, in this judgment.' Well, my poem would have been of that kind if it had appeared at that time. He comes on the scene in my poem, but He says nothing, only appears and passes on. Fifteen centuries have passed since He promised to come in His glory, fifteen centuries since His prophet wrote, 'Behold, I come quickly'; 'Of that day and that hour knoweth no man, neither the Son,

[5]Louis XI (1423–1483) was king of France from 1461 to 1483.

[6]Title of the eldest son of the king.

[7]French: The sound judgment of the very holy and gracious Virgin Mary.

[8]Peter the Great (1672–1725), tsar of Russia.

[9]A Mongol group who controlled much of Russia during the Middle Ages.

[10]The Virgin Mary.

[11]Trinity Sunday (the Sunday after Pentecost).

but the Father,' as He Himself predicted on earth.[12] But humanity awaits him with the same faith and with the same love. Oh, with greater faith, for it is fifteen centuries since man has ceased to see signs from Heaven.

> No signs from Heaven come today
> To add to what the heart doth say.

There was nothing left but faith in what the heart doth say. It is true there were many miracles in those days. There were saints who performed miraculous cures; some holy people, according to their biographies, were visited by the Queen of Heaven[13] herself. But the devil did not slumber, and doubts were already arising among men of the truth of these miracles. And just then there appeared in the north of Germany a terrible new heresy. 'A huge star like to a torch' (that is, to a church) 'fell on the sources of the waters and they became bitter.'[14] These heretics began blasphemously denying miracles. But those who remained faithful were all the more ardent in their faith. The tears of humanity rose up to Him as before, awaiting His coming, loved Him, hoped for Him, yearned to suffer and die for Him as before. And so many ages mankind had prayed with faith and fervor, 'O Lord our God, hasten Thy coming,' so many ages called upon Him, that in His infinite mercy He deigned to come down to His servants. Before that day He had come down, He had visited some holy men, martyrs, and hermits, as is written in their 'Lives.'[15] Among us, Tyutchev,[16] with absolute faith in the truth of his words, bore witness that

> Bearing the Cross, in slavish dress,
> Weary and worn, the Heavenly King
> Our mother, Russia, came to bless,
> And through our land went wandering.

And that certainly was so, I assure you.

"And behold, He deigned to appear for a moment to the people, to the tortured, suffering people, sunk in iniquity, but loving Him like children. My story is laid in Spain, in Seville, in the most terrible time

[12]Jesus' prophecy concerning his Second Coming (Matthew 24:36 and Mark 13:32).
[13]The Virgin Mary.
[14]Book of Revelation 8:10-11.
[15]Biographies.
[16]Fyodor Tyutchev (1803–1873), a Russian lyric poet.

of the Inquisition,[17] when fires were lighted every day to the glory of God, and 'in the splendid *auto-da-fé*[18] the wicked heretics were burned.' Oh, of course, this was not the coming in which He[19] will appear according to His promise at the end of time in all His heavenly glory, and which will be sudden 'as lightning flashing from east to west.' No, He visited His children only for a moment, and there where the flames were crackling round the heretics. In His infinite mercy He came once more among men in that human shape in which He walked among men for three years fifteen centuries ago.

"He came down to the 'hot pavement' of the southern town in which on the day before almost a hundred heretics had, *ad majorem gloriam Dei*,[20] been burned by the cardinal, the Grand Inquisitor,[21] in a magnificent *auto-da-fé*, in the presence of the king, the court, the knights, the cardinals, the most charming ladies of the court, and the whole population of Seville.

Imagined ✕ "He came softly, unobserved, and yet, strange to say, every one recognized Him. That might be one of the best passages in the poem. I mean, why they recognized Him. The people are irresistibly drawn to Him, they surround Him, they flock about Him, follow Him. He moves silently in their midst with a gentle smile of infinite compassion. The sun of love burns in His heart, light and power shine from His eyes, and their radiance, shed on the people, stirs their hearts with responsive love. He holds out His hands to them, blesses them, and a healing virtue comes from contact with Him, even with His garments. An old man in the crowd, blind from childhood, cries out, 'O Lord, heal me and I shall see Thee!' and, as it were, scales fall from his eyes and the blind man sees Him. The crowd weeps and kisses the earth under His feet. Children throw flowers before Him, sing, and cry hosannah.[22] 'It is He—it is He!' all repeat. 'It must be He, it can be no one but Him!' He stops at the steps of the Seville cathedral at the moment when the weeping mourn-

---

[17]The Inquisition, or the Congregation of the Holy Office (the official name), was charged with seeking out heresy (false beliefs) and punishing heretics. (The Inquisition was founded in the early thirteenth century and abolished in 1834. In the fifteenth and sixteenth centuries it raged most furiously in Spain, Portugal, and Italy.)

[18]Portuguese: act of faith. The phrase refers to the public sentencing and subsequent punishment of convicted (repentant and unrepentant) heretics.

[19]Jesus.

[20]Latin: to the greater glory of God.

[21]The high-ranking clergyman in charge of the Inquisition within a certain territory.

[22]A shout of praise to God: "Save, we pray!"

ers are bringing in a little open white coffin. In it lies a child of seven, the only daughter of a prominent citizen. The dead child lies hidden in flowers. 'He will raise your child,' the crowd shouts to the weeping mother. The priest, coming to meet the coffin, looks perplexed and frowns, but the mother of the dead child throws herself at His feet with a wail. 'If it is Thou, raise my child!' she cries, holding out her hands to Him. The procession halts, the coffin is laid on the steps at His feet. He looks with compassion, and His lips once more softly pronounce, 'Maiden, arise!' and the maiden arises. The little girl sits up in the coffin and looks round, smiling with wide-open wondering eyes, holding a bunch of white roses they had put in her hand.

"There are cries, sobs, confusion among the people, and at that moment the cardinal himself, the Grand Inquisitor, passes by the cathedral. He is an old man, almost ninety, tall and erect, with a withered face and sunken eyes, in which there is still a gleam of light. He is not dressed in his gorgeous cardinal's robes, as he was the day before, when he was burning the enemies of the Roman Church[23]—at that moment he was wearing his coarse, old, monk's cassock. At a distance behind him come his gloomy assistants and slaves and the 'holy guard.'[24] He stops at the sight of the crowd and watches it from a distance. He sees everything; he sees them set the coffin down at His feet, sees the child rise up, and his face darkens. He knits his thick grey brows and his eyes gleam with a sinister fire. He holds out his finger and bids the guards take Him. And such is his power, so completely are the people cowed into submission and trembling obedience to him, that the crowd immediately makes way for the guards, and in the midst of death-like silence they lay hands on Him and lead Him away. The crowd instantly bows down to the earth, like one man, before the old inquisitor. He blesses the people in silence and passes on. The guards lead their prisoner to the close, gloomy, vaulted prison in the ancient palace of the Holy Inquisition and shut Him in it. The day passes and is followed by the dark, burning 'breathless' night of Seville. The air is 'fragrant with laurel and lemon.' In the pitch darkness the iron door of the prison is suddenly opened and the Grand Inquisitor himself comes in with a light in his hand. He is alone; the door is closed at once behind him. He stands in the doorway and for a minute or two gazes into His face. At last he goes up slowly, sets the light on the table and speaks.

[23]Roman Catholic Church.
[24]Bodyguard.

"'Is it Thou? Thou?' but receiving no answer, he adds at once, 'Don't answer, be silent. What canst Thou say, indeed? I know too well what Thou wouldst say. And Thou hast no right to add anything to what Thou hadst said of old. Why, then, art Thou come to hinder us? For Thou hast come to hinder us, and Thou knowest that. But dost Thou know what will be tomorrow? I know not who Thou art and care not to know whether it is Thou or only a semblance of Him, but tomorrow I shall condemn Thee and burn Thee at the stake as the worst of heretics. And the very people who have today kissed Thy feet, tomorrow at the faintest sign from me will rush to heap up the embers of Thy fire. Knowest Thou that? Yes, maybe Thou knowest it,' he added with thoughtful penetration, never for a moment taking his eyes off the Prisoner."

"I don't quite understand, Ivan. What does it mean?" Alyosha, who had been listening in silence, said with a smile. "Is it simply a wild fantasy, or a mistake on the part of the old man—some impossible *quid pro quo*?"[25]

"Take it as the last," said Ivan, laughing, "if you are so corrupted by modern realism and can't stand anything fantastic. If you like it to be a case of mistaken identity, let it be so. It is true," he went on, laughing, "the old man was ninety, and he might well be crazy over his set idea. He might have been struck by the appearance of the Prisoner. It might, in fact, be simply his ravings, the delusion of an old man of ninety, over-excited by the *auto-da-fé* of a hundred heretics the day before. But does it matter to us after all whether it was a mistake of identity or a wild fantasy? All that matters is that the old man should speak out, should speak openly of what he has thought in silence for ninety years."

"And the Prisoner too is silent? Does He look at him and not say a word?"

"That's inevitable in any case," Ivan laughed again. "The old man has told Him He hasn't the right to add anything to what He has said of old. One may say it is the most fundamental feature of Roman Catholicism, in my opinion at least. 'All has been given by Thee to the Pope,' they say, 'and all, therefore, is still in the Pope's hands, and there is no need for Thee to come now at all. Thou must not meddle for the time, at least.' That's how they speak and write, too—the Jesuits,[26] at any rate. I

---

[25]One thing in exchange for another; a trade-off.

[26]Members of the Society of Jesus, which was viewed as the most aggressive and militant order of the Roman Catholic Church. The order was founded in 1534 by a former soldier, the Spaniard Ignatius of Loyola (1491–1556).

have read it myself in the works of their theologians. 'Hast Thou the right to reveal to us one of the mysteries of that world from which Thou hast come?' my old man asks Him, and answers the question for Him. 'No, Thou hast not; that Thou mayest not add to what has been said of old, and mayest not take from men the freedom which Thou didst exalt when Thou wast on earth. Whatsoever Thou revealest anew will encroach on men's freedom of faith; for it will be manifest as a miracle, and the freedom of their faith was dearer to Thee than anything in those days fifteen hundred years ago. Didst Thou not often say then, "I will make you free"? But now Thou hast seen these "free" men,' the old man adds suddenly, with a pensive smile. 'Yes, we've paid dearly for it,' he goes on, looking sternly at Him, 'but at last we have completed that work in Thy name. For fifteen centuries we have been wrestling with Thy freedom, but now it is ended and over for good. Dost Thou not believe that it's over for good? Thou lookest meekly at me and deignest not even to be wroth with me. But let me tell Thee that now, today, people are more persuaded than ever that they have perfect freedom, yet they have brought their freedom to us and laid it humbly at our feet. But that has been our doing. Was this what Thou didst? Was this Thy freedom?'"

"I don't understand again," Alyosha broke in. "Is he ironical, is he jesting?"

"Not a bit of it! He claims it as a merit for himself and his Church that at last they have vanquished freedom and have done so to make men happy. 'For now' (he is speaking of the Inquisition, of course) 'for the first time it has become possible to think of the happiness of men. Man was created a rebel; and how can rebels be happy? Thou wast warned,' he says to Him. 'Thou hast had no lack of admonitions, and warnings, but Thou didst not listen to those warnings; Thou didst reject the only way by which men might be made happy. But, fortunately, departing Thou didst hand on the work to us. Thou hast promised, Thou hast established by Thy word, Thou hast given to us the right to bind and to unbind, and now, of course, Thou canst not think of taking it away. Why, then, hast Thou come to hinder us?'"

"And what's the meaning of 'no lack of admonitions and warnings'?" asked Alyosha.

"Why, that's the chief part of what the old man must say."

"'The wise and dread Spirit,[27] the spirit of self-destruction and

[27]Devil.

nonexistence,' the old man goes on, 'the great spirit talked with Thee in the wilderness, and we are told in the books that he "tempted" Thee. Is that so? And could anything truer be said than what he revealed to Thee in three questions and what Thou didst reject, and what in the books is called "the temptation"?[28] And yet if there has ever been on earth a real stupendous miracle, it took place on that day, on the day of the three temptations. The statement of those three questions was itself the miracle. If it were possible to imagine simply for the sake of argument that those three questions of the dread spirit had perished utterly from the books, and that we had to restore them and to invent them anew, and to do so had gathered together all the wise men of the earth—rulers, chief priests, learned men, philosophers, poets—and had set them the task to invent three questions, such as would not only fit the occasion, but express in three words, three human phrases, the whole future history of the world and of humanity—dost Thou believe that all the wisdom of the earth united could have invented anything in depth and force equal to the three questions which were actually put to Thee then by the wise and mighty spirit in the wilderness? From those questions alone, from the miracle of their statement, we can see that we have here to do not with the fleeting human intelligence, but with the absolute and eternal. For in those three questions the whole subsequent history of mankind is, as it were, brought together into one whole, and foretold, and in them are united all the unsolved historical contradictions of human nature. At the time it could not be so clear, since the future was unknown; but now that fifteen hundred years have passed, we see that everything in those three questions was so justly divined and foretold, and has been so truly fulfilled, that nothing can be added to them or taken from them.

"'Judge Thyself who was right—Thou or he who questioned Thee then? Remember the first question; its meaning, in other words, was this: "Thou wouldst go into the world, and art going with empty hands, with some promise of freedom which men in their simplicity and their natural unruliness cannot even understand, which they fear and dread—for nothing has ever been more insupportable for a man and a human society than freedom. But seest Thou these stones in this parched and barren wilderness? Turn them into bread, and mankind will run after Thee like a flock of sheep, grateful and obedient, though

---

[28]The three temptations of Jesus as related in the Gospels: Matthew 4:1–11; Luke 4:1–13; Mark 1:12–13.

forever trembling, lest Thou withdraw Thy hand and deny them Thy bread." But Thou wouldst not deprive man of freedom and didst reject the offer, thinking, what is that freedom worth, if obedience is bought with bread? Thou didst reply that man lives not by bread alone. But dost Thou know that for the sake of that earthly bread the spirit of the earth will rise up against Thee and will strive with Thee and overcome Thee, and all will follow him, crying, "Who can compare with this beast? He has given us fire from heaven!" Dost Thou know that the ages will pass, and humanity will proclaim by the lips of their sages that there is no crime, and therefore no sin; there is only hunger? "Feed men, and then ask of them virtue!" that's what they'll write on the banner which they will raise against Thee, and with which they will destroy Thy temple. Where Thy temple stood will rise a new building; the terrible tower of Babel[29] will be built again, and though, like the one of old, it will not be finished, yet Thou mightest have prevented that new tower and have cut short the sufferings of men for a thousand years; for they will come back to us after a thousand years of agony with their tower. They will seek us again, hidden underground in the catacombs, for we shall be again persecuted and tortured. They will find us and cry to us, "Feed us, for those who have promised us fire from heaven haven't given it!" And then we shall finish building their tower, for he finishes the building who feeds them. And we alone shall feed them in Thy name, declaring falsely that it is in Thy name. Oh, never, never can they feed themselves without us! No science will give them bread so long as they remain free. In the end they will lay their freedom at our feet, and say to us, "Make us your slaves, but feed us." They will understand themselves, at last, that freedom and bread enough for all are inconceivable together, for never, never will they be able to share between them! They will be convinced, too, that they can never be free, for they are weak, vicious, worthless and rebellious. Thou didst promise them the bread of Heaven, but, I repeat again, can it compare with earthly bread in the eyes of the weak, ever-sinful and ignoble race of man? And if for the sake of the bread of Heaven thousands and tens of thousands shall follow Thee, what is to become of the millions and tens of thousands of millions of creatures who will not have the strength to forgo the earthly bread for the sake of the heavenly? Or dost Thou care

[29]According to the Old Testament (Genesis 11:1–9), a tower (and city) built in the plain of Shinar. The tower was to be so tall as to reach into heaven. However, God punished the builders for their pride by replacing their single language with many diverse tongues. Now unable to understand one another, the builders had to abandon their project.

only for the tens of thousands of the great and strong, while the millions, numerous as the sands of the sea, who are weak but love Thee, must exist only for the sake of the great and strong? No, we care for the weak, too. They are sinful and rebellious, but in the end they too will become obedient. They will marvel at us and look on us as gods, because we are ready to endure the freedom which they have found so dreadful and to rule over them—so awful it will seem to them to be free. But we shall tell them that we are Thy servants and rule them in Thy name. We shall deceive them again, for we will not let Thee come to us again. That deception will be our suffering, for we shall be forced to lie.

"'This is the significance of the first question in the wilderness, and this is what Thou hast rejected for the sake of that freedom which Thou hast exalted above everything. Yet in this question lies hidden the great secret of this world. Choosing "bread," Thou wouldst have satisfied the universal and everlasting craving of humanity—to find someone to worship. So long as man remains free he strives for nothing so incessantly and so painfully as to find someone to worship. But man seeks to worship what is established beyond dispute, so that all men would agree at once to worship it. For these pitiful creatures are concerned not only to find what one or the other can worship, but to find something that all would believe in and worship; what is essential is that all may be *together* in it. This craving for *community* of worship is the chief misery of every man individually and of all humanity from the beginning of time. For the sake of common worship they've slain each other with the sword. They have set up gods and challenged one another, "Put away your gods and come and worship ours, or we will kill you and your gods!" And so it will be to the end of the world, even when gods disappear from the earth; they will fall down before idols just the same. Thou didst know, Thou couldst not but have known, this fundamental secret of human nature, but Thou didst reject the one infallible banner which was offered Thee to make all men bow down to Thee alone—the banner of earthly bread; and Thou hast rejected it for the sake of freedom and the bread of Heaven. Behold what Thou didst further. And all again in the name of freedom! I tell Thee that man is tormented by no greater anxiety than to find someone quickly to whom he can hand over the gift of freedom with which the ill-fated creature is born. But only one who can appease their conscience can take over their freedom. In bread there was offered Thee an invincible banner; give bread, and man will worship Thee, for nothing is more certain than bread. But if someone else gains possession of his conscience—oh! then he will cast away Thy bread and follow after him who has ensnared his conscience. In that Thou wast right. For the secret of man's being is not only to live but to have something to live for. Without a stable conception of the object of life, man would not consent to go on living, and would rather destroy himself than remain on earth, though he had bread in abundance. That is true. But what happened? Instead of taking men's freedom from them, Thou didst make it greater than ever! Didst Thou forget that man prefers peace, and even death, to freedom of choice in the knowledge of good and evil? Nothing is more seductive for man than his freedom of conscience, but nothing is a greater cause of suffering. And behold, instead of giving a firm foundation for setting the conscience of man at rest forever, Thou didst choose all that is exceptional, vague and enigmatic; Thou didst choose what was utterly beyond the strength of men, acting as though Thou didst not love them at all—Thou who didst come to give Thy life for them! Instead of taking possession of man's freedom, Thou didst increase it, and burdened the spiritual kingdom of mankind with its sufferings forever. Thou didst desire man's free love, that he should follow Thee freely, enticed and taken captive by Thee. In place of the rigid, ancient law, man must hereafter with free heart decide for himself what is good and what is evil, having only Thy image before him as his guide. But didst Thou not know he would at last reject even Thy image and Thy truth, if he is weighed down with the fearful burden of free choice? They will cry aloud at last that the truth is not in Thee, for they could not have been left in greater confusion and suffering than Thou hast caused, laying upon them so many cares and unanswerable problems.

"'So that, in truth, Thou didst Thyself lay the foundation for the destruction of Thy kingdom, and no one is more to blame for it. Yet what was offered Thee? There are three powers, three powers alone, able to conquer and to hold captive forever the conscience of these impotent rebels for their happiness—those forces are miracle, mystery and authority. Thou hast rejected all three and hast set the example for doing so. When the wise and dread spirit set Thee on the pinnacle of the temple and said to Thee, "If Thou wouldst know whether Thou art the son of God then cast Thyself down, for it is written: the angels shall hold him up lest he fall and bruise himself, and Thou shalt know then whether Thou art the Son of God and shalt prove then how great is Thy faith in Thy Father." But Thou didst refuse and wouldst not cast Thyself down. Oh! of course, Thou didst proudly and well like God;

but the weak, unruly race of men, are they gods? Oh, Thou didst know then that in taking one step, in making one movement to cast Thyself down, Thou wouldst be tempting God and have lost all Thy faith in Him, and wouldst have been dashed to pieces against that earth which Thou didst come to save. And the wise spirit that tempted Thee would have rejoiced. But I ask again, are there many like Thee? And couldst Thou believe for one moment that men, too, could face such a temptation? Is the nature of men such that they can reject miracle, and at the great moments of their life, the moments of their deepest, most agonizing spiritual difficulties, cling only to the free verdict of the heart? Oh, Thou didst know that Thy deed would be recorded in books, would be handed down to remote times and the utmost ends of the earth, and Thou didst hope that man, following Thee, would cling to God and not ask for a miracle. But Thou didst not know that when man rejects miracles he rejects God too; for man seeks not so much God as the miraculous. And as man cannot bear to be without the miraculous, he will create new miracles of his own for himself, and will worship deeds of sorcery and witchcraft, though he might be a hundred times over a rebel, heretic and infidel. Thou didst not come down from the Cross when they shouted to Thee, mocking and reviling Thee, "Come down from the Cross and we will believe that Thou art He." Thou didst not come down, for again Thou wouldst not enslave man by a miracle, and didst crave faith given freely, not based on miracle. Thou didst crave for free love and not the base raptures of the slave before the might that has overawed him forever. But Thou didst think too highly of men therein, for they are slaves, of course, though rebellious by nature. Look round and judge; fifteen centuries have passed; look upon them. Whom hast Thou raised up to Thyself? I swear, man is weaker and baser by nature than Thou hast believed him! Can he, can he do what Thou didst? By showing him so much respect, Thou didst, as it were, cease to feel for him, for Thou didst ask far too much from him—Thou who hast loved him more than Thyself! Respecting him less, Thou wouldst have asked less of him. That would have been more like love, for his burden would have been lighter. He is weak and vile. What though he is everywhere now rebelling against our power, and proud of his rebellion? It is the pride of a child and a schoolboy. They are little children rioting and barring out the teacher at school. But their childish delight will end; it will cost them dear. They will cast down temples and drench the earth with blood. But they will see at last, the foolish children, that, though they are rebels, they are impotent rebels, unable to keep up their own rebellion. Bathed in their foolish tears, they will recognize at last that He who created them rebels must have meant to mock at them. They will say this in despair, and their utterance will be a blasphemy which will make them more unhappy still, for man's nature cannot bear blasphemy, and in the end always avenges it on itself. And so unrest, confusion and unhappiness—that is the present lot of man after Thou didst bear so much for their freedom! Thy great prophet tells in vision and in image that he saw all those who took part in the first resurrection and that there were of each tribe twelve thousand.[30] But if there were so many of them, they must have been not men but gods. They had borne Thy cross, they had endured scores of years in the barren, hungry wilderness, living upon locusts and roots—and Thou mayest indeed point with pride at those children of freedom, of free love, of free and splendid sacrifice for Thy name. But remember that they were only some thousands; and what of the rest? And how are the other weak ones to blame, because they could not endure what the strong have endured? How is the weak soul to blame that it is unable to receive such terrible gifts? Canst Thou have simply come to the elect and for the elect? But if so, it is a mystery and we cannot understand it. And if it is a mystery, we too have a right to preach a mystery, and to teach them that it's not the free judgment of their hearts, not love, that matters, but a mystery which they must follow blindly, even against their conscience. So we have done. We have corrected Thy work and have founded it upon *miracle, mystery* and *authority*. And men rejoiced that they were again led like sheep, and that the terrible gift that had brought them such suffering was, at last, lifted from their hearts. Were we right teaching them this? Speak! Did we not love mankind, so meekly acknowledging their feebleness, lovingly lightening their burden, and permitting their weak nature even sin with our sanction? Why hast Thou come now to hinder us? And why dost Thou look silently and searchingly at me with Thy mild eyes? Be angry. I don't want Thy love, for I love Thee not. And what use is it for me to hide anything from Thee? Don't I know to Whom I am speaking? All that I can say is known to Thee already. And is it for me to conceal from Thee our mystery? Perhaps it is Thy will to hear it from my lips. Listen, then. We are not working with Thee, but with *him*—that is our mystery. It's long—eight centuries—since we have been on *his* side and not on Thine. Just eight centuries ago, we

---

[30]A reference to a passage in the Book of Revelation (ascribed to John, the Evangelist), 7:4–8.

took from him what Thou didst reject with scorn, that last gift he offered Thee, showing Thee all the kingdoms of the earth. We took from him Rome and the sword of Caesar, and proclaimed ourselves sole rulers of the earth, though hitherto we have not been able to complete our work. But whose fault is that? Oh, the work is only beginning, but it has begun. It has long to await completion and the earth has yet much to suffer, but we shall triumph and shall be Caesars, and then we shall plan the universal happiness of man. But Thou mightest have taken even then the sword of Caesar. Why didst Thou reject that last gift? Hadst Thou accepted that last counsel of the mighty spirit, Thou wouldst have accomplished all that man seeks on earth—that is, someone to worship, someone to keep his conscience, and some means of uniting all in one unanimous and harmonious ant heap, for the craving for universal unity is the third and last anguish of men. Mankind as a whole has always striven to organize a universal state. There have been many great nations with great histories, but the more highly they were developed the more unhappy they were, for they felt more acutely than other people the craving for world-wide union. The great conquerors, Timours[31] and Genghis Khans,[32] whirled like hurricanes over the face of the earth, striving to subdue its people, and they too were but the unconscious expression of the same craving for universal unity. Hadst Thou taken the world and Caesar's purple,[33] Thou wouldst have founded the universal state and have given universal peace. For who can rule men if not he who holds their conscience and their bread in his hands? We have taken the sword of Caesar, and in taking it, of course, have rejected Thee and followed *him*. Oh, ages are yet to come of the confusion of free thought, of their science and cannibalism. For having begun to build their tower of Babel without us, they will end, of course, with cannibalism. But then the beast will crawl to us and lick our feet and spatter them with tears of blood. And we shall sit upon the beast and raise the cup, and on it will be written, "Mystery." But then, and only then, the reign of peace and happiness will come for men. Thou art proud of Thine elect, but Thou hast only the elect, while we give rest to all. And besides, how many of those

---

[31]Timour, or Tamerlane (*ca.* 1336–1405), was a Mongol conqueror, who, after he had made himself lord of Turkestan, took control of Persia and Central Asia and led armies deep into Russia, India, Syria and Asia Minor.

[32]Genghis Khan (1162–1227) was a Mongol conqueror whose hordes overran northern China, Korea, northern India, Iran, Iraq and parts of Russia.

[33]The symbol of imperial power in ancient Rome.

elect, those mighty ones who could become elect, have grown weary waiting for Thee, and have transferred and will transfer the powers of their spirit and the warmth of their heart to the other camp, and end by raising their *free* banner against Thee. Thou didst Thyself lift up that banner. But with us all will be happy and will no more rebel, nor destroy one another as under Thy freedom. Oh, we shall persuade them that they will only become free when they renounce their freedom to us and submit to us. And shall we be right or shall we be lying? They will be convinced that we are right, for they will remember the horrors of slavery and confusion to which Thy freedom brought them. Freedom, free thought and science, will lead them into such straits and will bring them face to face with such marvels and insoluble mysteries that some of them, the fierce and rebellious, will destroy themselves; others, rebellious but weak, will destroy one another, while the rest, weak and unhappy, will crawl fawning to our feet and whine to us: "Yes, you were right, you alone possess His mystery, and we come back to you, save us from ourselves!"

"'Receiving bread from us, they will see clearly that we take the bread made by their hands from them, to give it to them, without any miracle. They will see that we do not change the stones to bread, but in truth they will be more thankful for taking it from our hands than for the bread itself! For they will remember only too well that in old days, without our help, even the bread they made turned to stones in their hands, while since they have come back to us, the very stones have turned to bread in their hands. Too, too well they know the value of complete submission! And until men know that, they will be unhappy. Who is most to blame for their not knowing it, speak? Who scattered the flock and sent it astray on unknown paths? But the flock will come together again and will submit once more, and then it will be once for all. Then we shall give them the quiet humble happiness of weak creatures such as they are by nature. Oh, we shall persuade them at last not to be proud, for Thou didst lift them up and thereby taught them to be proud. We shall show them that they are weak, that they are only pitiful children, but that childlike happiness is the sweetest of all. They will become timid and will look to us and huddle close to us in fear, as chicks to the hen. They will marvel at us and will be awe-stricken before us, and will be proud at our being so powerful and clever, that we have been able to subdue such a turbulent flock of thousands of millions. They will tremble impotently before our wrath, their minds will grow fearful, they will be quick to shed tears like women and children, but they will be just as ready at a sign from us to pass to laughter and rejoicing, to happy mirth and childish song. Yes, we shall set them to work, but in their leisure hours we shall make their life like a child's game, with children's songs and innocent dance. Oh, we shall allow them even sin; they are weak and helpless, and they will love us like children because we allow them to sin. We shall tell them that every sin will be expiated, if it is done with our permission, that we allow them to sin because we love them, and the punishment for these sins we take upon ourselves. And we shall take it upon ourselves, and they will adore us as their saviors who have taken on themselves their sins before God. And they will have no secrets from us. We shall allow or forbid them to live with their wives and mistresses, to have or not to have children—according to whether they have been obedient or disobedient—and they will submit to us gladly and cheerfully. The most painful secrets of their conscience, all, all they will bring to us, and we shall have an answer for all. And they will be glad to believe our answer, for it will save them from the great anxiety and terrible agony they endure at present in making a free decision for themselves. And all will be happy, all the millions of creatures, except the hundred thousand who rule over them. For only we, we who guard the mystery, shall be unhappy. There will be thousands of millions of happy babes, and a hundred thousand sufferers who have taken upon themselves the curse of the knowledge of good and evil. Peacefully they will die, peacefully they will expire in Thy name, and beyond the grave they will find nothing but death. But we shall keep the secret, and for their happiness we shall allure them with the reward of heaven and eternity. Though if there were anything in the other world, it certainly would not be for such as they. It is prophesied that Thou wilt come again in victory, Thou wilt come with Thy chosen, the proud and strong, but we will say that they have only saved themselves, but we have saved all. We are told that the harlot who sits upon the beast, and holds in her hands the *mystery*, shall be put to shame, that the weak will rise up again, and will rend her royal purple and will strip naked her loathsome body. But then I will stand up and point out to Thee the thousand millions of happy children who have known no sin. And we who have taken their sins upon us for their happiness will stand up before Thee and say: "Judge us if Thou canst and darest." Know that I fear Thee not. Know that I too have been in the wilderness, I too have lived on roots and locusts, I too prized the freedom with which Thou hast blessed men, and I too was striving to stand among Thy elect, among the strong and powerful, thirsting "to make up the number." But I awakened and would not serve madness. I turned back and joined the ranks of those *who have corrected Thy work*. I left the proud and went back to the humble, for the happiness of the humble. What I say to Thee will come to pass, and our dominion will be built up. I repeat, tomorrow Thou shalt see that obedient flock who at a sign from me will hasten to heap up the hot cinders about the pile on which I shall burn Thee for coming to hinder us. For if anyone has ever deserved our fires, it is Thou. Tomorrow I shall burn Thee. *Dixi*.'"[34]

Ivan stopped. He was carried away as he talked and spoke with excitement; when he had finished, he suddenly smiled.

Alyosha had listened in silence; toward the end he was greatly moved and seemed several times on the point of interrupting, but restrained himself. Now his words came with a rush.

"But . . . that's absurd!" he cried, flushing. "Your poem is in praise of Jesus, not in blame of Him—as you meant it to be. And who will believe you about freedom? Is that the way to understand it? That's not the idea of it in the Orthodox Church.[35] . . . That's Rome, and not even the whole of Rome, it's false—those are the worst of the Catholics, the Inquisitors, the Jesuits! . . . And there could not be such a fantastic creature as your Inquisitor. What are these sins of mankind they take on themselves? Who are these keepers of the mystery who have taken some curse upon themselves for the happiness of mankind? When have they been seen? We know the Jesuits, they are spoken ill of, but surely they are not what you describe? They are not that at all, not at all. . . . They are simply the Romish army for the earthly sovereignty of the world in the future, with the Pontiff[36] of Rome for Emperor . . . that's their ideal, but there's no sort of mystery or lofty melancholy about it. . . . It's simple lust of power, of filthy earthly gain, of domination— something like a universal serfdom with them as masters—that's all they stand for. They don't even believe in God, perhaps. Your suffering Inquisitor is a mere fantasy."

"Stay, stay," laughed Ivan, "how hot you are! A fantasy you say, let it be so! Of course it's a fantasy. But allow me to say: do you really think that the Roman Catholic movement of the last centuries is actually

[34]Latin: I have said (all that I am going to); I have spoken.

[35]Russian Orthodox Church, the national church of tsarist Russia. (After the division of the ancient Roman Empire, the Christian Church, too, split into two main branches: Roman Catholicism in the West, and the Orthodox churches in the East.

[36]The pope.

nothing but the lust of power, of filthy earthly gain? Is that Father Paissy's[37] teaching?"

"No, no, on the contrary, Father Paissy did once say something rather the same as you . . . but of course it's not the same, not a bit the same," Alyosha hastily corrected himself.

"A precious admission, in spite of your 'not a bit the same.' I ask you why your Jesuits and Inquisitors have united simply for vile material gain? Why can there not be among them one martyr oppressed by great sorrow and loving humanity? You see, only suppose that there was one such man among all those who desire nothing but filthy material gain—if there's only one like my old Inquisitor, who had himself eaten roots in the desert and made frenzied efforts to subdue his flesh to make himself free and perfect. But yet all his life he loved humanity, and suddenly his eyes were opened, and he saw that it is no great moral blessedness to attain perfection and freedom, if at the same time one gains the conviction that millions of God's creatures have been created as a mockery, that they will never be capable of using their freedom, that these poor rebels can never turn into giants to complete the tower, that it was not for such geese that the great idealist dreamt his dream of harmony. Seeing all that, he turned back and joined—the clever people. Surely that could have happened?"

"Joined whom, what clever people?" cried Alyosha, completely carried away. "They have no such great cleverness and no mysteries and secrets. . . . Perhaps nothing but atheism,[38] that's all their secret. Your Inquisitor does not believe in God, that's his secret!"

"What if it is so! At last you have guessed it. It's perfectly true that that's the whole secret, but isn't that suffering, at least for a man like that, who has wasted his whole life in the desert and yet could not shake off his incurable love of humanity? In his old age he reached the clear conviction that nothing but the advice of the great dread spirit could build up any tolerable sort of life for the feeble, unruly, 'incomplete, empirical creatures created in jest.' And so, convinced of this, he sees that he must follow the counsel of the wise spirit, the dread spirit of death and destruction, and therefore accept lying and deception, and lead men consciously to death and destruction, and yet deceive them all the way so that they may not notice where they are being led, that the poor, blind creatures may at least on the way think themselves happy.

[37]Father Paissy, a learned monk.
[38]Denial of God's existence.

And note, the deception is in the name of Him in Whose ideal the old man had so fervently believed all his life long. Is not that tragic? And if only one such stood at the head of the whole army 'filled with the lust of power only for the sake of filthy gain'—would not one such be enough to make a tragedy? More than that, one such standing at the head is enough to create the actual leading idea of the Roman Church with all its armies and Jesuits, its highest idea. I tell you frankly that I firmly believe that there has always been such a man among those who stood at the head of the movement. Who knows, there may have been some such even among the Roman Popes. Who knows, perhaps the spirit of that accursed old man who loves mankind so obstinately in his own way is to be found even now in a whole multitude of such old men, existing not by chance but by agreement, as a secret league formed long ago for the guarding of the mystery, to guard it from the weak and the unhappy, so as to make them happy. No doubt it is so, and so it must be indeed. I fancy that even among the Masons[39] there's something of the same mystery at the bottom, and that that's why the Catholics so detest the Masons as their rivals breaking up the unity of the idea, while it is so essential that there should be one flock and one shepherd. . . . But from the way I defend my idea I might be an author impatient of your criticism. Enough of it."

"You are perhaps a Mason yourself!" broke suddenly from Alyosha. "You don't believe in God," he added, speaking this time very sorrowfully. He fancied besides that his brother was looking at him ironically. "How does your poem end?" he asked, suddenly looking down. "Or was it the end?"

"I meant it to end like this: When the Inquisitor ceased speaking, he waited some time for his Prisoner to answer him. His silence weighed down upon him. He saw the Prisoner had listened intently all the time, looking gently in his face and evidently not wishing to reply. The old man longed for Him to say something, however bitter and terrible. But He suddenly approached the old man in silence and softly kissed him on his bloodless, aged lips. That was all His answer. The old man shuddered. His lips moved. He went to the door, opened it, and said to Him 'Go, and come no more. . . . Come not at all, never, never!' And he let Him out into the dark alleys of the town. The Prisoner went away."

"And the old man?"

---

[39]Freemasons, a secret society formed for fraternal (and religious) purposes, which was outside the control of the Church.

"The kiss glows in his heart, but the old man adheres to his idea."

"And you with him, you too?" cried Alyosha, mournfully.

Ivan laughed.

"Why, it's all nonsense, Alyosha. It's only a senseless poem of a senseless student, who could never write two lines of verse. Why do you take it so seriously? Surely you don't suppose I am going straight off to the Jesuits, to join the men who are correcting His work? Good Lord, it's no business of mine. I told you, all I want is to live on to thirty, and then . . . dash the cup to the ground!"[40]

"But the little sticky leaves, and the precious tombs, and the blue sky, and the woman you love! How will you live, how will you love them?" Alyosha cried sorrowfully. "With such a hell in your heart and your head, how can you? No, that's just what you are going away for, to join them . . . if not, you will kill yourself, you can't endure it!"

"There is a strength to endure everything," Ivan said with a cold smile.

"What strength?"

"The strength of the Karamazovs—the strength of the Karamazov baseness."

"To sink into debauchery, to stifle your soul with corruption, yes?"

"Possibly even that . . . only perhaps till I am thirty I shall escape it, and then—"

"How will you escape it? By what will you escape it? That's impossible with your ideas."

"In the Karamazov way, again."

"'Everything is lawful,' you mean? Everything is lawful, is that it?"

Ivan scowled, and all at once turned strangely pale.

"Ah, you've caught up yesterday's phrase, which so offended Miusov[41]—and which Dmitri[42] pounced upon so naively and paraphrased!" he smiled queerly. "Yes, if you like, 'everything is lawful' since the word has been said. I won't deny it. And Mitya's[43] version isn't bad."

Alyosha looked at him in silence.

"I thought that going away from here I have you at least," Ivan said suddenly, with unexpected feeling; "but now I see that there is no place

---

[40] A poetic saying, meaning to end one's life.

[41] Peter Miusov, a relative of Ivan and Alyosha; a man of enlightened ideas.

[42] Half-brother of Ivan and Alyosha.

[43] Mitya is a variant name of Dmitri.

for me even in your heart, my dear hermit. The formula, 'all is lawful,' I won't renounce—will you renounce me for that, yes?"

Alyosha got up, went to him and softly kissed him on the lips.

"That's plagiarism,"[44] cried Ivan, highly delighted. "You stole that from my poem. Thank you, though. Get up, Alyosha, it's time we were going, both of us."

They went out, but stopped when they reached the entrance of the tavern.

"Listen, Alyosha," Ivan began in a resolute voice, "if I am really able to care for the sticky little leaves, I shall only love them remembering you. It's enough for me that you are somewhere here, and I shan't lose my desire for life yet. Is that enough for you? Take it as a declaration of love if you like. And now you go to the right and I to the left. And it's enough, do you hear—enough! I mean even if I don't go away tomorrow (I think I certainly shall go) and we meet again, don't say a word more on these subjects. I beg that particularly. And about Dmitri, too, I ask you especially never speak to me again," he added, with sudden irritation; "it's all exhausted, it has all been said over and over again, hasn't it? And I'll make you one promise in return for it. When, at thirty, I want to 'dash the cup to the ground,' wherever I may be I'll come to have one more talk with you, even though it were from America—you may be sure of that. I'll come on purpose. It will be very interesting to have a look at you, to see what you'll be by that time. It's rather a solemn promise, you see. And we really may be parting for seven years or ten. Come, go now to your Pater Seraphicus,[45] he is dying. If he dies without you, you will be angry with me for having kept you. Good-bye, kiss me once more; that's right, now go." . . .

*   *   *

---

[44]Stealing from the writing or ideas of another person.

[45]Father Zossima, the beloved and renowned elder at the monastery, was of great influence upon Alyosha.

27

Friedrich Nietzsche

The Genealogy of Morals

*F*RIEDRICH *Nietzsche (1844–*
1900) considered Dostoevsky the only one who had taught him anything about
human nature. And, as was the case with the Russian novelist, the true
greatness of this German philosopher has been recognized only in recent years,
when he has been acclaimed as the prophet of existentialism and psychoanalytic
doctrine. The earlier views of Nietzsche as a brilliant but incoherent iconoclast
and as the mad prophet of German Nazism have been abandoned as distortions.
Today, he is accorded a place as one of the original thinkers of the Western
tradition; he was one of the first to recognize the absurdity of human existence as
the necessary basis for creative life and to <u>stress the importance of irrational and
illusional factors in shaping human behavior.</u>

Nietzsche did not put forward a grand philosophical system. His ideas were
expressed in an elusive style, as brilliant aphorisms or in short paragraphs;
nevertheless, they framed a consistent and searching point of view. His writings
are the work of a lonely, sensitive man with profound convictions and integrity,
whose later life was marked by suffering and disease culminating in insanity. It
was as though Nietzsche strove by intellectual energy to overcome the obstacles
of his life and to derive bold, new visions from his plight. In any case, his work
has a supercharged quality that does not always make for clarity, but allows him
to strike off brilliant insights into the nature and condition of human beings.

Looking at the previous two thousand years of European history, Nietzsche
was certain that Europe had undergone a most harmful development and was
convinced that conditions had never been worse than in his own time, the late
nineteenth century. He believed that all kinds of institutions and movements
were engaged in reducing human beings to a still lower level of existence,
making everything ever smaller and more common; and that, accordingly, any
individual who displayed such qualities as strength, boldness, aggressiveness,

and power could expect to be vilified and shackled. Thus it was no wonder, suggested Nietzsche, that people living in the nineteenth century, as well as those of preceding ages, had not produced the many and mighty monuments they were capable of creating.

Nietzsche attributed the "wrong turn" in Western civilization to the influence of those Jews who, in the sixth century B.C., were held in captivity by the Babylonians. Rather than admit that their powerful captors must be the beloved of the deities, the subjugated Jews claimed that being a slave was a sure sign of divine favor and that thus they—powerless, humiliated, trampled, and weak—were the chosen people of God. Nietzsche saw in this claim the beginning of "slave" morality, the religious sanction under which slaves and losers of all sorts had ever since been ganging up on the strong and attempting to destroy the only genuine morality— "master" morality. Christianity, Judaism's successor, Nietzsche considered the embodiment of slave morality par excellence: it had not only succeeded in annihilating the Roman Empire but had held Europe in shackles ever afterward. Indeed, in Nietzsche's view of European history, whenever master morality had attempted to reassert itself, some embodiment of slave morality had sought to obliterate it. Thus, as Christianity had triumphed over the ideals of ancient warriors, the Reformation had triumphed over the Renaissance, and liberalism and socialism over feudal aristocracy. The Genealogy of Morals (1887), from which the following selection is taken, is Nietzsche's elaboration of these ideas.

Given the horrible uses made of his treatise by others, it is important to realize that, although he blamed the invention of slave morality on the ancient Jews, Nietzsche was never a religious persecutor. Nor did his heroes, among them the Renaissance soldier Cesare Borgia (1476–1507) and the French emperor Napoleon I (1769–1821), persecute or eliminate the weak and powerless. Those twentieth-century leaders who have dealt monstrously with Jews and other national minorities would have been abhorrent to Nietzsche.

• • •

By now the reader will have got some notion how readily the priestly system of valuations can branch off from the aristocratic and develop into its opposite. An occasion for such a division is furnished whenever

THE GENEALOGY OF MORALS   From *The Birth of Tragedy and the Genealogy of Morals* by Friedrich Nietzsche, trans. Francis Golffing. Copyright © 1956 by Doubleday & Company, Inc., 166–82, 185–87. Reprinted by permission of Doubleday & Company, Inc.

the priest caste and the warrior caste jealously clash with one another and find themselves unable to come to terms. The chivalrous and aristocratic valuations presuppose a strong physique, blooming, even exuberant health, together with all the conditions that guarantee its preservation: combat, adventure, the chase, the dance, war games, etc. The value system of the priestly aristocracy is founded on different presuppositions. So much the worse for them when it becomes a question of war! As we all know, priests are the most evil enemies to have—why should this be so? Because they are the most impotent. It is their impotence which makes their hate so violent and sinister, so cerebral and poisonous. The greatest haters in history—but also the most intelligent haters—have been priests. Beside the brilliance of priestly vengeance all other brilliance fades. Human history would be a dull and stupid thing without the intelligence furnished by its impotents. Let us begin with the most striking example. Whatever else has been done to damage the powerful and great of this earth seems trivial compared with what the Jews have done, that priestly people who succeeded in avenging themselves on their enemies and oppressors by radically inverting all their values, that is, by an act of the most spiritual vengeance.[1] This was a strategy entirely appropriate to a priestly people in whom vindictiveness had gone most deeply underground. It was the Jew who, with frightening consistency, dared to invert the aristocratic value equations good/noble/powerful/beautiful/happy/favored-of-the-gods and maintain, with the furious hatred of the underprivileged and impotent, that "only the poor, the powerless, are good; only the suffering, sick, and ugly, truly blessed. But you noble and mighty ones of the earth will be, to all eternity, the evil, the cruel, the avaricious, the godless, and thus the cursed and damned!" . . . We know who has fallen heir to this Jewish inversion of values. . . . In reference to the grand and unspeakably disastrous initiative which the Jews have launched by this most radical of all declarations of war, I wish to repeat a statement I made in a different context (*Beyond Good and Evil*),[2] to wit, that it was the Jews who started the slave revolt in morals; a revolt with two

---

[1]Nietzsche accused the ancient Jews of having undertaken a transformation of values while in Babylonian Captivity. (On three occasions, beginning with the year 597 B.C., the Babylonian King Nebuchadrezzar II [reigned 605–562 B.C.], having conquered Jerusalem, had its leading Jews deported to Babylon. This enforced stay of some fifty to seventy years is known as the Babylonian Captivity of the Jews. After conquering Babylon in 539 B.C., the Persian King Cyrus the Great [600–529 B.C.] permitted the Jews to return to their homeland.)

[2]One of Nietzsche's books, published in the preceding year, 1886.

millennia of history behind it, which we have lost sight of today simply because it has triumphed so completely.

• • •

You find that difficult to understand? You have no eyes for something that took two millennia to prevail? . . . There is nothing strange about this: all long developments are difficult to see in the round. From the tree trunk of Jewish vengeance and hatred—the deepest and sublimest hatred in human history, since it gave birth to ideals and a new set of values—grew a branch that was equally unique: a new love, the deepest and sublimest of loves. From what other trunk could this branch have sprung? But let no one surmise that this love represented a denial of the thirst for vengeance, that it contravened the Jewish hatred. Exactly the opposite is true. Love grew out of hatred as the tree's crown, spreading triumphantly in the purest sunlight, yet having, in its high and sunny realm, the same aims—victory, aggrandizement, temptation—which hatred pursued by digging its roots ever deeper into all that was profound and evil. Jesus of Nazareth, the gospel of love made flesh, the "redeemer," who brought blessing and victory to the poor, the sick, the sinners—what was he but temptation in its most sinister and irresistible form, bringing men by a roundabout way to precisely those Jewish values and renovations of the ideal? Has not Israel, precisely by the detour of this "redeemer," this seeming antagonist and destroyer of Israel, reached the final goal of its sublime vindictiveness? Was it not a necessary feature of a truly brilliant politics of vengeance, a farsighted, subterranean, slowly and carefully planned vengeance, that Israel had to deny its true instrument publicly and nail him to the cross like a mortal enemy, so that "the whole world" (meaning all the enemies of Israel) might naïvely swallow the bait? And could one, by straining every resource, hit upon a bait more dangerous than this? What could equal in debilitating narcotic power the symbol of the "holy cross," the ghastly paradox of a crucified god, the unspeakably cruel mystery of God's self-crucifixion for the benefit of mankind? One thing is certain, that in this sign Israel has by now triumphed over all other, nobler values.

• • •

—"But what is all this talk about nobler values? Let us face facts: the people have triumphed—or the slaves, the mob, the herd, whatever you wish to call them—and if the Jews brought it about, then no nation ever had a more universal mission on this earth. The lords are a thing of the past, and the ethics of the common man is completely triumphant. I don't deny that this triumph might be looked upon as a kind of blood poisoning, since it has resulted in a mingling of the races, but there can be no doubt that the intoxication has succeeded. The 'redemption' of the human race (from the lords, that is) is well under way; everything is rapidly becoming Judaized, or Christianized, or mob-ized—the word makes no difference. The progress of this poison throughout the body of mankind cannot be stayed; as for its tempo, it can now afford to slow down, become finer, barely audible—there's all the time in the world. . . . Does the Church any longer have a necessary mission or even a *raison d'être*?[3] Or could it be done without? *Quaeritur*.[4] It would almost seem that it retards rather than accelerates that progress. In which case we might consider it useful. But one thing is certain, it has gradually become something crude and lumpish, repugnant to a sensitive intelligence, a truly modern taste. Should it not, at least, be asked to refine itself a bit? . . . It alienates more people today than it seduces. . . . Who among us would be a freethinker, were it not for the Church? It is the Church which offends us, not its poison. . . . Apart from the Church we, too, like the poison. . . ." This was a "freethinker's" reaction to my argument—an honest fellow, as he has abundantly proved, and a democrat to boot. He had been listening to me until that moment, and could not stand to hear my silence. For I have a great deal to be silent about in this matter.

· · ·

The slave revolt in morals begins by rancor turning creative and giving birth to values—the rancor of beings who, deprived of the direct outlet of action, compensate by an imaginary vengeance. All truly noble morality grows out of triumphant self-affirmation. Slave ethics, on the other hand, begins by saying *no* to an "outside," an "other," a non-self, and that *no* is its creative act. This reversal of direction of the evaluating look, this invariable looking outward instead of inward, is a fundamental feature of rancor. Slave ethics requires for its inception a sphere different from and hostile to its own. Physiologically speaking, it requires an outside stimulus in order to act at all; all its action is reaction. The opposite is true of aristocratic valuations: such values grow and act spontaneously, seeking out their contraries only in order

[3]French: Reason (or justification) for being.
[4]Latin: The question arises.

to affirm themselves even more gratefully and delightedly. Here the negative concepts, *humble, base, bad*, are late, pallid counterparts of the positive, intense and passionate credo,[5] "We noble, good, beautiful, happy ones." Aristocratic valuations may go amiss and do violence to reality, but this happens only with regard to spheres which they do not know well, or from the knowledge of which they austerely guard themselves: the aristocrat will, on occasion, misjudge a sphere which he holds in contempt, the sphere of the common man, the people. On the other hand we should remember that the emotion of contempt, of looking down, provided that it falsifies at all, is as nothing compared with the falsification which suppressed hatred, impotent vindictiveness, effects upon its opponent, though only in effigy. There is in all contempt too much casualness and nonchalance, too much blinking of facts and impatience, and too much inborn gaiety for it ever to make of its object a downright caricature and monster. Hear the almost benevolent nuances the Greek aristocracy, for example, puts into all its terms for the commoner; how emotions of compassion, consideration, indulgence, sugar-coat these words until, in the end, almost all terms referring to the common man survive as expressions for "unhappy," "pitiable" (compare *deilos, deilaios, poneros, mochtheros*,[6] the last two of which properly characterize the common man as a drudge and beast of burden); how, on the other hand, the words *bad, base, unhappy* have continued to strike a similar note for the Greek ear, with the timbre "unhappy" preponderating. The "well-born" really felt that they were also the "happy." They did not have to construct their happiness factitiously by looking at their enemies, as all rancorous men are wont to do, and being fully active, energetic people they were incapable of divorcing happiness from action. They accounted activity a necessary part of happiness (which explains the origin of the phrase *eu prattein*).[7]

All this stands in utter contrast to what is called happiness among the impotent and oppressed, who are full of bottled-up aggressions. Their happiness is purely passive and takes the form of drugged tranquillity, stretching and yawning, peace, "sabbath," emotional slackness. Whereas the noble lives before his own conscience with confidence and frankness (*gennaîos* "nobly bred" emphasizes the nuance "truthful" and

[5]Creed (statement of beliefs).

[6]In sore distress, in sorry plight, wretched, villainous, rascally. This and the preceding descriptive Greek words have fine shades of meaning, extending from miserable to cowardly to villainous.

[7]Greek: To deal well, to do well.

perhaps also "ingenuous"), the rancorous person is neither truthful nor ingenuous nor honest and forthright with himself. His soul squints; his mind loves hide-outs, secret paths, and back doors; everything that is hidden seems to him his own world, his security, his comfort; he is expert in silence, in long memory, in waiting, in provisional self-depreciation, and in self-humiliation. A race of such men will, in the end, inevitably be cleverer than a race of aristocrats, and it will honor sharp-wittedness to a much greater degree, i.e., as an absolutely vital condition for its existence. Among the noble, mental acuteness always tends slightly to suggest luxury and overrefinement. The fact is that with them it is much less important than is the perfect functioning of the ruling, unconscious instincts or even a certain temerity to follow sudden impulses, court danger, or indulge spurts of violent rage, love, worship, gratitude, or vengeance. When a noble man feels resentment, it is absorbed in his instantaneous reaction and therefore does not poison him. Moreover, in countless cases where we might expect it, it never arises, while with weak and impotent people it occurs without fail. It is a sign of strong, rich temperaments that they cannot for long take seriously their enemies, their misfortunes, their *misdeeds*; for such characters have in them an excess of plastic curative power, and also a power of oblivion. (A good modern example of the latter is Mirabeau,[8] who lacked all memory for insults and meannesses done him, and who was unable to forgive because he had forgotten). Such a man simply shakes off vermin which would get beneath another's skin—and only here, if anywhere on earth, is it possible to speak of "loving one's enemy." The noble person will respect his enemy, and respect is already a bridge to love. . . . Indeed he requires his enemy for himself, as his mark of distinction, nor could he tolerate any other enemy than one in whom he finds nothing to despise and much to esteem. Imagine, on the other hand, the "enemy" as conceived by the rancorous man! For this is his true creative achievement: he has conceived the "evil enemy," the Evil One, as a fundamental idea, and then as a pendant he has conceived a Good One—himself.

• • •

The exact opposite is true of the noble-minded, who spontaneously creates the notion *good*, and later derives from it the conception of the

[8]Comte de Mirabeau (1749–91), an aristocratic French orator who was a leader in the French Revolution.

bad. How ill-matched these two concepts look, placed side by side: the bad of noble origin, and the *evil* that has risen out of the cauldron[9] of unquenched hatred! The first is a by-product, a complementary color, almost an afterthought; the second is the beginning, the original creative act of slave ethics. But neither is the conception of good the same in both cases, as we soon find out when we ask ourselves who it is that is really evil according to the code of rancor. The answer is: precisely the good one of the opposite code, that is the noble, the powerful—only colored, reinterpreted, reenvisaged by the poisonous eye of resentment. And we are the first to admit that anyone who knew these "good" ones only as enemies would find them evil enemies indeed. For these same men who, amongst themselves, are so strictly constrained by custom, worship, ritual, gratitude, and by mutual surveillance and jealousy, who are so resourceful in consideration, tenderness, loyalty, pride and friendship, when once they step outside their circle become little better than uncaged beasts of prey. Once abroad in the wilderness, they revel in the freedom from social constraint and compensate for their long confinement in the quietude of their own community. They revert to the innocence of wild animals: we can imagine them returning from an orgy of murder, arson, rape, and torture, jubilant and at peace with themselves as though they had committed a fraternity prank—convinced, moreover, that the poets for a long time to come will have something to sing about and to praise. Deep within all these noble races there lurks the beast of prey, bent on spoil and conquest. This hidden urge has to be satisfied from time to time, the beast let loose in the wilderness. This goes as well for the Roman, Arabian, German, Japanese nobility as for the Homeric heroes[10] and the Scandinavian vikings. The noble races have everywhere left in their wake the catchword "barbarian." And even their highest culture shows an awareness of this trait and a certain pride in it (as we see, for example, in Pericles'[11] famous funeral oration, when he tells the Athenians: "Our boldness has gained us access to every land and sea, and erected monuments to itself *for both good and evil*"). This "boldness" of noble races, so headstrong, absurd, incalculable, sudden, improbable (Pericles commends the Athenians especially for their *rathumia*),[12] their utter indifference to

[9]Boiling pot.

[10]The ancient heroes of Greek legend described by the poet Homer (*ca.* 800 B.C.) in his *Iliad* and *Odyssey*.

[11]Pericles was an Athenian general and statesman (died 429 B.C.).

[12]Greek: Relaxed temperament, nonchalance.

safety and comfort, their terrible pleasure in destruction, their taste for cruelty—all these traits are embodied by their victims in the image of the "barbarian," the "evil enemy," the Goth or the Vandal.[13] The profound and icy suspicion which the German arouses as soon as he assumes power (we see it happening again today) harks back to the persistent horror with which Europe for many centuries witnessed the raging of the blond Teutonic[14] beast (although all racial connection between the old Teutonic tribes and ourselves has been lost). I once drew attention to the embarrassment Hesiod[15] must have felt when he tried to embody the cultural epochs of mankind in the gold, silver, and iron ages. He could cope with the contradictions inherent in Homer's world, so marvelous on the one hand, so ghastly and brutal on the other, only by making two ages out of one and presenting them in temporal sequence; first, the age of the heroes and demigods of Troy[16] and Thebes,[17] as that world was still remembered by the noble tribes who traced their ancestry to it; and second, the iron age, which presented the same world as seen by the descendants of those who had been crushed, despoiled, brutalized, sold into slavery. If it were true, as passes current nowadays, that the real meaning of culture resides in its power to domesticate man's savage instincts, then we might be justified in viewing all those rancorous machinations by which the noble tribes, and their ideals, have been laid low as the true instruments of culture. But this would still not amount to saying that the *organizers* themselves represent culture. Rather, the exact opposite would be true, as is vividly shown by the current state of affairs. These carriers of the leveling and retributive instincts, these descendants of every European and extra-European slavedom, and especially of the pre-Aryan populations,[18] represent human retrogression most flagrantly. Such "instruments of culture" are a disgrace to man and might make one suspicious of culture altogether. One might be justified in fearing the wild beast lurking

[13]The Goths and the Vandals were barbarian Germanic tribes that ravaged the Roman Empire during the fourth and fifth centuries.

[14]Germanic.

[15]A Greek poet of the eighth century B.C..

[16]A famous ancient city located on the strait called Dardanelles, separating Europe from Asia Minor (near Istanbul); scene of the epic war between the Greeks and Trojans (*ca.* 1200 B.C.).

[17]An ancient city in Greece, some forty miles north of Athens; home of the ill-fated royal house of Laius and Oedipus.

[18]Those that lived in Europe before (about) 3000 B.C.

within all noble races and in being on one's guard against it, but who would not a thousand times prefer fear when it is accompanied with admiration to security accompanied by the loathsome sight of perversion, dwarfishness, degeneracy? And is not the latter our predicament today? What accounts for our repugnance to man—for there is no question that he makes us suffer? Certainly not our fear of him, rather the fact that there is no longer anything to be feared from him; that the vermin "man" occupies the entire stage; that, tame, hopelessly mediocre, and savorless, he considers himself the apex of historical evolution; and not entirely without justice, since he is still somewhat removed from the mass of sickly and effete creatures whom Europe is beginning to stink of today.

• • •

Here I want to give vent to a sigh and a last hope. Exactly what is it that I, especially, find intolerable; that I am unable to cope with; that asphyxiates me? A bad smell. The smell of failure, of a soul that has gone stale. God knows it is possible to endure all kinds of misery—vile weather, sickness, trouble, isolation. All this can be coped with, if one is born to a life of anonymity and battle. There will always be moments of re-emergence into the light, when one tastes the golden hour of victory and once again stands foursquare, unshakable, ready to face even harder things, like a bowstring drawn taut against new perils. But, you divine patronesses—if there are any such in the realm beyond good and evil—grant me now and again the sight of something perfect, wholly achieved, happy, magnificently triumphant, something still capable of inspiring fear! Of a man who will justify the existence of mankind, for whose sake one may continue to believe in mankind! . . . The leveling and diminution of European man is our greatest danger; because the sight of him makes us despond. . . . We no longer see anything these days that aspires to grow greater; instead, we have a suspicion that things will continue to go downhill, becoming ever thinner, more placid, smarter, cosier, more ordinary, more indifferent, more Chinese, more Christian—without doubt man is getting "better" all the time. . . . This is Europe's true predicament: together with the fear of man we have also lost the love of man, reverence for man, confidence in man, indeed the *will to man*. Now the sight of man makes us despond. What is nihilism[19] today if not that?

---

[19]The rejection of the certainties offered by religion and morality; in politics, the desire to overturn institutions and reduce them to nothing (Latin, *nihil*).

13

But to return to business: our inquiry into the origins of that other notion of goodness, as conceived by the resentful, demands to be completed. There is nothing very odd about lambs disliking birds of prey, but this is no reason for holding it against large birds of prey that they carry off lambs. And when the lambs whisper among themselves, "These birds of prey are evil, and does not this give us a right to say that whatever is the opposite of a bird of prey must be good?" there is nothing intrinsically wrong with such an argument—though the birds of prey will look somewhat quizzically and say, "*We* have nothing against these good lambs; in fact, we love them; nothing tastes better than a tender lamb."—To expect that strength will not manifest itself as strength, as the desire to overcome, to appropriate, to have enemies, obstacles, and triumphs, is every bit as absurd as to expect that weakness will manifest itself as strength. A quantum of strength is equivalent to a quantum of urge, will, activity, and it is only the snare of language (of the arch-fallacies of reason petrified in language), presenting all activity as conditioned by an agent—the "subject"—that blinds us to this fact. For, just as popular superstition divorces the lightning from its brilliance, viewing the latter as an activity whose subject is the lightning, so does popular morality divorce strength from its manifestations, as though there were behind the strong a neutral agent, free to manifest its strength or contain it. But no such agent exists; there is no "being" behind the doing, acting, becoming; the "doer" has simply been added to the deed by the imagination—the doing is everything. The common man actually doubles the doing by making the lightning flash; he states the same event once as cause and then again as effect. The natural scientists are no better when they say that "energy *moves*," "energy *causes*." For all its detachment and freedom from emotion, our science is still the dupe of linguistic habits; it has never yet got rid of those changelings called "subjects." The atom is one such changeling, another is the Kantian "thing-in-itself."[20] Small wonder, then, that the repressed and smoldering emotions of vengeance and hatred have taken advantage of this superstition and in fact espouse no belief more ardently than that it is within the discretion of the strong to be weak, of the bird of prey to be a lamb. Thus they assume the right of calling the bird of prey to account for being a bird of prey. We can hear the

---

[20]Immanuel Kant (1724–1804) was a German philosopher who desired to know what an object really *is* ("thing-in-itself"), rather than what human perception declares it to be.

oppressed, downtrodden, violated whispering among themselves with the wily vengefulness of the impotent, "Let us be unlike those evil ones. Let us be good. And the good shall be he who does not do violence, does not attack or retaliate, who leaves vengeance to God, who, like us, lives hidden, who shuns all that is evil, and altogether asks very little of life—like us, the patient, the humble, the just ones." Read in cold blood, this means nothing more than "We weak ones are, in fact, weak. It is a good thing that we do nothing for which we are not strong enough." But this plain fact, this basic prudence, which even the insects have (who, in circumstances of great danger, sham death in order not to have to "do" too much) has tricked itself out in the garb of quiet, virtuous resignation, thanks to the duplicity of impotence—as though the weakness of the weak, which is after all his essence, his natural way of being, his sole and inevitable reality, were a spontaneous act, a meritorious deed. This sort of person requires the belief in a "free subject" able to choose indifferently, out of that instinct of self-preservation which notoriously justifies every kind of lie. It may well be that to this day the subject, or in popular language the soul, has been the most viable of all articles of faith simply because it makes it possible for the majority of mankind—i.e., the weak and oppressed of every sort—to practice the sublime sleight of hand which gives weakness the appearance of free choice and one's natural disposition the distinction of merit.

．　．　．

Would anyone care to learn something about the way in which ideals are manufactured? Does anyone have the nerve? . . . Well then, go ahead! There's a chink through which you can peek into this murkey shop. But wait just a moment, Mr. Foolhardy; your eyes must grow accustomed to the fickle light. . . . All right, tell me what's going on in there, audacious fellow; now I am the one who is listening.

"I can't see a thing, but I hear all the more. There's a low, cautious whispering in every nook and corner. I have a notion these people are lying. All the sounds are sugary and soft. No doubt you were right; they are transmuting weakness into merit."

"Go on."

"Impotence, which cannot retaliate, into kindness; pusillanimity into humility; submission before those one hates into obedience to One of whom they say that he has commanded this submission—they call

him God. The inoffensiveness of the weak, his cowardice, his ineluct-
able standing and waiting at doors, are being given honorific titles such
as patience; to be *unable* to avenge oneself is called to be *unwilling* to
avenge oneself—even forgiveness ('for they know not what *they* do—
we alone know what *they* do'). Also there's some talk of loving one's
enemy—accompanied by much sweat."

"Go on."

"I'm sure they are quite miserable, all these whisperers and small-
time counterfeiters, even though they huddle close together for
warmth. But they tell me that this very misery is the sign of their
election by God, that one beats the dogs one loves best, that this misery
is perhaps also a preparation, a test, a kind of training, perhaps even
more than that: something for which eventually they will be compensated with tremendous interest—in gold? No, in happiness. They call
this *bliss*."

"Go on."

"Now they tell me that not only are they better than the mighty of
this earth, whose spittle they must lick (not from fear—by no means—
but because God commands us to honor our superiors), but they are
even better off, or at least they will be better off someday. But I've had
all I can stand. The smell is too much for me. This shop where they
manufacture ideals seem to me to stink of lies."

"But just a moment. You haven't told me anything about the
greatest feat of these black magicians, who precipitate the white milk of
loving-kindness out of every kind of blackness. Haven't you noticed
their most consummate sleight of hand, their boldest, finest, most
brilliant trick? Just watch! These vermin, full of vindictive hatred, what
are they brewing out of their own poisons? Have you ever heard
vengeance and hatred mentioned? Would you ever guess, if you only
listened to their words, that these are men bursting with hatred?"

"I see what you mean. I'll open my ears again—and stop my nose.
Now I can make out what they seem to have been saying all along: 'We,
the good ones, are also the just ones.' They call the thing they seek not
retribution but the triumph of justice; the thing they hate is not their
enemy, by no means—they hate injustice, ungodliness; the thing they
hope for and believe in is not vengeance, the sweet exultation of
vengeance ('sweeter than honey' as Homer said) but 'the triumph of
God, who is just, over the godless'; what remains to them to love on
this earth is not their brothers in hatred, but what they call their
'brothers in love'—all who are good and just."

"And what do they call that which comforts them in all their sufferings—their phantasmagoria[21] of future bliss?"

"Do I hear correctly? They call it Judgment Day, the coming of *their* kingdom, the 'Kingdom of God.' Meanwhile they live in 'faith,' in 'love,' in 'hope.'"

"Stop! I've heard enough."

• • •

Let us conclude. The two sets of valuations, good/bad and good/evil, have waged a terrible battle on this earth, lasting many millennia; and just as surely as the second set has for a long time now been in the ascendant, so surely are there still places where the battle goes on and the issue remains in suspension. It might even be claimed that by being raised to a higher plane the battle has become much more profound. Perhaps there is today not a single intellectual worth his salt who is not divided on that issue, a battleground for those opposites. The watchwords of the battle, written in characters which have remained legible throughout human history, read: "Rome vs. Israel, Israel vs. Rome." No battle has ever been more momentous than this one. Rome viewed Israel as a monstrosity; the Romans regarded the Jews as *convicted* of hatred against the whole of mankind—and rightly so if one is justified in associating the welfare of the human species with absolute supremacy of aristocratic values. But how did the Jews, on their part, feel about Rome? A thousand indications point to the answer. It is enough to read once more the Revelations of St. John,[22] the most rabid outburst of vindictiveness in all recorded history. (We ought to acknowledge the profound consistency of the Christian instinct in assigning this book of hatred and the most extravagantly doting of the Gospels to the same disciple. There is a piece of truth hidden here, no matter how much literary skulduggery may have gone on.) The Romans were the strongest and most noble people who ever lived. Every vestige of them, every least inscription, is a sheer delight, provided we are able to read the spirit behind the writing. The Jews, on the contrary, were the priestly, rancorous nation *par excellence*, though possessed of an une-

---

[21]Fantastic and idle dreams.

[22]The last book of the New Testament, supposedly written by St. John the Evangelist, who traditionally is also credited with writing the Gospel according to John.

qualed ethical genius; we need only compare with them nations of comparable endowments, such as the Chinese or the Germans, to sense which occupies the first rank. Has the victory so far been gained by the Romans or by the Jews? But this is really an idle question. Remember who it is before whom one bows down, in Rome itself, as before the essence of all supreme values—and not only in Rome but over half the globe, wherever man has grown tame or desires to grow tame: before three Jews and one Jewess (Jesus of Nazareth, the fisherman Peter, the rug weaver Paul, and Maria, the mother of that Jesus). This is very curious: Rome, without a doubt, has capitulated. It is true that during the Renaissance men witnessed a strange and splendid awakening of the classical ideal; like one buried alive, Rome stirred under the weight of a new Judaic Rome that looked like an ecumenical synagogue and was called the Church. But presently Israel triumphed once again, thanks to the plebeian rancor of the German and English Reformation, together with its natural corollary, the restoration of the Church—which also meant the restoration of ancient Rome to the quiet of the tomb. In an even more decisive sense did Israel triumph over the classical ideal through the French Revolution. For then the last political nobleness Europe had known, that of seventeenth- and eighteenth-century France, collapsed under the weight of vindictive popular instincts. A wilder enthusiasm was never seen. And yet, in the midst of it all, something tremendous, something wholly unexpected happened: the ancient classical ideal appeared incarnate and in unprecedented splendor before the eyes and conscience of mankind. Once again, stronger, simpler, more insistent than ever, over against the lying shibboleth[23] of the rights of the majority, against the furious tendency toward leveling out and debasement, sounded the terrible yet exhilarating shibboleth of the "prerogative of the few." Like a last signpost to an *alternative* route Napoleon[24] appeared, most isolated and anachronistic of men, the embodiment of the noble ideal. It might be well to ponder what exactly Napoleon, that synthesis of the brutish with the more than human, did represent. . . .

• • •

[23]A slogan or phrase associated with a particular group.

[24]Napoleon I (1769–1821), French emperor.

28

Henrik Ibsen

Hedda Gabler

*H*ENRIK *Ibsen (1828–1906), the distinguished Norwegian author, was a leading force in the shaping of modern Western drama. He was born in a small town southeast of Oslo, the capital of Norway. At the time of his birth, Ibsen's father was a prosperous merchant, but his business soon after declined and he was forced into bankruptcy. The failure of the business meant that Henrik would have little opportunity to receive the superior education required for one of the higher professions. Determined to succeed, nevertheless, he left the family home at age sixteen to work as a druggist's apprentice—while planning to study in his spare time for the university entrance examinations. In 1850 Henrik moved to Oslo to take these exams, and although he did not pass all of them successfully, he was permitted to enroll in medical courses at the University of Oslo. Ibsen, however, shortly abandoned the study of medicine, partly for financial reasons and partly because he found himself more attracted to courses in the liberal arts. Rather than pursuing his studies, he soon chose to work as a stage director, first in Oslo and then in other Scandinavian cities. As a director, he was able to learn about theater production from the ground up.*

While living in Oslo in the 1850s, Ibsen was drawn into two powerful social movements: nationalism and socialism. Both came to be important influences in his life and work. Norwegian nationalism reached a peak in the two decades following Ibsen's move to Oslo. Like developments elsewhere in Europe, this Norwegian awakening was rooted in a romanticized and idealized national past. Ibsen's dramas and poems written during that time reflect these sentiments, that is, the emotional experience of a people finding their identity in the events and monuments of a respected history.

While in his thirties, however, Ibsen became disenchanted with national and social developments in his own country. He left Norway in 1864 and thereafter spent most of his years in Germany, Italy, and Austria. (He did not return permanently to Oslo until 1891—at age sixty-three.) While residing in Germany, he noted to a greater degree than he had in Norway the distressing by-products of the Industrial Revolution—such as crushing poverty, misery, and despair. These conditions produced in him a deep compassion for the suffering class of laborers—reminding him, no doubt, of the deprived circumstances of his childhood.

In response, Ibsen was drawn to the political left, that is, to the cause of socialism. Certainly, Ibsen should not be viewed as an aggressive or doctrinaire fighter for any political party. Yet, throughout his life his commitment remained strong to those who had been squeezed to the fringes of existence by the workings of nineteenth-century industrialization. It is not surprising, then, that some of his plays reflect his wishes for a better and more just society, while at the same time painting bourgeois society as hypocritical, deceitful, and corrupt. He hoped that his plays would make some small contribution toward a better and more humane society. But Ibsen was also a realist; he was certain that no utopia would ever arrive.

The play Hedda Gabler, completed in 1890 and one of his last works, does not belong to Ibsen's group of social dramas. It is, rather, a psychological play. Because of the extreme individualism shown by the principal characters, it does not even seem to fit into the nineteenth century, but appears instead to belong to the second half of the twentieth century. Each personality, with perhaps the exception of Lovborg, has been molded by family upbringing or by the standards of the class into which each was born. They pursue their own selfish interests, using others for their purposes. Hedda is, of course, the central figure of the play—cold and ambitious—seeking power over other people's lives, even their destruction. Nevertheless, she continues over the years to fascinate readers and audiences with her striking qualities of determination, seductiveness, meanness, and proud defiance.

———————

Cast

GEORGE TESMAN
HEDDA TESMAN, *his wife*
MISS JULIA TESMAN, *his aunt*
MRS. THEA ELVSTED

JUDGE BRACK
EILERT LOVBORG
BERTA, *maid at the Tesmans'*

SCENE: *The action is Tesman's villa, in the west end of Oslo, Norway*

ACT I

SCENE: *A spacious, attractive, and tastefully furnished living room, decorated in dark colors. In the back, a wide doorway with curtains pulled back, leading into a smaller room decorated in the same style as the living room. In the right-hand wall of the front room, a folding door leading out to the hall. In the opposite wall, on the left, a glass door, also with curtains pulled back. Through the glass can be seen part of a veranda outside, and trees covered with autumn foliage. An oval table, with a cover on it, and surrounded by chairs, stands prominently forward. In front, by the wall on the right, a wide stove of dark procelain, a high-backed armchair, a cushioned footrest, and two footstools. A sofa with a small round table in front of it, fills the upper right-hand corner. In front, on the left, a little way from the wall, a sofa. Farther back than the glass door, a piano. On either side of the doorway at the back a set of small shelves with Italian pottery ornaments. Against the back wall of the inner room a sofa, with a table, and one or two chairs. Over the sofa hangs the portrait of a handsome elderly man in a General's uniform. Over the table a hanging lamp, with an opal glass shade. A number of bouquets are arranged about the living room, in vases and glasses. Others lie upon the tables. The floors in both rooms are covered with thick carpets. Morning light. The sun shines in through the glass door.*

[MISS JULIA TESMAN, *with her hat on and carrying a parasol, comes in from the hall, followed by* BERTA, *who carries a bouquet wrapped in paper.* MISS TESMAN *is an attractive and pleasant-looking lady of about sixty-five. She is nicely but simply dressed in a gray suit.* BERTA *is a middle-aged woman of plain and rather countrified appearance.*]

HEDDA GABLER   Adapted by editor from *Hedda Gabler* by Henrik Ibsen (trans. Edmund Gosse and William Archer), *Four Modern Plays* (New York: Rinehart & Co., Inc., 1957) 2–90.

MISS TESMAN [*Stops close to the door, listens, and says softly.*]   I do believe, they're not stirring yet!

BERTA [*Also softly.*]   I told you so, Miss. Remember how late the steamboat got in last night. And then, when they got home!—good Lord, what a lot the young mistress had to unpack before she could get to bed.

MISS TESMAN   Well, well—let them have their rest. But let us see that they get a good breath of the fresh morning air when they do appear. [*She goes to the glass door and throws it open.*]

BERTA [*Beside the table, at a loss what to do with the bouquet in her hand.*] My goodness, there isn't a bit of room left. I think I'll put it down here, Miss. [*She places it on the piano.*]

MISS TESMAN   So you've got a new mistress now, my dear Berta. Heaven knows it was hard for me to part with you.

BERTA [*On the point of weeping.*]   And do you think it wasn't hard for me, too, Miss? After all the happy years I've been with you and Miss Rina.

MISS TESMAN   We must make the best of it, Berta. There was nothing else to be done. George can't do without you, you see—he absolutely can't. He has had you to look after him ever since he was a little boy.

BERTA   Ah, but, Miss Julia, I can't help thinking of Miss Rina lying helpless at home there, poor thing. And with only that new girl, too! She'll never learn to take proper care of an invalid.

MISS TESMAN   Oh, I shall manage to train her. And, of course, you know I shall take most of it upon myself. You needn't be uneasy about my poor sister, my dear Berta.

BERTA   Well, but there's another thing, Miss. I'm so terribly afraid I won't be able to please the young mistress.

MISS TESMAN   Oh, well—just at first there may be one or two things . . .

BERTA   Most likely she'll be very particular in her ways.

MISS TESMAN   Well, you can't be surprised at that—General Gabler's daughter! Think of the sort of life she was accustomed to in her father's time. Don't you remember how we used to see her riding down the road along with the General? In that long black riding dress—and with feathers in her hat?

BERTA   Yes, indeed—I remember well enough!—But, good Lord, I should never have dreamed in those days that she and Mr. George would make a match of it.

MISS TESMAN   Nor I. But by the way, Berta—while I think of it: in the future you mustn't say Mr. George. You must say Dr. Tesman.

BERTA   Yes, the young mistress spoke of that, too—last night—the moment they set foot in the house. Is it true then, Miss?

MISS TESMAN   Yes, indeed it is. Just think, Berta—some foreign university has made him a doctor—while he has been abroad, you understand. I hadn't heard a word about it, until he told me himself at the pier.

BERTA   Well, well, he's smart enough for anything, he is. But I didn't think he'd have gone in for doctoring people, too.

MISS TESMAN   No, no, he's not that sort of doctor. [*Nods significantly.*] But let me tell you, we may have to call him something still grander before long.

BERTA   You don't say so! What can that be, Miss?

MISS TESMAN [*Smiling.*]   H'm—wouldn't you like to know! [*With emotion.*] Ah, dear, dear—if my poor brother could only look up from his grave now, and see what his little boy has grown into! [*Looks around.*] My goodness, Berta—why have you done this? Taken the covers off all the furniture?

BERTA   The mistress told me to. She can't stand covers on the chairs, she says.

MISS TESMAN   Are they going to make this their everyday living room then?

BERTA   Yes, that's what I understood—from the mistress. Mr. George—the doctor—he said nothing.

[GEORGE TESMAN *comes from the right into the inner room; humming to himself, and carrying an empty suitcase. He is a middle-sized,*
young-looking man of thirty-three, rather stout, with a round, open, cheerful face, fair hair and beard. He wears spectacles, and is somewhat carelessly dressed in comfortable indoor clothes.]

MISS TESMAN   Good morning, good morning, George.

TESMAN [*In the doorway between the rooms.*]   Aunt Julia! Dear Aunt Julia! [*Walks up to her and shakes hands warmly.*] Come all this way—so early!

MISS TESMAN   Why, of course I had to come and see how you were getting on.

TESMAN   In spite of your having had no good night's rest?

MISS TESMAN   Oh, that makes no difference to me.

TESMAN   Well, I suppose you got home all right from the pier?

MISS TESMAN   Yes, quite safely, thank goodness. Judge Brack was good enough to bring me right to my door.

TESMAN   We were so sorry we couldn't give you a seat in the carriage. But you saw what a pile of boxes Hedda had to bring with her.

MISS TESMAN   Yes, she certainly had plenty of boxes.

BERTA [*To* TESMAN.]   Shall I go in and see if there's anything I can do for the mistress?

TESMAN   No thank you, Berta—you needn't. She said she would ring if she wanted anything.

BERTA [*Walking toward the right.*]   Very well.

TESMAN   But look here—take this suitcase with you.

BERTA [*Taking it.*]   I'll put it in the attic.

[*She leaves by the hall door.*]

TESMAN   Imagine, Auntie—I had that suitcase packed full of copies of documents. You wouldn't believe how much I have picked up from all the archives I have been examining—curious old details that no one has had any idea of . . .

MISS TESMAN   Yes, you don't seem to have wasted your time on your wedding trip, George.

TESMAN   No, that I haven't. But do take off your hat, Auntie. Look here! Let me untie the strings.

MISS TESMAN [*While he does so.*]   Well, well—this is just as if you were still at home with us.

TESMAN [*With the hat in his hand, looks at it from all sides.*]   Why, what a gorgeous hat you've been investing in!

MISS TESMAN   I bought it because of Hedda.

TESMAN   Because of Hedda?

MISS TESMAN   Yes, so that Hedda needn't be ashamed of me if we happened to go out together.

TESMAN [*Patting her cheek.*]   You always think of everything, Aunt Julia. [*Puts the hat on a chair beside the table.*] And now, look here— suppose we sit comfortably on the sofa and have a little chat, till Hedda comes. [*They seat themselves. She places her parasol in the corner of the sofa.*]

MISS TESMAN [*Takes both his hands and looks at him.*]   What a delight it is to have you again, as large as life, before my very eyes, George! My George—my poor brother's own boy!

TESMAN   And it's a delight for me, too, to see you again, Aunt Julia! You, who have been father and mother to me.

MISS TESMAN   Oh yes, I know you will always keep a place in your heart for your old aunts.

TESMAN   And what about Aunt Rina? No improvement?

MISS TESMAN   Oh no—we can scarcely look for any improvement in her case, poor thing. There she lies, helpless, as she has lain for all these years. But heaven grant I may not lose her for awhile. For if I did, I don't know what I would do with my life, George—especially now that I haven't you to look after any more.

TESMAN [*Patting her back.*]   There, there, there . . . !

MISS TESMAN [*Suddenly changing her tone.*]   And to think that here you are a married man, George! And that you should be the one to carry off Hedda Gabler—the beautiful Hedda Gabler! Only think of it—she, who had so many admirers!

TESMAN [*Hums a little and smiles complacently.*]   Yes, I'm sure I have several good friends around town who would like to stand in my shoes.

MISS TESMAN   And then this fine long wedding trip you have had! More than five—nearly six months . . .

TESMAN   Well, for me it has been a sort of research trip as well. I have had to do so much digging among old records—and no end to reading either, Auntie.

MISS TESMAN   Oh yes, I suppose so. [*More confidentially, and lowering her voice a little.*] But listen now, George—have you nothing—nothing special to tell me?

TESMAN   As to our journey?

MISS TESMAN   Yes.

TESMAN   No, I don't know of anything except what I have told you in my letters. I had a doctor's degree conferred on me—but that I told you yesterday.

MISS TESMAN   Yes, yes, you did. But what I mean is—haven't you any—any—expectations . . . ?

TESMAN   Expectations?

MISS TESMAN   Why you know, George—I'm your old auntie!

TESMAN   Why, of course I have expectations.

MISS TESMAN   Ah!

TESMAN   I have every expectation of being a professor one of these days.

MISS TESMAN   Oh yes, a professor . . .

TESMAN   Indeed, I may say I am certain of it. But my dear Auntie—you know all about that already!

MISS TESMAN [*Laughing to herself.*]   Yes, of course I do. You are quite right there. [*Changing the subject.*] But we were talking about your journey. It must have cost a great deal of money, George?

TESMAN   Well, you see—my generous travel scholarship went a long way.

MISS TESMAN   But I can't understand how you made it go far enough for two.

TESMAN   No, that's not so easy to understand.

MISS TESMAN   And especially traveling with a lady—they tell me that makes it ever so much more expensive.

TESMAN   Yes, of course—it makes it a little more expensive. But Hedda had to have this trip, Auntie! She really had to. Nothing else would have done.

MISS TESMAN   No, no, I guess not. A wedding trip seems to be quite indispensable nowadays. But tell me now—have you gone thoroughly over the house yet?

TESMAN   Yes, you may be sure I have. I have been up ever since daylight.

MISS TESMAN   And what do you think of it all?

TESMAN   I'm delighted! Quite delighted! Only I can't think what we are to do with the two empty rooms between this inner room and Hedda's bedroom.

MISS TESMAN [*Laughing.*]   Oh my dear George, I'm sure you will find some use for them—in due time.

TESMAN   Why of course you are quite right, Aunt Julia! You mean as my library increases?

MISS TESMAN   Yes, quite so, my dear boy. It was your library I was thinking of.

TESMAN   I am specially pleased on Hedda's account. Many times, before we were engaged, she said that she would never care to live anywhere but in Secretary Falk's villa.[1]

MISS TESMAN   Yes, it was lucky that this very house should come on the market, just after you had left on your trip.

TESMAN   Yes, Aunt Julia, the luck was on our side, wasn't it?

MISS TESMAN   But the expense, my dear George! You will find it very expensive, all this.

TESMAN [*Looks at her, a little cast down.*]   Yes, I suppose I shall, Aunt!

MISS TESMAN   Oh, frightfully!

TESMAN   How much do you think? In round numbers?

MISS TESMAN   Oh, I can't even guess until all the bills are in.

TESMAN   Well, fortunately, Judge Brack has gotten the most favorable terms for me—so he said in a letter to Hedda.

---

[1] Falk was a Secretary in the national Cabinet.

MISS TESMAN   Yes, don't be uneasy, my dear boy. Besides, I have put up security for the furniture and all the carpets.

TESMAN   Security? You? My dear Aunt Julia—what sort of security could you give?

MISS TESMAN   I have taken out a mortgage on our annuity.

TESMAN [*Jumps up.*]   What! On your—and Aunt Rina's annuity!

MISS TESMAN   Yes, I knew of no other way, you see.

TESMAN [*Placing himself before her.*]   Have you lost your senses, Auntie! Your annuity—it's all that you and Aunt Rina have to live on.

MISS TESMAN   Well, well—don't get so excited about it. It's only a matter of form you know—Judge Brack assured me of that. It was he who was kind enough to arrange the whole affair for me. A mere matter of form, he said.

TESMAN   Yes, that may be all very well. But nevertheless . . .

MISS TESMAN   You will have your own salary to depend on now. And, good heavens, even if we did have to contribute a little . . . ! To assist a bit at the start . . . ! Why, it would be nothing but a pleasure to us.

TESMAN   Oh Auntie—will you never stop making sacrifices for me!

MISS TESMAN [*Rises and lays her hands on his shoulders.*]   Have I any other happiness in this world except to smooth your way for you, my dear boy? You, who have had neither father nor mother to depend on. And now we have reached the goal, George! Things have looked black enough for us, sometimes; but, thank heaven, now you have nothing to fear.

TESMAN   Yes, it is really marvelous how everything has turned out for the best.

MISS TESMAN   And the people who opposed you—who wanted to block your way—now you have them at your feet. They have fallen, George. Your most dangerous rival—his fall was the worst. And now he has to lie on the bed he has made for himself—poor misguided creature.

TESMAN   Have you heard anything of Eilert? Since I went away, I mean.

MISS TESMAN   Only that he is said to have published a new book.

TESMAN   What! Eilert Lovborg! Recently?

MISS TESMAN   Yes, so they say. Heaven knows whether it can be worth anything! Ah, when your new book appears—that will be another story, George! What is it to be about?

TESMAN   It will deal with the domestic industries of the Low Countries during the Middle Ages.

MISS TESMAN   Imagine—to be able to write on such a subject as that!

TESMAN   However, it may be some time before the book is ready. I have all these materials to arrange first, you see.

MISS TESMAN   Yes, collecting and arranging—no one can beat you at that. There you are my poor brother's own son.

TESMAN   I am looking forward eagerly to start working on it; especially now that I have my own delightful home to work in.

MISS TESMAN   And, most of all, now that you have won the wife of your heart, my dear George.

TESMAN [*Embracing her.*]   Oh yes, yes, Aunt Julia. Hedda—she is the best part of it all! [*Looks toward the doorway.*] I believe I hear her coming.

[*HEDDA enters from the left through the inner room. She is a woman of twenty-nine. Her face and figure show refinement and distinction. Her complexion is pale. Her steel-gray eyes express a cold, unruffled composure. Her hair is of an agreeable medium brown, but not particularly abundant. She is dressed in a tasteful, somewhat loose-fitting robe.*]

MISS TESMAN [*Going to meet* HEDDA.]   Good morning, my dear Hedda! Good morning, and a warm welcome!

HEDDA [*Holds out her hand.*]   Good morning, dear Miss Tesman! A visit so early? That is kind of you.

MISS TESMAN [*With some embarrassment.*]   Well—has the bride slept well in her new home?

HEDDA   Oh yes, thanks. Passably.

TESMAN [*Laughing.*]   Passably! Come, that's good, Hedda! You were sleeping like a log when I got up.

HEDDA   Fortunately. Of course one has always to accustom one's self to new surroundings, Miss Tesman—little by little. [*Looking toward the left.*] Oh—there the maid has gone and opened the veranda door, and let in a whole flood of sunshine.

MISS TESMAN [*Going toward the door.*]   Well, then we will close it.

HEDDA   No, no, not that! Tesman, please close the curtains. That will give a softer light.

TESMAN [*At the door.*]   All right—all right. There now, Hedda, now you have both shade and fresh air.

HEDDA   Yes, fresh air we certainly must have, with all these stacks of flowers . . . But—won't you sit down, Miss Tesman?

MISS TESMAN   No, thank you. Now that I have seen that everything is all right here—thank heaven!—I must be getting home again. My sister is lying waiting for me, poor thing.

TESMAN Give her my very best love, Auntie; and say I shall look in on her later in the day.

MISS TESMAN Yes, yes, I'll be sure to tell her. But by the way, George—[*feeling in her dress pocket*]—I had almost forgotten—I have something for you here.

TESMAN What is it, Auntie?

MISS TESMAN [*Produces a flat packet wrapped in newspaper and hands it to him.*] Look here, my dear boy.

TESMAN [*Opening the packet.*] Well, how about that? Have you really saved them for me, Aunt Julia! Hedda! Isn't this touching?

HEDDA [*Beside the small shelves on the right.*] Well, what is it?

TESMAN My old house shoes! My slippers.

HEDDA Really. I remember you often spoke of them while we were abroad.

TESMAN Yes, I missed them terribly. [*Walks to her.*] Now you shall see them, Hedda!

HEDDA [*Going toward the stove.*] Thanks, I really don't care about it.

TESMAN [*Following her.*] Just think—ill as she was, Aunt Rina embroidered these for me. Oh you can't know how many memories cling to them.

HEDDA [*At the table.*] Certainly not for me.

MISS TESMAN Of course not for Hedda, George.

TESMAN Well, but now that she belongs to the family, I thought . . .

HEDDA [*Interrupting.*] We shall never be able to manage with this maid, Tesman.

MISS TESMAN Not get on with Berta?

TESMAN Why, dear, what puts that in your head?

HEDDA [*Pointing.*] Look there! She has left her old hat lying about on a chair.

TESMAN [*Stunned, drops the slippers on the floor.*] Why, Hedda . . .

HEDDA Just think, if someone should come in and see it!

TESMAN But Hedda—that's Aunt Julia's hat.

HEDDA Is it!

MISS TESMAN [*Taking up the hat.*] Yes, indeed it's mine. And, what's more, it's not old, dear Hedda.

HEDDA I really did not look closely at it, Miss Tesman.

MISS TESMAN [*Trying on the hat.*] Let me tell you it's the first time I have worn it—the very first time.

TESMAN And a very nice hat it is too—quite beautiful!

MISS TESMAN Oh, it's no such great thing, George. [*Looks around her.*]

My parasol . . . ? Ah, here. [*Takes it.*] For this is mine too—
[*mutters*]—not Berta's.

TESMAN   A new hat and a new parasol! Just think, Hedda!

HEDDA   Very nice indeed.

TESMAN   Yes, isn't it? But Auntie, take a good look at Hedda before
you go! See how lovely she looks!

MISS TESMAN   Oh, my dear boy, there's nothing new in that. Hedda
was always lovely. [*She nods and goes toward the right.*]

TESMAN [*Following.*]   Yes, but have you noticed what splendid condition she is in? How she has filled out on the journey?

HEDDA [*Crossing the room.*]   Oh, do be quiet . . . !

MISS TESMAN [*Who has stopped and turned.*]   Filled out?

TESMAN   Of course you don't notice it so much now that she has that
robe on. But I, who can see . . .

HEDDA [*At the glass door, impatiently.*]   Oh, you can't see anything.

TESMAN   It must be the mountain air in the Tyrol . . .[2]

HEDDA [*Curtly, interrupting.*]   I am exactly as I was when I left.

TESMAN   So you insist; but I'm quite certain you are not. Don't you
agree with me, Auntie?

MISS TESMAN [*Who has been gazing at her with folded hands.*]   Hedda is
lovely—lovely—lovely. [*Walks to her, takes her head between both
hands, draws it downward, and kisses her hair.*] God bless and preserve
Hedda Tesman—for George's sake.

HEDDA [*Gently freeing herself.*]   Oh—! Let me go.

MISS TESMAN [*With quiet feeling.*]   I shall not let a day pass without
coming to see you.

TESMAN   No you won't, will you, Auntie?

MISS TESMAN   Good-bye—good-bye!

[*She leaves by the hall door.* TESMAN *accompanies her. The door remains
half open.* TESMAN *can be heard repeating his message to* AUNT RINA *and
his thanks for the slippers. In the meantime,* HEDDA *walks about the room,
raising her arms and clenching her hands as if in desperation. Then she flings
back the curtains from the glass door, and stands there looking out. Then*
TESMAN *returns and closes the door behind him.*]

TESMAN [*Picks up the slippers from the floor.*]   What are you looking at,
Hedda?

[2]The Tyrolean Mountains in Austria.

HEDDA [*Once more calm and in control of herself.*]   I am only looking at the leaves. They are so yellow—so withered.

TESMAN [*Wraps up the slippers and puts them on the table.*]   Well you see, we are well into September now.

HEDDA [*Again restless.*]   Yes, think of it! Already in—in September.

TESMAN   Don't you think Aunt Julia's behavior was strange, dear? Almost solemn? Can you imagine what was the matter with her?

HEDDA   I scarcely know her, you see. Isn't she often like that?

TESMAN   No, not as she was today.

HEDDA [*Leaving the glass door.*]   Do you think she was annoyed about the hat?

TESMAN   Oh, scarcely at all. Perhaps a little, just at the moment . . .

HEDDA   But what an idea, throwing her hat about in the living room! No one does that sort of thing.

TESMAN   Well you may be sure Aunt Julia won't do it again.

HEDDA   In any case, I shall manage to make my peace with her.

TESMAN   Yes, my dear, good Hedda, if you only would.

HEDDA   When you call on her this afternoon, you might invite her to spend the evening here.

TESMAN   Yes, I will. And there's one thing more you could do that would delight her.

HEDDA   What is it?

TESMAN   If you could only force yourself to be more friendly to her. For my sake, Hedda?

HEDDA   No, no, Tesman—you really mustn't ask that of me. I have told you so already. I shall try to call her "Aunt"; and you must be satisfied with that.

TESMAN   Well, well. Only I think now that you belong to the family, you . . .

HEDDA   H'm—I can't in the least see why . . . [*She walks toward the middle doorway.*]

TESMAN [*After a pause.*]   Is there anything the matter with you, Hedda?

HEDDA   I'm only looking at my old piano. It doesn't go at all well with all the other things.

TESMAN   The first time I get my salary, we'll see about exchanging it.

HEDDA   No, no—no exchanging. I don't want to part with it. Suppose we put it there in the inner room, and then get another here in its place. When it's convenient, I mean.

TESMAN [*A little startled.*] Yes—of course we could do that.

HEDDA [*Takes up the bouquet from the piano.*] These flowers were not here last night when we arrived.

TESMAN Aunt Julia must have brought them for you.

HEDDA [*Examining the bouquet.*] A visiting card. [*Takes it out and reads.*] "Shall return later in the day." Can you guess whose card it is?

TESMAN No. Whose?

HEDDA The name is "Mrs. Elvsted."

TESMAN Is it really? Sheriff Elvsted's wife? The former Miss Rysing.

HEDDA Exactly. The girl with the attractive hair, that she was always showing off. An old flame of yours I've been told.

TESMAN [*Laughing.*] Oh, that didn't last long; and it was before I knew you, Hedda. But imagine her being in town!

HEDDA It's odd that she should call upon us. I have scarcely seen her since we left school.

TESMAN I haven't seen her either for—heaven knows how long. I wonder how she can endure to live in such an out-of-the-way hole?

HEDDA [*After a moment's thought, says suddenly.*] Tell me, Tesman—isn't it somewhere near there that he—that—Eilert Lovborg is living?

TESMAN Yes, he is somewhere in that part of the country.

[BERTA *enters by the hall door.*]

BERTA That lady, ma'am, that brought some flowers a little while ago, is here again. [*Pointing.*] The flowers you have in your hand, ma'am.

HEDDA Ah, is she? Well, please show her in.

[BERTA *opens the door for* MRS. ELVSTED, *and leaves.*—MRS. ELVSTED *is a woman of fragile figure, with pretty, soft features. Her eyes are light blue, large, round, and somewhat prominent, with a startled, inquiring expression. Her hair is remarkably light, almost golden, and unusually abundant and wavy. She is a couple of years younger than* HEDDA. *She wears a dark dress, tasteful, but not quite in the latest fashion.*]

HEDDA [*Receives her warmly.*] How do you do, my dear Mrs. Elvsted? It's delightful to see you again.

MRS. ELVSTED [*Nervously, struggling for self-control.*] Yes, it's a very long time since we met.

TESMAN [*Gives her his hand.*] And we too.

HEDDA Thanks for your lovely flowers . . .

MRS. ELVSTED. Oh, not at all . . . I would have come straight here yesterday afternoon; but I heard that you were away . . .

TESMAN   Have you just come to town?

MRS. ELVSTED   I arrived yesterday, about midday. Oh, I was quite in despair when I heard that you were not at home.

HEDDA   In despair! How so?

TESMAN   Why, my dear Mrs. Rysing—I mean Mrs. Elvsted . . .

HEDDA   I hope that you are not in any trouble?

MRS. ELVSTED   Yes, I am. And I don't know another living soul here that I can turn to.

HEDDA [*Laying the bouquet on the table.*]   Come—let us sit here on the sofa . . .

MRS. ELVSTED   Oh, I am too upset to sit down.

HEDDA   Oh no, you're not. Come here. [*She pulls* MRS. ELVSTED *down on the sofa and sits at her side.*]

TESMAN   Well? What is it, Mrs. Elvsted . . . ?

HEDDA   Has anything particular happened to you at home?

MRS. ELVSTED   Yes—and no. Oh—I am so anxious you should not misunderstand me . . .

HEDDA   Then it is best to tell us the whole story, Mrs. Elvsted.

TESMAN   I guess that's what you have come for?

MRS. ELVSTED   Yes, yes—of course it is. Well then, I must tell you, if you don't already know, that Eilert Lovborg is in town, too.

HEDDA   Lovborg . . . !

TESMAN   What! Has Eilert Lovborg come back? Think of that, Hedda!

HEDDA   Well, well—I hear it.

MRS. ELVSTED   He has been here a week already. Just imagine—a whole week! In this dangerous town, alone! With so many temptations on all sides.

HEDDA   But, my dear Mrs. Elvsted—why does he concern you so much?

MRS. ELVSTED [*Looks at her with a startled air, and says rapidly.*]   He was the children's tutor.

HEDDA   Your children's?

MRS. ELVSTED   My husband's. I have none.

HEDDA   Your stepchildren's, then?

MRS. ELVSTED   Yes.

TESMAN [*Somewhat hesitatingly.*]   Then was he—I don't know how to express it—was he—sufficiently stable to do that kind of work?

MRS. ELVSTED   For the last two years his conduct has been beyond reproach.

TESMAN   Has it indeed? Hear that, Hedda!

HEDDA   I hear it.

MRS. ELVSTED   Absolutely beyond reproach. I assure you! In every respect. But all the same—now that I know he is here—in this big city—and with a large sum of money in his hands—I can't help being worried about him.

TESMAN   Why didn't he stay where he was? With you and your husband?

MRS. ELVSTED   After his book was published he was too restless and unsettled to stay with us.

TESMAN   Yes, by the way, Aunt Julia told me he had published a new book.

MRS. ELVSTED   Yes, a big book, dealing with the development of civilization—in broad outline, as it were. It came out about two weeks ago. And since it has sold so well, and has been so widely read—and become such a sensation . . .

TESMAN   Has it indeed? It must be something he has had lying around since his better days.

MRS. ELVSTED   Long ago, you mean?

TESMAN   Yes.

MRS. ELVSTED   No, he has written it all since he has been with us— within the last year.

TESMAN   Isn't that good news, Hedda? Think of that.

MRS. ELVSTED   Ah yes, if only it would last!

HEDDA   Have you seen him here in town?

MRS. ELVSTED   No, not yet. I have had the greatest difficulty in finding out his address. But this morning I discovered it at last.

HEDDA [*Looks searchingly at her.*]   Do you know, it seems to me a little odd of your husband—h'm . . .

MRS. ELVSTED [*Reacting nervously.*]   Of my husband! What?

HEDDA   That he should send you to town on such a mission—that he does not come himself and look after his friend.

MRS. ELVSTED   Oh no, no—my husband has no time. And besides, I—I had some shopping to do.

HEDDA [*With a slight smile.*]   Ah, that is a different matter.

MRS. ELVSTED [*Rising quickly and uneasily.*]   And now I beg and implore you, Mr. Tesman—receive Eilert Lovborg kindly if he comes to you! And that he is sure to do. Remember you were such good friends in the old days. And then you are interested in the same area—the same field of research—so far as I know.

TESMAN   We used to be, at any rate.

MRS. ELVSTED   That is why I beg so earnestly that you—you too—will keep a sharp eye on him. Oh, you will promise me that, Mr. Tesman—won't you?

TESMAN   With the greatest of pleasure, Mrs. Rysing . . .

HEDDA   Mrs. Elvsted.

TESMAN   I assure you I shall do everything I possibly can for Eilert. You may depend on me.

MRS. ELVSTED   Oh, how very, very kind of you! [*Presses his hands.*] Thanks, thanks, thanks! [*Frightened.*] You see, my husband is so very fond of him!

HEDDA [*Rising.*]   You ought to write to him, Tesman. Perhaps he may not care to come to you of his own accord.

TESMAN   Well, perhaps it would be the right thing to do, Hedda?

HEDDA   And the sooner the better. Why not at once?

MRS. ELVSTED [*Imploringly.*]   Oh, if you only would!

TESMAN   I'll write this very moment. Do you have his address, Mrs.—Mrs. Elvsted?

MRS. ELVSTED   Yes. [*Takes a slip of paper from her pocket, and hands it to him.*] Here it is.

TESMAN   Good, good. Then I'll go in . . . [*Looks about him.*] By the way—my slippers? Oh, here. [*Takes the packet, and is about to leave.*]

HEDDA   Be sure you write him a warm, friendly letter. And a good long one too.

TESMAN   Yes, I will.

MRS. ELVSTED   But please, please don't say a word to show that I have suggested it.

TESMAN   No, how could you think I would? [*He leaves to the right, through the inner room.*]

HEDDA [*Walks over to* MRS. ELVSTED, *smiles and says in a low voice.*]   There! We have killed two birds with one stone.

MRS. ELVSTED   What do you mean?

HEDDA   Couldn't you see that I wanted him to leave?

MRS. ELVSTED   Yes, to write the letter . . .

HEDDA   And that I might speak to you alone.

MRS. ELVSTED [*Confused.*]   About the same thing?

HEDDA   Precisely.

MRS. ELVSTED [*Apprehensively.*]   But there is nothing more, Mrs. Tesman! Absolutely nothing!

HEDDA   Oh yes, but there is. There is a great deal more—I can see that. Sit here—and we'll have a cozy, confidential chat. [*She forces* MRS. ELVSTED *to sit in the easy-chair beside the stove, and seats herself on one of the footstools.*]

MRS. ELVSTED [*Anxiously, looking at her watch.*]   But, my dear Mrs. Tesman—I was really getting ready to leave.

HEDDA   Oh, you can't be in such a hurry. Well? Now tell me something about your life at home.

MRS. ELVSTED   Oh, I don't want to talk about it.

HEDDA   But to me, dear . . . ? Why, weren't we schoolmates?

MRS. ELVSTED   Yes, but you were in the class above me. Oh, how terribly afraid of you I was then!

HEDDA   Afraid of me?

MRS. ELVSTED   Yes, terribly. For when we met on the stairs you used to pull my hair.

HEDDA   Did I, really?

MRS. ELVSTED   Yes, and once you said you would burn it off my head.

HEDDA   Oh, that was all nonsense, of course.

MRS. ELVSTED   Yes, but I was so silly in those days. And since then, too—we have drifted so far—far apart from each other. Our circles have been so entirely different.

HEDDA   Well then, we must try to drift together again. Now listen! At school we called each other by our first names . . .

MRS. ELVSTED   No, I am sure you must be mistaken.

HEDDA   No, not at all! I can remember quite distinctly. So now we are going to renew our old friendship. [*Pulls the footstool closer to* MRS. ELVSTED.] There now! [*Kisses her cheek.*] You must call me Hedda.

MRS. ELVSTED [*Presses and pats her hands.*]   Oh, how good and kind you are! I am not used to such kindness.

HEDDA   There, there, there! And I shall call you my dear Thora, as in the old days.

MRS. ELVSTED   My name is Thea.

HEDDA   Why, of course! I meant Thea. [*Looks at her compassionately.*] So you are not accustomed to goodness and kindness, Thea? Not in your own home?

MRS. ELVSTED   Oh, if I only had a home! But I haven't any; I have never had a home.

HEDDA [*Looks at her for a moment.*]   I almost suspected as much.

MRS. ELVSTED [*Gazing helplessly before her.*]   Yes—yes—yes.

HEDDA   I don't quite remember—was it not as housekeeper that you first went to Mr. Elvsted's?

MRS. ELVSTED   I really went as governess. But his wife—his late wife—was an invalid, and rarely left her room. So I had to look after the housekeeping as well.

HEDDA   And then—at last—you became mistress of the house.

MRS. ELVSTED [*Sadly.*]   Yes, I did.

HEDDA   Let me see—about how long ago was that?

MRS. ELVSTED   My marriage?

HEDDA   Yes.

MRS. ELVSTED   Five years ago.

HEDDA   To be sure; it must be that.

MRS. ELVSTED   Oh those five years . . . ! Or at least the last two or three of them! Oh, if you could only imagine, Mrs. Tesman.

HEDDA [*Giving her a little tap on the hand.*]   Mrs. Tesman? Not that, Thea!

MRS. ELVSTED   Yes, yes, I will try . . . well, if—you could only imagine and understand . . .

HEDDA [*Lightly.*]   Eilert Lovborg has been in your neighborhood about three years, hasn't he?

MRS. ELVSTED [*Looks at her doubtfully.*]   Eilert Lovborg? Yes—he has.

HEDDA   Had you known him before, in town here?

MRS. ELVSTED   Scarcely at all. I mean—I knew him by name of course.

HEDDA   But you saw a good deal of him in the country?

MRS. ELVSTED   Yes, he came to see us every day. You see, he gave the children lessons; for in the long run I couldn't manage it all myself.

HEDDA   No, that's clear. And your husband . . . ? I suppose he is often away from home?

MRS. ELVSTED   Yes. Being sheriff, you know, he has to travel about a good deal in his district.

HEDDA [*Leaning against the arm of the chair.*]   Thea—my poor, dear Thea—now you must tell me everything—exactly as it is.

MRS. ELVSTED   Well then, you must question me.

HEDDA   What sort of a man is your husband, Thea? I mean—you know—in everyday life. Is he kind to you?

MRS. ELVSTED [*Evasively.*]   I am sure he means well in everything.

HEDDA   I should think he must be altogether too old for you. There is at least twenty years' difference between you, isn't there?

MRS. ELVSTED [*Irritably.*]   Yes, that is true, too. Everything about him is repellent to me! We have nothing in common. We don't agree on anything—he and I.

HEDDA   But isn't he fond of you all the same? In his own way?

MRS. ELVSTED   Oh I really don't know. I think he regards me simply as a useful property. And then it doesn't cost much to keep me. I am not expensive.

HEDDA   That is stupid of you.

MRS. ELVSTED [*Shakes her head.*]   It cannot be otherwise—not with him. I don't think he really cares for anyone but himself—and perhaps a little for the children.

HEDDA   And for Eilert Lovborg, Thea.

MRS. ELVSTED [*Looking at her.*]   For Eilert Lovborg? How did you get that idea?

HEDDA   Well, my dear—I should say, when he sends you after him all the way to town . . . [*Smiling almost imperceptibly.*] And besides, you said so yourself, to Tesman.

MRS. ELVSTED [*With a little nervous twitch.*]   Did I? Yes, I guess I did. [*Vehemently, but not loudly.*] No—I may just as well make a clean breast of it at once! For it must all come out in any case.

HEDDA   Why, my dear Thea . . . ?

MRS. ELVSTED   Well, to make a long story short: My husband did not know that I was coming.

HEDDA   What! Your husband didn't know it!

MRS. ELVSTED   No, of course not. For that matter, he was away from home—he was traveling. Oh, I could bear it no longer, Hedda! I couldn't indeed—so utterly alone as I would have been up there now.

HEDDA   Well? And then?

MRS. ELVSTED   So I packed some of my things—what I needed most—as quietly as possible. And then I left the house.

HEDDA   Without a word?

MRS. ELVSTED   Yes—and took the train straight to town.

HEDDA   Why, my dear, good Thea—to think of you daring to do it!

MRS. ELVSTED [*Rises and moves about the room.*]   What else could I possibly do?

HEDDA   But what do you think your husband will say when you return home?

MRS. ELVSTED [*At the table, looks at her.*]   Back to him?

HEDDA   Of course.

MRS. ELVSTED   I shall never go back to him again.

HEDDA [*Rising and going toward her.*]   Then you have left your home—for good?

MRS. ELVSTED   Yes. There was nothing else to be done.

HEDDA   But then—to leave so openly.

MRS. ELVSTED   Oh, it's impossible to keep things like that secret.

HEDDA   But what do you think people will say of you, Thea?

MRS. ELVSTED   They may say what they like, for all I care. [*Seats herself wearily and sadly on the sofa.*] I only did what I had to do.

HEDDA [*After a short silence.*]   And what are your plans now? What are you going to do?

MRS. ELVSTED   I don't know yet. I only know this, that I must live here, where Eilert Lovborg is—if I am to live at all.

HEDDA [*Takes a chair from the table, seats herself beside her, and strokes her hands.*]   My dear Thea—how did this—this friendship—between you and Eilert Lovborg come about?

MRS. ELVSTED   Oh it developed gradually. I gained a sort of influence over him.

HEDDA   Really?

MRS. ELVSTED   He gave up his destructive habits. Not because I asked him to, for I never dared do that. But of course he saw how troubling they were to me; and so he stopped them.

HEDDA [*Concealing an involuntary smile of scorn.*]   Then you have reformed him—as the saying goes—my little Thea.

MRS. ELVSTED   So he says himself, at any rate. And he, on his side, has made a real human being of me—taught me to think, and to understand so many things.

HEDDA   Did he give you lessons too, then?

MRS. ELVSTED   No, not exactly lessons. But he talked to me—talked about many things. And then came the lovely, happy time when I began to share in his work—when he allowed me to help him!

HEDDA   Oh he did, did he?

MRS. ELVSTED   Yes! He never wrote anything without my assistance.

HEDDA   You were like two good comrades?

MRS. ELVSTED [*Eagerly.*]   Comrades! Yes, imagine, Hedda—that is the very word he used! Oh, I should feel perfectly happy; and yet I cannot; for I don't know how long it will last.

HEDDA   Are you no more certain of him than that?

MRS. ELVSTED [*Gloomily.*]   A woman's shadow stands between Eilert Lovborg and me.

HEDDA [*Looks at her anxiously.*]   Who can that be?

MRS. ELVSTED   I don't know. Someone he knew in his—in his past. Someone he has never been able entirely to forget.

HEDDA   What has he told you—about this?

MRS. ELVSTED   He has only once—quite vaguely—alluded to it. .

HEDDA   Well! And what did he say?

MRS. ELVSTED   He said that when they parted, she threatened to shoot him with a pistol.

HEDDA [*With cold composure.*]   Oh, nonsense! No one does that sort of thing here.

MRS. ELVSTED   No. And that is why I think it must have been that red-haired singing woman whom he once . . .

HEDDA   Yes, very likely.

MRS. ELVSTED   For I remember they used to say of her that she carried loaded firearms.

HEDDA   Oh—then of course it must have been she.

MRS. ELVSTED [*Wringing her hands.*]   And now just think, Hedda—I hear that this singing woman—that she is in town again! Oh, I don't know what to do . . .

HEDDA [*Glancing toward the inner room.*]   Sh! Here comes Tesman. [*Rises and whispers.*]   Thea—all this must remain between you and me.

MRS. ELVSTED [*Jumping up.*]   Oh yes—yes! For heaven's sake . . . !

[GEORGE TESMAN, *with a letter in his hand,*
comes from the right through the inner room.]

TESMAN   There now—the letter is finished.

HEDDA   That's right. Mrs. Elvsted is just leaving. Wait a moment— I'll walk with you to the garden gate.

TESMAN   Do you think Berta could mail the letter, Hedda dear?

HEDDA [*Takes it.*]   I will tell her to.

[BERTA *enters from the hall.*]

BERTA   Judge Brack wishes to know if Mrs. Tesman can see him.

HEDDA   Yes, ask Judge Brack to come in. And look here—mail this letter.

BERTA [*Taking the letter.*]   Yes, ma'am.

[*She opens the door for* JUDGE BRACK *and leaves.* BRACK *is a man of forty-five; stout, but well built and bouncy in his movements. His face is roundish with an aristocratic profile. His hair is short, still almost black, and carefully groomed. His eyes are lively and sparkling. His eyebrows thick. His mustache is also thick, with well-trimmed ends. He wears a well-tailored suit, a little too youthful for his age. He uses a monocle, attached to a chain, which he now and then lets drop.*]

JUDGE BRACK [*With his hat in his hand, bowing.*]   May one dare to call so early in the day?

HEDDA   Of course one may.

TESMAN [*shakes his hand.*]   You are welcome at any time. [*Introducing him.*] Judge Brack—Miss Rysing . . .

HEDDA   Oh . . . !

BRACK [*Bowing.*]   Ah—delighted . . .

HEDDA [*Looks at him and laughs.*]   It's nice to have a look at you by daylight, Judge!

BRACK   Do you find me—changed?

HEDDA   A little younger, I think.

BRACK   Thank you so much.

TESMAN   But what do you think of Hedda? Doesn't she look marvelous? She has actually . . .

HEDDA   Oh, do leave me alone. You haven't thanked Judge Brack for all the trouble he has gone to . . .

BRACK   Oh, nonsense—it was a pleasure for me . . .

HEDDA   Yes, you are a friend indeed. But here stands Thea all impatience to be off—so good-bye, Judge. I shall be back again shortly.

> [*Mutual good-byes.* MRS. ELVSTED *and* HEDDA
> *leave through the hall door.*]

BRACK   Well, is your wife sufficiently satisfied . . .

TESMAN   Yes, we can't thank you enough. Of course she talks of a little rearrangement here and there; and one or two things are still needed. We shall have to buy a few minor things.

BRACK   Really!

TESMAN   But we won't trouble you about these things. Hedda says she herself will look for what she wants. Shall we sit down?

BRACK   Thanks, for a moment. [*Seats himself beside the table.*] There is something I wanted to speak to you about, my dear Tesman.

TESMAN   Really? Ah, I understand! [*Seating himself.*] I suppose it's the business side of the house.

BRACK   Oh, the money question is not so very pressing; though, for that matter I wish we could have been a bit more economical.

TESMAN   But that would never have done, you know! Think of Hedda, my dear friend! You, who know her so well . . . I couldn't possibly ask her to put up with a simple style of living!

BRACK   No, no—that is just the difficulty.

TESMAN   And then—fortunately—it can't be long before I receive my appointment as professor.

BRACK Well, you see—such things often take their time.

TESMAN Have you heard anything definite?

BRACK Nothing really definite . . . [*Interrupting himself.*] But by the way—I have one piece of news for you.

TESMAN What?

BRACK Your old friend, Eilert Lovborg, has returned to town.

TESMAN I know that already.

BRACK Really? How did you find out?

TESMAN From that lady who left with Hedda.

BRACK Really? What was her name? I didn't quite catch it.

TESMAN Mrs. Elvsted.

BRACK Aha—Sheriff Elvsted's wife? Of course—he has been living up in their area.

TESMAN And think, I'm delighted to hear that he straightened out his life.

BRACK So they say.

TESMAN And then he has published a new book?

BRACK Yes, indeed he has.

TESMAN And I hear it has become a sensation!

BRACK Quite an unusual sensation.

TESMAN Just think—isn't that good news! A man of such extraordinary talents . . . It grieved me to think that he had ruined himself.

BRACK That was what everybody thought.

TESMAN But I cannot imagine what he will do now! How in the world will he be able to make a living?

[*During the last words,* HEDDA *has entered from the hall door.*]

HEDDA [*To* BRACK, *laughing with a touch of scorn.*] Tesman is forever worrying about how people are going to make their living.

TESMAN Well you see, dear—we were talking about poor Eilert Lovborg.

HEDDA [*Glancing at him quickly.*] Oh, indeed? [*Seats herself in the armchair beside the stove and asks casually.*] What is the matter with him?

TESMAN Well—no doubt he has squandered all his property long ago; and he can scarcely write a new book every year. So I really can't see what is to become of him.

BRACK Perhaps I can give you some information on that point.

TESMAN Really?

BRACK You must remember that his relatives have quite some influence.

TESMAN   Oh, his relatives, unfortunately, have entirely washed their hands of him.

BRACK   At one time they called him the hope of the family.

TESMAN   At one time, yes! But he has put an end to all that.

HEDDA   Who knows? [*With a slight smile.*] I hear they have reformed him at Sheriff Elvsted's . . .

BRACK   And then this book that he has published . . .

TESMAN   Well, well, I strongly hope that they may find something for him to do. I have just written to him. I asked him to come and see us this evening, Hedda dear.

BRACK   But my dear fellow, you are expected at my stag party this evening. You promised on the pier last night.

HEDDA   Had you forgotten, Tesman?

TESMAN   Yes, I had completely forgotten.

BRACK   But it doesn't matter, for you may be sure he won't come.

TESMAN   What makes you think that?

BRACK [*With a little hesitation, rising and resting his hands on the back of his chair.*]   My dear Tesman—and you too, Mrs. Tesman—I think I shouldn't keep you in the dark about something that—that . . .

TESMAN   That concerns Eilert . . . ?

BRACK   Both you and him.

TESMAN   Well, my dear Judge, out with it.

BRACK   You must be prepared to find your appointment deferred longer than you desired or expected.

TESMAN [*Jumping up uneasily.*]   Is there some hitch about it?

BRACK   The nomination may perhaps be made conditional on the result of a competition . . .

TESMAN   Competition! Think of that, Hedda!

HEDDA [*Sinking deeper into her chair.*]   Oh—no!

TESMAN   But who can my competitor be? Surely not . . . ?

BRACK   Yes, precisely—Eilert Lovborg.

TESMAN [*Clasping his hands.*]   No, no—it's quite inconceivable! Quite impossible!

BRACK   H'm—that is what it may come down to.

TESMAN   Well, but Judge Brack—it would show the most incredible lack of consideration for me. [*Wildly waving his arms.*] For—just think—I'm a married man! We have married on the fulfillment of these prospects, Hedda and I; and run deep into debt; and borrowed money from Aunt Julia too. Good heavens, they had as good as promised me the appointment.

BRACK Well, well, well—no doubt you will get it in the end; only after a contest.

HEDDA [*Motionless in her armchair.*] See, Tesman, this will be a kind of an exciting race.

TESMAN Why, my dearest Hedda, how can you be so indifferent about it?

HEDDA [*As before.*] I am not at all indifferent. I am most eager to see who wins.

BRACK In any case, Mrs. Tesman, it is best that you should know how matters stand. I mean—before you set about the little purchases I hear you are threatening.

HEDDA This can't make any difference.

BRACK Indeed! Then I have no more to say. Good-bye! [*To* TESMAN.] I shall look in on my way back from my afternoon walk, and take you home with me.

TESMAN Oh yes, yes—your news has quite upset me.

HEDDA [*Reclining, holds out her hand.*] Good-bye, Judge; and be sure you stop by again in the afternoon.

BRACK Many thanks. Good-bye, good-bye!

TESMAN [*Accompanying him to the door.*] Good-bye, my dear Judge! You must really excuse me . . .

[JUDGE BRACK *leaves through the hall door.*]

TESMAN [*Crosses the room.*] Oh Hedda—one should never rush into adventures.

HEDDA [*Looks at him, smiling.*] Do you do that?

TESMAN Yes, dear—there is no denying—it was adventurous to get married and set up house upon mere expectations.

HEDDA Perhaps you are right there.

TESMAN Well—at any rate, we have our lovely home, Hedda! Just think, the home we both dreamed of—the home we fell in love with.

HEDDA [*Rising slowly and wearily.*] It was part of our agreement that we were to be part of society—to entertain fashionably.

TESMAN Yes, if you only knew how I had been looking forward to it! Imagine—to see you as hostess—in a select circle! Well, well, well—for the present we shall have to get along without society, Hedda—only to invite Aunt Julia now and then. Oh, I intended for you to lead such an utterly different life, dear . . . !

HEDDA Of course I cannot have my butler just yet.

TESMAN   Oh no, unfortunately. It would be out of the question for us to keep a butler you know.

HEDDA   And the riding horse I was to have had . . .

TESMAN [*Aghast.*]   The riding horse!

HEDDA   . . . I suppose I must not think of that now.

TESMAN   Good heavens, no!—that's as clear as daylight.

HEDDA [*Crosses the room.*]   Well, I shall have one thing left at least to kill time with in the meanwhile.

TESMAN [*Beaming.*]   Oh thank heaven for that! What is it, Hedda?

HEDDA [*In the middle doorway, looks at him with hidden scorn.*] My pistols, George.

TESMAN [*In alarm.*]   Your pistols!

HEDDA [*With cold eyes.*]   General Gabler's pistols. [*She leaves through the inner room, to the left.*]

TESMAN [*Rushes up to the middle doorway and calls after her.*] No, for heaven's sake, Hedda darling—don't touch those dangerous things! For my sake, Hedda!

ACT II

SCENE: *The room at the* TESMANS' *as in the first act, except that the piano has been removed, and an elegant little writing table with bookshelves put in its place. A smaller table stands near the sofa on the left. Most of the bouquets have been taken away.* MRS. ELVSTED'S *bouquet is on the large table in front. It is afternoon.* HEDDA, *dressed to receive visitors, is alone in the room. She stands by the open glass door, loading a pistol. A matching pistol lies in an open case on the writing table.*

HEDDA [*Looks down into the garden, and shouts.*]   Glad to see you again, Judge!

BRACK [*Is heard calling from a distance.*]   Glad to see you, Mrs. Tesman!

HEDDA [*Raises the pistol and points.*]   Now I'm going to shoot you, Judge Brack!

BRACK [*Shouts unseen.*]   No, no, no! Don't aim at me!

HEDDA   This is what one gets for sneaking in the back way. [*She fires.*]

BRACK [*Nearer.*]   Are you out of your mind! . . .

HEDDA   Dear me—did I hit you?

BRACK [*Still outside.*]   I wish you would stop these pranks!

HEDDA   Come in then, Judge.

[JUDGE BRACK, *dressed somewhat gaudily for the stag party, enters by the glass door. He carries a light overcoat over his arm.*]

BRACK   What the devil—aren't you tired of that sport, yet? What are you shooting at?

HEDDA   Oh, I am only firing in the air.

BRACK [*Gently takes the pistol out of her hand.*]   Allow me, Madam! [*Looks at it.*] Ah—I know this pistol well! [*Looks around.*] Where is the case? Ah, here it is. [*Puts the pistol in it, and shuts it.*] Now we won't play that game any more today.

HEDDA   Then what in heaven's name would you have me do with myself?

BRACK   Have you had no visitors?

HEDDA [*Closing the glass door.*]   Not one. I suppose all our crowd is still out of town.

BRACK   And is Tesman not at home either?

HEDDA [*At the writing table, putting the pistol case in a drawer which she shuts.*]   No. He rushed off to his aunts' right after lunch; he didn't expect you this early.

BRACK   H'm—how stupid of me not to have thought of that!

HEDDA [*Turning her head to look at him.*]   Why stupid?

BRACK   Because if I had thought of it I would have come a little— earlier.

HEDDA [*Crossing the room.*]   Then you would have found no one to greet you; for I have been in my room changing my dress ever since lunch.

BRACK   And is there no little window in the door that we could have talked through?

HEDDA   You have forgotten to install one.

BRACK   That was another piece of stupidity.

HEDDA   Well, we must just settle down here—and wait. Tesman is not likely to be back for some time yet.

BRACK   Never mind; I shall not be impatient.

[HEDDA *seats herself in the corner of the sofa.* BRACK *puts his overcoat over the back of the nearest chair, and sits down, but keeps his hat in his hand. A short silence. They look at each other.*]

HEDDA   Well?

BRACK [*In the same tone.*]   Well?

HEDDA   I spoke first.

BRACK [*Leaning a little forward.*]   Come, let us have a cozy little chat, Mrs. Hedda.

HEDDA [*Leaning further back in the sofa.*]   Doesn't it seem like an eternity since our last talk? Of course I don't count those few words last evening and this morning.

BRACK   You mean since our last confidential talk? Our last cozy get-together?

HEDDA   Well, yes—since you put it that way.

BRACK   Not a day has passed that I haven't wished that you were back home again.

HEDDA   And I also have wished the same thing.

BRACK   You? Really, Mrs. Hedda? And I thought you had been enjoying your trip so much!

HEDDA   Oh, yes, you may be sure of that!

BRACK   But Tesman's letters spoke of nothing but happiness.

HEDDA   Oh, Tesman! You see, he thinks nothing so enjoyable as digging in libraries and making copies of old parchments, or whatever you call them.

BRACK [*With a touch of malice.*]   Well, that is his vocation in life—or part of it at any rate.

HEDDA   Yes, of course; and no doubt when it's your vocation . . . But *I*! Oh, my dear Mr. Brack, how dreadfully bored I have been.

BRACK [*Sympathetically.*]   Do you really mean it? Are you serious?

HEDDA   Yes, you can surely understand it . . . ! To go for six whole months without meeting a soul that knew anything of our circle, or could talk about the things we are interested in.

BRACK   Yes, yes—I, too, would feel deprived.

HEDDA   And then, what I found most intolerable of all . . .

BRACK   Well?

HEDDA   . . . was being constantly in the company of—one and the same person . . .

BRACK [*With a nod of understanding.*]   Morning, noon, and night, yes—at every moment.

HEDDA   I said "constantly."

BRACK   Just so. But I should have thought, with our excellent Tesman, one could . . .

HEDDA   Tesman is—a narrow specialist, my dear Judge.

BRACK   Undeniably.

HEDDA   And specialists are not at all fun to travel with. Not for so long at any rate.

BRACK   Not even—the specialist one happens to love?

HEDDA   Please—don't use that sickening word!

BRACK [*Taken aback.*]   What do you mean, Mrs. Hedda?

HEDDA [*Half laughingly, half irritated.*]   You should just try it! To hear of nothing but the history of civilization morning, noon, and night . . .

BRACK   Constantly.

HEDDA   Yes, yes, yes! And then all about the domestic crafts of the Middle Ages . . . ! That's the most disgusting part of it!

BRACK [*Looks searchingly at her.*]   But tell me—in that case, how am I to understand your . . . ? H'm . . .

HEDDA   My choosing George Tesman, you mean?

BRACK   Well, let us put it that way.

HEDDA   Good heavens, do you see anything so wonderful in that?

BRACK   Yes and no—Mrs. Hedda.

HEDDA   I had positively danced myself tired, my dear Judge. My youth was over . . . [*With a slight shudder.*] Oh, no—I won't say that; nor think it, either!

BRACK   You have certainly no reason to.

HEDDA   Oh, reasons . . . [*Watching him closely.*] And George Tesman—after all, you must admit that he is correctness itself.

BRACK   His correctness and respectability are beyond all question.

HEDDA   And I don't see anything ridiculous about him. Do you?

BRACK   Ridiculous? N—no—I shouldn't exactly say so . . .

HEDDA   Well—and his research efforts, at all times are untiring. I see no reason why he shouldn't one day be on top, after all.

BRACK [*Looks at her hesitatingly.*]   I thought that you, like everyone else, expected him to attain the highest distinction.

HEDDA [*With an expression of fatigue.*]   Yes, so I did—And then, since he was bent, at all cost, on being allowed to provide for me—there was really no reason why I shouldn't have accepted his offer.

BRACK   No—if you look at it in that way . . .

HEDDA   It was more than my other admirers were willing to do for me, my dear Judge.

BRACK [*Laughing.*]   Well, I can't answer for all the others; but as for myself, you know quite well that I have always entertained a—a certain respect for marriage—for marriage as an institution, Mrs. Hedda.

HEDDA [*Jokingly.*]   Oh, believe me I have never entertained any hopes with respect to you.

BRACK   All I ask for is a warm and intimate circle of friends, where I can make myself useful, and am free to come and go as—as a trusted friend . . .

HEDDA   Of the master of the house, do you mean?

BRACK [*Bowing.*]   Frankly—of the mistress first of all; but, of course, of the master, too, in the second place. Such a triangular friendship—if I may call it so—is really a great convenience for all parties, let me tell you.

HEDDA   Yes, I have many a time longed for someone to be the third person on our travels. Oh—how boring, just the two of us in those train compartments . . . !

BRACK   Fortunately your wedding trip is over now.

HEDDA [*Shaking her head.*]   Not by a long—long way. I have only arrived at a station on the line.

BRACK   Well, then the passengers get out and stretch their legs a little, Mrs. Hedda.

HEDDA   I never get out.

BRACK   Really?

HEDDA   No—because someone is always standing there to . . .

BRACK [*Laughing.*]   To look at your legs, do you mean?

HEDDA   Precisely.

BRACK   Well, but, my dear . . .

HEDDA [*With a gesture of disgust.*]   I won't have it. I would rather keep my seat where I happen to be—and continue the boring togetherness.

BRACK   But suppose a third person were to enter and join the couple.

HEDDA   Ah—that is quite another matter!

BRACK   A trusted, sympathetic friend . . .

HEDDA   . . . a captivating conversationalist on all kinds of intriguing topics . . .

BRACK   . . . and not the least bit of a narrow specialist!

HEDDA [*With an audible sigh.*]   Yes, that would be a relief, indeed.

BRACK [*Hears the front door open, and glances in that direction.*]   The triangle is completed.

HEDDA [*Half aloud.*]   And the train rolls on.

[GEORGE TESMAN, *in a gray suit, with a soft felt hat, enters from the hall. He has a number of unbound books under his arm and in his pockets.*]

TESMAN [*Walks to the table beside the corner sofa.*]   Wow—what a load for a warm day—all these books. [*Puts them on the table.*] I'm really perspiring, Hedda. Hello—are you here already, my dear Judge? Berta didn't tell me.

BRACK [*Rising.*]   I came in through the garden.

HEDDA   What books do you have there?

TESMAN [*Stands looking through them.*]   Some new books on my special
topic—quite indispensable to me.

HEDDA   Your special topic?

BRACK   Yes, books on his special topic, Mrs. Tesman.

[BRACK *and* HEDDA *exchange a confidential smile.*]

HEDDA   Do you need still more books on your special topic?

TESMAN   Yes, my dear Hedda, one can never have too many of them.
Of course, one must keep up with all that is written and published.

HEDDA   Yes, I guess one must.

TESMAN [*Searching among his books.*]   And look here—I have found a
copy of Eilert Lovborg's new book, too. [*Offering it to her.*] Perhaps
you would like to glance through it, Hedda?

HEDDA   No, thank you. Or rather—later perhaps.

TESMAN   I glanced at it on the way home.

BRACK   Well, what do you think of it—as a scholar?

TESMAN   I think it shows quite remarkable soundness of judgment.
He never wrote like that before. [*Putting the books together.*] Now I
shall take all these into my study. I'm eager to cut the pages . . . !
And then I must change my clothes. [*To* BRACK.] I suppose we
needn't leave just yet?

BRACK   Oh, dear, no—there is not the slightest hurry.

TESMAN   Well, then, I will take my time. [*Leaves with his books, but
stops in the doorway and turns.*] By the way, Hedda—Aunt Julia is
not coming this evening.

HEDDA   Not coming? Is it that incident of the hat that keeps her away?

TESMAN   Oh, not at all. How could you think such a thing of Aunt
Julia? The reason is that Aunt Rina is very ill.

HEDDA   She always is.

TESMAN   Yes, but today she is much worse than usual, poor dear.

HEDDA   Oh, then it's only natural that her sister should stay with her. I
must bear my disappointment.

TESMAN   And you can't imagine, dear, how delighted Aunt Julia
seemed to be—because you had come home looking so marvelous!

HEDDA [*Half aloud, rising.*]   Oh, those eternal aunts!

TESMAN   What?

HEDDA [*Walking toward the glass door.*]   Nothing.

TESMAN   Oh, all right. [*He walks through the inner room, out to the right.*]

BRACK   What hat were you talking about?

HEDDA   Oh, it was a little episode with Miss Tesman this morning. She had put her hat on the chair there—[*looks at him and smiles*]—and I pretended to think it was the maid's.

BRACK [*Shaking his head.*]   Now, my dear Mrs. Hedda, how could you do such a thing? To that dear old lady!

HEDDA [*Nervously crossing the room.*]   Well, you see—these impulses come over me all of a sudden; and I cannot resist them. [*Throws herself down in the armchair by the stove.*] Oh, I don't know how to explain it.

BRACK [*Behind the armchair.*]   You are not really happy—that is at the bottom of it.

HEDDA [*Looking straight ahead.*]   I know of no reason why I should be—happy. Perhaps you can give me one?

BRACK   Well—among other things, because you live in exactly the home you had set your heart on.

HEDDA [*Looks up at him and laughs.*]   Do you, too, believe in that fantasy?

BRACK   Is it not true, then?

HEDDA   Oh, yes, there is something to it.

BRACK   Well?

HEDDA   The truth is that I used Tesman to take me home from evening parties last summer . . .

BRACK   I, unfortunately, had to go a different way.

HEDDA   That's true. I know you were going a different way last summer.

BRACK [*Laughing.*]   Oh, Mrs. Hedda! Well, then—you and Tesman . . . ?

HEDDA   Well, we happened to pass here one evening; Tesman, poor fellow, was agonizing to make conversation; so I took pity on the learned man . . .

BRACK [*Smiles doubtfully.*]   You took pity? H'm . . .

HEDDA   Yes, I really did. And so—to help him out of his torment—I happened to say, in pure thoughtlessness, that I should like to live in this villa.

BRACK   No more than that?

HEDDA   Not that evening.

BRACK   But later?

HEDDA   Yes, my thoughtlessness had consequences, my dear Judge.

BRACK   Unfortunately that happens too often, Mrs. Hedda.

HEDDA   Thanks! You see it was this enthusiasm for Secretary Falk's villa that first formed a bond of sympathy between George Tesman and me. From that came our engagement and our marriage, and our wedding trip and all the rest of it. Well, well, my dear Judge—as you make your bed so you must lie, I could almost say.

BRACK   This is incredible! And you really didn't like it all the while?

HEDDA   No, heaven knows I didn't.

BRACK   But now? Now that we have made it so comfortable for you?

HEDDA   Ugh—the rooms all seem to smell of lavender and dried roseleaves. But perhaps it's Aunt Julia that has brought that scent with her.

BRACK [*Laughing.*]   No, I think it must be lingering from the late Mrs. Secretary Falk.

HEDDA   Yes, there is a smell of death about it. It reminds me of a bouquet—the day after the ball. [*Clasps her hands behind her head, leans back in her chair and looks at him.*] Oh, my dear Judge—you cannot imagine how horribly bored I shall be here.

BRACK   Why shouldn't you, too, find some kind of interest in life, Mrs. Hedda?

HEDDA   An interest—that should hold me?

BRACK   If possible, of course.

HEDDA   Heaven knows what sort of an interest that could be. I often wonder whether . . . [*Breaking off.*] But that would never do, either.

BRACK   Who can tell? Let me hear what it is.

HEDDA   Whether I might not get Tesman to go into politics, I mean.

BRACK [*Laughing.*]   Tesman? No, really now, political life is not the thing for him—not at all in his character.

HEDDA   No, I should say not. But if I could get him into it anyway?

BRACK   Why—what satisfaction could you find in that? If he is not suited for that sort of thing, why should you want to push him into it?

HEDDA   Because I am bored, I tell you! [*After a pause.*] Do you think it quite out of the question that Tesman should ever be a member of the Cabinet?

BRACK   H'm—you see, my dear Mrs. Hedda—to get into the Cabinet he would have to be quite a wealthy man.

HEDDA [*Rising impatiently.*]   Yes, that's just it! It is this stifling poverty I have managed to fall into . . . ! [*Crosses the room.*] That is what makes life so miserable! So utterly ludicrous!—For that's what it is.

BRACK   Now *I* should say the fault is elsewhere.

HEDDA   Where, then?

BRACK   You have never gone through any really exciting experience.

HEDDA   Anything serious, you mean?

BRACK   Yes, you may call it so. But now you may perhaps have one in store.

HEDDA [*Tossing her head.*] Oh, you're thinking of the annoyances about this wretched professorship! But that must be Tesman's own affair. I assure you I shall not waste a thought on it.

BRACK   No, no, I should say not. But suppose now that what people call—in elegant language—a noble responsibility were to come upon you? [*Smiling.*] A new responsibility, Mrs. Hedda?

HEDDA [*Angrily.*] Be quiet! Nothing of that sort will ever happen!

BRACK [*Warily.*] We will speak of this again a year from now—at the very latest.

HEDDA [*Curtly.*] I have no talent for anything of that sort, Judge Brack. No responsibilities for me!

BRACK   Are you so unlike the majority of women as to have no talent for duties which . . . ?

HEDDA [*Beside the glass door.*] Oh, be quiet, I tell you! I often think there is only one thing in the world I have any talent for.

BRACK [*Drawing near to her.*] And what is that, if I may ask?

HEDDA [*Stands looking out.*] Boring myself to death. Now you know it. [*Turns, looks toward the inner room, and laughs.*] Yes, as I thought! Here comes the Professor.

BRACK [*Softly, in a tone of warning.*] Come, come, come, Mrs. Hedda!

[GEORGE TESMAN, *dressed for the party, with his gloves and hat in his hand, enters from the right through the inner room.*]

TESMAN   Hedda, has no message come from Eilert Lovborg?

HEDDA   No.

TESMAN   Then you'll see he'll be here soon.

BRACK   Do you really think he will come?

TESMAN   Yes, I am almost sure of it. What you were telling us this morning must have been a mere passing rumor.

BRACK   You think so?

TESMAN   At any rate, Aunt Julia said she did not believe for a moment that he would ever stand in my way again.

BRACK   Well, then, that's all right.

TESMAN [*Placing his hat and gloves on a chair on the right.*] Yes, but you must let me wait for him as long as possible.

BRACK   We have plenty of time still. None of my guests will arrive before seven or half-past.

TESMAN   Then meanwhile we can keep Hedda company, and see what happens.

HEDDA [*Placing* BRACK'S *hat and overcoat on the corner sofa.*] And at the worst Mr. Lovborg can stay here with me.

BRACK [*Offering to take his things.*]   Oh, allow me, Mrs. Tesman! What do you mean by "at the worst"?

HEDDA   If he won't go with you and Tesman.

TESMAN [*Looks questioningly at her.*]   But, Hedda, dear—do you think it would be quite proper for him to stay with you? Remember, Aunt Julia can't come.

HEDDA   No, but Mrs. Elvsted is coming. The three of us can have a cup of tea together.

TESMAN   Oh, yes, that will be all right.

BRACK [*Smiling.*]   And that would perhaps be the safest plan for him.

HEDDA   Why so?

BRACK   Well, you know, Mrs. Tesman, how you used to poke fun at my little stag parties. You said they were fit only for men of the strictest principles.

HEDDA   But no doubt Mr. Lovborg's principles are strict enough now. A converted sinner . . .

[BERTA *appears at the hall door.*]

BERTA   There's a gentleman asking if you are at home, ma'am . . .

HEDDA   Well, show him in.

TESMAN [*Softly.*]   I'm sure it is he! Think of that!

[EILERT LOVBORG *enters from the hall. He is tall and slender; of the same age as* TESMAN, *but looks older and somewhat worn-out. His hair and beard are blackish brown, his face long and pale, but with patches of color on the cheekbones. He is dressed in a well-cut new black suit. He carries dark gloves and a silk hat in his hand. He stops near the door, and makes an awkward bow, seeming somewhat embarrassed.*]

TESMAN [*Walks toward him and warmly shakes his hand.*] Well, my dear Eilert—at long last we meet again!

EILERT LOVBORG [*Speaks in a quiet voice.*]   Thanks for your letter, Tesman. [*Approaching* HEDDA.] Will you, too, shake hands with me, Mrs. Tesman?

HEDDA [*Taking his hand.*]   I am glad to see you, Mr. Lovborg. [*With a motion of her hand.*] I don't know whether you two gentlemen . . . ?

LOVBORG [*Bowing slightly.*]   Judge Brack, I think.

BRACK [*Doing likewise.*]   Oh, yes—in the old days . . .

TESMAN [*To* LOVBORG, *with his hands on his shoulders.*]   And now you must make yourself completely at home, Eilert! Mustn't he, Hedda?—For I hear you are going to settle in town again?

LOVBORG   Yes, I am.

TESMAN   Quite right, quite right. Let me tell you, I just got hold of your new book; but I haven't had time to read it yet.

LOVBORG   You may save yourself the trouble.

TESMAN   Why so?

LOVBORG   Because there is very little in it.

TESMAN   How can you say that?

BRACK   But it has been highly praised, I hear.

LOVBORG   That was what I wanted; so I put nothing into the book except what everyone would agree with.

BRACK   Very clever of you.

TESMAN   Well, but, my dear Eilert . . . !

LOVBORG   For now I intend to regain my position—to make a fresh start.

TESMAN [*A little embarrassed.*]   Ah, that is what you wish to do?

LOVBORG [*Smiling, puts down his hat, and pulls a folder, which is in an envelope, from his coat pocket.*]   But when this one appears, George Tesman, you will have to read it. For this is the real book—the book I have put my true self into.

TESMAN   Indeed? And what is it?

LOVBORG   It is the sequel.

TESMAN   The sequel? Of what?

LOVBORG   Of the book.

TESMAN   Of the new book?

LOVBORG   Of course.

TESMAN   Why, my dear Eilert—doesn't it come up to the present time?

LOVBORG   Yes, it does; and this one deals with the future.

TESMAN   With the future! But, good heavens, we know nothing of the future!

LOVBORG   No; but there is a thing or two that may be said about it all the same. [*Opens the folder.*] Look here . . .

TESMAN   Why, that's not your handwriting.

LOVBORG   I dictated it. [*Turning the pages.*] It's divided into two parts. The first deals with the civilizing forces of the future. And here is the second—[*running through the pages toward the end*]—forecasting the probable course of development.

TESMAN   How strange! I would never have thought of writing anything of that sort.

HEDDA [*At the glass door, drumming on the glass.*]   H'm . . . I should say not.

LOVBORG [*Returning the manuscript to the folder and putting the envelope on the table.*]   I brought it, thinking I might read you a little of it this evening.

TESMAN   That was very good of you, Eilert! But this evening . . . ? [*Looking at* BRACK.] I don't quite see how we can arrange it . . .

LOVBORG   Well, then, some other time. There is no hurry.

BRACK   I must tell you, Mr. Lovborg—there is a little party at my house this evening—mainly in honor of Tesman, you know . . .

LOVBORG [*Looking for his hat.*]   Oh—then I won't keep you . . .

BRACK   No, but listen—won't you do me the favor of joining us?

LOVBORG [*Curtly and decidedly.*]   No, I can't—thank you very much.

BRACK   Oh, nonsense—do! We shall be quite a small group. And I assure you we shall have a "jolly time," as Mrs. Hed—as Mrs. Tesman says.

LOVBORG   I have no doubt about it. But nevertheless . . .

BRACK   And you might bring your manuscript with you, and read it to Tesman at my house. I could give you a room to yourselves.

TESMAN   Yes, think of that, Eilert—why shouldn't you?

HEDDA [*Interrupting.*]   But, Tesman, if Mr. Lovborg would really rather not! I am sure Mr. Lovborg would much rather stay here and have supper with me.

LOVBORG [*Looking at her.*]   With you, Mrs. Tesman?

HEDDA   And with Mrs. Elvsted.

LOVBORG   Ah . . . [*Lightly.*] I saw her for a moment this morning.

HEDDA   Did you? Well, she is coming this evening. So you see you are almost obliged to stay, Mr. Lovborg, or she will have no one to take her home.

LOVBORG   That's true. Many thanks, Mrs. Tesman—in that case I will stay.

HEDDA   In this case I have a few instructions to give to the maid . . .

[*She walks to the hall door and rings.* BERTA *enters.*
HEDDA *talks to her in a whisper, and points toward the inner room.*
BERTA *nods and leaves again.*]

TESMAN [*At the same time, to* LOVBORG.]   Tell me, Eilert—is it this new subject—the future—that you are going to lecture about?

LOVBORG   Yes.

TESMAN   They told me at the bookdealer's that you are going to deliver a series of lectures this fall.

LOVBORG   That is my intention. I hope you won't take it badly, Tesman.

TESMAN   Oh no, not in the least! But . . . ?

LOVBORG   I can quite understand that it must be unpleasant to you.

TESMAN [*Downcast.*]   Oh, I can't expect you, out of consideration for me, to . . .

LOVBORG   But I shall wait till you have received your appointment.

TESMAN   Will you wait? Yes, but—yes, but—are you not going to compete with me?

LOVBORG   No; it is only the scholarly recognition I care for.

TESMAN   Why, my word—then Aunt Julia was right after all! Oh, yes—I knew it! Hedda! Just think—Eilert Lovborg is not going to stand in our way!

HEDDA [*Curtly.*]   Our way? Please leave me out of that matter.

[*She walks toward the inner room, where* BERTA *is placing a tray with decanters and glasses on the table.* HEDDA *nods approvingly, and comes forward again.* BERTA *leaves.*]

TESMAN [*At the same time.*]   And you, Judge Brack—what do you say to this?

BRACK   Well, I say that a scholarly recognition—h'm—may be alright . . .

TESMAN   Yes, certainly. But all the same . . .

HEDDA [*Looking at* TESMAN *with a cold smile.*]   You stand there looking as if you were thunderstruck . . .

TESMAN   Yes—so I am—I almost think . . .

BRACK   Don't you see, Mrs. Tesman, a thunderstorm has just passed over?

HEDDA [*Pointing toward the inner room.*]   Won't you have a glass of cold punch, gentlemen?

BRACK [*Looking at his watch.*]   Just one. Yes, it wouldn't be a bad idea.

TESMAN   A great idea, Hedda! Just the right thing! Now that the weight has been taken off my mind . . .

HEDDA   Won't you join them, Mr. Lovborg?

LOVBORG [*With a gesture of refusal.*]   No, thank you. Nothing for me.

BRACK   But, my word—cold punch is surely not poison.

LOVBORG   Perhaps not for everyone.

HEDDA   I will keep Mr. Lovborg company in the meantime.

TESMAN   Yes, yes, Hedda dear, do.

[*He and* BRACK *go into the inner room, seat themselves, drink punch, smoke cigarettes, and carry on a lively conversation during the following scene.* LOVBORG *remains standing beside the stove.* HEDDA *walks to the writing table.*]

HEDDA [*Raising her voice a little.*]   Do you care to look at some pictures, Mr. Lovborg? You know Tesman and I took them on our trip through Tyrol on our way home?

[*She takes an album, and places it on the table beside the sofa, and then she seats herself at the far corner of the sofa.* LOVBORG *approaches, stops, and looks at her. Then he takes a chair and seats himself to her left, with his back toward the inner room.*]

HEDDA [*Opening the album.*]   Do you see this mountain range, Mr. Lovborg? It's the Ortler group. Tesman has written the name underneath. Here it is: "The Ortler group near Meram."

LOVBORG [*Who has never taken his eyes off her, says softly and slowly.*]   Hedda—Gabler!

HEDDA [*Glancing hastily at him.*]   Ah! Sh!

LOVBORG [*Repeats softly.*]   Hedda Gabler!

HEDDA [*Looking at the album.*]   That was my name in the old days— when we two knew each other.

LOVBORG   And I must remind myself never to say Hedda Gabler again—never, as long as I live.

HEDDA [*Still turning the pages.*]   Yes, you must. And I think you should start practicing now. The sooner the better, I should say.

LOVBORG [*In a tone of indignation.*]   Hedda Gabler married? And married to—George Tesman!

HEDDA   Yes—that's how things are.

LOVBORG   Oh, Hedda, Hedda—how could you throw yourself away!

HEDDA [*Looks sharply at him.*]   What? I can't allow this!

LOVBORG   What do you mean?

[TESMAN *comes into the room and walks toward the sofa.*]

HEDDA [*Hears him coming and says in a casual tone.*]   And this is a view from the Ampezzo Valley, Mr. Lovborg. Just look at these peaks! [*Looks affectionately up at* TESMAN.]   What's the name of these interesting peaks, dear?

TESMAN   Let me see. Oh, those are the Dolomites.

HEDDA   Yes, that's it! Those are the Dolomites, Mr. Lovborg.

TESMAN   Hedda, dear, I only wanted to ask whether I shouldn't bring you a little punch after all? For yourself, at any rate?

HEDDA   Yes, do, please; and perhaps a few cookies.

TESMAN   No cigarettes?

HEDDA   No.

TESMAN   Very well.

[*He walks into the inner room and out to the right.* BRACK *sits in the inner room, and keeps an eye from time to time on* HEDDA *and* LOVBORG.]

LOVBORG [*Softly, as before.*]   Answer me, Hedda—how could you do this?

HEDDA [*Apparently absorbed in the album.*]   If you continue to speak to me in such a familiar manner, I won't talk to you.

LOVBORG   May I not be familiar even when we are alone?

HEDDA   No. You may be in your thoughts but you mustn't in words.

LOVBORG   Ah, I understand. It is an offense against George Tesman, whom you love.

HEDDA [*Glances at him and smiles.*]   Love? What an idea!

LOVBORG   You don't love him then!

HEDDA   But I won't listen to any disloyalty! Remember that!

LOVBORG   Hedda—answer me one thing . . .

HEDDA   Sh!

[TESMAN *enters with a small tray from the inner room.*]

TESMAN   Here you are! Isn't this tempting?

[*He puts the tray on the table.*]

HEDDA   Why do you bring it yourself?

TESMAN [*Filling the glasses.*]   Because I think it's such fun to wait on you, Hedda.

HEDDA   But you have poured two glasses. Mr. Lovborg said he wouldn't have any . . .

TESMAN   No, but Mrs. Elvsted will soon be here, won't she?

HEDDA   Yes, later—Mrs. Elvsted . . .

TESMAN   Had you forgotten her?

HEDDA   We were so absorbed in these photographs. [*Shows him a picture.*] Do you remember this little village?

TESMAN   Oh, it's that one just below the Brenner Pass. It was there we spent the night . . .

HEDDA   . . . and met that noisy group of tourists.

TESMAN   Yes, that was the place. If we could only have had you with
us, Eilert!

[*He returns to the inner room and sits beside* BRACK]

LOVBORG   Answer me this one thing, Hedda . . .

HEDDA   What?

LOVBORG   Was there no love in your friendship for me, either? Not a
spark—not a trace of love in it?

HEDDA   I wonder if there was? To me it seems as though we were two
good friends—two thoroughly intimate friends. [*Smilingly.*] You
were completely candid.

LOVBORG   It was you who made me so.

HEDDA   As I look back upon it all, I think there was really something
beautiful, something fascinating—something daring—in—in that
secret intimacy—that friendship which no living soul dares to
dream of.

LOVBORG   Yes, yes, Hedda! Wasn't it?—When I used to come to your
father's in the afternoon—and the General sat by the window
reading his papers—with his back to us . . .

HEDDA   And we two on the corner sofa . . .

LOVBORG   Always with the same magazine in front of us . . .

HEDDA   Instead of an album, yes.

LOVBORG   Yes, Hedda, and when I made my confessions to you—
told you about myself, things that at that time no one else knew!
There I sat and told you about my escapades—my wild days and
nights. Oh, Hedda—what was the power in you that drove me to
confess these things?

HEDDA   Did I have that power?

LOVBORG   How else can I explain it? And all those—those indirect
questions you used to throw at me . . .

HEDDA   Which you understood so well . . .

LOVBORG   How could you sit and question me like that? Question me
quite frankly . . .

HEDDA   In indirect terms, please remember.

LOVBORG   Yes, but straightforward nevertheless. Cross-question me
about—all that sort of thing?

HEDDA   And you did answer, Mr. Lovborg?

LOVBORG   Yes, that is just what I can't understand—in looking back
upon it. But tell me now, Hedda—wasn't there love at the basis of
our friendship? On your side, didn't you feel as though you might
remove my stains—if I chose you as my confessor? Wasn't it so?

HEDDA   No, not quite.

LOVBORG   What was your motive, then?

HEDDA   Don't you think it quite understandable that a young girl—whenever possible—without anyone knowing . . .

LOVBORG   What?

HEDDA   . . . would be glad to have a peek, now and then, into a world which . . .

LOVBORG   Which . . . ?

HEDDA   . . . which she is forbidden to know anything about?

LOVBORG   So that was it?

HEDDA   Partly. Partly—I think.

LOVBORG   Friendship is the zest of life. But why couldn't that have continued?

HEDDA   It was your fault.

LOVBORG   You broke up with me.

HEDDA   Yes, when our friendship threatened to develop into something more serious. Shame on you, Eilert Lovborg! How could you think of betraying our—our friendship?

LOVBORG   [*Clenching his fists.*]   Oh, why didn't you carry out your threat? Why didn't you shoot me down?

HEDDA   Because I have such a fear of scandal.

LOVBORG   Yes, Hedda, you are a coward at heart.

HEDDA   A terrible coward. [*Changing her tone.*] But it was lucky for you. And now you have found plenty of consolation at the Elvsteds'.

LOVBORG   I know what Thea has told you.

HEDDA   And perhaps you have told her something about us?

LOVBORG   Not a word. She is too stupid to understand anything of that sort.

HEDDA   Stupid?

LOVBORG   She is stupid about matters of that sort.

HEDDA   And I am cowardly. [*Bends over toward him, without looking him in the face, and says more softly.*] But now I will tell you something.

LOVBORG [*Eagerly.*]   What?

HEDDA   The fact that I didn't dare shoot you down . . .

LOVBORG   Yes!

HEDDA   . . . that was not my greatest cowardice—that evening.

LOVBORG   [*Looks at her a moment, understands and whispers passionately.*]   Oh, Hedda! Hedda Gabler! Now I begin to see a hidden reason beneath our friendship! You and I . . . ! After all, then, it was your craving for life . . .

HEDDA [*Softly, with a sharp glance.*]   Take care! Believe nothing of the sort!

[*Twilight has begun to fall. The hall door is opened from the outside by* BERTA]

HEDDA [*Closes the album with a bang and calls smilingly.*] Ah, at last! My dear Thea—come in!

[MRS. ELVSTED *enters from the hall. She is in evening dress. The door is closed behind her.*]

HEDDA [*On the sofa, stretches out her arms toward her.*]   My dear Thea— you don't know how I have been looking forward to seeing you!

[MRS. ELVSTED, *in passing, exchanges passing greetings with the gentlemen in the inner room, then walks to the table and shakes* HEDDA'S *hand.* LOVBORG *stands. He and* MRS. ELVSTED *greet each other with a silent nod.*]

MRS. ELVSTED   Should I go in and talk to your husband for a moment?

HEDDA   Oh, not at all. Leave those two alone. They will soon be leaving.

MRS. ELVSTED   Are they going out?

HEDDA   Yes, to a stag party.

MRS. ELVSTED [*Quickly, to* LOVBORG.]   Aren't you going?

LOVBORG   No.

HEDDA   Mr. Lovborg stays with us.

MRS. ELVSTED [*Takes a chair and is about to seat herself at his side.*]   Oh, how nice it is here!

HEDDA   No, thank you, my dear Thea! Not there! You'll be good enough to come over here. I will sit between you.

MRS. ELVSTED   Yes, just as you wish.

[*She walks round the table and seats herself on the sofa on* HEDDA'S *right.* LOVBORG *seats himself on his chair.*]

LOVBORG [*After a short pause, to* HEDDA.]   Isn't she lovely to look at?

HEDDA [*Lightly stroking her hair.*]   Only to look at?

LOVBORG   Yes. For we two—she and I—we are two real friends. We have absolute faith in each other; so we can sit and talk with complete honesty . . .

HEDDA   Not indirectly, Mr. Lovborg?

LOVBORG   Well . . .

MRS. ELVSTED [*Leaning close to* HEDDA.]   Oh, how happy I am, Hedda! Just think, he says I have inspired him, too.

HEDDA [*Looks at her with a smile.*]   Ah! Does he say that, dear?

LOVBORG   And then she is so courageous, Mrs. Tesman!

MRS. ELVSTED   Good heavens—am I courageous?

LOVBORG   Exceedingly—where your comrade is concerned.

HEDDA   Ah, yes—courage! If one only had that!

LOVBORG   What then? What do you mean?

HEDDA   Then life would perhaps be worth living, after all. [*With a sudden change of tone.*] But now, my dearest Thea, you really must have a glass of cold punch.

MRS. ELVSTED   No, thanks—I never drink anything of that kind.

HEDDA   Well, then, you, Mr. Lovborg.

LOVBORG   Nor I, thank you.

MRS. ELVSTED   No, he doesn't, either.

HEDDA [*Stares at him.*]   But if I say you must?

LOVBORG   It would be no use.

HEDDA [*Laughing.*]   Then I, poor soul have no power over you?

LOVBORG   Not in that respect.

HEDDA   But seriously, I think you should—for your own sake.

MRS. ELVSTED   Why, Hedda . . . !

LOVBORG   Why so?

HEDDA   On account of other people.

LOVBORG   Really?

HEDDA   Otherwise people might suspect that—deep in your heart—you didn't feel quite secure—or confident in yourself.

MRS. ELVSTED [*Softly.*]   Oh, please, Hedda . . . !

LOVBORG   People may think what they like—for the present.

MRS. ELVSTED [*Joyfully.*]   Yes, let them!

HEDDA   I saw it plainly in Judge Brack's face a moment ago.

LOVBORG   What did you see?

HEDDA   His contemptuous smile, when you didn't dare to join them in the inner room.

LOVBORG   Didn't dare? Of course I preferred to stay here and talk to you.

MRS. ELVSTED   What could be more natural, Hedda?

HEDDA   But the Judge could not know that. And I saw, too, the way he smiled and glanced at Tesman when you didn't dare to accept his invitation to his wretched little party.

LOVBORG   Didn't dare? Do you say I don't dare?

HEDDA   I don't say it. But that was what Judge Brack thought.

LOVBORG   Well, let him.

HEDDA   Then you aren't going with them?

LOVBORG   I will stay here with you and Thea.

MRS. ELVSTED   Yes, Hedda—how can you doubt that?

HEDDA [*Smiles and nods approvingly to* LOVBORG.]   Firm as a rock! Faithful to your principles, now and forever! Ah, that is how a man should be! [*Turns to* MRS. ELVSTED *and pats her.*] Well, now, what did I tell you, when you came to us this morning in such a state of despair . . .

LOVBORG [*Surprised.*]   Despair?

MRS. ELVSTED [*Terrified.*]   Hedda—oh, Hedda . . . !

HEDDA   You can see for yourself! You haven't the slightest reason to feel such terror . . . [*Interrupting herself.*] There! Now we can all three enjoy ourselves!

LOVBORG [*Visibly shaken.*]   Ah—what do you mean, Mrs. Tesman?

MRS. ELVSTED   Oh, my God, Hedda! What are you saying? What are you doing?

HEDDA   Don't get excited! That horrid Judge Brack is watching you.

LOVBORG   So she was in despair? Because of me?

MRS. ELVSTED [*Softly whimpering.*]   Oh, Hedda—now you have ruined everything!

LOVBORG [*Stares at her for a moment. His face is tense.*] So that was my comrade's total trust in me?

MRS. ELVSTED [*Imploringly.*]   Oh, my dearest friend—only let me explain . . .

LOVBORG [*Takes one of the glasses of punch, raises it to his lips, and says in a low, husky voice.*]   To your health, Thea!

[*He empties the glass, puts it down, and takes the second.*]

MRS. ELVSTED [*Softly.*]   Oh, Hedda, Hedda—how could you do this?

HEDDA   *I* do it? *I?* Are you crazy?

LOVBORG   Here's to your health, too, Mrs. Tesman. Thanks for the truth. Hurrah for the truth!

[*He empties the glass and is about to refill it.*]

HEDDA [*Puts her hand on his arm.*]   Come, come—no more for the present. Remember you are going to a party.

MRS. ELVSTED   No, no, no!

HEDDA   Sh! They are sitting watching you.

LOVBORG [*Putting down the glass.*]   Now, Thea—tell me the truth . . .

MRS. ELVSTED   Yes.

LOVBORG   Did your husband know that you had come after me?

MRS. ELVSTED [*Wringing her hands.*]   Oh, Hedda—do you hear what he is asking?

LOVBORG   Was it arranged between you and him that you were coming to town and look after me? Perhaps it was the Sheriff himself that urged you to come? Aha, my dear—no doubt he wanted my help in his office. Or was it at the card table that he missed me?

MRS. ELVSTED [*Softly, in agony.*]   Oh, Lovborg, Lovborg . . . !

LOVBORG [*Grabs a glass and is on the point of filling it.*]   Here's a glass for the old Sheriff, too!

HEDDA [*Preventing him.*]   No more just now. Remember, you have to read your manuscript to Tesman.

LOVBORG [*Calmly, putting down the glass.*]   It was stupid of me, Thea— to take it in this way. Don't be angry with me, my dear, dear comrade. You shall see—both you and the others—that if I had fallen once—now I have risen again! Thanks to you, Thea.

MRS. ELVSTED [*Radiant with joy.*]   Oh, thank heaven . . . !

> [BRACK *has in the meantime looked at his watch.*
> *He and* TESMAN *return to the living room.*]

BRACK [*Takes his hat and overcoat.*]   Well, Mrs. Tesman, it's time to leave.

HEDDA   I guess it is.

LOVBORG [*Rising.*]   Time for me, too, Judge Brack.

MRS. ELVSTED [*Softly and imploringly.*]   Oh, Lovborg, don't do it!

HEDDA [*Pinching her arm.*]   They can hear you!

MRS. ELVSTED [*With a suppressed cry.*]   Ow!

LOVBORG [*To* BRACK.]   You were good enough to invite me.

BRACK   Well, are you coming after all?

LOVBORG   Yes, many thanks.

BRACK   I'm delighted . . .

LOVBORG [*To* TESMAN, *putting the envelope containing the manuscript in his pocket.*]   I should like to show you one or two things before I send it to the printers.

TESMAN   That will be delightful. But, Hedda dear, how will Mrs. Elvsted get home?

HEDDA   Oh, that can be arranged somehow.

LOVBORG [*Looking toward the ladies.*]   Mrs. Elvsted? Of course, I'll come back and get her. [*Approaching.*] Around ten, Mrs. Tesman? Will that do?

HEDDA   Certainly. That will be fine.

TESMAN   Well, then, that's all right. But you must not expect me that early, Hedda.

HEDDA   Oh, you may stay as long—as long as you please.

MRS. ELVSTED [*Trying to conceal her anxiety.*]   Well, then, Mr. Lovborg—I shall stay here until you return.

LOVBORG [*With his hat in his hand.*]   Please do, Mrs. Elvsted.

BRACK   And now let the fun begin, gentlemen! I hope we shall have a jolly time, as a certain lovely lady puts it.

HEDDA   Ah, if only the lovely lady could be present unseen . . . !

BRACK   Why unseen?

HEDDA   In order to hear a little of your frivolity at first hand, Judge Brack.

BRACK [*Laughing.*]   I should not advise the lovely lady to try it.

TESMAN [*Also laughing.*]   Come, you're a nice lady, Hedda!

BRACK   Well, good-bye, good-bye, ladies.

LOVBORG [*Bowing.*]   About ten o'clock then.

[BRACK, LOVBORG, *and* TESMAN *leave by the hall door. At the same time,* BERTA *enters from the inner room with a lighted lamp, which she puts on the living room table; she leaves the way she came.*]

MRS. ELVSTED [*Who has gotten up and is wandering restlessly about the room.*]   Hedda—Hedda—what will come of all this?

HEDDA   At ten o'clock—he will be back. I can see him already—with vine leaves[3] in his hair—flushed and fearless . . .

MRS. ELVSTED   Oh, I hope so.

HEDDA   And then, you see—then he will have regained control of himself. Then he will be a free man for the rest of his days.

MRS. ELVSTED   Oh, God!—if he would only return as you describe him!

HEDDA   He will return exactly as I say, and not otherwise. [*Rises and approaches* THEA.] You may doubt him as long as you please; *I* believe in him. And now we will try . . .

MRS. ELVSTED   You have some hidden motive in this, Hedda!

HEDDA   Yes, I have. For once in my life, I want the power to control the destiny of a human being.

MRS. ELVSTED   Don't you have the power?

HEDDA   I don't—and have never had it.

---

[3]Bacchus (Greek god of wine) wore vine leaves in his hair. For Hedda, the vine leaves symbolize defiance of convention, as well as a childhood image she carried into adulthood.

MRS. ELVSTED   Not even your husband?

HEDDA   Do you think that is worth the trouble? Oh, if you could only understand how poor I am. And fate has made you so rich. [*Embraces her wildly.*] I think I must burn your hair off, after all.

MRS. ELVSTED   Let me go! Let me go! I am afraid of you, Hedda!

BERTA [*In the middle doorway.*]   Tea is served in the dining room, ma'am.

HEDDA   Very well. We are coming.

MRS. ELVSTED   No, no, no! I would rather go home alone! At once!

HEDDA   Nonsense! First you shall have a cup of tea, you silly little girl. And then—at ten o'clock—Eilert Lovborg will be here—with vine leaves in his hair.

[*She drags* MRS. ELVSTED *almost by force toward the middle doorway.*]

ACT III

SCENE: *The room at the* TESMANS'. *The curtains are closed over the middle doorway, and also over the glass door. The lamp, half turned down, and with a shade over it, is burning on the table. In the stove, the door of which stands open, there has been a fire, which is now nearly burned out.*
MRS. ELVSTED, *wrapped in a large shawl, and with her feet upon a footrest, sits close to the stove, sunk back in the armchair.* HEDDA, *fully dressed, lies sleeping on the sofa, with a blanket over her.*

MRS. ELVSTED [*After a pause, suddenly sits up in her chair, and listens anxiously. Then she sinks back again wearily, moaning to herself.*] Not yet! Oh, God—oh, God—not yet!

[BERTA *slips quietly in by the hall door. She has a letter in her hand.*]

MRS. ELVSTED [*Turns and whispers anxiously.*]   Well—has anyone come?

BERTA [*Softly.*]   Yes, a girl has just brought this letter.

MRS. ELVSTED [*Quickly reaching for it.*]   A letter! Give it to me!

BERTA   No, it's for Dr. Tesman, ma'am.

MRS. ELVSTED   Oh, indeed.

BERTA   It was Miss Tesman's maid who brought it. I'll put it here on the table.

MRS. ELVSTED   Yes, do.

BERTA [*Puts down the letter.*]   I think I had better put out the lamp. It's smoking.

MRS. ELVSTED   Yes, put it out. It will soon be daylight.

BERTA [*Putting out the lamp.*]   It is daylight already, ma'am.

MRS. ELVSTED   Yes, broad daylight! And no one has come back yet . . . !

BERTA   Lord bless you, ma'am—I guessed it would happen that way.

MRS. ELVSTED   You guessed?

BERTA   Yes, when I saw that a certain person had come back to town—and that he went off with them. For we've heard enough about that gentleman by now.

MRS. ELVSTED   Don't speak so loud. You will wake up Mrs. Tesman.

BERTA [*Looks toward the sofa and sighs.*]   No, no—let her sleep, poor thing. Should I put some wood on the fire?

MRS. ELVSTED   Thanks, not for me.

BERTA   Oh, very well.

[*She leaves quietly by the hall door.*]

HEDDA [*Is awakened by the closing of the door, and looks up.*]   What's that . . . ?

MRS. ELVSTED   It was only the maid . . .

HEDDA [*Looking about her.*]   Oh, we're here . . . ! Yes, now I remember. [*Sits up straight, stretches herself, and rubs her eyes.*] What time is it, Thea?

MRS. ELVSTED [*Looks at her watch.*]   It's past seven.

HEDDA   When did Tesman come home?

MRS. ELVSTED   He hasn't come yet.

HEDDA   Not come home yet?

MRS. ELVSTED [*Rising.*]   No one has returned.

HEDDA   Think of our watching and waiting here till four in the morning . . .

MRS. ELVSTED [*Wringing her hands.*]   And how I watched and waited for him!

HEDDA [*Yawns, and says with her hand before her mouth.*] Well, well—we might have saved ourselves the trouble.

MRS. ELVSTED   Did you get some sleep?

HEDDA   Oh, yes; I believe I have slept quite well. Haven't you?

MRS. ELVSTED   Not for a moment. I couldn't Hedda!—not to save my life.

HEDDA [*Rises and walks toward her.*]   There, there, there! There's nothing to be so alarmed about. I know quite well what has happened.

MRS. ELVSTED   Well, what do you think? Please tell me.

HEDDA   Why, of course, it has been a very late party at Judge Brack's . . .

MRS. ELVSTED   Yes, yes—that is clear enough. But all the same . . .

HEDDA   And then, you see, Tesman didn't want to come home and disturb us in the middle of the night. [*Laughing.*] Perhaps he didn't want us to see him either—immediately after such a party.

MRS. ELVSTED   But in that case—where can he be?

HEDDA   Of course, he has gone to his aunts' and slept there. They keep his old room ready for him.

MRS. ELVSTED   No, he can't be with them; for a letter has just come for him from Miss Tesman. There it is.

HEDDA   Really? [*Looks at the address.*] Why, yes, it's addressed by Aunt Julia. Well, then, he stayed at Judge Brack's. And as for Eilert Lovborg—he is sitting, with vine leaves in his hair, reading his manuscript.

MRS. ELVSTED   Oh, Hedda, you are just saying things you really don't believe.

HEDDA   You really are a little blockhead, Thea.

MRS. ELVSTED   Oh, yes, I guess I am.

HEDDA   And how extremely tired you look.

MRS. ELVSTED   Yes, I am very tired.

HEDDA   Well, then, you must do as I tell you. You must go into my room and lie down for a little while.

MRS. ELVSTED   Oh, no, no—I wouldn't be able to sleep.

HEDDA   I am sure you will.

MRS. ELVSTED   Well, but your husband is certain to come home soon; and then I want to know at once . . .

HEDDA   I shall certainly let you know when he comes.

MRS. ELVSTED   Do you promise, Hedda?

HEDDA   Yes, trust me. Just go in and sleep.

MRS. ELVSTED   Thanks; I'll try to.

> [*She leaves through the inner room.* HEDDA *walks up to the glass door and opens the curtains. The bright daylight streams into the room. Then she takes a hand mirror from the writing table, looks at herself in it and arranges her hair. Next she walks to the hall door and presses the bell button.* BERTA *appears soon at the hall door.*]

BERTA   Did you want anything, ma'am?

HEDDA   Yes; you must put some more wood in the stove. I am shivering.

BERTA   Oh my—I'll build the fire at once. [*She rakes the embers together and puts a piece of wood on them; then stops and listens.*] There was a ring at the front door, ma'am.

HEDDA   Then go to the door. I will take care of the fire.

BERTA   It'll soon burn.

[*She leaves by the hall door.* HEDDA *kneels on the footrest and puts some more pieces of wood in the stove. After a short time,* GEORGE TESMAN *enters from the hall. He looks tired and rather serious. He tiptoes toward the middle doorway and is about to slip through the curtains.*]

HEDDA [*At the stove, without looking up.*]   Good morning.

TESMAN [*Turns.*]   Hedda! [*Approaching her.*] Good heavens—are you up so early?

HEDDA   Yes, I am up very early this morning.

TESMAN   And I thought sure you would be sound asleep! Think of that, Hedda!

HEDDA   Don't speak so loud. Mrs. Elvsted is resting in my room.

TESMAN   Has Mrs. Elvsted been here all night?

HEDDA   Yes, since no one came to get her.

TESMAN   Ah, of course.

HEDDA [*Closes the door of the stove and rises.*]   Well, did you enjoy yourselves at Judge Brack's?

TESMAN   Have you been worried about me?

HEDDA   No, I would never worry. But I asked if you had enjoyed yourself.

TESMAN   Oh, yes—part of the time. Especially in the beginning of the evening; when Eilert read me part of his book. We arrived more than one hour too early—imagine that! Brack had all kinds of arrangements to make—so Eilert read to me.

HEDDA [*Seating herself by the table on the right.*]   Well? Tell me, then . . .

TESMAN [*Sitting on a footstool near the stove.*]   Oh, Hedda, you can't imagine what a book that is going to be! I believe it is one of the most remarkable works that has ever been written. Imagine!

HEDDA   Yes, yes; I don't care about that . . .

TESMAN   I must make a confession to you, Hedda. When he had finished reading—a horrible feeling came over me.

HEDDA   A horrible feeling?

TESMAN   I felt jealous of Eilert because he was capable of writing such a book. Imagine, Hedda!

HEDDA   Yes, yes, I can imagine!

TESMAN   And then how pitiful to think that he—with all his talents—should be unsalvageable, after all.

HEDDA   I suppose you mean that he has more courage than all the rest?

TESMAN   No, not at all—I mean that he is unrestrained when indulging in pleasure.

HEDDA   And what did it all lead to?

TESMAN   Well, to tell the truth, I think it might best be described as an orgy, Hedda.

HEDDA   Did he have vine leaves in his hair?

TESMAN   Vine leaves? No, I saw nothing of the sort. But he made a long, rambling speech praising the woman who had inspired him in his work—that was the phrase he used.

HEDDA   Did he mention her name?

TESMAN   No, he didn't; but I think he meant Mrs. Elvsted. He must have.

HEDDA   Well—where did you leave him?

TESMAN   On the way to town. We separated at the same time—the last of us at any rate; and Brack came with us to get a breath of fresh air. And then, you see, we decided to take Eilert home; for he had far more to drink than was good for him.

HEDDA   I can believe that.

TESMAN   But now comes the strange part of it, Hedda; or, I should rather say, the sad part of it. I confess I am almost ashamed—on Eilert's account—to tell you . . .

HEDDA   Oh, go on . . . !

TESMAN   Well, as we were getting near town, you see, I happened to drop a little behind the others. Only for a minute or two— understand?

HEDDA   Yes, yes, yes, but . . . ?

TESMAN   And then, as I hurried after them—what do you think I found by the side of the road?

HEDDA   Oh, how should I know!

TESMAN   You mustn't tell a soul, Hedda! Do you hear? Promise me, for Eilert's sake. [*Pulls an envelope holding a folder from his coat pocket.*] Imagine, dear, I found this.

HEDDA   Isn't that the folder he had with him yesterday?

TESMAN   Yes, it is all of his precious, irreplaceable manuscript! And he had dropped it, and knew nothing about it. Oh, think of it Hedda! How deplorable!

HEDDA   But why didn't you give it back to him at once?

TESMAN   I didn't dare to—in the state he was in . . .

HEDDA   Didn't you tell the others that you had found it?

TESMAN   Oh, of course not! Can't you understand that, for Eilert's sake, I couldn't do that.

HEDDA   So no one knows that you have Lovborg's manuscript?

TESMAN   No. And no one must know it.

HEDDA   Then what did you say to him later?

TESMAN   I didn't talk to him again at all; as soon as we reached town, he and two or three of the fellows slipped away from us and disappeared. Can you believe that?

HEDDA   Really? They must have taken him home.

TESMAN   Yes, so it would appear. And Brack, too, left us.

HEDDA   And what have you been doing since?

TESMAN   Well, I, and some of the others, went home with one of the party, a jolly fellow, and drank our morning coffee with him; or perhaps I should rather call it our night coffee? But now, after a little rest, and when Eilert, poor fellow, has had some sleep, I must take this back to him.

HEDDA [*Holds out her hand for the folder.*]   No—don't give it to him! Don't be in such a hurry, I mean. Let me read it first.

TESMAN   No, my dearest Hedda, I mustn't, I really mustn't.

HEDDA   You must not?

TESMAN   No—for you can't imagine what a state of despair he will be in when he wakes up and misses the manuscript. He has no copy of it, you know! He told me so.

HEDDA [*Looking searchingly at him.*]   Can't it be reproduced? Written over again?

TESMAN   No, I don't think that would be possible. For the inspiration, you see . . .

HEDDA   Yes, yes—I suppose it depends on that . . . [*Lightly.*] But, by the way—here is a letter for you.

TESMAN   Really?

HEDDA [*Handing it to him.*]   It came early this morning.

TESMAN   It's from Aunt Julia! What can it be? [*He puts the folder on the other footstool, opens the letter, glances through it, and jumps up.*] Oh, Hedda—she says that poor Aunt Rina is dying!

HEDDA   Well, we were prepared for that.

TESMAN   And that if I wish to see her again, I must hurry. I'll run over at once.

HEDDA [*Suppressing a smile.*]   Run?

TESMAN   Oh, my dearest Hedda—if you only would come with me! Think about it!

HEDDA [*Rises and says wearily, rejecting the idea.*]   No, no, don't ask me. I will not look upon sickness and death. I loathe all sorts of ugliness.

TESMAN   Alright, then . . . ! [*Rushing about.*] My hat . . . ? My overcoat . . . ? Oh, in the hall . . . I do hope I won't be too late, Hedda!

HEDDA   Oh, if you run . . .

[BERTA *appears at the hall door.*]

BERTA   Judge Brack is at the door, and wishes to know if he may come in.

TESMAN   At this time! No, I can't possibly see him.

HEDDA   But I can. [*To* BERTA.] Ask Judge Brack to come in.

[BERTA *leaves.*]

HEDDA [*Quickly, whispering.*]   The folder, Tesman!

[*She snatches it up from the stool.*]

TESMAN   Yes, give it to me!

HEDDA   No, no, I will keep it till you return.

[*She walks to the writing table and puts it in the bookcase.* TESMAN,
who is in a state of haste, cannot get his gloves on.
JUDGE BRACK *enters from the hall.*]

HEDDA [*Nodding to him.*]   You are an early bird, I must say.

BRACK   Yes, don't you think so? [*To* TESMAN.] Are you on the move, too?

TESMAN   Yes, I must rush off to my aunts'. Imagine—the invalid aunt is lying at death's door, poor soul.

BRACK   Oh! Is she really? Then don't let me detain you. At such a critical moment . . .

TESMAN   Yes, I must really rush . . . Good-bye! Good-bye!

[*He hurries out by the hall door.*]

HEDDA [*Approaching.*]   You seem to have had a particularly jolly night of it at your place, Judge Brack.

BRACK   I assure you I have not had my clothes off, Mrs. Hedda.

HEDDA   Not you, either?

BRACK   No, as you may see. But what has Tesman been telling you of the night's adventures?

HEDDA   Oh, some boring story. Only that they left and had coffee somewhere.

BRACK   I have heard about that coffee party already. Eilert Lovborg was not with them, I guess?

HEDDA   No, they had taken him home before that.

BRACK   Tesman too?

HEDDA   No, but some of the others, he said.

BRACK [*Smiling.*]   George Tesman is really an innocent soul, Mrs. Hedda.

HEDDA   Yes, heaven knows he is. Then there is something behind all this?

BRACK   Yes, perhaps there may be.

HEDDA   Well then, sit down, my dear Judge, relax and tell me your story.

[*She seats herself to the left of the table.* BRACK *sits near her, at the long side of the table.*]

HEDDA   Now then?

BRACK   I had special reasons for keeping track of my guests—or rather of some of my guests—last night.

HEDDA   Of Eilert Lovborg among them, perhaps?

BRACK   Frankly—yes.

HEDDA   Now you make me really curious . . .

BRACK   Do you know where he and some of the others ended the night, Mrs. Hedda?

HEDDA   If it is not quite unmentionable, tell me.

BRACK   Oh no, it's not at all unmentionable. Well, they put in an appearance at an exciting place.

HEDDA   Of the lively kind?

BRACK   Of the very liveliest . . .

HEDDA   Tell me more of this, Judge Brack . . .

BRACK   Lovborg, as well as the others, had a previous invitation. I knew all about it. But he had declined the invitation; for now, as you know, he has become a new man.

HEDDA   Up at the Elvsteds', yes. But he went after all, didn't he?

BRACK   Well, you see, Mrs. Hedda—unhappily the spirit moved him at my place last evening . . .

HEDDA   Yes, I hear he found inspiration.

BRACK   Pretty violent inspiration. Well, I guess that changed his resolution; for we men are unfortunately not always so firm in our principles as we ought to be.

HEDDA   Oh, I am sure you are an exception, Judge Brack. But as to Lovborg . . . ?

BRACK   To make a long story short—he landed at last in Madam Diana's place.

HEDDA   Madam Diana's?

BRACK   It was Madam Diana who was giving the party to a select circle of her admirers and her lady friends.

HEDDA   Is she a red-haired woman?

BRACK   Precisely.

HEDDA   A sort of a—singer?

BRACK   Oh yes—in her leisure moments. And moreover a mighty huntress—of men—Mrs. Hedda. You have no doubt heard of her. Eilert Lovborg was one of her most enthusiastic admirers—in the days of his glory.

HEDDA   And how did all this end?

BRACK   Far from amicably, it appears. After a most affectionate beginning, they seem to have come to blows . . .

HEDDA   Lovborg and she?

BRACK   Yes. He accused her or her friends of having robbed him. He claimed that his wallet had disappeared—and other things as well. In short, he seems to have made a terrible disturbance.

HEDDA   And what came of it all?

BRACK   It climaxed in an all-out brawl, in which the ladies as well as the gentlemen participated. Fortunately the police finally appeared on the scene.

HEDDA   The police too?

BRACK   Yes. I'm afraid it will prove a costly escapade for Eilert Lovborg, foolish man that he is.

HEDDA   What do you mean?

BRACK   He seems to have put up violent resistance—to have hit one of the officers on the head and ripped the coat off his back. So they had to drag him off to the police station with the rest.

HEDDA   How have you learned all this?

BRACK   From the police.

HEDDA [*Gazing straight before her.*]   So that's what happened. Then he had no vine leaves in his hair.

BRACK   Vine leaves, Mrs. Hedda?

HEDDA [*Changing her tone.*]   But tell me now, Judge—what is your real reason for tracking Lovborg's movements so carefully?

BRACK   In the first place, I wouldn't remain totally unaffected if it should come out in court that he had come straight from my house.

HEDDA   Will the matter go to court?

BRACK   Of course. However, I wouldn't be so much concerned about that. But I thought that, as a friend of the family, it was my duty to give you and Tesman a full account of his nocturnal exploits.

HEDDA   Why, Judge Brack?

BRACK   Why, because I have the nagging suspicion that he intends to use you as a sort of cover.

HEDDA   Oh, how can you think such a thing!

BRACK   Good heavens, Mrs. Hedda—we are not blind. Mark .my words! This Mrs. Elvsted will be in no hurry to leave town again.

HEDDA   Well, even if there should be anything between them, I suppose there are plenty of other places where they could meet.

BRACK   Not a single home. From now on, as before, every respectable home will be closed to Eilert Lovborg.

HEDDA   And mine should be too, you mean?

BRACK   Yes. I confess it would be more than painful to me if he were to have free run of your house. How much in the way, how intrusive, he would be, if he were to force his way into . . .

HEDDA   . . . into the triangle?

BRACK   Precisely. It would simply mean that I should find myself homeless.

HEDDA [*Looks at him with a smile.*]   So you want to be the only rooster in the chicken coop—is that your aim?

BRACK [*Nods slowly and lowers his voice.*]   Yes, that is my aim. And for that I will fight—with every weapon at my command.

HEDDA [*Her smile vanishing.*]   I see you are a dangerous person—when your interests are threatened.

BRACK   Do you think so?

HEDDA   I am beginning to think so. And I am exceedingly glad to think—that you have no hold over me.

BRACK [*With a hollow laugh.*]   Well, well, Mrs. Hedda—perhaps you are right there. If I had, who knows what I might be capable of?

HEDDA   Come, come now, Judge Brack! That sounds almost like a threat.

BRACK [*Rising.*]   Oh, not at all! The triangle, you know, should if possible, come about naturally.

HEDDA   There I agree with you.

BRACK   Well, now I have said all I had to say; and I had better be getting back to town. Good-bye, Mrs. Hedda. [*He walks toward the glass door.*]

HEDDA [*Rising.*]   Are you going through the garden?

BRACK   Yes, it's a short cut for me.

HEDDA   And then it is a back way, too.

BRACK   Quite so. I have no objection to back ways. They may be intriguing enough at times.

HEDDA   When there is target practice going on, you mean?

BRACK [*In the doorway, laughing at her.*]   Oh, people don't shoot their tame roosters, I hope!

HEDDA [*Also laughing.*]   Oh no, especially when there is only one
   rooster in the coop.

[*They exchange laughing nods of farewell. He leaves. She closes the door
behind him.* HEDDA, *who has become quite serious, stands for a moment
looking out. Then she peeks through the curtain over the middle doorway.
Next she walks to the writing table, takes* LOVBORG'S *folder out of the
bookcase, and is about to look through it.* BERTA *is heard speaking loudly in
the hall.* HEDDA *turns and listens. Then she hastily locks up the folder in
the drawer, and puts the key on the pen tray.* EILERT LOVBORG, *with his
overcoat on and his hat in his hand, jerks open the hall door. He looks
somewhat confused and irritated.*]

LOVBORG [*Looking toward the hall.*]   And I tell you I must and will
   come in! There!

[*He closes the door, turns, sees* HEDDA,
at once regains his self-control, and bows.]

HEDDA [*At the writing table.*]   Well, Mr. Lovborg, this is rather a late
   hour to get Thea.

LOVBORG   You mean rather an early hour to visit you. Do pardon me!

HEDDA   How do you know that she is still here?

LOVBORG   They told me at her boarding house that she had been out
   all night.

HEDDA [*Going to the oval table.*]   Did you notice anything strange in
   their attitude when they gave you that information?

LOVBORG [*Looks inquiringly at her.*]   Notice anything strange?

HEDDA   I mean, did they seem to think it odd?

LOVBORG [*Suddenly understanding.*]   Oh yes, of course! I am dragging
   her down with me! However, I didn't notice anything.—I suppose
   Tesman is not up yet?

HEDDA   No—I don't think so . . .

LOVBORG   When did he come home?

HEDDA   Very late.

LOVBORG   Did he tell you anything?

HEDDA   Yes, I gathered that you had an exceedingly jolly evening at
   Judge Brack's.

LOVBORG   Nothing more?

HEDDA   I don't think so. However, I was so terribly sleepy . . .

[MRS. ELVSTED *enters through the curtains of the middle doorway.*]

MRS. ELVSTED [*Going toward him.*]   Ah, Lovborg! At last . . . !

LOVBORG   Yes, at last. And too late!

MRS. ELVSTED [*Looks anxiously at him.*]   What is too late?

LOVBORG   Everything is too late now. It is all over with me.

MRS. ELVSTED   Oh no, no—don't say that!

LOVBORG   You will say the same when you hear . . .

MRS. ELVSTED   I won't listen to anything!

HEDDA   Perhaps you would prefer to talk to her alone? If so, I will leave you.

LOVBORG   No, stay—you too. I beg you to stay.

MRS. ELVSTED   Yes, but I won't listen to anything, I tell you.

LOVBORG   It is not last night's adventures that I want to talk about.

MRS. ELVSTED   What is it then . . . ?

LOVBORG   I must tell you that now our ways must part.

MRS. ELVSTED   Part!

HEDDA [*Involuntarily.*]   I knew it!

LOVBORG   You can no longer help me, Thea.

MRS. ELVSTED   How can you stand there and say that! No more help to you! Why can't I help you now, as before? Aren't we going to work together?

LOVBORG   From now on I shall do no work.

MRS. ELVSTED [*Despairingly.*]   Then what am I to do with my life?

LOVBORG   You must try to live your life as if you had never known me.

MRS. ELVSTED   But you know I can't do that!

LOVBORG   Try, even if you think you can't, Гhea. You must go home again . . .

MRS. ELVSTED [*In vehement protest.*]   Never in this world! Where you are, there will I be also! I will not let myself be driven away like this! I will remain here! I will be with you when the book is published.

HEDDA [*Half aloud, in suspense.*]   Ah yes—the book!

LOVBORG [*Looks at her.*]   My book and Thea's; for it belongs to both of us.

MRS. ELVSTED   Yes, I feel that it does. And that is why I have a right to be with you when it appears! I will see with my own eyes how respect and honor come to you again. And the happiness—the happiness—oh, I must share it with you!

LOVBORG   Thea—our book will never appear.

HEDDA   Oh!

MRS. ELVSTED   Never appear!

LOVBORG   Can never appear.

MRS. ELVSTED [*In agonized foreboding.*]   Lovborg—what have you done with the manuscript?

HEDDA [*Looks anxiously at him.*]   Yes, the manuscript . . .

MRS. ELVSTED   Where is it?

LOVBORG   Oh Thea—don't ask me about it!

MRS. ELVSTED   Yes, yes, I must know. I demand to be told at once.

LOVBORG   The manuscript . . . Well then—I have torn the manuscript into a thousand pieces.

MRS. ELVSTED [*Shrieks.*]   Oh no, no . . . !

HEDDA [*Involuntarily.*]   But that's not . . .

LOVBORG [*Looks at her.*]   Not true, you think?

HEDDA [*Collecting herself.*]   Oh well, of course—since you say so. But it sounded so improbable . . .

LOVBORG   It is true, all the same.

MRS. ELVSTED [*Wringing her hands.*]   Oh God—oh God, Hedda—torn his own work to pieces!

LOVBORG   I have torn my own life to pieces. So why shouldn't I tear my life's work too . . . ?

MRS. ELVSTED   And you did this last night?

LOVBORG   Yes, I tell you! Tore it into a thousand pieces—and scattered them on the fjord[4]—far out. There is cool sea water there at any rate—let them drift upon it—drift with the current and the wind. And then they will sink—deeper and deeper—as I shall, Thea.

MRS. ELVSTED   Do you know, Lovborg, that what you have done with the book—I shall think of it to my dying day as though you had killed a little child.

LOVBORG   Yes, you are right. It is a kind of child murder.

MRS. ELVSTED   How could you, then . . . ! Did not the child belong to me too?

HEDDA [*Almost inaudibly.*]   Ah, the child . . .

MRS. ELVSTED [*Breathing heavily.*]   It is all over then. Well, well, now I will leave, Hedda.

HEDDA   But you are not leaving town?

MRS. ELVSTED   Oh, I don't know what I shall do. I see nothing but darkness before me. [*She leaves by the hall door.*]

HEDDA [*Stands waiting for a moment.*]   So you are not going to take her home, Mr. Lovborg?

---

[4]A deep inlet from the sea, with steep mountains on either side.

LOVBORG   I? Through the streets? Do you want people to see her walking with me?

HEDDA   Of course I don't know what else may have happened last night. But is it so utterly beyond repair?

LOVBORG   It will not end with last night—I know that perfectly well. And the truth is that now I have no desire for that sort of life either. I won't begin it anew. She has broken my courage and my strength to face life.

HEDDA [*Looking straight before her.*]   So that pretty little fool has had her fingers in a man's destiny. [*Looks at him.*] But all the same, how could you treat her so heartlessly?

LOVBORG   Oh, don't say that it was heartless!

HEDDA   To destroy what has filled her whole soul for months and years! You do not call that heartless!

LOVBORG   To you I can tell the truth, Hedda.

HEDDA   The truth?

LOVBORG   First promise me—give me your word—that what I now confess to you Thea shall never know.

HEDDA   I give you my word.

LOVBORG   Good. Then let me tell you that what I said just now was untrue.

HEDDA   About the manuscript?

LOVBORG   Yes. I have not torn it to pieces—nor thrown it into the fjord.

HEDDA   No, no . . . But—where is it then?

LOVBORG   I have destroyed it just the same—utterly destroyed it, Hedda!

HEDDA   I don't understand.

LOVBORG   Thea said that what I had done seemed to her like a child murder.

HEDDA   Yes, so she said.

LOVBORG   But to kill his child—that is not the worst thing a father can do to it.

HEDDA   Not the worst?

LOVBORG   No. I wanted to spare Thea from hearing the worst.

HEDDA   Then what is the worst?

LOVBORG   Suppose now, Hedda, that a man—in the early hours of the morning—came home to his child's mother after a night of wild drunkenness, and said: "Listen—I have been here and there—in this place and in that. And I have taken our child with me—to this place and to that. And I have lost the child—utterly lost it. The devil knows into what hands it may have fallen—who may have had their hands on it."

HEDDA   Well—but when all is said and done, you know—this was only a book . . .

LOVBORG   Thea's pure soul was in that book.

HEDDA   Yes, so I understand.

LOVBORG   And you can understand, too, that for us together there is no future.

HEDDA   What path do you mean to take then?

LOVBORG   None. I will only try to put an end to it all—the sooner the better.

HEDDA [*A step nearer him.*]   Eilert Lovborg—listen to me. Won't you try to—to do it beautifully?

LOVBORG   Beautifully? [*Smiling.*] With vine leaves in my hair, as you used to dream in the old days . . . ?

HEDDA   No, no. I have lost my faith in the vine leaves. But beautifully nevertheless! For now and forever! Good-bye! You must go now—and do not come here ever again.

LOVBORG   Good-bye, Mrs. Tesman. And give George Tesman my regards. [*He is about to leave.*]

HEDDA   No, wait! I must give you a token of remembrance.

[*She walks to the writing table and opens the drawer and the pistol case; then returns to* LOVBORG *with one of the pistols.*]

LOVBORG [*Looks at her.*]   This? Is this the token?

HEDDA [*Nodding slowly.*]   Do you recognize it? It was aimed at you once.

LOVBORG   You should have used it then.

HEDDA   Take it—and you use it now.

LOVBORG [*Puts the pistol in his breast pocket.*]   Thanks!

HEDDA   And beautifully, Eilert Lovborg. Promise me that!

LOVBORG   Good-bye, Hedda Gabler.

[*He leaves by the hall door.* HEDDA *listens for a moment at the door. Then she walks to the writing table, takes out the folder holding the manuscript, peeks under the cover, pulls a few of the sheets partially out, and looks at them. Next she walks over and seats herself in the armchair beside the stove, with the folder in her lap. Next she opens the stove door, and then the folder.*]

HEDDA [*Throws several pages into the fire and whispers to herself.*]   Now I am burning your child, Thea!—Burning it! [*Throwing more pages*

into the stove.] Your child and Eilert Lovborg's. [*Throws the rest in.*]
I am burning—I am burning your child.

ACT IV

SCENE: *The same rooms at the* TESMANS'. *It is evening. The living room
is in darkness. The back room is lighted by the hanging lamp over the table.
The curtains over the glass door are closed.* HEDDA, *dressed in black, walks
back and forth in the dark room. Then she walks into the back room and
disappears for a moment to the left. She is heard to strike a few chords on the
piano. Then she reappears, and returns to the living room.* BERTA *enters
from the right, through the inner room, with a lighted lamp, which she
places on the table in front of the corner sofa in the living room. Her eyes are
red from crying and she has black ribbons on her cap. She walks quietly to
the right.* HEDDA *walks up to the glass door, pulls the curtain partly aside,
and looks out into the darkness. Shortly afterward,* MISS TESMAN, *in
mourning, with a hat and veil on, enters from the hall.* HEDDA *walks
toward her and holds out her hand.*

MISS TESMAN   Yes, Hedda, here I am, in mourning and alone; for now
my poor sister has at last found peace.

HEDDA   I have heard the news already, as you see. Tesman sent me a
message.

MISS TESMAN   Yes, he promised me he would. But even so, I myself
wanted to deliver to Hedda—here in the house of life—the tidings
of death.

HEDDA   That was very kind of you.

MISS TESMAN   Ah, Rina should not have left us just now. This is not
the time for Hedda's house to be a house of mourning.

HEDDA [*Changing the subject.*]   She died quite peacefully, didn't she,
Miss Tesman?

MISS TESMAN   Oh, her end was so calm, so beautiful. And then she
had the unspeakable happiness of seeing George once more—and
telling him good-bye. Hasn't he come home yet?

HEDDA   No. He wrote that he might be delayed. But won't you sit
down?

MISS TESMAN   No thank you, my dear, dear Hedda. I should like to,
but I have so much to do. I must prepare my dear one for her rest as
well as I can. She shall go to her grave looking her best.

HEDDA   Can't I help you in some way?

MISS TESMAN   Oh, you must not trouble yourself. Hedda Tesman must not take part in such mournful work. Nor let her thoughts dwell on it either—not at this time.

HEDDA   One is not always in control of one's thoughts . . .

MISS TESMAN [*Continuing.*]   Ah yes, that's how it is. At my home we shall be sewing the burial clothes; and at this home there soon will be sewing too, I suppose—but of another kind, thank God!

[GEORGE TESMAN *enters by the hall door.*]

HEDDA   Ah, you have come at last!

TESMAN   You here, Aunt Julia? With Hedda?

MISS TESMAN   I was just leaving my dear boy. Well, have you done all you intended?

TESMAN   No; I'm really afraid I have forgotten half of it. I must see you again tomorrow. Today my mind is in such turmoil. I can't keep my thoughts together.

MISS TESMAN   Why, my dear George, you mustn't take it so hard.

TESMAN   Mustn't . . . ? How do you mean?

MISS TESMAN   Even in your sorrow you must rejoice, as I do—rejoice that she is at rest.

TESMAN   Oh yes, yes—you are thinking of Aunt Rina.

HEDDA   You will feel lonely now, Miss Tesman.

MISS TESMAN   Just at first, yes. But that will not last very long, I hope. I'm sure I shall soon find a renter for poor Rina's little room.

TESMAN   Really? Who do you think will take it?

MISS TESMAN   Oh, there's always some poor invalid in need of nursing, unfortunately.

HEDDA   Would you really take such a burden upon you again?

MISS TESMAN   A burden! Heavens no, Hedda—it hasn't been a burden to me.

HEDDA   But suppose you had a total stranger on your hands . . .

MISS TESMAN   Oh, one soon makes friends with people in need and it's an absolute necessity for me to have someone to live for. Well, thank heaven, there may soon be something in *this* house, too, to keep an old aunt busy.

HEDDA   Oh, don't trouble yourself about anything here.

TESMAN   Yes, think—what a nice time we three might have together, if . . . ?

HEDDA   If . . . ?

TESMAN [*Uneasily.*]   Oh, nothing. It will all come out right. Let us hope so.

MISS TESMAN   Well, well, undoubtedly you two want to talk to each other. [*Smiling.*] And perhaps Hedda may have something to tell you too, George. Good-bye! I must go home to Rina. [*Turning at the door.*] How comforting to think that now Rina is with me and with my poor brother as well!

TESMAN   Yes, think of that, Aunt Julia! [MISS TESMAN *leaves by the hall door.*]

HEDDA [*Looks at* TESMAN *coldly and searchingly.*]   I almost believe your Aunt Rina's death affects you more than it does your Aunt Julia.

TESMAN   Oh, it's not that alone. It's Eilert I am so terribly uneasy about.

HEDDA [*Quickly.*]   Is there anything new about him?

TESMAN   I looked in at his place this afternoon, intending to tell him the manuscript was in safe keeping.

HEDDA   Well, didn't you find him?

TESMAN   No. He wasn't at home. But afterward I met Mrs. Elvsted, and she told me that he had been here early this morning.

HEDDA   Yes, soon after you left.

TESMAN   And he said that he had torn his manuscript to pieces?

HEDDA   Yes, so he said.

TESMAN   Why, good heavens, he must have been completely out of his mind! And I suppose you thought it best not to give it back to him, Hedda?

HEDDA   No, he did not get it.

TESMAN   But of course you told him that we had it?

HEDDA   No. [*Quickly.*] Did you tell Mrs. Elvsted?

TESMAN   No; I thought I had better not. But you should have told him. Imagine, if, in desperation, he should harm himself! Let me have the manuscript, Hedda! I will take it to him at once. Where is it?

HEDDA [*Cold and unmoved, leaning on the armchair.*]   I haven't got it.

TESMAN   Haven't got it? What in the world do you mean?

HEDDA   I have burned it—every line of it.

TESMAN [*With a violent movement of terror.*]   Burned! Burned Eilert's manuscript!

HEDDA   Don't scream so. The maid might hear you.

TESMAN   Burned! Why, good God . . . ! No, no, no! It's impossible!

HEDDA   It is so, just the same.

TESMAN   Do you know what you have done, Hedda? It's unlawful appropriation of lost property. Think of it! Just ask Judge Brack, and he'll tell you what it is.

HEDDA   I advise you not to speak of it—either to Judge Brack, or to anyone else.

TESMAN   But how could you do anything so unheard of? What put it into your head? What possessed you? Answer me!

HEDDA [*Suppressing a slight smile.*]   I did it for your sake, George.

TESMAN   For my sake!

HEDDA   This morning, when you told me about what he had read to you . . .

TESMAN   Yes, yes—what of it?

HEDDA   You admitted that you envied him his work.

TESMAN   Oh, of course I didn't mean that literally.

HEDDA   No matter—I could not bear the idea that anyone should outshine you!

TESMAN [*In an outburst of mingled doubt and joy.*]   Hedda! Oh, is this true? But—but—you have never shown your love like that before. Imagine!

HEDDA   Well, I may as well tell you that—just at this time . . . [*Impatiently, breaking off.*] No, no; you can ask Aunt Julia. She will tell you, quickly enough.

TESMAN   Oh, I almost think I understand you, Hedda! [*Clasps his hands together.*] Great heavens! Do you really mean it?

HEDDA   Don't shout so. The maid might hear you.

TESMAN [*Laughing in irrepressible glee.*]   The maid! Why, how silly you are, Hedda. It's only my old Berta! Why, I'll tell Berta myself.

HEDDA [*Clenching her hands together in desperation.*]   Oh, it is killing me—it is killing me!

TESMAN   What is, Hedda?

HEDDA [*Coldly, controlling herself.*]   All this—absurdity—George.

TESMAN   Absurdity! Do you see anything absurd in my being overjoyed at the news! But after all—perhaps I had better not say anything to Berta.

HEDDA   Oh . . . why not?

TESMAN   No, no, not yet! But I certainly must tell Aunt Julia. And also that you have begun to call me George too! Imagine! Oh, Aunt Julia will be so happy—so happy!

HEDDA   When she hears that I have burned Eilert Lovborg's manuscript—for your sake?

TESMAN   No, by the way—that affair of the manuscript—of course nobody must know about that. But that you love me that much, Hedda—Aunt Julia really must share my joy in that! I wonder, now, whether this sort of thing is usual in young wives?

HEDDA   I think you had better ask Aunt Julia that question too.

TESMAN   I will indeed, some other time. [*Looks uneasy and downcast again.*] And yet the manuscript—the manuscript! Good God! It is terrible to think what will become of poor Eilert now.

[MRS. ELVSTED, *dressed as in the first act, with hat and coat enters by the hall door.*]

MRS. ELVSTED [*Greets them hurriedly, and says in visible excitement.*]   Oh, dear Hedda, forgive my coming again.

HEDDA   What is the matter, Thea?

TESMAN   Is it something about Eilert Lovborg again?

MRS. ELVSTED   Yes! I am so afraid something terrible has happened to him.

HEDDA [*Grabs her arm.*]   Ah—do you think so?

TESMAN   Why, good Lord—what makes you think that, Mrs. Elvsted?

MRS. ELVSTED   I heard them talking at my boardinghouse—just as I came in. Oh, the most incredible rumors are in the air about him today.

TESMAN   Yes, so I heard! And I can vouch that he went straight home to bed last night.

HEDDA   Well, what did they say at the boardinghouse?

MRS. ELVSTED   Oh, I couldn't make out anything clearly. Either they knew nothing definite, or else . . . They stopped talking when they saw me; and I didn't dare ask.

TESMAN [*Moving about uneasily.*]   We must hope—we must hope that you misunderstood them, Mrs. Elvsted.

MRS. ELVSTED   No, no; I am sure they were talking about him. And I heard something about the hospital or . . .

TESMAN   The hospital?

HEDDA   No—surely that cannot be!

MRS. ELVSTED   Oh, I was in such terror! I went to his place and asked for him.

HEDDA   You had the courage to do that, Thea!

MRS. ELVSTED   What else could I do? I really couldn't bear not knowing.

TESMAN   But you didn't find him either?

MRS. ELVSTED   No. And the people knew nothing about him. He hadn't been back since yesterday afternoon, they said.

TESMAN   Yesterday! Imagine, how could they say that?

MRS. ELVSTED   Oh, I am sure something terrible must have happene to him.

TESMAN   Hedda dear—how about my making some inquiries . . .

HEDDA   No, no—don't get mixed up in this affair.

[JUDGE BRACK, *with hat in hand, enters by the hall door, which* BERTA *opens, and closes behind him. He looks serious and bows in silence.*]

TESMAN   Oh, is that you, my dear Judge?

BRACK   Yes. It was absolutely necessary that I see you this evening.

TESMAN   I can see that you have heard the news about Aunt Rina?

BRACK   Yes, that among other things.

TESMAN   Isn't it sad?

BRACK   Well, my dear Tesman, that depends on how you look at it

TESMAN [*Looks questioningly at him.*]   Has anything else happened?

BRACK   Yes.

HEDDA [*In suspense.*]   Anything sad, Judge Brack?

BRACK   That, too, depends on how you look at it, Mrs. Tesman.

MRS. ELVSTED [*Unable to contain her anxiety.*]   Oh! It is somethin about Eilert Lovborg!

BRACK [*With a glance at her.*]   What makes you think that, Madam Perhaps you have already heard something . . . ?

MRS. ELVSTED [*In confusion.*]   No, nothing at all, but . . .

TESMAN   Oh, for heaven's sake, tell us!

BRACK [*Shrugging his shoulders.*]   Well, I regret to say Eilert Lovbor has been taken to the hospital. He is at the point of death.

MRS. ELVSTED [*Shrieks.*]   Oh God! Oh God . . . !

TESMAN   To the hospital! And at the point of death!

HEDDA [*Involuntarily.*]   So soon then . . .

MRS. ELVSTED [*Wailing.*]   And we parted in anger, Hedda!

HEDDA [*Whispers.*]   Thea—Thea—be careful!

MRS. ELVSTED [*Not heeding her.*]   I must hurry! I must see him alive!

BRACK   It is useless, Madam. No one can see him.

MRS. ELVSTED   Oh, at least tell me what has happened to him? How did it happen?

TESMAN   You don't mean to say that he has himself . . . ?

HEDDA   Yes, I am sure he has.

TESMAN   Hedda, how can you . . . ?

BRACK [*Keeping his eyes fixed on her.*]   Unfortunately you have guessec quite correctly, Mrs. Tesman.

MRS. ELVSTED   Oh, how horrible!

TESMAN   Himself, then! Imagine that!

HEDDA   Shot himself!

BRACK   Correct again, Mrs. Tesman.

MRS. ELVSTED [*With an effort at self-control.*]   When did it happen, Mr. Brack?

BRACK   This afternoon—between three and four.

TESMAN   But, good Lord, where did he do it?

BRACK [*With some hesitation.*]   Where? Well—I guess at the place where he stayed.

MRS. ELVSTED   No, that can't be; for I was there between six and seven.

BRACK   Well then, somewhere else. I don't know exactly. I only know that he was found . . . He had shot himself—in the chest.

MRS. ELVSTED   Oh, how terrible! That he should die like that!

HEDDA [*To* BRACK.]   Was it in the chest?

BRACK   Yes—as I told you.

HEDDA   Not in the temple?

BRACK   In the chest, Mrs. Tesman.

HEDDA   Well, well—the chest is a good place, too.

BRACK   What do you mean, Mrs. Tesman?

HEDDA [*Evasively.*]   Oh, nothing—nothing.

TESMAN   And the wound is serious, you say?

BRACK   Absolutely fatal. The end has probably already come.

MRS. ELVSTED   Yes, yes, I feel it. The end! The end! Oh, Hedda . . . !

TESMAN   But tell me, how have you learned all this?

BRACK [*Curtly.*]   Through one of the police. A man I once had business with.

HEDDA [*In a clear voice.*]   At last an act of courage!

TESMAN [*Terrified.*]   Good heavens, Hedda! What are you saying?

HEDDA   I say there is beauty in this.

BRACK   H'm, Mrs. Tesman . . .

TESMAN   Beauty! Think of that!

MRS. ELVSTED   Oh, Hedda, how can there be beauty in such an act!

HEDDA   Eilert Lovborg has settled his account with life. He has had the courage to do—the one right thing.

MRS. ELVSTED   No, you must never think that it happened like that! He must have been out of his mind when he did it.

TESMAN   In despair!

HEDDA   Not in despair. I am certain of that.

MRS. ELVSTED   Yes, yes! Out of his mind! Just as when he tore up our manuscript.

BRACK [*Startled.*]   The manuscript? Has he torn that up?

MRS. ELVSTED   Yes, last night.

TESMAN [*Whispers softly.*]   Oh, Hedda, we shall never get out of this.

BRACK   H'm, very extraordinary.

TESMAN [*Moving about the room.*]   To think of Eilert going out of the world in this way! And not leaving behind him the book that would have immortalized his name . . .

MRS. ELVSTED   Oh, if only it could be put together again!

TESMAN   Yes, if it only could! I don't know what I wouldn't give . . .

MRS. ELVSTED   Perhaps it can, Mr. Tesman.

TESMAN   What do you mean?

MRS. ELVSTED [*Searches in the pocket of her dress.*]   Look here. I have kept all the loose notes he used to dictate from.

HEDDA [*A step forward.*]   Ah . . . !

TESMAN   You have kept them, Mrs. Elvsted?

MRS. ELVSTED   Yes, I have them here. I put them in my pocket when I left home. Here they still are . . .

TESMAN   Oh, let me see them!

MRS. ELVSTED [*Hands him a bundle of papers.*]   But they are in such disorder—all mixed up.

TESMAN   Perhaps we could make something out of them, after all! Perhaps if we two put our heads together . . .

MRS. ELVSTED   Oh yes, at least let us try . . .

TESMAN   We will do it! We must! I will dedicate my life to this task.

HEDDA   You, George? Your life?

TESMAN   Yes, or rather all the time I can spare. My own work must wait. Hedda—you do understand, don't I owe this to Eilert's memory?

HEDDA   Perhaps.

TESMAN   And so, my dear Mrs. Elvsted, we must devote ourselves completely to it. There is no use in brooding over what can't be undone. We must try to control our grief as much as possible, and . . .

MRS. ELVSTED   Yes, yes, Mr. Tesman, I will do my best.

TESMAN   Well then, come here. I can't rest until we have looked through the notes. Where shall we sit? Here? No, in there, in the back room. Excuse me, my dear Judge. Come with me, Mrs. Elvsted.

MRS. ELVSTED   Oh, if only it could be done!

[TESMAN *and* MRS. ELVSTED *go into the back room. She takes off her hat and coat. They both sit at the table under the hanging lamp, and are soon absorbed in the examination of the papers.* HEDDA *walks to the stove and sits in the armchair. Then* BRACK *walks over to her.*]

HEDDA [*In a low voice.*]   Oh, what sense of liberation comes from this act of Eilert Lovborg.

BRACK   Liberation, Mrs. Hedda? Well, of course, it is a release for him . . .

HEDDA   I mean for me. It gives me a sense of liberation to know that an act of deliberate courage is still possible in this world—an act of spontaneous beauty.

BRACK [*Smiling.*]   H'm—my dear Mrs. Hedda . . .

HEDDA   Oh, I know what you are going to say. For you are a kind of specialist, too, like—you know!

BRACK [*Looking hard at her.*]   Eilert Lovborg meant more to you than perhaps you are willing to admit to yourself. Am I wrong?

HEDDA   I don't answer such questions. I only know that Eilert Lovborg has had the courage to live his life by his own rules. And then—the last great act, with its beauty! Ah! That he should have the will and the strength to turn away from the banquet of life—so early.

BRACK   I am sorry, Mrs. Hedda, but I fear I must dispel this romantic illusion.

HEDDA   Illusion?

BRACK   Which could not have lasted long in any case.

HEDDA   What do you mean?

BRACK   Eilert Lovborg did not shoot himself—voluntarily.

HEDDA   Not voluntarily!

BRACK   No. The thing didn't happen exactly as I told it.

HEDDA [*In suspense.*]   Have you concealed something? What is it?

BRACK   For poor Mrs. Elvsted's sake I changed the facts a little.

HEDDA   What are the facts?

BRACK   First, that he is already dead.

HEDDA   At the hospital?

BRACK   Yes—without regaining consciousness.

HEDDA   What more have you kept from us?

BRACK   This—the event did not happen at the place where he stayed.

HEDDA   Oh, that can't make any difference.

BRACK   Perhaps it may. For I must tell you—Eilert Lovborg was found shot in—in Madam Diana's apartment.

HEDDA [*Makes a motion as if to rise, but sinks back again.*]   That is impossible, Judge Brack! He can't have been there again today.

BRACK   He was there this afternoon. He went there, he said, to demand the return of something which they had taken from him. Talked wildly about a lost child . . .

HEDDA   Ah—so that was why . . .

BRACK   I thought probably he meant his manuscript; but now I hear. he destroyed that himself. So I guess it must have been his wallet.

HEDDA   Yes, no doubt. And there—there he was found?

BRACK   Yes, there. With a pistol in his breast pocket, discharged. The bullet lodged in a vital part.

HEDDA   In the chest—yes.

BRACK   No—in the belly.

HEDDA [*Looks up at him with an expression of disgust.*]   That, too! Oh, what curse is it that everything I touch becomes ludicrous and vulgar?

BRACK   There is something else, Mrs. Hedda—another puzzling feature of this affair.

HEDDA   And what is that?

BRACK   The pistol he carried . . .

HEDDA [*Breathless.*]   Well? What about it?

BRACK   He must have stolen it.

HEDDA [*Leaps up.*]   Stolen it! That isn't true! He didn't steal it!

BRACK   No other explanation is possible. He must have stolen it . . . Sh!

[TESMAN *and* MRS. ELVSTED *have risen from the table in the back room, and come into the living room.*]

TESMAN [*With the papers in both his hands.*]   Hedda, dear, it is almost impossible to see by that lamp. Think of that!

HEDDA   Yes, I am thinking.

TESMAN   Would you mind if we sit at your writing table?

HEDDA   If you like. [*Quickly.*] No, wait! Let me clear it first!

TESMAN   Oh, you needn't trouble, Hedda. There is plenty of room.

HEDDA   No, no, let me clear it, I insist! I will put these things on the piano. There!

[*She has picked up an object, covered with sheet music, from under the bookcase, puts additional pieces of music on it, and carries all of it into the inner room, to the left.* TESMAN *puts the scraps of paper on the writing table, and moves the lamp there from the corner table. He and* MRS. ELVSTED *sit down and proceed with their work.* HEDDA *returns.*]

HEDDA [*Behind* MRS. ELVSTED'S *chair, gently stroking her hair.*] Well, my dear Thea, how are things going with the memorial to Lovborg's scholarship?

MRS. ELVSTED [*Looks dejectedly at her.*]   Oh, it will be terribly hard to put in order.

TESMAN   We must succeed. I am determined. And putting other people's papers in order is just the work for me.

[HEDDA *walks over to the stove, and seats herself on one of the footstools.* BRACK *stands over her, leaning on the armchair.*]

HEDDA [*Whispers.*]   What did you say about the pistol?

BRACK [*Softly.*]   That he must have stolen it.

HEDDA   Why stolen it?

BRACK   Because every other explanation appears impossible, Mrs. Hedda.

HEDDA   Really?

BRACK [*Glances at her.*]   Of course, Eilert Lovborg was here this morning. Wasn't he?

HEDDA   Yes.

BRACK   Were you alone with him?

HEDDA   Part of the time.

BRACK   Didn't you leave the room while he was here?

HEDDA   No.

BRACK   Try to remember. Weren't you out of the room for even a moment?

HEDDA   Yes, perhaps just a moment—out in the hall.

BRACK   And where was your pistol case during that time?

HEDDA   I had it locked up in . . .

BRACK   Well, Mrs. Hedda?

HEDDA   The case was there on the writing table.

BRACK   Have you looked since, to see if both pistols are still there?

HEDDA   No.

BRACK   Well, you needn't. I saw the pistol that was found in Lovborg's pocket, and I knew at once it was the one I had seen yesterday—and before, too.

HEDDA   Do you have it with you?

BRACK   No, the police have it.

HEDDA   What will the police do with it?

BRACK   Search till they find the owner.

HEDDA   Do you think they will succeed?

BRACK [*Bends over her and whispers.*]   No, Hedda Gabler—not as long as I keep silent.

HEDDA [*Looks frightened.*]   And if you don't say anything—what then?

BRACK [*Shrugs his shoulders.*]   There is always the possibility that the pistol was stolen.

HEDDA [*Firmly.*]   Death is preferable to that.

BRACK [*Smiling.*]   People say such things—but they don't mean them.

HEDDA [*Expressing another thought.*]   And supposing the pistol was not stolen, and the owner is discovered? What then?

BRACK   Well, Hedda—then comes the scandal.

HEDDA   The scandal!

BRACK   Yes, the scandal—of which you are so horribly afraid. You will, of course, be brought before the court—both you and Madam Diana. She will have to explain how it happened— whether it was an accident or murder. Did the pistol go off as he was trying to take it out of his pocket, to threaten her with? Or did she grab the pistol out of his hand, shoot him, and push it back into his pocket? That would be more like her; for she is a strong and determined woman.

HEDDA   But *I* have nothing to do with all this repulsive business.

BRACK   No. But you will have to answer the question: Why did you give Eilert Lovborg the pistol? And what conclusions will people draw from the fact that you gave it to him?

HEDDA [*Drops her head.*]   That is true. I didn't think of that.

BRACK   Well, fortunately, there is no danger, as long as I keep silent.

HEDDA [*Looks up at him.*]   So I am in your power, Judge Brack. I am to be subservient to your every wish, from this time forward.

BRACK [*Whispers softly.*]   Dearest Hedda—believe me—I shall not abuse my advantage.

HEDDA   I am in your power just the same. Subject to your will and your demands. A slave, a slave then! [*Rises impulsively.*] No, I can't endure the thought of that! Never!

BRACK [*Looks half-mockingly at her.*]   People generally get used to the inevitable.

HEDDA [*Returns his look.*]   Yes, perhaps. [*She crosses to the writing table. Suppressing an involuntary smile, she imitates* TESMAN'S *way of speaking.*] Well? How is it coming along, George?

TESMAN   Heaven knows, dear. In any case it will take months to do the work.

HEDDA [*As before.*]   Think of that! [*Softly stroking* MRS. ELVSTED'S *hair.*] Doesn't it seem ironic to you, Thea? Here you are sitting with Tesman—just as you used to sit with Eilert Lovborg?

MRS. ELVSTED   Ah, if I could only inspire your husband in the same way!

HEDDA   Oh, that will come, too—in time.

TESMAN   Yes, you know, Hedda—I really think I begin to feel something of the kind. But please won't you go and sit with Brack again?

HEDDA   Is there nothing I can do to help you two?

TESMAN   No, nothing in the world. [*Turning his head.*] I trust you to keep Hedda company, my dear Brack.

BRACK [*With a glance at* HEDDA.]   With the greatest of pleasure.

HEDDA   Thanks. But I am tired this evening. I will go and lie down on the sofa.

TESMAN   Yes, do, dear.

[HEDDA *walks into the back room and closes the curtains. A short pause. Suddenly she is heard playing a wild dance on the piano.*]

MRS. ELVSTED [*Stiffens in her chair.*]   Oh—what is that?

TESMAN [*Runs to the doorway.*]   Why, my dearest Hedda—don't play dance music tonight! Just think of Aunt Rina! And of Eilert, too!

HEDDA [*Sticks her head out between the curtains.*]   And of Aunt Julia. And of all the rest of them. After this, I will be quiet. [*Closes the curtains again.*]

TESMAN [*At the writing table.*]   It's not good for her to see us at this sad work. I'll tell you what, Mrs. Elvsted—you must take the empty room at Aunt Julia's, and then I will come over in the evenings, and we can sit and work there.

HEDDA [*In the inner room.*]   I hear what you are saying, Tesman. But how am *I* to get through the evenings here all alone?

TESMAN [*Turning over the papers.*]   Oh, I'm sure Judge Brack will be so kind to look in now and then, even though I am out.

BRACK [*In the armchair, calls out gleefully.*]   Every blessed evening, with the greatest of pleasure, Mrs. Tesman! We shall get on famously together, we two!

HEDDA [*Speaking loud and clear.*]   Yes, isn't that what you were aiming for, Judge Brack? Now that you are the only rooster in the coop?

[*A shot is heard within.* TESMAN, MRS. ELVSTED, *and* BRACK *leap to their feet.*]

TESMAN   Oh, now she is playing with those pistols again.

[*He throws back the curtains and runs in, followed by* MRS. ELVSTED. HEDDA *lies stretched on the sofa, lifeless. Confusion and cries.* BERTA *enters in alarm from the right.*]

TESMAN [*Shrieks to* BRACK.]   Shot herself! Shot herself in the temple! Imagine that!

BRACK [*Half-fainting in the armchair.*]   Oh my God!—people just don't do such things.

29

Albert Einstein

My Views

ALBERT *Einstein (1879–1955),
the discoverer of many physical and mathematical principles, is for many
observers the greatest scientist who ever lived. When he was born in Ulm, a city
in southwestern Germany, the political unification of that country was not even
ten years old. Yet life in Germany, as well as political conditions in Europe,
appeared stable and the future predictable. Major wars in Europe seemed most
unlikely, and no one would have thought at Albert's cradle that he, as well as
millions of others of his generation, would someday witness drastic upheavals
that would turn many into refugees and exiles. In Einstein's life these profound
developments included the calamities of the First World War (1914–18); the
seizure of power in Germany by the National Socialists (Nazis) in 1933;
banishment from his homeland and exile in the United States; the Second World
War; and the post-war period of constant threat of nuclear annihilation.*

*Shortly after Einstein's birth, his father had moved the family to Munich; as
owner of a small business, he hoped for a better livelihood there. When Albert
reached the age for elementary education, he was sent to one of the local Roman
Catholic schools, although his family was Jewish in ethnic origin. With respect
to cultural ideals—in literature, poetry, and music—the family was anchored in
the best Germany had to offer. And since Einstein's mother insisted that he learn
to play the violin, he also developed a deep love for music that never left him.*

*It seems that many views which Einstein held to throughout his lifetime were
acquired in his early years. He did not, however, embrace ideas uncritically.
Possessing a keen and reflective mind, he readily discerned those things which
were of positive and universal value. When, as an adult, he came in contact with
various ideologies and party views, he, in like manner, identified their positive
features and tried to apply them for the benefit of humankind. Of necessity, his
independent views won him the applause of some and the hostility of others. But*

to commit himself totally to one ideology, whether nationalism, capitalism, or socialism, was impossible to him. Even Zionism, which he supported during the rise of anti-Semitism and Nazism, was not an ideology for him, but an effort, simply, to provide the Jewish people a land of their own—a haven of safety.

Mind-numbing drill was something Einstein abhorred throughout his life, whether it took the form of rote memorization in school or the rigid exercises of the military. He was only too happy when at age fifteen he was able to transfer from his German school—which he saw as an extension of Prussian drill—to a Swiss school that taught a student to think. This move to Switzerland was good for him, because the young individualist Einstein would have been ill-suited to an increasingly uniformed and militarized Germany.

The idea that Europeans someday would slaughter each other again on the battlefield was repulsive to Einstein. No wonder that after the First World War he declared himself a pacifist and supported various peace efforts, chiefly ones backed by the League of Nations. He hoped that eventually the League might succeed in preventing the barbarity of wars. It turned out to be one of the ironies of history that the pacifist Einstein, in the course of the Second World War, suggested to President Franklin D. Roosevelt the making of an atomic bomb.

When he accepted the professorial chair at the University of Berlin, Germany, in 1914, Einstein became internationally famous as a scientist. Following the First World War, he used this fame to support humanitarian causes. Regardless of his ever-increasing world stature and recognition, his lifestyle always remained a simple one; the pomp, material gain, and applause that this world has to offer held slight attraction for him. Einstein's life remained dedicated to the unlocking of the secrets of the universe and the beneficial application of scientific knowledge to the welfare of the human species.

THE WORLD AS I SEE IT[1]

How strange is the lot of us mortals! Each of us is here for a brief sojourn; for what purpose he knows not, though he sometimes thinks he senses it. But without deeper reflection one knows from daily life that one exists for other people—first of all for those upon whose smiles

[1]Probably written in 1930 and published in English in 1931.

MY VIEWS   Albert Einstein, *Ideas and Opinions* (based on *Mein Weltbild*, ed. by Carl Seelig, and other sources), new trans. and revisions by Sonja Bargmann. (New York: Crown Publishers, 1954) 8–11, 36–40, 356–59. Used by permission of publisher.

and well-being our own happiness is wholly dependent, and then for the many, unknown to us, to whose destinies we are bound by the ties of sympathy. A hundred times every day I remind myself that my inner and outer life are based on the labors of other men, living and dead, and that I must exert myself in order to give in the same measure as I have received and am still receiving. I am strongly drawn to a frugal life and am often oppressively aware that I am engrossing an undue amount of the labor of my fellow-men. I regard class distinctions as unjustified and, in the last resort, based on force. I also believe that a simple and unassuming life is good for everybody, physically and mentally.

I do not at all believe in human freedom in the philosophical sense. Everybody acts not only under external compulsion but also in accordance with inner necessity. Schopenhauer's[2] saying, "A man can do what he wants, but not want what he wants," has been a very real inspiration to me since my youth; it has been a continual consolation in the face of life's hardships, my own and others', and an unfailing well-spring of tolerance. This realization mercifully mitigates the easily paralyzing sense of responsibility and prevents us from taking ourselves and other people all too seriously; it is conducive to a view of life which, in particular, gives humor its due.

To inquire after the meaning or object of one's own existence or that of all creatures has always seemed to me absurd from an objective point of view. And yet everybody has certain ideals which determine the direction of his endeavors and his judgments. In this sense I have never looked upon ease and happiness as ends in themselves—this ethical basis I call the ideal of a pigsty. The ideals which have lighted my way, and time after time have given me new courage to face life cheerfully, have been Kindness, Beauty, and Truth. Without the sense of kinship with men of like mind, without the occupation with the objective world, the eternally unattainable in the field of art and scientific endeavors, life would have seemed to me empty. The trite objects of human efforts—possessions, outward success, luxury—have always seemed to me contemptible.

My passionate sense of social justice and social responsibility has always contrasted oddly with my pronounced lack of need for direct contact with other human beings and human communities. I am truly a "lone traveler" and have never belonged to my country, my home, my friends, or even my immediate family, with my whole heart; in the face of all these ties, I have never lost a sense of distance and a need for

[2]Arthur Schopenhauer (1788–1860), German philosopher of pessimism.

solitude—feelings which increase with the years. One becomes sharply aware, but without regret, of the limits of mutual understanding and consonance with other people. No doubt, such a person loses some of his innocence and unconcern; on the other hand, he is largely independent of the opinions, habits, and judgments of his fellows and avoids the temptation to build his inner equilibrium[3] upon such insecure foundations.

My political ideal is democracy. Let every man be respected as an individual and no man idolized. It is an irony of fate that I myself have been the recipient of excessive admiration and reverence from my fellow-beings, through no fault, and no merit, of my own. The cause of this may well be the desire, unattainable for many, to understand the few ideas to which I have with my feeble powers attained through ceaseless struggle. I am quite aware that it is necessary for the achievement of the objective of an organization that one man should do the thinking and directing and generally bear the responsibility. But the led must not be coerced, they must be able to choose their leader. An autocratic system of coercion, in my opinion, soon degenerates. For force always attracts men of low morality, and I believe it to be an invariable rule that tyrants of genius are succeeded by scoundrels. For this reason I have always been passionately opposed to systems such as we see in Italy and Russia today. The thing that has brought discredit upon the form of democracy as it exists in Europe today is not to be laid to the door of the democratic principle as such, but to the lack of stability of governments and to the impersonal character of the electoral system. I believe that in this respect the United States of America have found the right way. They have a President who is elected for a sufficiently long period and has sufficient powers really to exercise his responsibility. What I value, on the other hand, in the German political system is the more extensive provision that it makes for the individual in case of illness or need. The really valuable thing in the pageant of human life seems to me not the political state, but the creative, sentient[4] individual, the personality; it alone creates the noble and the sublime,[5] while the herd as such remains dull in thought and dull in feeling.

This topic brings me to that worst outcrop of herd life, the military system, which I abhor. That a man can take pleasure in marching in fours to the strains of a band is enough to make me despise him. He has only been given his big brain by mistake; unprotected spinal marrow was all he needed. This plague-spot of civilization ought to be abolished

---

[3]Balance, harmony.   [4]Feeling, conscious.   [5]Exalted, grand.

with all possible speed. Heroism on command, senseless violence, and all the loathsome nonsense that goes by the name of patriotism—how passionately I hate them! How vile and despicable seems war to me! I would rather be hacked in pieces than take part in such an abominable business. My opinion of the human race is high enough that I believe this bogey would have disappeared long ago, had the sound sense of the peoples not been systematically corrupted by commercial and political interests acting through the schools and the Press.

The most beautiful experience we can have is the mysterious. It is the fundamental emotion which stands at the cradle of true art and true science. Whoever does not know it and can no longer wonder, no longer marvel, is as good as dead, and his eyes are dimmed. It was the experience of mystery—even if mixed with fear—that engendered[6] religion. A knowledge of the existence of something we cannot penetrate, our perceptions of the profoundest reason and the most radiant beauty, which only in their most primitive forms are accessible to our minds—it is this knowledge and this emotion that constitute true religiosity; in this sense, and in this alone, I am a deeply religious man. I cannot conceive of a God who rewards and punishes his creatures, or has a will of the kind that we experience in ourselves. Neither can I nor would I want to conceive of an individual that survives his physical death; let feeble souls, from fear or absurd egoism, cherish such thoughts. I am satisfied with the mystery of the eternity of life and with the awareness and a glimpse of the marvelous structure of the existing world, together with the devoted striving to comprehend a portion, be it ever so tiny, of the Reason that manifests itself in nature.

• • •

RELIGION AND SCIENCE[7]

Everything that the human race has done and thought is concerned with the satisfaction of deeply felt needs and the assuagement[8] of pain. One has to keep this constantly in mind if one wishes to understand spiritual movements and their development. Feeling and longing are the motive force behind all human endeavor and human creation, in however exalted a guise the latter may present themselves to us. Now what are the feelings and needs that have led men to religious thought

[6]Produced, gave rise to.
[7]Written for the *New York Times Magazine*, where it was published on November 9, 1930.
[8]Easing, or reducing.

and belief in the widest sense of the words? A little consideration will suffice to show us that the most varying emotions preside over the birth of religious thought and experience. With primitive man it is above all fear that evokes religious notions—fear of hunger, wild beasts, sickness, death. Since at this stage of existence understanding of causal connections is usually poorly developed, the human mind creates illusory beings more or less analogous[9] to itself on whose wills and actions these fearful happenings depend. Thus one tries to secure the favor of these beings by carrying out actions and offering sacrifices which, according to the tradition handed down from generation to generation, propitiate[10] them or make them well disposed toward a mortal. In this sense I am speaking of a religion of fear. This, though not created, is in an important degree stabilized by the formation of a special priestly caste which sets itself up as a mediator between the people and the beings they fear, and erects a hegemony[11] on this basis. In many cases a leader or ruler or a privileged class whose position rests on other factors combines priestly functions with its secular authority in order to make the latter more secure; or the political rulers and the priestly caste make common cause in their own interests.

The social impulses are another source of the crystallization of religion. Fathers and mothers and the leaders of larger human communities are mortal and fallible. The desire for guidance, love, and support prompts men to form the social or moral conception of God. This is the God of Providence, who protects, disposes, rewards, and punishes; the God who, according to the limits of the believer's outlook, loves and cherishes the life of the tribe or of the human race, or even life itself; the comforter in sorrow and unsatisfied longing; he who preserves the souls of the dead. This is the social or moral conception of God.

The Jewish scriptures admirably illustrate the development from the religion of fear to moral religion, a development continued in the New Testament. The religions of all civilized peoples, especially the people of the Orient, are primarily moral religions. The development from a religion of fear to moral religion is a great step in people's lives. And yet, that primitive religions are based entirely on fear and the religions of civilized peoples purely on morality is a prejudice against which we must be on our guard. The truth is that all religions are a varying blend

---

[9]Comparable.
[10]Appease, gain favor from.
[11]Leadership.

of both types, with this differentiation: that on the higher levels of social life the religion of morality predominates.

Common to all these types is the anthropomorphic[12] character of their conception of God. In general, only individuals of exceptional endowments, and exceptionally high-minded communities, rise to any considerable extent above this level. But there is a third stage of religious experience which belongs to all of them, even though it is rarely found in a pure form: I shall call it cosmic religious feeling. It is very difficult to elucidate[13] this feeling to anyone who is entirely without it, especially as there is no anthropomorphic conception of God corresponding to it.

The individual feels the futility of human desires and aims and the sublimity and marvelous order which reveal themselves both in nature and in the world of thought. Individual existence impresses him as a sort of prison and he wants to experience the universe as a single significant whole. The beginnings of cosmic religious feeling already appear at an early stage of development, for example, in many of the Psalms of David and in some of the Prophets. Buddhism, as we have learned especially from the wonderful writings of Schopenhauer, contains a much stronger element of this.

The religious geniuses of all ages have been distinguished by this kind of religious feeling, which knows no dogma and no God conceived in man's image; so that there can be no church whose central teachings are based on it. Hence it is precisely among the heretics of every age that we find men who were filled with this highest kind of religious feeling and were in many cases regarded by their contemporaries as atheists, sometimes also as saints. Looked at in this light, men like Democritus,[14] Francis of Assisi,[15] and Spinoza[16] are closely akin to one another.

How can cosmic religious feeling be communicated from one person to another, if it can give rise to no definite notion of a God and no theology? In my view, it is the most important function of art and science to awaken this feeling and keep it alive in those who are receptive to it.

[12]Human-like.

[13]Explain.

[14]Democritus of Abdera (460–362 B.C.), Greek philosopher of the atomistic school.

[15]Francis of Assisi (1182–1226), Italian friar, saint, and founder of the Franciscan religious order.

[16]Baruch Spinoza (1632–1677), Dutch philosopher of pantheism who was of Jewish parentage.

We thus arrive at a conception of the relation of science to religion very different from the usual one. When one views the matter historically, one is inclined to look upon science and religion as irreconcilable antagonists, and for a very obvious reason. The man who is thoroughly convinced of the universal operation of the law of causation cannot for a moment entertain the idea of a being who interferes in the course of events—provided, of course, that he takes the hypothesis of causality really seriously. He has no use for the religion of fear and equally little for social or moral religion. A God who rewards and punishes is inconceivable to him for the simple reason that a man's actions are determined by necessity, external and internal, so that in God's eyes he cannot be responsible, any more than an inanimate[17] object is responsible for the motions it undergoes. Science has therefore been charged with undermining morality, but the charge is unjust. A man's ethical behavior should be based effectually on sympathy, education, and social ties and needs; no religious basis is necessary. Man would indeed be in a poor way if he had to be restrained by fear of punishment and hope of reward after death.

It is therefore easy to see why the churches have always fought science and persecuted its devotees. On the other hand, I maintain that the cosmic religious feeling is the strongest and noblest motive for scientific research. Only those who realize the immense efforts and, above all, the devotion without which pioneer work in theoretical science cannot be achieved are able to grasp the strength of the emotion out of which alone such work, remote as it is from the immediate realities of life, can issue. What a deep conviction of the rationality of the universe and what a yearning to understand, were it but a feeble reflection of the mind revealed in this world, Kepler[18] and Newton[19] must have had to enable them to spend years of solitary labor in disentangling the principles of celestial[20] mechanics! Those whose acquaintance with scientific research is derived chiefly from its practical results easily develop a completely false notion of the mentality of the men who, surrounded by a skeptical world, have shown the way to kindred spirits scattered wide through the world and the centuries. Only one who has devoted his life to similar ends can have a vivid

[17]Without life.

[18]Johannes Kepler (1571–1630), German astronomer and mathematician, discovered three laws of planetary motion.

[19]Isaac Newton (1642–1727), English mathematician and natural philosopher, discovered the principle of universal gravitation.

[20]Heavenly, pertaining to outer space.

realization of what has inspired these men and given them the strength to remain true to their purpose in spite of countless failures. It is cosmic religious feeling that gives a man such strength. A contemporary has said, not unjustly, that in this materialistic age of ours the serious scientific workers are the only profoundly religious people.

• • •

MESSAGE TO THE ITALIAN SOCIETY FOR THE ADVANCEMENT OF SCIENCE[21]

Let me first thank you most sincerely for your kindness in inviting me to attend the meeting of the "Society for the Advancement of Science." I should gladly have accepted the invitation if my health had permitted me to do so. All I can do under the circumstances is to address you briefly from my home across the ocean. In doing so, I am under no illusion that I have something to say which would actually enlarge your insight and understanding. However, we are living in a period of such great external and internal insecurity and with such a lack of firm objectives that the mere confession of our convictions may be of significance even if these convictions, like all value judgments, cannot be proven through logical deductions.

There arises at once the question: should we consider the search for truth or, more modestly expressed, our efforts to understand the knowable universe through constructive logical thought as an autonomous objective of our work? Or should our search for truth be subordinated to some other objective, for example, to a "practical" one? This question cannot be decided on a logical basis. The decision, however, will have considerable influence upon our thinking and our moral judgment, provided that it is born out of deep and unshakable conviction. Let me then make a confession: for myself, the struggle to gain more insight and understanding is one of those independent objectives without which a thinking individual would find it impossible to have a conscious, positive attitude toward life.

It is the very essence of our striving for understanding that, on the one hand, it attempts to encompass[22] the great and complex variety of man's experience, and that on the other, it looks for simplicity and economy in the basic assumptions. The belief that these two objectives can exist side by side is, in view of the primitive state of our scientific knowledge, a matter of faith. Without such faith I could not have a

---

[21]Sent to the forty-second meeting of that learned society in Lucca (Italy), 1950.
[22]Encircle, include.

strong and unshakable conviction about the independent value of knowledge.

This, in a sense, religious attitude of a man engaged in scientific work has some influence upon his whole personality. For apart from the knowledge which is offered by accumulated experience and from the rules of logical thinking, there exists in principle for the man in science no authority whose decisions and statements could have in themselves a claim to "Truth." This leads to the paradoxical situation that a person who devotes all his strength to objective matters will develop, from a social point of view, into an extreme individualist who, at least in principle, has faith in nothing but his own judgment. It is quite possible to assert that intellectual individualism and scientific eras emerged simultaneously in history and have remained inseparable ever since.

Someone may suggest that the man of science as sketched in these sentences is no more than an abstraction which actually does not exist in this world, not unlike the *homo oeconomicus*[23] of classical economics. However, it seems to me that science as we know it today could not have emerged and could not have remained alive if many individuals, during many centuries, would not have come very close to the ideal.

Of course, not everybody who has learned to use tools and methods which, directly or indirectly, appear to be "scientific" is to me a man of science. I refer only to those individuals in whom scientific mentality is truly alive.

What, then, is the position of today's man of science as a member of society? He obviously is rather proud of the fact that the work of scientists has helped to change radically the economic life of men by almost completely eliminating muscular work. He is distressed by the fact that the results of his scientific work have created a threat to mankind since they have fallen into the hands of morally blind exponents of political power. He is conscious of the fact that technological methods made possible by his work have led to a concentration of economic and also of political power in the hands of small minorities which have come to dominate completely the lives of the masses of people who appear more and more amorphous.[24] But even worse: the concentration of economic and political power in few hands has not only made the man of science dependent economically; it also threatens

[23]Latin: economic man. A concept of human beings motivated solely by economic concerns.

[24]Indistinguishable, shapeless.

his independence from within; the shrewd methods of intellectual and psychic influences which it brings to bear will prevent the development of really independent personalities.

Thus the man of science, as we can observe with our own eyes, suffers a truly tragic fate. Striving in great sincerity for clarity and inner independence, he himself, through his sheer superhuman efforts, has fashioned the tools which are being used to make him a slave and to destroy him also from within. He cannot escape being muzzled by those who have the political power in their hands. As a soldier he is forced to sacrifice his own life and to destroy the lives of others even when he is convinced of the absurdity of such sacrifices. He is fully aware of the fact that universal destruction is unavoidable since the historical development has led to the concentration of all economic, political, and military power in the hands of national states. He also realizes that mankind can be saved only if a supranational system, based on law, would be created to eliminate for good the methods of brute force. However, the man of science has slipped so much that he accepts the slavery inflicted upon him by national states as his inevitable fate. He even degrades himself to such an extent that he helps obediently in the perfection of the means for the general destruction of mankind.

Is there really no escape for the man of science? Must he really tolerate and suffer all these indignities? Is the time gone forever when, aroused by his inner freedom and the independence of his thinking and his work, he had a chance of enlightening and enriching the lives of his fellow human beings? In placing his work too much on an intellectual basis, has he not forgotten about his responsibility and dignity? My answer is: while it is true that an inherently[25] free and scrupulous person may be destroyed, such an individual can never be enslaved or used as a blind tool.

If the man of science of our own days could find the time and the courage to think over honestly and critically his situation and the tasks before him and if he would act accordingly, the possibilities for a sensible and satisfactory solution of the present dangerous international situation would be considerably improved.

• • •

---

[25]Basically.

30

Sigmund Freud

Why War?

*L*IKE *Marx and Darwin, Dr. Sigmund Freud (1856–1939) was a major influence on the modern view of human existence. What others had offered as poetic insights, Freud established by clinical observation and persuasive reasoning, as well as by shrewd leaps of the imagination. He provided a naturalistic explanation of the role of unconscious elements in human behavior and destroyed the old view of the self as (exclusively) a conscious rational entity. His huge influence is evident in modern psychiatry, literature, art, and social thought.*

An Austrian specialist in nervous disorders, Freud began his career in a conventional manner: in his treatment of disturbed patients, he used methods that were firmly in the tradition of nineteenth-century medical science. Increasingly, however, Freud came to rely on imaginative insights and on literary myths and symbols to clarify the deepest springs of human behavior. At the same time, he held to his faith in reason as the indispensable means of finding the truths that would enable individuals to be freed from the dark forces within the subconscious.

Freud applied his findings in the study of disturbed patients to normal individuals and to society as a whole. He explained that human behavior is largely the result of instinctual drives, such as sexual and aggressive urges, which must be controlled if humans wish to enjoy the benefits of civilization. In fact, society could not function even on the most rudimentary level if individuals gave free rein to their instinctual drives and desires. However, it was clear to Freud that these human impulses are never permanently eliminated or neutralized. They are merely repressed, driven underground—from where they can erupt with elemental force at any time. Civilization, thus, is but a thin crust floating precariously over an ocean of instincts and emotions. It can therefore be predicted that all societies will, from time to time, suffer violent eruptions.

For Freud, the First World War served as the chief example of such an eruption on a gigantic scale—that is, the total triumph of destructive instincts over reason. Interestingly, as declarations of war were exchanged in 1914 among the great powers of Europe, even Freud was drawn into the mass mania. He, like so many millions of Europeans, was carried away by the rolling wave of war enthusiasm. As a loyal citizen of Austria, he believed in a quick victory for the Central Powers (Austria-Hungary and Germany) over their enemies. No wonder, then, that Freud's three sons served and fought in the army of their native land. It was not until a few months after the war started that Freud reflected more soberly on what had happened to Europe. He then realized that the First World War—with its brutality, carnage, and mass graves—was proof that the insight he had gained from his clinical studies of human behavior was correct.

After the War, Europeans in general came to understand the extent of the calamity they had brought upon themselves. Some considered it extremely fortunate that their civilization had survived at all. Recalling the horrors of destruction and the ten million soldiers killed, some Europeans declared themselves now to be pacifists. Among them were two outstanding men of science, Albert Einstein and Sigmund Freud. Unfortunately, a much larger number of people continued to idealize war—notably Benito Mussolini of Italy and Adolf Hitler of Germany, who by 1930 had attracted millions of followers in their nations. (See selection 33.)

To strengthen the cause of peace and check the threat of a new war, Einstein suggested to Freud (in 1931) an exchange of open letters on the subject. This exchange was to be carried out under the sponsorship of the League of Nations, the international organization which both men supported. (Einstein suggested in a private letter to Freud that humankind might be spared future wars if the peace-loving intellectual leaders of every country would form free associations. These, he hoped, would bring pressure upon politicians and persuade them to pursue peaceful courses of action.)

Freud's reply to Einstein, written in September 1932, was well prepared and well developed because Freud had given much thought to the problem of war and peace for many years. With regard to the elimination of future wars, Freud expressed himself as hopeful but very cautious. Any chance for lasting peace, he believed, would depend on whether or not the human intellect would eventually be able to control the instinctual forces that for so long have directed human behavior. The following selection is Freud's letter of reply to Einstein's question of "Why War?"

Vienna, September, 1932

Dear Professor Einstein,

When I heard that you intended to invite me to an exchange of views on some subject that interested you and that seemed to deserve the interest of others besides yourself, I readily agreed. I expected you to choose a problem on the frontiers of what is knowable today, a problem to which each of us, a physicist and a psychologist, might have our own particular angle of approach and where we might come together from different directions upon the same ground. You have taken me by surprise, however, by posing the question of what can be done to protect mankind from the curse of war. I was scared at first by the thought of my—I had almost written 'our'—incapacity for dealing with what seemed to be a practical problem, a concern for statesmen. But I then realized that you had raised the question not as a natural scientist and physicist but as a philanthropist: you were following the promptings of the League of Nations[1] just as Fridtjof Nansen,[2] the polar explorer, took on the work of bringing help to the starving and homeless victims of the World War. I reflected, moreover, that I was not being asked to make practical proposals but only to set out the problem of avoiding war as it appears to a psychological observer. Here again you yourself have said almost all there is to say on the subject. But though you have taken the wind out of my sails I shall be glad to follow in your wake and content myself with confirming all you have said by amplifying it to the best of my knowledge—or conjecture.

You begin with the relation between Right[3] and Might.[4] There can be no doubt that that is the correct starting-point for our investigation. But may I replace the word 'might' by the balder and harsher word 'violence'? Today right and violence appear to us as antitheses.[5] It can easily be shown, however, that the one has developed out of the other;

---

[1]The forerunner of today's United Nations, founded in 1920. Among other functions, the League of Nations—with headquarters in Geneva, Switzerland—was to try to make war obsolete through international cooperation and a system of "collective security."

[2]Fridtjof Nansen (1861–1930), Norwegian explorer of the arctic regions, naturalist, and humanitarian.

[3]Moral Right, law and justice.

[4]Force and power.

[5]Opposites.

WHY WAR?   Sigmund Freud, *Collected Papers*, vol. 5, ed. James Strachey. (New York: Basic Books, Inc., 1959) 273–87. "Why War?" trans. by James Strachey. Used by permission.

and if we go back to the earliest beginnings and see how that first came about, the problem is easily solved. You must forgive me if in what follows I go over familiar and commonly accepted ground as though it were new, but the thread of my argument requires it.

— It is a general principle, then, that conflicts of interest between men are settled by the use of violence. This is true of the whole animal kingdom, from which men have no business to exclude themselves. In the case of men, no doubt, conflicts of *opinion* occur as well which may reach the highest pitch of abstraction and which seem to demand some other technique for their settlement. That, however, is a later complication. To begin with, in a small human horde,[6] it was superior muscular strength which decided who owned things or whose will should prevail. Muscular strength was soon supplemented and replaced by the use of tools: the winner was the one who had the better weapons or who used them the more skillfully. From the moment at which weapons were introduced, intellectual superiority already began to replace brute muscular strength; but the final purpose of the fight remained the same—one side or the other was to be compelled to abandon his claim or his objection by the damage inflicted on him and by the crippling of his strength. That purpose was most completely achieved if the victor's violence eliminated his opponent permanently, that is to say, killed him. This had two advantages: he could not renew his opposition and his fate deterred others from following his example. In addition to this, killing an enemy satisfied an instinctual inclination which I shall have to mention later. The intention to kill might be countered by a reflection that the enemy could be employed in performing useful services if he were left alive in an intimidated condition. In that case the victor's violence was content to subjugate him instead of killing him. This was a first beginning of the idea of sparing an enemy's life, but thereafter the victor had to reckon with his defeated opponent's lurking thirst for revenge and sacrificed some of his own security.

Such, then, was the original state of things: domination by whoever had the greater might—domination by brute violence or by violence supported by intellect. As we know, this regime[7] was altered in the course of evolution. There was a path that led from violence to right or law. What was that path? It is my belief that there was only one: the path which led by way of the fact that the superior strength of a single

---

[6]Organized group, such as a clan or tribe.
[7]System of control.

individual could be rivalled by the union of several weak ones. *'L'union fait la force.*[8] Violence could be broken by union, and the power of those who were united now represented law in contrast to the violence of the single individual. Thus we see that right is the might of a community. It is still violence, ready to be directed against any individual who resists it; it works by the same methods and follows the same purposes. The only real difference lies in the fact that what prevails is no longer the violence of an individual but that of a community. But in order that the transition from violence to this new right or justice may be effected, one psychological condition must be fulfilled. The union of the majority must be a stable and lasting one. If it were only brought about for the purpose of combating a single domineering individual and were dissolved after his defeat, nothing would have been accomplished. The next person who found himself superior in strength would once more seek to set up a dominion by violence and the game would be repeated *ad infinitum.*[9] The community must be maintained permanently, must be organized, must draw up regulations to anticipate the risk of rebellion and must institute authorities to see that those regulations—the laws—are respected and to superintend the execution of legal acts of violence. The recognition of a community of interests such as these leads to the growth of emotional ties between the members of a united group of people—feelings of unity which are the true source of its strength.

Here, I believe, we already have all the essentials: violence overcome by the transference of power to a larger unity, which is held together by emotional ties between its members. What remains to be said is no more than an expansion and a repetition of this.

The situation is simple so long as the community consists only of a number of equally strong individuals. The laws of such an association will determine the extent to which, if the security of communal life is to be guaranteed, each individual must surrender his personal liberty to turn his strength to violent uses. But a state of rest of that kind is only theoretically conceivable. In actuality the position is complicated by the fact that from its very beginning the community comprises elements of unequal strength—men and women, parents and children—and soon, as a result of war and conquest, it also comes to include victors and vanquished, who turn into masters and slaves. The justice of the

[8]French: union makes strength.
[9]Endlessly.

community then becomes an expression of the unequal degrees of power obtaining within it; the laws are made by and for the ruling members and find little room for the rights of those in subjection. From that time forward there are two factors at work in the community which are sources of unrest over matters of law but tend at the same time to a further growth of law. First, attempts are made by certain of the rulers to set themselves above the prohibitions which apply to everyone—they seek, that is, to go back from a dominion of law to a dominion of violence. Secondly, the oppressed members of the group make constant efforts to obtain more power and to have any changes that are brought about in that direction recognized in the laws—they press forward, that is, from unequal justice to equal justice for all. This second tendency becomes especially important if a real shift of power occurs within a community, as may happen as a result of a number of historical factors. In that case right may gradually adapt itself to the new distribution of power or, as is more frequent, the ruling class is unwilling to recognize the change, and rebellion and civil war follow, with a temporary suspension of law and new attempts at a solution by violence, ending in the establishment of a fresh rule of law. There is yet another source from which modifications of law may arise, and one of which the expression is invariably peaceful: it lies in the cultural transformation of the members of the community. This, however, belongs properly in another connection and must be considered later.

Thus we see that the violent solution of conflicts of interest is not avoided even inside a community. But the everyday necessities and common concerns that are inevitable where people live together in one place tend to bring such struggles to a swift conclusion and under such conditions there is an increasing probability that a peaceful solution will be found. But a glance at the history of the human race reveals an endless series of conflicts between one community and another or several others, between larger and smaller units—between cities, provinces, races, nations, empires—which have almost always been settled by force of arms. Wars of this kind end either in the spoliation or in the complete overthrow and conquest of one of the parties. It is impossible to make any sweeping judgment upon wars of conquest. Some, such as those waged by the Mongols and Turks, have brought nothing but evil. Others, on the contrary, have contributed to the transformation of violence into law by establishing larger units within which the use of violence was made impossible and in which a fresh system of law led to the solution of conflicts. In this way the conquests of the Romans gave the countries round the Mediterranean the priceless *pax Romana*,[10] and the greed of the French kings to extend their dominions created a peacefully united and flourishing France. Paradoxical as it may sound, it must be admitted that war might be a far from inappropriate means of establishing the eagerly desired reign of 'everlasting' peace, since it is in a position to create the large units within which a powerful central government makes further wars impossible. Nevertheless it fails in this purpose, for the results of conquest are as a rule short-lived: the newly created units fall apart once again, usually owing to a lack of cohesion between the portions that have been united by violence. Hitherto, moreover, the unifications created by conquest, though of considerable extent, have only been *partial*, and the conflicts between these have cried out for violent solution. Thus the result of all these warlike efforts has only been that the human race has exchanged numerous, and indeed unending, minor wars for wars on a grand scale that are rare but all the more destructive.

If we turn to our own times, we arrive at the same conclusion which you have reached by a shorter path. Wars will only be prevented with certainty if mankind unites in setting up a central authority to which the right of giving judgment upon all conflicts of interest shall be handed over. There are clearly two separate requirements involved in this: the creation of a supreme authority and its endowment with the necessary power. One without the other would be useless. The League of Nations is designed as an authority of this kind, but the second condition has not been fulfilled: the League of Nations has no power of its own and can only acquire it if the members of the new union, the separate States, are ready to resign it. And at the moment there seems very little prospect of this. The institution of the League of Nations would, however, be wholly unintelligible if one ignored the fact that here was a bold attempt such as has seldom (perhaps, indeed, never on such a scale) been made before. It is an attempt to base upon an appeal to certain idealistic attitudes of mind the authority (that is, the coercive influence) which otherwise rests on the possession of power. We have heard that a community is held together by two things: the compelling force of violence and the emotional ties (identifications is the technical name) between its members. If one of the factors is absent, the community may possibly be held together by the other. The ideas that are appealed

---

[10]Roman Peace. A relatively peaceful period of approximately 200 years between the reigns of the emperors Augustus (27 B.C.–14 A.D.) and Marcus Aurelius (161–180 A.D.).

to can, of course, only have any significance if they give expression to important concerns that are common to the members, and the question arises of how much strength they can exert. History teaches us that they have been to some extent effective. For instance, the Panhellenic[11] idea, the sense of being superior to the surrounding barbarians—an idea which was so powerfully expressed in the Amphictyonies,[12] the Oracles[13] and the Games[14]—was sufficiently strong to mitigate the customs of war among Greeks, though evidently not sufficiently strong to prevent warlike disputes between different sections of the Greek nation or even to restrain a city or confederation of cities from allying itself with the Persian foe in order to gain an advantage over a rival. In the same way, the community of feeling among Christians, powerful though it was, was equally unable at the time of the Renaissance[15] to deter Christian States, whether large or small, from seeking the Sultan's[16] aid in their wars with one another. Nor does any idea exist today which could be expected to exert a unifying authority of the sort. Indeed it is all too clear that the national ideals by which nations are at present swayed operate in a contrary direction. Some people are inclined to prophesy that it will not be possible to make an end of war until Communist ways of thinking have found universal acceptance. But that aim is in any case a very remote one today, and perhaps it could only be reached after the most fearful civil wars. Thus the attempt to replace actual force by the force of ideas seems at present to be doomed to failure. We shall be making a false calculation if we disregard the fact that law was originally brute violence and that even today it cannot do without the support of violence.

I can now proceed to add a gloss[17] to another of your remarks. You express astonishment at the fact that it is so easy to make men enthusiastic about a war and add your suspicion that there is something at work in them—an instinct for hatred and destruction—which goes halfway

[11]Embracing or including *all* of the ancient Greeks.

[12]Associations of neighboring Greek city-states to protect a religious center or shrine.

[13]Religious centers in ancient Greece where the deities—on request—revealed future events through their priests.

[14]Periodic athletic competitions considered part of Greek religious observances.

[15]The era between the Middle Ages and the modern European world, generally between the 14th and 16th century.

[16]The ruler of a Muslim country, usually a ruler of the Ottoman (Turkish) Empire.

[17]Commentary.

to meet the efforts of the warmongers. Once again, I can only express my entire agreement. We believe in the existence of an instinct of that kind and have in fact been occupied during the last few years in studying its manifestations. Will you allow me to take this opportunity of putting before you a portion of the theory of the instincts which, after much tentative groping and many fluctuations of opinion, has been reached by workers in the field of psychoanalysis?

According to our hypothesis human instincts are of only two kinds: those which seek to preserve and unite—which we call 'erotic', exactly in the sense in which Plato uses the word 'Eros' in his *Symposium*,[18] or 'sexual', with a deliberate extension of the popular conception of 'sexuality'—and those which seek to destroy and kill and which we class together as the aggressive or destructive instinct. As you see, this is in fact no more than a theoretical clarification of the universally familiar opposition between Love and Hate which may perhaps have some fundamental relation to the polarity of attraction and repulsion that plays a part in your own field of knowledge. We must not be too hasty in introducing ethical judgments of good and evil. Neither of these instincts is any less essential than the other; the phenomena of life arise from the operation of both together, whether acting in concert or in opposition. It seems as though an instinct of the one sort can scarcely ever operate in isolation; it is always accompanied—or, as we say, alloyed[19]—with an element from the other side, which modifies its aim or is, in some cases, what enables it to achieve that aim. Thus, for instance, the instinct of self-preservation is certainly of an erotic kind, but it must nevertheless have aggressiveness at its disposal if it is to fulfil its purpose. So, too, the instinct of love, when it is directed toward an object, stands in need of some contribution from the instinct of mastery if it is in any way to possess that object. The difficulty of isolating the two classes of instinct in their actual manifestations is indeed what has so long prevented us from recognizing them.

If you will follow me a little further, you will see that human actions are subject to another complication of a different kind. It is very rarely that an action is the work of a *single* instinctual impulse (which must in itself be compounded of Eros and destructiveness). In order to make an action possible there must be as a rule a *combination* of such compounded motives. . . . There is no need to enumerate them all. A lust for

[18]Plato's (427–347 B.C.) book (dialogue) discussing ideal love.
[19]Blended, mixed.

aggression and destruction is certainly among them: the countless cruelties in history and in our everyday lives vouch for its existence and its strength. The gratification of these destructive impulses is of course facilitated by their admixture with others of an erotic and idealistic kind. When we read of the atrocities of the past, it sometimes seems as though the idealistic motives served only as an excuse for the destructive appetites; and sometimes—in the case, for instance, of the cruelties of the Inquisition[20]—it seems as though the idealistic motives had pushed themselves forward in consciousness, while the destructive ones lent them an unconscious reinforcement. Both may be true.

I fear I may be abusing your interest, which is after all concerned with the prevention of war and not with our theories. Nevertheless I should like to linger for a moment over our destructive instinct, whose popularity is by no means equal to its importance. As a result of a little speculation, we have come to suppose that this instinct is at work in every living being and is striving to bring it to ruin and to reduce life to its original condition of inanimate matter. Thus it quite seriously deserves to be called a death instinct, while the erotic instincts represent the effort to live. The death instinct turns into the destructive instinct if, with the help of special organs, it is directed outward, on to objects. The living creature preserves its own life, so to say, by destroying an extraneous one. Some portion of the death instinct, however, remains operative *within* the living being, and we have sought to trace quite a number of normal and pathological phenomena to this internalization of the destructive instinct. We have even been guilty of the heresy[21] of attributing the origin of conscience to this diversion inward of aggressiveness. You will notice that it is by no means a trivial matter if this process is carried too far: it is positively unhealthy. On the other hand if these forces are turned to destruction in the external world, the living creature will be relieved and the effect must be beneficial. This would serve as a biological justification for all the ugly and dangerous impulses against which we are struggling. It must be admitted that they stand nearer to Nature than does our resistance to them, for which an explanation also needs to be found. It may perhaps seem to you as though our theories are a kind of mythology and, in the present case, not even an agreeable one. But does not every science come in the end to a

---

[20]Papal (Roman Catholic) tribunal founded in the 13th century for the purpose of searching out persons holding "false" religious beliefs and punishing those judged guilty.

[21]A view contrary to the accepted view of the times.

kind of mythology like this? Cannot the same be said today of your own Physics?

For our immediate purpose then, this much follows from what has been said: there is no use in trying to get rid of men's aggressive inclinations. We are told that in certain happy regions of the earth, where nature provides in abundance everything that man requires, there are races whose life is passed in tranquillity and who know neither compulsion nor aggressiveness. I can scarcely believe it and I should be glad to hear more of these fortunate beings. The Russian Communists, too, hope to be able to cause human aggressiveness to disappear by guaranteeing the satisfaction of all material needs and by establishing equality in other respects among all the members of the community. That, in my opinion, is an illusion. They themselves are armed today with the most scrupulous care and not the least important of the methods by which they keep their supporters together is hatred of everyone beyond their frontiers. In any case, as you yourself have remarked, there is no question of getting rid entirely of human aggressive impulses; it is enough to try to divert them to such an extent that they need not find expression in war.

Our mythological theory of instincts makes it easy for us to find a formula for *indirect* methods of combating war. If willingness to engage in war is an effect of the destructive instinct, the most obvious plan will be to bring Eros, its antagonist, into play against it. Anything that encourages the growth of emotional ties between men must operate against war. These ties may be of two kinds. In the first place they may be relations resembling those toward a loved object, though without having a sexual aim. There is no need for psychoanalysis to be ashamed to speak of love in this connection, for religion itself uses the same words: 'You shall love your neighbor as yourself.' This, however, is more easily said than done. The second kind of emotional tie is by means of identification. Whatever leads men to share important interests produces this community of feeling, these identifications. And the structure of human society is to a large extent based on them.

A complaint which you make about the abuse of authority brings me to another suggestion for the indirect combating of the propensity to war. One instance of the innate and ineradicable inequality of men is their tendency to fall into the two classes of leaders and followers. The latter constitute the vast majority; they stand in need of an authority which will make decisions for them and to which they for the most part offer an unqualified submission. This suggests that more care should be taken than hitherto to educate an upper stratum[22] of men with independent minds, not open to intimidation and eager in the pursuit of truth, whose business it would be to give direction to the dependent masses. It goes without saying that the encroachments made by the executive power of the State and the prohibition laid by the Church upon freedom of thought are far from propitious for the production of a class of this kind. The ideal condition of things would of course be a community of men who had subordinated their instinctual life to the dictatorship of reason. Nothing else could unite men so completely and so tenaciously, even if there were no emotional ties between them. But in all probability that is a Utopian[23] expectation. No doubt the other indirect methods of preventing war are more practicable, though they promise no rapid success. An unpleasant picture comes to one's mind of mills that grind so slowly that people may starve before they get their flour.

The result, as you see, is not very fruitful when an unworldly theoretician is called in to advise on an urgent practical problem. It is a better plan to devote oneself in every particular case to meeting the danger with whatever weapons lie to hand. I should like, however, to discuss one more question, which you do not mention in your letter but which specially interests me. Why do you and I and so many other people rebel so violently against war? Why do we not accept it as another of the many painful calamities of life? After all, it seems quite a natural thing, no doubt it has a good biological basis and in practice it is scarcely avoidable. There is no need to be shocked at my raising this question. For the purpose of an investigation such as this, one may perhaps be allowed to wear a mask of assumed detachment. The answer to my question will be that we react to war in this way because everyone has a right to his own life, because war puts an end to human lives that are full of hope, because it brings individual men into humiliating situations, because it compels them against their will to murder other men, and because it destroys precious material objects which have been produced by the labors of humanity. Other reasons besides might be given, such as that in its present-day form war is no longer an opportunity for achieving the old ideals of heroism and that owing to the perfection of instruments of destruction a future war might involve the extermination of one or perhaps both of the antagonists. All this is

[22]Level, class.
[23]An impossible dream of perfection.

true, and so incontestably true that one can only feel astonished that the waging of war has not yet been unanimously repudiated. No doubt debate is possible upon one or two of these points. It may be questioned whether a community ought not to have a right to dispose of individual lives; every war is not open to condemnation to an equal degree; so long as there exist countries and nations that are prepared for the ruthless destruction of others, those others must be armed for war. But I will not linger over any of these issues; they are not what you want to discuss with me, and I have something different in mind. It is my opinion that the main reason why we rebel against war is that we cannot help doing so. We are pacifists[24] because we are obliged to be for organic reasons. And we then find no difficulty in producing arguments to justify our attitude.

No doubt this requires some explanation. My belief is this. For incalculable ages mankind has been passing through a process of evolution of culture. (Some people, I know, prefer to use the term 'civilization.') We owe to that process the best of what we have become, as well as a good part of what we suffer from. Though its causes and beginnings are obscure and its outcome uncertain, some of its characteristics are easy to perceive. It may perhaps be leading to the extinction of the human race, for in more than one way it impairs the sexual function; uncultivated races and backward strata[25] of the population are already multiplying more rapidly than highly cultivated ones. The process is perhaps comparable to the domestication of certain species of animals and it is undoubtedly accompanied by physical alterations; but we are still unfamiliar with the notion that the evolution of culture is an organic process of this kind. The psychical modifications that go along with the cultural process are striking and unambiguous. They consist in a progressive displacement of instinctual aims and a restriction of instinctual impulses. Sensations which were pleasurable to our ancestors have become indifferent or even intolerable to ourselves; there are organic grounds for the changes in our ethical and aesthetic[26] ideals. Of the psychological characteristics of culture two appear to be the most important: a strengthening of the intellect, which is beginning to govern instinctual life, and an internalization of the aggressive impulses, with all its consequent advantages and perils. Now war is in the

[24]Persons opposed to war and the use of violence to settle disputes.
[25]Levels, classes.
[26]Relating to the sense of beauty.

crassest opposition to the psychical attitude imposed on us by the cultural process, and for that reason we are bound to rebel against it; we simply cannot any longer put up with it. This is not merely an intellectual and emotional repudiation; we pacifists have a constitutional intolerance of war, an idiosyncracy[27] magnified, as it were, to the highest degree. It seems, indeed, as though the lowering of aesthetic standards in war plays a scarcely smaller part in our rebellion than do its cruelties.

And how long shall we have to wait before the rest of mankind become pacifists too? There is no telling. But it may not be Utopian to hope that these two factors, the cultural attitude and the justified dread of the consequences of a future war, may result within a measurable time in putting an end to the waging of war. By what paths or by what side-tracks this will come about we cannot guess. But one thing we *can* say: whatever fosters the growth of culture works at the same time against war.

I trust you will forgive me if what I have said has disappointed you, and I remain, with kindest regards,

Yours sincerely,

SIGM. FREUD

---

[27]Special trait of character.

31

Carl G. Jung

Approaching the Unconscious

*F*OR *an ever larger number of follow-
ers, Carl G. Jung (1875–1961) is the leader who seems most capable of guiding
humanity through a confusing and unintelligible world. Today, when the fruits
of rationalism, that is, science and technology, threaten our world with disasters
(including ecological and nuclear), Jung offers the vision of a healed world with
humans integrated into a cosmic whole. To move toward such a world,
Jung sees little need for additional discoveries of scientific facts or acquisition of
technological know-how. Rather, he stresses the importance of rediscovering the
images (archetypes) of man's past—which, in turn, point toward the
divine (numinous).*

*Born in Switzerland to the family of a Swiss Reformed (Calvinist) pastor,
Jung became aware of himself and the world around him while still very young.
At an age when children ordinarily absorb their experiences in a matter-of-fact
fashion, Jung pondered his observations and dreams, seeking an explanation for
them. Even as a child he contemplated the existence of two worlds. One was the
world of facts, the realm of the sciences, which in school demanded his attention.
The other was the world of value, which gave meaning to what he had learned
and experienced. Having a dual personality of complementary traits, rather
than contradictory ones, Jung eventually had to choose between the sciences and
the humanities. Though both were appealing, the sciences prevailed; and he
decided to study medicine rather than archaeology or religion.*

*In 1900, while preparing for his final medical exam, Jung realized that
psychiatry was the special field to which he wanted to devote his life. Psychiatry
was then still in its infancy—groping for answers rather than offering them.
Among those who were also captivated by psychiatry was the Viennese physician Sigmund Freud (see selection 30). When Freud's pioneering work came to*

his attention in the same year, Jung was fascinated by Freud's penetrating perceptions and daring speculations. In 1906 the two men met for the first time, and shortly thereafter Freud decided that this younger man should be the person to preserve and continue his work. Jung, however, had begun his research into mythology, and he soon came to the conclusion that Freud's dogmatic nature and their differing intellectual orientations would keep him from carrying on the Freudian psychological heritage.

Indeed, signs of disharmony between Jung and Freud appeared as early as 1912. The break came over a number of issues: for example, the role of sexuality in infant behavior, and Freud's insistence that sexuality is the prime psychological force in the life of a human being. Jung judged the latter an unwarranted conclusion, especially in view of the fact that inquiry into the human psyche was then of very recent date and, in his view, needed to be pursued without restrictions. Another reason for disagreement was the fact that Freud focused on certain key events in a person's life, rather than considering them in relation to the person's cultural heritage. Elements of this heritage, especially myth, folklore, and long-standing religious practices, were of primary importance to Jung; whereas Freud assigned them to the realm of the occult.

While pursuing his studies, Jung noted that people in the West engage in many visible acts whose meaning has been either lost or forgotten. He attributed this loss to the fact that Western culture has valued reasoning and experience over feeling and intuition, or result and process over meaning and vision. Jung made the rediscovery of meaning and vision the center of his life's work. He believed that as one progresses in unlocking myth, religion, and philosophy, one discovers the ancient images and impressions common to all humankind—which he termed archetypes. *Jung came to the conclusion that dreams are often expressions of these repeated experiences of humankind. For Freud, on the other hand, dreams are responses, mainly, to sexual fantasies and certain disturbing experiences of particular individuals.*

Some people have found Jung's work vague and mystical, a relapse into a spirit-world long believed to have been overcome by reason, science and "enlightenment." Yet, for others, his message fills an inner emptiness—by restoring meaning *and* wholeness *to their lives.*

• • •

THE SOUL OF MAN

What we call civilized consciousness has steadily separated itself from the basic instincts. But these instincts have not disappeared. They have merely lost their contact with our consciousness and are thus forced to assert themselves in an indirect fashion. This may be by means of physical symptoms in the case of a neurosis,[1] or by means of incidents of various kinds, like unaccountable moods, unexpected forgetfulness, or mistakes in speech.

A man likes to believe that he is the master of his soul.[2] But as long as he is unable to control his moods and emotions, or to be conscious of the myriad secret ways in which unconscious factors insinuate themselves into his arrangements and decisions, he is certainly not his own master. These unconscious factors owe their existence to the autonomy of the archetypes.[3] Modern man protects himself against seeing his own split state by a system of compartments. Certain areas of outer life and of his own behavior are kept, as it were, in separate drawers and are never confronted with one another.

As an example of this so-called compartment psychology, I remember the case of an alcoholic who had come under the laudable influence of a certain religious movement, and, fascinated by its enthusiasm, had forgotten that he needed a drink. He was obviously and miraculously cured by Jesus, and he was correspondingly displayed as a witness to divine grace or to the efficiency of the said religious organization. But after a few weeks of public confessions, the novelty began to pale and some alcoholic refreshment seemed to be indicated, and so he drank again. But this time the helpful organization came to the conclusion that the case was "pathological"[4] and obviously not suitable for an intervention by Jesus, so they put him into a clinic to let the doctor do better than the divine Healer.

---

[1]An emotional or physical illness arising from unsolved conflicts between human drives and their environment.

[2]Mind, or essence of a human being.

[3]Subconscious images and impressions—tracing back to the earliest ages of the human species—which persons inherit, collectively, along with their physical traits.

[4]Caused by disease.

APPROACHING THE UNCONSCIOUS   Carl G. Jung et al., *Man and His Symbols*, ed. Carl G. Jung (New York: Dell Publishing, 1964), 72–78, 80–88, 90–94. Copyright © 1964 Aldus Books, Ltd., London. Used by permission of publisher.

This is an aspect of the modern "cultural" mind that is worth looking into. It shows an alarming degree of dissociation and psychological confusion.

If, for a moment, we regard mankind as one individual, we see that the human race is like a person carried away by unconscious powers; and the human race also likes to keep certain problems tucked away in separate drawers. But this is why we should give a great deal of consideration to what we are doing, for mankind is now threatened by self-created and deadly dangers that are growing beyond our control. Our world is, so to speak, dissociated like a neurotic, with the Iron Curtain marking the symbolic line of division. Western man, becoming aware of the aggressive will to power of the East, sees himself forced to take extraordinary measures of defense, at the same time as he prides himself on his virtue and good intentions.

What he fails to see is that it is his own vices, which he has covered up by good international manners, that are thrown back in his face by the communist world, shamelessly and methodically. What the West has tolerated, but secretly and with a slight sense of shame (the diplomatic lie, systematic deception, veiled threats), comes back into the open and in full measure from the East and ties us up in neurotic knots. It is the face of his own evil shadow that grins at Western man from the other side of the Iron Curtain.

It is this state of affairs that explains the peculiar feeling of helplessness of so many people in Western societies. They have begun to realize that the difficulties confronting us are moral problems, and that the attempts to answer them by a policy of piling up nuclear arms or by economic "competition" is achieving little, for it cuts both ways. Many of us now understand that moral and mental means would be more efficient, since they could provide us with psychic[5] immunity against the ever-increasing infection.

But all such attempts have proved singularly ineffective, and will do so as long as we try to convince ourselves and the world that it is only *they* (that is, our opponents) who are wrong. It would be much more to the point for us to make a serious attempt to recognize our own shadow and its nefarious doings. If we could see our shadow (the dark side of our nature), we should be immune to any moral and mental infection and insinuation. As matters now stand, we lay ourselves open to every infection, because we are really doing practically the same thing as *they*.

[5]Residing in the mind or soul.

Only we have the additional disadvantage that we neither see nor want to understand what we ourselves are doing, under the cover of good manners.

The communist world, it may be noted, has one big myth (which we call an illusion, in the vain hope that our superior judgment will make it disappear). It is the time-hallowed archetypal dream of a Golden Age (or Paradise), where everything is provided in abundance for everyone, and a great, just, and wise chief rules over a human kindergarten. This powerful archetype in its infantile form has gripped them, but it will never disappear from the world at the mere sight of our superior points of view. We even support it by our own childishness, for our Western civilization is in the grip of the same mythology. Unconsciously, we cherish the same prejudices, hopes, and expectations. We too believe in the welfare state, in universal peace, in the equality of man, in his eternal human rights, in justice, truth, and (do not say it too loudly) in the Kingdom of God on Earth.

The sad truth is that man's real life consists of a complex of inexorable opposites—day and night, birth and death, happiness and misery, good and evil. We are not even sure that one will prevail against the other, that good will overcome evil, or joy defeat pain. Life is a battleground. It always has been, and always will be; and if it were not so, existence would come to an end.

It was precisely this conflict within man that led the early Christians to expect and hope for an early end to this world, or the Buddhists to reject all earthly desires and aspirations. These basic answers would be frankly suicidal if they were not linked up with peculiar mental and moral ideas and practices that constitute the bulk of both religions and that, to a certain extent, modify their radical denial of the world.

I stress this point because, in our time, there are millions of people who have lost faith in any kind of religion. Such people do not understand their religion any longer. While life runs smoothly without religion, the loss remains as good as unnoticed. But when suffering comes, it is another matter. That is when people begin to seek a way out and to reflect about the meaning of life and its bewildering and painful experiences.

It is significant that the psychological doctor (within my experience) is consulted more by Jews and Protestants than by Catholics. This might be expected, for the Catholic Church still feels responsible for the *cura animarum* (the care of the soul's welfare). But in this scientific age, the psychiatrist is apt to be asked the questions that once belonged in the domain of the theologian. People feel that it makes, or would make, a great difference if only they had a positive belief in a meaningful way of life or in God and immortality. The specter of approaching death often gives a powerful incentive to such thoughts. From time immemorial, men have had ideas about a Supreme Being (one or several) and about the Land of the Hereafter. Only today do they think they can do without such ideas.

Because we cannot discover God's throne in the sky with a radiotelescope or establish (for certain) that a beloved father or mother is still about in a more or less corporeal form, people assume that such ideas are "not true." I would rather say that they are not "true" *enough*, for these are conceptions of a kind that have accompanied human life from prehistoric times, and that still break through into consciousness at any provocation.

Modern man may assert that he can dispense with them, and he may bolster his opinion by insisting that there is no scientific evidence of their truth. Or he may even regret the loss of his convictions. But since we are dealing with invisible and unknowable things (for God is beyond human understanding, and there is no means of proving immortality), why should we bother about evidence? Even if we did not know by reason our need for salt in our food, we should nonetheless profit from its use. We might argue that the use of salt is a mere illusion of taste or a superstition; but it would still contribute to our well-being. Why, then, should we deprive ourselves of views that would prove helpful in crises and would give a meaning to our existence?

And how do we know that such ideas are not true? Many people would agree with me if I stated flatly that such ideas are probably illusions. What they fail to realize is that the denial is as impossible to "prove" as the assertion of religious belief. We are entirely free to choose which point of view we take; it will in any case be an arbitrary decision.

There is, however, a strong empirical[6] reason why we should cultivate thoughts that can never be proved. It is that they are known to be useful. Man positively needs general ideas and convictions that will give a meaning to his life and enable him to find a place for himself in the universe. He can stand the most incredible hardships when he is con-

---

[6]Derived from experience and observation.

vinced that they make sense; he is crushed when, on top of all his misfortunes, he has to admit that he is taking part in a "tale told by an idiot."

It is the role of religious symbols to give a meaning to the life of man. The Pueblo Indians believe that they are the sons of Father Sun, and this belief endows their life with a perspective (and a goal) that goes far beyond their limited existence. It gives them ample space for the unfolding of personality and permits them a full life as complete persons. Their plight is infinitely more satisfactory than that of a man in our own civilization who knows that he is (and will remain) nothing more than an underdog with no inner meaning to his life.

A sense of a wider meaning to one's existence is what raises a man beyond mere getting and spending. If he lacks this sense, he is lost and miserable. Had St. Paul[7] been convinced that he was nothing more than a wandering weaver of carpets, he certainly would not have been the man he was. His real and meaningful life lay in the inner certainty that he was the messenger of the Lord. One may accuse him of suffering from megalomania,[8] but this opinion pales before the testimony of history and the judgment of subsequent generations. The myth that took possession of him made him something greater than a mere craftsman.

Such a myth, however, consists of symbols that have not been invented consciously. They have happened. It was not the man Jesus who created the myth of the god-man. It existed for many centuries before his birth. He himself was seized by this symbolic idea, which, as St. Mark[9] tells us, lifted him out of the narrow life of the Nazarene[10] carpenter.

Myths go back to the primitive storyteller and his dreams, to men moved by the stirring of their fantasies. These people were not very different from those whom later generations have called poets or philosophers. Primitive storytellers did not concern themselves with the origin of their fantasies; it was very much later that people began to wonder where a story originated. Yet, centuries ago, in what we now

---

[7]Former Saul of Tarsus, martyred (probably 67 A.D.). "Apostle to the Gentiles" and a founder of Christian theology.

[8]Having grandiose self-delusions.

[9]Supposedly the writer of the second (New Testament) Gospel, which many consider the most reliable report concerning the life of Jesus.

[10]Refers to Nazareth in northern Palestine, where Jesus spent his childhood years.

call "ancient" Greece, men's minds were advanced enough to surmise that the tales of the gods were nothing but archaic and exaggerated traditions of long-buried kings or chieftains. Men already took the view that the myth was too improbable to mean what it said. They therefore tried to reduce it to a generally understandable form. . . .

To the scientific mind, such phenomena as symbolic ideas are a nuisance because they cannot be formulated in a way that is satisfactory to intellect and logic. They are by no means the only case of this kind in psychology. The trouble begins with the phenomenon of "affect" or emotion, which evades all the attempts of the psychologist to pin it down with a final definition. The cause of the difficulty is the same in both cases—the intervention of the unconscious.

I know enough of the scientific point of view to understand that it is most annoying to have to deal with facts that cannot be completely or adequately grasped. The trouble with these phenomena is that the facts are undeniable and yet cannot be formulated in intellectual terms. For this one would have to be able to comprehend life itself, for it is life that produces emotions and symbolic ideas.

The academic psychologist is perfectly free to dismiss the phenomenon of emotion or the concept of the unconscious (or both) from his consideration. Yet they remain facts to which the medical psychologist at least has to pay due attention; for emotional conflicts and the intervention of the unconscious are the classical features of his science. If he treats a patient at all, he comes up against these irrationalities as hard facts, irrespective of his ability to formulate them in intellectual terms. It is, therefore, quite natural that people who have not had the medical psychologist's experience find it difficult to follow what happens when psychology ceases to be a tranquil pursuit for the scientist in his laboratory and becomes an active part of the adventure of real life. Target practice on a shooting range is far from the battlefield; the doctor has to deal with casualties in a genuine war. He must concern himself with psychic realities, even if he cannot embody them in scientific definitions. That is why no textbook can teach psychology; one learns only by actual experience.

We can see this point clearly when we examine certain well-known symbols:

The cross in the Christian religion, for instance, is a meaningful symbol that expresses a multitude of aspects, ideas, and emotions; but a cross after a name on a list simply indicates that the individual is dead.

The phallus[11] functions as an all-embracing symbol in the Hindu religion, but if a street urchin draws one on a wall, it just reflects an interest in his penis. Because infantile and adolescent fantasies often continue far into adult life, many dreams occur in which there are unmistakable sexual allusions. It would be absurd to understand them as anything else. But when a mason speaks of monks and nuns to be laid upon each other, or an electrician of male plugs and female sockets, it would be ludicrous to suppose that he is indulging in glowing adolescent fantasies. He is simply using colorful descriptive names for his materials. When an educated Hindu talks to you about the Lingam (the phallus that represents the god Siva in Hindu mythology), you will hear things we Westerns would never connect with the penis. The Lingam is certainly not an obscene allusion; nor is the cross merely a sign of death. Much depends upon the maturity of the dreamer who produces such an image.

The interpretation of dreams and symbols demands intelligence. It cannot be turned into a mechanical system and then crammed into unimaginative brains. It demands both an increasing knowledge of the dreamer's individuality and an increasing self-awareness on the part of the interpreter. No experienced worker in this field will deny that there are rules of thumb that can prove helpful, but they must be applied with prudence and intelligence. One may follow all the right rules and yet get bogged down in the most appalling nonsense, simply by overlooking a seemingly unimportant detail that a better intelligence would not have missed. Even a man of high intellect can go badly astray for lack of intuition or feeling.

When we attempt to understand symbols, we are not only confronted with the symbol itself, but we are brought up against the wholeness of the symbol-producing individual. This includes a study of his cultural background, and in the process one fills in many gaps in one's own education. I have made it a rule myself to consider every case as an entirely new proposition about which I do not even know the ABC. Routine responses may be practical and useful while one is dealing with the surface, but as soon as one gets in touch with the vital problems, life itself takes over and even the most brilliant theoretical premises become ineffectual words.

Imagination and intuition are vital to our understanding. And though the usual popular opinion is that they are chiefly valuable to

---

[11]Latin: penis.

poets and artists (that in "sensible" matters one should mistrust them), they are in fact equally vital in all the higher grades of science. Here they play an increasingly important role, which supplements that of the "rational" intellect and its application to a specific problem. Even physics, the strictest of all applied sciences, depends to an astonishing degree upon intuition, which works by way of the unconscious (although it is possible to demonstrate afterward the logical procedures that could have led one to the same result as intuition). . . .

THE ROLE OF SYMBOLS

When the medical psychologist takes an interest in symbols, he is primarily concerned with "natural" symbols, as distinct from "cultural" symbols. The former are derived from the unconscious contents of the psyche,[12] and they therefore represent an enormous number of variations on the essential archetypal images. In many cases they can still be traced back to their archaic roots—that is, to ideas and images that we meet in the most ancient records and in primitive societies. The cultural symbols on the other hand, are those that have been used to express "eternal truths," and that are still used in many religions. They have gone through many transformations and even a long process of more or less conscious development, and have thus become collective images accepted by civilized societies.

Such cultural symbols nevertheless retain much of their original numinosity[13] or "spell." One is aware that they can evoke a deep emotional response in some individuals, and this psychic charge makes them function in much the same way as prejudices. They are a factor with which the psychologist must reckon; it is folly to dismiss them because, in rational terms, they seem to be absurd or irrelevant. They are important constituents of our mental makeup and vital forces in the building up of human society; and they cannot be eradicated without serious loss. Where they are repressed or neglected, their specific energy disappears into the unconscious with unaccountable consequences. The psychic energy that appears to have been lost in this way in fact serves to revive and intensify whatever is uppermost in the unconscious—tendencies, perhaps, that have hitherto had no chance to

---

[12]Mind or soul, being.

[13]Awe-inspiring, incomprehensible divine power.

express themselves or at least have not been allowed an uninhibited existence in our consciousness.

Such tendencies form an ever-present and potentially destructive "shadow" to our conscious mind. Even tendencies that might in some circumstances be able to exert a beneficial influence are transformed into demons when they are repressed. This is why many well-meaning people are understandably afraid of the unconscious, and incidentally of psychology.

Our times have demonstrated what it means for the gates of the underworld to be opened. Things whose enormity nobody could have imagined in the idyllic harmlessness of the first decade of our century have happened and have turned our world upside down. Ever since, the world has remained in a state of schizophrenia.[14] Not only has civilized Germany disgorged its terrible primitivity, but Russia is also ruled by it, and Africa has been set on fire. No wonder that the Western world feels uneasy.

Modern man does not understand how much his "rationalism" (which has destroyed his capacity to respond to numinous symbols and ideas) has put him at the mercy of the psychic "underworld." He has freed himself from "superstition" (or so he believes), but in the process he has lost his spiritual values to a positively dangerous degree. His moral and spiritual tradition has disintegrated, and he is now paying the price for this break-up in worldwide disorientation and dissociation.

Anthropologists have often described what happens to a primitive society when its spiritual values are exposed to the impact of modern civilization. Its people lose the meaning of their lives, their social organization disintegrates, and they themselves morally decay. We are now in the same condition. But we have never really understood what we have lost, for our spiritual leaders unfortunately were more interested in protecting their institutions than in understanding the mystery that symbols present. In my opinion, faith does not exclude thought (which is man's strongest weapon), but unfortunately many believers seem to be so afraid of science (and incidentally of psychology) that they turn a blind eye to the numinous psychic powers that forever control man's fate. We have stripped all things of their mystery and numinosity; nothing is holy any longer.

In earlier ages, as instinctive concepts welled up in the mind of man, his conscious mind could no doubt integrate them into a coherent

[14]Split consciousness; a type of illness of the psyche.

psychic pattern. But the "civilized" man is no longer able to do this. His "advanced" consciousness has deprived itself of the means by which the auxiliary contributions of the instincts and the unconscious can be assimilated. These organs of assimilation and integration were numinous symbols, held holy by common consent.

Today, for instance, we talk of "matter." We describe its physical properties. We conduct laboratory experiments to demonstrate some of its aspects. But the word "matter" remains a dry, inhuman, and purely intellectual concept, without any psychic significance for us. How different was the former image of matter—the Great Mother— that could encompass and express the profound emotional meaning of Mother Earth. In the same way, what was the spirit is now identified with intellect and thus ceases to be the Father of All. It has degenerated to the limited ego-thoughts of man; the immense emotional energy expressed in the image of "our Father" vanishes into the sand of an intellectual desert. . . .

As scientific understanding has grown, so our world has become dehumanized. Man feels himself isolated in the cosmos, because he is no longer involved in nature and has lost his emotional "unconscious identity" with natural phenomena. These have slowly lost their symbolic implications. Thunder is no longer the voice of an angry god, nor is lightning his avenging missile. No river contains a spirit, no tree is the life principle of a man, no snake the embodiment of wisdom, no mountain cave the home of a great demon. No voices now speak to man from stones, plants, and animals, nor does he speak to them believing they can hear. His contact with nature has gone, and with it has gone the profound emotional energy that this symbolic connection supplied.

This enormous loss is compensated for by the symbols of our dreams. They bring up our original nature—its instincts and peculiar thinking. Unfortunately, however, they express their contents in the language of nature, which is strange and incomprehensible to us. It therefore confronts us with the task of translating it into the rational words and concepts of modern speech, which has liberated itself from its primitive encumbrances—notably from its mystical participation with the things it describes. Nowadays, when we talk of ghosts and other numinous figures, we are no longer conjuring them up. The power as well as the glory is drained out of such once-potent words. We have ceased to believe in magic formulas; not many taboos and similar restrictions are left; and our world seems to be disinfected of all such "superstitious" numina[15] as "witches, warlocks, and worricows," to say nothing of werewolves, vampires, bush souls, and all the other bizarre beings that populated the primeval forest.

To be more accurate, the surface of our world seems to be cleansed of all superstitious and irrational elements. Whether, however, the real inner human world (not our wish-fulfilling fiction about it) is also freed from primitivity is another question. Is the number of 13 not still taboo for many people? Are there not still many individuals possessed by irrational prejudices, projections, and childish illusions? A realistic picture of the human mind reveals many such primitive traits and survivals, which are still playing their roles just as if nothing had happened during the last 500 years.

It is essential to appreciate this point. Modern man is in fact a curious mixture of characteristics acquired over the long ages of his mental development. This mixed-up being is the man and his symbols that we have to deal with, and we must scrutinize his mental products very carefully indeed. Skepticism and scientific conviction exist in him side by side with old-fashioned prejudices, outdated habits of thought and feeling, obstinate misinterpretations, and blind ignorance.

Such are the contemporary human beings who produce the symbols we psychologists investigate. In order to explain these symbols and their meaning, it is vital to learn whether their representations are related to purely personal experience, or whether they have been chosen by a dream for its particular purpose from a store of general conscious knowledge.

Take, for instance, a dream in which the number 13 occurs. The question is whether the dreamer himself habitually believes in the unlucky quality of the number, or whether the dream merely alludes to people who still indulge in such superstitions. The answer makes a great difference to the interpretation. In the former case, you have to reckon with the fact that the individual is still under the spell of the unlucky 13, and therefore will feel most uncomfortable in Room 13 in a hotel or sitting at a table with 13 people. In the latter case, 13 may not mean any more than a discourteous or abusive remark. The "superstitious" dreamer still feels the "spell" of 13; the more "rational" dreamer has stripped 13 of its original emotional overtones.

This argument illustrates the way in which archetypes appear in practical experience: They are, at the same time, both images and

[15]Spirits.

emotions. One can speak of an archetype only when these two aspects are simultaneous. When there is merely the image, then there is simply a word-picture of little consequence. But by being charged with emotion, the image gains numinosity (or psychic energy); it becomes dynamic, and consequences of some kind must flow from it.

I am aware that it is difficult to grasp this concept, because I am trying to use words to describe something whose very nature makes it incapable of precise definition. But since so many people have chosen to treat archetypes as if they were part of a mechanical system that can be learned by rote, it is essential to insist that they are not mere names, or even philosophical concepts. They are pieces of life itself—images that are integrally connected to the living individual by the bridge of the emotions. That is why it is impossible to give an arbitrary (or universal) interpretation of any archetype. It must be explained in the manner indicated by the whole life-situation of the particular individual to whom it relates.

Thus, in the case of a devout Christian, the symbol of the cross can be interpreted only in its Christian context—unless the dream produces a very strong reason to look beyond it. Even then, the specific Christian meaning should be kept in mind. But one cannot say that, at all times and in all circumstances, the symbol of the cross has the same meaning. If that were so, it would be stripped of its numinosity, lose its vitality, and become a mere word.

Those who do not realize the special feeling tone of the archetype end with nothing more than a jumble of mythological concepts, which can be strung together to show that everything means anything—or nothing at all. All the corpses in the world are chemically identical, but living individuals are not. Archetypes come to life only when one patiently tries to discover why and in what fashion they are meaningful to a living individual. . . .

HEALING THE SPLIT

Our intellect has created a new world that dominates nature, and has populated it with monstrous machines. The latter are so indubitably useful that we cannot see even a possibility of getting rid of them or our subservience to them. Man is bound to follow the adventurous promptings of his scientific and inventive mind and to admire himself for his splendid achievements. At the same time, his genius shows the uncanny tendency to invent things that become more and more dangerous, because they represent better and better means for wholesale suicide.

In view of the rapidly increasing avalanche of world population, man has already begun to seek ways and means of keeping the rising flood at bay. But nature may anticipate all our attempts by turning against man his own creative mind. The H-bomb, for instance, would put an effective stop to overpopulation. In spite of our proud domination of nature, we are still her victims, for we have not even learned to control our own nature. Slowly but, it appears, inevitably, we are courting disaster.

There are no longer any gods whom we can invoke to help us. The great religions of the world suffer from increasing anemia,[16] because the helpful numina have fled from the woods, rivers, and mountains, and from animals, and the god-men have disappeared underground into the unconscious. There we fool ourselves that they lead an ignominious existence among the relics of our past. Our present lives are dominated by the goddess Reason, who is our greatest and most tragic illusion. By the aid of reason, so we assure ourselves, we have "conquered nature."

But this is a mere slogan, for the so-called conquest of nature overwhelms us with the natural fact of overpopulation and adds to our troubles by our psychological incapacity to make the necessary political arrangements. It remains quite natural for men to quarrel and to struggle for superiority over one another. How then have we "conquered nature"?

As any change must begin somewhere, it is the single individual who will experience it and carry it through. The change must indeed begin with an individual; it might be any one of us. Nobody can afford to look round and to wait for somebody else to do what he is loath to do himself. But since nobody seems to know what to do, it might be worth-while for each of us to ask himself whether by any chance his or her unconscious may know something that will help us. Certainly the conscious mind seems unable to do anything useful in this respect. Man today is painfully aware of the fact that neither his great religions nor his various philosophies seem to provide him with those powerful animating ideas that would give him the security he needs in face of the present condition of the world.

I know what the Buddhists would say: Things would go right if

[16]Reduction in vitality.

people would only follow the "noble eightfold path" of the *Dharma* (doctrine, law) and had true insight into the Self. The Christian tells us that if only people had faith in God, we should have a better world. The rationalist insists that if people were intelligent and reasonable, all our problems would be manageable. The trouble is that none of them manages to solve these problems himself.

Christians often ask why God does not speak to them, as he is believed to have done in former days. When I hear such questions, it always makes me think of the rabbi who was asked how it could be that God often showed himself to people in the olden days while nowadays nobody ever sees him. The rabbi replied: "Nowadays there is no longer anybody who can bow low enough."

This answer hits the nail on the head. We are so captivated by and entangled in our subjective consciousness that we have forgotten the age-old fact that God speaks chiefly through dreams and visions. The Buddhist discards the world of unconscious fantasies as useless illusions; the Christian puts his Church and his Bible between himself and his unconscious; and the rational intellectual does not yet know that his consciousness is not his total psyche. This ignorance persists today in spite of the fact that for more than 70 years the unconscious has been a basic scientific concept that is indispensable to any serious psychological investigation.

We can no longer afford to be so God-Almighty-like as to set ourselves up as judges of the merits or demerits of natural phenomena. We do not base our botany upon the old-fashioned division into useful and useless plants, or our zoology upon the naïve distinction between harmless and dangerous animals. But we still complacently assume that consciousness is sense and the unconscious is nonsense. In science such an assumption would be laughed out of court. Do microbes, for instance, make sense or nonsense?

Whatever the unconscious may be, it is a natural phenomenon producing symbols that prove to be meaningful. We cannot expect someone who has never looked through a microscope to be an authority on microbes; in the same way, no one who has not made a serious study of natural symbols can be considered a competent judge in this matter. But the general undervaluation of the human soul is so great that neither the great religions nor the philosophies nor scientific rationalism have been willing to look at it twice.

In spite of the fact that the Catholic Church admits the occurrence of *somnia a Deo missa* (dreams sent by God), most of its thinkers make no serious attempt to understand dreams. I doubt whether there is a Protestant treatise or doctrine that would stoop so low as to admit the possibility that the *vox Dei*[17] might be perceived in a dream. But if a theologian really believes in God, by what authority does he suggest that God is unable to speak through dreams?

I have spent more than half a century in investigating natural symbols, and I have come to the conclusion that dreams and their symbols are not stupid and meaningless. On the contrary, dreams provide the most interesting information for those who take the trouble to understand their symbols. The results, it is true, have little to do with such worldly concerns as buying and selling. But the meaning of life is not exhaustively explained by one's business life, nor is the deep desire of the human heart answered by a bank account.

In a period of human history when all available energy is spent in the investigation of nature, very little attention is paid to the essence of man, which is his psyche, although many researches are made into its conscious functions. But the really complex and unfamiliar part of the mind, from which symbols are produced, is still virtually unexplored. It seems almost incredible that though we receive signals from it every night, deciphering these communications seems too tedious for any but a very few people to be bothered with it. Man's greatest instrument, his psyche, is little thought of, and it is often directly mistrusted and despised. "It's only psychological" too often means: It is nothing.

Where, exactly, does this immense prejudice come from? We have obviously been so busy with the question of what we think that we entirely forget to ask what the unconscious psyche thinks about us. . . .

This modern standpoint is surely one-sided and unjust. It does not even accord with the known facts. Our actual knowledge of the unconscious shows that it is a natural phenomenon and that, like Nature herself, it is at least *neutral*. It contains all aspects of human nature—light and dark, beautiful and ugly, good and evil, profound and silly. The study of individual, as well as of collective, symbolism is an enormous task, and one that has not yet been mastered. But a beginning has been made at last. The early results are encouraging, and they seem to indicate an answer to many so far unanswered questions of present-day mankind.

· · ·

[17]Latin: voice of God.

32

V. I. Lenin

Imperialism AND State and Revolution

V LADIMIR *Ilyich Lenin (1870–1924),*
one of the most influential political figures of the twentieth century, was the archi-
tect of the Russian Bolshevik Revolution of 1917 and, from that time until his
death, the prime mover of the Soviet Socialist state. His radical, incisive ideas
and dynamic leadership have made him a guiding spirit of twentieth-century com-
munism and an inspiration for revolutionary movements throughout the world.

Lenin was trained to be a lawyer, but at age twenty-three he threw himself
into the revolutionary movement, becoming in time one of the leaders of the
Russian Socialist party. After imprisonment and exile in Siberia, he fled
Russia, not to return until after the outbreak of revolution in 1917. As the head
of the Bolsheviks, the left-wing faction of the socialists, he fought uncompro-
misingly against the theories and tactics of the moderate, democratic socialists and
organized the Bolshevik (Communist) seizure of power. From 1918 on, he led
the party and the nation in the building of a new political and economic system.

Leninism was an adaptation of Marxism to Russian conditions and the
Russian revolutionary tradition. In developing the ideas and organization of the
revolution, Lenin stressed the role of a professional revolutionary elite, orga-
nized in a centralized party, in leading the proletariat (industrial workers) in the
struggle against capitalism. This struggle, he insisted, was an expression of irrecon-
cilable class antagonisms and was to be carried on in both the political and the
economic spheres by violent as well as peaceful means. Once victorious, the communists
were to institute a dictatorship of the proletariat in order to effect the suppression
of the bourgeoisie and the destruction of the capitalist state—which was neces-
sary before the organization of a socialist and, eventually, a communist society.

Lenin also applied his theories to the advanced industrial countries. He
contended that capitalism has reached its final stage in such countries when
industrial and financial monopolies dominated the economy. After exhausting

the possibilities for economic growth at the domestic level, monopoly capitalists, or imperialists, are forced to seek political and economic control in backward areas of the world. According to Lenin, the resulting imperialistic rivalries lead inevitably to wars and the destruction of capitalism. Lenin elaborated these ideas in Imperialism, the Highest Stage of Capitalism *(1916), from which the first excerpt is taken.*

In his State and Revolution *(1917), from which the second excerpt is taken, Lenin expounds his theory of the state as the result of irreconcilable class conflict and as a coercive instrument of the ruling class. He saw revolution as the victory of the working-class state over the capitalistic state. Eventually, he predicted, when classes had been abolished in the communist society, the state as such would wither away.*

- - - -

• • •

IMPERIALISM

Imperialism as a Special Stage of Capitalism

We must now try to sum up and put together what has been said on the subject of imperialism. Imperialism emerged as the development and direct continuation of the fundamental attributes of capitalism in general. But capitalism only became capitalist imperialism at a definite and very high stage of its development, when certain of its fundamental attributes began to be transformed into their opposites, when the features of a period of transition from capitalism to a higher social and economic system began to take shape and reveal themselves all along the line. Economically, the main thing in this process is the substitution of capitalist monopolies for capitalist free competition. Free competition is the fundamental attribute of capitalism, and of commodity production generally. Monopoly is exactly the opposite of free competition; but we have seen the latter being transformed into monopoly before our very eyes, creating large-scale industry and eliminating small industry, replacing large-scale industry by still larger-scale industry, finally leading to such a concentration of production and capital that monopoly has been and is the result: cartels, syndicates and trusts, and, merging with them, the capital of a dozen or so banks manipulat-

IMPERIALISM   V. I. Lenin, *Imperialism, the Highest Stage of Capitalism* (New York: International Publishers, 1939), 88–89, 95–97, 123–27. Copyright 1939. Reprinted by permission of International Publishers Co., Inc.

ing thousands of millions. At the same time monopoly, which has grown out of free competition, does not abolish the latter, but exists over it and alongside of it, and thereby gives rise to a number of very acute, intense antagonisms, friction and conflicts. Monopoly is the transition from capitalism to a higher system.

If it were necessary to give the briefest possible definition of imperialism we should have to say that imperialism is the monopoly stage of capitalism. Such a definition would include what is most important, for, on the one hand, finance capital is the bank capital of a few big monopolist banks, merged with the capital of the monopolist combines of manufacturers; and, on the other hand, the division of the world is the transition from a colonial policy which has extended without hindrance to territories unoccupied by any capitalist power, to a colonial policy of monopolistic possession of the territory of the world which has been completely divided up.

But very brief definitions, although convenient, for they sum up the main points, are nevertheless inadequate, because very important features of the phenomenon that has to be defined have to be especially deduced. And so, without forgetting the conditional and relative value of all definitions, which can never include all the concatenations of a phenomenon in its complete development, we must give a definition of imperialism that will embrace the following five essential features:

1) The concentration of production and capital developed to such a high stage that it created monopolies which play a decisive role in economic life.

2) The merging of bank capital with industrial capital, and the creation, on the basis of this "finance capital," of a "financial oligarchy."

3) The export of capital, which has become extremely important, as distinguished from the export of commodities.

4) The formation of international capitalist monopolies which share the world among themselves.

5) The territorial division of the whole world among the greatest capitalist powers is completed. . . .

We notice three areas of highly developed capitalism with a high development of means of transport, of trade and of industry, the Central European, the British and the American areas. Among these are three states which dominate the world: Germany, Great Britain, the United States. Imperialist rivalry and the struggle between these countries have become very keen because Germany has only a restricted area and few colonies (the creation of "Central Europe" is still a matter for the future; it is being born in the midst of desperate struggles). For the moment the distinctive feature of Europe is political disintegration. In the British and American areas, on the other hand, political concentration is very highly developed, but there is a tremendous disparity between the immense colonies of the one and the insignificant colonies of the other. In the colonies, capitalism is only beginning to develop. The struggle for South America is becoming more and more acute.

There are two areas where capitalism is not strongly developed: Russia and Eastern Asia. In the former, the density of population is very low, in the latter it is very high; in the former political concentration is very high, in the latter it does not exist. The partition of China is only beginning, and the struggle between Japan, U.S.A., and so forth, in connection therewith is continually gaining in intensity. . . .

Finance capital and the trusts are increasing instead of diminishing the differences in the rate of development of the various parts of world economy. When the relation of forces is changed, how else, *under capitalism*, can the solution of contradictions be found, except by resorting to *violence*?

• • •

The Place of Imperialism in History

We have seen that the economic quintessence of imperialism is monopoly capitalism. This very fact determines its place in history, for monopoly that grew up on the basis of free competition, and precisely out of free competition, is the transition from the capitalist system to a higher social-economic order. We must take special note of the four principal forms of monopoly, or the four principal manifestations of monopoly capitalism, which are characteristic of the epoch under review.

Firstly, monopoly arose out of the concentration of production at a very advanced stage of development. This refers to the monopolist capitalist combines, cartels, syndicates and trusts. We have seen the important part that these play in modern economic life. At the beginning of the twentieth century, monopolies acquired complete supremacy in the advanced countries. And although the first steps toward the formation of the cartels were first taken by countries enjoying the protection of high tariffs (Germany, America), Great Britain, with her system of free trade, was not far behind in revealing the same basic phenomenon, namely, the birth of monopoly out of the concentration of production.

Secondly, monopolies have accelerated the capture of the most important sources of raw materials, especially for the coal and iron industries, which are the basic and most highly cartelized industries in capitalist society. The monopoly of the most important sources of raw materials has enormously increased the power of big capital, and has sharpened the antagonism between cartelized and non-cartelized industry.

Thirdly, monopoly has sprung from the banks. The banks have developed from modest intermediary enterprises into the monopolists of finance capital. Some three or five of the biggest banks in each of the foremost capitalist countries have achieved the "personal union" of industrial and bank capital, and have concentrated in their hands the disposal of thousands upon thousands of millions which form the greater part of the capital and income of entire countries. A financial oligarchy, which throws a close net of relations of dependence over all the economic and political institutions of contemporary bourgeois society without exception—such is the most striking manifestation of this monopoly.

Fourthly, monopoly has grown out of colonial policy. To the numerous "old" motives of colonial policy, finance capital has added the struggle for the sources of raw materials, for the export of capital, for "spheres of influence," namely, for spheres for profitable deals, concessions, monopolist profits and so on; in fine, for economic territory in general. When the colonies of the European powers in Africa, for instance, comprised only one-tenth of that territory (as was the case in 1876), colonial policy was able to develop by methods other than those of monopoly—by the "free grabbing" of territories, so to speak. But when nine-tenths of Africa had been seized (approximately by 1900), when the whole world had been divided up, there was inevitably ushered in a period of colonial monopoly and, consequently, a period of particularly intense struggle for the division and the redivision of the world.

The extent to which monopolist capital has intensified all the contradictions of capitalism is generally known. It is sufficient to mention the high cost of living and the oppression of the cartels. This intensification of contradictions constitutes the most powerful driving force of the transitional period of history, which began from the time of the definite victory of world finance capital.

Monopolies, oligarchy, the striving for domination instead of the striving for liberty, the exploitation of an increasing number of small or weak nations by an extremely small group of the richest or most powerful nations—all these have given birth to those distinctive characteristics of imperialism which compel us to define it as parasitic or decaying capitalism. More and more prominently there emerges, as one of the tendencies of imperialism, the creation of the "bondholding" (rentier) state, the usurer state, in which the bourgeoisie lives on the proceeds of capital exports and by "clipping coupons." It would be a mistake to believe that this tendency to decay precludes the possibility of the rapid growth of capitalism. It does not. In the epoch of imperialism, certain branches of industry, certain strata of the bourgeoisie and certain countries betray, to a more or less degree, one or other of these tendencies. On the whole, capitalism is growing far more rapidly than before. But this growth is not only becoming more and more uneven in general; its unevenness also manifests itself, in particular, in the decay of the countries which are richest in capital (such as England). . . .

In its turn, this finance capital which has grown so rapidly is not unwilling (precisely because it has grown so quickly) to pass on to a more "tranquil" possession of colonies which have to be seized—and not only by peaceful methods—from richer nations. In the United States, economic development in the last decades has been even more rapid than in Germany, and *for this very reason* the parasitic character of modern American capitalism has stood out with particular prominence. On the other hand, a comparison of, say, the republican American bourgeoisie with the monarchist Japanese or German bourgeoisie shows that the most pronounced political distinctions diminish to an extreme degree in the epoch of imperialism—not because they are unimportant in general, but because in all these cases we are discussing a bourgeoisie which has definite features of parasitism.

The receipt of high monopoly profits by the capitalists in one of the numerous branches of industry, in one of numerous countries, and so forth, makes it economically possible for them to corrupt certain sections of the working class, and for a time a fairly considerable minority, and win them to the side of the bourgeoisie of a given industry or nation against all the others. The intensification of antagonisms between imperialist nations for the division of the world increases this striving. And so there is created that bond between imperialism and opportunism, which revealed itself first and most clearly in England, owing to the fact that certain features of imperialist development were observable there much earlier than in other countries. . . .

From all that has been said on the economic nature of imperialism, it follows that we must define it as capitalism in transition, or, more precisely, as moribund capitalism. It is very instructive in this respect to note that the bourgeois economists, in describing modern capitalism, frequently employ terms like "interlocking," "absence of isolation," and so forth; "in conformity with their functions and course of development," banks are "not purely private business enterprises; they are more and more outgrowing the sphere of purely private business regulation." . . .

. . . But the underlying factor of this interlocking, its very base, is the changing social relations of production. When a big enterprise assumes gigantic proportions, and, on the basis of exact computation of mass data, organizes according to plan the supply of primary raw materials to the extent of two-thirds, or three-fourths of all that is necessary for tens of millions of people; when the raw materials are transported to the most suitable place of production, sometimes hundreds or thousands of miles away, in a systematic and organized manner; when a single center directs all the successive stages of work right up to the manufacture of numerous varieties of finished articles; when these products are distributed according to a single plan among tens and hundreds of millions of consumers (as in the case of the distribution of oil in America and Germany by the American "oil trust")—then it becomes evident that we have socialization of production, and not mere "interlocking"; that private economic relations and private property relations constitute a shell which is no longer suitable for its contents, a shell which must inevitably begin to decay if its destruction be delayed by artificial means; a shell which may continue in a state of decay for a fairly long period (particularly if the cure of the opportunist abscess is protracted), but which will inevitably be removed. . . .

STATE AND REVOLUTION

• • •

The State as the Product of the Irreconcilability of Class Antagonisms

Let us begin with the most popular of Engels'[1] works, *The Origin of the Family, Private Property, and the State.* . . . Summarizing his historical analysis Engels says:

> The state is therefore by no means a power imposed on
> society from the outside; just as little is it "the reality of the

---

[1]Friedrich Engels (1820–1895) was a German socialist, manufacturer, and writer, a lifelong friend and supporter of Karl Marx.

STATE AND REVOLUTION   V. I. Lenin, *State and Revolution* (New York: International Publishers, 1932, 1943), 8–10, 15–17, 71–80. Copyright 1932, 1943. Reprinted by permission of International Publishers Co., Inc.

moral idea," "the image and reality of reason," as Hegel[2] asserted. Rather, it is a product of society at a certain stage of development; it is the admission that this society has become entangled in an insoluble contradiction with itself, that it is cleft into irreconcilable antagonisms which it is powerless to dispel. But in order that these antagonisms, classes with conflicting economic interests, may not consume themselves and society in sterile struggle, a power apparently standing above society becomes necessary, whose purpose is to moderate the conflict and keep it within the bounds of "order"; and this power arising out of society, but placing itself above it, and increasingly separating itself from it, is the state.

Here we have, expressed in all its clearness, the basic idea of Marxism on the question of the historical role and meaning of the state. The state is the product and the manifestation of the *irreconcilability* of class antagonisms. The state arises when, where, and to the extent that the class antagonisms *cannot* be objectively reconciled. And, conversely, the existence of the state proves that the class antagonisms *are* irreconcilable.

It is precisely on this most important and fundamental point that distortions of Marxism arise along two main lines.

On the one hand, the bourgeois, and particularly the petty-bourgeois, ideologists, compelled under the pressure of indisputable historical facts to admit that the state only exists where there are class antagonisms and the class struggle, "correct" Marx[3] in such a way as to make it appear that the state is an organ for *reconciling* the classes. According to Marx, the state could neither arise nor maintain itself if a reconciliation of classes were possible. But with the petty-bourgeois[4] and philistine[5] professors and publicists, the state—and this frequently on the strength of benevolent references to Marx!—becomes a conciliator of the classes. According to Marx, the state is an organ of class *domination*, an organ of *oppression* of one class by another; its aim is the creation of "order" which legalizes and perpetuates this oppression by moderating the collisions between the classes. But in the opinion of the

[2]Georg Friedrich Wilhelm Hegel (1770–1831), a German philosopher, whose ideas had a profound influence on Karl Marx.

[3]Karl Marx (1818–1883), a German socialist philosopher and writer—sometimes with Engels—on economics and political philosophy.

[4]Shopkeeping class.

[5]Smugly conventional and narrow.

petty-bourgeois politicians, order means reconciliation of the classes, and not oppression of one class by another; to moderate collisions does not mean, they say, to deprive the oppressed classes of certain definite means and methods of struggle for overthrowing the oppressors, but to practice reconciliation. . . .

On the other hand, the "Kautskyist"[6] distortion of Marx is far more subtle. "Theoretically," there is no denying that the state is the organ of class domination, or that class antagonisms are irreconcilable. But what is forgotten or glossed over is this: if the state is the product of the irreconcilable character of class antagonisms, if it is a force standing *above* society and "increasingly separating itself from it," then it is clear that the liberation of the oppressed class is impossible not only without a violent revolution, *but also without the destruction* of the apparatus of state power, which was created by the ruling class and in which this "separation" is embodied.

• • •

The "Withering Away" of the State and Violent Revolution

Engels' words regarding the "withering away" of the state enjoy such popularity, they are so often quoted, and they show so clearly the essence of the usual adulteration by means of which Marxism is made to look like opportunism, that we must dwell on them in detail. Let us quote the whole passage [from *Anti-Duehring*][7] from which they are taken.

> The proletariat seizes state power, and then transforms the means of production into state property. But in doing this, it puts an end to itself as the proletariat, it puts an end to all class differences and class antagonisms, it puts an end also to the state as the state. Former society, moving in class antagonisms, had need of the state, that is, an organization of the exploiting class at each period for the maintenance of its external conditions of production; therefore, in particular, for the forcible holding down of the exploited class in the conditions of oppression (slavery, bondage or serfdom, wage-labor) determined by the

[6]Karl Johann Kautsky (1854–1938) was a German Social Democratic leader and writer. (Kautsky argued that state power could be "taken over" by the working classes through political means. It was chiefly to refute this "revisionist" view that Lenin argues in this document for the necessity of the forceful *seizure* of power.)

[7]Friedrich Engels, *Herr Eugen Duehring's Revolution in Science* (1878), a work commonly known as *Anti-Duehring*.

existing mode of production. The state was the official representative of society as a whole, its embodiment in a visible
corporate body; but it was this only in so far as it was the state of
that class which itself, in its epoch, represented society as a
whole: in ancient times, the state of the slave-owning citizens;
in the Middle Ages, of the feudal nobility; in our epoch, of the
bourgeoisie. When ultimately it becomes really representative
of society as a whole, it makes itself superfluous. As soon as
there is no longer any class of society to be held in subjection; as
soon as, along with class domination and the struggle for
individual existence based on the former anarchy of production, the collisions and excesses arising from these have also
been abolished, there is nothing more to be repressed, and a
special repressive force, a state, is no longer necessary. The first
act in which the state really comes forward as the representative
of society as a whole—the seizure of the means of production in
the name of society—is at the same time its last independent act
as a state. The interference of a state power in social relations
becomes superfluous in one sphere after another, and then
becomes dormant of itself. Government over persons is replaced by the administration of things and the direction of the
processes of production. The state is not "abolished," *it withers
away*. It is from this standpoint that we must appraise the phrase
"people's free state"—both its justification at times for agita-
tional purposes, and its ultimate scientific inadequacy—and
also the demand of the so-called Anarchists[8] that the state
should be abolished overnight. . . .

In the first place, Engels at the very outset of his argument says that,
in assuming state power, the proletariat by that very act "puts an end to
the state as the state." One is "not accustomed" to reflect on what this
really means. Generally, it is either ignored altogether, or it is considered as a piece of "Hegelian weakness" on Engels' part. As a matter of
fact, however, these words express succinctly the experience of one of
the greatest proletarian revolutions—the Paris Commune of 1871,[9] of
which we shall speak in greater detail in its proper place. As a matter of

[8]The anarchists struggled against and endeavored to abolish any and all forms of power of
human beings over human beings. They were so called after the Greek word *anarchos*,
meaning without a ruler—hence, absence of government. (See selection 24.)

[9]An uprising, in March 1871, of radical, republican, and "socialist" Paris against the
pro-monarchistic National Assembly and the kind of France it seemed to foreshadow.
The lower classes were further enraged by the fact that the Assembly had too readily
accepted the peace terms ending the Franco-Prussian war. The uprising was ruthlessly
stamped out by troops of the National Assembly before the end of May 1871.

fact, Engels speaks here of the destruction of the bourgeois state by the proletarian revolution, while the words about its withering away refer to the remains of *proletarian* statehood *after* the Socialist revolution. The bourgeois state does not "wither away," according to Engels, but is "put an end to" by the proletariat in the course of the revolution. What withers away after the revolution is the proletarian state or semistate.

Secondly, the state is a "special repressive force." This splendid and extremely profound definition of Engels is given by him here with complete lucidity. It follows from this that the "special repressive force" of the bourgeoisie for the suppression of the proletariat, of the millions of workers by a handful of the rich, must be replaced by a "special repressive force" of the proletariat for the suppression of the bourgeoisie (the dictatorship of the proletariat). It is just this that constitutes the destruction of "the state as the state." It is just this that constitutes the "act" of "the seizure of the means of production in the name of society." And it is obvious that such a substitution of one (proletarian) "special repressive force" for another (bourgeois) "special repressive force" can in no way take place in the form of a "withering away."

Thirdly, as to the "withering away" or, more expressively and colorfully, as to the state "becoming dormant," Engels refers quite clearly and definitely to the period *after* "the seizure of the means of production [by the state] in the name of society," that is, *after* the Socialist revolution. We all know that the political form of the "state" at that time is complete democracy. But it never enters the head of any of the opportunists who shamelessly distort Marx that when Engels speaks here of the state "withering away," or "becoming dormant," he speaks of *democracy*. At first sight this seems very strange. But it is "unintelligible" only to one who has not reflected on the fact that democracy is *also* a state and that, consequently, democracy will *also* disappear when the state disappears. The bourgeois state can only be "put an end to" by a revolution. The state in general, that is, most complete democracy, can only "wither away."

• • •

Transition from Capitalism to Communism

> Between capitalist and Communist society—Marx [writes]—lies the period of the revolutionary transformation of the former into the latter. To this also corresponds a political

> transition period, in which the state can be no other than *the*
> *revolutionary dictatorship of the proletariat.*

This conclusion Marx bases on an analysis of the role played by the proletariat in modern capitalist society, on the data concerning the evolution of this society, and on the irreconcilability of the opposing interests of the proletariat and the bourgeoisie.

Earlier the question was put thus: to attain its emancipation, the proletariat must overthrow the bourgeoisie, conquer political power and establish its own revolutionary dictatorship.

Now the question is put somewhat differently: the transition from capitalist society, developing toward Communism, toward a Communist society, is impossible without a "political transition period," and the state in this period can only be the revolutionary dictatorship of the proletariat.

What, then, is the relation of this dictatorship to democracy?

We have seen that the *Communist Manifesto* simply places side by side the two ideas: the "transformation of the proletariat into the ruling class" and the "establishment of democracy." On the basis of all that has been said above, one can define more exactly how democracy changes in the transition from capitalism to Communism.

In capitalist society, under the conditions most favorable to its development, we have more or less complete democracy in the democratic republic. But this democracy is always bound by the narrow framework of capitalist exploitation, and consequently always remains, in reality, a democracy for the minority, only for the possessing classes, only for the rich. Freedom in capitalist society always remains just about the same as it was in the ancient Greek republics: freedom for the slave-owners. The modern wage-slaves, owing to the conditions of capitalist exploitation, are so much crushed by want and poverty that "democracy is nothing to them," "politics is nothing to them"; that, in the ordinary peaceful course of events, the majority of the population is debarred from participating in social and political life. . . .

Democracy for an insignificant minority, democracy for the rich—that is the democracy of capitalist society. If we look more closely into the mechanism of capitalist democracy, everywhere, both in the "petty"—so-called petty—details of the suffrage (residential qualification, exclusion of women, and so forth), and in the technique of the representative institutions, in the actual obstacles to the right of assembly (public buildings are not for "beggars"!), in the purely capitalist organization of the daily press, and so forth—on all sides we see restriction after restriction upon democracy. These restrictions, exceptions, exclusions, obstacles for the poor, seem slight, especially in the eyes of one who has himself never known want and has never been in close contact with the oppressed classes in their mass life (and nine-tenths, if not ninety-nine hundredths, of the bourgeois publicists and politicians are of this class), but in their sum total these restrictions exclude and squeeze out the poor from politics and from an active share in democracy.

Marx splendidly grasped this *essence* of capitalist democracy, when, in analyzing the experience of the Commune,[10] he said that the oppressed were allowed, once every few years, to decide which particular representatives of the oppressing class should be in parliament to represent and repress them!

But from this capitalist democracy—inevitably narrow, subtly rejecting the poor, and therefore hypocritical and false to the core—progress does not march onward, simply, smoothly and directly, to "greater and greater democracy," as the liberal professors and petty-bourgeois opportunists would have us believe. No, progress marches onward, that is, toward Communism, through the dictatorship of the proletariat; it cannot do otherwise, for there is no one else and no other way to *break the resistance* of the capitalist exploiters.

But the dictatorship of the proletariat—that is, the organization of the vanguard of the oppressed as the ruling class for the purpose of crushing the oppressors—cannot produce merely an expansion of democracy. *Together* with an immense expansion of democracy which *for the first time* becomes democracy for the poor, democracy for the people, and not democracy for the rich folk, the dictatorship of the proletariat produces a series of restrictions of liberty in the case of the oppressors, the exploiters, the capitalists. We must crush them in order to free humanity from wage-slavery; their resistance must be broken by force; it is clear that where there is suppression there is also violence, there is no liberty, no democracy.

Engels expressed this splendidly in his letter to Bebel[11] when he said, as the reader will remember, that "as long as the proletariat still *needs* the state, it needs it not in the interests of freedom, but for the purpose of crushing its antagonists; and as soon as it becomes possible to speak of freedom, then the state, as such, ceases to exist."

[10]The Paris Commune (see footnote 9).

[11]August Bebel (1840–1913), a German Social Democratic leader who shared the political position of Karl Kautsky (see footnote 6).

Democracy for the vast majority of the people, and suppression by force, namely, exclusion from democracy, of the exploiters and oppressors of the people—this is the modification of democracy during the *transition* from capitalism to Communism.

Only in Communist society, when the resistance of the capitalists has been completely broken, when the capitalists have disappeared, when there are no classes (that is, there is no difference between the members of society in their relation to the social means of production), *only then* "the state ceases to exist," and "*it becomes possible to speak of freedom.*" Only then a really full democracy, a democracy without any exceptions, will be possible and will be realized. And only then will democracy itself begin to *wither away* due to the simple fact that, freed from capitalist slavery, from the untold horrors, savagery, absurdities and infamies of capitalist exploitation, people will gradually *become accustomed* to the observance of the elementary rules of social life that have been known for centuries and repeated for thousands of years in all school books; they will become accustomed to observing them without force, without compulsion, without subordination, without the *special apparatus* for compulsion which is called the state.

The expression "the state *withers away*," is very well chosen, for it indicates both the gradual and the elemental nature of the process. Only habit can, and undoubtedly will, have such an effect; for we see around us millions of times how readily people get accustomed to observe the necessary rules of life in common, if there is no exploitation, if there is nothing that causes indignation, that calls forth protest and revolt and has to be *suppressed*.

Thus, in capitalist society, we have a democracy that is curtailed, poor, false; a democracy only for the rich, for the minority. The dictatorship of the proletariat, the period of transition to Communism, will, for the first time, produce democracy for the people, for the majority, side by side with the necessary suppression of the minority— the exploiters. Communism alone is capable of giving a really complete democracy, and the more complete it is the more quickly will it become unnecessary and wither away of itself.

In other words: under capitalism we have a state in the proper sense of the word, that is, special machinery for the suppression of one class by another, and of the majority by the minority at that. Naturally, for the successful discharge of such a task as the systematic suppression by the exploiting minority of the exploited majority, the greatest ferocity and savagery of suppression are required, seas of blood are required, through which mankind is marching in slavery, serfdom, and wage-labor.

Again, during the *transition* from capitalism to Communism, suppression is *still* necessary; but it is the suppression of the minority of exploiters by the majority of the exploited. A special apparatus, special machinery for suppression, the "state," is *still* necessary, but this is now a transitional state, no longer a state in the usual sense, for the suppression of the minority of exploiters, by the majority of the wage slaves *of yesterday*, is a matter comparatively so easy, simple and natural that it will cost far less bloodshed than the suppression of the risings of slaves, serfs or wage laborers, and will cost mankind far less. This is compatible with the diffusion of democracy among such an overwhelming majority of the population, that the need for *special machinery* of suppression will begin to disappear. The exploiters are, naturally, unable to suppress the people without the most complex machinery for performing this task; but *the people* can suppress the exploiters even with very simple "machinery," almost without any "machinery," without any special apparatus, by the simple *organization of the armed masses*. . . .

Finally, only Communism renders the state absolutely unnecessary, for there is *no one* to be suppressed—"no one" in the sense of a *class*, in the sense of a systematic struggle with a definite section of the population. We are not Utopians,[12] and we do not in the least deny the possibility and inevitability of excesses on the part of *individual persons*, nor the need to suppress *such* excesses. But, in the first place, no special machinery, no special apparatus of repression is needed for this; this will be done by the armed people itself, as simply and as readily as any crowd of civilized people, even in modern society, parts a pair of combatants or does not allow a woman to be outraged. And, secondly, we know that the fundamental social cause of excesses which consist in violating the rules of social life is the exploitation of the masses, their want and their poverty. With the removal of this chief cause, excesses will inevitably begin to "*wither away*." We do not know how quickly and in what succession, but we know that they will wither away. With their withering away, the state will also *wither away*.

Without going into Utopias, Marx defined more fully what can *now* be defined regarding this future, namely, the difference between the lower and higher phases (degrees, stages) of Communist society.

---

[12]Idealists dreaming of a society of perfect harmony.

First Phase of Communist Society

. . . Marx gives a sober estimate of exactly how a Socialist society will have to manage its affairs. Marx undertakes a *concrete* analysis of the conditions of life of a society in which there is no capitalism, and says:

> What we are dealing with here [analyzing the programme of the party] is not a Communist society which has *developed* on its own foundations, but, on the contrary, one which is just *emerging* from capitalist society, and which therefore in all respects— economic, moral and intellectual—still bears the birthmarks of the old society from whose womb it sprung.

And it is this Communist society—a society which has just come into the world out of the womb of capitalism, and which, in all respects, bears the stamp of the old society—that Marx terms the "first," or lower, phase of Communist society.

The means of production are no longer the private property of individuals. The means of production belong to the whole of society. Every member of society, performing a certain part of socially-necessary work, receives a certificate from society to the effect that he has done such and such a quantity of work. According to this certificate, he receives from the public warehouses, where articles of consumption are stored, a corresponding quantity of products. Deducting that proportion of labor which goes to the public fund, every worker, therefore, receives from society as much as he has given it.

"Equality" seems to reign supreme. . . .

"Equal right," says Marx, we indeed have here; but it is *still* a "bourgeois right," which, like every right, *presupposes inequality*. Every right is an application of the *same* measure to *different* people who, in fact, are not the same and are not equal to one another; this is why "equal right" is really a violation of equality, and an injustice. In effect, every man having done as much social labor as every other, receives an equal share of the social products (with the above-mentioned deductions).

But different people are not alike: one is strong, another is weak; one is married, the other is not; one has more children, another has less, and so on.

> With equal labor—Marx concludes—and therefore an equal share in the social consumption fund, one man in fact receives more than the other, one is richer than the other, and so forth. In order to avoid all these defects, rights, instead of being equal, must be unequal.

The first phase of Communism, therefore, still cannot produce justice and equality; differences, and unjust differences, in wealth will still exist, but the *exploitation* of man by man will have become impossible, because it will be impossible to seize as private property the *means of production*, the factories, machines, land, and so on. In tearing down Lassalle's[13] petty-bourgeois, confused phrase about "equality" and "justice" *in general*, Marx shows the *course of development* of Communist society, which is forced at first to destroy *only* the "injustice" that consists in the means of production having been seized by private individuals, and which *is not capable* of destroying at once the further injustice consisting in the distribution of the articles of consumption "according to work performed" (and not according to need). . . .

Marx not only takes into account with the greatest accuracy the inevitable inequality of men; he also takes into account the fact that the mere conversion of the means of production into the common property of the whole of society ("Socialism" in the generally accepted sense of the word) *does not remove* the defects of distribution and the inequality of "bourgeois right" which *continue to rule* as long as the products are divided "according to work performed."

> But these defects—Marx continues—are unavoidable in the first phase of Communist society, when, after long travail, it first emerges from capitalist society. Justice can never rise superior to the economic conditions of society and the cultural development conditioned by them.

And so, in the first phase of Communist society (generally called Socialism) "bourgeois right" is *not* abolished in its entirety, but only in part, only in proportion to the economic transformation so far attained, that is, only in respect of the means of production. "Bourgeois right" recognizes them as the private property of separate individuals. Socialism converts them into common property. *To that extent*, and to that extent alone, does "bourgeois right" disappear.

However, it continues to exist as far as its other part is concerned; it remains in the capacity of regulator (determining factor) distributing the products and allotting labor among the members of society. "He who does not work, shall not eat"—this Socialist principle is *already* realized; "for an equal quantity of labor, an equal quantity of products"—this Socialist principle is also *already* realized. However, this is not yet Communism, and this does not abolish "bourgeois right,"

[13]Ferdinand Lassalle (1825–1864) was a German socialist and the founder of the German Social Democratic Party.

which gives to unequal individuals, in return for an unequal (in reality unequal) amount of work, an equal quantity of products.

This is a "defect," says Marx, but it is unavoidable during the first phase of Communism; for, if we are not to fall into Utopianism, we cannot imagine that, having overthrown capitalism, people will at once learn to work for society *without any standards of right*; indeed, the abolition of capitalism *does not immediately lay* the economic foundations for *such* a change.

And there is no other standard yet than that of "bourgeois right." To this extent, therefore, a form of state is still necessary, which, while maintaining public ownership of the means of production, would preserve the equality of labor and equality in the distribution of products.

The state is withering away in so far as there are no longer any capitalists, any classes, and, consequently, no *class* can be suppressed.

But the state has not yet altogether withered away, since there still remains the protection of "bourgeois right" which sanctifies actual inequality. For the complete extinction of the state, complete Communism is necessary.

Higher Phase of Communist Society

Marx continues:

> In a higher phase of Communist society, when the enslaving subordination of individuals in the division of labor has disappeared, and with it also the antagonism between mental and physical labor; when labor has become not only a means of living, but itself the first necessity of life; when, along with the all-round development of individuals, the productive forces too have grown, and all the springs of social wealth are flowing more freely—it is only at that stage that it will be possible to pass completely beyond the narrow horizon of bourgeois rights, and for society to inscribe on its banners: from each according to his ability; to each according to his needs!

Only now can we appreciate the full correctness of Engels' remarks in which he mercilessly ridiculed all the absurdity of combining the words "freedom" and "state." While the state exists there is no freedom. When there is freedom, there will be no state.

The economic basis for the complete withering away of the state is that high stage of development of Communism when the antagonism between mental and physical labor disappears, that is to say, when one of the principal sources of modern *social* inequality disappears—a source, moreover, which it is impossible to remove immediately by the mere conversion of the means of production into public property, by the mere expropriation of the capitalists.

This expropriation will make a gigantic development of the productive forces *possible*. And seeing how incredibly, even now, capitalism *retards* this development, how much progress could be made even on the basis of modern technique at the level it has reached, we have a right to say, with the fullest confidence, that the expropriation of the capitalists will inevitably result in a gigantic development of the productive forces of human society. But how rapidly this development will go forward, how soon it will reach the point of breaking away from the division of labor, of removing the antagonism betweeen mental and physical labor, of transforming work into the "first necessity of life"—this we do not and *cannot* know.

Consequently, we have a right to speak solely of the inevitable withering away of the state, emphasizing the protracted nature of this process and its dependence upon the rapidity of development of the *higher phase* of Communism; leaving quite open the question of lengths of time, or the concrete forms of withering away, since material for the solution of such questions is *not available*.

The state will be able to wither away completely when society has realized the rule: "From each according to his ability; to each according to his needs," namely, when people have become accustomed to observe the fundamental rules of social life, and their labor is so productive, that they voluntarily work *according to their ability*. "The narrow horizon of bourgeois rights," which compels one to calculate, with the hard-heartedness of a Shylock,[14] whether he has not worked half an hour more than another, whether he is not getting less pay than another—this narrow horizon will then be left behind. There will then be no need for any exact calculation by society of the quantity of products to be distributed to each of its members; each will take freely "according to his needs."

From the bourgeois point of view, it is easy to declare such a social order "a pure Utopia," and to sneer at the Socialists for promising each the right to receive from society, without any control of the labor of the individual citizen, any quantity of truffles, automobiles, pianos, and so

[14]The greedy and merciless moneylender in Shakespeare's play *The Merchant of Venice*.

forth. Even now, most bourgeois "savants"[15] deliver themselves of such sneers, thereby displaying at once their ignorance and their self-seeking defense of capitalism.

Ignorance—for it has never entered the head of any Socialist to "promise" that the highest phase of Communism will arrive; while the great Socialists, in *foreseeing* its arrival, presupposed both a productivity of labor unlike the present and a person not like the present man in the street, capable of spoiling, without reflection, like the seminary students in Pomyalovsky's[16] book, the stores of social wealth, and of demanding the impossible.

Until the "higher" phase of Communism arrives, the Socialists demand the *strictest* control, *by society and by the state*, of the quantity of labor and the quantity of consumption; only this control must *start* with the expropriation of the capitalists, with the control of the workers over the capitalists, and must be carried out, not by a state of bureaucrats, but by a state of *armed workers*. . . .

---

[15]Learned men; here used satirically, as "wiseacres."

[16]Nikolai Pomyalovsky (1835–1863) was a Russian writer who had been a theology student before turning to literature. In his *Sketches from the Seminary*, published in 1859, he rendered a shocking and disenchanting description of life in a theological school.

33

Adolf Hitler

My Struggle

*T*HE First World War and the Bolshe-
*vik Revolution were severe blows to the European liberal order. The destruction
of the traditional social system and its values and the spiritual uprooting of the
European masses gave rise to a widespread popular reaction against liberalism,
democracy, and the complex urban-industrial revolution that had nurtured
them. Adolf Hitler (1889–1945) became the demonic prophet and leader of this
counterrevolution.*

*As a young man, Hitler led an aimless existence in prewar Austria and
Germany. After the war, in which he served with great personal satisfaction, he
devoted his life to political affairs, joining the National Socialist (Nazi)
German Workers' Party and soon becoming its leader (Führer). In 1923 he led
an unsuccessful revolt against the government, for which he served a short term
in prison; but he went on to transform the Nazi party into the mass movement
that would, within a decade, dominate Germany. In doing so, he played on the
frustrations of a people in defeat and economic depression and, for the most part,
in distress over the dislocations brought on by industrialization and urbaniza-
tion. The party he headed won allegiance through mass propaganda and terror,
and in 1933 he became dictator of the nation. As head of state he instituted a
nationalist, collectivist, and militarist regime based on romantic notions of
people (Volk) and race, and led the Germans into a series of annexations and
invasions that developed into the Second World War.*

*Hitler had expounded his program in an exciting but confused book called
Mein Kampf (My Struggle), which was written during his prison term and
published sometime between 1925 and 1927. Supposedly the story of his early
life and the development of his ideas and the Nazi movement, the book is a
mixture of half truths, big lies, scurrilous attacks, and idealistic emotional
appeals intended to arouse in the reader resentment and hatred toward others. He*

denounces Marxism, Jews, bourgeois liberals, and democracy as the sources of Germany's ills; and he calls for a "regenerated" German nation, attached to its sacred soil, purified in its racial make-up, and devotedly following its leaders to world supremacy. The "bible" of Nazi Germany, the book remains a classic exhibition of violent hatred and irrationality.

The following selection from Mein Kampf—in which sections have been rearranged for the sake of clarity—illustrates Hitler's views on what he believed to be a Marxist-Jewish conspiracy against the German people; the natural inequality of races and the superiority of the Aryan race; the Volk as the natural human unit and the primacy of the German Volk; the nature and purposes of propaganda in the creation of a successful mass movement dedicated to the achievement of Nazi objectives; and the need for Germany to conquer more soil for its people. Though largely discredited at present, some of Hitler's ideas still have appeal among those disenchanted with the course of Western civilization and those who feel uncomfortable in a pluralistic society.

* * *

MARXISM

I began to make myself familiar with the founders of [Marxism] in order to study the foundations of the movement. If I reached my goal more quickly than at first I had perhaps ventured to believe, it was thanks to my newly acquired, though at that time not very profound, knowledge of the Jewish question. This alone enabled me to draw a practical comparison between the reality and the theoretical flim-flam of the founding fathers of Social Democracy, since it taught me to understand the language of the Jewish people, who speak in order to conceal or at least to veil their thoughts; their real aim is not therefore to be found in the lines themselves, but slumbers well concealed between them.

For me this was the time of the greatest spiritual upheaval I have ever had to go through.

I had ceased to be a weak-kneed cosmopolitan and become an anti-Semite.[1] . . .

---

[1]One who hates Jews and Jewish things.

MY STRUGGLE   Adolf Hitler, *Mein Kampf*, trans. Ralph Manheim (Boston: Houghton Mifflin, 1943), 51, 64–65, 107, 118–19, 177–81, 214–15, 231, 286, 288, 290, 294, 305–306, 314–16, 318–20, 324–27, 382–85, 391, 393–94, 402–405, 623, 642–43, 645–46, 652–54, 661, 682.

The Jewish doctrine of Marxism rejects the aristocratic principle of Nature and replaces the eternal privilege of power and strength by the mass of numbers and their dead weight. Thus it denies the value of personality in man, contests the significance of nationality and race, and thereby withdraws from humanity the premise of its existence and its culture. As a foundation of the universe, this doctrine would bring about the end of any order intellectually conceivable to man. And as, in this greatest of all recognizable organisms, the result of an application of such a law could only be chaos, on earth it could only be destruction for the inhabitants of this planet.

If, with the help of his Marxist creed, the Jew is victorious over the other peoples of the world, his crown will be the funeral wreath of humanity and this planet will, as it did thousands of years ago, move through the ether devoid of men.

Eternal Nature inexorably avenges the infringement of her commands.

Hence today I believe that I am acting in accordance with the will of the Almighty Creator: *by defending myself against the Jew, I am fighting for the work of the Lord.* . . .

Only a knowledge of the Jews provides the key with which to comprehend the inner, and consequently real, aims of Social Democracy.

The erroneous conceptions of the aim and meaning of this party fall from our eyes like veils, once we come to know this people, and from the fog and mist of social phrases rises the leering grimace of Marxism. . . .

Marxist doctrine is a brief spiritual extract of the philosophy of life that is generally current today. And for this reason alone any struggle of our so-called bourgeois world against it is impossible, absurd in fact, since this bourgeois world is also essentially infected by these poisons, and worships a view of life which in general is distinguished from the Marxists only by degrees and personalities. The bourgeois world is Marxist, but believes in the possibility of the rule of certain groups of men (bourgeoisie), while Marxism itself systematically plans to hand the world over to the Jews. . . .

. . . A Germany saved from these mortal enemies of her existence and her future would possess forces which the whole world could no longer have stifled. *On the day when Marxism is smashed in Germany, her fetters will in truth be broken forever.* For never in our history have we been defeated by the strength of our foes, but always by our own vices and by the enemies in our own camp. . . .

JEWS

The Jew of all times has lived in the states of other peoples, and there formed his own state, which, to be sure, habitually sailed under the disguise of 'religious community' as long as outward circumstances made a complete revelation of his nature seem inadvisable. But as soon as he felt strong enough to do without the protective cloak, he always dropped the veil and suddenly became what so many of the others previously did not want to believe and see: the Jew.

The Jew's life as a parasite in the body of other nations and states explains a characteristic which once caused Schopenhauer[2]. . . to call him the 'great master in lying.' Existence impels the Jew to lie, and to lie perpetually, just as it compels the inhabitants of the northern countries to wear warm clothing.

His life within other peoples can only endure for any length of time if he succeeds in arousing the opinion that he is not a people but a 'religious community,' though of a special sort.

And this is the first great lie. . . .

The Jew has always been a people with definite racial characteristics and never a religion; only in order to get ahead he early sought for a means which could distract unpleasant attention from his person. And what would have been more expedient and at the same time more innocent than the 'embezzled' concept of a religious community? For here, too, everything is borrowed or rather stolen. Due to his own original special nature, the Jew cannot possess a religious institution, if for no other reason because he lacks idealism in any form, and hence belief in a hereafter is absolutely foreign to him. And a religion in the Aryan[3] sense cannot be imagined which lacks the conviction of survival after death in some form. . . .

The Jew also becomes liberal and begins to rave about the necessary progress of mankind.

Slowly he makes himself the spokesman of a new era.

Also, of course, he destroys more and more thoroughly the foundations of any economy that will really benefit the people. By way of

[2]Arthur Schopenhauer (1788–1860), a German philosopher and chief expounder of pessimism.

[3]Indo-European, as differentiated from Jewish. (The Indo-European peoples, as a large *language* group, were believed to have originated in north-central Europe and to have dispersed westward, southward, and eastward beginning around 3000 B.C. Some race theorists, followed by Hitler, insisted that the Indo-Europeans constituted a distinctive and superior *racial* group, which they called "Aryans.")

stock shares he pushes his way into the circuit of national production which he turns into a purchasable or rather tradable object, thus robbing the enterprises of the foundations of a personal ownership. Between employer and employee there arises that inner estrangement which later leads to political class division.

Finally, the Jewish influence on economic affairs grows with terrifying speed through the stock exchange. He becomes the owner, or at least the controller, of the national labor force.

To strengthen his political position he tries to tear down the racial and civil barriers which for a time continue to restrain him at every step. To this end he fights with all the tenacity innate in him for religious tolerance. . . .

He always represents himself personally as having an infinite thirst for knowledge, praises all progress, mostly, to be sure, the progress that leads to the ruin of others; for he judges all knowledge and all development only according to its possibilities for advancing his nation, and where this is lacking, he is the inexorable mortal enemy of all light, a hater of all true culture. He uses all the knowledge he acquires in the schools of other peoples, exclusively for the benefit of his race. . . .

His ultimate goal . . . is the victory of 'democracy,' or, as he understands it: the rule of parliamentarianism. It is most compatible with his requirements; for it excludes the personality—and puts in its place the majority characterized by stupidity, incompetence, and last but not least, cowardice. . . .

. . . While on the one hand he organizes capitalist methods of human exploitation to their ultimate consequence, [the Jew] approaches the very victims of his spirit and his activity and in a short time becomes the leader of their struggle against himself. 'Against himself' is only figuratively speaking; for the great master of lies understands as always how to make himself appear to be the pure one and to heap the blame on others. Since he has the gall to lead the masses, it never even enters their heads that this might be the most infamous betrayal of all times.

And yet it was.

Scarcely has the [proletariat] grown out of the general economic shift than the Jew, clearly and distinctly, realizes that it can open the way for his own further advancement. First, he used the bourgeoisie as a battering-ram against the feudal world, then the worker against the bourgeois world. If formerly he knew how to swindle his way to civil rights in the shadow of the bourgeoisie, now he hopes to find the road to his own domination in the worker's struggle for existence.

From now on the worker has no other task but to fight for the future of the Jewish people. Unconsciously he is harnessed to the service of the power which he thinks he is combating. He is seemingly allowed to attack capital, and this is the easiest way of making him fight for it. In this the Jew keeps up an outcry against international capital and in truth he means the national economy which must be demolished in order that the international stock exchange can triumph over its dead body. . . .

Thus there arises a pure movement entirely of manual workers under Jewish leadership, apparently aiming to improve the situation of the worker, but in truth planning the enslavement and with it the destruction of all non-Jewish peoples.

The general pacifistic paralysis of the national instinct of self-preservation . . . in the circles of the so-called intelligentsia[4] is transmitted to the broad masses and above all to the bourgeoisie by the activity of the big papers which today are always Jewish. Added to these two weapons of disintegration comes a third and by far the most terrible, the organization of brute force. As a shock and storm troop, Marxism is intended to finish off what the preparatory softening up with the first two weapons has made ripe for collapse. . . .

Here [the Jew] stops at nothing, and in his vileness he becomes so gigantic that no one need be surprised if among our people the personification of the devil as the symbol of all evil assumes the living shape of the Jew.

The ignorance of the broad masses about the inner nature of the Jew, the lack of instinct and narrow-mindedness of our upper classes, make the people an easy victim for this Jewish campaign of lies. . . .

With satanic joy in his face, the black-haired Jewish youth lurks in wait for the unsuspecting girl whom he defiles with his blood, thus stealing her from her people. With every means he tries to destroy the racial foundations of the people he has set out to subjugate. Just as he himself systematically ruins women and girls, he does not shrink back from pulling down the blood barriers for others, even on a large scale. It was and it is Jews who bring the Negroes into the Rhineland,[5] always with the same secret thought and clear aim of ruining the hated white race by the necessarily resulting bastardization, throwing it down from its cultural and political height, and himself rising to be its master.

For a racially pure people which is conscious of its blood can never be

---

[4]The educated class, the intellectuals.

[5]A reference to the French occupation of the Rhineland after the First World War; some of the French troops were blacks from French colonial Africa.

enslaved by the Jew. In this world he will forever be master over bastards and bastards alone.

And so he tries systematically to lower the racial level by a continuous poisoning of individuals.

And in politics he begins to replace the idea of democracy by the dictatorship of the proletariat.

In the organized mass of Marxism he has found the weapon which lets him dispense with democracy and in its stead allows him to subjugate and govern the peoples with a dictatorial and brutal fist.

He works systematically for revolutionization in a twofold sense: economic and political.

Around peoples who offer too violent a resistance to attack from within he weaves a net of enemies, thanks to his international influence, incites them to war, and finally, if necessary, plants the flag of revolution on the very battlefields.

In economics he undermines the states until the social enterprises which have become unprofitable are taken from the state and subjected to his financial control.

In the political field he refuses the state the means for its self-preservation, destroys the foundations of all national self-maintenance and defense, destroys faith in the leadership, scoffs at its history and past, and drags everything that is truly great into the gutter.

Culturally he contaminates art, literature, the theater, makes a mockery of natural feeling, overthrows all concepts of beauty and sublimity, of the noble and the good, and instead drags men down into the sphere of his own base nature.

Religion is ridiculed, ethics and morality represented as outmoded, until the last props of a nation in its struggle for existence in this world have fallen.

Now begins the great last revolution. In gaining political power the Jew casts off the few cloaks that he still wears. The democratic people's Jew becomes the blood-Jew and tyrant over peoples. In a few years he tries to exterminate the national intelligentsia and by robbing the peoples of their natural intellectual leadership makes them ripe for the slave's lot of permanent subjugation.

The most frightful example of this kind is offered by Russia, where he killed or starved about thirty million people with positively fanatical savagery, in part amid inhuman tortures, in order to give a gang of Jewish journalists and stock exchange bandits domination over a great people.

The end is not only the end of freedom of the peoples oppressed by the Jew, but also the end of this parasite upon the nations. After the death of his victim, the vampire sooner or later dies too. . . .

The Jewish train of thought in all this is clear. The Bolshevization of Germany[6]—that is, the extermination of the national folkish . . . intelligentsia to make possible the sweating of the German working class under the yoke of Jewish world finance—is conceived only as a preliminary to the further extension of this Jewish tendency of world conquest. As often in history, Germany is the great pivot in the mighty struggle. If our people and our state become the victim of these blood-thirsty and avaricious Jewish tyrants of nations, the whole earth will sink into the snares of this octopus; if Germany frees herself from this embrace, this greatest of dangers to nations may be regarded as broken for the whole world. . . .

. . . The striving of the Jewish people for world domination . . . is just as natural as the urge of the Anglo-Saxon to seize domination of the earth. And just as the Anglo-Saxon pursues this course in his own way and carries on the fight with his own weapons, likewise the Jew. He goes his way, the way of sneaking in among the nations and boring from within, and he fights with his weapons, with lies and slander, poison and corruption, intensifying the struggle to the point of blood-ily exterminating his hated foes. *In Russian Bolshevism[7] we must see the attempt undertaken by the Jews in the twentieth century to achieve world domination.* . . .

RACE AND THE FOLKISH PHILOSOPHY

For me and all true National Socialists there is but one doctrine: people and fatherland.

What we must fight for is to safeguard the existence and reproduction of our race and our people, the sustenance of our children and the purity of our blood, the freedom and independence of the fatherland, so that our people may mature for the fulfillment of the mission allotted it by the creator of the universe.

Every thought and every idea, every doctrine and all knowledge, must serve this purpose. And everything must be examined from this point of view and used or rejected according to its utility. Then no theory will stiffen into a dead doctrine, since it is life alone that all things must serve. . . .

No more than Nature desires the mating of weaker with stronger

---

[6]The turning of Germany into a Communist state on the Russian Bolshevik model.
[7]Soviet communism.

individuals, even less does she desire the blending of a higher with a lower race, since, if she did, her whole work of higher breeding, over perhaps hundreds of thousands of years, might be ruined with one blow.

Historical experience offers countless proofs of this. It shows with terrifying clarity that in every mingling of Aryan blood with that of lower peoples the result was the end of the cultured people. North America, whose population consists in by far the largest part of Germanic elements who mixed but little with the lower colored peoples, shows a different humanity and culture from Central and South America, where the predominantly Latin immigrants often mixed with the aborigines on a large scale. By this one example, we can clearly and distinctly recognize the effect of racial mixture. The Germanic inhabitant of the American continent, who has remained racially pure and unmixed, rose to be master of the continent; he will remain the master as long as he does not fall a victim to defilement of the blood.

The result of all racial crossing is therefore in brief always the following:

(a) Lowering of the level of the higher race;

(b) Physical and intellectual regression and hence the beginning of a slowly but surely progressing sickness.

To bring about such a development is, then, nothing else but to sin against the will of the eternal creator. . . .

Everything we admire on this earth today—science and art, technology and inventions—is only the creative product of a few peoples and originally perhaps of *one* race. On them depends the existence of this whole culture. If they perish, the beauty of this earth will sink into the grave with them. . . .

It is idle to argue which race or races were the original representative of human culture and hence the real founders of all that we sum up under the word 'humanity.' It is simpler to raise this question with regard to the present, and here an easy, clear answer results. All the human culture, all the results of art, science, and technology that we see before us today, are almost exclusively the creative product of the Aryan. This very fact admits of the not unfounded inference that he alone was the founder of all higher humanity, therefore representing the prototype of all that we understand by the word 'man.' He is the Prometheus[8] of mankind from whose bright forehead the divine spark

---

[8]In Greek mythology, an ancient god who stole fire from heaven and gave it to humankind.

of genius has sprung at all times, forever kindling anew that fire of knowledge which illumined the night of silent mysteries and thus caused man to climb the path to mastery over the other beings of this earth. Exclude him—and perhaps after a few thousand years darkness will again descend on the earth, human culture will pass, and the world turn to a desert.

If we were to divide mankind into three groups, the founders of culture, the bearers of culture, the destroyers of culture, only the Aryan could be considered as the representative of the first group. From him originate the foundations and walls of all human creation, and only the outward form and color are determined by the changing traits of character of the various peoples. He provides the mightiest building stones and plans for all human progress and only the execution corresponds to the nature of the varying men and races. . . .

. . . Just as in the life of the outstanding individual, genius or extraordinary ability strives for practical realization only when spurred on by special occasions, likewise in the life of nations the creative forces and capacities which are present can often be exploited only when definite preconditions invite.

We see this most distinctly in connection with the race which has been and is the bearer of human cultural development—the Aryans. As soon as Fate leads them toward special conditions, their latent abilities begin to develop in a more and more rapid sequence and to mold themselves into tangible forms. The cultures which they found in such cases are nearly always decisively determined by the existing soil, the given climate, and—the subjected people. This last item, to be sure, is almost the most decisive. The more primitive the technical foundations for a cultural activity, the more necessary is the presence of human helpers who, organizationally assembled and employed, must replace the force of the machine. Without this possibility of using lower human beings, the Aryan would never have been able to take his first steps toward his future culture; just as without the help of various suitable beasts which he knew how to tame, he would not have arrived at a technology which is now gradually permitting him to do without these beasts. . . .

The folkish[9] philosophy finds the importance of mankind in its basic racial elements. In the state it sees on principle only a means to an end and construes its end as the preservation of the racial existence of man.

[9]Originating from the people (*Volk*) and benefiting them.

Thus, it by no means believes in an equality of the races, but along with their difference it recognizes their higher or lesser value and feels itself obligated, through this knowledge, to promote the victory of the better and stronger, and demand the subordination of the inferior and weaker in accordance with the eternal will that dominates this universe. Thus, in principle, it serves the basic aristocratic idea of Nature and believes in the validity of this law down to the last individual. It sees not only the different value of the races, but also the different value of individuals. From the mass it extracts the importance of the individual personality, and thus, in contrast to disorganizing Marxism, it has an organizing effect. It believes in the necessity of an idealization of humanity, in which alone it sees the premise for the existence of humanity. But it cannot grant the right to existence even to an ethical idea if this idea represents a danger for the racial life of the bearers of a higher ethics; for in a bastardized and niggerized world all the concepts of the humanly beautiful and sublime, as well as all ideas of an idealized future of our humanity, would be lost forever. . . .

And so the folkish philosophy of life corresponds to the innermost will of Nature, since it restores that free play of forces which must lead to a continuous mutual higher breeding, until at last the best of humanity, having achieved possession of this earth, will have a free path for activity in domains which will lie partly above it and partly outside it.

We all sense that in the distant future humanity must be faced by problems which only a highest race, become master people and supported by the means and possibilities of an entire globe, will be equipped to overcome. . . .

It is self-evident that so general a statement of the meaningful content of a folkish philosophy can be interpreted in thousands of ways. And actually we find hardly a one of our newer political formations which does not base itself in one way or another on this world view. And, by its very existence in the face of the many others, it shows the difference of its conceptions. And so the Marxist world view, led by a unified top organization, is opposed by a hodge-podge of views which even as ideas are not very impressive in face of the solid, hostile front. Victories are not gained by such feeble weapons! Not until the international world view—politically led by organized Marxism—is confronted by a folkish world view, organized and led with equal unity, will success, supposing the fighting energy to be equal on both sides, fall to the side of eternal truth.

A philosophy can only be organizationally comprehended on the basis of a definite formulation of that philosophy, and what dogmas represent for religious faith, party principles are for a political party in the making.

Hence an instrument must be created for the folkish world view which enables it to fight, just as the Marxist party organization creates a free path for internationalism.

This is the goal pursued by the National Socialist German Workers' Party. . . .

THE STATE

All these views have their deepest root in the knowledge that the forces which create culture and values are based essentially on racial elements and that the state must, therefore, in the light of reason, regard its highest task as the preservation and intensification of the race, this fundamental condition of all human cultural development. . . .

It is, therefore, the first obligation of a new movement, standing on the ground of a folkish world view, to make sure that its conception of the nature and purpose of the state attains a uniform and clear character.

Thus the basic realization is: *that the state represents no end, but a means. It is, to be sure, the premise for the formation of a higher human culture, but not its cause, which lies exclusively in the existence of a race capable of culture.* Hundreds of exemplary states might exist on earth, but if the Aryan culture-bearer died out, there would be no culture corresponding to the spiritual level of the highest peoples of today. We can go even farther and say that the fact of human state formation would not in the least exclude the possibility of the destruction of the human race, provided that superior intellectual ability and elasticity would be lost due to the absence of their racial bearers. . . .

This glorious creative ability was given only to the Aryan, whether he bears it dormant within himself or gives it to awakening life, depending whether favorable circumstances permit this or an inhospitable Nature prevents it.

From this the following realization results:

The state is a means to an end. Its end lies in the preservation and advancement of a community of physically and psychically homogeneous creatures. This preservation itself comprises first of all existence as a race and thereby permits the free development of all the forces dormant in this race. Of them a part will always primarily serve the preservation of physical life, and only the remaining part the promotion of a further spiritual development. Actually the one always creates the precondition for the other.

States which do not serve this purpose are misbegotten, monstrosities in fact. The fact of their existence changes this no more than the success of a gang of bandits can justify robbery. . . .

Thus, the highest purpose of a folkish state is concern for the preservation of those original racial elements which bestow culture and create the beauty and dignity of a higher mankind. We, as Aryans, can conceive of the state only as the living organism of a nationality which not only assures the preservation of this nationality, but by the development of its spiritual and ideal abilities leads it to the highest freedom.

But what they try to palm off on us as a state today is usually nothing but a monstrosity born of deepest human error, with untold misery as a consequence. . . .

Anyone who does not want the earth to move toward [racial mixing] must convert himself to the conception that it is the function above all of the Germanic states first and foremost to call a fundamental halt to any further bastardization.

The generation of our present notorious weaklings will obviously cry out against this, and moan and complain about assaults on the holiest human rights. *No, there is only one holiest human right, and this right is at the same time the holiest obligation, to wit: to see to it that the blood is preserved pure and, by preserving the best humanity, to create the possibility of a nobler development of these beings.*

A folkish state must therefore begin by raising marriage from the level of a continuous defilement of the race, and give it the consecration of an institution which is called upon to produce images of the Lord and not monstrosities halfway between man and ape.

The protest against this on so-called *humane* grounds is particularly ill-suited to an era which on the one hand gives every depraved degenerate the possibility of propagating, but which burdens the products themselves, as well as their contemporaries, with untold suffering, while on the other hand every drug store and our very street peddlers offer the means for the prevention of births for sale even to the healthiest parents. In this present-day state of law and order in the eyes of its representatives, this brave, bourgeois-national society, the prevention of the procreative faculty in sufferers from syphilis, tuberculosis, hereditary diseases, cripples, and cretins is a crime, while the actual suppression of the procreative faculty in millions of the very best people is not regarded as anything bad and does not offend against the morals of this hypocritical society, but is rather a benefit to its short-sighted mental laziness. For otherwise these people would at least be forced to rack their brains about providing a basis for the sustenance and preservation of those beings who, as healthy bearers of our nationality, should one day serve the same function with regard to the coming generation.

How boundlessly unideal and ignoble is this whole system! People no longer bother to breed the best for posterity, but let things slide along as best they can. If our churches also sin against the image of the Lord, whose importance they still so highly emphasize, it is entirely because of the line of their present activity which speaks always of the spirit and lets its bearer, the man, degenerate into a depraved proletarian. Afterwards, of course, they make foolish faces and are full of amazement at the small effect of the Christian faith in their own country, at the terrible 'godlessness,' at this physically botched and hence spiritually degenerate rabble, and try with the Church's Blessing, to make up for it by success with the Hottentots and Zulu Kaffirs.[10] While our European peoples, thank the Lord, fall into a condition of physical and moral leprosy, the pious missionary wanders off to Central Africa and sets up Negro missions until there, too, our 'higher culture' turns healthy, though primitive and inferior, human beings into a rotten brood of bastards.

It would be more in keeping with the intention of the noblest man in this world if our two Christian churches, instead of annoying Negroes with missions which they neither desire nor understand, would kindly, but in all seriousness, teach our European humanity that where parents are not healthy it is a deed pleasing to God to take pity on a poor little healthy orphan child and give him father and mother, than themselves to give birth to a sick child who will only bring unhappiness and suffering on himself and the rest of the world.

The folkish state must make up for what everyone else today has neglected in this field. *It must set race in the center of all life. It must take care to keep it pure. It must declare the child to be the most precious treasure of the people. It must see to it that only the healthy beget children; that there is only one disgrace: despite one's own sickness and deficiencies, to bring children into the world, and one highest honor: to renounce doing so. And conversely it must be considered reprehensible: to withhold healthy children from the nation. Here the state must act as the guardian of a millennial future in the face of which the wishes and the selfishness of the individual must appear as nothing and submit. It must put the most modern medical means in the service of this knowledge. It*

---

[10]African tribes (representing all such "primitive" peoples), whom Hitler loathed.

must declare unfit for propagation all who are in any way visibly sick or who have inherited a disease and can therefore pass it on, and put this into actual practice. Conversely, it must take care that the fertility of the healthy woman is not limited by the financial irresponsibility of a state regime which turns the blessing of children into a curse for the parents. It must put an end to that lazy, nay criminal, indifference with which the social premises for a fecund[11] family are treated today, and must instead feel itself to be the highest guardian of this most precious blessing of a people. Its concern belongs more to the child than to the adult. . . .

In the folkish state, finally, the folkish philosophy of life must succeed in bringing about that nobler age in which men no longer are concerned with breeding dogs, horses, and cats, but in elevating man himself, an age in which the one knowingly and silently renounces, the other joyfully sacrifices and gives.

That this is possible may not be denied in a world where hundreds and hundreds of thousands of people voluntarily submit to celibacy,[12] obligated and bound by nothing except the injunction of the Church.

Should the same renunciation not be possible if this injunction is replaced by the admonition finally to put an end to the constant and continuous original sin of racial poisoning, and to give the Almighty Creator beings such as He Himself created? . . .

PROPAGANDA

The broad masses of the people can be moved only by the power of speech. And all great movements are popular movements, volcanic eruptions of human passions and emotional sentiments, stirred either by the cruel Goddess of Distress or by the firebrand of the word hurled among the masses; they are not the lemonade-like outpourings of literary aesthetes and drawing-room heroes.

Only a storm of hot passion can turn the destinies of peoples, and he alone can arouse passion who bears it within himself.

It alone gives its chosen one the words which like hammer blows can open the gates to the heart of a people.

But the man whom passion fails and whose lips are sealed—he has not been chosen by Heaven to proclaim its will. . . .

In general the art of all truly great national leaders at all times consists among other things primarily in not dividing the attention of a people,

---

[11]Fertile, capable of procreating many children.
[12]Unmarried state.

but in concentrating it upon a single foe. The more unified the application of a people's will to fight, the greater will be the magnetic attraction of a movement and the mightier will be the impetus of the thrust. It belongs to the genius of a great leader to make even adversaries far removed from one another seem to belong to a single category, because in weak and uncertain characters the knowledge of having different enemies can only too readily lead to the beginning of doubt in their own right.

Once the wavering mass sees itself in a struggle against too many enemies, objectivity will put in an appearance, throwing open the question whether all others are really wrong and only their own people or their own movement are in the right.

And this brings about the first paralysis of their own power. Hence a multiplicity of different adversaries must always be combined so that in the eyes of the masses of one's own supporters the struggle is directed against only one enemy. This strengthens their faith in their own right and enhances their bitterness against those who attack it. . . .

The function of propaganda does not lie in the scientific training of the individual, but in calling the masses' attention to certain facts, processes, necessities, and so forth, whose significance is thus for the first time placed within their field of vision.

The whole art consists in doing this so skillfully that everyone will be convinced that the fact is real, the process necessary, the necessity correct, and so forth. But since propaganda is not and cannot be the necessity in itself, since its function, like the poster, consists in attracting the attention of the crowd, and not in educating those who are already educated or who are striving after education and knowledge, its effect for the most part must be aimed at the emotions and only to a very limited degree at the so-called intellect.

All propaganda must be popular and its intellectual level must be adjusted to the most limited intelligence among those it is addressed to. Consequently, the greater the mass it is intended to reach, the lower its purely intellectual level will have to be. But if, as in propaganda for sticking out a war, the aim is to influence a whole people, we must avoid excessive intellectual demands on our public, and too much caution cannot be exerted in this direction.

The more modest its intellectual ballast, the more exclusively it takes into consideration the emotions of the masses, the more effective it will be. And this is the best proof of the soundness or unsoundness of a propaganda campaign, and not success in pleasing a few scholars or young aesthetes.

The art of propaganda lies in understanding the emotional ideas of the great masses and finding, through a psychologically correct form, the way to the attention and thence to the heart of the broad masses. The fact that our bright boys do not understand this merely shows how mentally lazy and conceited they are.

Once we understand how necessary it is for propaganda to be adjusted to the broad mass, the following rule results:

It is a mistake to make propaganda many-sided, like scientific instruction, for instance.

The receptivity of the great masses is very limited, their intelligence is small, but their power of forgetting is enormous. In consequence of these facts, all effective propaganda must be limited to a very few points and must harp on these in slogans until the last member of the public understands what you want him to understand by your slogan. As soon as you sacrifice this slogan and try to be many-sided, the effect will piddle away, for the crowd can neither digest nor retain the material offered. In this way the result is weakened and in the end entirely cancelled out.

Thus we see that propaganda must follow a simple line and correspondingly the basic tactics must be psychologically sound. . . .

. . . The magnitude of a lie always contains a certain factor of credibility, since the great masses of the people in the very bottom of their hearts tend to be corrupted rather than consciously and purposely evil, and that, therefore, in view of the primitive simplicity of their minds, they more easily fall a victim to a big lie than to a little one, since they themselves lie in little things, but would be ashamed of lies that were too big. . . .

FOREIGN POLICY AND WAR

When the nations on this planet fight for existence—when the question of destiny, 'to be or not to be,' cries out for a solution—then all considerations of humanitarianism or aesthetics crumble into nothingness; for all these concepts do not float about in the ether, they arise from man's imagination and are bound up with man. When he departs from this world, these concepts are again dissolved into nothingness, for Nature does not know them. . . .

But all such concepts become secondary when a nation is fighting for its existence; in fact, they become totally irrelevant to the forms of the struggle as soon as a situation arises where they might paralyze a struggling nation's power of self-preservation. And that has always been their only visible result.

As for humanitarianism, Moltke[13] said years ago that in war it lies in the brevity of the operation, and that means that the most aggressive fighting technique is the most humane.

But when people try to approach these questions with drivel about aesthetics, and so forth, really only one answer is possible: where the destiny and existence of a people are at stake, all obligation toward beauty ceases. The most unbeautiful thing there can be in human life is and remains the yoke of slavery. . . .

The foreign policy of the folkish state must safeguard the existence on this planet of the race embodied in the state, by creating a healthy, viable natural relation between the nation's population and growth on the one hand and the quantity and quality of its soil on the other hand.

As a healthy relation we may regard only that condition which assures the sustenance of a people on its own soil. Every other condition, even if it endures for hundreds, nay, thousands of years, is nevertheless unhealthy and will sooner or later lead to the injury if not annihilation of the people in question.

Only an adequately large space on this earth assures a nation of freedom of existence.

Moreover, the necessary size of the territory to be settled cannot be judged exclusively on the basis of present requirements, not even in fact on the basis of the yield of the soil compared to the population. For . . . *in addition to its importance as a direct source of a people's food, another significance, that is, a military and political one, must be attributed to the area of a state.* If a nation's sustenance as such is assured by the amount of its soil, the safeguarding of the existing soil itself must also be borne in mind. This lies in the general power-political strength of the state, which in turn to no small extent is determined by geomilitary considerations.

Hence, the German nation can defend its future only as a world power. . . .

If the National Socialist movement really wants to be consecrated by history with a great mission for our nation, it must be permeated by knowledge and filled with pain at our true situation in this world; boldly and conscious of its goal, it must take up the struggle against the aimlessness and incompetence which have

---

[13]Helmuth von Moltke (1800–1891), a German general, remembered for his contributions to the unification of Germany (1864–71).

hitherto guided our German nation in the line of foreign affairs. Then, without consideration of 'traditions' and prejudices, it must find the courage to gather our people and their strength for an advance along the road that will lead this people from its present restricted living space to new land and soil, and hence also free it from the danger of vanishing from the earth or of serving others as a slave nation.

The National Socialist Movement must strive to eliminate the disproportion between our population and our area—viewing this latter as a source of food as well as a basis for power politics—between our historical past and the hopelessness of our present impotence. . . .

And I must sharply attack those folkish pen-pushers who claim to regard such an acquisition of soil as a 'breach of sacred human rights' and attack it as such in their scribblings. One never knows who stands behind these fellows. But one thing is for certain, that the confusion they can create is desirable and convenient to our national enemies. By such an attitude they help to weaken and destroy from within our people's will for the only correct way of defending their vital needs. For no people on this earth possesses so much as a square yard of territory on the strength of a higher will or superior right. Just as Germany's frontiers are fortuitous frontiers, momentary frontiers in the current political struggle of any period, so are the boundaries of other nations' living space. And just as the shape of our earth's surface can seem immutable as granite only to the thoughtless soft-head, but in reality only represents at each period an apparent pause in a continuous development, created by the mighty forces of Nature in a process of continuous growth, only to be transformed or destroyed tomorrow by greater forces, likewise the boundaries of living spaces in the life of nations.

State boundaries are made by man and changed by man. . . .

But we National Socialists must go further. *The right to possess soil can become a duty if without extension of its soil a great nation seems doomed to destruction.* And most especially when not some little nigger[14] nation or other is involved, but the Germanic mother of life, which has given the present-day world its cultural picture. *Germany will either be a world power or there will be no Germany.* And for world power she needs that magnitude which will give her the position she needs in the present period, and life to her citizens.

• • •

[14]Hitler's term of contempt for any small, non-Aryan country.

34

Jean-Paul Sartre

Existentialism

*E*XISTENTIALISM *is a contemporary intellectual movement that has found expression in philosophy, literature, religion, and politics. Though its roots lie in the nineteenth century, in the writings of Sören Kierkegaard, Dostoevsky, and Nietzsche, it flowered in the years after the Second World War. Essentially, it is a response of Westerners to an age of anxiety, an age in which war, collectivism, and technological innovation have weakened the traditional belief in progress and destroyed the generally accepted standards for determining the good and the true. The existentialist movement is an attempt to find new grounds of truth and value for the modern human being—"a lonely anguished being in an ambiguous world."*

The most popular and influential exponent of existentialism is Jean-Paul Sartre (1905–1980), a French philosopher, novelist, playwright, and political activist. Sartre's form of existentialism has a secular orientation; it rejects any belief in God or the supernatural. Starting from and centered on the human situation, it may be characterized as a contemporary version of humanism.

Like all existentialists, Sartre rejects abstract, rationalistic views of the world that are concerned with defining human essence or being and then deducing the purpose and values of human existence. He insists that existence is prior to essence. It is our condition—our actions and total experience—that define human nature. We are what we make of ourselves. Individual humans are the creators of all values and whatever meaning there may be in human life. But they must act; they must exercise their choice. Only by so acting, in the face of preponderant force, evil, despair, and death, can individuals be truly free. And freedom for Sartre is the greatest good. It is not, however, merely a negative release. It is a dreadful responsibility, for individuals by their choices not only determine their own existence but legislate for all. They endow the universe with values by their actions. Sartre, in short, proposes a courageous, irrational affirmation of responsible life and truth against meaninglessness and death.

Sartre's own life was a heady and controversial amalgam of belief and action. A professor of philosophy at the outset of the Second World War, Sartre later fought in the French resistance and was taken prisoner by the Germans. After his release he wrote Being and Nothingness *(1943), his major philosophical work. He later expounded his existentialist concepts in a number of plays, the best known and most performed being* No Exit *(1945). In 1964, Sartre declined the coveted Nobel Prize for literature because of what he believed to be the political implications of the award. An unorthodox Marxist, he was a critical supporter of postwar communist causes.*

The following selection is taken from lectures Sartre gave in Paris in 1945. It is a pointed response to his critics and a popular and stimulating exposition of his existentialist views.

———————

. . . What can be said from the very beginning is that by existentialism we mean a doctrine which makes human life possible and, in addition, declares that every truth and every action implies a human setting and a human subjectivity. . . .

. . . What complicates matters is that there are two kinds of existentialist; first, those who are Christian, among whom I would include Jaspers[1] and Gabriel Marcel,[2] both Catholic; and on the other hand the atheistic existentialists, among whom I class Heidegger,[3] and then the French existentialists and myself. What they have in common is that they think that existence precedes essence, or, if you prefer, that subjectivity must be the starting point.

Just what does that mean? Let us consider some object that is

———

[1]Karl Jaspers (1883–1969), a German philosopher and psychologist who (after 1948) taught at Basel, Switzerland.

[2]Gabriel Marcel (1889–1973), a French writer and an exponent of a form of Christian existentialism. His philosophy stands in sharp opposition to Sartre's, especially regarding the problem of death.

[3]Martin Heidegger (1889–1976), a German philosopher; his important work *Being and Time* was published in 1927.

EXISTENTIALISM   Jean-Paul Sartre, *Existentialism*, trans. Bernard Frechtman (New York: Philosophical Library, 1947), 10, 12–40, 49–51.

manufactured, for example, a book or a paper-cutter: here is an object which has been made by an artisan whose inspiration came from a concept. He referred to the concept of what a paper-cutter is and likewise to a known method of production, which is part of the concept, something which is, by and large, a routine. Thus, the paper-cutter is at once an object produced in a certain way and, on the other hand, one having a specific use; and one can not postulate a man who produces a paper-cutter but does not know what it is used for. Therefore, let us say that, for the paper-cutter, essence—that is, the ensemble of both the production routines and the properties which enable it to be both produced and defined—precedes existence. Thus, the presence of the paper-cutter or book in front of me is determined. Therefore, we have here a technical view of the world whereby it can be said that production precedes existence.

When we conceive God as the Creator, He is generally thought of as a superior sort of artisan. Whatever doctrine we may be considering, whether one like that of Descartes[4] or that of Leibnitz,[5] we always grant that will more or less follows understanding or, at the very least, accompanies it, and that when God creates He knows exactly what He is creating. Thus, the concept of man in the mind of God is comparable to the concept of paper-cutter in the mind of the manufacturer, and, following certain techniques and a conception, God produces man, just as the artisan, following a definition and a technique, makes a paper-cutter. Thus, the individual man is the realization of a certain concept in the divine intelligence.

In the eighteenth century, the atheism of the *philosophes*[6] discarded the idea of God, but not so much the notion that essence precedes existence. To a certain extent, this idea is found everywhere; we find it in Diderot,[7] in Voltaire,[8] and even in Kant.[9] Man has a human nature; this human nature, which is the concept of the human, is found in all men, which means that each man is a particular example of a universal

[4]René Descartes (1596–1650), a French philosopher and mathematician. (See selection 3.)

[5]Gottfried Wilhelm von Leibnitz (1646–1716), a German philosopher, scientist, and mathematician.

[6]The philosophers of the French Enlightenment.

[7]Denis Diderot (1713–1784), a French philosopher and author who was a co-editor of the monumental *Encyclopedia*.

[8]The literary name of François Marie Arouet (1694–1778), French writer, historian, and philospher. (See selection 9.)

[9]Immanuel Kant (1724–1804), a German critical and moral philosopher.

concept, man. In Kant, the result of this universality is that the wild-man, the natural man, as well as the bourgeois, are circumscribed by the same definition and have the same basic qualities. Thus, here too the essence of man precedes the historical existence that we find in nature.

Atheistic existentialism, which I represent, is more coherent. It states that if God does not exist, there is at least one being in whom existence precedes essence, a being who exists before he can be defined by any concept, and that this being is man, or, as Heidegger says, human reality. What is meant here by saying that existence precedes essence? It means that, first of all, man exists, turns up, appears on the scene, and, only afterward, defines himself. If man, as the existentialist conceives him, is indefinable, it is because at first he is nothing. Only afterward will he be something, and he himself will have made what he will be. Thus, there is no human nature, since there is no God to conceive it. Not only is man what he conceives himself to be, but he is also only what he wills himself to be after this thrust toward existence.

Man is nothing else but what he makes of himself. Such is the first principle of existentialism. It is also what is called subjectivity, the name we are labeled with when charges are brought against us. But what do we mean by this, if not that man has a greater dignity than a stone or table? For we mean that man first exists, that is, that man first of all is the being who hurls himself toward a future and who is conscious of imagining himself as being in the future. Man is at the start a plan which is aware of itself, rather than a patch of moss, a piece of garbage, or a cauliflower; nothing exists prior to this plan; there is nothing in heaven; man will be what he will have planned to be. Not what he will want to be. Because by the word "will" we generally mean a conscious decision, which is subsequent to what we have already made of ourselves. I may want to belong to a political party, write a book, get married; but all that is only a manifestation of an earlier, more spontaneous choice that is called "will." But if existence really does precede essence, man is responsible for what he is. Thus, existentialism's first move is to make every man aware of what he is and to make the full responsibility of his existence rest on him. And when we say that a man is responsible for himself, we do not only mean that he is responsible for his own individuality, but that he is responsible for all men.

The word subjectivism has two meanings, and our opponents play on the two. Subjectivism means, on the one hand, that an individual chooses and makes himself; and, on the other, that it is impossible for man to transcend human subjectivity. The second of these is the essential meaning of existentialism. When we say that man chooses his own self, we mean that every one of us does likewise; but we also mean by that that in making this choice he also chooses all men. In fact, in creating the man that we want to be, there is not a single one of our acts which does not at the same time create an image of man as we think he ought to be. To choose to be this or that is to affirm at the same time the value of what we choose, because we can never choose evil. We always choose the good, and nothing can be good for us without being good for all.

If [moreover] existence precedes essence, and if we grant that we exist and fashion our image at one and the same time, the image is valid for everybody and for our whole age. Thus, our responsibility is much greater than we might have supposed, because it involves all mankind. If I am a workingman and choose to join a Christian trade union rather than be a communist, and if by being a member I want to show that the best thing for man is resignation, that the kingdom of man is not of this world, I am not only involving my own case—I want to be resigned for everyone. As a result, my action has involved all humanity. To take a more individual matter, if I want to marry, to have children; even if this marriage depends solely on my own circumstances or passion or wish, I am involving all humanity in monogamy and not merely myself. Therefore, I am responsible for myself and for everyone else. I am creating a certain image of man of my own choosing. In choosing myself, I choose man.

This helps us understand what the actual content is of such rather grandiloquent words as anguish, forlornness, despair. As you will see, it's all quite simple.

First, what is meant by anguish? The existentialists say at once that man is anguish. What that means is this: the man who involves himself and who realizes that he is not only the person he chooses to be, but also a lawmaker who is, at the same time, choosing all mankind as well as himself, can not help escape the feeling of his total and deep responsibility. Of course, there are many people who are not anxious; but we claim that they are hiding their anxiety, that they are fleeing from it. Certainly, many people believe that when they do something, they themselves are the only ones involved, and when someone says to them, "What if everyone acted that way?" they shrug their shoulders and answer, "Everyone doesn't act that way." But really, one should always ask himself, "What would happen if everybody looked at things that way?" There is no escaping this disturbing thought except by a kind of double-dealing. A man who lies and makes excuses for himself by saying "not everybody does that" is someone with an uneasy conscience, because the act of lying implies that a universal value is conferred upon the lie.

Anguish is evident even when it conceals itself. This is the anguish that Kierkegaard[10] called the anguish of Abraham. You know the story:[11] an angel has ordered Abraham to sacrifice his son; if it really were an angel who has come and said, "You are Abraham, you shall sacrifice your son," everything would be all right. But everyone might first wonder, "Is it really an angel, and am I really Abraham? What proof do I have?"

There was a madwoman who had hallucinations; someone used to speak to her on the telephone and give her orders. Her doctor asked her, "Who is it who talks to you?" She answered, "He says it's God." What proof did she really have that it was God? If an angel comes to me, what proof is there that it's an angel? And if I hear voices, what proof is there that they come from heaven and not from hell, or from the subconscious, or a pathological condition? What proves that they are addressed to me? What proof is there that I have been appointed to impose my choice and my conception of man on humanity? I'll never find any proof or sign to convince me of that. If a voice addresses me, it is always for me to decide that this is the angel's voice; if I consider that such an act is a good one, it is I who will choose to say that it is good rather than bad.

Now, I'm not being singled out as an Abraham, and yet at every moment I'm obliged to perform exemplary acts. For every man, everything happens as if all mankind had its eyes fixed on him and were guiding itself by what he does. And every man ought to say to himself, "Am I really the kind of man who has the right to act in such a way that humanity might guide itself by my actions?" And if he does not say that to himself, he is masking his anguish.

There is no question here of the kind of anguish which would lead to quietism,[12] to inaction. It is a matter of a simple sort of anguish that anybody who has had responsibilities is familiar with. For example,

[10]Sören Kierkegaard (1813–1855), a Danish theologian and philosopher. Sartre is referring to Kierkegaard's important work *Fear and Trembling*, published in 1843.

[11]The story of the readiness of Abraham to kill his son, Isaac, if it is God's will that he do so (Genesis 22:1–14).

[12]A kind of mysticism that demanded that a person surrender totally to God. The extinction of human will and passion was considered a prerequisite for God's entrance into the human vessel. Those who separated themselves from this world and calmly and passively meditated on God and divine things received divine grace.

when a military officer takes the responsibility for an attack and sends a certain number of men to death, he chooses to do so, and in the main he alone makes the choice. Doubtless, orders come from above, but they are too broad; he interprets them, and on this interpretation depend the lives of ten or fourteen or twenty men. In making a decision he can not help having a certain anguish. All leaders know this anguish. That doesn't keep them from acting; on the contrary, it is the very condition of their action. For it implies that they envisage a number of possibilities, and when they choose one, they realize that it has value only because it is chosen. We shall see that this kind of anguish, which is the kind that existentialism describes, is explained, in addition, by a direct responsibility to the other men whom it involves. It is not a curtain separating us from action, but is part of action itself.

When we speak of forlornness, a term Heidegger was fond of, we mean only that God does not exist and that we have to face all the consequences of this. The existentialist is strongly opposed to a certain kind of secular ethics which would like to abolish God with the least possible expense. About 1880, some French teachers tried to set up a secular ethics which went something like this: God is a useless and costly hypothesis; we are discarding it; but, meanwhile, in order for there to be an ethics, a society, a civilization, it is essential that certain values be taken seriously and that they be considered as having an *a priori*[13] existence. It must be obligatory, *a priori*, to be honest, not to lie, not to beat your wife, to have children, and so forth. So we're going to try a little device which will make it possible to show that values exist all the same, inscribed in a heaven of ideas, though otherwise God does not exist. In other words—and this, I believe, is the tendency of everything called reformism in France—nothing will be changed if God does not exist. We shall find ourselves with the same norms of honesty, progress, and humanism, and we shall have made of God an outdated hypothesis which will peacefully die off by itself.

The existentialist, on the contrary, thinks it very distressing that God does not exist, because all possibility of finding values in a heaven of ideas disappears along with Him; there can no longer be an *a priori* Good, since there is no infinite and perfect consciousness to think it. Nowhere is it written that the Good exists, that we must be honest, that we must not lie because the fact is we are on a plane where there are only men. Dostoevsky[14] said, "If God didn't exist, everything would be

---

[13]Preceding and independent.
[14]Fyodor Dostoevsky (1821–1881), a Russian novelist.

possible." That is the very starting point of existentialism. Indeed, everything is permissible if God does not exist, and as a result man is forlorn, because neither within him nor without does he find anything to cling to. He can't start making excuses for himself.

If existence really does precede essence, there is no explaining things away by reference to a fixed and given human nature. In other words, there is no determinism, man is free, man is freedom. On the other hand, if God does not exist, we find no values or commands to turn to which legitimize our conduct. So, in the bright realm of values, we have no excuse behind us, nor justification before us. We are alone, with no excuses.

That is the idea I shall try to convey when I say that man is condemned to be free. Condemned, because he did not create himself, yet, in other respects is free; because, once thrown into the world, he is responsible for everything he does. The existentialist does not believe in the power of passion. He will never agree that a sweeping passion is a ravaging torrent which fatally leads a man to certain acts and is therefore an excuse. He thinks that man is responsible for his passion.

The existentialist does not think that man is going to help himself by finding in the world some omen by which to orient himself. Because he thinks that man will interpret the omen to suit himself. Therefore, he thinks that man, with no support and no aid, is condemned every moment to invent man. Ponge,[15] in a very fine article, has said, "Man is the future of man." That's exactly it. But if it is taken to mean that this future is recorded in heaven, that God sees it, then it is false, because it would really no longer be a future. If it is taken to mean that, whatever a man may be, there is a future to be forged, a virgin future before him, then this remark is sound. But then we are forlorn.

To give you an example which will enable you to understand forlornness better, I shall cite the case of one of my students who came to see me under the following circumstances: his father was on bad terms with his mother, and, moreover, was inclined to be a collaborationist,[16] his older brother had been killed in the German offensive of 1940, and the young man, with somewhat immature but generous feelings, wanted to avenge him. His mother lived alone with him, very much upset by the half-treason of her husband and the death of her older son; the boy was her only consolation.

[15]Francis Ponge (1899–), a French writer and poet.

[16]One of a minority of French people, who, following the fall of France in the Second World War (1940), willingly collaborated (cooperated) with the German (Nazi) occupation forces.

The boy was faced with the choice of leaving for England and joining the Free French Forces[17]—that is, leaving his mother behind—or remaining with his mother and helping her to carry on. He was fully aware that the woman lived only for him and that his going-off—and perhaps his death—would plunge her into despair. He was also aware that every act that he did for his mother's sake was a sure thing, in the sense that it was helping her to carry on, whereas every effort he made toward going off and fighting was an uncertain move which might run aground and prove completely useless; for example, on his way to England he might, while passing through Spain, be detained indefinitely in a Spanish camp; he might reach England or Algiers and be stuck in an office at a desk job. As a result, he was faced with two very different kinds of action: one, concrete, immediate, but concerning only one individual; the other concerned an incomparably vaster group, a national collectivity, but for that very reason was dubious, and might be interrupted en route. And, at the same time, he was wavering between two kinds of ethics. On the one hand, an ethics of sympathy, of personal devotion; on the other, a broader ethics, but one whose efficacy was more dubious. He had to choose between the two.

Who could help him choose? Christian doctrine? No. Christian doctrine says, "Be charitable, love your neighbor, take the more rugged path, and so forth." But which is the more rugged path? Whom should he love as a brother? The fighting man or his mother? Which does the greater good, the vague act of fighting in a group, or the concrete one of helping a particular human being to go on living? Who can decide *a priori*?[18] Nobody. No book of ethics can tell him. The Kantian ethics says, "Never treat any person as a means, but as an end." Very well, if I stay with my mother, I'll treat her as an end and not as a means; but by virtue of this very fact, I'm running the risk of treating the people around me who are fighting, as means; and, conversely, if I go to join those who are fighting, I'll be treating them as an end, and, by doing that, I run the risk of treating my mother as a means.

If values are vague, and if they are always too broad for the concrete and specific case that we are considering, the only thing left for us is to trust our instincts. That's what this young man tried to do; and when I saw him, he said, "In the end, feeling is what counts. I ought to choose

---

[17]French soldiers who, from places outside France (either England or North Africa), continued to struggle against the German occupation until France was liberated.

[18]Without knowing all the facts or the final result.

whichever pushes me in one direction. If I feel that I love my mother enough to sacrifice everything else for her—my desire for vengeance, for action, for adventure—than I'll stay with her. If, on the contrary, I feel that my love for my mother isn't enough, I'll leave."

But how is the value of a feeling determined? What gives his feeling for his mother value? Precisely the fact that he remained with her. I may say that I like so-and-so well enough to sacrifice a certain amount of money for him, but I may say so only if I've done it. I may say "I love my mother well enough to remain with her" if I have remained with her. The only way to determine the value of this affection is, precisely, to perform an act which confirms and defines it. But, since I require this affection to justify my act, I find myself caught in a vicious circle.

On the other hand, Gide[19] has well said that a mock feeling and a true feeling are almost indistinguishable; to decide that I love my mother and will remain with her, or to remain with her by putting on an act, amount somewhat to the same thing. In other words, the feeling is formed by the acts one performs; so, I can not refer to it in order to act upon it. Which means that I can neither seek within myself the true condition which will impel me to act, nor apply to a system of ethics for concepts which will permit me to act. You will say, "At least, he did go to a teacher for advice." But if you seek advice from a priest, for example, you have chosen this priest; you already knew, more or less, just about what advice he was going to give you. In other words, choosing your adviser is involving yourself. The proof of this is that if you are a Christian, you will say, "Consult a priest." But some priests are collaborating, some are just marking time, some are resisting. Which to choose? If the young man chooses a priest who is resisting or collaborating, he has already decided on the kind of advice he's going to get. Therefore, in coming to see me he knew the answer I was going to give him, and I had only one answer to give: "You're free, choose, that is, invent." No general ethics can show you what is to be done; there are no omens in the world. The Catholics will reply, "But there are." Granted—but, in any case, I myself choose the meaning they have.

When I was a prisoner, I knew a rather remarkable young man who was a Jesuit.[20] He had entered the Jesuit order in the following way: he had had a number of very bad breaks; in childhood, his father died, leaving him in poverty, and he was a scholarship student at a religious

---

[19]André Gide (1869–1951), a French writer and moralist.
[20]A member of the Society of Jesus, a Roman Catholic religious order.

institution where he was constantly made to feel that he was being kept out of charity; then, he failed to get any of the honors and distinctions that children like; later on, at about eighteen, he bungled a love affair; finally, at twenty-two, he failed in military training, a childish enough matter, but it was the last straw.

This young fellow might well have felt that he had botched everything. It was a sign of something, but of what? He might have taken refuge in bitterness or despair. But he very wisely looked upon all this as a sign that he was not made for secular triumphs, and that only the triumphs of religion, holiness, and faith were open to him. He saw the hand of God in all this, and so he entered the order. Who can help seeing that he alone decided what the sign meant?

Some other interpretation might have been drawn from this series of setbacks; for example, that he might have done better to turn carpenter or revolutionist. Therefore, he is fully responsible for the interpretation. Forlornness implies that we ourselves choose our being. Forlornness and anguish go together.

As for despair, the term has a very simple meaning. It means that we shall confine ourselves to reckoning only with what depends upon our will, or on the ensemble of probabilities which make our action possible. When we want something, we always have to reckon with probabilities. I may be counting on the arrival of a friend. The friend is coming by rail or street-car; this supposes that the train will arrive on schedule, or that the street-car will not jump the track. I am left in the realm of possibility; but possibilities are to be reckoned with only to the point where my action comports with the ensemble of these possibilities, and no further. The moment the possibilities I am considering are not rigorously involved by my action, I ought to disengage myself from them, because no God, no scheme, can adapt the world and its possibilities to my will. When Descartes said, "Conquer yourself rather than the world," he meant essentially the same thing.

The Marxists[21] to whom I have spoken reply, "You can rely on the support of others in your action, which obviously has certain limits because you're not going to live forever. That means: rely on both what others are doing elsewhere to help you, in China, in Russia, and what they will do later on, after your death, to carry on the action and lead it to its fulfillment, which will be the revolution. You even *have* to rely upon that, otherwise you're immoral." I reply at once that I will always

---

[21]Marxian socialists.

rely on fellow fighters insofar as these comrades are involved with me in a common struggle, in the unity of a party or a group in which I can more or less make my weight felt; that is, one whose ranks I am in as a fighter and whose movements I am aware of at every moment. In such a situation, relying on the unity and will of the party is exactly like counting on the fact that the train will arrive on time or that the car won't jump the track. But, given that man is free and that there is no human nature for me to depend on, I can not count on men whom I do not know by relying on human goodness or man's concern for the good of society. I don't know what will become of the Russian revolution;[22] I may make an example of it to the extent that at the present time it is apparent that the proletariat plays a part in Russia that it plays in no other nation. But I can't swear that this will inevitably lead to a triumph of the proletariat. I've got to limit myself to what I see.

Given that men are free and that tomorrow they will freely decide what man will be, I can not be sure that, after my death, fellow fighters will carry on my work to bring it to its maximum perfection. Tomorrow, after my death, some men may decide to set up Fascism,[23] and the others may be cowardly and muddled enough to let them do it. Fascism will then be the human reality, so much the worse for us.

Actually, things will be as man will have decided they are to be. Does that mean that I should abandon myself to quietism? No. First, I should involve myself; then, act on the old saw, "Nothing ventured, nothing gained." Nor does it mean that I shouldn't belong to a party, but rather that I shall have no illusions and shall do what I can. For example, suppose I ask myself, "Will socialization, as such, ever come about?" I know nothing about it. All I know is that I'm going to do everything in my power to bring it about. Beyond that, I can't count on anything. Quietism is the attitude of people who say, "Let others do what I can't do." The doctrine I am presenting is the very opposite of quietism, since it declares, "There is no reality except in action." Moreover, it goes further, since it adds, "Man is nothing else than his plan; he exists only

---

[22]The Russian revolution began as a bourgeois revolution in the spring of 1917 and climaxed with the seizure of power by the Bolsheviks (Communists) in early November of that year. Its ultimate form is, of course, unknown to Sartre.

[23]A twentieth-century political ideology that is characterized by elitism, one-party rule and dictatorship, and persecution of racial and religious minorities. Its growth was most pronounced after the First World War in the states of Italy and Germany. Fascism (called Nazism in Germany) was crushed militarily in the course of the Second World War.

to the extent that he fulfills himself; he is therefore nothing else than the ensemble of his acts, nothing else than his life."

According to this, we can understand why our doctrine horrifies certain people. Because often the only way they can bear their wretchedness is to think, "Circumstances have been against me. What I've been and done doesn't show my true worth. To be sure, I've had no great love, no great friendship, but that's because I haven't met a man or woman who was worthy. The books I've written haven't been very good because I haven't had the proper leisure. I haven't had children to devote myself to because I didn't find a man with whom I could have spent my life. So there remains within me, unused and quite viable, a host of propensities, inclinations, possibilities, that one wouldn't guess from the mere series of things I've done."

Now, for the existentialist there is really no love other than one which manifests itself in a person's being in love. There is no genius other than one which is expressed in works of art; the genius of Proust[24] is the sum of Proust's works; the genius of Racine[25] is his series of tragedies. Outside of that, there is nothing. Why say that Racine could have written another tragedy, when he didn't write it? A man is involved in life, leaves his impress on it, and outside of that there is nothing. To be sure, this may seem a harsh thought to someone whose life hasn't been a success. But, on the other hand, it prompts people to understand that reality alone is what counts, that dreams, expectations, and hopes warrant no more than to define a man as a disappointed dream, as miscarried hopes, as vain expectations. In other words, to define him negatively and not positively. However, when we say, "You are nothing else than your life," that does not imply that the artist will be judged solely on the basis of his works of art; a thousand other things will contribute toward summing him up. What we mean is that a man is nothing else than a series of undertakings, that he is the sum, the organization, the ensemble of the relationships which make up these undertakings.

When all is said and done, what we are accused of, at bottom, is not our pessimism, but an optimistic toughness. If people throw up to us our works of fiction in which we write about people who are soft, weak, cowardly, and sometimes even downright bad, it's not because

---

[24]Marcel Proust (1871–1922), a French novelist renowned for his work *Remembrance of Things Past.*

[25]Jean Baptiste Racine (1639–1699), a French dramatist.

these people are soft, weak, cowardly, or bad; because if we were to say, as Zola[26] did, that they are that way because of heredity, the workings of environment, society, because of biological or psychological determinism, people would be reassured. They would say, "Well, that's what we're like, no one can do anything about it." But when the existentialist writes about a coward, he says that this coward is responsible for his cowardice. He's not like that because he has a cowardly heart or lung or brain; he's not like that on account of his physiological make-up; but he's like that because he has made himself a coward by his acts. There's no such thing as a cowardly constitution; there are nervous constitutions; there is poor blood, as the common people say, or strong constitutions. But the man whose blood is poor is not a coward on that account, for what makes cowardice is the act of renouncing or yielding. A constitution is not an act; the coward is defined on the basis of the acts he performs. People feel, in a vague sort of way, that this coward we're talking about is guilty of being a coward, and the thought frightens them. What people would like is that a coward or a hero be born that way.

One of the complaints most frequently made about *The Ways of Freedom*[27] can be summed up as follows: "After all, these people are so spineless, how are you going to make heroes out of them?" This objection almost makes me laugh, for it assumes that people are born heroes. That's what people really want to think. If you're born cowardly, you may set your mind perfectly at rest; there's nothing you can do about it; you'll be cowardly all your life, whatever you may do. If you're born a hero, you may set your mind just as much at rest; you'll be a hero all your life; you'll drink like a hero and eat like a hero. What the existentialist says is that the coward makes himself cowardly, that the hero makes himself heroic. There's always a possibility for the coward not to be cowardly any more and for the hero to stop being heroic. What counts is total involvement; some one particular action or set of circumstances is not total involvement.

Thus, I think we have answered a number of the charges concerning

[26]Émile Zola (1840–1902), a French novelist whose main theme is that people are the helpless creatures of their biological make-up and their physical and social environment. Zola is also remembered for his courageous defense of Alfred Dreyfus, a Jewish captain in the French army, falsely and viciously accused of treason.

[27]*The Ways of Freedom*, Sartre's trilogy of novels: *The Age of Reason*, 1945, *The Reprieve*, 1945, and *Troubled Sleep*, 1949.

existentialism. You see that it can not be taken for a philosophy of quietism, since it defines man in terms of action; nor for a pessimistic description of man—there is no doctrine more optimistic, since man's destiny is within himself; nor for an attempt to discourage man from acting, since it tells him that the only hope is in his acting and that action is the only thing that enables a man to live. Consequently, we are dealing here with an ethics of action and involvement.

Nevertheless, on the basis of a few notions like these, we are still charged with immuring man in his private subjectivity. There again we're very much misunderstood. Subjectivity of the individual is indeed our point of departure, and this for strictly philosophic reasons. Not because we are bourgeois, but because we want a doctrine based on truth and not a lot of fine theories, full of hope but with no real basis. There can be no other truth to take off from than this: *I think; therefore, I exist.*[28] There we have the absolute truth of consciousness becoming aware of itself. Every theory which takes man out of the moment in which he becomes aware of himself is, at its very beginning, a theory which confounds truth, for outside the Cartesian[29] *cogito*,[30] all views are only probable, and a doctrine of probability which is not bound to a truth dissolves into thin air. In order to describe the probable, you must have a firm hold on the true. Therefore, before there can be any truth whatsoever, there must be an absolute truth; and this one is simple and easily arrived at; it's on everyone's doorstep; it's a matter of grasping it directly.

Secondly, this theory is the only one which gives man dignity, the only one which does not reduce him to an object. The effect of all materialism is to treat all men, including the one philosophizing, as objects, that is, as an ensemble of determined reactions in no way distinguished from the ensemble of qualities and phenomena which constitute a table or a chair or a stone. We definitely wish to establish the human realm as an ensemble of values distinct from the material realm. But the subjectivity that we have thus arrived at, and which we have claimed to be truth, is not a strictly individual subjectivity, for we have demonstrated that one discovers in the *cogito* not only himself, but others as well.

[28]The starting point in Descartes' philosophical search for certainty and truth.

[29]From Cartesius, a Latinized form of Descartes' name.

[30]Latin: I think.

The philosophies of Descartes and Kant to the contrary, through the *I think* we reach our own self in the presence of others, and the others are just as real to us as our own self. Thus, the man who becomes aware of himself through the *cogito* also perceives all others, and he perceives them as the condition of his own existence. He realizes that he can not be anything (in the sense that we say that someone is witty or nasty or jealous) unless others recognize it as such. In order to get any truth about myself, I must have contact with another person. The other is indispensable to my own existence, as well as to my knowledge about myself. This being so, in discovering my inner being I discover the other person at the same time, like a freedom placed in front of me which thinks and wills only for or against me. Hence, let us at once announce the discovery of a world which we shall call intersubjectivity; this is the world in which man decides what he is and what others are.

Besides, if it is impossible to find in every man some universal essence which would be human nature, yet there does exist a universal human condition. It's not by chance that today's thinkers speak more readily of man's condition than of his nature. By condition they mean, more or less definitely, the *a priori*[31] limits which outline man's fundamental situation in the universe. Historical situations vary; a man may be born a slave in a pagan society or a feudal lord or a proletarian. What does not vary is the necessity for him to exist in the world, to be at work there, to be there in the midst of other people, and to be mortal there. The limits are neither subjective nor objective, or, rather, they have an objective and a subjective side. Objective because they are to be found everywhere and are recognizable everywhere; subjective because they are *lived* and are nothing if man does not live them, that is, freely determine his existence with reference to them. And though the configurations may differ, at least none of them are completely strange to me, because they all appear as attempts either to pass beyond these limits or recede from them or deny them or adapt to them. Consequently, every configuration, however individual it may be, has a universal value.

Every configuration, even the Chinese, the Indian, or the Negro, can be understood by a Westerner. "Can be understood" means that by virtue of a situation that he can imagine, a European of 1945 can, in like manner, push himself to his limits and reconstitute within himself the

[31]Predetermined.

configuration of the Chinese, the Indian, or the African. Every configuration has universality in the sense that every configuration can be understood by every man. This does not at all mean that this configuration defines man forever, but that it can be met with again. There is always a way to understand the idiot, the child, the savage, the foreigner, provided one has the necessary information.

In this sense we may say that there is a universality of man; but it is not given, it is perpetually being made. I build the universal in choosing myself; I build it in understanding the configuration of every other man, whatever age he might have lived in. This absoluteness of choice does not do away with the relativeness of each epoch. At heart, what existentialism shows is the connection between the absolute character of free involvement, by virtue of which every man realizes himself in realizing a type of mankind, an involvement always comprehensible in any age whatsoever and by any person whosoever, and the relativeness of the cultural ensemble which may result from such a choice; it must be stressed that the relativity of Cartesianism and the absolute character of Cartesian involvement go together. In this sense, you may, if you like, say that each of us performs an absolute act in breathing, eating, sleeping, or behaving in any way whatever. There is no difference between being free, like a configuration, like an existence which chooses its essence, and being absolute. There is no difference between being an absolute temporarily localized, that is, localized in history, and being universally comprehensible.

· · ·

I've been reproached for asking whether existentialism is humanistic. It's been said, "But you said in *Nausea*[32] that the humanists were all wrong. You made fun of a certain kind of humanist. Why come back to it now?" Actually, the word humanism has two very different meanings. By humanism one can mean a theory which takes man as an end and as a higher value. Humanism in this sense can be found in Cocteau's[33] tale *Around the World in Eighty Hours* when a character, because he is flying over some mountains in an airplane, declares, "Man is simply amazing." That means that I, who did not build the airplanes, shall personally benefit from these particular inventions, and that I, as man, shall personally consider myself responsible for, and honored by,

---

[32]*La Nausée*, a philosophical novel by Sartre published in 1938.
[33]Jean Cocteau (1889–1963), a French novelist and playwright.

~cts of a few particular men. This would imply that we ascribe a value to man on the basis of the highest deeds of certain men. This humanism is absurd, because only the dog or the horse would be able to make such an over-all judgment about man, which they are careful not to do, at least to my knowledge.

But it can not be granted that a man may make a judgment about man. Existentialism spares him from any such judgment. The existentialist will never consider man as an end because he is always in the making. Nor should we believe that there is a mankind to which we might set up a cult in the manner of Auguste Comte.[34] The cult of mankind ends in the self-enclosed humanism of Comte, and, let it be said, of fascism. This kind of humanism we can do without.

But there is another meaning of humanism. Fundamentally, it is this: man is constantly outside of himself; in projecting himself, in losing himself outside of himself, he makes for man's existing; and, on the other hand, it is by pursuing transcendent goals that he is able to exist, man, being in this state of passing-beyond, and seizing upon things only as they bear upon this passing-beyond, is at the heart, at the center of this passing-beyond. There is no universe other than a human universe, the universe of human subjectivity. This connection between transcendency, as a constituent element of man—not in the sense that God is transcendent, but in the sense of passing beyond—and subjectivity, in the sense that man is not closed in on himself but is always present in a human universe, is what we call existentialist humanism. Humanism, because we remind man that there is no lawmaker other than himself, and that in his forlornness he will decide by himself; because we point out that man will fulfill himself as man, not in turning toward himself, but in seeking outside of himself a goal which is just this liberation, just this particular fulfillment.

From these few reflections it is evident that nothing is more unjust than the objections that have been raised against us. Existentialism is nothing else than an attempt to draw all the consequences of a coherent atheistic position. It isn't trying to plunge man into despair[35] at all. But if one calls every attitude of unbelief despair, like the Christians, then the word is not being used in its original sense. Existentialism isn't so atheistic that it wears itself out showing that God doesn't exist. Rather,

---

[34]A French philosopher and mathematician (1798–1857), who was the founder of the "religion of humanity," a cult that establishes *humanity* as the Supreme Being.

[35]A key concept in Christian existentialism.

it declares that even if God did exist, that would change nothing. There you've got our point of view. Not that we believe that God exists, but we think that the problem of His existence is not the issue; [what man needs is to find himself again, and to understand that nothing can save him from himself, not even a valid proof of the existence of God]. In this sense existentialism is optimistic, a doctrine of action, and it is plain dishonesty for Christians to make no distinction between their own despair and ours and then to call us despairing.

• • •

35

Virginia Woolf

A Room of One's Own

*T*HE *brilliant English author, Virginia Woolf (1882–1941), was the third child of Leslie and Julia Stephen. Their marriage, the second for both, produced four talented children—Vanessa, Thoby, Virginia, and Adrian. Virginia was undoubtedly the most gifted of them. By the time these children arrived, Leslie—through his work as author, editor, and scholar—had gained sufficient financial means to assure the family a comfortable style of living. He could also promise his children a secure future— naturally, within the bounds approved by English society.*

In practical terms, this meant that the two boys would receive their formal education in one of England's excellent private boarding schools and then advance to one of the places of higher learning, preferably Cambridge University. On the other hand, the current rules of society demanded that girls should be taught at home, with marriage and motherhood as the goal and climax of their mature lives. From the earliest days and throughout her life, Virginia resented the idea that a person's sex should determine his or her future. Fortunately for Virginia and her sister, Vanessa, their parents were well educated and intellectually alive, so that they could discuss with them many important issues and topics. In addition, both girls had access to their large and excellent home library, where they could educate themselves, especially in the subjects of literature, history, and art.

Upon reaching college age, Virginia longed to study at Cambridge, but being female stood in the way. Even as late as 1929, Cambridge (as well as Oxford) was still seen as a place reserved for male students—although women were no longer barred from enrolling. (Later in life, after she became famous, several universities offered her honorary degrees. Without exception, she declined them all.)

Though deprived of advanced formal education, Virginia did become, indeed, a cultivated "intellectual." While she would ultimately express important ideas concerning literary theory, and write hundreds of book reviews, her first love was writing novels. *Her imagination soared above reality, and she found the highest enjoyment of life in her world of fiction. Her most notable early novels included* The Voyage Out *(1915) and* Night and Day *(1919).*

In 1912 Virginia married the kind and loving Leonard Woolf, who had been an officer of the British colonial civil service. He, too, became a writer and editor, and in 1917 he and Virginia founded the Hogarth Press in London—which thereafter published Virginia's books. Following Night and Day, *she sought to* experiment with various forms of writing novels. *One of these new forms involved the "stream of consciousness" technique; it appears, for example, in* The Waves *(1931).*

Along with writing about women in fiction, Virginia had strong views about their personal and social life in the real world. The selection from her works included here is not taken from one of her novels, but, rather, from a long essay published under the title, A Room of One's Own *(1929). The book reads like a* lecture *to a female audience—because it is an extension and development of a lecture she had actually delivered at two colleges for women (Newnham and Girton, residential colleges of Cambridge University). Woolf had been asked to speak there on the topic, "Women and Fiction," but she turned her lecture into a far broader and deeper presentation.*

The effectiveness of her essay lies in the fact that Woolf expresses her views in a committed and passionate language without becoming shrill or vengeful. She convincingly points out how much humankind has lost by holding down the vast majority of women to an inferior status, while buttressing male "superiority." Sadly, this shackled condition, which has lasted through the ages, remained in force into and through her own days. Woolf was aware that she was unusually fortunate to have risen above the traditional level of female existence. She felt, further, that this good fortune placed a special obligation upon her to speak out for all ordinary women (whom she refers to collectively as a fictional "Mrs. Seton")—as well as for those born with the genius of a "Judith Shakespeare." To a degree, she identified personally with both.

Woolf demanded that women be freed from their shackles so that they could (at long last) be free to develop their talents and participate in all aspects of social life—as men have been free to do for very long. She was convinced that women would contribute something unique because of who they are. Women should not, therefore, try to imitate men or view them as the opposing faction. In the future, she visualized women cooperating with men, thus contributing to each other's happiness. Woolf was certain, however, that no woman will ever have any claim to being free or a man's equal until she has "a room of her own"—and "five hundred pounds sterling a year," sufficient for a modest living. To be free, in other words, a woman must have her very own place and be financially independent. Here, then, is the selection—a work of literary art and a moving appeal for women's liberation.

———————

But, you may say, we asked you to speak about women and fiction— what has that got to do with a room of one's own? I will try to explain. When you asked me to speak about women and fiction I sat down on the banks of a river and began to wonder what the words meant. They might mean simply a few remarks about Fanny Burney[1]; a few more about Jane Austen[2]; a tribute to the Brontës[3] and a sketch of Haworth Parsonage[4] under snow; some witticisms if possible about Miss Mitford[5]; a respectful allusion to George Eliot[6]; a reference to Mrs. Gaskell[7] and one would be done. But at second glance the words seemed not so simple. The title women and fiction might mean, and you may have meant it to mean, women and what they are like; or it might mean women and the fiction that they write; or it might mean women and the fiction that is written about them; or it might mean that somehow all three are inextricably mixed together and you want me to consider them in that light. But when I began to consider the subject in this last way, which seemed the most interesting, I soon saw that it had one fatal drawback. I should never be able to come to a conclusion. I should never be able to fulfil what is, I understand, the first duty of a lecturer—to hand you after an hour's discourse a nugget of pure truth to wrap up between the pages of your notebooks and keep on the

[1]Frances Burney (1752–1840), English novelist.

[2]Jane Austen (1775–1815), English novelist.

[3]Charlotte (1816–1855), Emily Jane (1818–1848), and Anne (1820–1849) Brontë. Three sisters and English novelists.

[4]The home of the Brontë family.

[5]Mary Russell Mitford (1787–1855), English novelist and writer of dramas.

[6]George Eliot, pseudonym of Mary Ann Evans (1819–1880), English novelist and poet.

[7]Elizabeth Cleghorn Gaskell (1810–1865), English novelist.

mantelpiece forever. All I could do was to offer you an opinion upon one minor point—a woman must have money and a room of her own if she is to write fiction; and that, as you will see, leaves the great problem of the true nature of woman and the true nature of fiction unsolved. I have shirked the duty of coming to a conclusion upon these two questions—women and fiction remain, so far as I am concerned, unsolved problems. But in order to make some amends I am going to do what I can to show you how I arrived at this opinion about the room and the money. I am going to develop in your presence as fully and freely as I can the train of thought which led me to think this. Perhaps if I lay bare the ideas, the prejudices, that lie behind this statement you will find that they have some bearing upon women and some upon fiction. At any rate, when a subject is highly controversial—and any question about sex is that—one cannot hope to tell the truth. One can only show how one came to hold whatever opinion one does hold. One can only give one's audience the chance of drawing their own conclusions as they observe the limitations, the prejudices, the idiosyncracies[8] of the speaker. Fiction here is likely to contain more truth than fact. Therefore I propose, making use of all the liberties and licenses of a novelist, to tell you the story of the two days that preceded my coming here—how, bowed down by the weight of the subject which you have laid upon my shoulders, I pondered it, and made it work in and out of my daily life. I need not say that what I am about to describe has no existence; Oxbridge[9] is an invention; so is Fernham[10]; "I" is only a convenient term for somebody who has no real being. Lies will flow from my lips, but there may perhaps be some truth mixed up with them; it is for you to seek out this truth and to decide whether any part of it is worth keeping. If not, you will of course throw the whole of it into the wastepaper basket and forget all about it.

$\bullet \quad \bullet \quad \bullet$

I went, therefore, to the shelf where the histories stand and took down one of the latest, Professor Trevelyan's[11] *History of England*. Once

[8]Special traits of character.

[9]A composite name derived from Ox(ford) and (Cam)bridge *universities*. Oxbridge also stands for male learning and teaching, male superiority, and the study of a world made by males.

[10]Fernham (the name is similar to Newnham) is the invented name of a *college* for females. This institution is poor and without recognition or fame.

[11]George Macaulay Trevelyan (1876–1962), English historian. *History of England* was published in 1926.

more I looked up Women, found "position of," and turned to the pages indicated. "Wife-beating," I read, "was a recognized right of man, and was practiced without shame by high as well as low. . . . Similarly," the historian goes on, "the daughter who refused to marry the gentleman of her parents' choice was liable to be locked up, beaten and flung about the room, without any shock being inflicted on public opinion. Marriage was not an affair of personal affection, but of family avarice, particularly in the 'chivalrous' upper classes. . . . Betrothal often took place while one or both of the parties was in the cradle, and marriage when they were scarcely out of the nurses' charge." That was about 1470, soon after Chaucer's time.[12] The next reference to the position of women is some two hundred years later, in the time of the Stuarts.[13] "It was still the exception for women of the upper and middle class to choose their own husbands, and when the husband had been assigned, he was lord and master, so far at least as law and custom could make him. Yet even so," Professor Trevelyan concludes, "neither Shakespeare's women nor those of authentic seventeenth-century memoirs, like the Verneys and the Hutchinsons, seem lacking in personality and character." Certainly, if we consider it, Cleopatra must have had a way with her; Lady Macbeth, one would suppose, had a will of her own; Rosalind, one might conclude, was an attractive girl. Professor Trevelyan is speaking no more than the truth when he remarks that Shakespeare's women do not seem lacking in personality and character. Not being a historian, one might go even further and say that women have burned like beacons in all the works of all the poets from the beginning of time—Clytemnestra, Antigone, Cleopatra, Lady Macbeth, Phaedra, Cressida, Rosalind, Desdemona, the Duchess of Malfi, among the dramatists; then among the prose writers: Millamant, Clarissa, Becky Sharp, Anna Karenina, Emma Bovary, Madame de Guermantes—the names flock to mind, nor do they recall women "lacking in personality and character." Indeed, if woman had no existence save in the fiction written by men, one would imagine her a person of the utmost importance; very versatile; heroic and mean; splendid and sordid; infinitely beautiful and hideous in the extreme; as great as a man, some think even greater. But this is woman in fiction. In fact, as Professor Trevelyan points out, she was locked up, beaten and flung about the room.

A very queer, composite being thus emerges. Imaginatively she is of

[12]Geoffrey Chaucer (1340–1400), English poet famous for *The Canterbury Tales*.
[13]Family of 17th century English monarchs.

the highest importance; practically she is completely insignificant. She pervades poetry from cover to cover; she is all but absent from history. She dominates the lives of kings and conquerors in fiction; in fact she was the slave of any boy whose parents forced a ring upon her finger. Some of the most inspired words, some of the most profound thoughts in literature fall from her lips; in real life she could hardly read, could scarcely spell, and was the property of her husband.

It was certainly an odd monster that one made up by reading the historians first and the poets afterward—a worm winged like an eagle; the spirit of life and beauty in a kitchen chopping up suet. But these monsters, however amusing to the imagination, have no existence in fact. What one must do to bring her to life was to think poetically and prosaically at one and the same moment, thus keeping in touch with fact—that she is Mrs. Martin, aged thirty-six, dressed in blue, wearing a black hat and brown shoes; but not losing sight of fiction either—that she is a vessel in which all sorts of spirits and forces are coursing and flashing perpetually. The moment, however, that one tries this method with the Elizabethan woman, one branch of illumination fails; one is held up by the scarcity of facts. One knows nothing detailed, nothing perfectly true and substantial about her. History scarcely mentions her. And I turned to Professor Trevelyan again to see what history meant to him. I found by looking at his chapter headings that it meant—

"The Manor Court and the Methods of Open-field Agriculture . . . The Cistercians and Sheep-farming . . . The Crusades . . . The University . . . The House of Commons . . . The Hundred Years' War . . . The Wars of the Roses . . . The Renaissance Scholars . . . The Dissolution of the Monasteries . . . Agrarian and Religious Strife . . . The Origin of English Sea-power . . . The Armada . . ." and so on. Occasionally an individual woman is mentioned, an Elizabeth, or a Mary; a queen or a great lady. But by no possible means could middle-class women with nothing but brains and character at their command have taken part in any one of the great movements which, brought together, constitute the historian's view of the past. Nor shall we find her in any collection of anecdotes. Aubrey[14] hardly mentions her. She never writes her own life and scarcely keeps a diary; there are only a handful of her letters in existence. She left no plays or poems by which we can judge her. What one wants, I thought—and why does not some brilliant student at Newnham or Girton[15] supply it?—is a mass of

---

[14]John Aubrey (1626–1697), English writer who portrayed the lives of famous Englishmen.

[15]Two colleges for women in Cambridge University, where Woolf delivered this lecture.

information; at what age did she marry; how many children had she as a rule; what was her house like; had she a room to herself; did she do the cooking; would she be likely to have a servant? All these facts lie somewhere, presumably, in parish registers and account books; the life of the average Elizabethan woman must be scattered about somewhere, could one collect it and make a book of it. It would be ambitious beyond my daring, I thought, looking about the shelves for books that were not there, to suggest to the students of those famous colleges that they should re-write history, though I acknowledge that it often seems a little queer as it is, unreal, lop-sided; but why should they not add a supplement to history? calling it, of course, by some inconspicuous name so that women might figure there without impropriety? For one often catches a glimpse of them in the lives of the great, whisking away into the background, concealing, I sometimes think, a wink, a laugh, perhaps a tear. And, after all, we have lives enough of Jane Austen; it scarcely seems necessary to consider again the influence of the tragedies of Joanna Baillie[16] upon the poetry of Edgar Allan Poe[17]; as for myself, I should not mind if the homes and haunts[18] of Mary Russell Mitford were closed to the public for a century at least. But what I find deplorable, I continued, looking about the book-shelves again, is that nothing is known about women before the eighteenth century. I have no model in my mind to turn about this way and that. Here am I asking why women did not write poetry in the Elizabethan age, and I am sure how they were educated; whether they were taught to write; whether they had rooms to themselves; how many women had children before they were twenty-one; what, in short, they did from eight in the morning till eight at night. They had no money evidently; according to Professor Trevelyan they were married whether they liked it or not before they were out of the nursery, at fifteen or sixteen very likely. It would have been extremely odd, even upon this showing, had one of them suddenly written the plays of Shakespeare, I concluded, and I thought of that old gentleman, who is dead now, but was a bishop, I think, who declared that it was impossible for any woman, past, present, or to come, to have the genius of Shakespeare. He wrote to the papers about it. He also told a lady who applied to him for information that cats do not as a matter of fact go to heaven, though they have, he added, souls of a sort. How much thinking those old

---

[16]Joanna Baillie (1762–1851), Scottish poetess and writer of dramas.

[17]Edgar Allan Poe (1809–1849), American writer of stories and poems.

[18]Places frequented by that author.

gentlemen used to save one! How the borders of ignorance shrank back at their approach! <u>Cats do not go to heaven</u>. Women cannot write the plays of Shakespeare.

Be that as it may, I could not help thinking, as I looked at the works of Shakespeare on the shelf, that the bishop was right at least in this; it would have been impossible, completely and entirely, for any woman to have written the plays of Shakespeare in the age of Shakespeare. Let me imagine, since facts are so hard to come by, what would have happened had Shakespeare had a wonderfully gifted sister, called Judith, let us say. Shakespeare himself went, very probably—his mother was an heiress—to the grammar school, where he may have learned Latin—Ovid, Virgil and Horace[19]—and the elements of grammar and logic. He was, it is well known, a wild boy who poached rabbits, perhaps shot a deer, and had, rather sooner than he should have done, to marry a woman in the neighborhood, who bore him a child rather quicker than was right. That escapade sent him to seek his fortune in London. He had, it seemed, a taste for the theater, he began by holding horses at the stage door. Very soon he got work in the theater, became a successful actor, and lived at the hub of the universe, meeting everybody, knowing everybody, practicing his art on the stage, exercising his wits in the streets, and even getting access to the palace of the queen. Meanwhile his extraordinarily gifted sister, let us suppose, remained at home. She was as adventurous, as imaginative, as eager to see the world as he was. But she was not sent to school. She had no chance of learning grammar and logic, let alone of reading Horace and Virgil. She picked up a book now and then, one of her brother's perhaps, and read a few pages. But then her parents came in and told her to mend the stockings or mind the stew and not moon about with books and papers. They would have spoken sharply but kindly, for they were substantial people who knew the conditions of life for a woman and loved their daughter—indeed, more likely than not she was the apple of her father's eye. Perhaps she scribbled some pages up in an apple loft on the sly, but was careful to hide them or set fire to them. Soon, however, before she was out of her teens, she was to be betrothed to the son of a neighboring wool-stapler. She cried out that marriage was hateful to her, and for that she was severely beaten by her father. Then he ceased to scold her. He begged her instead not to hurt him, not to shame him in this matter of her marriage. He would give her a chain

---

[19]Ancient Roman poets.

of beads or a fine petticoat, he said; and there were tears in his eyes. How could she disobey him? How could she break his heart? The force of her own gift alone drove her to it. She made up a small parcel of her belongings, let herself down by a rope one summer's night and took the road to London. She was not seventeen. The birds that sang in the hedge were not more musical than she was. She had the quickest fancy, a gift like her brother's, for the tune of words. Like him, she had a taste for the theater. She stood at the stage door; she wanted to act, she said. Men laughed in her face. The manager—a fat, loose-lipped man— guffawed. He bellowed something about poodles dancing and women acting—no woman, he said, could possibly be an actress. He hinted— you can imagine what. She could get no training in her craft. Could she even seek her dinner in a tavern or roam the streets at midnight? Yet her genius was for fiction and lusted to feed abundantly upon the lives of men and women and the study of their ways. At last—for she was very young, oddly like Shakespeare the poet in her face, with the same grey eyes and rounded brows—at last Nick Greene the actor-manager took pity on her; she found herself with child by that gentleman and so— who shall measure the heat and violence of the poet's heart when caught and tangled in a woman's body?—killed herself one winter's night and lies buried at some crossroads where the omnibuses now stop outside the Elephant and Castle.[20]

That, more or less, is how the story would run, I think, if a woman in Shakespeare's day had had Shakespeare's genius. But for my part, I agree with the deceased bishop, if such he was—it is unthinkable that any woman in Shakespeare's day should have had Shakespeare's genius. For genius like Shakespeare's is not born among laboring, uneducated, servile people. It was not born in England among the Saxons and the Britons. It is not born today among the working classes. How, then, could it have been born among women whose work began, according to Professor Trevelyan, almost before they were out of the nursery, who were forced to it by their parents and held to it by all the power of law and custom? Yet genius of a sort must have existed among women as it must have existed among the working classes. Now and again an Emily Brontë or a Robert Burns[21] blazes out and proves its presence. But certainly it never got itself on to paper. When, however, one reads

---

[20]Elephant and Castle was a pub (tavern) in south London.

[21]Robert Burns (1759–1796), Scottish farmer whose poetry has become much loved and very popular.

of a witch being dunked, of a woman possessed by devils, of a wise woman selling herbs, or even of a very remarkable man who had a mother, then I think we are on the track of a lost novelist, a suppressed poet, of some mute and inglorious Jane Austen, some Emily Brontë who dashed her brains out on the moor or mopped and mowed about the highways crazed with the torture that her gift had put her to. Indeed, I would venture to guess that Anon,[22] who wrote so many poems without signing them, was often a woman. It was a woman Edward Fitzgerald,[23] I think, suggested, who made the ballads and the folk songs, crooning them to her children, beguiling her spinning with them, or the length of the winter's night.

This may be true or it may be false—who can say?—but what is true in it, so it seemed to me, reviewing the story of Shakespeare's sister as I had made it, is that any woman born with a great gift in the sixteenth century would certainly have gone crazed, shot herself, or ended her days in some lonely cottage outside the village, half witch, half wizard, feared and mocked at. For it needs little skill in psychology to be sure that a highly gifted girl who had tried to use her gift for poetry would have been so thwarted and hindered by other people, so tortured and pulled asunder by her own contrary instincts, that she must have lost her health and sanity to a certainty. No girl could have walked to London and stood at a stage door and forced her way into the presence of actor-managers without doing herself a violence and suffering an anguish which may have been irrational—for chastity may be a fetish invented by certain societies for unknown reasons—but were none the less inevitable. Chastity had then, it has even now, a religious importance in a woman's life, and has so wrapped itself round with nerves and instincts that to cut it free and bring it to the light of day demands courage of the rarest. To have lived a free life in London in the sixteenth century would have meant for a woman who was poet and playwright a nervous stress and dilemma which might well have killed her. Had she survived, whatever she had written would have been twisted and deformed, issuing from a strained and morbid imagination. And undoubtedly, I thought, looking at the shelf where there are no plays by women, her work would have gone unsigned. That refuge she would have sought certainly. It was the relic of the sense of chastity that

[22]Anonymous, that is, an author of unknown identity.
[23]Edward Fitzgerald (1809–1883), English poet.

dictated anonymity to women even so late as the nineteenth century. Currer Bell,[24] George Eliot,[25] George Sand,[26] all the victims of inner strife as their writings prove, sought ineffectively to veil themselves by using the name of a man. Thus they did homage to the convention, which if not implanted by the other sex was liberally encouraged by them (the chief glory of a woman is not to be talked of, said Pericles,[27] himself a much-talked-of man), that publicity in women is detestable. Anonymity runs in their blood. The desire to be veiled still possesses them. They are not even now as concerned about the health of their fame as men are, and, speaking generally, will pass a tombstone or a signpost without feeling an irresistible desire to cut their names on it, as Alf, Bert or Chas. must do in obedience to their instinct. . . .

• • •

. . . It is fairly evident that even in the nineteenth century a woman was not encouraged to be an artist. On the contrary, she was snubbed, slapped, lectured and exhorted. Her mind must have been strained and her vitality lowered by the need of opposing this, of disproving that. For here again we come within range of that very interesting and obscure masculine complex which has had so much influence upon the woman's movement; that deep-seated desire, not so much that *she* shall be inferior as that *he* shall be superior, which plants him wherever one looks, not only in front of the arts, but barring the way to politics too, even when the risk to himself seems infinitesimal and the suppliant humble and devoted. Even Lady Bessborough, I remembered, with all her passion for politics, must humbly bow herself and write to Lord Granville Leveson-Gower[28]: ". . . notwithstanding all my violence in politics and talking so much on that subject, I perfectly agree with you that no woman has any business to meddle with that or any other serious business, farther than giving her opinion (if she is asked)." And so she goes on to spend her enthusiasm where it meets with no obstacle whatsoever upon that immensely important subject, Lord Granville's

[24]Pseudonym of Charlotte Brontë (1816–1855), English novelist.
[25]Pseudonym of Mary Ann Evans (1819–1880), English novelist and poet.
[26]Pseudonym of Amadine Dudevant Dupin (1804–1876), French novelist.
[27]Pericles (495–429 B.C.), Athenian general and statesman.
[28]Leveson-Gower, Lord Granville (1773–1846), English diplomat and politician.

maiden speech in the House of Commons.[29] The spectacle is certainly a strange one, I thought. The history of men's opposition to women's emancipation is more interesting perhaps than the story of that emancipation itself. An amusing book might be made of it if some young student at Girton or Newnham would collect examples and deduce a theory—but she would need thick gloves on her hands, and bars to protect her of solid gold.

• • •

... The pressure of convention decrees that every speech must end with a peroration.[30] And a peroration addressed to women should have something, you will agree, particularly exalting and ennobling about it. I should implore you to remember your responsibilities, to be higher, more spiritual; I should remind you how much depends upon you, and what an influence you can exert upon the future. But those exhortations can safely, I think, be left to the other sex, who will put them, and indeed have put them, with far greater eloquence than I can achieve. When I rummage in my own mind I find no noble sentiments about being companions and equals and influencing the world to higher ends. I find myself saying briefly and prosaically that it is much more important to be oneself than anything else. Do not dream of influencing other people, I would say, if I knew how to make it sound exalted. Think of things in themselves.

And again I am reminded by dipping into newspapers and novels and biographies that when a woman speaks to women she should have something very unpleasant up her sleeve. Women are hard on women. Women dislike women. Women—but are you not sick to death of the word? I can assure you that I am. Let us agree, then, that a paper read by a woman to women should end with something particularly disagreeable.

But how does it go? What can I think of? The truth is, I often like women. I like their unconventionality. I like their subtlety. I like their anonymity. I like—but I must not run on in this way. . . . Let me then adopt a sterner tone. Have I, in the preceding words, conveyed to you sufficiently the warnings and reprobation of mankind? I have told you the very low opinion in which you were held by Mr. Oscar

[29]The principal house of the British Parliament.
[30]Summing-up.

Browning.[31] I have indicated what Napoleon once thought of you and what Mussolini[32] thinks now. Then, in case any of you aspire to fiction, I have copied out for your benefit the advice of the critic about courageously acknowledging the limitations of your sex. I have referred to Professor X and given prominence to his statement that women are intellectually, morally and physically inferior to men. I have handed on all that has come my way without going in search of it, and here is a final warning—from Mr. John Langdon-Davies.[33] Mr. John Langdon-Davies warns women "that when children cease to be altogether desirable, women cease to be altogether necessary." I hope you will make a note of it.

How can I further encourage you to go about the business of life? Young women, I would say, and please listen, for the peroration is beginning, you are, in my opinion, disgracefully ignorant. You have never made a discovery of any sort of importance. You have never shaken an empire or led an army into battle. The plays of Shakespeare are not by you, and you have never introduced a barbarous race to the blessings of civilization. What is your excuse? It is all very well for you to say, pointing to the streets and squares and forests of the globe swarming with black and white and coffee-colored inhabitants, all busily engaged in traffic and enterprise and love-making, we have had other work on our hands. Without our doing, those seas would be unsailed and those fertile lands a desert. We have borne and bred and washed and taught, perhaps to the age of six or seven years, the one thousand six hundred and twenty-three million human beings who are, according to statistics, at present in existence, and that, allowing that some had help, takes time.

There is truth in what you say—I will not deny it. But at the same time may I remind you that there have been at least two colleges for women in existence in England since the year 1866; that after the year 1880 a married woman was allowed by law to possess her own property; and that in 1919—which is a whole nine years ago—she was given a vote? May I also remind you that the most of the professions have

---

[31]Oscar Browning (1837–1923), English writer on history and education. He had concluded that among university students "the best woman was intellectually the inferior of the worst man."

[32]Benito Mussolini (1883–1945), Italian Fascist dictator. He and Napoleon I (1769–1821) insisted that women were inferior to men.

[33]John Langdon-Davies (1897–1971), English journalist and author. He wrote *A Short History of Women*, published in 1927.

been open to you for close to ten years now? When you reflect upon these immense privileges and the length of time during which they have been enjoyed, and the fact that there must be at this moment some two thousand women capable of earning over five hundred a year in one way or another, you will agree that the excuse of lack of opportunity, training, encouragement, leisure and money no longer holds true. Moreover, the economists are telling us that Mrs. Seton[34] has had too many children. You must, of course, go on bearing children, but, so they say, in twos and threes, not in tens and twelves.

Thus, with some time on your hands and with some book learning in your brains—you have had enough of the other kind, and are sent to college partly, I suspect, to be un-educated—surely you should embark upon another stage of your very long, very laborious and highly obscure career. A thousand pens are ready to suggest what you should do and what effect you will have. My own suggestion is a little fantastic, I admit; I prefer, therefore, to put it in the form of fiction.

I told you in the course of this paper that Shakespeare had a sister; but do not look for her in Sir Sidney Lee's[35] life of the poet. She died young—alas, she never wrote a word. She lies buried where the omnibuses now stop, opposite the Elephant and Castle. Now my belief is that this poet who never wrote a word and was buried at the crossroads still lives. She lives in you and in me, and in many other women who are not here tonight, for they are washing up the dishes and putting the children to bed. But she lives; for great poets do not die; they are continuing presences; they need only the opportunity to walk among us in the flesh. This opportunity, as I think, it is now coming within your power to give her. For my belief is that if we live another century or so—I am talking of the common life which is the real life and not of the little separate lives which we live as individuals—and have five hundred[36] a year each of us and rooms of our own; if we have the habit of freedom and the courage to write exactly what we think; if we escape a little from the common living room and see human beings not always in their relation to each other but in relation to reality; and the sky, too, and the trees or whatever it may be in themselves; if we look past

[34]A fictional name, meaning the average English housewife.
[35]Sidney Lee (1859–1926), English biographer.
[36]Pounds sterling.

Milton's bogey,[37] for no human being should shut out the view; if we face the fact, for it is a fact, that there is no arm to cling to, but that we go alone and that our relation is to the world of reality and not only to the world of men and women, then the opportunity will come and the dead poet who was Shakespeare's sister will put on the body which she has so often laid down. Drawing her life from the lives of the unknown who were her forerunners, as her brother did before her, she will be born. As for her coming without that preparation, without that effort on our part, without that determination that when she is born again she shall find it possible to live and write her poetry, that we cannot expect, for that would be impossible. But I maintain that she would come if we worked for her, and that so to work, even in poverty and obscurity, is worth-while.

---

[37]John Milton (1608–1674), English poet and writer, most famous for his long poem, *Paradise Lost*. "Bogey" appears to mean his great reputation as a poet which might overawe and discourage young writers.

36

Modern Poetry

MODERN *literature cannot be understood apart from the intellectual crisis of Western culture. These times have seen the alienation of human beings from their environment and from themselves, as well as the fragmentation of the concepts of self and society, with accompanying uncertainty, anxiety, and despair. In addition, many young poets of the early twentieth century were sent into the cauldron of the First World War. The intensity of their experiences compelled them to convey to others the infernal scenes they were forced to witness.*

Modern poets, in trying to cope with a hostile world and their own alienation from it, have written with relentless, analytic frankness, often tinged with mockery of humanity's tragic plight. They have discarded traditional techniques and have experimented freely, while insisting on the need for a rigorous poetic discipline. Many have used a new vocabulary that aims at both precision and allusiveness; this dual character has often made their poems difficult, requiring the reader's most careful and informed attention. The following selection of poets and poems offers a considerable range of modern subjects and styles.

Robert Lee Frost *(1874–1963), the renowned American poet and educator, wrote "After Apple-Picking" (1914), an excellent example of his art. The poem appears to be a realistic account of a rural New England scene. It is written in the ordinary rhythms of speech, but its surface simplicity is deceiving. The poem skillfully suggests, through the metaphor of apple harvesting, one individual's weariness with life and his growing sense of wonder about his mortality.*

The poem titled "In Flanders Fields" became the most famous and memorable English poem to come out of the First World War. It was written by John McCrae *(1872–1918), a Canadian physician who felt, a few weeks into the war, that his services were needed in the Allied war effort. Urged on by his patriotism, he sailed to Europe and was assigned as a medical officer to a Canadian artillery unit. In 1915 this unit was operating in Flanders (western Belgium), where it suffered heavy losses to a powerful German sweep toward Paris. The soldiers' sacrifices seemed to McCrae to serve an important and noble purpose: had the Germans taken Paris, the Allies could have lost the war. The poem holds to this heroic note and calls upon others to join the war effort—in order to keep faith with the dead soldiers.*

As the murderous trench warfare ground on at the western front, the tone of war poetry changed decisively. This is displayed in the work of Siegfried Sassoon *(1886–1967), a decorated English infantry officer. His poem "A Working Party," was written in 1916, while Sassoon was in France, fighting against the Germans. As the struggle dragged on, devouring young men like an insatiable monster, Sassoon concluded that the war had become one of aggression and conquest, prolonged by those who held power in England. Following the publication of his anti-war views, he was sent to a hospital in Scotland to recover from "shell shock." While there he wrote more poems about different aspects of the war. One of them, titled "Glory of Women," was a biting comment on the role of women on the home front.*

Wilfred Owen *(1893–1918) picked up the theme of bitterness toward the unending slaughter. As the cynical poem "Dulce et Decorum Est" (1917) so vividly describes, death and suffering were ever present—be it through bullets, poison gas, or bursting artillery shells. In June 1917, Owen (like Sassoon) was sent to a hospital in Scotland because of shell shock. While back home, he saw many young men whom war had reduced to a pitiable state—as portrayed in his poem "Disabled" (1917). The brutality of war had robbed these men of a meaningful future and of everything that makes life worthwhile and enjoyable. (Owen himself was ordered back to frontline duty in 1918 and was killed on November 4, exactly one week before the Armistice took effect.)*

Yvan Goll *(1891–1950) was born in Alsace and grew up in Lorraine, the two provinces situated between France and Germany, and claimed by both over many centuries. It is not surprising, then, that Goll grew up bi-culturally, writing with equal skill in both languages. Seeing the nations of Europe tearing savagely into each other during the First World War caused the poet pain, despair, and compassion for all those whose lives had been damaged.*

Goll *expressed his anguish in a number of poems, among them eleven that bear the title "Recitative" (1916). The poem numbered "VIII" tells about the cruelty and misery of war, the staggering number of casualties, and the never-ending succession of battles. For even in the worst days of the war there were on each side enough politicians and generals who, claiming to see light at the end of the tunnel, persuaded the nation to send their sons into yet another battle—to their deaths.*

The shock and depression from the war persisted even after its end in 1918 William Butler Yeats (1865–1939), the Irish poet and nationalist, expressed in his poem "The Second Coming" (1921) a grim view of the future in harsh, broken rhythms and astringent, symbolic language. Turning from the sentimental, Christian hope for an age of peace, Yeats sees beyond the chaos of his times the coming of an iron age of anarchy and brutality.

Among the literary figures in America after the war, Louis Untermeyer (1885–1977) claims a prominent place. Much of his long and productive life was given to writing poetry, biographies, children's books, and the publishing of anthologies. The topics of Untermeyer's poems—generally insightful and friendly, on occasion humorous—range across the entire spectrum of human experience. The poem "The Flaming Circle" (1923) reflects a particular strand of thought among some modern philosophers, namely, that humans remain strangers to each other. Even intimate union between them is but temporary, followed by separation and aloneness.

Wystan Hugh (W.H.) Auden (1907–1973) proved to be one of the most prolific writers of his century. Among his many literary creations are poems, plays, texts for operas and films, as well as travel reports. Auden was the son of a well-to-do English physician who provided him with an excellent education. While in his teens, Auden began to write poetry, and soon it became clear to him that writing, and above all the writing of poems, was to be his life's work.

Much of Auden's inspiration came from his travels—which carried him to Germany, Iceland, Spain, China, and the United States. He remained in America from 1939 to 1948 and became a citizen in 1946. The 1920s and 1930s were plagued with political problems, social and economic dislocations, and bitter ideological controversies. Auden found these a rich source of themes which he expressed in his poems, and he also participated actively in several movements for social reform.

The poem "The Unknown Citizen" was written in 1939, with its title suggested by the Tomb of the Unknown Soldier. It is a caricature of the sheeplike organization man—who, like millions of others, has become submerged in modern bureaucratic mass society. The hero of this poem is the "well-adjusted," conforming person—devoid of critical thinking or independent action. Auden is saying here that a person of this type, though well intentioned and well cared for by the state, fails as a creative human being.

ROBERT FROST

After Apple-Picking

My long two-pointed ladder's sticking through a tree
Toward heaven still,
And there's a barrel that I didn't fill
Beside it, and there may be two or three
Apples I didn't pick upon some bough.
But I am done with apple-picking now.
Essence of winter sleep is on the night,
The scent of apples: I am drowsing off.
I cannot rub the strangeness from my sight
I got from looking through a pane of glass
I skimmed this morning from the drinking trough
And held against the world of hoary grass.
It melted, and I let it fall and break.
But I was well
Upon my way to sleep before it fell,
And I could tell
What form my dreaming was about to take.
Magnified apples appear and disappear,
Stem end and blossom end,
And every fleck of russet showing clear.
My instep arch not only keeps the ache,
It keeps the pressure of a ladder-round.
I feel the ladder sway as the boughs bend.
And I keep hearing from the cellar bin
The rumbling sound
Of load on load of apples coming in.
For I have had too much
Of apple-picking: I am overtired
Of the great harvest I myself desired.
There were ten thousand thousand fruit to touch,
Cherish in hand, lift down, and not let fall.

For all
That struck the earth,
No matter if not bruised or spiked with stubble,
Went surely to the cider-apple heap
As of no worth.
One can see what will trouble
This sleep of mine, whatever sleep it is.
Were he not gone,
The woodchuck could say whether it's like his
Long sleep, as I describe its coming on,
Or just some human sleep.

JOHN McCRAE

In Flanders Fields

In Flanders fields the poppies blow
Between the crosses, row on row,
    That mark our place; and in the sky
    The larks, still bravely singing, fly
Scarce heard amid the guns below.

We are the Dead. Short days ago
We lived, felt dawn, saw sunset glow,
    Loved and were loved, and now we lie
        In Flanders fields.

Take up our quarrel with the foe:
To you from failing hands we throw
    The torch; be yours to hold it high.
    If ye break faith with us who die
We shall not sleep, though poppies grow
        In Flanders fields.

MODERN POETRY   John McCrae, "In Flanders Fields," from *The Penguin Book of First World War Poetry*, ed. Jon Silkin. New York: Viking Penguin, Inc., 1981. Copyright ©
Jon Silkin, 1979, 1981. Page 85.

SIEGFRIED SASSOON

A Working Party

Three hours ago he blundered up the trench,
Sliding and poising, groping with his boots;
Sometimes he tripped and lurched against the walls
With hands that pawed the sodden bags of chalk.
He couldn't see the man who walked in front;
Only he heard the drum and rattle of feet
Stepping along barred trench boards, often splashing
Wretchedly where the sludge was ankle-deep.

Voices would grunt 'Keep to your right—make way!'
When squeezing past some men from the front-line:
White faces peered, puffing a point of red;
Candles and braziers glinted through the chinks
And curtain-flaps of dug-outs; then the gloom
Swallowed his sense of sight; he stooped and swore
Because a sagging wire had caught his neck.

A flare went up; the shining whiteness spread
And flickered upward, showing nimble rats
And mounds of glimmering sand-bags, bleached with
    rain;
Then the slow silver moment died in dark.
The wind came posting by with chilly gusts
And buffeting at corners, piping thin.
And dreary through the crannies; rifle-shots
Would split and crack and sing along the night,
And shells came calmly through the drizzling air
To burst with hollow bang below the hill.

Three hours ago he stumbled up the trench;
Now he will never walk that road again:
He must be carried back, a jolting lump
Beyond all need of tenderness and care.

He was a young man with a meagre wife
And two small children in a Midland town;
He showed their photographs to all his mates,
And they considered him a decent chap
Who did his work and hadn't much to say,
And always laughed at other people's jokes
Because he hadn't any of his own.

That night when he was busy at his job
Of piling bags along the parapet,[1]
He thought how slow time went, stamping his feet
And blowing on his fingers, pinched with cold.
He thought of getting back by half-past twelve,
And tot[2] of rum to send him warm to sleep
In draughty dug-out frowsty[3] with the fumes
Of coke,[4] and full of snoring weary men.

He pushed another bag along the top,
Craning his body outward; then a flare
Gave one white glimpse of No Man's Land and wire;
And as he dropped his head the instant split
His startled life with lead, and all went out.

Glory of Women

You love us when we're heroes, home on leave,
Or wounded in a mentionable place.
You worship decorations; you believe
That chivalry redeems the war's disgrace.
You make us shells. You listen with delight,
By tales of dirt and danger fondly thrilled.
You crown our distant ardors while we fight,
And mourn our laurelled memories when we're killed.

[1]Earthen embankment shielding the top of the trench.
[2]Small drink.
[3]Stuffy, musty.
[4]A solid fuel made from coal.

MODERN POETRY "Glory of Women," from *The Collected Poems of Siegfried Sassoon* by Siegfried Sassoon. Copyright 1918, 1920 by E. P. Dutton & Co.; 1936, 1946, 1947, 1948 by Siegfried Sassoon. Reprinted by permission of Viking Penguin, Inc.

You can't believe that British troops 'retire'
When hell's last horror breaks them, and they run,
Trampling the terrible corpses—blind with blood.
    O German mother dreaming by the fire,
    While you are knitting socks to send your son
    His face is trodden deeper in the mud.

WILFRED OWEN

Dulce et Decorum Est

Bent double, like old beggars under sacks,
Knock-kneed, coughing like hags, we cursed through sludge,
Till on the haunting flares we turned our backs
And towards our distant rest began to trudge.
Men marched asleep. Many had lost their boots
But limped on, blood-shod. All went lame; all blind;
Drunk with fatigue; deaf even to the hoots
Of gas shells dropping softly behind.

Gas! GAS! Quick, boys!—An ecstasy of fumbling,
Fitting the clumsy helmets just in time;
But someone still was yelling out and stumbling,
And flound'ring like a man in fire or lime . . .
Dim, through the misty panes[5] and thick green light,
As under a green sea, I saw him drowning.

In all my dreams, before my helpless sight,
He plunges at me, guttering, choking, drowning.

If in some smothering dreams you too could pace
Behind the wagon that we flung him in,
And watch the white eyes writhing in his face,
His hanging face, like a devil's sick of sin;
If you could hear, at every jolt, the blood
Come gargling from the froth-corrupted lungs,

[5]Goggles fitted in the gas mask.

MODERN POETRY   Wilfred Owen, "Dulce et Decorum Est," from *The Penguin Book of First World War Poetry*, ed. Jon Silkin. New York: Viking Penguin, Inc., 1981. Copyright © Jon Silkin, 1979, 1981. Pp. 182–83.

Obscene as cancer, bitter as the cud
Of vile, incurable sores on innocent tongues,—
My friend, you would not tell with such high zest
To children ardent for some desperate glory,
The old Lie: Dulce et decorum est
Pro patria mori.[6]

Disabled

He sat in a wheeled chair, waiting for dark,
And shivered in his ghastly suit of grey,
Legless, sewn short at elbow. Through the park
Voices of boys rang saddening like a hymn,
Voices of play and pleasure after day,
Till gathering sleep had mothered them from him.

· · ·

About this time Town used to swing so gay
When glow-lamps budded in the light blue trees,
And girls glanced lovelier as the air grew dim,
—In the old times, before he threw away his knees.
Now he will never feel again how slim
Girls' waists are, or how warm their subtle hands.
All of them touch him like some queer disease.

· · ·

There was an artist silly for his face,
For it was younger than his youth, last year.
Now, he is old; his back will never brace;
He's lost his color very far from here,
Poured it down shell-holes till the veins ran dry,

[6]"Dulce . . . mori." Latin, by the Roman poet Horace (65–8 B.C.): "It is sweet and fitting to die for one's country."

MODERN POETRY Wilfred Owen, "Disabled," from *The Penguin Book of First World War Poetry*, ed. Jon Silkin. New York: Viking Penguin, Inc., 1981. Copyright © Jon Silkin, 1979, 1981. Pp. 184–85.

And half his lifetime lapsed in the hot race
And leap of purple spurted from his thigh.

• • •

One time he liked a bloodsmear down his leg,
After the matches, carried shoulder-high.
It was after football, when he'd drunk a peg,
He thought he'd better join.—He wonders why.
Someone had said he'd look a god in kilts,
That's why; and maybe, too, to please his Meg,
Aye, that was it, to please the giddy jilts
He asked to join. He didn't have to beg;
Smiling they wrote his lie: aged nineteen years.
Germans he scarcely thought of; all their guilt,
And Austria's,[7] did not move him. And no fears
Of Fear came yet. He thought of jewelled hilts
For daggers in plaid socks; of smart salutes;
And care of arms; and leave; and pay arrears;
Esprit de corps;[8] and hints for young recruits.
And soon, he was drafted out with drums and cheers.

• • •

Some cheered him home, but not as crowds cheer Goal.
Only a solemn man who brought him fruits
Thanked him; and then inquired about his soul.

• • •

Now, he will spend a few sick years in institutes,
And do what things the rules consider wise,
And take whatever pity they may dole.
Tonight he noticed how the women's eyes
Passed from him to the strong men that were whole.
How cold and late it is! Why don't they come
And put him into bed? Why don't they come?

---

[7]Austria and Germany were allies in the First World War.
[8]French, the spirit of comradeship and related ideals shared by a group.

YVAN GOLL

Recitative (VIII)

Like a grey wall around Europe
The long battle ran.
The never-ending battle, the bogged-down battle, the softening-up
battle,
The battle that was never the final battle.
Oh, the monotony of trench-warfare! Oh, trench-grave! Oh, sleep
of starvation!
The bridges built of corpses!
The roads surfaced with corpses!
The walls cemented with corpses!
For months on end the horizon stared mysteriously and glassily like
a dead man's eye.
For years on end the distance rang like the same old passing-bell.
The days were as alike as a pair of graves.
Oh, you heroes!
Crawling out on wet nights, mewling in the bitter cold, you from
your all-electric cities!
The sentry swapped ten nights' sleep for one cigarette; whole
regiments gambled away eternity for ten yards of wasteland.
Full-blooded curses spat into the starlit mire. Damp cellars littered
with tinny booty captured from the enemy.
Oh, you Greek dancers, dwarfed in lousy caverns! Popping up like
Indians in fancy-dress when the drums sounded the attack:
Before sticking your bayonet into his groin, did not one of you see
the Christ-like look of his opponent, did not one of you notice
that the man over there had a kingly heart full of love?
Did not one of you still believe in his own and mankind's
conscience?
You brothers, fellow-men! Oh, you heroes!

MODERN POETRY   Yvan Goll, "Recitative (VIII)," trans. from the German and reprinted by permission of Patrick Bridgwater. From *The Penguin Book of First World War Poetry*, ed. Jon Silkin. Copyright © Jon Silkin, 1979, 1981. (New York: Viking Penguin, Inc., 1981) Page 242.

WILLIAM BUTLER YEATS

The Second Coming[9]

Turning and turning in the widening gyre[10]
The falcon cannot hear the falconer;[11]
Things fall apart; the center cannot hold;
Mere anarchy is loosed upon the world,
The blood-dimmed tide is loosed, and everywhere
The ceremony of innocence is drowned;
The best lack all conviction, while the worst
Are full of passionate intensity.

Surely some revelation is at hand;
Surely the Second Coming is at hand.
The Second Coming! Hardly are those words out
When a vast image out of Spiritus Mundi[12]
Troubles my sight: somewhere in sands of the desert
A shape with lion body and the head of a man,
A gaze blank and pitiless as the sun,
Is moving its slow thighs, while all about it
Reel shadows of the indignant desert birds.
The darkness drops again; but now I know
That twenty centuries of stony sleep
Were vexed to nightmare by a rocking cradle,
And what rough beast, its hour come round at last,
Slouches towards Bethlehem to be born?

[9]The biblical prophecy of the Second Coming of Jesus is used as the poem's underlying theme.

[10]Circular, or spiral, motion.

[11]Christ.

[12]Latin: World Spirit.

MODERN POETRY   William Butler Yeats, "The Second Coming." Reprinted with permission of Macmillan Publishing Company from *Collected Poems* by William Butler Yeats. Copyright 1924 by Macmillan Publishing Company, renewed 1952 by Bertha Georgie Yeats. Pp. 346–47.

LOUIS UNTERMEYER

The Flaming Circle

Though for fifteen years you have chaffed[13] me across the table,
  Slept in my arms and fingered my plunging heart,
I scarcely know you; we have not known each other.
  For all the fierce and casual contacts, something keeps us apart.

Are you struggling, perhaps, in a world that I see only dimly,
  Except as it sweeps toward the star on which I stand alone?
Are we swung like two planets, compelled in our separate orbits,
  Yet held in a flaming circle far greater than our own?

Last night we were single, a radiant core of completion,
  Surrounded by flames that embraced us but left no burns,
Today we are only ourselves; we have plans and pretensions;
  We move in dividing streets with our small and different concerns.

Merging and rending, we wait for the miracle. Meanwhile
  The fire runs deeper, consuming these selves in its growth.
Can this be the mystical marriage—this clash and communion;
  This pain of possession that frees and encircles us both?

W. H. AUDEN

The Unknown Citizen

To JS/07/M/378
This Marble Monument is Erected by the State

He was found by the Bureau of Statistics to be
One against whom there was no official complaint,
And all the reports on his conduct agree

---

[13]Good-natured teasing.

MODERN POETRY   "The Flaming Circle" from *Roast Leviathan* by Louis Untermeyer. (New York: Harcourt, Brace and Co., 1923). Copyright 1923 by Harcourt Brace Jovanovich, Inc.; renewed 1951 by Louis Untermeyer. Reprinted by permission of the publisher. Pp. 25–26.

MODERN POETRY   "The Unknown Citizen." Copyright 1940 and renewed 1968 by W. H. Auden. Reprinted from *W. H. Auden: Collected Poems*, ed. Edward Mendelson. by permission of Random House, Inc. Pp. 85–86.

That, in the modern sense of an old-fashioned word, he was a saint,
For in everything he did he served the Greater Community.
Except for the War till the day he retired
He worked in a factory and never got fired,
But satisfied his employers, Fudge Motors Inc.
Yet he wasn't a scab or odd in his views,
For his Union reports that he paid his dues,
(Our report on his Union shows it was sound)
And our Social Psychology workers found
That he was popular with his mates and liked a drink.
The Press are convinced that he bought a paper every day
And that his reactions to advertisements were normal in every way.
Policies taken out in his name prove that he was fully insured,
And his Health-card shows he was once in hospital but left it cured.
Both Producers Research and High-Grade Living declare
He was fully sensible to the advantages of the Installment Plan
And had everything necessary to the Modern Man,
A gramophone, a radio, a car and a frigidaire.
Our researchers into Public Opinion are content
That he held the proper opinions for the time of year;
When there was peace, he was for peace; when there
                                                was war, he went.
He was married and added five children to the population,
Which our Eugenist[14] says was the right number for a parent of
                                                his generation,
And our teachers report that he never interfered with their education.
Was he free? Was he happy? The question is absurd:
Had anything been wrong, we should certainly have heard.

[14]An official charged with supervising the improvement of the genetic qualities of the population.